D1569198

Nationalism and Federalism in Yugoslavia, 1962–1991

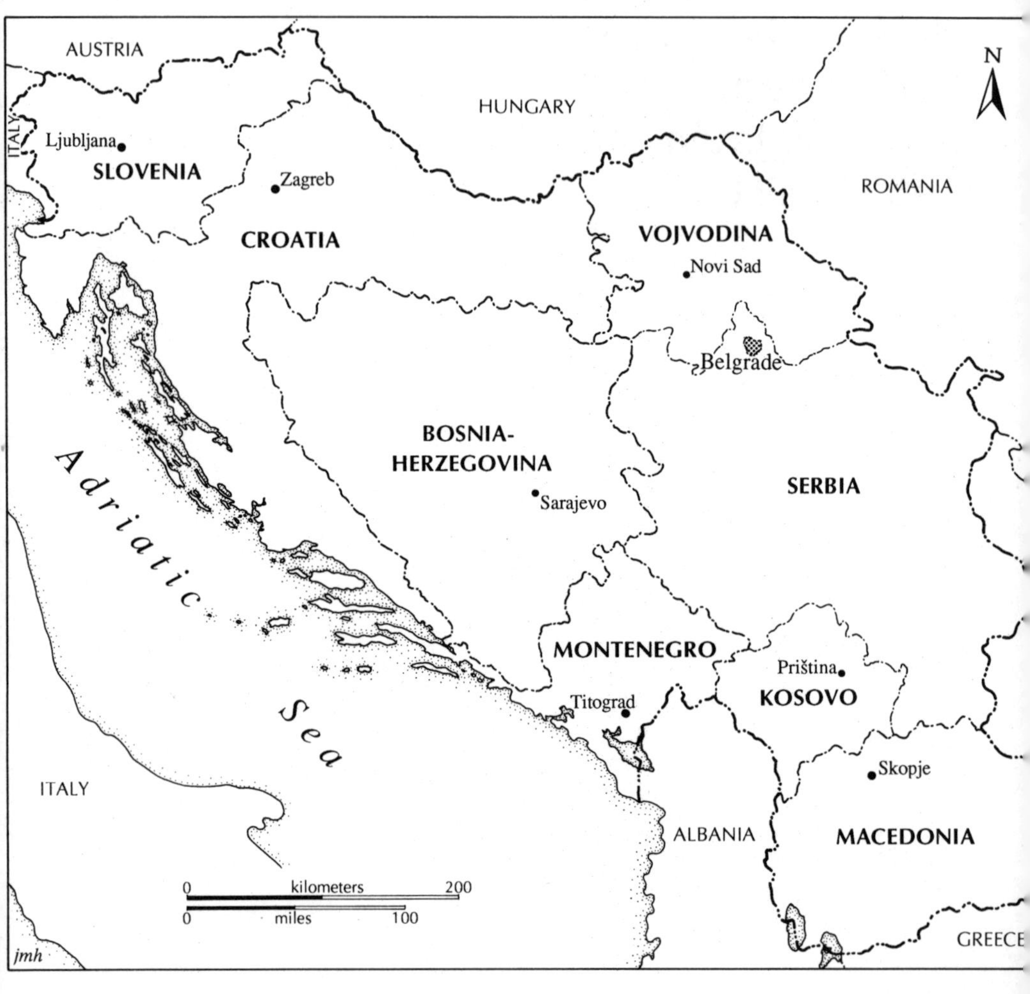

AUSTRIA
HUNGARY
N
ITALY
Ljubljana
SLOVENIA
Zagreb
ROMANIA
CROATIA
VOJVODINA
Novi Sad
Belgrade
BOSNIA-
HERZEGOVINA
Adriatic
SERBIA
Sarajevo
MONTENEGRO
Priština
Titograd
KOSOVO
Sea
Skopje
ITALY
ALBANIA
MACEDONIA
0
kilometers
200
0
miles
100
GREECE
jmh

Nationalism and Federalism in Yugoslavia, 1962–1991

SECOND EDITION

Sabrina P. Ramet

INDIANA UNIVERSITY PRESS

BLOOMINGTON AND INDIANAPOLIS

Manufactured in the United States of America

Library of Congress Cataloging-in-Publication Data

Ramet, Sabrina P., date.
Nationalism and federalism in Yugoslavia, 1962–1991 / Sabrina P. Ramet. — 2nd ed.
p. cm.
Rev. ed. of: Nationalism and federalism in Yugoslavia, 1963–1983. 1984.
Includes bibliographical references and index.
ISBN 0-253-34794-7 (cloth). — ISBN 0-253-20703-7 (paper)
I. Ramet, Sabrina P., date. Nationalism and federalism in Yugoslavia, 1963–1983. II. Title.
DR1302.R36 1992
320.5′09497—dc20 91-23623

1 2 3 4 5 96 95 94 93 92

For Christine, with love.
Com' è bella, questa vita!

Contents

TABLES

APPENDIX TABLES

PREFACE

The reissue of this book in a second edition is a happy occasion for me. It gives me the opportunity to return to what was my first book and to add to it a great deal of new information picked up over the succeeding years. In its original incarnation, this book grew out of my Ph.D. dissertation research at UCLA, under the mentorship of Andrzej Korbonski. I began work on the manuscript in 1978 and spent a year in Yugoslavia, 1979–80, thanks to a Fulbright-Hayes fellowship, doing the major part of the research for the first edition. A third trip to Yugoslavia in 1982 (my first trip had been in 1978), funded by a grant from the American Council of Learned Societies, allowed me to supplement my research with extensive interviews.

Since the publication of the first edition, I have made several return visits to Yugoslavia (specifically in 1987, 1988, and 1989), conducting extensive interviews with people in many walks of life, including government officials, economists, journalists, feminist sociologists, clergymen, rock performers, and dissidents. That broad interview data has given me insights and ideas I could not have gleaned from interviews only with politicians and economists and has given me a better sense of the spirit and mood of the country. The 1989 visit was funded by grants from the University of Washington Graduate School Research Fund and from IREX.

My professors at UCLA—Andrzej Korbonski and Bariša Krekić—were an inspiration to me in my work on this book and helped me fashion my research skills. I am also indebted to Robin Alison Remington and Dennison I. Rusinow, who read early drafts for the first edition and provided many thoughtful recommendations.

Some of the material in this book has been published earlier. The section on Albanian nationalism in chapter 9 is a considerably revised and updated version of "Problems of Albanian Nationalism in Yugoslavia," which appeared originally in *Orbis* (vol. 25, no. 2 [Summer 1981]). The section on the Slovenian syndrome, in the same chapter, is a revised and extended version of a section of "Yugoslavia 1987: Stirrings from Below," originally published in *South Slav Journal* (vol. 10, no. 3 [Autumn 1987]). Chapter 11 originally appeared under the title, "Serbia's Slobodan Milošević: A Profile," in *Orbis* (vol. 35, no. 1 [Winter 1991]). My thanks to *Orbis* and to *South Slav Journal* for their permission to reuse this material.

Finally, a personal note: The first edition of this book appeared under the byline of Pedro Ramet, and the second edition appears under the byline of Sabrina P. Ramet. I have always felt female, from about age ten, if not before.

After unending cycles of deep depression, starting about age twelve and coming at a rhythm of every three to six months, I finally accepted myself, in December 1989, for who and what I am and began the long process of transformation to bring my physical sex into harmony with my psychic gender. I am happier now and know greater peace of mind than I have ever known.

Sabrina Petra Ramet
Seattle, Washington

ABBREVIATIONS

AP—Autonomous Province
AVNOJ—Antifašističko vijeće narodnog oslobodjenja Jugoslavije (Antifascist Council of National Liberation of Yugoslavia)
BOAL—Basic Organization of Associated Labor
CC—central committee
CD—cognitive dissonance
CEP—Council for Environmental Protection
CPP—Croatian Peasant party
CPSU—Communist Party of the Soviet Union
CPY—Communist Party of Yugoslavia (until 1952); see LCY
CRO—Community of Railroad Organizations
CRP—Chamber of Republics and Provinces
CSCE—Conference on Security and Cooperation in Europe
EEC—European Economic Community
FADURK—Federal Fund for the Accelerated Development of the Underdeveloped Republics and the Province of Kosovo
FBIS—Foreign Broadcast Information Service
FREDUD—Republican Fund for Encouraging the Development of the Underdeveloped Districts
HT—Hrvatski tjednik (Croatian Weekly)
IAA—Inex Adria Aviopromet (Slovenian airline)
IRCS—Interrepublican committee system
JAT—Jugoslovenski Aerotransport (Serbian airline)
JNA—Yugoslav National Army
LC—League of Communists
LC B-H—League of Communists, Bosnia-Herzegovina
LCC—League of Communists of Croatia
LCK—League of Communists of Kosovo
LCY—League of Communists of Yugoslavia; see CPY
NDH—Nezavisna Država Hrvatska (Croatian Independent State during World War II)
NR—*narodna republika*
NSK—Neue slowenische Kunst
RFE—Radio Free Europe
SAP—Socialist autonomous province
SAWP—Socialist Alliance of Working People

SAWPY—Socialist Alliance of Working People of Yugoslavia
SFRY—Socialist Federated Republic of Yugoslavia
SIV—Savezno Izvršno Veće (Federal Executive Council)
SIZ—Samoupravne Interesne Zajednice (Self-Managing Interest Community)
SR—Socialist Republic
UDBa—Uprava Državne Bezbednosti (State Security Administration)

INTRODUCTION

Yugoslavia is a new country of old peoples. Slavic tribes settled in what is now Yugoslavia during the sixth century and ruled themselves until the Ottoman Turks began their Balkan expansion in the twelfth century. After the collapse of the medieval kingdoms of Croatia, Bosnia, and Serbia, the South Slavs (*južni slaveni* or *jugoslaveni*) were ruled variously by Austrians, Hungarians, Italians, and Turks. The division between the jurisdictions of the Christian powers and the empire of the Muslim Turks marked a major cultural divide that reinforced the earlier cleavage between Catholic and Orthodox South Slavs. By the time the South Slavs were brought into a common state in 1918, they had become accustomed to thinking of themselves as Slovenes, Croats, Serbs, and Montenegrins—that is, as distinct peoples. The additional presence of certain non-Slavic peoples (Hungarians, Albanians, Germans, and Italians), together with Slavic Bulgarians and Macedonians, further complicated the picture and helped to make the so-called national question a burning issue for the interwar Kingdom of Yugoslavia. It has remained a central issue for postwar Yugoslavia.

Because Yugoslavia is a new country, ties of ethnicity have continued to exert greater hold on its people than do ties of political loyalty to the state. The interwar kingdom foundered on its misconceived denial of these differences among its Slavic peoples (treating them as members of a single "Yugoslav nation"); Yugoslavia's postwar communist regime succeeded in assuaging ethnic sensitivities not by eroding their bases but by creating ethnic republics of Slovenia, Croatia, Serbia, Macedonia, and Montenegro within the political body of Yugoslavia and conceding vast jurisdiction to these republics. Yugoslav politics in the years prior to 1989 was correspondingly shaped by a delicate balance of power among the federal units, a balance in which issues have been heavily colored by the ethnic factor.

In two cases—Bosnia and Vojvodina—the local populations were so heterogeneous that the Communist party hesitated to establish them as separate republics. Vojvodina was therefore established as an autonomous province, a unit that, at least initially, had less self-governing power than the republics. Bosnia was, after some hesitation, established as a republic, but its Croats, Serbs, and "ethnic Muslims" were declared to have equal title to the republic. Finally, in the southern part of Yugoslavia, in a region that Hitler had granted to Albania and Tito's partisans had wrenched back by force, the Yugoslav communists established the autonomous region of Kosovo-Metohija, juridically a notch below Vojvodina. Kosovo's population, then as now, was predominantly Albanian.

If the sundry federal units were themselves ethnically homogeneous—for example, if Serbia were 100 percent Serbian and Croatia 100 percent Croatian—the political landscape would already be complex. But it is further complicated by the dispersion of nationalities throughout the country. Thus, for example, 14 percent of the population of Croatia is ethnically Serbian and 17 percent of the population of Macedonia is ethnically Albanian—two diasporas that have played volatile roles during the past fifteen years, inflaming relations among ethnic groups and among the federal units. Some of the dispersed ethnic groups, moreover, have played a role out of proportion to their numbers. The Croatian Serbs, for instance, were long overrepresented in the Croatian party, police, and militia. Serbs have also long played a disproportionate role in the governing apparatus of Albanian-populated Kosovo.

Despite its federal form, the Yugoslav political system was initially tightly centralized on the Stalin model. The Sixth Party Congress in 1952, at which the Communist party of Yugoslavia (CPY) assumed its new name, the League of Communists of Yugoslavia (LCY), began a process of decentralization that would prove distinctive among communist systems. Since decentralization, the republics and autonomous provinces increasingly became spokespersons of their titular nationalities (except, obviously, in the cases of Bosnia, Vojvodina, and, perhaps, Kosovo). The interrepublican policy struggles that have become the lodestone of Yugoslav politics were played out on four levels: among the republics themselves in those areas where republics have exclusive jurisdiction; within the arena of the federal center (government and party) on issues in which the jurisdiction of the center is pivotal; between groups of republics, with the federal center taking one side in the struggle; and among various factions within the sundry republics, with a faction from one republic allying with a kindred group in another republic to defeat legislation proposed by its antagonists. Major policy departures, such as the legitimation of a separate Muslim nationality in 1968, have always required the sanction of the center and, often, the initiative of factions at the center.

President Josip Broz Tito ruled Yugoslavia for more than thirty-five years. His death in May 1980 was perceived by most Yugoslavs as the end of an era. Some observers believed further that his death would catalyze revolt throughout the country and mark the end of Yugoslavia as such. Instead, the transition to post-Tito Yugoslavia was smooth, and change was initially imperceptible. One symptom of the gradual transition was that long after Tito's death (itself following a four-month coma), Yugoslav newspapers continued to adorn their pages with large and prominent pictures of the deceased leader, sustaining the illusion that Tito was somehow still active. Only some four months after his death did the papers begin to run fewer pictures of the former president.

On the political level, the collective leadership fashioned by Tito loudly insisted on its determination to follow "Tito's path," but it proved unable to prevent a loosening of the system for at least four reasons. First, without Tito, the LCY lacked an ultimate arbiter and was therefore tangibly weaker than before. The divided party leadership could not assert itself because, in many cases, "the will of the party" could not even be determined. Second, important power centers within the party wanted change (albeit change disguised as continuity) and pressed for a measure of relaxation. Such relaxation as did take place probably exceeded the limits of what these party "liberals" had in mind, since a retrenchment that was set in motion in the summer of 1982 met no serious overt resistance within the party. Third, the tangible economic deterioration that began in 1979 threw the entire system into disarray, and numerous officials blamed the federal balance, that is, the distribution of powers between the federation and the federal units, for the country's economic problems. Although some suggested that the country suffered from too much decentralization, others took a divergent position and argued that only extensive decentralization enabled Yugoslavia to function as well as it did. And, fourth, the explosion of violence in Kosovo in April 1981, when discontented Albanians burned cars and attacked Serbs, produced a nationalist backlash throughout Yugoslavia. Kosovo was placed under military occupation, and the episode reopened the question of the utility of federalism as a solution for interethnic tensions and distrust.

These sundry problems gradually eroded the legitimacy and political capacity of the system, and by 1989 Slovenia was talking of secession, Serbia was trying to eliminate its autonomous provinces, and the Serbian minority in Croatia was becoming restive. After free elections in Slovenia and Croatia in spring 1990, Yugoslavia was in the unique situation of being "two-thirds communist"—with noncommunist governments in the two aforementioned republics and lameduck communist governments in the other four republics. Slovenia and Croatia were actively pushing for the country's transformation into a full-fledged confederation—an eventuality that, as of September 1990, seemed likely.

This book seeks to demonstrate that, with the multifaceted reform set in motion between 1963 and 1965, the Yugoslav political system acquired, domestically, the basic features of an international balance-of-power system. It will show that these features account for the basic pattern and dynamics of Yugoslav politics to the present day. In this spirit, I will outline, in the pages that follow, a theory that synthesizes the insights of several balance-of-power theorists, including Morton A. Kaplan and Dina A. Zinnes.

Part I explores the dynamics of nationalism and the nature of the problems posed by ethnic nationalism; empirical hypotheses are set forth regarding the behavior of ethnically constituted political units in a multipolar system. Chapter 2 highlights the main problems associated with ethnic nationalism in Yugoslavia. Chapter 3 explores the putative linkage between ethnic problems and federalism as a tentative solution in light of the evolution of Yugoslav thinking on the subject. It also traces the origins of Yugoslav policy from the influence of Marx and the Austro-Marxists to the positions of Edvard Kardelj and the LCY.

The hypotheses set forth in Part I presume wide autonomy on the part of the federal units. Evidence for this assumption is provided in Part II, which also outlines the basic structure of the federal system.

In Part III, the hypotheses are tested by application to case studies of interethnic and interrepublican conflict. Some cases are macrocases that placed the entire system under strain: the reform crisis of 1962–71, the Croatian crisis of 1967–72, and the violent eruptions of Albanian nationalism in 1968 and in the spring of 1981 must be viewed as crises of the first magnitude. Other cases—such as the controversy over the identity of the Muslims and the struggle over the level and method of assistance to the economically underdeveloped south—are salient medium-level controversies. Still other case studies examined—such as the controversy over the Belgrade-Bar railway and the debate about the proliferation of airlines (both covered in chapter 9)—are microcases, albeit with system-wide importance. It is hoped that the mix of macro-, micro-, and medium-level cases will give the reader a balanced perspective on Yugoslav political reality and provide a sensible proportion of evidence for hypotheses intended to be applicable at different levels of conflict. Chapters 10–12 trace the rise of nationalism and the disintegration of the system in the course of the 1980s. Chapter 13 examines the course of the civil war, as far as October 1991.

PART I
Interethnic Relations in an Interrepublican Context

1

The Multinational State as an International System

In a trailblazing essay published in 1963, Chadwick F. Alger proposed that the bifurcation of political science into the two great spheres of intranational politics (or comparative politics) and international relations might, to a far greater extent than is generally acknowledged, be arbitrary and even unnecessary. Alger specifically charged that "the lack of 'governments' in international systems does not preclude wider application of knowledge and concepts from intranational politics to the study of international politics."[1] His conclusion was that theory generated in the realm of comparative politics—for example, notions of interest aggregation and articulation—might serve useful explanatory functions if transplanted to the field of international relations.

My intention here is to demonstrate that the converse proposition also has merit, that is, that theory generated in international relations can throw light on processes that constitute the natural subject matter of comparative politics, and, in particular, that Kaplan's typology of systems of international behavior provides a useful framework for the study of a multiethnic state.[2] The notion that political behavior has universal characteristics, whether it takes place between or within states, is not novel by any means. Hobbes drew the parallel between the hypothetical state of nature that prevailed among men in any given society prior to the establishment and legitimation of authority and the actual state of nature that characterizes relations among sovereign states. Harold Lasswell, in *World Politics and Personal Insecurity*, pointed out analogies between domestic and international balance-of-power politics. John Bassett Moore's *International Law and Some Current Illusions* draws attention to "relations of mutual support" among diverse sectors of the United States in the era preceding system breakdown in the American Civil War.[3] And, although Kaplan has cautioned that "the actors [on the international stage] are more highly particularized than are actors within the domestic arena,"[4] we may observe that (1) as Edward Vose Gulick has pointed out, Europe during the golden age of the "balance of power" had a shared heritage that embraced common religious, aesthetic, legal, and cultural traditions,[5] and (2) Kaplan himself gave his imprimatur to the efforts of two colleagues to apply some of his concepts germane to the field of international relations to what can, at the very least, be termed regional subsystems.[6]

I am attempting here to be a bit bolder, since the presence of a central government apparatus that is firmly in control places obvious constraints on the regional actors within the state. I propose to demonstrate that there are striking parallels between the patterns of interstate behavior in eighteenth- and nineteenth-century Europe and those of interrepublican behavior in contemporary Yugoslavia. I believe that the term *balance of power*, generally applied to the former pattern, is an accurate characterization of Yugoslav politics as well.

Most of the numerous attempts to provide a meaningful structural analysis of interethnic relations in multiethnic states have necessarily emphasized the differences in the number of actors in the system. Yet the typologies of Clifford Geertz, Alvin Rabushka and Kenneth A. Shepsle, and Crawford Young—three of the best known discussions of this subject—are purely arithmetic, lacking any behavioral dimension.[7] These models are purely descriptive and have little explanatory or predictive power. Moreover, except for Young's typology, these approaches cannot account for change in the pattern of ethnic relations. Kaplan's typology of international systems remedies these deficiencies by taking account of varying degrees of integration and calling attention to structural dynamics. Thus, on the first count, he arrays the unit-veto, balance-of-power, universal, and hierarchical systems in that order, from least integrated to most integrated. On the second count, Kaplan's models remind us that assessment of system interaction entails not only a tally of major actors (as is implied, for instance, in Geertz's typology) but also the determination of alignment patterns, cleavage lines, and axes of conflict. Kaplan's typology also promises (1) to provide empirical "rules" of behavior, (2) to provide guidelines for the transformations of systems, and (3) to facilitate prediction of the effects of deviations from his rules on the other actors and the system as a whole. Application of this framework to the study of multinational states offers tantalizing conceptual possibilities.

To apply a modified version of Kaplan's typology to Yugoslavia, I will designate ethnic groups, rather than states, as actors in the system and treat the state, rather than a group of states, as the conceptual system. Thus, I will view Yugoslavia as a system of interethnic behavior and will attempt to identify patterns of interaction among its national units. The intrastate system offers some analogies with other aspects found in Kaplan's model of the interstate system, including parallels for bloc actors and universal actors, alliance formation, and dominance relations.

In the interstate universe, according to Kaplan, only the loose bipolar and balance-of-power systems have actually had historical manifestations, at least for the last two hundred years. The other four systems that Kaplan mentions—the tight bipolar, unit-veto, universal, and hierarchical systems—are intended as analytical constructs for probabilistic projection. But in the intrastate system, five of the six have had historical referents—only the unit-veto system has not. Austria-Hungary (1867–1918)—with separate stamps, currency, parliaments, tax collections, and judicial, educational, and transportation systems—is perhaps one of the clearest historical examples of a tight bipolar system. The Austrian and Hungarian halves of the empire regularly clashed over questions of foreign policy and engaged in continual rivalry within the state. The Soviet

Union closely resembles the universal system, described by Kaplan as a semi-unified political system under a world government, in which a central actor dominates peripheral actors enrolled on a formally voluntary basis. In the Soviet Union, the Great Russians dominate a multiethnic realm in which the non-Russian republics enjoy the formal right of secession. Switzerland figures as Kaplan's hierarchical system, in which national actors (in this case the German, French, and Italian language groups) cease to be primary foci of loyalty and function instead as territorial subdivisions or intermediate levels of organization.[8] Yugoslavia, finally, evolved gradually from a configuration that paralleled a loose bipolar system (1918–63) to a balance-of-power system (since 1965).

I hope that the use of the balance-of-power model as an analytical framework will help to bring into focus the patterns of interethnic politics in Yugoslavia, shed light on the nature of transformations in the patterns of ethnic interaction, illustrate how specific behavioral patterns of ethnic group behavior are determined by the degree of institutional integration and patterns of institutional interaction, and illuminate why a nationalities policy that worked in one country at a certain time may not be successful or relevant in other times and places. Thus, to illustrate the last point, decentralization may work in a nonbipolar system, because the system's crosscutting cleavages are also bonds of common interest. But, though decentralization may form the basis for stable interregional relations in a nonbipolar state, it is likely to aggravate tensions in a bipolar system by providing potential separatists with political resources. Finally, I will argue that the principles governing the political behavior of collective units are more universal than hitherto believed and that it is possible to apply insights gained in the study of international politics to subject matter germane to comparative politics (and, by implication, the reverse—provided that caution and good sense are exercised). As a theory of interunit behavior, the approach is perhaps relevant only to systems in which administrative units are organized on ethnic or quasi-ethnic lines.

Loose Bipolar System

Perhaps the most common historical pattern, both among and within states, is the loose bipolar system, which generally presumes two permanently hostile core powers around which lesser powers cluster in a non-random fashion that approximates equal distribution of allies. Within a multinational state, this configuration results if ethnic groups are polarized on a salient and durable issue or issues and divide into two fairly stable camps or, in a state constituted by a number of regional ethnic units, if two predominant units command the allegiance of various smaller units and each power views the other as its chief competitor, neither being able to gain lasting control of state policy (for instance, by obtaining control of appointments to the state bureaucracy). Axes along which an ethnically diverse state may polarize include religion, alphabet, language, urban/rural, center/periphery (in the sense that outlying areas may perceive certain provinces as constituting a geographic and political center from which they are excluded), and, prominently, economic diversity, whether this involves rich/poor distinctions or simply differences in the economic bases of the respective sectors of the society. When the society is riddled with reinforced cleavages (as in Yugoslavia, where the prosperous, Catholic, ex-Habsburg, Latin-alphabet, industrialized north vies with the underdeveloped, Orthodox and Muslim, ex-Ottoman, Cyrillic-alphabet south) and when one actor (Serbia in the interwar period) attempts to spread its language and culture and to dominate the rest of the population, a bipolar configuration is a natural result.

According to Kaplan, the bipolar system is characterized by polarization, with most significant actors adhering to one of the two blocs and a universal actor presiding over the inevitable conflicts of interest. He argues that neither bloc can permit its rival to achieve preponderant strength; that each bloc seeks to further its own interests first, but will support the universal actor (the central government) when such support will help to weaken or constrain the rival; and that the universal actor will seek, through mediation and whatever coercive capability it possesses, to resolve or dampen interbloc conflicts and to assuage differences between the blocs.[9] Kaplan adds that, if unchecked, the universal actor will strive to impose a directive, monolithic unity on the system.

It is well known that Kaplan meant this description to elucidate the processes of the Cold War system, with the United Nations in the role of universal actor. And it must be stressed that bipolar politics in no way presumes, a priori, the presence of a universal actor. Yet, at the same time, Kaplan intended his model to have a degree of universality that would transcend mere description of U.S.-Soviet competition. The League of Communists of Yugoslavia, with headquarters in Belgrade, functioned as a kind of universal actor within the Yugoslav system, but, unlike the U.N., which can always be paralyzed by veto, the central party of Yugoslavia long retained considerable powers, even during the devolutionary days of 1966–71 and certainly until the death of Tito.

Between 1918 and 1941 and again from 1945 to 1963, Yugoslavia functioned as a loose bipolar system. Interwar Yugoslav politics was monopolized by the Serbs and Croats, whose electoral aspirations were championed, respectively, by the Serbian Radical party under Nikola Pašić and the Croatian Peasant party (CPP) led by Stjepan Radić. A third group, Stojan Pribičević's Democratic party, outpolled its rivals but cooperated with the Radicals in pushing through a centralist program that often entailed Serbianization. Radić and the CPP clamored for Croatian secession and withdrew their support for the constitution in 1921. They were followed in this by the Slovene Popular party, another political machine that catered exclusively to the interests of a single ethnic group and opposed the program of cultural homogenization. By contrast, Yugoslavia's Muslim population, consisting of Bosniaks, Albanians, and Turks, tended to back the centralist regime. The flight of Ante Pavelić and a group of militant Croats (organized into the fascist *Ustaše* party) after the imposition of royal dictatorship in 1929 was symptomatic of the increasing bifurcation of

Yugoslav politics into centralists and decentralists, and by 1934 only the Slovenes and Dalmatians had failed to develop significant secessionist movements.

Interwar Yugoslavia, though not a Serbian creation, was in fact dominated by the Serbs, who staffed the new government with the leaders of the old Serbian kingdom. The Serbs denied the national identity of the Macedonians and Montenegrins, viewed Croats and Slovenes as no more than regional "tribes" of the Serbian nation, and attempted to run the state on a unitary basis. As early as February 1919, however, Radić supported Croatian secession. The Croatian question lay at the heart of the constitutional debate, and Croatian politicians exerted pressure on Belgrade to make some accommodations. Toward the end of 1924, pressured by the Croatian Peasant party, Nikola Pašić, the Serbian prime minister, briefly entertained the possibility of cutting off Croatia and permitting the CPP to establish an independent republic there.[10] By 1934, even King Alexander was convinced of the untenability of the political status quo and may have been planning to divide Yugoslavia into a Serbian unit and a Croatian unit when an *Ustaše* assassin cut him down.[11]

Although Serbian-Croatian rivalry was a fixed feature of the interwar period, the sentiments of the other ethnic groups were not entirely predictable. Although the Slovenian Clerical Populist party under Antun Korošec cooperated closely with the Serbs, the Slovenes overwhelmingly recoiled from the Serbian-dominated centralist apparatus, and Korošec accordingly maintained close liaison with Vladko Maček, Radić's successor at the head of the CPP.[12] Similarly, though the Yugoslav Muslim Organization (YMO) by and large supported Belgrade, Mehmed Spaho did lead the YMO into alignment with the so-called Opposition Front in February 1935, thus putting the YMO in partnership with the CPP and other alienated parties.

It appears that group interests may be treated as de facto monolithic, at least within the context of intergroup conflict, for regardless of what the particular interests of Croatian peasants, merchants, sailors, priests, and intellectuals may have been, they united to support the same program in the conviction that their principal foe was one and the same (Serbian hegemonism). Maček's endorsement of the *Ustaše* confirms the principle that the interests of the ethnic actor may—with certain qualifications and exceptions to be noted later—be treated as monolithic. Maček, in fact, actively collaborated with Pavelić and the *Ustaše* from July 1928 (when Radić approved the pro-Italian policy) to June 1930 (when Maček was put on trial for separatism and accordingly softened his approach somewhat). By late 1928, Maček and other leading figures of the Croatian Peasant party (such as Ante Trumbić) had already made contact with Hungarian and Italian plenipotentiaries, soliciting support for the "eventual amputation of Croatia."[13] Maček was in fact involved in the decision to establish the *Ustaše*, and though the Peasant party and the *Ustaše* operated independently of one another abroad, inside Yugoslavia their activities were coordinated through a body called the "Directory," in which certain Italians were involved.[14] Moreover, in October 1929, August Košutić, the foreign policy expert of the

CPP, and Ante Pavelić traveled to Rome for consultations with Roberto Forges Davanzati and Paolo Cortese. They presented a combined CPP-*Ustaše* plan for the establishment of an independent Croatia.[15] Relations between the CPP and the *Ustaše* became strained in 1932, with an open break occurring in 1934/35, partly as a result of Maček's new policies vis-à-vis Italy and Belgrade. But Pavelić's and Maček's goals remained essentially identical. In fact, Maček's agents were actively negotiating with Mussolini as late as March 1939 with a view to establishing an independent Croatia under Italian protection.[16] When Pavelić came to power, Maček told his adherents to cooperate and then retired to Dugo Selo. Although he did not actually collaborate with the so-called Independent State of Croatia (NDH), his endorsement gave Pavelić what he needed—the support of a good 50 percent of CPP members.[17]

The identical viewpoints of Maček and the *Ustaše* can be illustrated by a comparison of their statements on the central question of Bosnia's relationship to the Serbian-Croatian rivalry and, thus, to the system as a polarized whole. Maček had this to say in 1936: "The Croatian Peasant party, as the political organization of the entire Croatian nation, considers the Bosnian Muslims the purest part of the Croatian nation, by origin, by history, and by dialect."[18] Ante Pavelić said much the same thing in July 1938: "It is not permissible to speak of Bosnia and Herzegovina as if they were countries in their own right or to distinguish the Muslims from the Croatian nation, because Bosnia is the heart of the Croatian state, and the Muslim tribes, part of the Croatian nation."[19] Accordingly, the Cvetković-Maček *Sporazum* (agreement) of August 26, 1939, divided Bosnia between Croatia and Serbia. Under the *Sporazum*, the *banovina* (province) of Croatia became internally autonomous, linked to the rest of the country only in finance and banking, foreign affairs, and joint legislation.[20] Maček's party "was not interested in the federalization of the remaining Yugoslav lands"[21]—a project that had its proponents in Montenegro—and sought only to obtain for Croatia the maximum possible benefit. Meanwhile, certain sectors in Zagreb, the Catholic Church, and extremist factions in the Croatian Peasant party were calling for the incorporation of all of Bosnia and Herzegovina into *banovina* Croatia. And Pavelić, in power, ceded Dalmatia to Italy, assuring himself a free hand in Bosnia.[22] With the intervention of Nazi Germany in 1941 and the accession of Pavelić to the head of the new Independent State of Croatia, the Croats brought the inherent fissiparous tendency of the system to fruition, and the fledgling state immediately undertook the systematic extermination of Serbs within its borders. The earlier attempt at Serbianization was now being answered by a brutal Croatianization campaign. More than 5 percent of the Yugoslav population died as a result of Serbian and Croatian reprisals. Pavelić and his *Ustaše* henchmen alone were responsible for the liquidation of some 350,000 Serbs.[23]

In the immediate postwar period, after the reconstitution of a unified Yugoslavia under Marshal Tito, the state authorities revived the centralist solution and resumed the attempt to forge a Yugoslav identity, albeit one that was intended to transcend mere Serbian ethnic identity. Belgrade attempted to "reduce the incompatibility between the blocs," as called for under Kaplan's rule 14.[24] The chief problems faced by the fledgling regime were the legacy of bitterness from the period of fratricidal warfare and the extreme concentration of wealth in the northern areas. To remedy the latter problem, the federal government initiated a program of economic redistribution that included the establishment of unprofitable factories in the less industrialized areas and the transfer of capital from north to south. Yet Croatia and Slovenia remained economically dominant in a country of 22 million inhabitants. Belgrade, as the capital, also has its share of industry. Montenegro, Macedonia, Bosnia-Herzegovina, southeast Serbia, and the autonomous province of Kosovo have remained relatively backward and underdeveloped. It was in the postwar period that rivalry ensued between the richer northern areas and the poorer southern areas for the direction of federal policy. The picture had become quite different from what it had been in the interwar years: the issues had changed (economics were of greater concern), and previously unacknowledged groups (such as Macedonians, Bosniaks, and the Albanians of Kosovo) were granted de jure recognition and, with it, some institutional instruments for interest articulation. Yet, despite these changes, the system remained bipolar, and Croatia and Serbia remained the major actors in the system. To employ a distinction drawn by Kaplan, there had been *equilibrium* change but not, as yet, *system* change.

The poorer republics complained of the discrepancies in income levels and distribution of industry. In 1963, for instance, the average per capita income in Slovenia was 95 percent above the national average, whereas the Macedonian average was 36 percent below the national average.[25] Worse yet, the gap between them had been growing rather than shrinking. Croatia and Slovenia were dominant in most industries, including tourism and manufactures of all kinds, and enjoyed a virtual monopoly on production of consumer goods and export items. The more prosperous republics expressed discontent at being shackled to the underdeveloped areas and insisted on wider autonomy. Protests were voiced that economic development in the north was hampered by connection with the south. A key point of dispute was the Special Fund for Crediting the Development of the Underdeveloped Republics and Provinces, whereby funds raised through general taxation were distributed to the less developed regions.

Balance-of-Power System

The fundamental principle of balance-of-power politics is that no single actor has sufficient power to dictate terms unilaterally to the other actors. In Stanley Hoffmann's words, a balance-of-power system is "a *system* of international politics in which the pattern of relations among the actors tends to curb the ambitions or the opportunities of the chief rivals and to preserve an approximate equilibrium of power among them."[26] And, as we shall see momentarily, equilibrium and equality are not interchangeable concepts.

It is often assumed that, when the balance of power is construed as a system, there must be at least five national actors: this, at least, is the argument made by Kaplan, Arthur Lee Burns, Patrick J. McGowan and Robert M. Rood, and Zinnes.[27] Charles R. Schleicher and Hoffmann consider it possible to have analogous behavior, and thus a balance-of-power system, with only two major powers present.[28] Richard E. Quandt appears willing to allow for the functioning of the system with four major actors; Hsi-sheng Chi describes balance-of-power politics in a Chinese warlord system that, for several years, contained only three essential actors; George Orwell's *1984* conjures a futuristic international system in which balance-of-power politics are played by just three actors; and Burns sees five as not only minimal but, in fact, the ideal number to ensure system stability.[29] To the extent that alliance behavior is considered an important aspect of the system, four would seem to be just barely adequate and probably highly unstable; the system would be most stable with five to seven essential actors.

These essential actors must have comparable power, but equality of power is relatively unimportant to the maintenance of the balance-of-power system, according to Gulick.[30] Talleyrand lent his authority to this viewpoint in his *Memoirs*: "an absolute equality of forces among all the states," he wrote, "aside from the fact that it can never exist, is not necessary to the political equilibrium, and would perhaps in some respects be harmful to it."[31] The essential characteristic of the system is that no single actor can impose its will on all other actors in the system. As Zinnes has pointed out, at least six configurations meet this requirement and are capable of ensuring the defense of the integrity and interests of each of the essential actors:

(1) no alliances, all states roughly equal in power
 $A = B = C = D = E$
(2) two alliances, roughly equal in overall power
 $A + B = C + D + E$
(3) two equal alliances, one nonaligned state
 $A + B = C + D, E$
(4) two unequal alliances, one nonaligned state holding the balance
 $A + B \neq C + D, E$
 $A + B + E > C + D$
 $A + B < C + D + E$
 [and $E < A + B$, $E < C + D$]
(5) no alliances, power of each state is less than the power of the remaining states combined
(6) one state is more powerful than any other individual state, but less powerful than the power of the remaining states combined.[32]

Thus, according to Zinnes, alliance flexibility is a possible but nonessential aspect of the system. Equality of the actors and the presence of a balancer are also nonessential (for example, systems 3 and 4 involve a nonaligned state that functions in the absence of a balancer).

Sir Eyre Crowe, England's permanent undersecretary for foreign affairs, was eager to claim the role of balancer for England and, thus, to win for his country exclusive credit for thwarting powers with hegemonic ambitions. Roger D. Masters, among others, has honored this claim and considered that the balancer was an essential ingredient in the balance-of-power system and that the role was monopolized by England.[33] Neither proposition is true. In the international politics of eighteenth- and nineteenth-century Europe, at least until the Franco-Prussian War, all of the major actors were "available": there were no "marriages made in heaven," not even the culturally reinforced Austro-German connection. After all, Austria and England had many interests in common, including the maintenance of the Ottoman empire, and Germany and England were entering the early stages of what would become a fierce naval race. Germany and Russia felt similarly close, whereas Austria and Russia were competing for influence, domination, and territorial acquisitions in the Balkans. Thus, every state in the system was a balancer, at least until the hardening of alliances in the early years of this century.

European politics did not assume a static configuration from the time of the Hundred Years War. On the contrary, the balance of power was played in different forms in different periods, though largely according to the same rules. In Zinnes's typology (above), sixteenth-century power relations fit the contours of configuration 3—two roughly equal alliances, with one nonaligned state—except that in this case we are dealing with *two* nonaligned states. The major confrontational states were Bourbon France and the Habsburg crown territories (Austria and Spain, briefly united under a single monarch). Initially, England, under Henry VIII, found itself more often supporting the Habsburgs against France, but, as Spain grew stronger, Elizabeth I realigned with France. At the same time, Venice operated as a balancer in the Mediterranean between Habsburg Austria and Bourbon France. There is nothing mysterious or sanctimonious about this: England and Venice simply feared to allow either empire to grow too powerful.

In the course of the eighteenth century, European interstate politics came closer to configuration 5—no permanent alliances, with the power of each state less than the power of the remaining states combined. No alliance was guaranteed to last longer than the duration of the war for which it was contracted, if it lasted even that long.[34] This system came to an end with the creation of the Napoleonic empire, which transformed the system into configuration 4. Napoleon's republicanism, transmogrified into imperialism, threatened stability because it challenged the legitimacy of the internal order under the *ancien régime*. The result was the coalescence of two blocs, with Austria and Russia holding the balance and floating from one side to the other.

The penetration of reformist ideas and the increasing influence of ideologies in politics had their effect, although it was not immediate. For the interim, Metternich was able to achieve a restoration of something resembling the status quo ante, that is, system 1 instead of system 5, with a concert mechanism imposed on it. The rise of England and Prussia, the simultaneous decay of the

Habsburg and Ottoman empires, and the continued decline of Spain and Portugal contributed to the polarization of politics that also owed much to the revolutions of 1848, the growing Austro-Russian acrimony (which arose from Austria's failure to repay a debt in 1856, as well as from Austro-Russian rivalry in the Balkans), and the Franco-Prussian War. This polarization was incompatible with either system 5 or 1 and hence completed the breakdown begun by Napoleon. The resulting system corresponded to configuration 2—two alliances roughly equal in power. Superficially, this looks like a bipolar system, but the key difference (and that which defines the balance of power, Zinnes notwithstanding) is the persistence of a flexibility that defies even alliances. The defection of Germany's treaty allies, Italy and Romania, in World War I is consistent with this interpretation of balance-of-power theory; the defection would be anomalous in a tight or loose bipolar system. Finally, the pivotal role played by the U.S. in World War I suggests that it is possible to view the international system of 1914–17 as an example of Zinnes's configuration 4, with the U.S. holding the balance in the role of nonaligned state (E).

Essential to this overview is the concept that the particular configuration can change without altering the basic contours of the system. As long as alliances do not freeze, the most important *behavioral* variable of the system is present. (Obviously any precise definition of freezing will have an arbitrary element.) System flexibility can, however, be assured in ways other than alliance switching. (These alternatives should probably be seen as options rather than potential substitutes for alliance switching.) The most important such method is the overlapping of alliances. Zinnes conjures the following alliance configurations in a five-state universe to suggest the problem of cross-pressures in situations of multiple memberships:

(1) ABC / DE
(2) ABC / BCD / CDE / DEA
(3) AB / AC / AD / AE
(4) ABCDE (collective security).[35]

"In 1833," Zinnes writes, "Austria, Prussia, and Russia each belonged to two alliances," a pattern that was common in balance-of-power Europe. In fact, she continues, "the one-alliance-per-nation assumption is only valid for 22 of the 130 years [discussed by Singer and Small in an earlier article in the *Journal of Peace Research*]: from 1824 to 1832, 1849, 1860 to 1862, 1865, 1871 to 1876, [and] 1879 to 1880."[36]

Such a system's stability thus rests on three major factors: the existence of five or more essential actors, their mutual acceptability in a context of flexible and impermanent alignments, and the tendency for states to react with fear to the undue self-aggrandizement of one of their number. Guaranteed by those factors, the system manifests itself in different configurations. The inexorable conclusion is that the system must be amenable to description in terms of behavioral constants. This is exactly what Kaplan set out to do.

Kaplan assumes a distinction between stability and equilibrium and starts from the premise that a system will remain in equilibrium until shaken by a major disturbance.[37] In Kaplan's terminology, the Napoleonic wars resulted in equilibrium change, whereas the combination of World Wars I and II brought system change. The basic behavioral constants or "essential rules" (as Kaplan prefers to call them) change only in the latter instance. In Kaplan's version of the balance-of-power system, there is *no* universal or supranational actor capable of marshaling authoritative legitimacy (the U.N. does so only occasionally), winning elite consensus (as did Metternich's Concert of Europe), or effectively utilizing armed force (for example, the U.N. in Korea). Any national actor that strives to transform itself into a supranational actor by attempting to launch an incipient world state (for example, Napoleon I or Maximilian I [Habsburg]) is opposed by those capable of resistance.

The six behavioral constants that Kaplan developed are well known but deserve recapitulation here. According to Kaplan, each of the five or six essential actors must

(1) act to increase capabilities but negotiate rather than fight;
(2) fight rather than pass up an opportunity to increase capabilities;
(3) stop fighting rather than eliminate an essential national actor;
(4) act to oppose any coalition or single actor which tends to assume a position of predominance with respect to the rest of the system;
(5) act to constrain actors who subscribe to supranational organizing principles;
(6) permit defeated or constrained essential national actors to reenter the system as acceptable role partners or act to bring some previously inessential actor within the essential actor classification; treat all essential actors as acceptable role partners.[38]

Winfried Franke suggested the addition of a seventh behavioral constant when dealing with regional subsystems, such as the Italian city-state system of the fourteenth and fifteenth centuries. In his view, an essential actor in such a system must also

(7) oppose any potentially permanent or disruptive invasion of the subsystem by environmental actors and discourage alliances between subsystem actors and environmental actors that may lead to such an invasion.[39]

In the Peloponnesian system, for example, Persia represented an outside environmental actor, alliance with which threatened to catalyze (and, in fact, did produce) ultimate invasion. The Ottoman empire is a somewhat more recent example of an environmental actor proscribed from active alliance by the members of the (European) international system.

The adapted model I shall use consists of discrete behavioral constants for the component republics and autonomous provinces of Yugoslavia (the essential actors) and for the central government (the universal actor). Component republics will

(1) act to increase capabilities, specifically by seeking to ensure the adoption of federal policies favorable to themselves, and negotiate rather than provoke a crisis;
(2) provoke a crisis rather than forego an opportunity to increase capabilities;
(3) act to oppose any coalition of republics or provinces or any single republic that tends to assume a position of predominance with respect to the rest of the system;
(4) resist any republic seeking to establish its titular nationality as the ascendant nationality to which other groups are to be assimilated and act to constrain any republic seeking the abolition of the federal system;
(5) treat all republics or provinces as acceptable coalition partners, abandon partners whose ambitions become threatening to their interests or to the maintenance of the system and cooperate, where interest dictates, with republics that may have held antagonistic positions on earlier issues;
(6) oppose any potentially permanent or disruptive invasion of the subsystem by any external power or combination of external powers and discourage tacit understandings, cooperative arrangements, and contacts of any kind between republics (or autonomous provinces) and external powers that might lead to such an invasion.

Note that behavioral constants 1 through 5 correspond to Kaplan's constants 1, 2, 4, 5, and 6, and my constant 6 corresponds to Franke's 7. The option of eliminating a fellow republic was not open to the republics until Serbia's Slobodan Milošević changed the rules of the game in 1990–91 and went to war against Croatia. Serbia's former power to abolish its autonomous provinces was abrogated by Tito, who denied Serbia the power to change the borders of the two autonomous provinces lying within its juridical frontiers without their consent. Therefore, there is no equivalent for Kaplan's behavioral constant 3.

According to my adapted system, the Belgrade regime will

(1) retain the ultimate authority on policy questions of systemwide importance, including but not restricted to matters of foreign policy and defense;
(2) work to reduce the power disparities among the republics;
(3) resolve any dispute between republics that threatens to upset the stability of the system.

There can be no dispute that the presence of a universal actor (the central government) will make a difference in the operation of the system. Yet the Metternichean concert affected the operation of Europe's balance-of-power system in an analogous fashion, and the Concert of Europe was similar in intent, if less effective than the interrepublican structures of decision making in Yugoslavia. As I suggested earlier, I am inclined to view the so-called concert system not as a system in its own right but as a mechanism that can be superimposed on any other system, be it the balance-of-power system of early nineteenth-century Europe or a bipolar system of some other age. This view is compatible with Gulick's approach, although there is some suggestion that Gulick wants to equate the balance-of-power system and the concert mechanism. This interpretation would make the concert mechanism an integral and essential part of the system—a claim that I must reject for reasons already given.

The concert mechanism did provide the occasion for the great powers to work out solutions to their common problems on the principle of unanimity, but it stopped short of anything that could impugn the ultimate sovereignty of its members. The concert's very existence enshrined the distinction between great powers, which were not to be humiliated, and lesser powers, which were expendable. In the Yugoslav framework one might note a three-tier hierarchy of ethnic groups: (1) titular nationalities of the republics (Serbs, Croats, Slovenes, Macedonians, and Montenegrins), (2) autonomous-province nationalities (Hungarians and Albanians), and (3) ethnic minorities lacking any politically recognized territorial unit, with Muslims and Yugoslavs as special cases. The Yugoslav regime has not condoned secession (the ultimate exercise of national sovereignty), though the constitution nominally permits it, but the regime has gone a long way toward satisfying ethnic demands. The various ethnic minorities of Yugoslavia have for some time enjoyed the opportunity to obtain education in their own languages, and students in minority-language schools are also required to study the language (not necessarily Serbo-Croatian) of the republic in which they reside.

For the sake of convenience, we may restate the behavioral constants in the form of hypotheses.

Hypothesis 1: The republics and autonomous provinces will seek to maximize their individual gains even at the expense of Yugoslavia as a whole.

Hypothesis 2: The republics and autonomous provinces will negotiate when possible but provoke a crisis when negotiations deadlock on a matter of fundamental importance. The republics, except Serbia, may threaten to secede.

Hypothesis 3: The republics and autonomous provinces will oppose any encroachment on their autonomy, resist ethnic assimilation as a threat to their raison d'être, and unite in coalitions to oppose any republic or coalition of republics and provinces that threatens to establish a hegemonic hold on the system.

Hypothesis 4: The republics and autonomous provinces will treat all actors in the system as acceptable coalition partners and shift alignment when interest dictates.

Hypothesis 5: The republics and autonomous provinces will oppose the conclusion of any pact between a member of the system (e.g., Serbia) and an external power (e.g., the U.S.S.R.) that threatens to result in foreign occupation or in the forcible reconstitution of the system.

Hypothesis 6: The federal government will work to reduce the disparities in power and wealth among the other actors.

Hypothesis 7: The federal government will retain ultimate authority in questions of systemwide importance and intervene to resolve interrepublican disputes that threaten to upset the system.

It is readily apparent that hypothesis 1 (H1) derives from the first behavioral constant (BC1) for republics, H2 from BC1 and BC2 for republics, H3 from BC3 and BC4 for republics, H4 from BC5 for republics, H5 from BC6 for republics, H6 from BC2 for the Belgrade regime, and H7 from BC1 and BC3 for the Belgrade regime.

Two more hypotheses compatible with the model, though not, strictly speaking, derived from it, may be included here:

Hypothesis 8: The federal government will strive to preserve cultural neutrality and eschew identification with any of the component ethnic groups or their republics (e.g., with the Serbs).

Hypothesis 9: In a system electrified by exclusivist nationalisms, the only alternative to devolution is civil strife. Hence, social mobilization will increase pressures for decentralization and local autonomy or, alternatively, for conflict.

Socialist Yugoslavia evolved a particular system of conflict regulation and social integration through devolution, seeking to assure communal loyalty through the abandonment of nation building and the provision of far-reaching autonomy to the federal units. Yugoslavia's path to balance-of-power politics lay in the rise of political consciousness in federal units other than Serbia and Croatia and in the massive devolution of power to the republics during the series of crises in the late 1960s, which enabled republics other than Serbia and Croatia to wield autonomous power in the political arena. The economic reforms of 1963–65 began the devolutionary process, which was largely completed by the constitutional amendments of 1967–71.

In the early years of the 1960s, Serbia's hope was to establish itself as the leader of a bloc of underdeveloped republics within Yugoslavia. Such a bloc would isolate Slovenia and Croatia and permit the pursuit of a policy of effective economic aid to the underdeveloped regions, concentration of industries in Serbia, centralization of the political system, and reassertion of Serbian hegemony within a federal context. Since the autonomous provinces had, at that time, little authorized or institutionalized political power and since Montenegro was culturally close to Serbia, Serbian party bosses predicted a favorable alignment (table 1) and assumed that policy debates could be kept at the economic level.

Table 1. *Predicted Alignment of Yugoslav Federal Units on Reform Issue, 1963*

Proreform	*Antireform*
Croatia	Serbia
Slovenia	Kosovo
	Vojvodina
	Montenegro
	Bosnia-Herzegovina
	Macedonia

The expected alignment on economic grounds, however, did not materialize. Slovenian and Croatian liberals were able to exploit fears of Greater Serbian chauvinism and woo southern liberals, who were partial to devolution and greater reliance on market mechanisms in the economy. Thus, although economic interest had traditionally linked the Macedonians to Serbia's centralist program, at least in the postwar period, the Macedonians were, for primarily political reasons, drawn to Croatia's side. Rusinow recounts that

> by 1964 younger Macedonian leaders like Krsto Crvenkovski and Kiro Gligorov—the former a rising star not hitherto counted as a liberal and the latter already with a reputation as a bright and liberal economic specialist in the Federal Government—were as outspokenly in favour of *deetatizacija* as any Slovene or Croat. Even the Albanians of the Kosmet were audibly restive under a Serbian and UDBa domination which had brought them few economic benefits.[40]

The Croats and Slovenes transformed economic issues—decentralization of economic decision making, dismantling of central planning, and curtailment of aid to unprofitable enterprises in the south—into political issues—opposition to Serbian hegemony and support of "liberalization." The result was that Macedonia and Kosovo both took positions antithetical to their economic interests (producing the alignment shown in table 2). Vojvodina's position on the reforms was less clearly defined in the early stages, though by the later 1960s, Vojvodina was unmistakably supporting Croatian economic proposals. Outgunned by the so-called liberal bloc, the Serbs had no choice but to acquiesce in far-reaching reforms.

Although the first crisis (1963–65) had been precipitated as much by the Slovenes as by the Croats, the Croatian Communist party leadership took the lead in bringing on a second crisis in 1967. With their political motives then predominant, Croatian leaders concentrated on further decentralization of the party. Backed by the Slovenes and the Macedonians, the Croats were able to keep momentum on their side. The Ninth Party Congress registered the victory of the Croatian-led national-liberal coalition by devolving further power to the republican parties. Members of the LCY presidium were henceforth to be selected by the republican party congresses rather than hand-picked by Bel-

Table 2. *Actual Alignment of Yugoslav Federal Units in Reform Crisis, 1963–65*

Proreform	*Antireform*
Croatia	Serbia
Slovenia	Montenegro
Macedonia	
Bosnia-Herzegovina	
Kosovo	
Vojvodina	

grade, and the republican parties were also extended the right to draw up their own party statutes.

The national-liberal coalition was based on premises of common interest and mutual trust. These evaporated after 1969, as the Croatian party leadership escalated its demands and sought far-reaching reforms that went beyond the desires of its coalition partners.[41] Having lent Croatia support in two previous confrontations with Serbia, Vojvodina and, later, Slovenia and Macedonia backed away from their erstwhile Croatian ally. Miko Tripalo, secretary of the Croatian League of Communists, and Savka Dabčević-Kučar, president of the Croatian central committee, allowed their supporters to push them further to the political right and espoused ever more radical nationalist positions. They were unable to dissociate themselves from their more radical supporters, who demanded Croatia's secession and even aggrandizement of Croatian territory at the expense of other republics. Defusing the crisis entailed the removal of Tripalo and Dabčević-Kučar and the bridling of Croatia's radical students.

The balance-of-power model predicts that an actor who goes too far and whose ambitions threaten the territorial integrity or economic interests of the other members of the system will be isolated and brought to heel. The Croatian crisis of 1971 confirms this principle. Moreover, in this crisis, as in the previous two crises cited, the federal units displayed autonomy, flexibility, and the power to affect federal policy.

Much later, in 1987–89, the Serbian party—by then under the leadership of the avowedly nationalist Slobodan Milošević—again set itself on a course of alliance-building and again hoped to isolate Slovenia and Croatia. Milošević's ultimate goal was to reverse thirty years of steady devolution and to heavily reconcentrate power in Belgrade. But, as in the early 1960s, Serbia's course alienated Macedonia and Bosnia as well, and even the Kosovar party apparatus, which Milošević tried to pack with loyal supporters, proved impossible to control. Milošević cut through the Gordian Knot by arresting the members of Kosovo's provincial Assembly and by reshuffling the Kosovar leadership until he obtained the docility he wanted. Milošević forged an alliance with the Serb-dominated officer corps of the JNA, armed Serbian civilian militias with stolen army weaponry, and mobilized both the JNA and the militias in a war against Croatia in summer 1991. In so doing, Milošević shattered the balance-of-power system and set Serbia on a clear quest for complete hegemony.

2

Nationalism, Regionalism, and the Internal Balance of Power

Aggregations are wholes, yet not wholes—brought together, yet carried asunder; in accord, yet not in accord; [in] all, one; [in] one, all.

HERACLITUS

Yugoslavia from the devolutions of the early 1960s until 1989 could be seen as a nine-actor balance-of-power system that consisted of a federal actor (the federal government or, alternatively, the LCY), six socialist republics (Bosnia-Herzegovina, Croatia, Macedonia, Montenegro, Serbia, and Slovenia), and two socialist autonomous provinces (Kosovo and Vojvodina) that, while within the socialist republic of Serbia, were, in fact, autonomous actors. Within this universe, regional demands were aggregated along ethnic lines and articulated by republican and provincial authorities.

In a multiethnic state, diverse social problems also manifest themselves as interethnic problems. The involvement of ethnicity and the possibility for the mobilization of group loyalty and group resources transmogrify political processes. Social antagonisms are expressed differently in a multiethnic state from the way in which they are expressed in an ethnically homogeneous or binational state. Politics in a multiethnic state is essentially different from politics in a nation-state. Multiethnicity becomes the justification for introducing a federal system in which ethnic and republic boundaries coincide. Middle-level interest groups tend to follow the lead of their republican leaders during times of intercommunal crisis, since intercommunal stability is, to a large extent, hinged on the viability of the federal system as a mechanism of conflict regulation and crisis management.

Ethnically, Yugoslavia is one of the most heterogeneous polities in the world (see table 3). The largest group, the Serbs, makes up less than 40 percent of the population, and the second largest group, the Croats, represents roughly 20 percent of the total population. Although the three largest groups share a common language (known, alternatively, as Serbo-Croatian or Croato-Serbian), roughly one-fifth of all Yugoslavs are not native speakers of Serbo-Croatian, and many never learn the language. (This is especially true in the rural areas of the non-Serbo-Croatian-speaking federal units.) Yugoslavia also contains pockets of national minorities from all of its neighbors, although the numbers of Austrians and Greeks are minuscule.

Table 3. *Population of Yugoslavia by Ethnic Group, 1981*

	Number	*Percent*
Serbs	8,136,578	36.3
Croats	4,428,135	19.7
Muslims	2,000,034	8.9
Slovenes	1,753,605	7.8
Albanians	1,731,252	7.7
Macedonians	1,341,420	6.0
"Yugoslavs"	1,216,463	5.4
Montenegrins	577,298	2.6
Hungarians	426,865	1.9
Gypsies	148,604	0.7
Turks	101,328	0.5
Slovaks	80,300	0.4
Romanians	54,721	0.2
Bulgarians	36,642	0.2
Vlahs	32,071	0.1
Ruthenes	23,320	0.1
Czechs	19,609	0.1
Italians	15,116	0.1
Ukrainians	12,809	0.1
Undeclared	46,716	0.2
TOTAL (including other categories not listed above)	22,418,331	

Source: *Statistički kalendar Jugoslavije 1982* (Belgrade: Savenzni zavod za statistiku, February 1982), 28:37.

Yugoslavia had some 22,418,331 inhabitants as of March 31, 1981, with Serbia, Croatia, and Bosnia-Herzegovina the most populous units. Although Bosnia and Vojvodina are both highly heterogeneous, their heterogeneity tends, with the exception of the largest towns, to be *pluralist*—that is, the two federal units are ethnically mixed, but most of their villages and smaller towns are ethnically homogeneous. In all of the other federal units, the titular nationality constitutes at least two-thirds of the population (in four of these, the titular nationality accounts for at least 75 percent of the population). For this reason, republican policy continues to be identified (in every federal unit except, arguably, Bosnia) with the interests of the principal ethnic group. This did not apply to Kosovo until the 1970s, but after the riots in 1968 and 1969, positions of authority in Kosovo were steadily relinquished by Serbs and Montenegrins and turned over to Albanians. As table 4 makes clear, all the federal units, except for Slovenia and Serbia, are relatively heterogeneous. In Bosnia, Vojvodina, and Macedonia no ethnic group composes more than two-thirds of the population. In Croatia, moreover, the Serbian minority (11.6 per cent in 1981) played a pivotal role in exacerbating interethnic tensions in 1970–71.

Table 4. *Population of Yugoslavia by Republic, 1981*

	Number of inhabitants in thousands	*Percentage of largest nationality*
YUGOSLAVIA	22,418	—
Bosnia-Herzegovina	4,128	39.5[a]
Croatia	4,582	75.4
Macedonia	1,921	66.7
Montenegro	585	68.2
Serbia	5,673	85.7
Slovenia	1,887	90.1
Kosovo	1,595	76.9[b]
Vojvodina	2,029	54.6[c]

a = Muslims
b = Albanians
c = Serbs

Sources: *Statistički kalendar Jugoslavije 1982* (Belgrade: Savenzni zavod za statistiku, February 1982), 28:33; and author's calculations from *NIN*, no. 1626, February 28, 1982, pp. 19–20.

Ethnicity and Ethnocentrism

Today *ethnicity* is usually understood in two senses—as the objective characteristics that distinguish and define a group of people (common language, consciousness of being a group, sense of territorial homeland, and, sometimes, common religion) and also as the subjective response to the fact of collective identity, that is, as the pure phenomenon of group consciousness. Collective identity itself signifies the formation of an interest group in which the preservation of group characteristics and the safeguarding of territorial lines become invested with emotive value.

Ethnicity need not be accompanied by ethnocentrism. It is the presence of a perceived cultural threat—intensified by ethnic mixing—that gives rise to ethnocentrism. *Ethnocentrism* may be defined here as an attitudinal orientation that inclines one to condemn the culture, language, and customs of another ethnic group as inferior and "wrong." Ethnocentrism is reinforced by stereotypes both of one's own group and of other groups.

Every society has a degree of ethnocentrism, but the intensity may vary widely among groups within a single society. Religion plays an important role in nurturing ethnocentrism, and certain religious groups, such as Muslims, have shown a marked predisposition toward ethnocentrism. The dramatically lower incidence of intermarriage between members of Yugoslavia's Muslim community and members of other ethnoreligious communities may indicate a greater ethnocentrism rating for that community.[1]

Peter Klinar, in a 1971 study, found that Yugoslavia's national groups display a strong proclivity to engage in ethnic stereotyping. The Croatian self-image is, of course, a flattering one and emphasizes the Croats' love of justice, the peace-loving nature of the Croatian nation, its thousand-year-old culture, and Croatia's "Westernness." The Serbian self-image focuses on the heroic character of the Serbs and paints the Serbian nation as the guardian of Yugoslavia. The Croats and Serbs do not share such high regard for each other, however. The Croats tend to view the Serbs as expansionistic and arrogant, and the Serbs portray the Croats as passive, timid to the point of cowardice, and inclined to collaborate with (foreign) subversive elements. The Slovenes' self-image contains some feelings of superiority (love of order, efficiency at work, and cleanliness) and of inferiority (principally in connection with their lack of a historical tradition of independent statehood). The Slovenes also have a tendency to look down on other Yugoslavs for their inefficiency and allegedly irrational use of resources. The Slovenes themselves are viewed by other Yugoslavs as unsociable, unfriendly, "Germans."[2]

The Yugoslavs realized, even before Milošević, that ethnocentrism remained a problem for them. Stipe Šuvar, criticizing ethnocentrism among Croats, noted that during 1976–77, Croatian theaters did not present a single work written by a dramatist from another republic, and only one book was translated into Croatian from the language of another Yugoslav nationality.[3] Ethnocentrism is deeply ingrained and is reflected in a panoply of variables. For instance, there is a strong tendency for marriages to involve members of the same ethnic or language group (for example, Serbs often marry Croats). Those most likely to intermarry with members of other ethnic groups are members of the smaller minorities (particularly Italians, Ruthenes, and Bulgarians).[4] Ethnocentrism may also lead a group to change its customs and behavior, accentuating or even creating differences to distinguish itself from a group with which it has confrontations. Šuvar wrote in 1978 that "a number of ignorant Serbs in Croatia have [recently] started to speak ekavian [spoken by the Serbs in Serbia], even though their mothers had taught them ijekavian," the other principal variant of Serbo-Croatian.[5]

Yugoslavia's brief flirtation with multicandidate elections confirmed the prominence of ethnocentrism in political choice. In local elections held in Derventa during July and August of 1968, for instance, voters overwhelmingly cast their ballots along ethnic lines—Serbs supporting Serbs, Croats voting for Croats, and Muslims for Muslims. As might be expected, however, very few (about 3 percent), when asked about their voting patterns, would admit that ethnicity had anything to do with their choices.[6]

Nationalism

Early theorists of modernization, especially Marxists, assumed that nationalism was obsolescent and moribund. The advancing integration of world culture was expected to result in an erosion of ethnic consciousness, and nationalism as a divisive force was often rated as secondary in importance to class conflicts and the urban/rural cleavage. But ethnicity, not ideology or class, appears to provide the ultimate source of political identity in intergroup conflict.

Yugoslavia's Marxists have gradually accepted the permanence of the ethnic factor and now concede that, far from witnessing the unraveling of national consciousness, the contemporary period has seen the deepening of ethnic loyalties and a retrenchment among nationality groups.[7] Some have gone even further, admitting that neither the content nor the role of a nation or nationality group is at all changed by socialist revolution.[8]

Nationalism can assume many forms within a multiethnic state. It may foster separatism, stimulate unitarism, provide a transregional focus of loyalty, or drive the component ethnic groups into civil strife. During the late eighteenth and nineteeth centuries, the nationalist awakening spread to all groups in the Habsburg empire except the Ruthenes, yet each group reacted in a different fashion. The Pan-Germans dreamt of union with the rest of the German nation. The Italians worked actively for secession. The Czechs strove for federalist concessions and attempted to move all of Austria in a federalist direction. The Poles enjoyed their autonomy, oppressed the Ruthenes, and cautiously waited, fearful that a miscalculation would undo the privileges they enjoyed and catapult them into the culturally and politically depressed condition of the Russian and Prussian Poles. The Croats worked calmly for autonomy. The Magyars, for their part, were bent on the Magyarization of their subjects and the revival of the Kingdom of St. Stephen. Nationalism clearly is not a constant that can be plugged into any equation with predictable effects. On the contrary, it is a variable whose influence may be critical at some times and under certain circumstances, and only marginally significant in other times and conditions.

Following E. K. Francis, *nationalism* will be understood here as collective affectivity "extolling the nation as a supreme value and representing it as a dominant principle of societal organization,"[9] that is, as politicized ethnicity. Obviously, nationalism is potentially threatening to a multinational state. Hence, elites in multinational states have often tried to create transnational bases for collective consciousness. Soviet leaders were long fond of speaking of the "Soviet" people. The principle of *Kaisertreue* served a similar function in the Habsburg empire. In postwar Europe it was hoped that institutional cooperation would promote European unity, but it was also apprehended that nationalism was a divisive element that had to be overcome if support for a European state was to burgeon. Similarly, in Yugoslavia the Communist party originally hoped to erase all ethnic attachments, not only to the groups as they are currently defined—Serbs, Croats, Slovenes, and so forth—but also to the South Slav conglomerate.

But Serbia easily relapsed into the role of "big brother" in postwar Yugoslavia. Despite Stipe Šuvar's assurance that "the Serbian people . . . has outgrown nationalism and is characterized by general internationalism,"[10] non-Serbs felt threatened, not only because of memories of the Great Serbianism of the interwar period but also because assimilation of any kind, whether to a Serbian or to a Yugoslav model, was abhorrent both to culture-conscious elements and to regional politicians who had a stake in federalism. Yet the Serbs have felt comfortable in their self-appointed role. That Serbian chauvinism lives is not only readily verifiable, but was also admitted by politicians in the Serbian League of Communists (LC). Thus, Vladimir Jovičić, a member of the executive committee of the central committee of the Serbian LC, told the weekly news magazine *NIN* in 1978 that Serbian chauvinism, existing "beyond rationality," remained a serious problem.[11] A high proportion of the lower- and middle-ranking civil servants in the federal government were, naturally, drawn from the Serbian community in the area surrounding Belgrade. Yet, whatever the reasons, the proliferation of Serbs in the federal government added to the wariness of a non-Serb population that has learned to identify the Belgrade regime with the interests of the Serbian nation. Indeed, it was in the hope of breaking this identification that the proposal was entertained, in the immediate postwar years, to move the federal capital to Sarajevo. The dismissal of Aleksandar Ranković from his post as chief of security in July 1966 and the subsequent purge of the secret police represented a decisive dissociation of the federal government from Serbian interests, and the crisis was generally viewed as a defeat for the Serbs. Later, in the wake of the Croatian crisis of 1971, Tito purged not only the Croatian party but also the Serbian party: such high-ranking Serbian liberals as Marko Nikezić and Latinka Perović were among the heavy casualties suffered by the Serbian party at that time.

Two questions may be raised, then, about the function of nationalism in Yugoslavia: (1) Was nationalism perceived as a problem by the LCY? and (2) Was nationalism the guiding impulse in republican policies, economic or otherwise? The most radical interpretation would answer both questions in the affirmative and conclude, as Milovan Djilas did in 1974, that Yugoslavia might not survive long beyond 2024.[12] In the most extreme view, nationalism is considered so intense and so rampant in Yugoslavia that the unity of the state is preserved only by authoritarian means and Yugoslavia is believed to be threatened by "the eventual anarchy of unstructured conflict as a result of primordial distrust."[13]

Perhaps no one will dispute the importance of nationalism on the regime's agenda. Public life regularly reverberates with its pulses. In the summer of 1978 a wave of Croatian nationalism forced a number of concessions in the selection of plays for the Split Summer Festival, for instance. *Slobodna Dalmacija* singled out Šoljan's play, "A Romance about Three Loves," as a well-known but mediocre piece of nationalist drama. Evidently, attempts were also made to include plays by completely unknown authors in the program, simply because they were nationalistic.[14] In the early 1980s, the regime made clear its fear of nationalistic manifestations and its determination not to let matters get out of hand. The LCY took regional nationalism most seriously. In February 1975, for instance, fifteen Croats were sentenced to terms of up to twelve years in jail for having formed a terrorist organization designed to bring about the secession of Croatia from Yugoslavia.[15] Albanian nationalists were also rounded up and jailed in the course of 1975 and again in 1979, and in December 1975 Croatian separatist Miljenko Hrkac was sentenced to death for having planted a bomb in a Belgrade theater in July 1968.[16] It could be argued that in these cases it was the violence employed or the advocacy of secession, rather than nationalism, that provoked sharp government reaction. Yet, in other instances, the LCY displayed a hostility to expressions of nationalism that stopped short of these extremes. In 1974, for instance, the semiofficial newspaper *Oslobodjenje* warned that Muslim nationalism was neither naive nor harmless and attacked the importance accorded Islam.[17] Again, in February 1982, a Bosnian Muslim received a two-year prison sentence for having publicly claimed that there was ethnic discrimination in Bosnia and Kosovo.[18] Nor have the Serbs been immune from antinationalist thrusts. On December 5, 1977, for instance, the LCY weekly, *Komunist*, upbraided the prominent Serbian author, Dobrica Ćosić, for insisting that the Serbs were being exploited and denigrated by the other Yugoslav nationalities and for making other inflammatory nationalistic statements.[19]

Nationalism is a very real phenomenon in Yugoslavia and animates much of social life. Tensions have reached the boiling point in nearly every republic in recent years. Typically, sporting events provide a ready spark for outbursts of ethnic hatred, and, according to *NIN*, Serb-Croat competitions such as basketball games and soccer matches are still frequently marred by outbursts of ethnic slurs and name calling. In Split, after one such sports match, young Croats pushed several cars bearing Belgrade license plates into the sea.[20] Even the old Serbian military and patriotic songs have resurfaced—beginning in 1965—although they have been banned since 1945. Surprisingly, as late as March 1966, Vladimir Bakarić, then president of the League of Communists of Croatia, seemed uncertain as to how important nationalism was and, at one point in the course of a long interview, blithely dismissed the importance of nationalism. "The 'national question,' " he told *Borba*, "plays a very small role in the ordinary world. The youth are not very interested. And I think it can be said that nationalism, as a mass phenomenon, does not exist, and that it appears in the first place among the bureaucrats, [and] among the intelligentsia in our elites."[21] A few years later, however, a disabused Bakarić confessed that under socialism Yugoslavia had witnessed a reanimation of ethnic consciousness and ethnonationalism.[22]

By the late 1960s, nationalism had once again become the central question in Yugoslav politics, and it remains of fundamental importance today. I had a chance to see this for myself while visiting Yugoslavia for the first time in August and September of 1978. I recall in particular one conversation that took place when I was visiting the island of Pag, off the Dalmatian coast. A middle-aged Croat heatedly insisted that Serbian and Croatian were "two completely different languages" and that "there is no such thing as Serbo-Croatian." The idea that a self-respecting Croat should admit to having something as basic as language in common with the Serbs was a complete anathema to him.

However vital nationalism may be, and however important in molding people's attitudes, whether it is the guiding impulse in the formulation of the republics' policies or plays only a pivotal role in setting their context is an entirely different question. Certainly the feeling of relative deprivation had become strong among many Croats, including Croatian leaders and intellectuals, by 1971; moreover, ethnic prejudice impeded not only interrepublican migration but also interregional circulation of investment capital—hurting resource-rich, capital-poor regions in the south.[23] This has been a serious problem since, as William Zimmerman has noted, "some parts of Yugoslavia—Kosovo and Montenegro in particular—are barely integrated into [the] Yugoslav market."[24]

In multinational states, not only interregional rivalry but also "regional opposition against centralized political power tends to be expressed and mobilized in ethnic terms."[25] Regional leaders in Yugoslavia have frequently adopted this tactic, even though economic and ethnic interests are not always equally well served by the same solutions. Regional elites deliberately play the role of national (i.e., ethnic) leaders and present issues in ethnic terms: Croatian leaders have done this vis-à-vis the Serbs, Kosovar-Albanian leaders vis-à-vis the Serbs, Macedonian party leaders vis-à-vis the Serbs, and Serbian leaders vis-à-vis almost everyone else. But Yugoslav politics is not reducible to Serb versus non-Serb, as we shall see in the course of this study. The Serbs, for instance, share many common interests with the Montenegrins as well as with the Macedonians, and they have repeatedly courted the Bosnian party as a natural ally. Nor would it be accurate to leave the impression that non-Serbs constitute a "camp." Croats, for instance, became (at one time) increasingly worried about the steady Slovene infiltration of the northwest corner of Croatia's Istrian peninsula, along the border with Slovenia. This was, at least in part, an economic issue, but the apprehension was ethnic in source and was voiced in ethnic terms.

Thus, Yugoslavia's federal system, like the international state system, fixed boundaries, oriented the communication system, provided the pattern for economic life, restricted and channeled population movement, and set the parameters for political life and political conflict. The importance of the institutional framework must not be underestimated, since it can both reinforce and muffle inherent lines of conflict.

In this multipolar context there will be instances in which the nature of the issues will be unintelligible except in the light of nationalism. But, in this connection, it is important to remember that cultural and communications elites may have a vested interest in fueling cultural nationalism. Djilas himself denied that national feeling was the basis for interrepublican rivalry; rather, he felt that the elites manipulated national feelings to maximize their power. Yet five of the six republics (Serbia, Croatia, Slovenia, Macedonia, and Montenegro) were created around their regional ethnic majorities, and the federal system itself was a creature of the multinational configuration of Yugoslavia. Thus, whether primary or secondary, ethnicity is wedded to regionalism in Yugoslavia.

Cleavage in a Multiethnic State

The contours of politics are often defined or molded by lines of cleavage that lay the basis or set the framework for conflict behavior and accommodation. Cleavage may be economic, cultural, religious, linguistic, racial, or regional. It may be appropriate here to register an important caveat. Kaplan has warned that no pattern of international politics is permanent. Comparative power levels fluctuate, cultural affinities lose or gain importance, and ethnic conflict, which may be the crucial factor at one point, may be mere window dressing at another point. Even "the definition of groups is in constant flux."[26] Thus, for instance, the Macedonian nationality, which never enjoyed recognition under the inter-war government and did not enjoy Communist party recognition until November 1942, obtained republican status at the end of World War II and has been the object of serious courting by a Bulgarophobic Belgrade. Again, the Muslims, once regarded strictly as a religious group by the regime, later came into their own as a major Yugoslav nationality group.

In 1971, R. V. Burks argued that Yugoslavia was characterized by the polarization of northern provinces, which enjoyed economies comparable to Austria, and southern provinces, whose economies were similar to those of Albania or southern Italy. Burks associated the deep conflict of regional interests with differences in the levels and rates of development, among other things, and defined the north as Slovenia, Croatia-Slavonia, Vojvodina, and Belgrade, and the south as Dalmatia, Bosnia-Herzegovina, Serbia proper, Montenegro, Kosovo, Macedonia, and Croatia south of the Sava River.[27] After the war, however, industrial production in Montenegro grew at a rate that far eclipsed growth rates in other republics. Montenegro has modern airports at Titograd and Tivat; Titograd has now been connected by railway both with Nikšić and with Bar. The economy of Dalmatia, moreover, was so completely transformed in the 1970s, mostly as a result of the construction of the Adriatic highway and the development of the tourist industry there, that it came to be considered part of the developed north.[28] Yet, despite these changes, it can be argued that the basic problem in Yugoslavia remained the same, namely, how does a developed industrial region coexist in the same polity with an underdeveloped region that desires further industrialization? The dividing line between rich and poor still corresponds almost exactly to the old military frontier that once divided the Habsburg and Ottoman empires.

Politically, the so-called northerners have tended to be liberal, partial to decentralization, and opposed to programs that have been geared to the redistribution of resources, whereas the southerners have tended to be conservative, partial to centralized disbursement of investment funds, and hostile to anything smacking of laissez-faire economics. The Tito regime expressly recognized the cleavage and, for redistribution purposes, designated certain areas as "underdeveloped."

The differences in social product are reflected in table 5 and regional differ-

Table 5. *Regional Economic Disparities in Yugoslavia, 1990*
Five measures of relative advantage

	% total population	*% total area*	*% total social product*	*% total exports to the convertible area*	*% total unemployed*
Serbia	41.1	34.5	38.3	28.9	47.4
Croatia	23.2	22.1	25.3	21.2	11.7
Bosnia	16.7	20.0	13.6	12.3	22.6
Slovenia	8.8	7.9	15.0	32.2	1.6
Macedonia	7.7	10.1	5.7	4.0	13.2
Montenegro	2.5	5.4	2.1	1.4	3.6

Source: *Danas*, no. 459 (4 December 1990), p. 18.

ences in net personal income are shown in table 6. Given the tremendous disparity in wealth, it is perhaps not surprising that conflict over policy directions has flared up regularly. But the Serb-Croat rivalry that (for reasons a cursory examination of table 3 should make clear) remains the pivot of ethnic competition in Yugoslavia is widely viewed by both Serbs and Croats in religious terms. The identification of the churches with nationalism goes back to the time of the Ottoman occupation, when, under the millet system, the Orthodox churches were the guardians of national culture as well as the political viceroys. In independent Montenegro, too, the Orthodox Church arrogated to itself the role of protector of the Montenegrin nation. At the same time, the Catholic Church in Croatia, which had been absorbed into the Habsburg empire, maintained a political role. Thus, for example, when Orthodox Serbs in Dalmatia formed a political party in 1879, the Catholic Serbs replied by forming a movement of their own under the leadership of Baron Frano Gundulić of Dubrovnik. The chief ideologue of this movement was Ivo Stojanović, a Catholic priest. More significant, when the exclusionist Croatian Rights party of Ante Starčević began to expand its activities into Bosnia and Herzegovina in the 1880s, its leading proponents in the region were none other than the Franciscan friars of Herzegovina, who were eager to transform Bosnian Muslims into Croatian Catholics. Nor should one fail to mention the church's involvement in the creation of the Croatian Agricultural Bank in 1900, whose raison d'être was resistance to the encroachment of Hungarian capital. Subsequently, in World War II, the Croatian-fascist government of Ante Pavelić found a ready ally in the Catholic Church. During the war, priests on both sides of the barricades played active roles in fomenting the mutual slaughter of Serbs and Croats. And in the 1980s, communist officials would complain that Croatianness tends to be identified with Catholicity and Serbianness with Orthodoxy. Contrary to what one would expect in a modernizing society, namely, secularization, Yugoslavia experienced a waxing xenophobia and a recrudescence of religious sentiment among the young in the late 1960s, especially in Slovenia and Croatia.[29] That this tumescent affectivity was associated with a reassertion of nationalist feelings and was, in both instances, centered in Slovenia and Croatia, underlines the closeness of the ethnic-religious relationship.

Conflict of Interest

So deep were the divisions in Yugoslav society in 1945 that the Communist party had little with which to hold the country together except the partisan myth, promises of a future cornucopia, and coercive force. The break with the Cominform certainly helped in this respect, for even anticommunists rallied to Tito rather than risk Sovietization. But the promises remained important. The regime had pledged, for example, to intensify industrialization—a clearly perceived need—and to level interregional economic disparities. This was to be done by funneling a disproportionate amount of new investments into the poorer regions of the south.

This early period was, of course, also the period of the Stalinist model—with or without Stalin—and the decision to emphasize heavy industry naturally gave preference to the southern regions that were rich in such basic raw materials as minerals and energy sources. Kosovo is rich in minerals, with its mines at Trepča alone producing 25 percent of Europe's lead and 13 percent of Europe's zinc.[30] Bosnia-Herzegovina has important reserves of coal, iron ore, and lumber, and sizeable potential sources of hydroelectric power. Thus, it made good economic sense to locate heavy industry in the south. But, as Kardelj himself noted in 1960, the overall effect of this was "to contribute indirectly more to the rise in national income in other regions with developed manufacturing by supplying them with raw materials from less developed areas."[31] Slovenia, Croatia, and the Belgrade environs—and, to a lesser extent, Vojvodina[32]—continued to be preferentially favored with the development of light and consumer industries. Understandably, politicians in the underdeveloped republics saw parallels to the classic model of imperialism. In addition, income differentials were widening. Macedonian per capita income, for instance, dipped from 31 percent below the national average in 1947 to 36 percent below the average in 1963, while, during the same period, the average per capita income in Slovenia soared from 62 percent above the national average to almost twice the national average.[33]

Yet the more advanced republics were also dissatisfied. In addition to investments in raw material extraction and processing, the south was also the recipient of certain investments demonstratively made on political rather than economic grounds; Croatia and Slovenia were particularly irked by the duplication of industries already flourishing in their own republics. Furthermore, these new industries often proved glaringly inefficient. Thus, with the shift of the center of steel production from Slovenia to Bosnia, it became cheaper to

Table 6. *Net Personal Income by Republic*
(In new dinars)

	Average income over 12 months		
	1968	*1973*	*1978*
Slovenia	997	2,242	5,903
Croatia	904	2,083	5,432
YUGOSLAVIA	862	1,938	5,075
Serbia proper	845	1,831	4,937
Vojvodina	797	1,871	4,904
Bosnia-Herzegovina	797	1,863	4,671
Montenegro	766	1,689	4,404
Macedonia	750	1,647	4,220
Kosovo	749	1,617	4,084

Source: *Statistički Godišnjak 1979* (Belgrade, July 1979), p. 431.

import steel than to produce it in Yugoslavia. The market reform of 1965 "revealed that 600,000 industrial workers, nearly half the industrial labor force, were employed in enterprises that operated at a loss."[34] Croatia's share in the total Yugoslav industrial potential dropped from 33 percent in 1925 to 29 percent in 1946 and plunged to 19 percent in 1965.[35] Of course, since Croatia's industry was expanding during this period and since percentages reflect a relationship to a greater whole, these figures do not necessarily mean that Croatia was being "oppressed"; the important point is that many people thought the figures did mean just that. Croatian scholars like Šime Djodan and Marko Veselica lashed out at the alleged exploitation of Croatia (and Slovenia). Djodan, who was later imprisoned, often hinted at secession. The Croats did not deny that Croatia had made progress under communism, but they adamantly maintained that progress would have been far greater had the Croatian economy not been milked to succor the less developed republics.

As early as 1957, Bosnia's share in industrial investment began to slip as investment in heavy industry (and, more particularly, in raw material extraction) reached the saturation point. Bosnia's share of federal investment funds had declined from 19.4 percent under the first five-year plan to 12.6 percent under the second. Serbia's share, meantime, jumped from 31.3 percent to 41.7 percent—the only increase among the six republics. Serbia was now garnering between 50 and 60 percent of all new investments in metalwork, machine-building, nonferrous metallurgy, and chemical industries. These facts convinced Joseph Bombelles that it was no longer possible to "speak of a conscious government policy of aiding underdeveloped republics after 1956. Rather, the western republics were now supposed to subsidize the eastern republics without regard to the level of development."[36] The entire system of investments was overhauled in the 1965 reforms (to be treated in detail in chapter 6), and profitability became the crucial criterion. The central government ceased to channel funds to the south under a planned system, and, despite continued

Table 7. *Relative Importance of Heavy and Light Industry, 1977* (In percent)

	Social product		*Employment*	
	Heavy industry	*Light industry*	*Heavy industry*	*Light industry*
YUGOSLAVIA	24.0	76.0	14.90	85.1
Slovenia	15.0	85.0	11.0	89.0
Croatia	22.5	77.5	10.7	89.3
Vojvodina	17.1	82.9	6.9	93.1
Serbia proper	22.2	77.8	14.4	85.6
Macedonia	27.6	72.4	17.1	82.9
Bosnia	34.6	65.4	24.6	75.4
Montenegro	53.3	46.7	30.70	69.3
Kosovo	49.2	50.8	40.2	59.8
Underdeveloped regions	41.0	59.0	10.7	89.3

Source: Momir Ćećez, "O efikasnosti društvenih sredstava u privredno nedovoljno razvijenim područjima," *Pregled* 70 (1) (January 1980): 34–35.

payments of subsidies to certain industries and the invocation of "special case" tax consideration for investments in the south, the reform generally favored the developed regions.

It is certainly not insignificant that the four most prosperous republics are precisely those that have the highest proportions of light industry, whether this is measured, on the one hand, in terms of contribution to the social product or, on the other, in terms of employment (see table 7). The two federal units most reliant on heavy industry are the two poorest units, Kosovo and Montenegro. Clearly this complementarity might furnish the basis for identical policy aims. Yet a more detailed breakdown of the structure of industry (table 8), although it omits certain branches of light industry, fails to reveal any obvious axes of potential cooperation or competition.

Conflict Behavior

Despite the hypotheses originally set forth, we have seen that Yugoslavia's regions can be divided into "developed" and "underdeveloped" categories. If this rift is the basis for the polarization of the political system, Yugoslavia ought to be analyzed as a loose bipolar, not a balance-of-power, system. The old Serbian-Croatian friction has not become suddenly irrelevant either. The Serb-Croat civil war (1941–45) provides support for viewing pre-1965 Yugoslav politics in bipolar terms. War, the great polarizer, did in fact drive Serbs and Croats further apart. At the same time, however, there are reasons for thinking that the bipolar model is not relevant to the 1965–89 period. One might note, among other things, that the north-south divide does not explain enough to warrant

Table 8. *Structure of Industry as Percent of Social Product, 1977* (In percent)

	YUGO.	*Bosn.*	*Mont.*	*Croa.*	*Mace.*	*Slov.*	*Serb.*	*Koso.*	*Vojv.*
Electric	6.9	8.9	17.8	7.2	4.7	4.1	8.5	11.1	4.0
Coal and coke	2.9	9.7	1.8	0.4	—	2.2	2.9	15.5	—
Petroleum	3.0	2.1	—	6.8	—	0.4	0.6	—	8.6
Ferrous metals	3.8	10.6	14.8	3.0	6.0	3.9	0.9	3.6	0.4
Nonferrous	3.8	2.8	8.4	1.3	6.4	2.6	7.7	16.3	0.5
Nonmetals	2.5	2.3	1.5	1.8	4.8	2.3	3.1	3.8	1.8
Metal ind.	19.8	18.2	10.9	13.4	7.1	22.1	29.6	7.7	21.2
Shipbuilding	1.4	—	2.6	4.3	—	0.1	0.7	—	0.9
Chemicals	7.7	4.4	1.0	9.9	8.3	9.0	7.3	6.1	5.6
Bldg. materials	4.6	3.4	2.1	5.8	7.9	2.9	4.0	6.1	5.6
Lumber	6.4	11.4	9.2	6.1	3.7	9.6	2.7	2.5	4.9
Paper	1.7	2.6	2.4	1.4	0.6	2.5	1.2	1.3	0.8
Textiles	1.5	9.5	9.4	11.7	18.6	13.1	8.9	11.6	12.5
Leather	2.7	3.5	2.5	2.4	2.7	3.9	1.5	2.1	2.6
Rubber	1.2	0.1	0.8	1.6	0.2	1.8	1.6	2.1	0.2
Food processing	9.2	5.6	6.1	10.9	9.4	7.5	6.7	2.5	21.7
Print and publ.	3.1	1.3	2.3	3.8	2.0	2.2	4.5	0.9	3.9
Tobacco	2.3	1.5	2.3	2.0	14.5	1.4	1.6	5.2	0.4
Other	0.5	—	—	0.5	0.1	0.9	0.7	—	0.4
TOTAL	100.0	100.0	100.0	100.0	100.0	100.0	100.0	100.0	100.0

Source: Momir Ćećez, "O efikasnosti društvenih sredstava u privredno nedovoljno razvijenim područjima," *Pregled* 70 (1) (January 1980): 32–33.

the term *bipolarity* and that there are enough crossovers to justify construing Yugoslavia as a system characterized by flexible coalitions among its eight federal units.

William A. Gamson, in "A Theory of Coalition Formation," outlined four conditions required for the flexible formation of coalitions: (1) there are issues to be resolved by three or more interested parties, each of whom stands to lose if the outcome assumes a given configuration; (2) no single possible outcome would maximize the payoff to all actors; (3) no single actor has the resources to impose a decision; and (4) no participant enjoys a veto power that would require that it be included in any winning coalition.[37] I would argue that these conditions were met in communist Yugoslavia and that, because of the degree of decentralism, republican leaders were in the position to strike bargains on national legislation.

On the basis of the north-south cleavage and the information provided in tables 5 and 6, we might graphically depict Yugoslavia as a four-box set:

Figure 1

	W	E
N	Slovenia Croatia	Vojvodina Serbia
S	Bosnia-Herz. Montenegro	Kosovo Macedonia

The upper left-hand box contains those actors that, during most of their history, had formed a part of the Austrian empire. The lower left-hand box contains actors liberated from Ottoman rule in the nineteenth century. Bosnia-Herzegovina was placed under Austrian administration in 1878, the same year in which Montenegro achieved its independence from Istanbul. The lower right-hand box contains actors that remained under Ottoman rule until 1912: members of this set, as suggested by appendix 3, showed the most marked and consistent pattern of economic retrogression as measured by total investment in fixed assets. The upper right-hand box is less homogeneous: Serbia won its independence in 1878, having enjoyed internal autonomy since the early part of the nineteenth century, whereas Vojvodina constituted an integral part of the Kingdom of Hungary until the Peace of Trianon. These historical differences were reinforced by systematic geographic variations. Moreover, differences in political history also made for differences in economic development, cultural life, work ethic, and religious traditions.

The northerners in the upper half of the box—Slovenia, Croatia, Vojvodina, and Serbia—were the more developed regions and had the highest social products and per capita incomes. The southerners in the lower half of the box—Bosnia-Herzegovina, Montenegro, Kosovo, and Macedonia—were officially designated "underdeveloped areas" after 1965. Between 1956 and 1964, however, it appeared that the notion of underdevelopment was being manipulated by Serbian elements so that, in Bombelles's words, "the policy of aid to underdeveloped republics was changed to a policy of aiding [the] eastern republics."[38] Indeed, between 1961 and 1964 the republic of Bosnia-Herzegovina was considered "developed" for funding purposes, while portions of Serbia proper were redesignated as "underdeveloped" (albeit along with sections of Slavonia). During this period frequent complaints were heard about Serbian banking and industrial monopolies, especially vis-à-vis the concentration of corporations in Belgrade and its vicinity. Thus, an alternative, at least for the 1956–64 period, is to view the cleavage as an east-west split, with the republic of Serbia (including Vojvodina and Kosovo), Macedonia, and possibly Montenegro—the easterners—exploiting the westerners—Croatia, Slovenia, and Bosnia-Herzegovina.

The diagram in figure 1 predicts that policy alignments that cross diagonally should be rare. That is, if the system is bipolar and not balance of power, we will not expect to find Slovenia and Kosovo aligned, say, against Serbia and Montenegro. What we find, however, is exactly the opposite. We find flexible, ephemeral alignments; a tendency for republics to align in opposition to whichever federal unit is seen to threaten the stability of the system (whether Serbia, Croatia, or even Kosovo); and alignments that confute any simple predictions on the basis of cleavages.

This is not surprising in the least. After all, by May 1940 the CPY had denounced the *Sporazum*, under which Croatia had finally gained a degree of administrative and political autonomy in the old kingdom. The party depicted the agreement as a compact between Serbian and Croatian bourgeoisies made at the expense not only of the working classes but also of the other republics. Although the partisans probably never intended to go that far, the adoption of a federal constitution was an unmistakable concession (a) to nationalist sentiment and (b) to the balance-of-power principle. In this vein, the recognition of Montenegrins as a distinct nationality in the 1946 constitution makes sense from the perspective of balance-of-power politics. "It has been suggested that the creation of a Montenegrin republic, rather than the inclusion of Montenegro in Serbia, was intended to allay fears of Serbian hegemony in other republics."[39] With Montenegro incorporated into Serbia, the Serbian republic would have been given a superordinate position in the new federation, but, established as a separate republic, Montenegro was available as an alignment partner to all other actors, even though the close cultural affinity and commonly shared economic interests continued to incline Montenegro to align, virtually automatically, with Serbia. Another factor, however, was at work—the postwar reemergence of the anti-Serbian faction of the Montenegrin elite. The CPY took advantage of this current to strengthen Montenegro as an independent republic.

Conflict Accommodation

As noted in chapter 1, the Tito regime (1945–80) was the ultimate arbiter in this system and, thus, was both the realm in which conflict accommodation most often took place and the chief agent for such accommodation. After Tito's death, the federal center started to decay—at first slowly, but after 1987, rapidly. By 1989, the federal government was no longer capable of playing the role of rule-enforcer, and Serbia's Milošević stepped into the vacuum.

Tito had come to believe in decentralization, and he generally preferred to let the republics govern themselves, and, under Tito's immediate successors, the federal government relinquished its position of preponderance and participated in interrepublican negotiations, if at all, as an equal (or, perhaps, as primus inter pares). The practical import is that conflict accommodation is accomplished by the parties in the conflict. This has certain drawbacks in terms of speed. It took the nine negotiating parties (the eight federal units and a federal deputy) a full year to agree on the level of aid to be provided to Montenegro for damage caused by the April 1979 earthquake. And the debate on the establishment of new criteria for the disbursement of resources from the Fund for the Accelerated Development of the Underdeveloped Republics and Kosovo (FADURK) missed two deadlines, forcing the parties to operate the program, temporarily at least, in the absence of formal criteria. Again, the debate on the balance-of-payments deficit, which was supposed to wind up in December 1979, dragged on to July 1980. Yet the process of interrepublican conflict accommodation expressed in the Serbo-Croatian words *dogovaranje* (literally "coming to an agreement" or, as I have translated it, "negotiation") and *usaglašavanje* (literally "harmonization of views" or, as I have translated it, "mutual accommodation") has been relatively successful. The "concert" style of accommodation has reduced the incidence and intensity of resentment at policy decisions, since those affected by the decisions have been consulted.

In a fragmented system with reinforced cleavages, whose federal units enjoy extensive powers, the danger of escalation of policy differences into crises is great. Yugoslavia has been characterized by reinforced cleavages, conflicts of interest that frequently follow cleavage lines, and conflict behavior that does not always follow lines of cleavage. Yet, as long as the communists were in charge, the system did not get out of control.

Conflict Regulation

Having set out to investigate the viability of democracy in plural societies, Rabushka and Shepsle concluded that differing ethnic groups tend to be self-segregating and intermingle only "in the marketplace"; force is necessary to maintain order in plural societies; crosscutting cleavages do not eliminate the political importance of ethnic distinctions; only balanced competition affords the possibility of working democracy; and, as a result, stable democracy is impossible in fragmented societies. In short, as sociologist Pierre van den Berghe concluded, in despair, "generally, the more pluralistic the society as a whole and the political institutions in particular, the more tyrannical the polity."[40]

At the same time, it is a well-known principle that repression, especially if unevenly or inefficiently applied, tends to provoke resistance, obstruction, and violence. Neither the repressive Serbian centralism of the interwar period nor the hegemonistic unitarism of the postwar period (1946–66) succeeded in producing the modicum of stability essential for the orderly functioning of Yugoslav society. Neither formula, in short, was adequate to the requirements of conflict regulation in multiethnic Yugoslavia. Yugoslavia's post-1971 solution was to wed decentralization to democratization in a one-party context and to make that marriage the basis for conflict regulation. The Yugoslav experiment was based on the premise that conflict could be regulated if there was pluralism *within* the party, even if genuine pluralism was proscribed *outside* the party.

In a sense, conflict accommodation is subsumed under the broader category of conflict regulation. In this context, however, I have distinguished between them in order to highlight two discrete functions necessary for the survival of the system. By *conflict accommodation*, I mean the working out of solutions satisfactory to the major parties to a conflict. By *conflict regulation*, I mean the prevention, containment, and management of conflict in such a way that the basic parameters of the system are maintained. If the ground rules of the system have to be rewritten, a section of the society attempts violent secession, the society explodes in massive and sustained violence, or the very survival of the system becomes a matter of widespread doubt, then conflict regulation has failed. Conflict-regulating practices are those measures that make possible the normal functioning of the society. When conflict regulation fails, as happened in Yugoslavia in 1971, the result is *system crisis*. The rules of the system are called into question, and the orderly functioning of the system cannot be restored without a restructuring of system relationships and institutionalized patterns of behavior. The explosion of ethnic riots in Kosovo in 1981 proved to be an adumbration of impending system crisis.

Eric A. Nordlinger, whose 1972 study has given us a perspicacious analysis of conflict regulation, outlined six typical conflict-regulating practices: (1) a stable government coalition in which the political parties of all major ethnic groups are represented according to a fixed formula; (2) the principle of proportionality, according to which the representation accorded to each ethnic group in the ruling coalition is roughly proportional to its share in the overall population; (3) the mutual veto, which allows any coalition partner to veto legislation; (4) the purposive depoliticization of public policy areas of direct concern to the constituent ethnic groups qua separate groups, that is, the endeavor to treat them as administrative problems of the entire country rather than as political contests pitting one group against another; (5) reliance on compromise as a means to draw antagonists to a common solution; and (6) the encouragement of concessions as a method of compromise.[41] Nordlinger claimed that at least one of these six practices had to be employed for conflict regulation to be successful.

The Yugoslav socialist polity, in fact, employed five of the six practices listed above (all but the first—unless the LCY itself is interpreted as a stable coalition). Proportional representation was more or less faithfully adhered to in the party, the government, and even, within limits, in the army officer corps and party organization (see table 9). The republics and provinces enjoyed equal representation in the collective presidency, the federal Executive Council, the Constitutional Court of Yugoslavia, and various other bodies. The mutual veto was also incorporated into the Communist system of decision making, which spurned majoritarianism as a species of tyranny and sought to ensure solutions satisfactory to all by requiring unanimity among delegations in the two houses of the *Skupština*. To make this practical, the Yugoslavs spent a great deal of time in committees hammering out compromises acceptable to all.

In the early postwar years, when all decisions of any consequence were made by the CPY politburo, and the republics had to be satisfied with consultation

Table 9. *National Composition of Office-Holders*

	% of pop. (1981)	*% of federal organs of administration (1969)*	*% of delegates to conference (1989)*	*% of party membership in army (1989)*
Serbs	36.3	39.4	54.0	52.07
Croats	19.7	19.1	12.67	13.4
Muslims	8.9	5.1	4.0	5.54
Slovenes	7.8	10.0	5.33	1.98
Albanians	7.7	0.8	1.33	0.7
Macedonians	6.0	7.8	4.67	6.37
Montenegrins	2.6	15.1	5.33	5.83
Hungarians	1.0	0.2	0.67	0.72
Others	9.1	2.5	0.67*	11.94*

* = Romanians

Sources: Gary K. Bertsch, "Ethnicity and Politics in Socialist Yugoslavia," in *Annals of the American Academy of Political and Social Science* (September 1977), 433: 97; Slobodan Stanković, "On the Eve of the 12th Yugoslav Party Congress," *Radio Free Europe Research*, June 25, 1982, p. 4; and Tanjug (November 24, 1989), trans. in Foreign Broadcast Information Service, *Daily Report* (Eastern Europe), December 14, 1989, p. 89.

on questions affecting their interests, the Yugoslavs hoped to "depoliticize politics" by breaking down the sense of separateness that divided Croats from Serbs, Slovenes from Macedonians. But the endeavor failed, and by the late Tito era, the Yugoslavs were trying a new tack, namely, to purposively depoliticize public policy areas impinging on the basic values and interests of the chief nationality groups. Devolution was the technique whereby this was accomplished, since the greater the policy domain within the jurisdiction of the federal units, the fewer the occasions for dispute at the federal level. Where a common strategy was necessary, the decision-making style of *usaglašavanje*, incorporating the mutual veto, was at hand.

For all the talk of class struggle and class interests, the Yugoslavs realized—no thanks to Marx and Engels—that the interests of the working class are not monolithic and that sections of the working class may have strongly vested interests that conflict with the interests of another section of the working class. The Yugoslavs therefore embraced the un-Marxist concept of compromise. "At this point in our socioeconomic development," wrote Mahmut Mujačić, a candidate member of the central committee of the LCY, in 1978, "compromise (*kompromis*) is an extremely important means of reconciling viewpoints and a necessary element in the harmonization of interests among the republics and provinces."[42] It became, in fact, a routine element in interrepublican negotiation. Finally, the Yugoslav modus operandi also embraced the last item on Nordlinger's list—the use of concessions offered to the less fortunate or weaker republics.

Nordlinger pointedly excluded federalism and semiautonomy from his list. Both, he claimed, may more properly be viewed as the goals of certain actors in the system rather than as processes assuring conflict regulation, and, far from regulating conflict, they might exacerbate it.[43] The Yugoslavs, however, disputed this assessment and placed the dual policy of federalism and far-reaching autonomy at the very heart of their solution to the problems of interethnic distrust and interregional rivalry—the key, in other words, to conflict regulation in Yugoslavia.[44]

Conflict regulation in an international balance-of-power system involves the use of analogous and often identical techniques. Bearing in mind that the mechanism for conflict regulation in a balance-of-power system is the so-called concert system, it is apparent that such a mechanism presumes unanimity among the great power concert-participants (the mutual veto), assumes the use of compromises and concessions, and honors the principle of proportionality in the sense of one great power, one vote.

It should not be forgotten, however, that the Yugoslav communists were not elected to power but seized it, and they have never won free elections in any part of Yugoslavia. Nor should it be forgotten that, for all the talk of the sovereignty of the republics, the LCY was always determined to hold Yugoslavia together by whatever means necessary. Ultimately, Yugoslav stability has rested on force and the threat of force. The LCY never hesitated to use force when deemed necessary; it resolutely sent armed troops and tanks into Croatia in 1971 and into Kosovo in 1981. Similarly, in the weeks after Tito's death, extraordinary security measures were taken in Bosnia, where a Croatian nationalist putsch was not ruled out. The events of 1991 are also of clear relevance here.

Behavioral Constants in a Balance-of-Power System

To present Yugoslavia as a balance-of-power system is neither to deny the reality of the deterioration of interethnic relations in the mid-1960s nor to assume that the antipathy that has sometimes characterized interethnic relations is a permanent, if periodically latent, feature of the system. I do not contend that it is merely because of the ethnic divisions that the federal system operates as a balance-of-power system. Yet, certainly, ethnicity is a potent factor that influences the choice of alliance partners and the endurance of coalitions, especially where the dictates of economic interest are ambiguous. This need not be a weakness; by a kind of Madisonian logic, it may even be a strength. This is evidently the interpretation that the president of the Chamber of Nationalities wished to place on things when he wrote, in 1967, that he considered "the existence of several peoples and nationalities in Yugoslavia . . . an advantage for our socialist community, rather than a necessary evil which has to be disposed of as soon as possible by some kind of supranational structures."[45] No system of interactor behavior—whether international, interethnic, or interregional—is permanent, but an understanding of the prevailing patterns may help us predict likely outcomes of system breakdown, as Kaplan foresaw. When Djilas wrote that, by 2024, "Yugoslavia will become a confederation of four states: Slovenia, Croatia, Macedonia, and Serbia, with Serbia itself being a federative state,"[46] he was extrapolating current trends in an attempt to identify those that, of a number of contradictory tendencies, will prevail. Systems analysis does not start with what is possible and work backwards to link the future with the present; it starts with what is essential and derives models of change on the basis of institutionalized power. Thus, Djilas's four emergent states were all expected to evolve from then-existing socialist republics. But there is not only an institutional dimension to Djilas's prognostications; there is also an ethnic dimension. Djilas predicted that both Montenegro and Bosnia-Herzegovina would disappear as autonomous territories—the former, presumably, because of the close ethnic affinity between Serbs and Montenegrins and the latter, perhaps, because Muslim national self-consciousness is neither as developed nor as tenacious as the Serbian, the Croatian, or the Slovene. In the first edition of this book, I concluded this chapter by observing:

> An awareness of the wide-ranging autonomy enjoyed by the federal units is sufficient to permit prediction of evolution in the direction of loose confederation. Establishing the precise patterns of interrepublican behavior would enable us—in the event we wished to undertake such an enterprise—to forecast, with some confidence, how many states might emerge from system breakdown and what their likely alignments would be.[47]

Events have proven the accuracy of this forecast, just as they have highlighted the dangers associated with the resultant clash between centrifugal and centripetal forces.

3

Yugoslav Nationalities Policy

> Then there is difference of race or nation, which remains a source of dissension until such time as the two groups learn to live together. This may be a long process; for just as a state cannot be made out of any and every collection of people, so neither can it be made at any time at will.
>
> ARISTOTLE, *Politics*, Book V

In mobilization systems like the Leninist one-party systems that operated in Eastern Europe and the Soviet Union until the end of the 1980s, interregional politics, like every other political aspect, could not be abstracted from its ideological milieu. This is especially true of interethnic and interrepublican relations, which were framed and channeled by an explicit, developed nationalities policy based on and derived from the underlying ideological presumptions of the system. The very federal arrangement that permitted the wide degree of autonomy enjoyed by Yugoslavia's republics had first to be hammered out on the ideological-polemical plane; it had to be justified before it could be advanced.

The concept of policy presumes purpose, coherence, consistency, and application. A *nationalities policy* may accordingly be defined as a unified, purposeful, and coherent program that is potentially consistent and that infuses specific decisions and actions of state. The Yugoslavs long claimed to have a nationalities policy. This claim meant, first of all, that the Yugoslavs viewed their multiethnic composition as—at least potentially—problematic and considered political involvement in this sphere legitimate.

The Yugoslavs made a further claim that is far more interesting: they claimed to have "resolved" the nationalities question, at least in the terms in which they considered the question to have been posed.[1] This claim can be understood in either of two ways: (1) that nationalism, as politicized ethnicity, had been by and large eliminated or (2) that institutionalized patterns of cooperation and mutual accommodation had become a stable part of the political landscape, allowing nationalist excesses to be contained, defused, or even bypassed. The former interpretation, as we shall see, is the way in which the Yugoslav communists themselves understood their claim until the Eighth Congress of the LCY (1964). After that, however, the second interpretation dominated Yugoslav thinking on the subject until the late 1980s. That is to say, the second Yugoslav claim amounted to the faith that under so-called self-managing socialism, conditions were created that would make possible a solution in the future. That it ought to be understood in this light is suggested by a party official's ridicule, in late 1982, of those who somehow clung to the belief that the national question was, by definition, already solved.[2] This remark also reflected the new candor and modesty that characterized Yugoslav statements on the subject of nationalism after the Kosovo riots of April 1981; bolder claims would have lacked credibility. Still, even the more modest assertions—that Yugoslavia was "on the right track" and that it had devised a system that gave the groups free rein to advance their separate interests and (according to the Yugoslavs) thus to draw together around a common interest—are worth examining, for they represent a claim to have devised a model of political organization worthy of emulation. Yet, though declaring that the combination of authentic federalism and self-managing socialism enabled the national question to be "correctly formulated"—the precondition for political resolution—and even to be correctly treated, the Yugoslavs nonetheless conceded that insofar as "general human emancipation has not yet been realized, . . . the problem of . . . interethnic relations in a multiethnic . . . community remains actual."[3] Socialism, born in dialectics, was ever forward-looking, ever conscious of itself as an unstable phenomenon that would give way to other forms—either deformations (such as bureaucratic statism—in the Yugoslav view) or purified forms (some form of communism). Hence, it was neither possible nor necessary to claim that socialism would result in the forthright achievement of interethnic harmony. Rather, it was claimed that "with the achievement of socialist revolution in a series of countries is created the possibility of the final resolution of the national question. In socialism the objective preconditions for the actual equality of nations are, in principle, laid down."[4] Hedged though it may be, it was nonetheless a bold claim, since it carried the implication that only under some form of socialism was interethnic harmony possible.

Marx's Formulation of the National Question

Marx was the first writer to consider the existence of ethnically heterogeneous communities as a problem to be resolved. That it *was* a problem had become clear for the Habsburg empire, which had suppressed a vigorous Hungarian revolution in 1848–49. True, Hegel had already outlined a view of history in which lower ethnic forms of life gave way to higher forms and heterogeneity was expected to melt away before the waxing *Volksgeist* of "historical peoples." But before Marx no one had raised ethnic heterogeneity from the level of a policy question a posteriori to status as a question a priori. Marx's formulation of the question at once implied and required an answer, a resolution, a correct approach.

This approach to multinationality stemmed in part from the dialectical view of history, in which each historical stage manifests internal contradictions and tensions that are resolved at a higher stage, thus propelling history forward. It also grew from the Marxist presumption that true conflict is economically motivated—the corollary being that ethnic strife is a sham, a veneer behind which the exploitative middle classes can mobilize and manipulate their proletarian and peasant populations. Nationalism, rooted in ethnic prejudice and collective consciousness based on a shared language, was linked with the so-called bourgeois-capitalist stage of historical development, eventually to be transcended by the passage to socialism. In this view, proletarian internationalism is not problematic but automatic, even ineluctable. Little wonder that Marx spent little time on it. His supposition that national differences would dissolve with modernization and political and economic unification is the natural corollary of the Marxist premise that the nation is an expression or form of the social organization of the market. But it is far from obvious that Marx drew from this the inference imputed to him by the Soviets, namely, that nationalism and internationalism are opposed. Rather, Marx seems to have viewed proletarian nationalism (or the authentic nationalism of a socialist country) and internationalism as being in some sense symbiotic. And, thus, "Marx's . . . aphorism . . . 'the worker has no country' . . . was not, as is sometimes supposed, either a boast or a program. It was a protest against the exclusion of the proletariat from the privilege of full membership of the nation."[5] It is worth noting here that Stipe Šuvar, who, until 1989, represented Yugoslav officialdom, concurs with this interpretation of the Marxist dictum, with the result that Šuvar can insist that nationality is indeed an important factor in the consciousness of the working class, that "the working class still is national."[6]

If this seems to lead directly to "national communism," which has been treated rather as a profligate stepchild by Soviet Marxists, it is nevertheless consistent with the tradition in which Marx was working. Jaures and Bernstein were much closer to Marx's spirit than Plekhanov and Lenin in holding that internationalism and national socialism were consonant.[7] Yet, it is clear from the *Communist Manifesto* that Marx and Engels thought that national consciousness and nationalism would evaporate as a result of modernization. This stems from the underlying assumption of Marxism that change of behavior will lead to change of mental attitude—an assumption held in common with the behaviorists—and, thus, that the elimination of conflicts rooted in class society will stimulate cooperation across ethnic lines and create positive feelings among ethnic groups within the system.

But it is not obvious that Marx and Engels thought that the world would eventually be speaking only one language. (The current universality of English proves no more than did the earlier universality of Latin; that is, it demonstrates only that people of different states require some medium, and it is likely to be the language of the dominant, or hitherto dominant, power.) And, although Marx and Engels welcomed the subjugation of "less civilized, unhistorical peoples" (e.g., Slavs and Mexicans) by the more advanced Caucasian races (e.g.,

Germans and Americans), they stopped short of explicit advocacy of coercive ethnic assimilation.[8]

The Austro-Marxists

The Yugoslavs are not heirs to an unmediated Marxist legacy, and one cannot consider Marx's theories regarding nationality without also considering the ideas of the Austro-Marxists—chiefly Karl Renner and Otto Bauer—and of Lenin and Stalin. Indeed, Yugoslavia's communists spent more time with the texts of these exegetes than with the few original Marxist discussions of the national question. Yugoslav nationalities policy can only be understood as a reaction to, development of, and repudiation of ideas carried forward by Renner, Bauer, Lenin, and Stalin.

The so-called Austro-Marxists were the first Marxists to articulate a political program dealing with the creation of harmony in an ethnically diverse state. They were inspired in this endeavor by their desire, as Austrians, to prop up the faltering multinational Habsburg realm. The Austro-Marxists designed a centralist scheme with concessions to cultural autonomy and guarantees of free use of language. Renner, drawing on the writings of Matija Majer (1865), who had undertaken to divorce "purely ethnic" questions from politics, described the nation as a "spiritual and cultural community" and emphasized the centrality of language in the formation of group consciousness. Bauer, in his magnum opus, *Die Nationalitätenfrage und die Sozialdemokratie* (1907), underlined national character as a social bond and spoke of the nation as a collective with a common culture and a shared destiny. Bauer's definition of *nation* as "an aggregate of people bound into a community of character by a common destiny"[9] not only blurred the distinction between state and nation, citizenship and nationality, but also implied a minimization of the importance of compact territory. This implication was made explicit by Renner, who, writing under the pseudonym of Rudolf Springer, declared that "nationality is not essentially connected with territory; [rather, nations] are autonomous unions of persons."[10]

The Austro-Marxist formulations were closer in spirit to Hegelianism than to Marxism, allowing for the intrusion of the semimystical concepts of "character," "culture," "consciousness," "spiritual community," and "destiny." The Austro-Marxists considered nationality to be basically a matter of folk culture and language and were therefore content to offer reassurances of cultural autonomy, withholding both administrative and political autonomy as potentially disintegrative concessions.

Stalin's Critique of the Austro-Marxists

The ideas of Renner and Bauer were first subjected to Marxist critique by Josef Strasser in his essay "Worker and Nation" and then by Anton Pannekock in "Class Struggle and Nation." Rejecting the Austro-Marxist stress on language and culture and proceeding from an uncompromising if misguided interpretation of internationalism, Strasser and Pannekock made a fetish of class in order to disparage national feeling. They allowed that nationality might be tolerated only in the manner in which Marxists tolerate religion.[11]

Stalin was influenced by Strasser and Pannekock when he undertook, on Lenin's request, to produce an analysis of ethnicity as a political factor. His final product, "Marxism and the National Question" (1913), is largely a synthesis of the ideas of other writers concerning the national question. In it, Stalin concentrated his attacks on the abstractions of the Austro-Marxist approach to the issue. He warned that exclusive stress on national character was leading Bauer and company away from the essence of nationality, which is a complex phenomenon emerging not only on the basis of a shared language but also within a compact territory and within the context of a common economic life. "What is national character," Stalin asked,

> if not a reflection of the conditions of life, a coagulation of impressions derived from environment? How can one limit the matter to national character alone, isolating and divorcing it from the soil that gave rise to it? . . . Bauer's point of view, which identifies a nation with its national character, divorces the nation from its soil and converts it into an invisible, self-contained force. The result is not a living and active nation, but something mystical, intangible and supernatural.[12]

It is not consciousness that molds life but life that determines consciousness.

Given this premise and the Marxist tenet that modernization not only creates a world culture (Coca-Cola and blue jeans) but also results in the disintegration of distinct national cultures and the evaporation of national antagonisms, Stalin was easily led to the conclusion that the notion of cultural autonomism, infused with notions of preservation of culture, was inherently reactionary. Hence, he not only considered the concept to be founded on a seriously flawed analysis of nationality, but also deemed it politically nefarious. Stalin was, however, unable to trumpet centralism, since such a policy had unmistakably failed in tsarist Russia and because the liberation of the proletariat could not be allowed to entail the constriction of the self-determination of any self-conceived nationality group. Stalin, therefore, offered as the ideal solution a system of regional or territorial autonomy. This, he believed, would permit the nationalities to enjoy their rights of self-administration and self-determination without obstructing the drawing together of nations that is concomitant with the creation of a unified market and is stimulated by modernization.

Development of CPY Policy vis-à-vis the National Question

The Titoists were fond of claiming that their policy on the national question had, at least since 1925, been more or less consistent.[13] It is possible, however, to outline a series of phases in the evolution of Yugoslav nationalities policy, in the course of which the Yugoslav communists reexamined and altered several of their basic premises. These phases are (1) 1919–23, advocacy of centralism and unitarism, buttressed by the concept of the tri-named people; (2) 1923–28, internal contention between left and right wings of the party; (3) 1928–34, the Comintern period, marked by submission to the Comintern dictum that Yugoslavia should be broken into separate, homogeneous nation-states; (4) 1934–43, recognition of the right of national self-determination, accompanied by the desire to preserve the unity of a socialist Yugoslavia; (5) 1943–64, formal federalism, characterized by the disjunction of republics and nationalities and the concept of "Yugoslavism"; and (6) 1964–89, abandonment of Yugoslavism and the emergence of genuine federalism, expressed by the equation of republics and nationalities and, thus, of interrepublican and interethnic relations. It can be argued that a seventh phase was inaugurated in 1974 with the passage of the new constitution and the introduction of the principle of collective leadership. Certainly the post-1974 period saw a renewed emphasis on what is called "Yugoslav socialist patriotism" as well as a conscious restructuring of decision making, particularly via the self-managing interest communities and various interrepublican bodies. The new structure moved in the direction of consensualism—in effect creating a concert system in Yugoslavia.

The working assumptions among Marxists at the time of the founding of the CPY (in April 1919) included the following: (1) nationalism is a capitalist phenomenon, a projection of the needs of the unified national market; (2) nations will wither away, just as the state will wither away, under socialism-communism; (3) only socialism can ensure ethnic harmony; (4) class identity and political allegiance give content to political life, national culture is mere coloring, and, therefore, nationality is a matter of form, not content (and, hence, also Stalin's phrase, "national in form, socialist in content"); and (5) the only suitable form of political organization for an incipient socialist state is centralized dictatorship by the Communist party in the name of the industrial working class.

The Serbian Social Democratic party (SDP), reflecting the outlook of most Serbs, viewed the newborn Yugoslav state as an extension of Serbia. At its First Party Congress (Belgrade, November 25, 1918) it declared: "Serbs, Croats, and Slovenes are one nation, because they have one language and indistinguishable ethnic traits. They feel themselves to be one nation and desire unification."[14] When, a few months later, the left wing of the Serbian SDP split off and reconstituted itself as the Socialist Workers party of Yugoslavia—Communist (it became the Communist party of Yugoslavia [CPY] in 1923), it retained this Greater Serbian orientation, snubbed the national question, and fully supported centralism as the most progressive distribution of power. The party endorsed the concept of the "tri-named people," which held that "Serb," "Croat," and "Slovene" were three names for one nation, and it continued to treat Slovenian as a dialect of Serbo-Croatian. And even though the party's Second National Conference, held in Vienna in May 1923, abandoned the thesis of national homogeneity, it nonetheless referred to Yugoslavia as a nation in the process of being created.[15] The inexorable wheels of modernization were expected to adjust reality to suit the needs of administration and policy.

Until then, the party had been divided between those who wanted to adhere to the Second Socialist International and those who proposed adherence to the new, communist Muscovite Third International (the Comintern). At the Second Party Conference, the latter group prevailed, and, in the flush of excited anticipation of the world revolution that was expected to wash across Europe within a matter of months if not weeks, the conference declared, in its program, that the soon-to-be-established "Soviet Republic of Yugoslavia must join in fraternal union with all neighboring peoples in order to establish a Soviet Federation of Balkan-Danubian Lands that will be a constituent part of the [emergent] international federation of soviet republics."[16] This made the working out of an articulate nationalities policy seem even less important. Soviet Yugoslavia would be just one small part of the world communist state, whose federal arrangement would atrophy forthwith. Hence, it appeared unlikely that Soviet Yugoslavia would be faced with the task of dealing with the national question on an autonomous basis.

With the dimming of the prospects of world revolution, however, came disillusionment with the earlier analysis and a realization that Yugoslavia's ethnic problems might have to be attacked at the Yugoslav level. But ideological differences could not so easily be plastered over once the issues ceased to be academic.

Partly as a result of the introduction of a federal form of government in Soviet Russia in 1923, which clouded the hitherto relatively translucent ideological waters, and partly as a result of tensions and conflicts within Yugoslavia itself, the party now found itself once more riven into factions—the right wing or "softs" advocating continued support of centralism and a gradualist approach to social reform, and the left wing or "hards" favoring more radical measures. Sima Marković, archdeacon of the softs, published a series of works, among them *Komunizam u Jugoslaviji*, *Nacionalno pitanje u svetlosti marksizma*, and *Ustavno pitanje i radnička klasa Jugoslavije*, in which he argued that ethnic harmony in Yugoslavia could be achieved by legal guarantees and institutional mechanisms and emphasized the need for constitutional reform. Though opposed to the Greater Serbian orientation of the fledgling state, Marković was likewise hostile to federalism—which, in his view, might at best serve the interests of segments of the rival Serbian, Croatian, and Slovenian bourgeoisies—and he argued that the objective conditions for ethnic equality could be realized within a unitary state. Writing in 1923 in defense of what had been the party line, Marković declared it a matter of indifference whether Serbs, Croats, and Slovenes were three nations or one. "This question . . . ," he wrote, "has no practical relevance." Closely related as they indisputably are, the three nations were bound, in his opinion, to merge in time into a single nation. Lingering on questions of ethnicity threatened to distract the party from its tasks and to lead it into reactionary positions: "national demands are [merely] the ideological forms in which the class interests of the national bourgeoisie are expressed." It followed, for Marković, that the only sensible policy was to slake the ephemeral thirst of national groups for self-expression by the grant of wide administrative and even political autonomy within the framework of a unitary, that is, nonfederal, state.[17]

But Marković went further, appearing to assign the resolution of the national question to the capitalist rather than to the socialist epoch and inviting the CPY to become engaged in the constitutional debate that had not been calmed but inflamed by passage of the Vidovdan Constitution. "Only in certain *special* circumstances can the national question be conceived of as a constitutional question," Marković conceded. But, he continued,

> as long as the Croats and Slovenes want to preserve the unity of the contemporary state, the national question presents itself as a question of internal organization of the state, i.e., as a constitutional question. However, . . . the desire of the Croats and Slovenes to remain in community with the Serbs is not *absolute*. . . . The primary condition that they set for the survival of the community is *complete internal democracy*.[18]

Two elements in Marković's argument were unacceptable to the party's left wing—his tacit endorsement of Serbianization and ostensible willingness to postpone agitation for the violent overthrow of the contemporary political order. Both propositions put Marković at odds with the Soviet and Comintern line, and pressure was brought to bear on him to confess his errors. In particular, Marković's stance on the question of unitarism and Serbianization signified a rejection of Lenin's revision of Marxism, a preference for orthodoxy over emulation of the Soviet path (increasingly becoming the new orthodoxy), and a stubborn adherence to Marx's doctrine of "historical peoples" at a time when the Russian communists were finding it better to allow and even stimulate a renaissance of national cultures through the multinational Soviet state. Marković's insistence on the superiority of unitarism at the very time the new orthodoxy had legitimized federalism seemed incomprehensible. Simo Miljuš, challenging Marković in the pages of *Radnik-Delavec* (September 1923), denied that partial palliatives would suffice and urged that Croats, Slovenes, and even Macedonians (!) be enabled to exercise the right of self-determination, even if that would mean the creation of separate independent states.[19]

Marković's asseveration that the national question might be solved by the simple device of guaranteeing the national, cultural, and linguistic rights of the minorities (i.e., nationalities other than Serbs, Croats, or Slovenes) drew the most blistering volleys from the left. For the party left (A. Cesarec, Dj. Cvijić, Moše Pijade, Kosta Novaković, T. Kaclerović, and others), Marković's reduction of the national question to a constitutional question was tantamount to suggesting that problems of social forces were soluble in terms of legal formulas. "The national question is not, for us, a constitutional question, as comrade Marković supposes, but a question of the direct conflict between oppressive forces and the oppressed," wrote Novaković in an article for *Radnik-Delavec*.[20]

Logically, alignments followed ethnic lines: Serbs backed centralism, which reinforced their hegemony, while Croats and Slovenes worked for federalization. The same phenomenon manifested itself inside the party, where the unitarism of the right wing attracted its chief support among Serbs, and the left wing's recognition of the national rights and distinctiveness of the non-Serbian peoples drew to its flank most of the Croatian and Slovenian members.[21]

At this point, the Comintern intervened and attempted to pressure the softs into adopting a more cooperative stance. Zinoviev, in an inflammatory speech at the Third Plenum of the Comintern (Moscow, June 12–23, 1923), repudiated the "rightist" notion that the bourgeoisie could make any headway against its nationality problems and pressed the CPY to renounce its constitutionalist delusions.[22] Neither the right nor the left supported federalism at this time, despite its introduction in the Soviet Union and despite the cardinal Comintern dogma that the future world communist state would be federal in form. But in polemics during the course of 1927, the left accused the right of trying to exploit the separatist and federalist ideas of certain minority factions in Croatia in order to mobilize an anti-Zagreb front that could be given a unitarist and pro-Serbian thrust. Indeed, for Marković, the entire issue of centralism versus federalism was in reality only a dimension of the rivalry between competing centers of monopoly capital (Belgrade and Zagreb, with the banks cast as the chief culprits). Calling Marković to account, Stalin pointed out that "the Bolsheviks never separated the national question from the general question of revolution, either before October or after October." Stalin claimed that Marković's portrayal of the national question as a struggle between rival bourgeoisies prevented his apprehending the national question as a peasant question and insisted that the CPY incorporate federalism into its program.[23] Despite Stalin's pressure, however, Marković, still party secretary, stalled. But in November and December 1927, with Marković and Laza Stefanović (another prominent rightist) in jail, the party left quickly called a plenum of the central committee and pushed through a resolution assigning exclusive blame for the intraparty crisis to the right and condemning right-wing sectarianism.

The issue was not yet over, however, and in January 1928 the Comintern felt constrained to order the central committee of the CPY to send a delegation of both left and right factions to Moscow for "counseling." Zinoviev told the Yugoslav delegation that even militant support for the revision of the constitution was insufficiently revolutionary and backed the leftist contention that it was a matter of obligation that Yugoslavia be splintered into individual homogeneous entities. In fact, the Comintern had been urging this line at least since its Fifth Congress (June 17–July 8, 1924), when it had resolved that "the general slogan of the right of nations to self-determination, to which the CPY subscribes, must be expressed in the form of separating Croatia, Slovenia, and Macedonia from the body of Yugoslavia and creating, from them, independent republics."[24] Crumbling under Muscovite pressure, the CPY assembled for its Fourth Congress in November 1928 and accepted Comintern demands for the creation of independent socialist states of Croatia, Slovenia, and Montenegro; the unification of all Macedonian lands (both those within Yugoslavia and those within Bulgaria) into a single republic; the transfer of the Hungarian sections of Vojvodina to the imminent Hungarian socialist republic; and the surrender to Albania of all territories inhabited predominantly by Albanians.[25]

The CPY had, thus, been gradually nudged further and further to the left. In 1920 Ilija Mikić, CPY delegate, could tell the Comintern that there was no national question in Yugoslavia, since the country was essentially homogeneous ethnically and its nationalities differed only in religious affiliation. By its Third Conference (Belgrade, 1923), the CPY, already somewhat intimidated by the Comintern and also faced with growing evidence of interethnic antagonisms, recognized only the possibility of creating a single homogeneous nation. But, defying the Comintern, the conference continued to insist that "the union of the Serbian, Croatian, and Slovenian nations is historically progressive and in the class interest of the struggle of the proletariat.[26] Finally, after 1928, the CPY, cowed into submission, functioned as little more than a Comintern mouthpiece, parroting the Moscow line that Yugoslavia had to be broken up as a prelude to the creation of a Balkan federation of worker-peasant republics.

This remained CPY policy until 1934. After the triumph of the Nazis in Germany, however, the Comintern reviewed its entire strategy, concluded that it had been misconceived, and sought, above all, to prevent any further spread of fascism. A critical reappraisal of the nationalities aspect of Comintern strategy was also undertaken. The result was that the CPY concluded, at its Fourth National Party Conference (December 1934), "that the [national] question could be successfully resolved within the framework of a Yugoslav state."[27] The possibility of a *Yugoslav* solution entailed necessarily the soft-pedaling of the notion of the Balkan federation. Although the CPY simultaneously determined to establish Communist party organizations for Croatia, Slovenia, and Montenegro, this decision was tempered by the continued adherence to the principle of party centralization. Secession was no doubt a right, but it was no longer seen as inherently progressive: the danger was all too great that separatism might play into the hands of the fascists (witness the Croatian *Ustaše* state). Thus, Kardelj, in his 1938 classic, *Razvoj slovenačkog nacionalnog pitanja*, warned that "although it is necessary to recognize the right of the Slovenes and Croats to self-determination, [it is a fact] nevertheless [that] every separatist action that at this moment attempts to break up Yugoslavia is in reality a preparation for a new enslavement, and not for self-determination."[28]

Leon Gešković claims that the CPY favored federalism by the mid-1930s.[29] But as late as the Fifth National Party Conference (Zagreb, November 1940), the CPY, while recognizing the campaign for national equality to be one of the most important tasks ahead, shrank from formal endorsement of federalism, an alternative that was discussed at that time. It was only in its second session at Jajce on November 29, 1943, that the Antifascist Council of the National Liberation of Yugoslavia (AVNOJ), in which the CPY was heavily represented, promised a federal order for postwar Yugoslavia. (AVNOJ had previously appointed a provisional government from among its members.)

Yet, despite the agonizing appraisals and reappraisals that had punctuated the CPY's torturous groping to this point, the party adopted a relatively bland attitude to the national problem immediately after the war. "The national question here has been settled," Tito told a Slovenian audience in 1948, "and very well settled, to the general satisfaction of all our peoples. It has been settled on the lines of Lenin's teaching. . . . The reason why we were able to settle the nationalities question so thoroughly is to be found in the fact that it had begun to be settled in a revolutionary way in the course of the liberation war."[30] It was generally assumed, in the early postwar period, that a new socialist nation was in the process of being created.[31] Therefore, the federal system set up was presumed to be largely an ephemeral formality and relinquished little authority to the republics. The national heterogeneity was the sole raison d'être for the establishment of federalism, with each republic except Bosnia-Herzegovina named after and consecrated as the official political embodiment of a discrete national group. The anticipated processes of homogenization would, therefore, erode the basis for the federal system. No doubt in the ripeness of time national differences would wither away—a prerequisite for the withering away of either federalism or the state.[32]

During the 1950s, "Yugoslav" was touted sometimes as an ethnic/national category in its own right, sometimes as a supranational category. This Yugoslavism (*Jugoslovenstvo*) campaign reached its culmination at the Seventh Congress of the LCY in 1958. Although the party program adopted on that occasion denied the intention of assimilating the composite groups into a homogeneous Yugoslav nation, the concept of "Yugoslav culture" endorsed by the congress implied an expectation of homogenization.[33]

It was at this point that Kardelj issued his *Razvoj slovenačkog nacionalnog pitanja* in a revised second edition that criticized Stalin's analysis of the national question and specifically modified the Stalinist definition of "nation." According to Kardelj, "a nation (*nacija*) is . . . a specific folk (*narodna*) community arising on the basis of the social division of labor in the epoch of capitalism . . . on a compact national (*nacionalnog*) territory, in the framework of a common language and a close ethnic and cultural relationship in general."[34] This is, in fact, Stalin's old definition, with the additional specification that the national community arises *on the basis of the social division of labor*. This addition appeared to allow for the forging of what Edmund S. Glenn has called the "state-nation"—a nation formed on the basis of a unified market within the context of a unified polity.[35] But, again, Kardelj demurred from driving the argument forward to this conclusion and drew, instead, a distinction between nation-building—the consolidation of a sense of national community—and assimilation:

> The merging of nations . . . does not mean the same thing as the merging of languages, of national particularities in culture, etc., or the forced assimilation of the small nations. On the contrary, . . . the independent social and cultural development of the nation [is] the prerequisite for the ever closer cooperation among and drawing together (*zbližavanje*) of nations.[36]

Kardelj's conclusion was paradoxical or—if you will—dialectical. On the one hand, Kardelj accorded a legitimate place to the national consciousness of the titular nationalities and of the smaller nationality groups. On the other hand, he warned that such nationalism is inherently reactionary, stultifying, and even culturally crippling unless it is associated with a strong sense of "Yugoslav socialist patriotism."[37] As Predrag Matvejević would later write,

> without a corresponding consciousness of community, i.e., without a *common Yugoslav consciousness*, we cannot further any sort of interrepublican relations, and, of course, not cultural relations. . . . The idea has taken root that it is enough to be a good Slovene or Croat, a good Serb or Macedonian, etc., and that by that very virtue one becomes equally also a good Yugoslav.

This idea, said Matvejević, is "fallacious" and "misguided."[38]

Consistent with this trend in Yugoslav thinking, the 1961 census introduced the category "Yugoslav" as an ethnic alternative. Only 317,124 persons, however, declared themselves to be Yugoslavs rather than Serbs, Croats, or any of the other traditional groups. The Croats and Slovenes in particular, but also the Muslims and other nationalities, felt threatened by the specter of renewed Serbian unitarism thought to be lurking under the robes of this ambiguous "Yugoslavism." They countered this notion of *integral Yugoslavism* (the notion, championed by Ranković, that there was a Yugoslav nation in the process of formation) with the idea of *organic Yugoslavism.* The emergent controversy between the two rival interpretations remained unresolved until the Eighth Congress of the LCY (December 1964), when the party finally and resolutely disavowed any assimilationist intent. Speaking at the Eighth Congress, Veljko Vlahović warned that the insistence on the withering away of Yugoslavia's nations, voiced in the wake of the Seventh Congress by advocates of integral Yugoslavism, reflected narrow-minded chauvinism and creeping crypto-unitarism. Tito condemned "the confused idea that the unity of our peoples means the elimination of nationalities and the creation of something new and artificial."[39] In the end, the congress adopted a firm resolution announcing that

> the erroneous opinions that our nations have, in the course of our socialist social development, become obsolete and that it is necessary to create a unified Yugoslav nation [are] expression[s] of bureaucratic centralism and unitarism. Such opinions usually reflect ignorance of the political, social, economic, and other functions of the republics and autonomous provinces.[40]

This was unquestionably a turning point both for Yugoslav nationalities policy and for interrepublican relations. Henceforth, it was no longer assumed that Yugoslavia's nations were in the process of disintegration and Yugoslav socialist patriotism was clearly disjointed from Yugoslavism.[41] As a consequence, the republics at last came into their own as fully legitimate agents of popular sovereignty; at last, federalism was accepted by the party as legitimate. This congress thus laid the basis for subsequent political decentralization. A change in nationalities policy provided the preliminary thrust toward the transformation of Yugoslavia into a system in which the republics could advance their distinct interests in an autonomous way—a balance-of-power system.

The Eighth Party Congress was the occasion of the first open discussion of the nationalities question in postwar Yugoslavia. No longer was it pretended that Yugoslavia's national groups were somehow different from other national groups either in consciousness or in behavior, and Stalin's distinction between bourgeois and socialist nations was openly repudiated as an un-Marxist doctrinal innovation. "The Yugoslav nations . . . behave and react as all other nations in the world and feel their interests just as much as any other nation. Therefore, they neither can nor will resolve the problems of their mutual relations in any other way than that in which all other nations do so."[42] "The same objective laws are valid in their mutual relations as in those among other nations."[43]

It was now openly acknowledged that ethnic prejudice and national antagonisms continued to plague socialist Yugoslavia, and the existence of conflicts of interest among the nationalities was recognized as legitimate. One spokesman even conceded that ethnic antagonisms were so deeply rooted that "it is an illusion [to expect] that the national question can be solved once and for all."[44] And some quarters dared to suggest that the nationalism of the separate nationality groups had a positive role to play in socialist society—a viewpoint that nonetheless remained heretical within the Yugoslav context.[45]

The reassessment of Yugoslavism created doubts in certain quarters about the whole notion of such a self-identification. In June 1969, *NIN* conducted a survey asking people what they thought it meant to be a "Yugoslav." By September 1969, the resulting article was under fire for unitarism, suprastatism, and negation of the equality of the peoples of Yugoslavia.[46] The question of Yugoslavism was again the subject of discussion at a joint meeting of the executive committee and presidency of the Federal Conference of the Socialist Alliance of Working People of Yugoslavia (SAWPY) on June 12, 1970. Certain members present urged that the "Yugoslav" category be dropped from the census forms in the forthcoming census, with Vlado Beznik, secretary of the Republican Conference of the SAWP of Slovenia, arguing that

> Yugoslavism as a nationality is not only inappropriate but implies also the existence of some sort of supernation. But the overcoming of nationality . . . cannot be realized in our society by creating yet another artificial nation but exclusively by the drawing together and binding together (*zbližavanjem i povezivanjem*) of all the national collectivities that live in our community.[47]

Replying to Beznik and others, Enver Redžić called Yugoslavism a natural and progressive product of the shared experience of the country's peoples. He vehemently objected to the proposed deletion of the "Yugoslav" ethnic category from the 1971 census forms. "Elimination of the category 'Yugoslav' from the forthcoming census," Redžić argued, "would amount to impeding an incontrovertibly live historical process that continues in conditions of self-managing and democratic socialist society."[48] Others (such as Puniša Perović) pointed out that many self-designated "Yugoslavs" were the offspring of ethnically mixed marriages and argued that deletion would in effect deny certain people their right of national self-expression. The category was therefore retained. As it turned out, however, only 273,077 persons availed themselves of this option in the 1971 census and declared themselves to be ethnically "Yugoslav"—a 14 percent decline from 1961. Doubts remained as to whether it reflected anything more than mixed marriage or, as in many cases, the sentiment of unpoliticized Muslims. As for the supposition that there was something immanently progressive about calling oneself a "Yugoslav"—this, too, was called into question. Vida Tomšić, for instance, told *VUS* that she would be insulted if someone thought himself more patriotic simply because he declared himself a Yugoslav while she registered as a Slovene.[49]

In the 1981 census, however, some 1,216,463 citizens of Yugoslavia declared themselves "Yugoslavs" by nationality—a substantial increase over the 1971 figure. This development led some members of the party to applaud, but provoked doubts and skepticism in other quarters. Dušan Bilandžić, a member of the central committee of the Croatian party, pointedly assailed the notion that Yugoslav nationality was somehow "superior" to Croatian, Serbian, and so on. In an article for the Croatian newspaper *Vjesnik*, he wrote that "there is absolutely no possibility of a Yugoslav nation being formed." Further, Bilandžić accused some newly converted Yugoslavs of antifederalist motives expressed in admiration of centralized administration. Bilandžić implied that this process of Yugoslavization was working specifically against the Croats and noted the "disappearance" of 30,000 Croats in Vojvodina.[50] In a second article for the newspaper, Bilandžić openly discarded the classical Marxist thesis of the withering away of nationality under communism and argued that the reasons for affirming a Yugoslav nationality were insufficient and therefore not persuasive.

Bilandžić's articles awakened a chorus of criticism. His critics found it impossible (or perhaps merely inconvenient) to defend the problematic concept of Yugoslav nationality, concerning which the party itself admitted considerable ambiguity. But they were evidently discomfited by Bilandžić's claim that Yugoslavism reflected centralist tendencies and quickly replied in kind. The critics insinuated that Bilandžić's real concern was shown in his lamentation over the decline of Croats in Vojvodina; in short, Bilandžić's doubts about Yugoslavism were portrayed as latent Croatian nationalism.

In the wake of the Croatian crisis of 1971 came a renewed emphasis on Yugoslav socialist patriotism, now unequivocally given an *organic* interpretation. Whether this signaled a new phase in Yugoslav nationalities policy is disputable. Certainly, since the early 1970s there has been more talk of the cohesiveness of the society. Yugoslav socialist patriotism lacks the supranational, assimilationist property of the earlier Yugoslavism campaign and is described, rather, as "the identification with, feeling for, and love of the socialist self-managing community." In this role, it is said to represent "a moral force for the unity of the socialist self-managing community of nations and nationalities of Yugoslavia."[51] The sentiment is thus ordinarily construed as the emotive bond that ties the individual to the collective. But at least one writer has urged that Yugoslav socialist patriotism be understood to involve collective affectivity at two levels: (1) devotion toward the "narrow" homeland, that is, one's republic, and (2) devotion toward the "wider" homeland, that is, Yugoslavia as a whole. In this way, wider patriotism not only does not exclude narrow patriotism but presumes it, and ethnonationalism, thrown out the front door, is quietly allowed entry through the rear.[52]

Components and Practice of Yugoslav Nationalities Policy

In the era of Titoism—which extended for several years beyond the lifespan of its creator—Yugoslav nationalities policy had eight chief components. First, the system recognized the ethnic particularity and full equality of all nationality groups and embodied the right of cultural-linguistic self-determination. Second, the system was organized as a federation with extensive decentralization and the right of political self-determination, including, in theory, the right of secession. Third, the party asserted the need to equalize economic conditions throughout the federal units and recognized the equal claim of all nationalities to economic resources and standards. Fourth, ethnic tensions were defused through self-management, a system for defusing social issues at the lowest level possible. Fifth, religious organizations were advised to abstain from outspoken involvement on behalf of particular nationality groups (though the creation of an autocephalous Macedonian Orthodox Church in 1967 enjoyed active party support because it provided an institutional symbol of Macedonian ethnicity in the face of claims that Macedonians are merely Bulgarians). Sixth, decentralization translated interethnic relations into interrepublican relations. Seventh, dual consciousness was affirmed—ethnic consciousness and Yugoslav consciousness ("Yugoslav socialist patriotism"). And, eighth, separatism and unitarism were considered two forms of the same perilous deviation.

Titoist Yugoslav nationalities policy thus combined radical decentralization and generous guarantees to the ethnic cultures with a terror of nationalism that often found expression in shrill denunciations of "neofascist nationalism" and "antisocialist chauvinism."[53] In fact, the operating assumption of Titoist nationalities policy was that any exclusivist nationalist sentiment was "anti-self-management," that is, that any revival of excessive ethnic pride (such as might be manifested in the singing of certain songs) was by definition anticommunist and potentially prosecessionist. The reason for this fear of nationalism is, at least in part, that the Titoists, as Marxists, viewed nationalism not primarily as a spirit with which a nation is infused (nor even perhaps as "a political doctrine extolling the nation as a supreme value and representing it as a dominant principle of societal organization"[54]) but as a relationship between two or more national societies, in which at least one society aspires to dominate, exploit, or despoil the other. For Yugoslavia's Marxists, hence, nationalism was a social relationship in which distinct national communities faced each other with mutually exclusive demands fired by collective arrogance and tinged with resentment of the unmatched gains of the other.[55] Under the circumstances, it is understandable that Tihomir Vlaškalić, president of the central committee of the League of Communists (LC) of Serbia, should have told his colleagues in 1976 that "to be a nationalist today, in conditions of national freedom and equality, means to be against the national freedoms of others, to be against equality, and, finally, to be against even the freedom of one's own nation, because nationalism today can only serve interests in favor of hegemony and exploitation, and that is certainly not the working class."[56]

Yet this horror of nationalism (whether urging separatism or hegemonism) was balanced by a scrupulous respect for the national sensitivities, linguistic rights, and cultural needs of all of Yugoslavia's national groups. Titoist nationalities policy recognized two broad categories here: (1) the "peoples" (*narodi*), consisting of Serbs, Croats, Slovenes, Macedonians, Montenegrins, and, after 1971, Muslims, and (2) the "protected nationalities" (*narodnosti*), of whom Gazmend Zajmi lists nine—Albanians, Hungarians, Turks, Slovaks, Bulgarians, Romanians, Ruthenes/Ukrainians, Czechs, and Italians, amounting to 2,200,000 persons or 10.8 percent of the total population in 1971.[57] But, in fact, Yugoslavia's record on national rights in the period 1969–81 was commendable for all groups except Gypsies. (Only Macedonia's constitution accorded the Gypsies equal status with the other national groups: in all the other federal units, the Gypsies, though guaranteed their legal rights "as individuals," were treated as outcasts and denied any collective rights.)[58]

To take one example, about 60,000 Bulgarians live in Yugoslavia, most of them in the *opštinas* (districts) of Dimitrovgrad, Vosiljgrad, Surdulica, and Babušnica. They have enjoyed daily broadcasts in Bulgarian, courtesy of Radio Niš, and several Bulgarian-language publications—among them, the weekly *Bratstvo* (now twenty-five years old); *Drugarčer*, a magazine for youth; and *Most*, a journal for literature, science, and culture.[59] Children of all nationalities are provided the option of schooling in their native languages through the high school or technical school level. Children attending such schools also study one of the Yugoslav languages. There are also bilingual schools. Until recently, all Yugoslav pupils were obliged to study a Yugoslav language other than their own. The revocation of this requirement resulted in massive loss of interest in Serbo-Croatian among Slovenian pupils and students.[60]

Guarantees to minority national groups are especially evident in the more heterogeneous autonomous provinces. In Kosovo, until the changes brought about by Slobodan Milošević in 1989, all provincial laws and regulations were published in authentic texts in three languages—Albanian, Serbo-Croatian, and Turkish—and state organs conducted public procedures in either Serbo-Croatian or Albanian or, if specified by statute in a given locality or enterprise, in Turkish. Official use of Albanian in Kosovo, however, only dated from the early 1970s and was disallowed in 1989. In Vojvodina, provincial laws, declarations, and proposals, including the social plan, appear in Serbo-Croatian, Hungarian, Slovak, Romanian, and Ruthenian.[61] All the republics guarantee their minority national groups the right to establish organizations to promote their communal interests and exercise their cultural rights. The Italian cultural association in Croatia has been one of the most active.

Yugoslavia recognized three official languages: Serbo-Croatian, Slovenian, and Macedonian. Because of mutual sensitivity to differences of orthography, spelling, and vocabulary, the Serbian and Croatian variants of Serbo-Croatian were usually both given, that is to say, they were treated as distinct languages for legal purposes. Thus, all treaties between Yugoslavia and other states were published in at least four languages—Serbian, Croatian, Slovenian, and Macedonian—and the constitution and other legal documents have also been published in Hungarian and Albanian. All federal buildings in Belgrade are scrupulously identified in all four languages, and the ingredients or instructions of many household commodities—such as canned fruit, detergent, and chocolate bars—were, by law, painstakingly given in the four languages.

Language policy in Yugoslavia was oriented to the protection of the homelands.[62] Two court cases involving Slovenia will serve to illustrate the point. The first arose in the early 1970s, when a certain resident Croat, accused of a criminal offense, objected that her language rights were being violated through the refusal of the municipal court to read its verdict in Serbo-Croatian. Her unusual suit came before the district court in Maribor, which, in a decision handed down in 1973, upheld the constitutionality of the Slovenian practice and declared that courts in Slovenia were not bound to issue their verdicts in any language but Slovenian.[63] The second case arose in 1974, when the Cinema Enterprise Maribor challenged the constitutionality of a republican law that prescribed that movies that were not made in or dubbed into Slovenian could not be shown in the socialist republic (SR) of Slovenia. The case came before the Constitutional Court of Yugoslavia, which, acting on the case in October 1977, declared that the Slovenian Law on Movies was not in discord with Article 246 of the Yugoslav Constitution (which deals with the equality of languages). The court upheld Slovenia's right to prescribe conditions for the public showing of films in its territory.[64] The essence of these cases was the protection of republican sovereignty as the best defense of the non-Serbian nationalities against Yugoslavization.

The national groups were also safeguarded in other ways. The 1974 constitution guaranteed the proportional representation of nationalities within the officer corps of the Yugoslav National Army (JNA)—though in 1970 figures made public clearly showed Serbian domination of the officer corps—and made important concessions to the national banks of the republics (Articles 260–265). The republics, moreover, were guaranteed participation in international treaties affecting their interests (Article 271).

The federal units played an important role in nationalities policy, not only in the administration of the various cultural/educational programs but also through the extension of substantial subsidies to minority institutions. For example, despite belt tightening and a restrained growth in the overall republican budget of only 14.7 percent, the Croatian republic increased subsidies for its national minorities by 20 percent for 1980, bringing the total allotted for this purpose to 50 million dinars. Of this total, 21.2 million dinars were earmarked for the Hungarian, Czech, Slovak, Ruthene, and Ukrainian councils; for newspapers in those languages; and for the support of the Italian Union and Italian-language drama in Croatia. Another 27.8 million dinars were assigned for the support of the newspaper *Edit* (of Rijeka).[65] Under Amendment 4 to the Croatian constitution (1971), a republic Committee for Interethnic Relations was established as a watchdog for minority rights. Similar committees were created subsequently in the other federal units.

Yugoslav nationalities policy necessarily assumed an economic dimension because of the Marxist dictum that political equality is impossible without economic equality. Given the vast differences in economic development between the northern and southern republics (to be discussed in further detail in chapter 8), the establishment of institutional mechanisms for channeling resources to the underdeveloped regions was viewed as a political imperative. As early as the Fifth Congress of the CPY (1948), Boris Kidrić declared that "it is clear that we would not be able to speak of a totally final resolution of the national question if the republics were to remain economically unequal."[66] This has been a recurrent theme, especially since the inflammation of Albanian nationalism in Kosovo has given the aid program for the south a sense of urgency. In a typical statement, the party presidency agreed (April 22, 1970) that "the reversal of the relative regression in Kosovo's development and the creation of conditions for the gradual diminution of the relative differences in the level of development is an essential condition for the realization of the principle of national equality . . . and a cohesive force in the Yugoslav socialist community."[67] Hence, it is not surprising that Yugoslavia's social plans have underlined the need to accelerate development in Kosovo and the underdeveloped republics. The social plan for the 1976–80 period, for instance, observed that "the policy of the faster development of the economically insufficiently developed republics and SAP [Socialist Autonomous Republic] Kosovo has special meaning for the further promotion of interethnic relations and for the strengthening of the unity of the working class, the equality of the nations and nationalities, republics and provinces."[68]

Titoist nationalities policy, thus, mounted a multifaceted assault on the roots of internal discord and a comprehensive program of socialization to Yugoslav socialist norms of brotherhood and unity (*bratstvo i jedinstvo*—a catch phrase incorporating equality, patriotism, and self-management). Self-management was often depicted as the necessary presupposition for the attainment of equality among the nationality groups and ethnic harmony in general. The linkage between self-management and nationalities policy occurred because the former was seen as a basic mechanism for decentralization and "de-etatization." And, though Titoist nationalities policy clearly tackled problems at the economic base, this was not in itself considered sufficient to effect the desired metamorphosis of the superstructure. Hence, far from resolutely snuffing out all traces of neo-Hegelian idealism, Kardelj, in one of his last works, conceded that interethnic problems cannot be extracted from their roots in group consciousness. *The German Ideology* notwithstanding, he concluded, changes in group behavior follow and often require changes in group consciousness. Therefore, it is not enough to introduce constitutional and institutional changes; changes must also take place in collective consciousness.[69]

PART II
The Institutional Context in Yugoslavia

4

Institutional Mechanisms of Interrepublican Cooperation and Policy Making

Despite the plethora of forms of political organization with which history is littered, the modern age comprehends, in essence, only three forms in which power may be organized: confederalism, federalism, and unitarism. The first can be dated to ancient times, with the Delian League in ancient Greece as perhaps the earliest example and the Swiss Confederation (1291–1848, with a brief interruption during the Napoleonic period) as the most enduring and best known example. Under confederative arrangements, member units retain absolute sovereignty over their respective territories, and even the forms of government of the confederal units may be heterogeneous (as was the case in the Swiss Confederation). Confederacies, by laying claim only to unified and coordinated foreign policy, scarcely amount to more than well-developed alliances.

Unitarism—which rejects any division of power, and, instead, concentrates authority in a single, unitary central government—is of similarly ancient vintage. Pharaonic Egypt and ancient Babylonia were unitary states, as was the Roman empire. So, too, have been most polities throughout history.

Federalism, however, is a distinctly modern phenomenon, unknown before the establishment of the American federal state in 1787. It was viewed then as a compromise between the unitary principle (which was unacceptable to most of the state delegates) and the confederative principle, which had proven unworkable in its pure form, embodied in the Articles of Confederation that had provided the constitutional basis for the North American Confederation during its brief six-year existence. The bicameral legislative structure that provided the underpinnings for the nascent system itself represented a compromise between the concept of representation proportional to population (the Virginia Plan, a de facto kind of unitarism) and the concept of equal representation for each federal unit (the New Jersey Plan, which reflected confederal ways of thinking).[1] Federalism is also a compromise in the sense that, although federal states permit the federal units autonomy in administration, the states have always demanded that their units adopt the same form of self-government. This feature applies as much to the Soviet and Yugoslav cases as to the American.

The U.S. was the only federal state until 1848, when confederal Switzerland followed the American example and adopted a federal constitution. Argentina followed suit in 1853, Mexico in 1857, Venezuela in 1864, Canada in 1867, Germany in 1871, Brazil in 1891, and Australia in 1900. Today, half the population of the world lives under one federal system or another. The popularity of federalism must be ascribed to its unique suitability as a mechanism for coping with problems that have only recently become so serious as to pose impediments to the establishment of modern political order. The reasons for adopting a federal order can be subsumed under three general categories: (1) *traditional*, which means simply that people who have traditionally enjoyed self-rule and who think of themselves as different or as having different interests from other groups with whom they share a common state may desire autonomy in order to safeguard their distinct culture and interests—the U.S. and Switzerland have this origin, and the establishment of the Autonomous Province of Vojvodina was similarly inspired by the distinct culture and group consciousness of Vojvodina's Serbian population as well as by the presence of the Hungarian minority; (2) *economic/geographic*, where differences of economic interest (e.g., one region may be highly industrialized, another largely agrarian) or the presence of geographic barriers that produce impediments to communication and transportation dictate a decentralized arrangement—as was the case in Mexico, Venezuela, Argentina, and Brazil; and (3) *ethnic/religious*, where the presence of linguistic, religious, racial-national, or other cultural differences, inflamed by the political awakening associated with modernization, militates against the imposition of a unitary political order.

Nineteenth-century federalism was a liberal construct, premised on the Madisonian argument that the division of power afforded the surest protection against tyranny. Nineteenth-century liberalism created what has been called *dual federalism*, which comprehends federation and federal unit as discrete, disjointed elements presiding over autonomous realms and not impinging on each other's domain. Dual federalism was appropriate to the nineteenth century and met the needs of that period. The growing demands placed on government, however, which generally meant the tumescent growth of *central* government, created a "crisis of federalism," in which federal states chose either to curtail the powers of the federal units and evolve in a unitarist direction or to seek a new solution for extracting themselves from untenable circumstances. The alternative conception that was generated came to be known as *cooperative federalism* and designates a system in which the isolation of the federal units from each other and from the federal government is viewed as unworkable, leading to a style of political management that depends heavily on cross-jurisdictional cooperation. Cooperative federalism entails two basic elements—cooperation between the federal units and the federal government and cooperation among the federal units themselves.[2] Of these two, the second is without question the more important. Indeed, one might say that mutual consultation and the coordination of policies among the federal units outside the framework of the central government is the keynote of cooperative federalism. Cooperative federalism is, therefore, a new type of federalism, a strain adapted and appropriate to the conditions of the twentieth century.

The Yugoslavs claimed to have created, within the context of their self-managing socialism, a cooperative federal system.[3] "Contemporary Yugoslavia is no longer a classic federation," wrote Edvard Kardelj in 1971.

> Nor can it be a classic confederation, but rather a socialist, self-managing community of nations, which to a great extent introduces simultaneously an essentially new category in interethnic relations. The independence of nations in such a community grows greater than in classic federations and confederations, but at the same time the processes of integration are opened wider in all areas where the common interest of the nations and working people is made manifest and where the conditions for equality are assured.[4]

In such a system, federation and confederation may be, in fact, anomalous. Stane Kavčić told *Politika* in 1968 that the question of federation or confederation was inappropriate, since these are *bourgeois* concepts representing political arrangements that arise in capitalist systems.[5] But if it was neither a classic federation nor a confederation as such, Titoist Yugoslavia nonetheless blended elements of both. This, in fact, was the view articulated by most participants at a symposium on federalism held in Novi Sad early in 1971.[6] Yugoslav cooperative federalism was said to depend on the pivotal role played by interrepublican cooperation. The validity of the Yugoslav claim to have generated an advanced form of cooperative federalism is one of the propositions to be examined in the course of this study. Ultimately, I will argue that the Yugoslav claim was *justified*, and this conclusion will be harnessed to the theory spelled out in Part I to infer a tight analogy between Yugoslav cooperative federalism and the nineteenth-century balance of power as realized in the Concert of Europe. But, as we shall see, this cooperative federalism contained within itself the seeds of its own transformation into a confederation, with all the associated risks.

Marxism and Federalism

The transplantation of federalism to a Marxist-Leninist system posed an ideological hurdle insofar as Marx's writings are unmistakably hostile to federalism. Marx and Engels believed that the interests of the proletariat would be better served in a unitary state than in a federal system, and the *Eighteenth Brumaire*, for one, is replete with praise for the efficiency and progressiveness of centralized power. Marx was convinced that decentralization could only serve the interests of regional bourgeois elites. He argued that centralization would create the preconditions for its own transcendence and, thus, for the withering away of the state. In opposition to the liberal democrats who were backing federation, Marx told the Communist League in 1850 that "the workers must use their influence not only for the one and indivisible German republic, but for a decisive centralization of force within it in the hands of the state power."[7] Similarly, Engels, despairing of federalism as costly, unwieldy, torpid, and corruptible, held that "the proletariat can make use only of the form of the one and indivisible republic."[8]

Lenin originally preserved the hostility of his German mentors toward federalism. He was categorically opposed to it and wrote, in a letter to S. Shauman in 1913, "We are in principle against federalism—it weakens economic links, it is an unsuitable model for any state."[9] Stalin echoed these sentiments in an article of March 1917 entitled "Against Federalism." Reiterating the Marxist maxims about the preferability of centralism, Stalin concluded: "federalism in Russia does not and cannot solve the national question; . . . it merely confuses and complicates it with quixotic ambitions to turn back the wheel of history."[10] Up to the very eve of the October Revolution, Lenin considered the right of secession a sufficient guarantee for the composite nationalities of the Russian empire. *State and Revolution*, written shortly before the Bolsheviks came to power, represents a turning point in Lenin's thinking on this subject. Although he still noted that federalism was in general "a hindrance to development," he insisted that it might represent "a 'step forward' in certain special conditions" and that "among these special conditions the national question appears prominently."[11]

Although Soviet federalism was compromised by a refusal to extend the principle to the Communist party of the Soviet Union (CPSU)—as enshrined in a resolution of the Eighth Party Congress (1919) that the central committees of the Ukraine, Latvia, and Lithuania had no legitimate basis on which to stake out autonomous realms—it nonetheless quickly became a point of doctrine. Surprisingly, in the early years after the left wing of the Serbian Social Democratic party broke off and reconstituted itself as the CPY, the party, as we have seen, snubbed the Soviet example. It was only in the wake of the adoption of the popular front policy at the Comintern's Seventh Congress (July–August 1935) that the CPY abandoned its program of seeking to break up Yugoslavia into small national states and began to move in the direction of an endorsement of federalism itself.[12]

It is true, of course, that Yugoslav Marxism was not married to the federal principle. Hamdija Pozderac, former president of the Bosnian republic's *skupština*, for example, cautioned that "federalism . . . is not a final ideal, but [merely] a necessary step in the process of the socialist development of a multiethnic state, in the process of its withering away."[13] Yet, at the same time, federalism remained an integral component of what Kardelj called "the pluralism of self-managing interests," the Yugoslavs were convinced that federalism necessarily entailed democratization, and they made an articulate defense of federalism in a Marxist state.[14] But, faithful to their dialectical view of history, they refused to imbue political forms with absolute value. "Federalism is not the culmination of political history and the ideal condition of relation among nations and people in the future. . . . Every idealization and absolutization of federalism is [therefore] antihistorical and unscientific, and in practice may betray a proclivity toward utopianism."[15] What the Titoists did claim for their system was what any good Marxist would wish to claim, namely, that the existing system of cooperative federalism was the most advanced political arrangement possible for the given level of the evolution in the organization of modes of production. Whether it would speed its own dissolution when the time was ripe for the introduction of a more progressive order—the sort of expectation that might sprout forth on the basis of *The German Ideology*—or whether federalism was a permanent feature of the Yugoslav political landscape remained a point of contention. The issue was connected to the overall policy adopted vis-à-vis the national question. On the one hand, if the nationalities would disappear in time, as Balša Špadijer, for example, has argued, then the basic rationale for federalism was of transitory relevance.[16] Gazmend Zajmi, on the other hand, contested the notion that the nationalities would necessarily wither away and disputed the legitimacy of connecting this notion with the Marxist concept of the withering away of the state.[17] And, if the nationalities of Yugoslavia would not dissolve in time into a larger group and their separate consciousness would not wither away, then Yugoslav federalism, it followed, was also permanent.

The Chamber of Republics and Provinces of the Federal *Skupština*

The focal point of interrepublican cooperation and the chief arena for interrepublican controversies was the Federal Assembly (*Skupština*), in particular, the Chamber of Republics and Provinces. The 1974 constitution described the *Skupština* as "the highest organ of government within the framework of the rights and responsibilities of the federation" (Article 282). Working through consultation and mutual agreement among the republics and provinces, particularly through the republican *skupštinas*, it served as the most important policy-making governmental institution in Yugoslavia. Under the 1974 constitution, the *Skupština* passed the Yugoslav social plan and the federal budget, discussed and set basic internal policies and foreign policy, was ultimately responsible for amendments to the federal constitution, and figured prominently in the determination of developmental policy and foreign trade relations.[18]

The forerunner of the contemporary Chamber of Republics and Provinces was the Chamber of Nationalities, established in 1946 within the framework of a bicameral legislative structure. The federal structure in this period was pure façade, and the Chamber of Nationalities had no real decision-making capacity. It was little surprise that, under the Basic Law of 1953, the Chamber of Nationalities was swallowed by the Federal Chamber and an independent Chamber of Producers was set up. This was entirely consistent with the ideological expectation of the day that the republics would wither away (producing a fully centralized state) before the state itself would disappear. The 1963 constitution, however, reorganized the *Skupština* as a pentacameral body and, in the waxing struggle between the centralist forces and the rising nationalist forces allied with nascent technocratic interests, the Chamber of Nationalities proved to be not only the logical arena in which to press for reform but also the key to political reform. De facto federalization of a de jure federal state demanded, above all, the invigoration of that chamber in which the federal units enjoyed representation. The turning point came in April 1967 when the first of forty-one amendments changed the system of election to the Chamber of Nationalities and broadened its rights and autonomy. For the first time since 1953, the Chamber of Nationalities met separately, in its own right. Amendment 8, passed the following year, eliminated the Federal Chamber, once the linchpin of the legislative system, and the Chamber of Nationalities, reconstituted as the Chamber of Delegates of the Republics and Autonomous Provinces, became the body with basic responsibility for legislation. About this time, a demand was also raised in various quarters that Kosovo and Vojvodina be represented by their own delegations in the Chamber of Nationalities rather than through wings of the Serbian delegation—a demand granted by the end of the year.[19]

Under a standing rule of the Chamber of Nationalities, legislation could be initiated on the proposal of any group of eight delegates. In effect, this meant that any republic could avail itself of this prerogative, but the autonomous provinces could not, since the former were represented by eight delegates each and the latter had only five delegates. The second-class standing of the autonomous provinces was, however, rendered purely formal by a subsequent change that, while leaving the procedural rule intact, permitted each republic to send twelve delegates to the Chamber of Republics and Provinces (CRP) and each autonomous province, eight. Amendment 38 (passed in 1971) required the concurrence of the federal units (or of their appropriate organs) before the federal *Skupština* could pass the Yugoslav social plan or other laws affecting the Yugoslav economy. Yugoslav federalism was increasingly becoming a "contract and participant interrepublican system," in which decision-making power emanates from the periphery rather than the center.[20]

Article 286 of the Yugoslav Constitution of 1974 outlined the prerogatives, powers, and responsibilities of the CRP as they were until the system disintegrated between 1989 and 1990. Under this article, the CRP, with the assent of the assemblies of the republics and provinces (1) passed the Yugoslav social plan; (2) established policy and passed legislation in the areas of the monetary system, foreign trade, credit and other economic relations with foreign countries, tariff protection, social control of prices of products and services, the fund for the more rapid development of the less developed areas, and the federal budget; (3) decided on the establishment of federal funds and the incurring of federal obligations; (4) ratified international agreements that would require alterations in legislation in areas within its jurisdiction; and (5) determined the expenses of the federation each year. Autonomously, the CRP (1) passed laws concerning temporary measures; (2) established, on the recommendation of the presidency of the Socialist Federated Republic of Yugoslavia (SFRJ), the sources and amount of credits and other obligations to be undertaken in connection with national defense and state security; (3) mediated in conflicts of jurisdiction between federal organs and republican or provincial organs; (4) ratified international agreements that required alterations in republican or provincial law; and (5) approved the extension of mandates of delegates to the *Skupština*.

Delegates to the Chamber of Republics and Provinces were chosen by the republican and provincial assemblies *from among their own ranks*, and continued, during their terms of office at the center, to retain their seats in the assemblies that they represented. Delegates were not mere "transmission belts" for the policy positions of their respective federal units, but were empowered to play a "creative role" in lawmaking.[21] The delegates played this *trustee* role, however, only in the initial drafting stages. In the later stages of legislative bargaining and negotiation, each delegation acted as a bloc, and each delegate was required to adhere to the policy position agreed on by the delegation as a whole and determined in consultation with the home base, the republican *skupština*.

Any republican delegation or working body of the CRP, the *skupština* of any federal unit, or the federal Executive Council (SIV) was permitted to propose legislation. On certain questions that the republican *skupština* considered of categorical importance, the delegation was usually not allowed to deviate from the official platform without consulting its *skupština*. Quite often, however, the assemblies of the republics and autonomous provinces authorized their delegations to act in their name with regard to approving draft legislation (as is permitted under Article 300 of the constitution).

From this point on, the delegations were responsible for coming to an agreement, since, except for emergency measures, all legislation required the assent of every delegation. Before the process of mutual accommodation began in the CRP committees (*odbori*), however, the delegations met separately to review the positions of the other republican and provincial assemblies. Once that was completed, the process of *usaglašavanje* (literally, the harmonization of viewpoints) began in earnest, advancing by means of compromise, alliance formation, and logrolling. The principle of unanimity took its toll in the protraction of negotiations in controversial areas. The CRP Committee for the Monetary-Credit System, for instance, met eleven times between January 24 and March 9, 1977, to discuss the scope and conditions of economic assistance to Kosovo through 1980. SIV's proposal was that, over the period 1977–80, Kosovo receive a grant of 400 million dinars. This proposal was initially supported by five delegations, namely, Bosnia-Herzegovina, Montenegro, Kosovo, Macedonia, and Serbia. At the beginning of March, Vojvodina switched ranks and also supported the SIV draft. The delegations of Slovenia and Croatia, however, insisted that the sum should be a loan rather than a grant. At the ninth session, the Croatian and Slovenian delegations jointly introduced a new proposal, which stipulated that the money be given as a loan, to be repaid over a twenty-five year period. Two further meetings failed to unite the parties around a common draft, and SIV finally intervened with a proposal that increased the amount of aid flowing to Kosovo (pacifying the bloc of less developed units) while specifying that the sum was to be a loan (thus offering some satisfaction to Slovenia and

Croatia). The specific terms outlined a loan of 1.6 billion dinars (four times the original figure), to be repaid at 3 percent annual interest but without a fixed term for repayment. These terms were adopted by the CRP shortly after the Slovenian delegation, though still voicing discontent, backed down and accepted the compromise draft.[22]

The Federal Chamber of the Federal *Skupština*

Whereas the Chamber of Republics and Provinces legislated in areas of economic policy, the federal Chamber—the other house of the bicameral assembly—independently legislated in areas of internal politics and foreign policy without the direct participation of the republican and provincial assemblies.[23] Decentralization, however, went so far (as we will see in the next chapter) that, in effect, the federal Chamber did *not* have a major role to play in policy making. It comes as little surprise, then, to learn that in the fall of 1971 the Yugoslavs even entertained scrapping the bicameral idea altogether and setting up a unicameral legislature: such an assembly would probably have functioned like an expanded CRP, since the republican delegations appeared likely to play the dominant role in this complex house.[24]

The federal Chamber consisted principally of representatives of self-managing organizations and sociopolitical organizations (including the Socialist Alliance of Working People of Yugoslavia [SAWPY] and the veterans' organization), but the republics and autonomous provinces also had delegations here that were obliged to hold to the positions of their respective federal units—thus replicating the pattern in the CRP. The delegates were apportioned so that there were thirty delegates from the self-managing organizations and sociopolitical communities of each republic and twenty from each autonomous province. Whereas the CRP operated on the basis of achieved unanimity, the federal Chamber carried decisions by majority vote—another clue to the lesser importance of this body in a system where every federal unit wanted a veto on important policy decisions.

The Interrepublican Committee System

Legislation passed in 1971 created a system of five interrepublican committees that dealt with various facets of economic policy. The five committees were for (1) developmental policy, (2) the monetary system, (3) foreign trade and hard currency, (4) the market, and (5) finance. Under the present arrangement, the rough outlines of legislation were usually established first in working groups and coordination bodies of the CRP and then passed on to the interrepublican committees to work out the details.[25]

Between May 1974 (when the new constitution was adopted) and the end of 1976, the interrepublican committees held some 125 meetings and considered some 450 questions on various subjects.[26] The Interrepublican Committee for

Market and Prices, for example, reached a concrete agreement about price policy in 1978; again, in the spring of 1980, the Interrepublican Committee for Planning and Development succeeded in hammering out a social compact (*društveni dogovor*) to stimulate the development of private enterprise and increase production in cooperatives in Yugoslavia.[27]

The SFRJ Presidency

Finally, the Titoist system created a collective state presidency, which served as the executive head of the complicated political apparatus that functioned after the death of Tito in May 1980. This collective body brought together delegates of the federal units (one per federal unit), who rotated annually in the office of "president of the presidency." The members of the SFRJ presidency were responsible to the assemblies of their respective federal units, which in fact elected them, and therefore lacked a common vision.

By 1990, Serbia's Slobodan Milošević had reduced Montenegro, Vojvodina, and Kosovo to mere satellites of Serbia, and, accordingly, controlled four of the eight votes in the collective presidency. Milošević's ability to produce deadlocks in the presidency at will was, however, only one symptom of the disintegration of the federal system, which was far advanced by the end of 1990.

5

Limited Sovereignty: The Autonomy of the Federal Units

The lines between the federated states in a federal Yugoslavia are not lines of separation, but of union.

TITO (shortly after the liberation of Zagreb)

The utility of the balance-of-power model is predicated here on the supposition that the actors in the system enjoy considerable autonomy. This chapter will endeavor to establish that such autonomy has existed in the Yugoslav system during the period under discussion. Before exploring the operation of the system in detail, I will demonstrate that the federal units have used that autonomy to promote their own interests, in accordance with behavioral constants 1 and 5 (see chap. 1, pp. 13–14).

By the end of 1990, the Communist party in Yugoslavia was in an advanced state of decay. In Slovenia and Croatia, many local party organizations had closed down. In Slovenia itself, the Communist party seceded from the League of Communists of Yugoslavia (LCY) in early 1990 and renamed itself the Party for Democratic Renewal. Simultaneously, it abrogated all obligations to the LCY, including those of a financial nature. In Croatia and Serbia, the local communist parties fused with local "Socialist Alliances" to create supposedly new socialist parties—the latter electing Communist party boss Slobodan Milošević in June 1990 to continue as head of the Socialist party of Serbia.[1]

Moreover, after the free elections in Slovenia and Croatia in early 1990 and the election of noncommunist governments in those republics, evolution into a full-fledged confederation seemed the only peaceful option. As of early 1991, *autonomy* seemed too weak a word to describe the wide-ranging powers effectively wielded by the republics. *Sovereignty*—a word employed by the governments of Slovenia, Croatia, and Bosnia—seemed more appropriate. In these conditions, the relevance of a balance-of-power analogy is, I should think, self-evident.

Yet even prior to the collapse of the center—a process that quickened after the polarizing appearance of Serbian party boss Slobodan Milošević on the political scene in 1987—the balance-of-power model had relevance. In 1969 (at the party's Ninth Congress), the LCY introduced collective leadership in the form of the executive bureau of the presidency, with fourteen members—two from each republic and one from each of the two autonomous provinces.

This body replaced the central committee, which, for the time being, was abolished. This collective principle was soon after extended to the other sociopolitical organizations, such as the Socialist Alliance, the Labor Union, the Veterans Organization, and the Youth Organization.[2] As a result of this and other restructuring, the League of Communists ceased to be a unified body. One can say, without exaggeration, that after 1969 there was no national communist party organization in Yugoslavia. What unity the party had it owed to the unifying and commanding presence of Josip Broz Tito, Yugoslavia's longtime president, and the powers he, uniquely, enjoyed.

The League of Communists of Yugoslavia was literally that—a league comprising six republican and two provincial party organizations. Each of these eight regional parties held its own party conferences, which, after 1969, were scheduled before rather than after the LCY congresses (indicating that they did more than rubber-stamp LCY policies). Each party set up its own presidium and its own executive bureau. Beginning in 1969, the republican organizations, at their congresses, passed their own statutes. These developments were followed by the adoption, at the Ninth Party Congress of the LCY (also in 1969), of a resolution calling for the further strengthening of the role and responsibilities of the republic party organizations.[3] Significantly, the republican parties also came to enjoy autonomous control of cadres policy in their own organizations. These autonomous party organizations were united only at the level of the federal presidium and remained both autochthonous and authoritative in their respective realms. As a result, in the Tito era Yugoslav politicians tended to eschew removal to the center, so that the real talent generally remained at the republican level. This practice set the pattern for the post-Tito era as well.

Autonomy of the Republics

Contrary to popular belief, Yugoslav decentralization did not originate in 1965. The Communist party of Yugoslavia (CPY) became the LCY in 1952, and that transformation expanded the jurisdiction enjoyed by republican and local party organizations over economic enterprises and projects. As early as 1950, the textile and leather industries had been transferred from federal to republican control; coal, electrical, chemical, and certain consumer-goods industries soon followed, and by the end of 1952, it was possible to speak of effective economic decentralization (though the republics were not the only beneficiaries, since they had to share the spoils with workers' councils and local party administrators).[4] By 1965, the federal government no longer had any direct means of control over enterprises, and the republics exercised considerably more control, although often mediated through local governments. Autarkic tendencies developed as each republic sought to develop its economic independence, even if it compromised the free market. Unnecessary duplications of services as well as productive capability occurred, although the interests of the federal government and of the country at large suffered. One example was the lack of coordination of bus services, which were even then consigned to the jurisdiction of the republics. Again, Slovenia's establishment of her own airline, Aviopromet, was motivated more by reasons of political competition than by economic requirements. Finally, severe constraints were placed on companies that attempted to open outlets or compete for contracts across republican boundaries. In the early 1960s, as Paul Shoup notes, " . . . decisions in the Central Committee of the League of Communists . . . were taken by a majority vote and often not implemented if they were considered contrary to republic interests."[5] Even during the crucial months during 1965–66, when the struggle against Ranković was coming to a head, Croatia put preservation of its autonomy ahead of certain ends that could have been achieved through cooperation with the federal center. Thus, despite contrary instructions from Belgrade, the Croatian secret police, responsible to the Croatian ministry of the interior, was instructed not to turn over reports to Belgrade and to continue its own independent investigation of Ranković. The Croatian secret police also refused Belgrade's demands to provide reports of meetings of the central committee of the Croatian LC at which the national question had been discussed.[6]

The republican party organizations had obtained control of economic organizations within their territories and acquired influence over questions of personnel in enterprises, banks, and social services. They enjoyed growing financial leverage and the ability to retain talented cadres. The determination of republican party apparatuses to pursue their own interests was demonstrated in 1967 in Slovenia. The Slovenian premier, Janko Smole, an ex-officio member of the federal government, compromised with other federal officials and introduced a bill calling for a cut in expenditures on social insurance. The Slovenian Social and Health Chamber, which had opposed any such reduction, vetoed this proposal, which resulted in Smole's resignation as premier. The republics viewed themselves as rival centers of legitimate interests. Thus, Miko Tripalo, just a few months before his fall from power, said, "SR [Socialist Republic] Croatia is [now] a state; so it is necessary to behave like statesmen."[7]

The federal units obtained an effective veto in many areas of federal legislation, the federal budget came to require the unanimous consent of the six republics and two autonomous provinces, and most of the functions formerly accorded the federal secretariat for internal affairs were, by the early 1970s, vested in the republics. The republics therefore ceased to be interested in appointments to the secretariat, as even federal secret police came to depend on cooperation from the republican ministries. So entrenched did republic interests become that one British observer was moved to declare it "unlikely that the LCY in fact exercises fully effective control over the present system."[8]

At this writing, Yugoslavia is still technically governed under its fourth (1974) constitution. All but the second (1953) have guaranteed the republics the right of secession. That this guarantee could be taken seriously became clear in 1989,[9] but even earlier, during the period of the struggle against Ranković, several influential Slovenes urged the invocation of this article and the secession of their republic.

But, though the 1946 constitution recognized the right of the republics to secede in their own name, the constitutions of 1963 and 1974 accorded this right to "the peoples of Yugoslavia," that is, to the Serbs, Croats, Slovenes, Macedonians, Montenegrins, and Muslims. (Under the Titoist formulas, the Hungarians and Albanians were considered "nationalities," not "peoples," and were denied the right of secession.) Whether this guarantee should be seen to have been intended as a kind of "devolution" or recentralization (insofar as the right is guaranteed to the people rather than to their representatives) is debatable. Regardless of the terminology employed in this article, however, it is certain that under Article 110 of the 1963 constitution, the republics gained the right to engage in cooperative ventures among themselves without any role being played by the federal government. (This had already been happening in practice, for example, in certain cultural agreements between the Serbian and Montenegrin republics.) This right was not rescinded. Even more important for the assurance of republican autonomy—indeed, the sine qua non of regional autonomy—is the absence of a federal power to transfer republic-level personnel from one republic to another. Such lateral transfers were long common in the U.S.S.R. (at least until Gorbachev's accession). But in Titoist Yugoslavia, offices in any given republic were filled solely by citizens of that republic. Of course, this meant that Serbs born and living in Croatia were eligible to serve in the Croatian, rather than in the Serbian, party apparatus.

The constitutional legislation of 1971–74 sharply reduced the legislative and economic functions of the federal government. In 1977, a law on hard currency guaranteed the republics the right to dispose of hard currency earnings, thus assuring them of fiscal sovereignty. From that point on, the only important economic functions left to the federal government (aside from preventing the erection of internal tariff barriers and coordinating economic relations abroad and with the World Bank) were its supervision of the Federal Fund for the Accelerated Development of the Underdeveloped Republics and the Province of Kosovo (FADURK) and the minting of coins and printing of currency. The federal units were the chief beneficiaries of this devolution.[10] The republics obtained exclusive jurisdiction in regulating, among other things, the following: the use of agricultural farmlands; mining, transport, forestry, urban planning; the planning and erection of investment objects; education, science, culture, health, public safety, environmental protection; the residence of citizens; public meetings; the legal status of religious communities; and marriage and family, guardianship, parent–child relations, inheritance, residential life, and employment. Criminal law was also assigned to the jurisdiction of the republics and provinces but was coordinated via interrepublican mechanisms. Economic planning was to be carried out by each federal unit in coordination with both federal and district planning agencies, and each republic was to determine its own budget with complete autonomy.

For a number of years, many prices subject to regulation in Yugoslavia were regulated not by the federal government but by the governments of the federal units. Thus, in 1979, when an increase in slaughtering of cows presaged a reduced supply of milk and signaled the need for higher milk prices, some republics (Slovenia and the Socialist Autonomous Province [SAP] of Vojvodina) reacted quickly and approved the price hikes sought by the dairy industry, resulting in an assured supply of milk. Others, such as Croatia and Serbia, were slow to approve higher prices. Croatian and Serbian dairies responded by sending their milk out of the republic in search of higher prices, thus producing milk shortages in their own republics. By the end of the year, patience had worn thin, and Dragutin Jurko, Croatian secretary for agriculture, forestry, and food industry, revealed that discussions were underway to establish a uniform nationwide price for milk.[11] Then, on December 28, straining under the dual pressure of rising inflation and foreign trade imbalances, the federal Executive Council (SIV) upbraided those republics that, during November and December, had granted permission for hefty price increases for various products and services. The council announced that prices should not be allowed to rise without interrepublican agreement. Gojko Ubiparip, vice president of SIV, said that this behavior imperiled the policy of economic stabilization, and he demanded that the federal units sign an agreement synchronizing price policy for 1980. A special working body was created, and by early February, the federal government had its agreement—limiting price inflation to 25 percent for 1980. Although the federal government obviously initiated the agreement, it is important to note that the agreement was reached by mutual consultation of the republics, not imposed by federal diktat.

Interrepublican coordination was seen, at least until the Serbs broke off economic relations with Slovenia in December 1989, as a basic necessity in the decentralized polity. Hence, for example, when the federal Secretariat for Transport was shut down in 1975, it was replaced by an interrepublican coordinating committee for transport.

The republics gradually became aware of built-in social and institutional factors that militated toward a degree of uniformity in both economic and noneconomic sectors. For example, in the mid-1970s, Vojvodina abolished the pre-graduation exam administered to high school seniors. All the other federal units, however, retained this exam, and the universities in all federal units other than Vojvodina continued to require passage of this exam as a condition for admission. Graduates of Vojvodina's high schools had no option but to attend the University of Novi Sad. Thereupon, the Vojvodinan *skupština* repealed the law and restored the exam.

Whatever the imperatives of coordination, the republics clearly enjoyed vast political, cultural, and administrative autonomy. Indeed, under the 1974 constitution, the federal units enjoyed quasi-confederal autonomy. Yet, despite the constriction of federal functions, the exclusion of the federal government from various sectors, the strengthening of the direct (via republican assemblies) and indirect (via republican representatives in the federal Assembly) participation of the federal units in the passage of federal law, and the deepening autonomy of the republics and provinces effected by the 1974 constitution, a cautionary note may be appropriate. For, despite the overhaul carried out between 1971 and 1974, Djordji J. Caca could still write, in 1977, that

> [the first] three years of experience in applying the new constitution do not fully confirm the suppositions and expectations [that had accompanied its passage]. Undoubtedly policy is more in conformity with the essence and norms of the constitution than was earlier policy, but this is still uncertain because again it is not rare to find federal laws spelling out norms on certain questions both fully and in detail. We can no longer regard that as inertia.[12]

Bearing that caveat in mind, the republics were, nonetheless, already at that time, genuinely autonomous centers of power.

In July 1990, the Slovenian parliament proclaimed the sovereignty of Slovenia and declared that federal law would be valid in Slovenia only if approved by Slovenian legislators and if federal law did not conflict with Slovenian laws. Tone Persak, a member of the Slovenian parliament, commented: "By this declaration, the Slovenian Parliament de jure created a sovereign Slovenian state that is no longer a part of the Yugoslav federation. The declaration created a confederal relationship."[13]

Role of the Republics in Foreign Relations

With the passage of republican constitutional amendments in January 1969, the republics acquired the right to participate autonomously in the foreign policy of the Yugoslav federation, that is, to engage in unmediated contacts with foreign states.[14] Croatia and Slovenia were quick to exercise their new prerogatives and established close contacts with Austria. Other early examples of independent foreign policy contacts include the dispatch by Croatia of emissaries to Hungary in 1969 and 1971 in pursuit of economic and cultural links and the visit by a Croatian delegation to Munich in November 1971 to conduct bilateral discussions with deputies of the "Free State of Bavaria."[15] Such contacts have continued to the present day.

Certain "unreconstructed" centralists attempted to abort this development, calling the move another token of Yugoslavia's "degeneration into a confederation."[16] But, ten years later, each federal unit had its own Bureau of Foreign Relations and its own Coordination Commission for Economic Relations Abroad, and bilateral contacts between Yugoslavia's federal units and foreign states had become commonplace. In addition to contacts arranged at the intergovernmental level, the republican and provincial organizations of SAWPY likewise played a role, until 1989, in maintaining contacts with regional organizations of neighboring countries as well as with the organizations of Croatian and Slovenian minorities in Austria and Italy.

Autonomy of the Autonomous Provinces

When first called into being by the constitution of 1946, the Autonomous Province of Vojvodina and the Autonomous Region of Kosovo-Metohija (as it was then designated) were little more than administrative divisions of Serbia. They enjoyed no independent representation in federal bodies, and their borders were subject to modification at Serbia's discretion. Even after Kosovo was granted the more dignified rank of autonomous province, the two units were, until the end of the 1960s, unmistakably inferior to the six socialist republics, as illustrated by their having statutes, rather than constitutions, under the 1963 constitutional arrangement.

By the latter half of the 1960s, however, Kosovo and Vojvodina, supported by Croatian nationalist-liberals (such as Djodan) and Slovenian liberals, were pressing for more equal treatment, with certain circles even attempting to obtain equality of representation in the Chamber of Nationalities.[17] Nonetheless, not until 1968 were some of these desiderata granted. Amendment 16 to the Yugoslav Constitution finally guaranteed that the boundaries of the provinces could not be changed without the consent of their *skupštinas* (a guarantee subsequently incorporated also into the constitution of SR Serbia), and their statutes were given the legal status of constitutions. This latter change made possible the establishment of constitutional-judicial branches of the supreme courts of Vojvodina and Kosovo, which performed the same functions as the republican constitutional courts. But the formal establishment in the autonomous provinces of the constitutional courts—which the republics had had since 1963—was delayed until 1972, by which time, through the passage of further constitutional amendments in 1971, the autonomous provinces had acquired extensive additional legislative and judicial powers and enjoyed the same degree of administrative autonomy as the republics.[18] Moreover, by the early 1980s, changes to the constitutions of Vojvodina and Kosovo were being made entirely autonomously, with no provision for either review or recommendative proposal on the part of any Serbian organ; the provincial assemblies of Vojvodina and Kosovo were, in effect, empowered to make amendments without consulting with the Serbs.

There has long been a provision in the Serbian constitution (Article 301) for enacting legislation for the entire territory of the Serbian republic (i.e., including Vojvodina and Kosovo) on the basis of the mutual agreement of the assemblies of all three units. The article also provided that should the assembly of one autonomous province approve a Serbian-sponsored measure rejected by the other autonomous province, the bill would become law only in Serbia proper and the province that approved it. Similarly, though another article of the Serbian constitution (Article 296) authorized the Serbian republic to communicate directly with lower organs of the autonomous provinces "in matters of national defense, state security and . . . in other circumstances in which irreparable damage might ensue"[19] (provided only that the provincial government be apprised), this article was, for all practical purposes, a dead letter from the time the fourth constitution was passed (1974) to the seizure of power in Serbia by Slobodan Milošević in 1987. Milošević would claim that Serbia had the right to legislate unilaterally on the territory of the provinces and that the provinces had usurped their autonomy "illegally." But when Milošević began to curtail the powers of the APs (autonomous provinces), their assent was not freely given.

The general Yugoslav view in the late Titoist and early post-Titoist period was that Vojvodina and Kosovo were republics in everything but name. The differences between the SRs and the SAPs through the late 1970s and most of the 1980s amounted to this: Vojvodina and Kosovo had no provincial flags, no provincial citizenship (natives of the SAPs have automatically received Serbian citizenship), and no legal claim to the right of secession (a guarantee always reserved for the republics). In addition, the autonomous provinces have had less representation on certain federal bodies, such as in the Chamber of Republics and Provinces (where they have eight delegates each instead of the twelve to which a republic is entitled) and the Federal Chamber (where they have twenty delegates instead of thirty). Since it required only eight delegates, acting as a block, to introduce or veto bills in the Chamber of Republics and Provinces, the difference in delegation size was without consequence. In fact, the purely symbolic character of the differences between the republics and the provinces until 1989 confirms the conclusion that they were, for all practical purposes, equivalent.

By the same token, to the extent that the socialist republics can be treated as autonomous actors, the socialist autonomous provinces functioned in the same way until the end of the 1980s. That the autonomous provinces participated in federal policy making on a par with the republics was demonstrated in March 1978, for instance, in a discussion of a draft law on the customs tariff that took place in the CRP's Committee for Economic Relations with Foreign Countries. On this occasion, Croatia clashed with Kosovo over a 15 percent increase in the tariff on imported equipment. Rajko Savić, the Kosovar delegate, wanted only a 7 percent increase. Regional interest, of course, dictated the differences in policy proposals. A compromise tariff rate was finally worked out by the other republics and Vojvodina.[20] Clearly, in this discussion, Kosovo and Vojvodina negotiated on equal terms with the republics.

Article 292 of Vojvodina's constitution and Article 293 of Kosovo's authorized the autonomous provinces to make contact and enter into agreements with "organs and organizations" of foreign states. Both provinces exercised this right and engaged in unmediated negotiations with foreign states. Of the two, Vojvodina was the more active in pursuing foreign economic relations, though Kosovo maintained active contacts with neighboring Albania, including a steady flow of faculty and cultural groups between the University of Tirana and the University of Priština, until the Albanian-nationalist riots of the spring of 1981 prompted Belgrade authorities to cancel the exchange program.

In the latter part of 1981, in the wake of accusations of cover-up by provincial officials in Kosovo, authorities of the Serbian republic began to talk of downgrading the autonomous provinces and reclaiming powers that the SAPs had obtained "unconstitutionally." Vojvodinan officials reacted vehemently, however, complaining that Serbia was overreacting to events that had nothing to do with Vojvodina. A full-blown dispute erupted between Vojvodina and Serbia over the autonomy of the APs, especially in the realms of national defense, civil defense, economic planning, and foreign trade.[21] Serbia also wanted to retract authority over citizenship in the SAPs from the ministries of internal affairs in the provinces to the Serbian ministry and tried for two years to persuade Kosovo and Vojvodina to acquiesce in the transfer of authority. Finally, in early 1983, having failed to obtain the assent of the SAPs, Serbia simply promulgated the new law unilaterally (in breach of their own republican constitution).[22]

In the course of 1988, Slobodan Milošević removed many provincial leaders in Kosovo and Vojvodina and replaced them with his own people. In February 1989, he pushed through a series of amendments to the constitution of SR Serbia that eliminated the provinces' authority to pass their own legislation and established the Supreme Court of SR Serbia as the highest judicial court of appeal for Kosovo, prior to appeal to the federal level. Later, in summer 1990, Kosovo was placed under direct rule from Belgrade. As a result of these moves, the APs effectively disappeared as autonomous actors from the Yugoslav political scene.

PART III

Yugoslavia as a Balance-of-Power System

6

The Reform Crisis, 1962–71

At the dawn of the 1960s, Yugoslavia was run by a small circle of functionaries. Aside from President Tito, this circle included Aleksandar Ranković (a Serb), head of the secret police, who became vice president of the country in 1963; Edvard Kardelj (a Slovene), vice president of the federal Executive Council, president of the Committee for Legislation and the Building of People's Power, and the chief architect of the social system; Mijalko Todorović (a Serbian liberal), who exercised leading authority in the economic sphere after 1958; Svetozar Vukmanović-Tempo (a Montenegrin), president of the Labor Union; Ivan Gošnjak (a Croat), state secretary for national defense; and Koča Popović (a Serb), state secretary for foreign relations. To this group, one might add the name of Vladimir Bakarić (a Croat), secretary of the League of Communists of Croatia. Although Bakarić eschewed removal to the center, he was nonetheless a senior figure in the party and played a larger role than other regional barons. Although these figures presented a unified front to the outside world, they were torn by serious internal differences. Kardelj, in particular, was the leading advocate of political reform, and, under his influence, the federal Assembly passed a series of laws in March 1961, setting up, at the same time, joint commissions of representatives of several federal bodies to carry out reforms in the economic sector.[1]

In mid-March 1962, the executive bureau of the LCY central committee held a closed session to discuss the political directions of the system. The session saw sharp political conflicts but ultimately produced a decision to take concrete steps to address certain problems and shortcomings. Among these problems were localism, chauvinism, and national particularism.[2] The session unleashed an ideological-political campaign against these and other problems, and party members were placed on "alert." On May 6, 1962, Tito delivered an important address in Split, highlighting the dangers associated with localism and telling his audience that there was a real danger that each republic was just out for itself, ignoring the interests of the Yugoslav community as a whole.[3]

The importance of this early evidence of internationality and interrepublican frictions cannot be overemphasized since it gives the lie to claims by later advocates of recentralization that these problems were "created" by decentralization. On the contrary, decentralization was undertaken in order to address this issue, and in this regard, decentralization was partially successful. Ultimately, the stronger pressures have been for continued and deeper decentralization rather than for the reverse.

Tito and Kardelj warned about corruption in economic management and about the diversion of investment funds into politically motivated projects. Commissions and committees were set up, and work on "the Reform" began.

The reform began as a series of ad hoc adjustments to the economic administrative mechanism and blossomed in 1965 into a full-fledged assault on economic inefficiency, unprofitable enterprises, inflationary development, and distorted prices. "Centrally planned investment [had become] impossible in Yugoslavia because it was no longer possible to agree politically about such planning."[4] The alternative adopted was to reduce the role of the federal government, scrap central planning, and allow greater say in economic planning and administration to the local decision makers, that is, the federal units, *opštinas*, and enterprises. The chief beneficiaries of this devolution were the federal units.

The motivations for the reform were, at first, purely economic. The overriding issue was that of efficiency, and partisans of all sides addressed this key issue, marshaling pertinent economic arguments. The debate quickly took on an ideological character, however, when the loose alliance of liberals, technocrats, and enterprise managers met more ideologically conservative opponents, who appealed as much to socialist values as to economic criteria. Liberals considered it "an illusion [to think] that it is possible to build socialism in an autarkic fashion."[5] Some even dared to summon Adam Smith in defense of the proposition that every nation and every republic should produce whatever goods and services it can produce best and most cheaply and import whatever it cannot produce well, cheaply, or efficiently.[6] Moreover, as opinions hardened on each side, the controversy surrounding the reform took on interrepublican characteristics, with Croatia leading the proreform coalition and Serbia the most energetic opponent of reform.

The Eighth Congress of the LCY, held in December 1964, had the task of assuaging the surfacing tensions in interrepublican relations. The Eighth Congress was the occasion for the first open discussion of the national question and for a somewhat nebulously worded agreement to undertake economic reform. The Croats began arguing the case for economic "optimalization," that is, the use of profit criteria in investment, and questioned the lack of circumspection with which General Investment Fund (GIF) resources had been funneled into the south. Drawing on support from Slovenia and Macedonia, the Croats achieved a partial victory at this congress. But the consensus reached was flimsy and even superficial, since, in practice, rival and contradictory economic orientations were incorporated into resolutions adopted at the Eighth Congress.[7]

The reform and the subsequent political devolution, along with the resultant institutional configuration of Yugoslavia, were, to a considerable extent, the handiwork of the liberals, who won them by wrenching control of the system from the old-style conservatives. In time, however, the liberals lost the reins of power to a coalition of new-style conservatives and party centrists ("Titoists").

The Yugoslavs in power from 1971 to 1980 did not refer to themselves as "conservatives" any more than they called themselves "unitarists" (a term of abuse in Yugoslavia since at least the mid-1960s). The regime had a tendency to concatenate the label "liberal" with another one—normally considered unrelated in Western thought—namely, "anarchist." This produces the hybrid "anarcho-liberalism." Although in Western usage anarchists are usually considered to occupy a niche far to the left in the political spectrum, the Titoists condemned anarcho-liberals for right-wing deviationism. Anarcho-liberals were said to favor the establishment of a multiparty system (though anarchists, of course, propose to do away with all government) and were said to be hostile to self-management on principle.

A related difficulty is that the meaning assigned by the Yugoslavs to the word "liberal" is fluid. In 1970 and 1971 the term was generally applied to the programmatic current represented by Croats Miko Tripalo and Savka Dabčević-Kučar, Slovene Stane Kavčić, and Macedonians Krste Crvenkovski and Slavko Milosavlevski, as well as by Serbs Marko Nikezić and Mirko Čanadanović. It was considered respectable at that time to be liberal, and such liberalism distinguished its adherents from the more centralistically oriented line that "conservatives" had favored. By the late 1970s, however, the term "liberal" was more often applied to dissident intellectuals, including Ljubomir Tadić, Milovan Djilas, and others. The identification of liberalism with dissent was obvious from the title of the two-volume work *Liberalism from Djilas to Today* (*Liberalizam od Djilasa do danas*). By the time of the Twelfth Party Congress (in June 1982), liberalism had once again become a respectable, even fashionable, epithet, and a leading hard-liner was so bold as to inform me, two weeks after the congress, that "*we liberals* won a great victory at the Twelfth Party Congress."

Every selection of terminology involves a compromise. Some terms may be more precise but suffer from unfavorable political overtones. Other terms may be more neutral but also less precise. I have decided to use the terms "liberal" and "conservative" to identify the principal currents in Yugoslav politics in the 1970s and 1980s, realizing that these terms may call forth associations irrelevant to the Yugoslav context.

By "liberal" in the Yugoslav context I mean someone who favored (1) decentralization and the deepening of federalism, (2) emphasis on profitability in investments, (3) a more open society with greater respect for human rights, (4) loose party supervision of society, (5) pluralism *within* the party, and (6) the placing of priority on the needs of one's own republic. This is not to say that everyone I identify as "liberal" necessarily favors all six liberal planks. But it does presume that she or he identifies with at least three or four of the six liberal stands and that she or he cooperates with other liberals, some of whom advocate the other liberal planks listed.

By "conservative" in the Yugoslav context I mean someone who favored (1) a strong central government or party, (2) emphasis on the political goals to be accomplished through investments (e.g., equalization of living standards), (3) a less open society with tighter censorship and social controls, (4) tight party control of all sociopolitical organizations, (5) democratic centralism (operational party discipline), and (6) the rendering of priority to federal needs (or the needs of the LCY) over the needs of individual federal units *in all cases*.

Not all party officials fall into one of these two categories, however. In addition to these two groups, there is a fluid group of "brokers" who may hold the balance and who attempt to find a middle ground between the liberals and the conservatives. Tito, Vladimir Bakarić, and Branko Mikulić were all prominent brokers. In practice, the brokers were usually closer to the conservatives than to the liberals, though most brokers, Tito included, identified with the liberals during the 1966–71 period.

Economic Reform as a Stimulus of System Change

It is a cliché among Marxists that political development tends to lag behind socioeconomic transformation and that changes in the latter sphere create irresistible imperatives for changes in the former. Whether universally true or not, the axiom appears to fit the Yugoslav case in the mid-1960s. Prior to 1963, Yugoslavia was a centralized state with a federal veneer. After 1963, however, changes began to take place in the behavior of the federal units, changes that bubbled up from the realm of economics into the political world and impelled ultimate institutional overhaul. By 1971 various observers, both Yugoslav and American, believed that decentralization had gone so far that Yugoslavia was on the verge of reconstituting itself as a confederacy. The economic reform, by unleashing certain political forces, proved a stimulus of system change.

More significant than the occurrence of system change is the fact that its essence was *depolarization*. As the triplex program of "de-etatization," decentralization, and democratization advanced, four important changes took place in the system: (1) the Serb-Croat rivalry ceased to be the lodestone of intra-Yugoslav politics; (2) the north/south split ceased to provide a reliable basis for predicting the alignment of federal units in issues; (3) the other six federal units, though demographically and (aside from Slovenia) economically outgunned by Croatia and Serbia, began to mobilize in the political arena and to assert their demands; and (4) the republics began to oppose the federal government in areas where their interests were threatened. Slovenia was the first republic to openly oppose a federal decision (in the Slovenian road controversy of 1969), but the phenomenon would later become quite common in Yugoslav politics.

The years immediately prior to the economic reform of 1965 were riddled with difficulties. Industrial plants had often been built more for political, that is, cosmetic or palliative, reasons than with an eye to economic rationality, and inventories of unwanted goods were rising. Unused capacities in industrial production were accompanied by the unprofitable records of many "political factories." All this was aggravated by growing inflationary pressure and by perennial balance-of-payment deficits.[8] When the economic reform began, it was conceived, as such things usually are, as a simple adjustment to enable the existing system to function more smoothly. Its origins were piecemeal adjustments that prompted further adjustments. Three reform measures were introduced in 1961: opening the Yugoslav economy to the world market, reorganizing the financial markets, and relaxing wage controls. "The reform measures were, however, insufficiently prepared and hastily implemented," as a World Bank report notes.[9] Economic problems continued to mount, with inflation quickening after 1962, and they compelled a major reexamination of the premises of the system.

Between 1964 and 1965, a series of policy decisions were made that reflected the outlook of the economic liberals, that is, the system's discontents. Among the chief elements of this reform were

(1) the transfer of considerable responsibility for administration of the economy from the federal government to the republics;
(2) the repudiation of the concept of regional autarkic development (the concept that *every* Yugoslav republic should be self-supporting);
(3) the adoption of a more realistic exchange rate, permitting greater participation by Yugoslavia in world trade;
(4) the complete revision of price ratios, marked by steep hikes in the prices of raw materials, agricultural goods, and certain other commodities and services;
(5) the aggrandizement of the role of banks and economic enterprises (susceptible to republican pressure and manipulation), at the expense of the federal government; and
(6) the abolition of the federally controlled General Investment Fund (GIF).

The reform had an unmistakable devolutionary character: its main features were the strengthening of the role of the periphery (the republics and enterprises) at the expense of the center (the federal government and the Belgrade banking monopoly). But by turning the resources of the defunct GIF over to the large central banks, the reformers failed to carry the reform through to its logical conclusion. Thus, they aggravated certain latent antagonisms in the system, stimulating a growing conflict between the central banks, insurance companies, and foreign trade organizations on the one side and their republican counterparts on the other. This conflict increasingly took on political overtones and in time assumed nationalist garb as a conflict between the assimilationist conservatives gathered around Ranković and the partial and egoistic interests of the national communities, especially Croatia.[10]

As Crane Brinton has noted in his classic study of revolution, collective cognitive dissonance does not set in during a period of sustained oppression or exploitation but, rather, as a formerly oppressive or exploitative regime begins to reform itself.[11] Once given better conditions, citizen-subjects inevitably ask why conditions could not have been better *sooner* and why they could not be *better yet*. In Yugoslavia, the suppression had been perceived in regional terms and, therefore, the heightened consciousness produced by the relaxation of federal control was also framed in regional-ethnic terms. Cognitive dissonance (CD) was expressed in group terms—as Croatian CD, Montenegrin CD, or

Kosovar/Albanian CD, but never as *Yugoslav* cognitive dissonance per se. Miko Tripalo, then a member of the executive council of the presidency of the LCY, recognized this when he told *Borba* in 1970 that "nationalism of all sorts is one of the negative reactions to unitarism. Its essence is *etatism*, but at the level of the republic."[12]

The Croatian crisis was, in fact, revolutionary in character and signaled the surfacing of long-repressed resentments. It was natural, therefore, that this sentiment should carry over into the political realm, that is, Croats, perceiving themselves to be economically exploited, should champion not only further economic liberalization but also political reform. Some Yugoslavs recognized this tendency quite early; shortly after the fall of Ranković (July 1966), one disgruntled conservative pointed to the futility of trying to contain reform in the economic sphere. At the same time, this revolutionary character impelled the Croatian leaders to pose as leaders of the Croatian *Volk* and as progressive leaders of the Yugoslav community. In the process, the transformation of intergroup behavior made system change not only necessary but possible.

Politicization of the Reform

If the recession that struck Yugoslavia in 1961–62 served as a spur to economic reform, it was also the irritant that inflamed Yugoslav politics. Slovenes and Croats argued that central planning was no longer relevant to their level of development. But the Yugoslav south lagged considerably behind this standard, and some argued that the use of a centralized mechanism to distribute resources was still a boon to the less developed parts of the country. The northerners complained that gross investment figures disguised the true advantage enjoyed by the south, since large sums had to be spent in the north for maintenance and replacement of existing equipment, while the admittedly lower gross amounts for the south could largely be funneled into new projects and direct expansion. The southerners replied that development of the south was the most rational strategy over the long run, because the wealth and natural resources were there and it would be cheaper to process natural resources in the south than to transport them elsewhere.[13] Kosta Mihailović, for instance, in a 1962 article for *Ekonomist*, claimed that the eastern republics (the "Danubian zone") were more suitable targets for Yugoslav investment, that that region was economically more dynamic, and that for the next thirty years it would not be necessary to build *anything* on the Adriatic coast![14] But, as Deborah D. Milenkovitch has pointed out, "few really believed that rapid development of the less developed regions was also a maximum growth policy for the nation, and fewer still believed that their rapid development was economically more beneficial to the already advanced areas than an equivalent amount of investment in the advanced areas would have been."[15] The northerners complained of excessive waste in southern investment and noted the higher marginal capital coefficients (i.e., the greater investment necessary to produce a given income) and the lower labor efficiency prevailing in the underdeveloped areas.[16]

Šime Djodan, then a prominent Croatian economist, outlined three alternative models of economic development applicable to a country with heterogeneously developed zones: accelerated development of the underdeveloped areas to equalize all areas, concentration on further development of the better developed areas, and development according to the principle of economic rationality. We have already seen that the first approach was associated with the so-called Danubian concept of development and that the third model was espoused by advocates of the "Adriatic concept." Conservatives like Stipe Šuvar unfairly attempted to identify the liberals with the second model. But, in fact, there was another faction, small and not very vocal, that believed the second model to be a suitable framework. This faction espoused a "Slovenian concept" that called for the intensification of investment in the most advanced areas: not surprisingly, advocates of the "Slovenian concept" tended to be Slovenes.[17]

Under the third (Adriatic) model, optimal economic results are the guiding criterion; for example, it would favor development of nonferrous metallurgy in Serbia, Kosovo, and Macedonia and of aluminum, bauxite, and hydroelectric industries in Croatia and Bosnia. In a key argument, Djodan claimed that the less developed republics suffered as much from the errors of the Danubian concept as did the Adriatic republics. If the development of Slovenia, Croatia, and Vojvodina had not been hindered by advocates of the Danubian concept, he argued, "the development of the underdeveloped districts would be a far more tractable problem today than it is."[18] Unfortunately, charged the Croatian liberal critics, Yugoslavia had operated on the basis of the first model. Too many factories had been built in the south without economic justification—and the phenomenon of the "political factories" was said to be worst in Kosovo and Bosnia-Herzegovina.[19] Djodan, like many other Croats at this time, concluded that "if one considers regional development on the territory of Yugoslavia as a whole over the preceding period, one must confess that it was understood as the development of the insufficiently developed regions."[20] Some demanded that a federally appointed agency be created to supervise investments in the south and assure that funds were sensibly spent. (Djodan's arguments will be taken up at greater length in the following chapter, in the context of the Djodan-Šuvar debate.)

The LCY tried to hold the line against the growing criticism. Answering the charge that northern money was being squandered on the construction of "political factories" in the south, Kardelj asked a Slovenian audience:

> But is it really true that there are no irrational investments in Slovenia and Croatia? I will not cite instances of such failures and misses, because you yourselves know them well, but I would pose the following question: what would be the reaction in Slovenia if someone were to demand that predetermined federal organs should evaluate the rationality of Slovenian investments and the economic policies of the organs of the republic of Slovenia? There is no doubt that such a demand would

> be bitterly repulsed and that it would be viewed as an attack on the independence of the Slovenian nation. I think that such a reaction would be legitimate. Is it not clear, then, that the same things cannot be measured with different measures? And is it not clear that the use of such different criteria [for Slovenia and Croatia on the one hand, and the underdeveloped areas on the other] would lead not only to the undermining of the equality of the Yugoslav peoples, but also—in that event—to the economic and political dependence of the economically less developed nations and republics on the more developed?[21]

But the underdeveloped republics showed no sign of catching up with the developed republics, and, thus, it could be (and was) convincingly argued that, if equalization was indeed the aim, a new approach was necessary.

These arguments, and the presence of liberals like Crvenkovski in the leaderships of the underdeveloped republics, converted this rich-poor debate, which might have produced a simple economic polarization under other circumstances, into a political question. It provided the basis for an anti-Serbian coalition, as we have seen in chapter 1 (see, in particular, tables 1 and 2). Bakarić was instrumental in bringing about a change in Croatian tactics, designed to appeal to the non-Serbian underdeveloped areas. The Croats actively began to woo the south and, as early as 1961, Croats began to talk of de-etatization rather than decentralization. Evidently, Bakarić indeed believed that the underdeveloped areas could profit economically from decentralization and de-etatization; he was staunchly antinationalist and consistently opposed expressions of ethnic particularism, especially in his native Croatia.[22]

The liberals (the decentralists) and the conservatives (the centralists) now began to look about for allies. The liberals' identification with Croatian-Slovenian interests and conservatism's association with the interests of the Serbian republic became a complicating factor. Macedonia and Croatia both had a stake in federalism and had resisted suggestions made in the early 1950s, during the Yugoslavism campaign, that nominal federalism be dumped and replaced by open unitarism.[23] Croatian and Macedonian elites, both motivated by the desire to maximize republican autonomy, reached a working understanding. The Serbs concentrated on courting the underdeveloped republics and, in the case of Montenegro, had some success: in December 1963, Serbia and Montenegro announced the integration of their respective industries; cooperation in communications, foreign trade, and long-term joint planning; and the conclusion of an agreement to complete the Belgrade-Bar railway. In the course of 1964 and 1965, the Serbian and Montenegrin parties signed additional protocols for economic and cultural cooperation.[24] These actions collectively constituted the domestic equivalent of a treaty. They also signified the abandonment of any pretense to neutrality on the part of the Serbs. (It might be recalled, in this connection, that Šuvar, among others, had at one time claimed that the Serbs were uniquely "internationalistic," that is, culturally neutral, and that Serbs were ready to become "Yugoslavs.") The Serbo-Montenegrin protocols and

Serbian wooing of other underdeveloped federal units signaled Serbian identification with the conservative southeastern bloc. But the simple polarization that the Serbs envisaged did not materialize; instead, the situation proved much more complex. A stable national-liberal coalition began to take shape, composed of Slovenia, Croatia, and Macedonia, with Vojvodina as a kind of associate partner.[25]

This national-liberal coalition, applying pressure both through its representatives in Belgrade and through vigorous self-assertion within the areas of its collective geographic jurisdiction, was able to push the reform forward between 1965 and 1966, dramatically reducing the prerogatives of the federal government in the economic sector. Federal subsidies to industry were slashed—a clear victory for Croatia and Slovenia and an unmistakable setback for the centralists, whose strongholds lay not only in Serbia but also, at that time, in Kosovo and Montenegro. Profitability became the chief criterion for the allocation of resources. The market reform of 1965 effectively ended the golden age of "political factories," and central investment planning was abandoned. Yet the Serbs were not unconditional losers in this round of battle, since they continued to dominate the national banks and since the reforms were not inimical to Belgrade's larger corporations. Moreover, the distinction between advocacy of pluralistic decision making through syndicalist mechanisms or along territorial/ethnic lines was blurred by the temporary alliance of proponents of both approaches in the fight against unitarism.[26]

At the same time, concern over the slide toward political pluralism was growing among Serbs. The Serbs were sensitive to accusations of Serbian hegemony and harbored lingering resentment against the Croats for the establishment of an independent Croatia in World War II and the concomitant *Ustaše* massacres of Serbs. It is important to remember that the LCY established itself on the wreckage of the Serbian Chetniks, who had waged rather lackadaisical guerrilla warfare against the Germans, actually collaborating with them in the end. This commixture of historically rooted emotions is combined with the conviction of many Serbs that centralism provides the greatest good for the greatest number—shades of Jeremy Bentham—and that Serbs, the only true internationalists in Yugoslavia, have been abused and exploited by the other nationalities.[27]

Passage of the reform did not, therefore, signify the end of the issue. For one thing, the Macedonian League of Communists (LCM) was internally divided. Many in the LCM were as bitterly opposed as their colleagues in the LC Serbia to the decision, made by the Third Plenum of the LCY central committee in early March 1966 to reduce federal investment, support economic reform, and permit enterprises to invest throughout Yugoslavia. For another thing, the centralists, still in control of many of the levers of command, were sabotaging the reform through a combination of studied perversion, perfervid Švejkism, and outright noncompliance. "Individual measures were frustrated, sometimes mysteriously, or else pushed to ridiculous extremes. . . . There were always sound reasons for deviations, vehemently and sometimes apparently unwittingly argued by politicians and an increasingly disputatious and regionally or functionally partisan press."[28] By midwinter 1966, the liberals were dispirited. "It's like punching a rubber wall," one despondent liberal confided to an American observer, "you seem to make an impression, but then it's just like it was." Another reformer was even more disheartened and announced grimly in January 1966: "the Reform is dead."[29]

The Serbian party was taking a hard line. Men like Jovan Veselinov and Vojin Lukić, both party secretaries and the latter a close confidant of Ranković, were determined to block devolution and reform to the furthest possible extent. Ranković, as head of the state security service, had carved out a small empire for himself and had long opposed Kardelj's more liberal, polycentric visions with his own neo-Stalinist centralism.

In March 1966, *Komunist* reported discussions (of March 10) "of a markedly political character" between representatives of the executive committees of the party central committees of Macedonia and Serbia. Though the parties met in part to explore possibilities for widening bilateral interrepublican cooperation in the fields of economics and culture, the contacts also represented an effort to dampen lingering Macedonian suspicions toward Great Serbian chauvinism (the kind that had labeled the Macedonians "South Serbs" during the interwar period). The discussants hoped to lure Macedonia away from the liberal and back into the conservative orbit.[30] This gambit failed, however, and Macedonia clung fast to its coalition with Slovenia and Croatia. Note, however, that this kind of direct contact between the Serbian and Macedonian parties, like the earlier contact between the Serbian and Montenegrin parties, is exactly what is expected within the framework of the model.

The Fall of Ranković

In 1959, there was an attempt on Kardelj's life. Kardelj was seriously wounded but survived. Although nothing was proven, Kardelj's wife, Pepca, let it be known that she blamed the Serbian leadership, that is, Ranković, for the assassination attempt.[31] Her suspicion makes clear the depth of enmity existing between the two men. They were not merely rivals—they were deadly enemies. The incident was passed over but not forgotten.

Meanwhile, Ranković was making enemies in other ways. His use of methods of intimidation and his surveillance of leading party functionaries, including the collection of intimate details of their lives, angered many.[32] Kardelj and his liberal allies prepared the field of battle in early 1965, when they obtained the reassignment of Ranković's loyal ally, Vojin Lukić, who was now moved from his post as federal secretary for internal affairs to a less sensitive job as organizational secretary of the Serbian party.[33] By spring 1966, the liberal bloc had finally persuaded Tito that Ranković had to go. The final decision seems to have been made suddenly, and the "investigation" of Ranković was rushed through in order to deny him any possibility to respond.

Only on June 16, 1966, was a special commission appointed by the executive bureau of the LCY central committee, with the task of preparing the case against Ranković. The commission was chaired by Krste Crvenkovski of Macedonia. Its other members were Blažo Jovanović, Djuro Pucar, Dobrivoje Radosavljević, and most interestingly, Miko Tripalo (of Croatia) and France Popit (of Slovenia). The commission worked in secret, with the responsibility of producing a full report within six days.[34] Although not members of the commission, the powers behind this commission were liberals Kardelj, Vladimir Bakarić, and Petar Stambolić (of Serbia).[35] They would be among the chief beneficiaries, ultimately, of Ranković's removal. Crvenkovski and Tripalo would also soon show liberal colors.

Ranković was kept in the dark about the commission's work until the last minute and only received the documentation amassed against him on the eve of the Brioni plenum, at the same time that this documentation was also made available to the other delegates invited to the meeting.[36]

In session, Tito accused Ranković of deviating from party policy as early as 1964 and of forming a political clique with the objective of taking power. Ranković and his adherents were specifically accused of "dragging their feet in carrying out the decisions of the Eighth Congress—in fact, they have as much as completely forgotten about the decisions altogether."[37] Ranković was stripped of his posts and expelled from the central committee. His deputy, Svetislav Stefanović, was likewise stripped of his posts and expelled from the party, as was Vojin Lukić.

Serbs reacted to Ranković's ouster as though the Serbian nation itself had been defeated. *Borba* (September 15, 1966) cited lamentations that LCY policy had become anti-Serb and that the Serbs no longer had anyone to defend their interests. UDBa itself was shaken up, and many key security personnel were transferred to large trading corporations in Belgrade.

Although Ranković's fall in July 1966 essentially ended the crisis, there was an interesting sequel—interesting, that is, from the perspective of coalition theory. The provincial committee of Kosovo was angered by the revelations of UDBa misconduct and by the "gentleness" with which the Great Serbian unitarist Ranković was being coddled. Alienated from its former "protector," Kosovo demanded his expulsion, also, from the LCY—a demand seconded by the central committees of the LC Montenegro, LC Bosnia, and LC Macedonia and passed by the Fifth Plenum on April 10, 1967. The composition of this anti-Ranković group seemed to symbolize the solidarity of the underdeveloped republics with the Croatia-Slovenia axis and betray a certain amount of opportunistic maneuvering. Possibly it also indicated a postreform switch of Montenegro from the conservative to the liberal camp. The establishment of this broadly based, anti-Serbian coalition suggests to me that Yugoslavia was transformed, in the course of this crisis, from a loose bipolar system, polarized along economic lines, into a balance-of-power system.

Ascendancy of the National-Liberal Coalition

At this juncture, there were three obvious alternative paths of development: recentralization, further devolution culminating in the transformation of Yugoslavia into a loose confederation, and shoring up of the status quo on the basis of interrepublican consensus. Such consensus was lacking. Throughout this period the national-liberal coalition (Croatia-Slovenia-Macedonia) concentrated on further decentralization and "democratization" both of the LCY and of society. A key issue was federal control of the greater part of earned foreign currency. In championing the federalist principle, the Croatian party was supported by the Slovenes, who had common economic interests and favored currency reforms; by the Macedonians, fearful, above all, of a revival of Serbian chauvinism; and even by some members of the new Serbian leadership who were hostile to centralism.

There was some support for centralism throughout the less developed regions, but all of these areas, especially Macedonia, saw the Serbian republic as minatory to the autonomy of the other republics. Serbia, it was thought, viewed its own interests as tantamount to the interests of the whole and tended to benefit disproportionately from centralism. The disjunction of the LCY from Serbian interests, if not its actual neutrality in the controversy, was attested by an article in *Komunist* (February 3, 1966) that referred to Serbia as the center of antireform resistance.

Throughout 1967 and 1968 there was considerable furor over whether republican delegates to the Chamber of Nationalities ought to be free to act on their own opinions (thus allowing for compromise with opponents and a possible failure to assure the interests of their respective federal units) or whether delegates ought to be bound by an "imperative mandate" to observe the strictures and instructions of their republics and autonomous provinces. In vain Miloš Žanko, a Croatian representative in the chamber and vice president of the federal Assembly, urged deputies to transcend the parochial interests of their respective republics and to adopt policy stances consonant with the interests of Yugoslavia as a whole. Žanko was reported to have said that "deputies in the Assembly [must] make decisions according to their own convictions. . . . No deputy is answerable only to his own [republic]. Every deputy is answerable to all the peoples of our country."[38] For this, and for openly criticizing the laxity of Zagreb in dealing with Croatian nationalism, Žanko was recalled by the Croatian party and relieved of his posts.

This was the period of liberal ascendancy, which reached its high-water mark in the summer of 1971 (i.e., after the national-liberal coalition had fallen apart) with the passage of a series of amendments to the constitution. Together, these amendments amounted to the reconstitution of Yugoslavia as a confederative republic. They included the conversion of the office of the presidency into an interrepublican collective presidency, albeit still presided over by Tito. Throughout this period there was a tendency for liberals to identify centralism with Great Serbian assimilationism, resulting (as forecast under hypothesis 3) in the formation of a stable anti-Serbian coalition.

This was also a period in which various circles indulged in what, under the circumstances, can only be judged to have been idle fantasies. Stevan Vračar, for example, seeing in the breath of liberalism an opportunity to dismantle the dictatorial superstructure altogether, openly advocated installation of a two-party system in Yugoslavia, his only proviso being that both parties be committed to socialism—a notion Crvenkovski was said to have favored.[39] Certain unnamed individuals allegedly tried to seize control of SAWPY in order to use it as the nucleus for an opposition party parallel to the LCY.[40] Milosavlevski, in a 1966 article for *Gledišta*, urged that SAWPY be empowered to reach its own conclusions independent of LCY direction and even to differ with the LCY over policy matters.[41]

Not even the LCY appeared, at first, to be immune to the reformist contagion. A commission was set up as early as September 1966 to consider the possibility of a reorganization of the LCY throughout the country, with the Macedonians perhaps in the forefront of the campaign. Even the official party journal, *Socijalizam*, published an article by Tomislav Čokrevski in October 1967 that argued that the Leninist conception of democratic centralism had been devised to meet the needs of an underground party in tsarist Russia and that Yugoslav party organization had to reflect changed historical and social conditions.[42] Party reform appeared, for a while, to be a logical extension of the reform, and, indeed, party structure was reorganized in October 1966. Even Radio Belgrade would state, in June 1967, that "the reform of the League of Communists is a component part [of] and vital presupposition for the implementation of economic and social reform goals."[43] It soon became clear that what the reformers wanted was no less than the complete and official federalization of the party. The LCY could not be satisfied with the faithful representation of the "general interest" of the working class, the reformers argued. According to Stojan Tomić, a high-ranking party member in the LC Bosnia, "the League of Communists must also realize partial interests," and, accordingly, the LC Bosnia was obliged to represent specifically Bosnian interests just as the LC Macedonia ought to represent specifically Macedonian interests.[44] Tomić added the understandable qualification that the "partial interests" of the republics should not be pursued at the expense of the general interest of Yugoslavia. Seeking to strengthen the ability of the republican parties to defend precisely such partial interests, Macedonian Mito Hadži Vasilev tried to obtain for the republican parties a veto power over the decisions of federal party organs. In a daringly blunt repudiation of the concept of democratic centralism, Vasilev argued that "no majority, no matter how overwhelming, can, in and for itself, justify a decision—we say within the League of Communists of Yugoslavia—when it is clear that even a single republican organization cannot accept and implement this decision."[45] That this demand was no idiosyncratic fluke was clear from its subsequent reiteration at the Fifth Congress of the LC Macedonia (Skopje, November 18–20, 1968), when Milosavlevski unreservedly came out in favor of the extension of federalism to all political sectors, including the LCY. Among the Montenegrins, the anti-Serbian faction also appeared to be ascendant in the post-Ranković phase. Budislav Šoškić, candidate member of the LCY presidium representing Montenegro, fully expressed the waxing federal spirit when he declared, in December 1968, that the republican party organizations were no mere "transmission belts" for LCY policy.[46]

This anti-Leninist talk elicited resistance from those unwilling to equate party democratization and party federalization. Dragomir Drašković, denouncing such talk of federalization on behalf of the Serbs, declared that communism must be proletarian, not national, in content and that proletarian interests would only be diluted, fractionalized, and prejudiced by allowing the ethnic factor into the political calculus in this respect.[47] The issue was still a live one when the Ninth Congress of the LCY met in March 1969, and the participants carried the debate into the halls of that congress.[48] Yet, while the national-liberal coalition showed itself to be all for democratization of the party as long as this strengthened the autonomy of the republic organizations, once that process threatened to factionalize the republican party organizations, the coalition resurrected the old dictum of democratic centralism.[49] Neither side, thus, challenged democratic centralism per se; the dispute raged over its appropriate application. And, though the Ninth Congress ended up being purposefully vague in some of its resolutions, republican party congresses were empowered to select members of the LCY presidium and to draw up their own party statutes. The more active role that the national-liberal coalition was claiming for the republican party organizations was accorded a degree of legitimacy when the Ninth Congress resolved that "instead of binding them in a centralized fashion, the League of Communists of Yugoslavia realizes a creative ideopolitical synthesis of the conceptions, opinions, activities, and initiatives of the Leagues of Communists of the socialist republics."[50] Although Aleksandar Fira, then a professor at the University of Novi Sad, fired back that "the League of Communists is not a league of leagues of communists, but a league of communists of Yugoslavia,"[51] the tethers seemed to be slackening, the transformation was complete, and the movement for economic reform had been metamorphized into a movement for political reform.

Disintegration of the Coalition

The Ninth Congress was perhaps the highpoint of the national-liberal coalition. Within a few months, the Slovenes became enraged at their coalition partners for pusillanimous support or outright desertion on an issue of vital importance to the republic of Slovenia, the Croatian and Macedonian parties were engaged in open polemics, and the coalition drifted apart.

The Third Session of the LCY presidency, held on May 29, 1969, just two months after the Ninth Party Congress, signaled the first crack in the national-liberal coalition. The session highlighted the inner tension in the alliance of actors with divergent economic interests. Serbian liberal Mijalko Todorović had already thrown the issue into relief by venting his concern over expressions of exclusivist nationalism in the publications of Matica Hrvatska (the Croatian Culture Society). More potent yet was Crvenkovski's denunciation of Croatian economic nationalism as a kind of separatism. Crvenkovski called for a retreat from economic decentralization, arguing that the persistence of Yugoslavia's economic woes was due to the inadequate integration of the Yugoslav economy. Tripalo, speaking on behalf of the Croatian party, rejected Crvenkovski's analysis and insisted that economic troubles could best be cured by more thorough decentralization.[52]

The strains in the alliance were subsequently exacerbated by the Slovenian road affair, during which alliance partners Croatia and Macedonia declined to share the cuts in highway construction that Slovenia was expected to shoulder. Generally, by the time a foreign credit or foreign aid package is formally tendered to Yugoslavia, the republics have already agreed on the dispersal and disposal of the funds, and project work can therefore proceed without a hitch. In the summer of 1969, however, after the World Bank had announced the award of extensive credits to Yugoslavia for structural development, including road construction, the Yugoslav federal Executive Council (SIV) revised its project package, provoking sharp Slovenian reaction.

In July 1968, Belgrade had applied to the World Bank for assistance in financing a highway construction program. A World Bank appraisal mission visited Yugoslavia in October and November of 1968 and agreed to finance three road projects (one each in Croatia, Slovenia, and Macedonia) and to consider the financing of further roads in Serbia and elsewhere at a later date. The Slovenian sections, which would link that republic with Austria, were deemed by bank experts to be an economically wise investment in view of the potential for developing the tourist industry in the northeast.

On June 5, 1969, Yugoslavia signed the agreement with the World Bank for a loan of $30 million (the so-called Third Highway Project) and allocated the funds according to a formula acceptable to all concerned parties.[53] In mid-July, however, the SIV unilaterally decided to shelve construction on the Šentilj-Nova Gorica road temporarily, in order to apply the funds designated for that stretch of road against works in other republics. This meant that the Hoče-Lovec and Postojna-Razdrto segments were temporarily being scrapped and that Slovenia would have to wait. The decision sent a shock wave through Slovenia, and citizens of that republic convened meetings to protest the decision. The Slovenes had counted on support for what all concerned recognized to be a high priority project. Instead, their project had been trimmed back in order to fund projects that the Slovenes deemed to be of lesser consequence. Since these other projects included a stretch of road that would ultimately link Croatia and Serbia, the Slovenes concluded that a Serbian-Croatian deal had taken place. The executive council of the Slovenian assembly took up the issue that same day and issued an acerbic protest, insisting that the project was of "extraordinary significance."[54] The executive council declared that the project would constitute the optimal road connection between Yugoslavia and the West and requested that the project be restored to the agenda. The following day (August 1), the secretariat of the central committee of the LC Slovenia, chaired by Andrej Marinc, convened again to consider SIV's road decision. The Slovenes complained that the decision was contrary to the spirit of the Ninth Congress insofar as the decision was made unilaterally, without any consultation with the republic. Indeed, the Slovenes had not even been told that SIV would take up the question of the road project and the bank loan at its July meeting. The Slovenian central committee warned of negative consequences for relations between the republics and the federal government if this decision were not reversed and once more asked the federal Executive Council to reconsider.[55]

The move was unprecedented. As Bilandžić has noted, this was the first time that a republic had dared to remonstrate against a federal decision.[56] Croatia quickly lent its support to the Slovenes, despite the Slovenes' heated allegation of a deal between Serbia and Croatia. Not so sympathetic were the Serbs, whose condemnation of the Slovenian protests came as a surprise to no one. The harshness of Crvenkovski's castigation of the Slovenes for "republican egoism" and weakness of Yugoslav socialist patriotism was unexpected and produced another fissure in the national-liberal coalition.[57] The federal Executive Council responded, finally, on August 7, when it sharply upbraided the Slovenes—embittering them—and adamantly refused to revise the new disbursement schedule. The secretariat of the central committee of the League of Communists of Slovenia was still discussing the "road affair," as it came to be called, at its meetings of August 25–26, but there was nothing more to be done. Still, Slovenian tempers had become so inflamed that France Popit, president of the LC Slovenia, felt compelled to explain that Slovenia had no intention of seceding from the Yugoslav federation—a sure sign that the subject had been raised unofficially.[58]

The project, as it was finally carried out, involved the following sections: (1) in Croatia, a highway from Zagreb to Karlovac with access roads in Zagreb and Karlovac, which accounted for 34 percent of project costs; (2) in Slovenia, a highway from Vrhnika to Postojna, which accounted for 54 percent of project costs; and (3) in Macedonia, a highway from Gostivar to Kičevo, which accounted for 12 percent of project costs. Thus, although the losers in their struggle with the federal Executive Council, the Slovenes still garnered the lion's share of the loan. Ironically, the Croatian and Slovenian roads, segments of the international highway system that had been expected to see considerable use, actually had less traffic than anticipated, largely because they were operated as toll roads. The Macedonian highway, however, which replaced a low-grade, mountainous road, experienced greater traffic than anticipated. (By way of a footnote to this episode, it should be noted that the Slovenes did get credit support for the two outstanding stretches of highway under a World Bank loan contracted on June 18, 1971 [the "Fifth Highway Project"], which were completed by the end of 1977.)[59]

Thus, in terms of what roads were ultimately constructed, the crisis had no effect whatsoever. But it had moliminous ramifications in the political system in two respects: (1) it changed expectations of republican behavior and, despite Belgrade's sharp condemnation, set a precedent that expanded the realm of legitimate action, and (2) by stirring Slovenian resentment against the Croats and pitting the Macedonians against the Slovenes, it effectively shattered the erstwhile trilateral coalition. After the Slovenian road affair, the Slovenian leadership became increasingly tepid in its support of Croatian demands for reform, even if their interests were similar. The national-liberal coalition had become a Croatian-Macedonian alliance, and that nexus was itself increasingly strained.

There were other changes in republican orientations. Vojvodina, which had been associated with Croatian and Slovenian demands for further decentralization of the banking system and reform of the foreign currency exchange systems, began to back off in mid-1969. Montenegro—as we shall see in the following chapter—steadily took on a more clearly anti-Serbian, if not exactly pro-Croatian, hue. And Croatia, shorn of support to the north and east, began actively courting Kosovo.

The Slovenes had been more or less cowed by the response to their own half-conscious bending of the rules of the system. The Croatian leadership, however, set out to change those rules. Tripalo, already at the head of this movement, published an article in *Socijalizam* in November 1969, in which he cautioned:

> Social praxis, events, and experiences since the Fourth Plenum of the central committee of the LCY up to now clearly show that our system cannot work without a reorganization of the League of Communists. . . . The League of Communists cannot realize its vanguard role if it plays the lackey of corporate management or some sort of propaganda machine for higher organs of power and representative bodies. But, in the same way, the League of Communists must have the powers to resist demagogic, *petit bourgeois*, and primitive conceptions of one section of the working class and of working people in general.[60]

At the Tenth Session of the Croatian central committee, amid criticisms of unitarism—which was said to underestimate the seriousness of the national question—the Croats launched a campaign aimed at further devolution of authority to the republics.[61] The Croats became the primary advocates for adoption of the principle of unanimity in decision making in governmental and party organs. They inherited the task that the Macedonians had earlier pursued with such vigor and that the Slovenes had given up after the road crisis. In this they were successful, moreover, and, in April 1970, the LCY party presidium accepted the principle of unanimity in decision making, effectively granting the coalition's demand for a veto power.

7

The Croatian Crisis, 1967–72

A balance-of-power system is a system in unstable equilibrium, where countervailing forces hold each other in suspension. The decision of a major actor to defy the rules of the system *in hope of overthrowing or revolutionizing that system* may, under appropriate conditions, evoke an antirevolutionary coalition fearful of the risks of system change. Yugoslavia in the 1960s was in a particularly unstable equilibrium because the republics had not been able to agree on the basic premises of federal policy. The successes of the national-liberal coalition had built up an expectation of change among the coalition's remaining—and, by attrition, ever more radical—activists. The intersection of economic grievances with the perception of cultural threat eventually propelled the Croatian leadership beyond the bounds of tolerable political behavior, provoking a systemwide crisis.

Economic Exploitation

The economic reform has come down, in historical memory, as a partial success. After all, it made possible the economic boom of the late 1970s. But in the short run the reform produced disappointment. Economic growth slowed from 9.7 percent annually in the prereform period (1954–65) to 6.0 percent annually in the immediate postreform period (1966–70). The rate of increase of employment also slowed—from 5.9 percent annually in the earlier period to 1.0 percent in the subsequent period. At the same time, however, labor productivity rose measurably.[1]

In Croatia, the economic reform was disappointing. Croats found their expectations often unfulfilled, and in some cases, their economic position actually deteriorated. A leading Croatian economist claimed, further, that economic resources and credits were more concentrated in Belgrade after the reform (specifically, in 1967) than before.[2] The reform had been forged by the forces of devolution but seemed only to have served to further advance the centralization of resources. Even four years after the reform, Belgrade's banks had a stranglehold on the Yugoslav economy, controlling more than half of total credits and some 81.5 percent of foreign credits. As of 1969, according to a Croatian economist, Croatia brought in about 50 percent of all foreign capital but controlled—between Zagreb, Split, and Rijeka—scarcely more than 15 percent of total credits. Belgrade's foreign trade companies, moreover, were said to enjoy a virtual monopoly, garnering 77.1 percent of Yugoslav income in this sector, with Ljubljana accounting for most of the rest (19.4 percent) and Zagreb for a mere 2.4 percent.[3]

In the course of September and November of 1971, *Hrvatski tjednik*, the weekly newspaper of Matica Hrvatska, published a series of articles that gave detailed information about the secret contents of the so-called Green Book (*Analyses of the Conditions of Crediting the Hotel-Touristic Organizations in the Coastal Region of Croatia*). The book attempted to show how Belgrade's banks had monopolized credit in Dalmatia and squeezed out the indigenous Croatian banks. Belgrade export firms were also exploiting Croatia unfairly, *Hrvatski tjednik* charged. For instance, Progress, a trade corporation in Belgrade, illegitimately reaped huge profits at Croatia's expense throughout 1971 by the sale of ships earmarked for the Croatian merchant fleet, using, as a cover, fictitious companies registered in Liberia and Luxembourg.[4] It was bad enough that the Serbs were penetrating the Croatian hotel industry; worse yet was the Croats' growing perception that their resources were being drained away by Serbia. Thus, during the 1965–69 period, the very time when investments in the Croatian hotel and tourist industry began to climb at a fast pace, profitability slumped: the reason, charged *Hrvatski tjednik*, was Serbian manipulation of investment credits and terms.[5] In some of the most controversial cases, Serbian corporations allegedly applied political pressure in order to obtain long-term agreements of a colonial character. In other cases, bribery may have been involved. Generalexport, for instance, whose main offices are in Belgrade, secured ten-year agreements with Croatian hotels in Jelsa and Primošten and a twenty-year agreement with one in Cavtat. According to *Hrvatski tjednik*, Generalexport obtained these agreements through political pressure and, though putting up only 10 percent of the capital in each case, assured itself of the legal right to lay claim to at least 50 percent of the foreign currency earnings of each of the two enterprises. It also established "service committees" that exercised wide authority in the management of the hotels without being bound by explicit regulations. In every case, Generalexport was assured a fixed dividend even if the enterprise went into the red. Nor was this an isolated case. Belgrade's Jugoslovenska Poljoprivredna Banka similarly extracted foreign currency privileges as terms of agreement with the Veruda enterprise in Pula and the Plava laguna enterprise in Poreč.[6]

It was impossible to divorce economics from politics because it seemed clear to an increasing number of Croats not only that they were being exploited but also that they were being exploited *as Croats*. The Croats noted that Generalexport, the same Belgrade company that was knee-deep in the Croatian hotel industry, "was permitted to set up its own airline long before permission for a Croatian airline was granted."[7] Since this was Serbia's second airline, the Croats could only conclude that the forces of unitarism were still entrenched. More disturbing to Croats was Šime Djodan's argument that Croatia had been forced to accept a deficit in trade with every other republic in the Yugoslav federation, even while netting a sizeable surplus in foreign trade.[8]

Djodan, an economist by training and a leading Croatian nationalist, identified Croatia's interests with liberalism and associated Yugoslav conservatives, insofar as they were partial to centralism, with "opposition to self-management."[9] By so doing, Djodan laid claim to the primal source of legitimacy in the system and forced his opponents to reply. The opening volley in the anti-Djodan campaign was fired in 1969 by Croatian conservative Stipe Šuvar. Writing in *Naše teme*, Šuvar maintained that Djodan's evident dissatisfaction with economic policy had political implications that were damaging to interethnic relations in Yugoslavia.[10] Through his prism, Šuvar saw three *idées fixe* in Djodan's writings: (1) the harmfulness of the policy of favoring the accelerated development of the underdeveloped areas; (2) the domination of Yugoslavia by Belgrade, federalism being only a façade to cloak the "Yugocrat bureaucracy" that really ran the country; and (3) the economic and biological impoverishment of Croatia as a result of central policies.[11] But a fairer account would probably judge that Djodan's first contention was not that the policy of aid to the underdeveloped regions was "harmful" but that it was inefficient and, insofar as Bosnia was left out, mismanaged. Djodan put it like this: "The Fund for the Development of the Underdeveloped [Republics and Kosovo] is inefficient. It would perhaps be better to establish a bank for the development of all undeveloped regions, with its seat in Sarajevo, because Bosnia-Herzegovina is the greatest undeveloped area, and that bank would . . . work according to economic criteria."[12] Djodan scored Belgrade for an iniquitous economic policy vis-à-vis Bosnia-Herzegovina, Croatia, Slovenia, and Vojvodina and for an inefficiency that undermined whatever benefits might have accrued to Macedonia or Kosovo. In Šuvar's distorted account, however, we read only that Djodan believed that "Slovenia and Croatia, and by the same virtue Vojvodina, have sacrificed their faster development for the benefit of the undeveloped sectors."[13] Šuvar's version obscured Djodan's commitment to the underdeveloped regions, and Djodan emerged as the champion of the haves against the have-nots. It was only one step further for Šuvar to find that Djodan's entire argument cast "aspersions" on the Serbian nation and was one with the gallimaufry of Croatian "petit bourgeois" nationalism.[14]

Others defamed Djodan and attempted to undercut his growing authority as a guru among Croatian youth. In May 1969, certain hostile agents appeared before the executive committee of the central committee of the League of Communists of Croatia to press a case that Djodan was trying to assure that new investments would occur only west of the Drina, that is, in Bosnia, Croatia, and Slovenia exclusively (though Šuvar himself admitted that this allegation was unfounded).[15]

In an article entitled "Where Dr. Stipe Šuvar 'Discovers' Nationalism and Where He Does Not See It," Djodan categorically denied Šuvar's allegation that he had questioned the policy of aiding the underdeveloped regions. Djodan reiterated the central issue, the unworkability of the autarkic model of development. He also underlined his conviction that in some ways Bosnia was the great unsung victim of Serbian "internal imperialism," for that republic had failed to receive what Djodan felt was its fair share of industrial investments.[16]

Quoting at length from articles he had published up to six years earlier (i.e., as early as 1963), Djodan countered that he had not expressed concern solely for Croatian interests; he did, in fact, believe that economic assistance to Yugoslavia's underdeveloped regions should be *intensified*.[17] Djodan won this round but, after the fall of the Tripalo–Dabčević-Kučar–Pirker triumvirate, he was arrested and jailed. He was unable to publish anything after that for some twenty years. Šuvar, by contrast, remained the Croatian secretary for education, culture, and athletics, and was later elevated to the central committee of the LC Croatia. Eventually Šuvar became secretary of the LCY with a one-year mandate. Šuvar's legendary arrogance, however, and his firmly established reputation as the great antinationalist stigmatized him in his native Croatia for many years.

Cultural and Demographic Threat

It is a well-known constant of social psychology that perception of a threat incites collective affectivity and stimulates recourse to countervailing action. There is no surer way to rally any group around a flag than to convince its members that they are menaced by some other group and that their most cherished values are endangered. Threat perception may, thus, be manipulated. In the Croatian case, however, it seems not to have been manipulated, at least not consciously: those nationalists who anxiously warned Croats of impending Serbianization were convinced that the threat was real.

The Serbian threat was thought to take three forms: the demographic displacement of Croats by Serbs, the catering to Dalmatian sentiment in order to split Croatia in two, and the Serbianization of the Croatian language. It is interesting that these three phenomena should have been read by the overwhelming majority of Croats as symptoms of a Serbian threat. Population movements can, after all, be explained as strictly economic phenomena, and linguistic homogenization is a typical epiphenomenon of modernization. Even the stirrings of Dalmatian ethnic self-identity might have been interpreted as a genuine manifestation of endogenous currents. The public did not, however, view these developments as isolated features, and increasingly the talk was of Croatia's need to defend itself.

Linguistic Homogenization and Its Foes

In December 1954, the cultural associations of those federal units in which Serbo-Croatian is the lingua franca convened in Novi Sad to make arrangements for collaboration on the creation of a common orthography for the entire country and to produce a definitive Serbo-Croatian dictionary. Although an official document dating from 1945 had seemed to accord distinct status to Serbian and Croatian (or Serbo-Croatian and Croato-Serbian, as they had sometimes been called), Matica Srpska, the Serbian cultural association, had succeeded in persuading other participants that creation of a unified standard dictionary and orthography was in the interests of Serbs, Croats, and Montenegrins alike.[18]

When the first two volumes of this dictionary were finally published in 1967, however, they inflamed the informed Croatian public. Common Croatian vocabulary and expressions were either excluded or relegated to the status of a local dialect; everywhere the Serbian variant was presented as the standard, the Croatian as the deviation. This consistency was more remarkable and objectionable insofar as a certain Dr. Miloš S. Moskovljević had been reprimanded the previous year for putting out an allegedly chauvinistic dictionary that had no entry for *Hrvat* (Croat), though *Srbin* (Serb) and related words (e.g., *Srbovati* [to act like a real Serb]) were well represented. Croatian linguists in Zagreb severely criticized the orientation of the new dictionary and issued a declaration of protest in the March 17 edition of the Zagreb newspaper *Telegram*. This "Declaration concerning the Characterization and Status of the Croatian Literary Language" demanded that Croatian and Serbian be considered two distinct languages and that recognition of this fact be incorporated into a reformulated Article 131 of the constitution, so that all laws and treaties would have to be published in four languages instead of three (i.e., Serbian, Croatian, Slovenian, and Macedonian instead of Serbo-Croatian, Slovenian, and Macedonian). The declaration continued by demanding that the government "guarantee the consistent usage of the Croatian literary language in schools, in the press, in public and political life, on the radio and television, wherever one is dealing with Croats, and that civil servants, teachers, and officials, without regard to their place of origin, use in their official functions the literary language of the area in which they are working."[19] This last clause was unmistakably aimed at the large number of Serbian bureaucrats working in Croatia, and the entire declaration had an overtly anti-Serbian flavor. Inevitably, the declaration aroused Serbian tempers and elicited an angry rebuttal only two days later. It also signaled the beginning of the "Croatian national renaissance," which was to last just over four and a half years.

The declaration did not, however, resolve the immediate issue. Throughout the late 1960s, the cultural organizations Matica Hrvatska and Matica Srpska engaged in protracted discussions over the cooperative project. The central committees of the communist parties of Croatia, Serbia, Bosnia-Herzegovina, and Montenegro conducted lengthy joint discussions concerning language policy.[20] Failing to obtain satisfaction in a joint enterprise, the Croats set about compiling a new *Croatian* orthography and dictionary and began the "purification" of Croatian from Serbian infiltration. Challenged by skeptics, Ljudevit Jonke, president of Matica Hrvatska, wrote in *Kritika* (1968) that the Broz-Iveković *Dictionary of the Croatian Language*, first published in 1901 but still generally considered authoritative in 1968, actually relied heavily on Serbian materials and cited Serbian roots as the sources of 90 percent of its words—an unacceptable device, according to Jonke.[21] Serbian recalcitrance and Croatian dissatisfaction finally prompted Matica Hrvatska, the Croatian cultural association, to unilaterally withdraw from the joint project on November 22, 1970.

Matica Hrvatska declared, on that occasion, that it saw no point in further cooperation in the writing of a *Serbian* dictionary.

Matica Hrvatska's position had been stiffened by Matica Srpska's adamant insistence that Croatian is only a dialect of Serbian. But, when the Croats went their own way, the Serbs loudly protested. In January 1971, Matica Srpska objected that "The mechanical division of this language, which results from their [Matica Hrvatska's] . . . decisions, is not only scientifically ungrounded but also unjust to our two republics as well as to the Croats in SR Serbia and the Serbs in SR Croatia."[22] Reinforcing the battlements, Mirko Čanadović argued in *Politika*, three days later, that the language of the Serbs, Croats, Montenegrins, and Bosniak Muslims is a single language with negligible variations. Mate Šimundić replied in *Kritika* that Čanadović's program would stifle the autonomous development of Croatian, Montenegrin, and so forth.[23] From a purely linguistic point of view, one might observe that Serbo-Croatian was "obviously" a single language; this was, however, a political, not a linguistic-scientific, controversy.

At approximately the same time, Matica Hrvatska issued another proclamation declaring that the Novi Sad agreement was "null and void" from the beginning and condemning Matica Srpska's endeavors to systematically suppress the Croatian language. Professor Jonke was able to obtain an interview with *Komunist* and stated simply, "Matica Srpska says that we have a single uniform language, and we say that that is not the case . . . it is one language, but it is not uniform."[24] Whatever conciliation seemed implied in Jonke's concession that Serbian and Croatian were "one language," the lines of battle were nonetheless drawn. In autumn 1971 the publication of the *Croatian Orthography (Hrvatski pravopis)* with a new dictionary of the "Croatian language" precipitated Serbian condemnations. *NIN* warned that the publication would exacerbate growing ethnic tensions between Croats and Serbs, not help to heal them.[25]

Threat of Demographic Displacement

At the same time that the Novi Sad agreement was disintegrating, Croatian demographers began to speak of a demographic threat. To begin with, Croatia's population was proportionately older than that of any other republic except Slovenia.[26] The Croatian mortality rate of 11.6 per thousand was second only to Vojvodina's rate of 11.8 per thousand, and its birth rate (in 1972) was the third lowest, behind Vojvodina and Serbia.[27] Later, in the period between the 1971 and 1981 censuses, Croatia recorded the lowest birth rate (3.3 percent) of all the Yugoslav federal units—lower than Vojvodina's 3.8 percent (second place) and far below Kosovo's 27.4 percent.[28]

Moreover, the large emigration of Croatian workers to Western Europe, which had formerly been construed as economic opportunity, was suddenly viewed as a Serbian plot to move able-bodied Croats out of their homeland. An official Yugoslav source recorded that 9.6 percent of the Croatian labor force was employed abroad in 1971—the highest proportion of all the federal units, and significantly higher than the Yugoslav average of 6.6 percent. Bosnia was a close second with 9.2 percent of its labor force employed as *Gastarbeiter*, but Serbia and Slovenia were far behind with rates of 3.7 percent and 5.4 percent, respectively.[29] Djodan claimed that more than half of Yugoslavia's émigré workers in 1968 were ethnic Croats and that Croats' net rate of emigration more than canceled out the rate of increase in the Croatian population.[30] Sociologist M. Rendulić, addressing a 1971 conference in Zagreb on "Population, Emigration, and Employment," warned that the rate of natural increase in Croatia was declining and gradually approaching zero.[31] These projections and forebodings were perhaps borne out by the results of the 1981 census, which showed that the number of Croats living in Croatia actually decreased from 3,513,647 in 1971 to 3,454,661 in 1981, while the number of Croats living in Yugoslavia as a whole declined from 4,526,782 to 4,428,135 during the same period.[32]

This situation was compounded by another variable—the increasing influx of Serbs into Croatia. These Serbian immigrants were believed to be taking the places relinquished by the Croatian *Gastarbeiter*. As early as 1967—the same year in which the *Telegram* declaration turned the tide in linguistic trends—a certain Minić addressed an open letter to Miko Tripalo. "We want you to prevent any more Serbs from moving into Croatia," he said plainly. "They are already talking of a Serbia [extending] all the way to Omiš. The Croatian nation will not pardon you!"[33] Simultaneously, concerned Croats organized to "reclaim" immigrants of earlier centuries who had hitherto been written off as Serbian. The immigrants were recast (as they had been during the war) as "Orthodox Croats," thus confounding the traditional shibboleth that a Croat is Catholic and a Serb is Orthodox.[34]

The Campaign to Split Off Dalmatia

As early as the end of the eighteenth century, when I. Kreljanović published his book *Dalmazia autonoma*, there was an articulate coterie of Slavs who viewed Dalmatia as distinct from the rest of Croatia. "Autonomists," then as now, were fond of emphasizing the Mediterranean, even Italian, character of the Dalmatian culture and people. During the nineteenth century, autonomism found followers chiefly among the wealthier families of Dalmatia—merchants, entrepreneurs, bankers, and landowners—and the notion, which originally had a largely cultural hue, took on political overtones. In *Ai Dalmati* (1861), N. Tommaseo, a Dalmatian of Italian extraction, opposed the unification of Dalmatia with the rest of Croatia. He argued that the Dalmatian name was older than the Croatian and that Dalmatian culture was of a higher level, with dialect and customs that differed from those of other Croats. Hence, Dalmatian autonomists were pleased with the outcome of the Austro-Hungarian *Ausgleich* of 1867, because Dalmatia was allotted to Austria although the rest of Croatia fell to Hungary.[35]

Most early Dalmatian autonomists were foreigners "together with a handful of native renegades schooled in Italy and Vienna," as one Croatian nationalist put it.[36] The Dalmatian idea did not clash with the Croatian idea in an organic sense but, on the contrary, fed Italian irredentism as it was manifested during and after World War I. With the establishment of the Kingdom of the Serbs, Croats, and Slovenes, Dalmatian consciousness came to be seen in a new light. Nikola Pašić, the prime minister of Serbia and later of Yugoslavia, claimed in a 1914 telegram that "Dalmatia wants to be annexed to Serbia—that is its ideal, that is what its interests require, and it is the longstanding drive of the Serbo-Croatian nation."[37] The concept is scarcely surprising, since it is well known that Pašić and his cohorts believed that Croats, Slovenes, and Macedonians were all in fact Serbs (the "tri-named people") and that they all spoke dialects of Serbo-Croatian. Pašić's separate reference to Dalmatia is interesting, for it is suggestive of what proved to be regime policy until the Maček-Cvetković *Sporazum*, namely, to divide the Croats into as many parts as possible and attempt to make those divisions permanent by cultivating and encouraging the development of local identity among Dalmatians, Istrians, Slavonians, Kordunians, and so forth.

The Serbian Orthodox Church has always resented the tenth-century transfer of Dalmatia from Byzantium's jurisdiction to the jurisdiction of Rome. A Serbian textbook on the church, approved by the Main Educational Council in 1927 for use in the secondary and professional schools, referred to medieval Dalmatia as the "Serbian West," counting as Serbian the bishoprics of Ston, Dubrovnik, and Kotor.[38] As the 1970s began, Serbian interest in Dalmatia was more openly expressed. The Serbian Orthodox Church, for one, published a book entitled *Serbs and Orthodoxy in Dalmatia and Dubrovnik (Srbi i pravoslavlje u Dalmaciji i Dubrovniku)* in 1971.[39] *Srbi u prošlosti*, a book written by Josip Potkozarac and published by a Smederevo publishing house in 1969, was belatedly banned by civil authorities in 1970 for its alleged effort to prove that the populations of Dalmatia, Bosnia, and other regions are purely Serbian and that "the borders of Serbia extend from Djevdjelija to Split."[40] During 1971, a ring of Serbian nationalists that included Slobodan Subotić and Radisav Mičić printed and distributed pamphlets that called for the immediate organization of autonomous Serbian provinces in Dalmatia and elsewhere in Croatia and for the subsequent removal of these areas from Croatia.[41] There were reports of "Serbian chauvinists" singing Chetnik songs in Dalmatia, and, as early as 1970, the central committee of the Croatian League of Communists considered it necessary to condemn Dalmatian autonomism as a "unitarist," anti-Croatian ruse.[42]

Croatian nationalists thus had reason to believe that Dalmatian autonomism was reviving in the 1960s, and Serbian interference was tangibly present. A contemporary Croatian writer observed that

> autonomism has . . . persistently tried to drive a wedge into Croatia and to split off Dalmatia, the historical cradle of the Croatian state, from upper Croatia, dividing the Croatian nation into "Dalmatians" and Croats. But this would be only

> the first phase of the master plan, because afterwards the unitarists . . . would press for like autonomy for Lika, Banija, Kordun, Istria, Slavonia, etc., and the question arises whether, in their opinion, Croatia comprises even the area from Karlovac to Varaždin. Shattering the integrity of the Croatian lands and reducing Croats to a semination, they would at last be able to speak with ease of one language as the presupposition of the theory of a single nation—and all that as the condition for a single unitarist state.[43]

The Dalmatians continue, to be sure, to view themselves as distinct from other Croats—but in most cases this feeling is as harmless as the Texan's pride in being Texan. But the Croatian central committee took pains to make it absolutely clear that in its view no province in Croatia had any ethnic or historical basis for seeking autonomous status nor had it the right to do so.[44] Dalmatian autonomism could lay no claim to any kind of legitimacy, because it was nothing less than "treason" against the Croatian nation.[45]

The Croatian Backlash

Threatened, as they saw it, with the suppression of their language, the obliteration of their people, and the usurpation of their land, the Croats reacted strongly. They repudiated the antimony of nationalism and patriotism and challenged the socialist doctrine that the latter is immeasurably superior to the former. They also began to look for institutional-legal measures to safeguard the Croatian nation from the Serbs. The argument made was that "the Croatian nation will cease to be manipulated and exploited only if it realizes its statehood, that it will be truly equal only insofar as it attains its sovereignty. If that is not achieved, then it will [continue to] serve as a plaything for other actors."[46] And, in a classic expression of balance-of-power thinking, one Croat even argued that "Croatia must be set as the criterion at every moment, in every undertaking. Nothing can be done to benefit others that would at the same time be contrary to Croatia's interests."[47] The dividing line between statehood and secession or self-interest and rejection of fellow Yugoslavs was often fuzzy.

Early in 1969, Petar Šegedin, president of the Croatian Literary Society, wrote an article for *Kolo* (the bimonthly journal published by Matica Hrvatska) and spelled out Croatian grievances in detail. His chief complaints were (1) Croats are treated as illegal residents in their own country; (2) Croatian interests are subordinate to the interests of Serbia; (3) to feel Croatian under current circumstances is to be worthy of pity; (4) to lose one's language is to lose one's (separate) ethnic identity; (5) the Croatian nation has, by various nefarious means, been portrayed as criminal; (6) Croatia is still being equated with the *Ustaše*; (7) Belgrade is attempting to assimilate the Croats, that is, to Serbianize Croatia; (8) Croatia has become a "no-man's land"; (9) Croatia has lost everything essential to the preservation of its culture: its native Croatian intelligentsia has been exterminated and Croatia is becoming a "science-less" land of ignorant peasants; and (10) the Serbs have a definite program designed to assimilate Croatian youth and to cause the Croatian nation to disappear without a trace.[48]

Although the leaderships of Slovenia and Vojvodina supported the Croatian leadership until mid-1969 in its demands for further decentralization of the banking system and reform of the foreign currency exchange systems, the catch phrase "5 to 1" began to acquire currency among Croats as early as 1968.[49] The phrase signified the widely held view that Croatia's demands for progressive change were always opposed by the other five Yugoslav republics and that Croatia therefore stood alone.

Šuvar, brimming with antipathy toward these currents, blasted nationalism as an emotional, irrational mysticism "dragged up from the trash heap of history" (Trotsky's pet phrase).[50] In response, he was deluged with letters, both signed and unsigned, and was personally upbraided by friends and acquaintances for being a "Serbophile, a Yugo-agent, a unitarist, a Rankovićite." Šuvar refused to budge, however, and condemned the revival of "Croatian *petit bourgeois* nationalism." Croatian nationalism, he said, was characterized by the conviction that all of Croatia's misfortunes are due to the activities of the other Yugoslav nations (especially the Serbs); by dependence on, and willingness to serve, various foreign imperialist forces, thus betraying the indigenous peoples; by a mystic belief in the superiority of the Croatian nation; and by the tenet that Croatian nationalism, like Macedonian, Slovenian, *and even Serbian* (!) nationalism, can only blossom with the carving up of Yugoslavia.[51] The thrust of Šuvar's portrayal is unmistakable: Croatian nationalism is misguided, ethnocentric, and dangerous. But Šuvar's ability to influence Croatian public opinion was minimal.

The Croats began to behave like a new "master race," displaying the arrogant attitude that "we solve our economic problems by ourselves, why can't you solve yours by yourselves?" "Many Croats, especially intellectuals," and certain high-ranking party officials

> behaved with unalloyed obtuseness toward their non-Croat colleagues, especially vis-à-vis the Serbs. For example, at a meeting of the Yugoslav Council on Visual Arts, the Croatian delegates walked out when they were defeated by a 5-to-1 vote on the issue of moving the administrative headquarters to a different republic capital every two years at the time of biennial meetings. They dismissed the arguments of their colleagues from the other republics that biennial shifts were not only uneconomical, but self-defeating since close contact with foreign cultural groups and exhibitions—one of the organization's principal purposes—could best be handled in Belgrade where all the embassies are located.[52]

Visiting academicians coming to Zagreb to attend scholarly conferences were likely to find themselves being corrected by militant Croatophiles for use of Serbian words instead of Croatian. In the summer of 1971, the Croats set about compiling their new orthography for literary Croatian. The result was a dictionary stuffed with archaisms and exotic neologisms designed to eliminate anything that might be construed as a Serbianism. At the same time, a meeting of teachers and textbook writers demanded the revision of school history books to give greater emphasis to specifically Croatian achievements and called for devoting two-thirds of the time allotted to history lessons to Croatian culture and history.[53]

Matica Hrvatska, whose championing of the Croatian language had made it the darling of Croatia, became the focal point of the nationalist revival. *Hrvatski književni list (Croatian Literary Gazette)*, a weekly publication, took up Croatia's cause early in the burgeoning crisis, and its subscription list accordingly swelled. Had a free election been held in Croatia in 1969 or 1970, Šime Djodan, himself closely affiliated with Matica Hrvatska, would indisputably have been elected to high office.

But the Croatian leadership was internally divided, and those leaders who were unfavorably disposed toward these developments attempted to abort the Croatian revival and to resist demands for greater autonomy. In a series of articles for *Borba* (February 14–20, 1969), Miloš Žanko, the prominent Croatian conservative, attacked the nationalistically inclined *Hrvatski književni list*. Immediately thereafter, the Third Plenum of the central committee of LC Croatia (February 21, 1969), roundly condemned the gazette for its nationalist orientation and put it on "probation." The Zagreb city council of the League of Communists, still in the hands of the conservatives, observed on July 20 that

> The so-called *Croatian Literary Gazette* has been appearing in Zagreb for more than a year. Through an analysis of the issues that have appeared thus far, one can establish, without any great efforts, that the editorial board of *Hrvatski književni list* has formulated a political program that is directly contrary to the policy of the League of Communists and that is at variance with the basic interests of the Croatian nation and of all the nations of Yugoslavia.[54]

Within a matter of weeks, *Hrvatski književni list* was silenced and nationalist elements in the Emigrant Society (Matica Iseljenika) and the Institute for the History of the Workers Movement were neutralized. But that act scarcely deprived the nationalists of a forum, and *Studentski list*, *Hrvatsko sveučilište*, *Kritika*, *Kolo*, *Dubrovnik*, and *Vidik* continued to espouse nationalist viewpoints. Two periodicals catering to the youth, *Tlo* and *Omladinski tjednik*, also joined the nationalist ranks, and *Hrvatski gospodarski glasnik* adopted a nationalist stance in May 1971. In April 1971, Matica Hrvatska inaugurated *Hrvatski tjednik*, whose reportage far surpassed *Hrvatski književni list*'s in the radicalism of its approach. Its subscription list quickly outstripped all competitors, *Vjesnik* included. Even *Vjesnik* and Radio-Television Zagreb, though formally the organs of the SAWP of Croatia, actually figured as de facto agents of the nationalists as the crisis built.[55] Little surprise, then, that the suppression of *Hrvatski književni list* met with a welter of open criticism. In November 1969, *Borba*, unnerved by the continued criticism of this and other policies that was emanating from *Kolo*, *Kritika*, and *Dubrovnik*, warned that "there is a system to all this [nationalistic] lunacy."[56]

The Turning Point

Until the end of 1969, the Croatian party leadership had not taken a clear stand on the nationalist revival, principally because neither of its two principal factions had been able to get the upper hand. Žanko, who was at that time vice president of the federal *Skupština*, publicly attacked Petar Šegedin, Šime Djodan, Vlado Gotovac, Marko Veselica, and other prominent Croatian liberals, and, in a series of articles for *Borba*, charged that exclusivist nationalism was on the rise in Croatia.[57] Advocating a principle diametrically opposed to good balance-of-power logic, he exhorted delegates of the Chamber of Republics and Provinces to keep the interests of the entire community uppermost in their minds and to subordinate *Croatian* interests to *Yugoslav* interests.[58] As a result, he polarized the Croatian party, alienated most of his passive supporters, and provoked a counterattack. This came at the Tenth Plenum of the central committee of the LC Croatia (January 15–17, 1970), on which occasion Savka Dabčević-Kučar herself led the attack on Žanko. She claimed that the struggle against unitarism and the struggle against nationalism were two sides of the same coin but that, because of the influence of demented unitarists like Žanko, the LC Croatia had devoted its energies exclusively to the struggle against nationalism. She concluded that, far from concentrating on problems of nationalism, the Croatian party organization would have to devote greater attention to combating unitarism. Dabčević-Kučar interpreted Žanko's behavior as disloyal, betraying an intention to topple the republican leadership and necessarily implying a readiness to mobilize intervening forces from outside the republic in order to achieve that end.[59] The LC Croatia rebuffed Žanko for antiparty views, stripped him of his posts, and attested that "the struggle against nationalism cannot be waged from unitarist battlements."[60] From this point on, the Croatian party leadership drew steadily closer to the ideology of Matica Hrvatska and the nationalists. An internal alliance was being forged to replace the moribund interrepublican alliance with Slovenia, Vojvodina, and Macedonia. The Tenth Plenum was a turning point in another sense: it was the first time that a republican central committee had rendered an assessment of problems of further development (and of the state of interethnic relations) independently of central party organs. The republican leadership was coming into its own, speaking for Croatia as a body of Croatian politicians.

A new mood prevailed, a sense that the tide had been turned and that the unitarists were on the defensive. Two manifestations of this mood were a seminar held in Zagreb the following month on the theme "Socialism and the National Question" and a large symposium in Krapinske Toplice in March focusing on "The Relation of Class and Nation in Contemporary Socialism." Participants at the latter event displayed a candor that would have been unthinkable a few years earlier. Most significant, this symposium all but ratified nationalism as a legitimate ideology. Zdenko Roter, one of those in attendance, was most explicit on this score, avowing that "it is necessary to accept nationalism as a positive phenomenon that makes possible the creativity and faster integration of a nation."[61] Others, including Esad Ćimić, echoed his sentiments. Anton Marušić went still further, portraying nationalism as a presupposition of democratic society and opposing nationalism to totalitarianism. More important still, the leadership identified itself with these currents. Tripalo remarked that "It would be good if we could disabuse ourselves of the habit of using the term 'nationalism' only in a pejorative sense, for . . . nationalism can have various contents. I think that nationalism is our foe only when it develops into chauvinism."[62]

The Croatian revival reclaimed the heroes of the past. Croats began reexamining their history, searching for "lost heroes" who had been swept under the carpet by the communist regime. Stjepan Radić (d. 1928), founder of the Croatian Peasant party, became overnight the most popular politician in Croatia, with Miko Tripalo, the engaging secretary of the central committee, in second place, and Tito, possibly, a distant third.[63] In August 1971, the culture committee of the presidency of the League of Students of Croatia put up a commemorative plaque in honor of Radić on the façade of the Zagreb house in which he had lived and died. Subsequently, a statue of Stjepan Radić (Yugoslavia's first) was unveiled in Metković, and there was even talk of erecting a monument to Radić in Zagreb.[64] The coastal town of Šibenik, swept along by the euphoria, canceled plans to erect a monument to the victims of fascism and decided to construct instead a statue of the Croatian king, Petar Kresimir IV.[65]

More daring were efforts to rehabilitate a nineteenth-century Croatian military governor, Josip Jelačić, and restore him to the Valhalla of Croatian gods and heroes. Marx had savagely condemned Jelačić for his "reactionary" support of the Austrian kaiser in the suppression of the "progressive" Hungarian rebellion of 1848–49. The CPY had manifestly identified itself with Marx's censure by renaming Zagreb's Jelačić Square (*Trg Jelačića*) the "Square of the Republic" (*Trg Republike*). Nevertheless, in the spring of 1971, Zvonimir Kulundžić demanded that the LCY admit that it had erred in debunking Jelačić and he called on the party to erect a public statue to Jelačić, "the symbol of old Zagreb."[66] The subsequent wave of letters to the editor of *Hrvatski tjednik* suggested broad support and enthusiasm for the proposal. The entire atmosphere changed —almost overnight. As Miko Tripalo recalled much later, "the whole political life, which had been closed to the public, now opened up and people started to speak their minds, both about the way things were then and about how things had been in the past."[67]

During Croatia's flourishing national exultation, the (officially proscribed) traditional patriotic songs of the Croatian homeland were revived and could often be heard publicly in Croatia's restaurants. Vice Vukov became Croatia's most popular singer in the course of 1971, and also its most controversial. His specialty was songs of Croatia, and at least two of his concerts were banned by a nervous regime fearful of nationalist outbursts.

Matica Hrvatska went on the offensive, bent on "de-Serbianizing" the Croatian language. In June 1971, Matica Hrvatska organized an open meeting to discuss the *Zadar Review (Zadarska revija)*. The discussion became intense and bitter, with Matica Hrvatska complaining that the *Review*'s language was "impure," a concatenation created by the contributions of a staff drawn not merely from Croatia but from various parts of the country.[68] Matica Hrvatska also pressured Yugoslav Railways, objecting that its exclusive use of the ekavian variant (Serbian) was prejudicial to the Croatian language. Under additional pressure applied by Zagreb, Yugoslav Railways agreed that by September 1, 1971, all railway notices, schedules, and forms would be printed in the ijekavian variant (Croatian) as well.[69] *Hrvatski tjednik*, always in the midst of the fray, complained that the buses servicing the Zagreb airport were marked "Jugoslovenski Aerotransport"—correct Serbian—rather than "Jugoslavenski Aerotransport"—correct Croatian.[70] *Hrvatski tjednik* even initiated a column devoted to distinguishing correct Croatian from common Serbian infiltrations. Croatia was awash with nationalist euphoria, and the team of Dabčević-Kučar and Tripalo, firmly in the saddle, was riding the crest of the wave. But they had not solved the problem of how to reconcile Croatian nationalism with the imperatives of coalition politics.

The Catholic Church and the Nation

The Croatian spring—as it came to be called in the West—found considerable support in the ranks of Catholic clergy.[71] Perhaps most clergy welcomed the new role being played by Matica Hrvatska, and especially in the towns of Rijeka, Split, Zadar, and Zagreb, Catholic priests became active in the national movement. Some Franciscans gathered data on the number of Croats holding political office in Herzegovina,[72] others accused the party of discrimination against Croatia. Two priests published a "Croatian prayer" in a 1971 issue of *Vjesnik Sv. Nikole Tavelića*, portraying Croatia as "wretched and nameless."[73] Split's Archbishop Frane Franić himself took the initiative to organize a "double anniversary of the Croatian people" in Solin, in commemoration of the thirteen hundredth anniversary of Croatian Christianity and the thousandth anniversary of the construction of the first Croatian university at Solin. A huge contingent of seven cardinals, thirty bishops, and 300 priests turned out to attend the ceremonies. A decade later—in 1981—the regime turned down a church proposal to establish a "Catholic Croatian Day," with the explanation that this would only incite national hatred between Croats and Serbs.[74]

Revision of Croatia's Constitution

Throughout the gathering maelstrom, the Serbs living in Croatia—who comprised some 15 percent of the republic's population—occupied a unique and rather precarious niche. Their economic interests were inseparable from the interests of the Croatian republic and they were represented in the federal *Skupština* by the delegation from Croatia. Moreover, most of these Serbs spoke ijekavian or a mixture of ijekavian and ekavian, not the pure ekavian of their kin in SR Serbia. But the Croatian renaissance displayed systematic anti-Serbian overtones, and it was impossible for Croatia's Serbs to be unaffected by this. The result was a growing controversy surrounding the status of the Serbs in Croatia and the impact of heightened Croatian national consciousness on their rights of national self-expression.

Inevitably, there were currents that gave the nationalist awakening the most negative interpretation possible. Before the end of the year, *Hrvatski tjednik* found it necessary to warn of the development of a campaign "to convince the Serbs in Croatia of two big lies": that the aesthetic self-development of Croatian serves the exclusive purpose of setting Croatian apart from Serbian and that by means of this "artificial, exclusivist, anti-Serbian language and orthography, the Croats mean to oppress the Serbs in Croatia."[75] But the explanation that the Croats were only embarking on "the elimination of what was by coercion and pressure forced on the Croatian language" failed to assuage the fears of Croatia's Serbian community.[76] It searched for allies among Croatian conservatives and initiated a campaign to incorporate cosovereignty for Serbs in the Croatian constitution.

Professor Mihailo Djurić, a member of the law faculty in Belgrade, told a colloquium at the law school in March 1971 that Croatia's Serbs needed special constitutional guarantees to safeguard their rights of national self-expression.[77] The Serbs zeroed in on the opening paragraphs of the Croatian constitution. Article 1 in the 1963 version read, "The Socialist Republic of Croatia is the socialist democratic state community of the Croatian nation (*narod*), established on the power of the working people and self-management."[78] This article was preceded by an apparently innocuous section of "general principles" that began, "The Croatian nation, in harmony with its historical aspirations, proceeding from the right of self-determination, including also the right of secession, in common struggle with the other nations of Yugoslavia . . . united with the other nations of Yugoslavia in a federal republic of free and equal nations and nationalities."[79] The Serbs perceived that they were excluded from participation in the "socialist democratic community" and denied explicit credit for their role in the "common struggle." They therefore proposed to rectify these oversights with the following draft Amendment 1:

1. The Croatian nation, in harmony with its historical aspirations, *in common struggle with the Serbian nation and the nationalities in Croatia* and with the other nations and nationalities of Yugoslavia, realized, in the national liberation war and in the socialist revolution, its own national state—the Socialist Republic of Croatia—and, proceeding from the right of self-determination, including even the right of secession, in the free expression of its own will and in order to protect its national independence and freedom, to build socialism and advance multifaceted social and national development,

conscious that the further strengthening of the fraternity and unity of the nations and nationalities of Yugoslavia was in their common interest, voluntarily united with the other nations and nationalities in the Socialist Federated Republic of Yugoslavia.

2. The Socialist Republic of Croatia is the sovereign national state of the Croatian nation, *the state of the Serbian nation in Croatia*, and the state of the nationalities that live in it.[80]

The insertions made explicit the rights of the Serbs in Croatia, but they also compromised the national status of the Croatian republic.

Matica Hrvatska immediately sprang forward with a detailed critique of the draft amendment. The very first sentence, said Matica Hrvatska, showed no cognizance of the fact that Croatian statehood is centuries old: "the Croatian nation . . . did not have merely historical aspirations—it had as well a state." The draft, moreover, revealed traces of unitarism in speaking of Croatia's having "*united (ujedinjenja)* with the other nations and nationalities in . . . Yugoslavia," although the principle of federalism precludes unification. A better formulation would have been to speak of Croatia's having chosen to *associate (udruživati)* with the other nations and nationalities. Again, the very order of presentation, albeit a carryover from the 1963 version, was open to objection: the first point, said Matica Hrvatska, should be an affirmation of the sovereignty of the Croatian national state, and only then should the text speak of Croatia's voluntary association with Yugoslavia. The given order seemed, to Matica Hrvatska, designed to undercut the formal right of secession, even to contradict the literal meaning of the words themselves. Finally, Matica Hrvatska opened fire on the pivotal change being proposed:

> Sovereignty is one, indivisible, inalienable, and imperishable—that is the classic characterization and the only proper one. If then SR Croatia is the national state of the Croatian nation, it is Croatian sovereignty that is one, indivisible, inalienable, and imperishable. And, in that case, SR Croatia cannot be at the same time the national Croatian state and the state of the Serbian nation in Croatia and the state of all the other peoples that inhabit it. . . . *We resolutely support the position that SR Croatia is the unique national state of the Croatian nation and that Croatian sovereignty is one, indivisible, inalienable, and imperishable.*[81]

Hrvatski tjednik dredged up a fifteen-year-old statement by jurist Jovan Stefanović to the effect that it would be erroneous to conclude, on the basis of "the regulation . . . regarding the equality of Serbs in Croatia, . . . that NR [*narodna republika*] Croatia is the republic of Croats and Serbs. It is the republic of the Croatian nation."[82] The paper complained that the draft reduced Croatia to a quasi-federation of nationalities. By contrast, the first constitution of NR Croatia (1947) had forthrightly described Croatia as the Croatian "national state of republican form."

The effect of this confrontation was electric: all Croatia was fired into a state of excited agitation, and support for the concept of the Croatian national state became a fundamental test of republican and ethnic loyalty. One disconcerted reader of *Hrvatski tjednik* expressed his wonderment that the "unitarists" and Serbophiles had not yet proposed renaming the republic "Serbo-Croatia" (*Srbo-Hrvatska*).[83] Consistent application of the principle implied in the draft amendment would require redefining Macedonia as the state of the Macedonians, Turks, Albanians, and Bulgarians; Serbia as the state of the Serbs, Gypsies, Albanians, Hungarians, and others; Montenegro as the state of the Montenegrins, Albanians, Muslims, and Serbs; and so on.

Matica Hrvatska countered with its own draft of Amendment 1 for Croatia's constitution:

> Article 1. SR Croatia is the national state of the Croatian nation. National sovereignty—one, indivisible, inalienable, and imperishable—belongs, in SR Croatia, to the Croatian nation and it realizes it through its deputies and by direct expressions of its will.
>
> Article 2. SR Croatia is a self-managing community of working people led by the working class. The self-managing rights of the working people are founded on their right to dispose of their [working] conditions, their resources, and the products of their labor, and on the political power of the working class. The self-managing rights of the working people are inviolable, inalienable, and imperishable.
>
> Article 3. SR Croatia is a democratic system in which all citizens have equal rights. Citizens of SR Croatia are equal in their rights and duties, without regard to nationality, race, religion, or conviction. Citizens' rights in SR Croatia are inviolable, inalienable, and imperishable.
>
> Article 4. The principles of SR Croatia are: freedom, social justice, equality, fraternity and unity, solidarity.
>
> Article 5. The national anthem of SR Croatia is "Our Beautiful Homeland" (*Lijepa naša domovina*). The official language of SR Croatia is Croatian. The capital city of SR Croatia is Zagreb.
>
> Article 6. By its struggle for national liberation and its socialist revolution and in united struggle together with the Serbs in Croatia and members of other nations that live with them in the common Croatian homeland, and with the remaining Yugoslav peoples, the Croatian nation secured its right of self-determination, including also the right of secession, and founded its national state, which is a continuation of a centuries-old political-legal tradition of the Croatian state and homeland. Proceeding from its right of self-determination, including also the right of secession, and in order to assure its national independence, the building of a socialist society, and multifaceted national development, the Croatian nation voluntarily associated with (the) other peoples in the Socialist Federated Republic of Yugoslavia.[84]

However popular this version may have been with the majority of Croats, the Croatian conservatives still controlled a number of levers of power, and even some of those sympathetic to the concept of the national state feared that Matica Hrvatska might have gone too far. Members of the executive committee of the republic conference of the SAWP of Croatia, the executive committee of the central committee of the LC Croatia, and participants in the sessions of the Republic Coordination Committee for Promoting Discussion of the Amendments reacted vehemently to Matica Hrvatska's proposed modifications of the draft amendments. *Vjesnik* sprang to the defense of the clause defining Croatia as "the sovereign state of the Croats [and] the Serbs in Croatia" and argued that "Serbian people live in Croatia, but very few Croats live in Serbia."[85] It quickly became obvious—if it had not been clear from the beginning—that Matica Hrvatska's original version was incapable of passage. In its issue of November 5, 1971, *Hrvatski tjednik* extended an olive branch and proposed a compromise set of constitutional amendments. The key changes in its proposals were (1) a change in the order of the introductory, fundamental principles, so that the founding of the Croatian republic and its right of self-determination would now be mentioned first and only subsequently would it be set forth that Croatia is "the sovereign national state of the Croatian people"; and (2) incorporation of explicit mention of "Serbs in Croatia" into Article 3, describing Croatia as the "homeland of all its citizens, Croats, Serbs in Croatia, and the members of other nations and nationalities who inhabit it."[86]

Matica Hrvatska lost this round, however, and the official governmental draft amendments were ultimately passed. Hence, from that point until the Croatian constitutional amendments of 1990, "the Socialist Republic of Croatia [was] the national state of the Croatian nation, the state of the Serbian nation in Croatia, and the state of the nationalities inhabiting it."[87]

Spread of Nationalism to Other Republics

Every federal unit was struck by nationalist outbursts in these years and, among all the non-Serbian nationalities, there were strong anti-Serbian feelings. The fall of Ranković had been a cathartic catalyst because, by branding the arch-Serb as arch-villain, it legitimized the release of pent-up frustrations even as it made their expression more practical. Nationalist discontent was most visible in Croatia and Kosovo, followed, in declining intensity, by Serbia, Montenegro, Bosnia-Herzegovina, Macedonia, Slovenia, and Vojvodina. The typical pattern was that ethnocentric behavior on the part of Serbian bureaucrats provided the stimulus for remonstration. There were even hints of this in pacific Vojvodina, where the so-called Rehák affair signaled the beginning of a breakdown in the Serbian-Hungarian equilibrium. Laszlo Rehák, an active member of the LCY, had complained in the Serbian republic assembly (in 1967) that the University of Novi Sad was dragging its feet in setting up the approved Hungarian Studies Institute; in response, the Serbian press hauled him over the coals for "nationalism" and mobilized forces sufficient to block his election as vice president of the executive council of SR Serbia. Though in some ways the most pacific of Yugoslavia's minorities, the Hungarians of Vojvodina were ruffled by this development and affected by the train of events in Croatia. In an article for *Uj Symposion* (Novi Sad, August 1971), Sándor Rósza, a student at the University of Novi Sad, charged that Hungarians were victims of overt discrimination and that shopkeepers in Novi Sad were loathe to speak Hungarian. Rósza's charges reached the absurd degree of portraying the Hungarians as the "niggers" of Yugoslavia, and the regime reacted swiftly and vengefully. Rósza lost his scholarship and his post as Hungarian-language program coordinator of the Novi Sad Youth Council and was sentenced to three years of strict imprisonment. Oto Tolnak was fired from the editorship of *Uj Symposion* and sentenced to one year in prison. Finally, *Uj Symposion*, under a new editor, had to print an apology for permitting publication of the offending article in the first place.[88] Nor was this an isolated instance. Indeed, as early as 1968, Dobrica Ćosić had cautioned the Fourteenth Plenary Session of the central committee of the LC Serbia that the problem of Hungarian nationalism in Vojvodina ought not be underestimated.

A far more serious flare-up of nationalism occurred in Montenegro, where, during this period, the anti-Serbian faction temporarily prevailed over its pro-Serbian colleagues. The latter group had traditionally been inclined to stress the close kinship, if not outright identity, of Montenegrins and Serbs; the former, in affirming the distinctiveness of the Montenegrin nation, made hostility to Serbia the core of its program. The Montenegrin Literary Society, following in Matica Hrvatska's footsteps, became embroiled in various nationalist disputes, and the review *Ovdje* and the journal *Stvaranje* provided forums for nationalist discontent. Certain problems were revived and reexamined with great interest, including the ethnogenesis and formation of the Montenegrin nation (a politically sensitive subject even in 1982); the relation of the Montenegrin nation to the Serbian nation; the relationship of a possible Montenegrin variant to Serbo-Croatian (or Croato-Serbian); and various issues regarding the content of textbooks in Montenegro.

But, unlike Croatia, where officialdom represented the only stronghold for pockets of conservatives, in Montenegro the pro-Serb faction had deep social roots and recourse to alternative institutions. Forcefully resisting Montenegrin nationalist currents, a Serbian Orthodox Church symposium, meeting at Kosjerevo in the spring of 1970, alleged that the so-called Montenegrins had been forced to identify themselves as Montenegrins but were, in essence, Serbs.[89] But when Patriarch German began a speech shortly thereafter by saying, "We Serbs—of course, I believe that Montenegrins are also Serbs,"[90] even the conservatives were dismayed. *NIN* sprang to the attack and upbraided the patriarch for the "negation of the national sovereignty of certain nations," a stance that, said *NIN*, derived from the tenet held by "certain elements" in the Serbian Orthodox Church that ethnic affiliation is only *artificially* distinguished from confessional affiliation.[91]

Nationalism even made certain inroads in Slovenia, though, lacking any tradition as a separate state, the Slovenes were somewhat more disposed to docility. All the same, the pattern was a familiar one. A prominent Slovenian writer and chairman of the League of Yugoslav Novelists voiced an early protest, complaining, in February 1967, that Slovenian resources had been siphoned off to build up the south and that this policy was contrary to Slovenian interests in both the long and the short run. Another Slovenian novelist, Marjan Rožanc, received a six-month prison term in October 1967 for having written an article for the Slovenian-language journal *Most* (which appeared in Trieste), in which he described the Slovenian nation as a sacrificial offering on the altar of Yugoslavism.[92] Such sentiments spread to the general public of Slovenia, and there were reports of Slovenian workers noisily protesting the showing of films with Serbo-Croatian subtitles.[93] Not surprisingly, Stane Kavčić, head of the Slovenian government in 1970–71, tried to wrest as much political liberty for Slovenia as possible, gave preference to the construction of transportation links with the north and west rather than with Zagreb and Belgrade, and allied himself with the liberals in Croatia. Kavčić was opposed in Ljubljana by Sergej Krajger (in 1982 vice president of the Yugoslav collective presidency) and by France Popit (president of the League of Communists of Slovenia), both hostile to massive decentralization.[94] Although Kavčić himself clearly opposed secession, Mitja Ribičič, a member of the Slovenian party's executive committee, had warned in 1967 of an incipient frondescence of separatist sentiment in Slovenia.[95] Alojz Vindiš later claimed that certain groups in Slovenia took advantage of the uncertainties of the early 1970s, "coquetted" with the idea of Slovenian secession from Yugoslavia, and envisioned the establishment of an independent neutral state based on the Swiss model and oriented to the West.[96]

Nationalist chauvinism was, in a sense, most serious among Serbs—partly because, paradoxically, they considered themselves almost by definition immune to chauvinism. Yet, as early as February 1966, that is, even before the fall of Ranković, *Komunist* had charged that "some members of the LC Serbia have not studied the materials of the Eighth Congress of the LCY and the Fifth Congress of the LCS, in which all the aspects and problems of interethnic relations in our socialist community are treated very clearly and openly." They continued to act, *Komunist* observed, as if they were a special caste whose voice had a certain priority.[97] Chauvinistic behavior has remained a problem where Serbs are concerned, and in January 1978, for example, *Komunist* was again castigating the forces of Serbian reaction.[98]

Serbian nationalism was a particular problem among the Serbs of Croatia. It escalated at this time partly in response to the wave of Croatian nationalism, partly as an adjunct of persistent Great Serbian chauvinism centered in the Serbian republic, and partly as a reflection of the traditional, religiously derived distrust that Croatia's Serbs have long felt toward their Croatian cousins. Prosvjeta, the Serbian cultural society in Croatia that was created in 1944, started to change its character around 1969 and became a stronghold for Serbian nationalists and a forum for former Chetniks.[99] Exploiting this institutional base, Croatia's Serbian nationalists sought in 1970 to create a Serbian autonomous province within Croatia and demanded the establishment of a separate network of special Serbian schools; those further to the right even broached the idea of seceding from SR Croatia and attaching themselves to SR Serbia.[100] In one of its last meetings in 1971, the executive committee of Prosvjeta demanded (1) that Croatian and Serbian be recognized as official languages of SR Croatia and that all republican legislative acts be published both in Croatian and in Cyrillic-Serbian; (2) that a Chamber for Interethnic Relations be formed within the framework of the Croatian *Sabor* (Assembly), with the delegates from each national group chosen exclusively by the members of that group; and (3) that this chamber play a deciding role in all questions relevant to the equality of nationalities and that its decisions require the assent of *all* delegations.[101] (Recall also that the Serbs were the first to be reprimanded by the federal government for having produced a chauvinistic dictionary—Moskovljević's *Dictionary of the Modern Serbo-Croatian Language* [1966].)

Symptomatic of the same syndrome, experimentation with semifree elections in 1967 and 1969 led in Serbia to the election of opposition nationalists to the federal Assembly. Nationalism animated a large portion of the Serbian population, from the peasantry to those on the rungs of power. Thus, in a story recounted by Carl Gustaf Ströhm, Slobodan Penezić-Krcun, Ranković's onetime deputy, even sought to pay Tito a compliment by saying that he had only one shortcoming—he was not a Serb![102]

All of these regional parties—whether one thinks of Slovenia or Croatia or Bosnia or Montenegro or Macedonia or Serbia—were internally divided, and typically the two chief political camps were liberals and conservatives. (This picture had local nuances in Bosnia and Montenegro.) In Serbia, the party was temporarily under the leadership of Marko Nikezić and Latinka Perović. Their position seems to have been that if the Serbian party could not control the center, it was better to maximize republic etatism (autonomy). Internally, the Nikezić-Perović group was associated with a degree of liberalization.

The Battle at the Center

After the passage of some nineteen amendments during 1967–68 that trimmed the prerogatives of the federal government, enhanced the status and powers of the republics, and granted the autonomous provinces near parity with the republics, a movement emerged to transform the federal government itself into an interrepublican agency. The chief advocates of this movement were Stane Kavčič, Slavko Milosavlevski, and Miko Tripalo, and the means of transformation were to be the network of interrepublican committees that had finally been established in mid-1971. One of the movement's more alacritous adherents, Dražen Budiša, even suggested redesignating Yugoslavia the "League of Yugoslav Socialist Self-Managing Republics" as an explicit token of the system's imminent metamorphosis into a confederation.[103]

Although part of a package of twenty-three more amendments passed on June 30, 1971, stripping the federal government of most of its remaining prerogatives (limiting its powers in foreign affairs, defense, foreign trade, and the common currency and guaranteeing a common tariff system and the free flow of goods throughout the country), the committees themselves seem to have been conceived in a spirit of experimentation.[104] Amendment 33, adopted at this time, specified that economic questions of general interest were to be resolved through direct consultation with deputies of the republics. This was the legal foundation for the committees. In the last week of June 1971, Djemal Bijedić was asked to form a new government, and it fell to his administration to inaugurate the new committee system. By the end of August, the newly constituted Federal Executive Council (SIV) had managed to form most of its working bodies and had announced its determination to complete all appointments to the nascent interrepublican committees by September 2.

Five interrepublican committees were created: for developmental policy, the monetary system, foreign trade and hard currency, the market, and finance. Each committee would consist of nine members, one from each federal unit and a chairman selected by SIV from among its own ranks. Under Article 2 of the executive act that brought the interrepublican committees into legal existence, the new committee system was described as the mechanism whereby the republics and provinces participate in "the establishment of federal policy and in the passage of federal laws and other acts, as well as in the passage of regulations for the execution of federal laws and other acts if the mutual accommodation (*usaglašavanje*) of positions is prescribed in [the areas of] those laws or acts."[105] They were authorized to consider any questions lying within their jurisdiction either at the request of SIV or on their own initiative, even if their involvement was not technically and specifically prescribed by the constitution. At the time of the committees' birth, their creators argued that they would quicken the legislative process without impinging on the jurisdiction of SIV or of the federal *Skupština*. The committees were to render their evaluations to SIV and to the executive councils of the federal units. But the positions of an interrepublican committee could be overruled only if SIV could obtain the specific assent of the executive councils of the federal units (Article 12). This meant that the new committees would become the ultimate repository of power where economics was concerned.

A Coordination Committee was also established to act as a kind of supervisory board over the activities of the interrepublican committee system (IRCS). This commission is made up of the president of SIV, the presidents of the executive councils of the federal units, and eight members of SIV (one from each federal unit).

Before they came into being, while the procedures under which they would operate were still being discussed, the interrepublican committees were already under fire. Entrenched interests in the decision-making process feared that the new institution would result in the curtailment of their prerogatives. Critics repeatedly charged that establishment of the committees would unnecessarily complicate interrepublican negotiation and create, in effect, a three-phase legislative process (republics, interrepublican committees, and *Skupština*)—whereas previously the *Skupština* had handled matters in one phase.[106]

But, far from producing a bottleneck in the system, the interrepublican committees proved very efficient. At the time the IRCS was created, there were some 124 questions of interrepublican importance that had not been resolved, even after months of debate. IRCS disposed of all these questions within five months—ninety-two of them in the committees themselves, thirty-two in the Coordination Commission. Satisfied with what was at least partly his handiwork, Bijedić told the Twenty-eighth Session of the presidency of the LCY: "I am convinced that, in our phase of development, we could not discover and pass decisions so quickly without accommodation via the committees and Coordination Commission."[107] Dragutin Kosovac, president of the executive council of Bosnia-Herzegovina and ipso facto a member of the Coordination Commission, was even more rhapsodic and raved that the IRCS assured "the most rational decisions and these, in essence, represent the optimal interest of the whole."[108]

So smoothly did the committees do their work that other organs of decision making found themselves to the sidelines. Even the Federal Executive Council's meetings merely ratified the decisions and conclusions of the Coordination Commission, now alternatively dubbed the "Supreme InterRepublican Committee" or the "Super-Government" (*super-vlada*).[109] The confederal character of this institution was unmistakable. Yet the system's proponents looked forward to the further expansion of the powers of the IRCS. Ksente Bogoev, president of the executive council of Macedonia, argued that IRCS served to "neutralize manifestations of narrow economic nationalism, which periodically accompany positive tendencies" in the strengthening of the autonomy of the federal units. He urged that more intensive use be made of the committees and suggested that questions arising in the spheres of education, science, culture, and health also be turned over to the committees for resolution.[110]

Ilija Bakić, president of Kosovo's executive council, echoed these sentiments and even thought that the committees might be engaged in the formulation of issues at an earlier stage, relieving the presidents of the executive councils of responsibility for all but the most crucial questions.[111] Such suggestions were naturally disconcerting to the conservatives, who were already in retreat.

Croatia Declares War

The various factions in the Yugoslav debate over the federalization of the LCY—democratizers, liberals, nationalists, humanists, and conservatives—had their counterparts within the League of Communists of Croatia (LCC). There were the "liberals," such as Savka Dabčević-Kučar, Miko Tripalo, and their coterie, together with technocrats and other economic reformers; the "nationalists," such as Šime Djodan, Marko Veselica, and the exploding membership of Matica Hrvatska; and the band of centralist-humanists known as the "Praxis group." In addition to these three groups were the conservatives, including such persons as Miloš Žanko (by now discredited), Stipe Šuvar, Veljko Rus, Dušan Dragosavac, Jure Bilić, J. Radojčević, and Milutin Baltić (Radojčević, Dragosavac, and Baltić, significantly, were Croatian Serbs).

The nationalists had, by early 1971, found natural ideological allies in the liberals. When, in February 1971, the conservative members of the Croatian executive committee demanded that resolute action be taken against Matica Hrvatska, Dabčević-Kučar and Pirker—supported by liberal loyalists Tripalo, Dragutin Haramija, Ivan Šibl, Marko Koprtla, and Srečko Bijelić (president of the city conference of the LCC of Zagreb)—blocked them. Encouraged by this and similar signs of strength, *Omladinski tjednik* and *Hrvatski tjednik* floated the idea of convoking an extraordinary session of the LCC, hoping to strengthen the hands of the liberals further.

Conservative strength was, however, scarcely spent, and the antinationalist factions in the Croatian party scored a victory on July 23, when they succeeded in having Šime Djodan and Marko Veselica expelled from the party as "ringleaders" of ethnocentric turmoil. This decision was made by the presidency of the city conference of the LCC, where, Bijelić notwithstanding, the conservatives still had strength. But this victory was an isolated triumph, for the tide was turning against the conservatives. Bakarić, no conservative but no nationalist either, was retired to the back benches. Membership in Matica Hrvatska soared to 41,000 members in fifty-five branches by November 1971 (up from 2,323 members in thirty branches in November 1970).[112] And the nationalists steadily made inroads among establishment news organs. Among the local newspapers that became outspoken advocates of "Croatia first" were *Slobodna Dalmacija*, the weeklies *Varaždinske vijesti, Brodski list, Vinkovačke novosti, Imotska krajina, VUS*, and the clerically oriented *Požeski list*. In time, *Vjesnik* likewise drew closer to the nationalists. Radio-Television Zagreb began to carry all speeches of Savka Dabčević-Kučar in their entirety, while systematically curtailing programming from other Yugoslav stations and information regarding other parts of the country—except for material pertaining to the federal government.

During the summer of 1971, the periodicals of Belgrade and Zagreb engaged in polemics over a series of incidents and provocations, many of which were undoubtedly blown out of proportion if not essentially fabricated. The best known of these incidents is probably the "Podravska Slatina" affair, a story that broke on May 11, 1971, when Belgrade's *Politika* reported obstructive activities by members of Matica Hrvatska on their way to a society meeting. The article portrayed the members as anti-Yugoslav Croatian nationalists—they were said to have been flying only Croatian colors lacking the red star on their car antennae (an allegation they denied)—and accused them of trying to break up a meeting of old partisans in the town of Podravska Slatina in Slavonia. The article was immediately lambasted by Croatia's *Glas Slavonije* (May 13), which described the *Politika* article as "fabricated disinformation" that distorted an insignificant event so as to make it appear to *Politika*'s Serbian readers that the Croats were getting completely out of control. Yet the *Politika* version was also picked up by *Komunist, Vjesnik*, and *Večernje Novosti*, a Belgrade tabloid. By the following day (i.e., May 14), *Glas Slavonije* was nervously drawing the conclusion that *Politika*'s provocation was designed to undermine Matica Hrvatska's prestige and legitimacy, throttle the reform movement, and abort passage of the constitutional amendments by portraying their chief exponents (the Croats) as nationalistic zealots.[113] The central committee of the LCC appointed an investigative commission to look into the various allegations pertaining to the Podravska Slatina affair. After two weeks the commission concluded (on May 30) "that there had been no provocation of the meeting of partisans on the part of [Matica Hrvatska]" and that claims that the Matica cars were flying Croatian, not Yugoslav, colors were groundless.[114] As the summer drew on, Matica Hrvatska became convinced that there was a determined campaign to paint it "as a nationalistic, even chauvinistic, organization"—a conviction that only deepened when, immediately after the Brioni meeting, party conservatives demanded that the organization be put in a straitjacket.[115]

In this politically fluid situation, the Croatian conservatives employed any and all available means in their struggle for control of the Croatian party. Ironically, they found natural allies in the so-called humanists of the Praxis group, who felt an ideologically rooted antipathy toward decentralization, nationalism, and even federalism (which the humanists viewed as an unnecessary compromise with dogma). When the Sisak district court banned the May–August 1971 issue of *Praxis* because of an article by Milan Kangrga that contained, among other things, "the most searing indictment hitherto printed in *Praxis* of the rising nationalist movement in Yugoslavia (and especially in Croatia), linking it intimately with the efforts of a new middle class to consolidate its position," the conservatives took the issue to the republic's Supreme Court.[116] Both sides in the contest knew exactly how *Praxis* figured in the struggle. Thus,

> the consistently outspoken and hostile attacks of the *Praxis* collaborators on the spirit of nationalism had made it increasingly urgent for the nationalist ideologues to discredit *Praxis* in the public eye and to impair, insofar as possible, its further activity. . . . It is unlikely, therefore, that *Praxis*'s strategic value in the struggle against "nationalist deformations" went unnoticed by the federal authorities, and it cannot be doubted that calculations such as these played some role in the Croatian Supreme Court's 1971 decision to overturn the Sisak District Court's ban on the contested issue of *Praxis*.[117]

By that point, the Serbs were putting pressure on Tito to curb the Croatian liberals,[118] and Tito himself was watching developments in Croatia with increasing concern. Early in July, he traveled to Zagreb to talk with Croatia's leadership. At a closed meeting, Tito revealed his misgivings that Croatia was sliding back to the atmosphere of the prewar era and implied that the republican leadership was losing control of the situation. "Are we going to have 1941 all over again?" Tito asked. "That would be a catastrophe." Of special concern to Tito was the cult of Stjepan Radić. "Radić's organization was a kulak organization," Tito snapped. "He hated communists and did not represent the interests of the working class. We offered to cooperate with him, but he didn't want to have anything to do with us."[119] Tito also criticized efforts to bring back

Jelačić's statue, calling Jelačić a reactionary and condemning him for having helped suppress Louis Kossuth's "progressive" revolution; indeed, Tito stated firmly that he would not permit any monument to Jelačić on the Trg Republike (Zagreb's main square, casually referred to by Zagrebers, even today, as the "Trg Jelačića"). Tito even offered to make Tripalo prime minister of Yugoslavia in order to get him out of Croatia and away from the Croatian nationalists. But Tripalo declined. Clearly, Tito remained the ultimate arbiter in interrepublican and—so it seemed—intrarepublican affairs; when he brought the full force of pressure to bear, a republican leadership almost always had to yield ground, at least temporarily. But, since Tito was increasingly considering that Yugoslav stability was best guaranteed when Yugoslavia operated as a "self-regulating" system of broadly autonomous federal units, the republics, in practice, perceived his interventions as setting the limits of legitimate activity rather than aborting independent decision making.

Hence, the response of Croatia's "national communists" to Tito's July 4 lecture was not to cave in but to conclude that Tito was "poorly informed" and that it was necessary "to select proper representatives of the Croatian nation who will converse with Comrade Tito."[120] The district (*općina*) committee of the LCC of Zadar circulated a letter among the presidency of the central committee of the LCC and all regional political organizations that questioned the sense of political responsibility of Baltić, Bilić, Dragosavac, Derosi-Bjelajac, and Radojčević (all Croatian conservatives) because of their interference in the efforts of the nationalists to capture the channels of political communication.[121] The conservatives had to be neutralized, and Tito had to be wooed and convinced that, far from being a "key problem," as he had claimed, Croatia was politically healthy. This the nationalists managed to do by mid-September, in a carefully orchestrated reception for Tito in Zagreb. Tito made an about-face and told his Zagreb audience on September 14, "I have been able to convince myself [on this visit] just how absurd certain stories about Croatia are—that there is no unity here, that people here think differently, that chauvinism blossoms and thrives here. None of that is true."[122]

Croatian nationalism now took a dangerous turn, however, riveting its attention on ethnically mixed Bosnia to the south. In the gathering storm, it was inevitable that Croatian eyes should turn to Bosnia—a territory that many Croats continued to believe was rightfully theirs. This territory had been a part of Croatia during the heyday of *Ustaše* Croatia, and some 20 percent of its population consisted of ethnic Croats. By now it had been openly admitted that, under Ranković, the state security apparatus had systematically persecuted Croats in Bosnia.[123] Matica Hrvatska claimed that Croats were still being denied their rights in Bosnia and other republics and, therefore, sought to set up branches in Bosnia and Vojvodina to cater to the needs of Croats in those areas. Viewing this as a kind of cultural imperialism, however, neither Bosnia nor Vojvodina would permit it.[124] Bakarić's earlier charge that Matica Hrvatska was comporting itself as a shadow government was proving accurate.[125] Meantime—so claimed *Oslobodjenje*—Ante Paradžik, president of the League of

Students of Croatia (LSC), with other members of the LSC leadership, was traveling around the districts of Herzegovina, organizing student meetings and attempting to court support for the recently expelled Veselica and Djodan.[126]

In November 1971, *Hrvatski tjednik* added fuel to the fire by publishing statistics on the ethnic affiliation of members of elite bodies in Bosnia-Herzegovina. The paper charged that Croats were systematically underrepresented at all except the highest levels of republican administration, where they enjoyed pro forma proportional parity. Under the 1961 census—then the most recent set of population statistics available—the population of Bosnia consisted of 42.9 percent Serbs, 25.7 percent Muslims, 21.7 percent Croats, and 9.7 percent other nationalities. Yet Croats comprised only 11.1 percent of the Higher Economic Court of Bosnia, 16.6 percent of the republican constitutional court, 7.6 percent of the public prosecutor's office, 12.5 percent of the undersecretaries, 15.3 percent of republican chiefs of inspectorates, and 17.8 percent of the republican secretariat for internal affairs. All presiding members in the judicial branch were Serbs, as was the republic's secretary for national defense. And, though the Croats were generously represented among republican secretaries and their assistants, no republican secretary of Croatian nationality sat on the executive council (as against four Serbs and one Muslim), and there were no Croats in the republican secretariat for national defense or among directors of republican agencies. The trend penetrated into the media as well, where Croats comprised only 17 percent of the editorial board of *Oslobodjenje* and had only one of the six seats on the Board of Documentation. The general director of Radio-Television Sarajevo, the director of Sarajevo Television, the editor and director of *Odjek*, the director of the National Library of Bosnia-Herzegovina, and the president of the Bosnian Academy of Arts and Sciences were all Serbs, and the director of Sarajevo Radio, the director of *Zadruga*, and the editors of *Život*, *Izraz*, and *Pregled* were all Muslims. The only important positions held by Croats in the media were the directorship of joint services of Radio-Television Sarajevo and the editorship of television programming—both clearly subordinate. The pattern was replicated in the structure of the bank directorates where, of thirty-two directors, directorate chiefs, and division chiefs, only three were Croats. The pattern even extended to the composition of the League of Communists of Bosnia-Herzegovina (LC B-H), where the Serbs were clearly overrepresented and the Croats drastically underrepresented. Citing 1966 figures, *Hrvatski tjednik* claimed that the LC B-H consisted of 57.14 percent Serbs, 26.30 percent Muslims, and 12.05 percent Croats.[127] (Remember that Bosnia's Croats and Muslims played a large role in *Ustaše* activity and that the Serbs were the first to join the partisan ranks in World War II.)

But, waving aside Croatian objections that they were underrepresented in the Bosnian political structure, Hamdija Pozderac, member of the presidency of the central committee of the LCY and a prominent Bosnian politician, replied facilely that "no one is responsible for his work only 'to some nation of his' but rather to the working class and to all the peoples and nationalities in our self-managing socialist community."[128] As the figures in table 10 make clear, the

Table 10. *Membership of the LC of Bosnia-Herzegovina by Nationality*

	Muslims	*Croats*	*Serbs*	*Total membership (including members of other nationalities)*	*% Croats*
1965	34,496	15,857	75,749	132,696	11.95
1966	35,049	15,693	76,069	133,273	11.78
1967	35,459	15,221	73,463	130,846	11.63
1968	41,455	17,885	86,962	158,110	11.31
1969	39,505	17,130	84,257	152,232	11.25
1970	39,588	15,993	77,737	142,313	11.24
1971	39,787	15,619	75,300	140,735	11.10
1972	41,901	15,259	73,612	138,833	10.99
1973	46,087	16,160	77,099	148,061	10.91
. . . .					
1981	138,929	48,010	172,205	391,244	12.27
1984	142,606	47,298	172,887	410,000	11.53

Sources: Othmar Nikola Haberl, *Parteiorganisation und nationale Frage in Jugoslawien* (Berlin: Otto Harrassowitz, 1976), p. 209; *Oslobodjenje*, May 17, 1982, p. 5; and *Oslobodjenje*, March 29, 1984, pp. 2–3.

proportion of Croats in the Bosnian party declined steadily in the late 1960s and early 1970s, and even the somewhat higher tally recorded for 1981 (12.27 percent) was still drastically lower than the proportion of the Bosnian population consisting of Croats—18.38 percent in 1981.[129] Gradually, Croatian nationalists became convinced that the only solution was to incorporate the "expatriate" Croats into an expanded Croatian republic. Therefore, they demanded the attachment of the western part of Bosnia-Herzegovina to Croatia. Ironically, Serbian nationalists responded to this not by aligning themselves with Bosnia in a show of solidarity but rather by claiming the southeastern sections of Bosnia-Herzegovina for themselves.[130] One is reminded of Poland's response to Hitler's annexation of Bohemia: ultimately dependent on French and British support against the German menace, Poland nonetheless did not shrink from claiming the Teschen enclave for itself. Yet, by clamoring for territorial expansion at Bosnia's expense, the Croatian nationalists had in effect "declared war" on Bosnia and on the federation itself.

Croatia's actions in 1971 mirrored Napoleon's actions as he moved from defending France to his new project of conquering Europe. "The European states would have accepted Napoleon had he been willing to play according to the rules of the game."[131] In the same way, the Croatian party had good relations with the parties of Slovenia and Macedonia as long as Croatia was perceived to be "playing by the rules of the game." Indeed, in the 1970–71 period, the Croats went to great lengths to establish a special relationship with Kosovo.

This included the stimulation of historical research designed to reveal and emphasize traditional historical links between parts of Croatia and the Kosovo region. These efforts bore some fruit, and, on the occasion of one particular visit to Kosovo, Croatia's Dabčević-Kučar was greeted as a queen by enthusiastic Kosovars. A certain solidarity also developed of its own accord between Croatian and Kosovar students. This spontaneous and natural solidarity, rooted in common resentment of the Serbs, was brought out, for instance, at a dinner for delegations from student organizations from all parts of Yugoslavia that convened in conjunction with a student conference in Ljubljana (May 13–14, 1971). When certain students began singing nostalgic songs about Ranković, the Croatian and Kosovar students predictably arose and left together.[132] Yet, ultimately, by their excessive demands and intransigence, the Croatian leadership intimidated other republican leaderships and persuaded them that Croatia had become a greater threat to the system than Serbia. As usual, there were differences of opinion within the various republican elites. Crvenkovski and Kavčič refused to abandon the Croats, continued to lend them strong support, and were later removed from their leadership posts.

Earlier on, the Croatian leadership had begun to campaign for reforms of the banking, foreign trade, and foreign currency systems—reforms that were unacceptable to the leaderships of Kosovo, Montenegro, Bosnia-Herzegovina, and Serbia. Friction between the Croatian and Serbian leaderships became so grave that, at a meeting in Brioni in April 1971, the Slovenian and Bosnian representatives urged a public airing of the differences between the Serbian and Croatian leaderships in an effort to assuage them. The Slovenian and Macedonian leaders were particularly concerned about the implications of Croatia's nationalistic fever as well as the growing intransigence of the Croatian leadership.[133] But the Croatian leaders could not back down at this point; they believed that compromising with the "centralists" would cost them their local support and, thus, their jobs in Zagreb.

On November 5, 1971, the Croatian central committee heard a report from President Dabčević-Kučar on Croatia's foreign currency earnings, economic grievances, and economic woes in general. The Croatian government took a strong stand on increased retention of foreign currency earnings—a stand that was, at first, backed by the Slovenian party. Matica Hrvatska, of course, played an instrumental role in propelling the Croatian leadership further to the right. In an article that appeared in Matica Hrvatska's journal, *Kritika*, Peter Šegedin, president of the Croatian society of novelists, repeated that Croatian policy must be predicated on self-interest and *not* on the interests of Yugoslavia as a whole.[134] Matica Hrvatska then called for use of Croatian as the language of command for military units stationed in Croatia, or, alternatively, if Serbian was retained as the language of command for the army, the establishment of Croatian as the language of command for the navy (on the grounds that 90 percent of the Yugoslav navy operates in Croatian waters). By the summer of 1971, Matica Hrvatska had lent its voice to demands for the enlargement of Croatian territory at the expense of both Herzegovina and Montenegro and had begun to mobilize ethnic Croats both in Bosnia and in Vojvodina.[135] By failing to suppress Matica Hrvatska at this juncture, the Croatian party leaders lost their chance to save themselves. In threatening the territorial integrity of two fellow federal units and alienating a third (Serbia) by their minatory pose vis-à-vis Serbs residing in Croatia, the Croats lapsed into a Napoleonic role. They had gone too far; thus, the appearance of an anti-Croatian coalition was to be expected. This coalition, of course, was not responsible for the defeat of the "Croatia first" movement, but its presence permitted the effective quashing of the movement by the federal government in league with the Croatian conservatives.

To replace the national-liberal coalition (with Slovenia and Macedonia) that had been united in the advocacy of specific liberal planks, the Croats sought to create an anti-Serbian coalition (with Kosovo and Montenegro) that was united by an aversion to the assimilationist policies associated with Ranković and, at least where Kosovo was concerned, by the desire for expanded political autonomy vis-à-vis Belgrade.[136] But these new partners were not as influential, useful, or even as reliable as Croatia's former alliance partners, and the fragility of the new alliance would be demonstrated soon enough, when the slogan of "5 to 1" became a self-fulfilling prophecy.

Nor could there any longer be doubt as to the ideological coloration of the Croatian troika: at the Twentieth Plenum of the central committee of the LCC (May 13–14, 1971), Miko Tripalo openly identified with the Croatian national movement led by Matica Hrvatska and *Hrvatski tjednik*. The intense and broadly based popularity that this generated for the troika was amply demonstrated when, in August 1972, the funeral of the former secretary of the Croatian party's central committee, Pero Pirker, prompted a massive demonstration by more than 100,000 supporters.

The Croats began to press their demands with determination. Not only should the foreign currency retention system be renegotiated so that Croatia might retain a larger chunk of its earnings; it was even suggested that a separate Croatian currency be created.[137] Not only was the Croatian district of the JNA to become, in effect, a Croatian army, but also the Supreme Headquarters of the National Navy must be relocated to Split. Not only was there a need to further decentralize and reform the banking system, but Croatia should also have its own Croatian national bank with a governor appointed by the republican leadership and empowered to negotiate foreign loans independently.[138] Not only was republican statehood to be "more precisely" defined, but also—more concretely—the Croatian national *Sabor* was to be recognized as the highest organ of power in Croatia (relegating the LCC to, at best, second place).[139] Economist Hrvoje Šošic demanded that Croatia be represented in the United Nations.[140] Vladimir Loknar lodged a demand for the passage of an endogenous Croatian legal code.[141] Others clamored for the printing of Croatian postage stamps.[142] Ultimately, the nationalist group gathered around Matica Hrvatska explicitly raised the cry for complete Croatian independence: secession was fast becoming mainstream political sentiment in Croatia.[143] In ethnically heterogeneous communities, friction between Croats and Serbs became commonplace, and there were reports that in some communities residents were "arming themselves in anticipation of a physical showdown."[144]

Ironically, despite their huge popularity and the symbolic leadership of both the mass movement and the LCC, the national troika (Tripalo, Dabčević-Kučar, and Pirker) actually controlled neither. The popular movement, under the guidance of Matica Hrvatska, was antipathetic toward the key desiderata of the entrenched conservative faction in the LCC. The troika was thus confronted with an ineluctable choice between (1) allying with Matica Hrvatska against the conservatives and gambling that Tito's confidence could be retained or the conservatives could be outmaneuvered, and (2) seeking a compromise with the conservatives and moving to bridle Matica Hrvatska. But the latter option was unpalatable because the liberals and the conservatives were separated by an unbridgeable distrust and because the liberals and the nationalists continued to share a number of common positions, especially where economic complaints were concerned. When Dabčević-Kučar addressed the Twenty-second Session of the Croatian central committee on November 5, it was abundantly clear that the choice had been confronted and the dilemma decisively resolved in favor of the national mass movement.

Collapse of the House of Cards

The Croatian conservatives were gathering their forces, plotting how best to administer the coup de grace to the liberal troika. In late October, Bakarić journeyed to Sarajevo to court Bosnian support. He hoped to escalate the intra-Croatian party contest to the federal level in order to defeat the coalition of Croatian liberals and nationalists there. Branko Mikulić, a Bosnian Croat and president of the Bosnian party, was sensitive to the nationalistic propaganda washing over from Croatia and receptive to Bakarić's wooing. Almost at the same time, Tito, closeted with Yugoslav army leaders at a secret meeting in Bugojno, Bosnia, was being shown "suppressed TV reels of Croatian Communist mass meetings, with only Croatian flags [missing the Communist red star] and with nationalist and anti-Tito slogans, songs, shouts and signs."[145] Unnerved by the obvious exacerbation of the intraparty conflict, Tripalo made a show of force, telling a gathering in Vela Luka at the end of November "the policy that we are pursuing in Croatia cannot be changed. Our opponents think that that policy can be changed by replacing a few leaders. In order to achieve that, it would be necessary to replace thousands of leaders in Croatia. . . . We have taken our fate in our hands and we will keep it in our hands."[146]

The public did not know—but Matica Hrvatska and the student leaders apparently did—that the Croatian conservatives had undertaken a concerted effort to enlist Tito's support in throttling the liberals.[147] At this point the Croatian Students Union, in a dramatic gambit designed to demonstrate support for the troika and outbid the conservatives, organized a massive strike, hoping to undermine the conservative move by making clear that conservatism lacked a popular base. Some three thousand students met in Zagreb on November 22, 1971, and unanimously voted to begin a strike at 9 A.M. the following day to protest the existing federal regulations governing hard currency, banking, and commerce.[148] At Paradžik's prompting, the union also aligned behind the various linguistic, military, and political demands outlined above.[149] Interestingly, representatives of the Native Macedonian Students Club and of the Native Club of Kosovar Students, who were present at the meeting, firmly supported the Croatian students.

The following day, student meetings were held at many university departments in Zagreb and strike committees were formed. At 7 P.M., a plenum of the Croatian Students Union unanimously passed a resolution calling for a strike at all institutions of higher education in Croatia, and faculty deans, meeting in Zagreb, expressed solidarity with the students. Two months earlier, the student prorector, Ivan Zvonimir Čičak, had advised this very tactic when, on the occasion of the one hundredth anniversary of the birth of Stjepan Radić, he had told a university crowd that "students must be prepared to demonstrate, rebel, and strike, because their youth and their radicalism are the only guarantee to their nation for a better and brighter future."[150] Nor did the liberal establishment wish to risk estrangement from the mass movement by distancing itself from the strike. Dabčević-Kučar commented, "I am deeply convinced that the motives of the greatest portion of the students who have undertaken this strike were positive and well meaning and progressive."[151]

On November 25, the League of Students of Split convened an emergency plenum and enthusiastically endorsed the resolutions passed by the students in Zagreb. In Rijeka, students began circulating a petition for use of a chamber in which to convene a similar meeting. In Dubrovnik, the presidency of the Dubrovnik Student Union came out in support of the Zagreb resolutions. Within a matter of days, at least 30,000 university students across Croatia were on strike. By the beginning of December, students at the Zagreb law school had demanded the expulsion of all unitarists from the LCC, specifically naming Dragosavac (secretary of the central committee), Baltić (central committee secretary for SR Croatia as of 1980) and Bilić (president of the Croatian *Sabor*), together with Ema Derossi-Bjelajac and Čedo Grbić.[152]

Until the autumn of 1971, Tito had hoped that it would be possible to effect a compromise with the forces in power in Croatia and to let things develop more or less on their own.[153] If the suppressed newsreel footage was not enough, the student strike helped convince Tito that compromise was impossible.[154]

Liberalization, decentralization, and appeasement of Croatia had only fed the Croats' ever-increasing hunger for autonomy. Indeed, military intelligence later uncovered evidence that some of the party leaders had been in contact with Croatian *Ustaše* émigré groups in West Germany.[155] At first, Tito considered sending troops into Croatia; eventually he decided to simply decapitate the Croatian party leadership. On December 1, Tito convened a joint meeting of the party presidiums of the LCY and the LCC at Karadjordjevo, Vojvodina.

On this occasion, the famous Twenty-first Session of the LCY presidency, it became obvious just how isolated Croatia had become. The Serbian and Croatian conservatives led the charge, supported by ideological bedfellows from Vojvodina and Montenegro. Bosnia, Slovenia, and even Kosovo criticized the waxing exclusivist nationalism and called for stern measures against it.[156] Latinka Perović, Serbia's spokesperson at the session, declared that "Yugoslavia will emerge from this crisis only if nationalism is *wiped out* in every constituent national group."[157] Only the Macedonian representative, Angel Čemerski, showed any readiness to treat the Croatian liberals mildly.[158] The Croatian leaders were treated to a tongue-lashing for "unhealthy liberalism," nonchalance with respect to counterrevolutionary groups, and use of student groups to advance their political aims. The Croats were told to put their house in order, but, given the denunciation of the policy pursued by the liberal troika, the Twenty-first Session could only strengthen the hand of the conservatives on the Croatian central committee.

Despite this, there was a scurry of activity designed to avert the inevitable. At a meeting of the city conference of the LCC of Zagreb on December 4, immediately after the Twenty-first Session of the LCY presidency, conference president Šrecko Bijelić omitted any mention of "nationalism" or "counterrevolutionary activity" in discussing the session's resolutions and employed only bland and ambiguous references to "anti-self-management" and "antidemocratic forces." He proposed the relatively mild remedy of meeting with representatives of Matica Hrvatska in order to sort things out.[159] Mirko Dragović and Pero Kriste, chairman and deputy chairman respectively of the LCC interdistrict conference for Dalmatia, made an attempt to stem the tide loosed by the Twenty-first Session. Kriste, after a hastily arranged meeting with Tripalo, assembled a number of political functionaries in Dubrovnik, told them that it seemed the Croatian leadership might be changed, blamed the forthcoming changes on the fact that Tito was "probably poorly informed" about the situation in Croatia, urged the mobilization of strong support for the troika, and suggested convoking an extraordinary congress in order to underline that support. Simultaneously, Dragović invited various leaders from Zadar (Sarić, Pera, Zanki, and Festini) to Hotel Solaris on the outskirts of Šibenik, where he also warned that Tito was poorly informed, the state security apparatus was behind the uproar, and the Croatian leadership required rescue.[160] *Vjesnik* (December 6, 1971) reported that working collectives and local assemblies in Croatia were voicing their implicit faith in and strong support of the troika. At the Twenty-second Session of the LCY presidency (December 9), Dabčević-Kučar defended herself and claimed that she and her cohorts would faithfully undertake such actions as were necessary *in the spirit of the Twenty-first Session.*[161]

Meanwhile, the Croatian conservatives demanded that they be provided a copy of the stenographic record of the Twenty-first Session (held December 1–2). The liberal troika, still formally holding the reins, tried to submit only an edited transcript. Finally, on December 12, the house of cards collapsed: Tripalo, Dabčević-Kučar, Pirker, and Marko Koprtla, hitherto a member of the executive committee, resigned their posts under pressure. In protest of Tripalo's resignation, five hundred student militants demonstrated for four days in downtown Zagreb and demanded creation of a separate Croatian state—a response that only served to further implicate Tripalo and strengthen Tito's hand. Helmeted riot police were sent in to occupy strategic points in Zagreb, while helicopters surveyed the streets from above. If necessary, the army was prepared to move in. A follow-up conference to the Twenty-first Session declared that "nationalism has become . . . the focal point for everything in our society that is reactionary, anti-socialist and anti-democratic, bureaucratic, and Stalinist."[162]

In the aftermath of the crisis, literally tens of thousands of members were expelled from the party, most for failure to toe the party line.[163] In the higher echelons of political authority, 741 persons were stripped of their posts and expelled from the party, another 280 party members were merely compelled to resign their posts, and yet another 131 functionaries were demoted. Of this total, the greatest number were to be found in Osijek, Zagreb, and Split (in that order).[164] Others—Djodan, Čičak, Marko Veselica, Hrvoje Šošic, Franjo Tudjman (the former partisan general), and Gotovac, editor of *Hrvatski tjednik*, were sentenced to long prison terms. Altogether some two to three thousand persons were imprisoned for political reasons in Croatia in the wake of the fall of Tripalo and Dabčević-Kučar; thousands more were held administratively (without formal charges) for two to three months.[165] Matica Hrvatska was shut down and its fourteen periodical publications (including the popular *Hrvatski tjednik* and *Kolo*) were put out of commission. *Tlo* survived only a few months longer—long enough to publish four 1972 issues. *Dubrovnik* was placed under provisional ban. Within a fortnight, the party removed the director of Radio Dubrovnik and the editors of *Vjesnik*, *Vjesnik u srijedu*, *Vidici*, *Pitanja*, *Tlo*, *Jež*, and *Omladinski tjednik*, and the staff of Radio Pula was obliged to engage in self-criticism. Wayward student publications in other republics were also "cleansed": the editors of *Student* (Belgrade), *Bota e Re* (Kosovo), and a Macedonian student paper were replaced, and the editor of the Ljubljana student paper, *Tribuna*, was reprimanded. On May 8, 1971, the Twenty-eighth Session of the League of Communists of Croatia, meeting in Zagreb, adopted a resolution expelling Dabčević-Kučar, Tripalo, Pirker, and Koprtla from the party. The backlash continued through 1973, reaching a climax in October and November with the continued purge of writers, filmmakers, university professors, and former liberal leaders.[166] The Roman Catholic Church, whose adherents are concentrated in Croatia and Slovenia, also came under press attack during 1973 for alleged nationalism.

At the same time, however, Tito moved to undercut the popular bases of the Croatian nationalists by granting many of the nationalist demands. Thus, export firms were allowed to retain 20 percent of foreign exchange earnings instead of 7 to 12 percent, and tourist enterprises were permitted to retain 45 percent of their earnings instead of 12 percent.[167] In addition, the dinar was devalued (by 18.7 percent) for the second time in a year, boosting the value of Croatia's foreign currency earnings and complicating the importation of goods and materials into less developed areas in Serbia, Montenegro, and Macedonia. Belgrade was even willing to concede that, in a sense, Croatia *had* been exploited; it admitted that Croatia's contribution to the federal budget had been proportionately largest. *Ekonomska politika* noted that whereas, in 1970, Slovenia freely disposed of 62.2 percent of its social product, Serbia of 59.2 percent, Bosnia of 62.1 percent, Montenegro of 60.1 percent, Macedonia of 59.2 percent, Vojvodina of 59.0 percent and Kosovo of 59.7 percent, Croatia disposed of only 58.3 percent of its own income—the lowest figure among the eight federal units.[168]

The Yugoslav federation had, to be sure, weathered the crisis—but not without demonstrating the flimsiness of system support founded only on groups' perceived self-interest. Without an emotional attachment to the political aggregate, a multiethnic state is condemned to survive at best as a collection of jealous, warring competitors.

Disembowelment of the Interrepublican Committees

Despite the defeat suffered by the nationalist-liberals not only in Croatia but also in Slovenia and Macedonia, the interrepublican committee system, a byproduct of the liberal ascendancy, lingered on. The committees had been conceived, from the beginning, as a sort of experiment. But though the liberals and those who favored decentralization of decision making claimed that the experiment was a success in that it speeded legislation and furthered devolution, the conservatives condemned it as a failure, complaining that it had fundamentally altered the way in which the legislative process took place.

The conservative opposition to the IRCS was at first somewhat intimidated by its successes, though not complacent about them. Those outside the IRCS feared the growing power of the committees, and rumblings of discontent could be heard in the capital about the committees' bypassing of the "self-managing structures" of decision making. More threatening to IRCS's political survival was the growing perception that reliance on the interrepublican committees would lead to the atrophy of the *Skupština*, which would merely formalize decisions already arrived at in the committees. Mijalko Todorović, president of the federal *Skupština*, was one of the leaders of the opposition to the burgeoning new institution. "The *Skupština* is even today in an unfavorable situation," he told *Ekonomska politika*, "above all because we have a kind of dual system in our sociopolitical system today. . . . We have neutralized all other democratic self-managing mechanisms and relations [including even the *Skupština*], with the result that the entire Yugoslav public waits, so to speak, to see what these committees will decide, waits to see what will happen."[169] The public, in short, was reduced to a passive spectator. Some members of the *Skupština* voiced resentment that the work of drawing up preliminary drafts had now been turned over to the committees. In their opinion, this reduced the *Skupština* to a kind of rubber stamp. The danger, said Todorović, was that the interrepublican committees would monopolize the decision-making process and, as another member of the *Skupština* warned, "how can one speak of a parliamentary system where the parliament is reduced to a purely symbolic function?"[170] The committees, moreover, tended to closet themselves, leaving the *Skupština* in ignorance as to their deliberations. Avgustin Lah, president of the Cultural-Educational Chamber of the federal *Skupština*, complained, "They don't tell us anything. I am a member of the *Skupština* and president of one of its working bodies and all I know is what I read in the newspapers."[171]

The impression increasingly took hold that the IRCS was a potential shadow government that was gradually usurping the real power in the system and that the federation was about to be swallowed up by an explicitly confederal body. The Coordination Commission was repeatedly charged with bypassing regular government channels and with "taking over the affairs of state." The IRCS had resolved the practical issues that had been laid before it, but in the process it had threatened most of the vested interests in the *status quo ante*. Increasingly, the talk was of muzzling the IRCS before it was too late.

IRCS advocates were quick to spring to its defense. "It would be harmful to destroy the current institutions of interrepublican negotiation (*dogovaranje*)," Stane Kavčič pleaded in *Politika*. "What is necessary is to perfect the existing forms and to adjust them to the demands and conditions of social development." The committees, said Kavčič, were

> the most important element in the changes that we have brought about in recent years in our socioeconomic system. . . . [The interrepublican committees] represent significantly more than mere agreement in the area[s] of the questions concerned. Their meaning consists also in that they have very positive consequences for stability and for interethnic relations. In them I see a potent form of the struggle against nationalism, because they make it possible for all questions to be dealt with and solved legally—which contributes to the strengthening of interrepublican understanding.[172]

For a while it seemed that the advocates of the committees might prevail. Kardelj even offered consolation, urging that

> it is necessary now to oppose the frontal attacks on interrepublican negotiation and on the interrepublican committees, because every objective analysis has confirmed that the positive results achieved through this form of work outweigh the negative, especially if we have in view the earlier period when the federation and the republics were in reality paralyzed because of conflicts flaring up during the legislative process.[173]

Yet, at the same time, Kardelj thought it advisable to subject the committees to "greater public supervision and control" and expressed doubts as to "whether they have been sufficiently protected from sundry bureaucratic distortions."[174] Before the end of 1972, the interrepublican committees were already in retreat.

The Interrepublican Committee for Developmental Policy was abolished and its functions were transferred to the Federal Committee for Social Planning. The remaining interrepublican committees were, shortly thereafter, significantly downgraded. Under Article 333 of the draft constitution (published in June 1973), they were no longer described as the arenas for the working out of interrepublican differences and the reconciliation of viewpoints—the function originally assigned to them under Amendment 33—but were defined merely as agents for the representation of the federal units (and of their executive agencies) "in the passage of regulations to accompany laws and other general acts."[175]

This wording was preserved in the executive act of June 1974, whereby the federal Executive Council formally demoted the interrepublican committees to their current status. Under this act, the committees were said to have been formed to ensure "the participation and consent of republican and provincial organs in the passage of regulations for the execution of laws, other regulations, and other general acts that are adopted by the Chamber of Republics and Provinces of the *Skupština* SFRJ" where such participation and consent were required by law.[176] The new wording absolved the committees of their former role in "the establishment of federal policy and in the passage of federal laws" and reduced them to consultative bodies where policy proposals could be sounded out. They continued to draw up legislation for the Chamber of Republics and Provinces (CRP), but even here the interrepublican committees had to yield an expanded role to a network of CRP committees. As Caca has observed, the proposals of the committees were often ratified without emendation by the federal Executive Council.[177] Legislation would henceforth no longer start in the IRCS but rather in the CRP, with the IRCS usually serving to smooth out the rough edges. The committees were indisputably subordinated both to SIV and to the CRP, and, even within their constricted domain, they no longer enjoyed decision-making authority.

Once the fulcrum of decision making, the IRCS committees were now a cog in the legislative machine. Ironically, at the end of 1978, the Federal Committee for Social Planning (FCSP) was abolished and its functions returned to a resurrected Interrepublican Committee for Social Planning and Development, restoring the original constellation of five committees.

Conclusions

Though only Croatia fell into the "Napoleonic syndrome," the purge affected not only Croatia but also Croatia's erstwhile fellow travelers in the other republics—including Kavčič and Leopold Krese in Slovenia, Crvenkovski and Milosavlevski in Macedonia, and those who, like Serbia's Marko Nikezić, had fallen afoul of the conservatives for their "anarcho-liberal" temperaments.[178] But instead of leading to a return to centralism, this purge only prepared the way for still greater decentralization.

The entire period of the Croatian crisis may be viewed as one in which the political actors were testing the limits of legitimate political behavior and, in some cases, attempting to transcend them. It was also a period in which the processes of alliance building are exceedingly clear. Alliances existed as tangible understandings and were consciously pursued: indeed, alliance partners, among the federal units, were viewed as indispensable. Thus, when Slovenia and Macedonia backed away from the Croatian nexus, Croatia sought new allies in Kosovo and Montenegro.

But interrepublican conflict cannot be characterized one-dimensionally. On the contrary, the Croatian crisis case study suggests that in a multinational state, fundamental conflict is likely to be manifested on three levels: (1) the *federal* (or central) level, as a conflict between republican actors within a federal context; (2) the *interrepublican* level, as an unmediated conflict between the units themselves; and (3) the *intrarepublican* level, as a struggle between factions within the "Napoleonic" unit and a confrontation between cross-migrated diasporas (such as the Croatian Serbs or the Bosnian Croats) and their host cultures.

8

Controversies in the Economic Sector, 1965–90

It is a well-known constant of political life that even slight differences in interregional economic standards may awaken sharp feelings of resentment that catalyze, where they coincide with ethnic divisions, surges of nationalism. Jealousy kindles collective affectivity and ethnocentric behavior, often resulting in violence and even civil war. In Western analyses, however, economic differences accentuate but do not themselves generate nationalist feelings. Leninism pushes the analysis one step further and claims that all nationalism has its wellsprings in oppression, exploitation, and inequality: liquidate the bourgeoisie and eliminate economic inequality among national groups, and nationalist attachments will lose their hold. The infusion of tangible economic aid and the application of large doses of industrialization should, accordingly, offer the prospect of alleviating Serb-Albanian tensions in Kosovo.[1] Indeed, as we saw in chapter 3, the policy of aid to the underdeveloped regions of Yugoslavia was viewed by the Tito regime and the Titoists who ruled Yugoslavia after his death from 1980 to 1987, as the key to eliminating the nationalities question altogether. Alternatively, the failure to ease interregional economic inequalities, it was argued, "would threaten the integrity of the Yugoslav community and throw into question the common interests of all its regions and nationalities."[2] Interethnic relations are colored by economic differentials, and interethnic harmony is incapable of realization in the presence of collective cognitive dissonance. None of the republican leaderships challenged this principle.

Aid for the Underdeveloped Regions

There are two basic strategies of directed economic development: (1) *sector* development, emphasizing the optimal development of each sector of the economy, with a view to the well-being of the entire country; and (2) *regional* development, treating each of a plurality of regional units as a discrete subject of policy and giving rise to tendencies toward autarky. Although the former strategy has the advantage by utilitarian calculations, it confronts the difficulty, in multiethnic environments, of alienating entire nationality groups. Thus, it was the latter orientation that found expression in the policy decisions taken in early postwar Yugoslavia, the assumption being that equality could not be differentiated from uniformity. Yet, although the first (abortive) five-year plan (1947–51) and the tenuous period of the one-year plans (1953–56) showed some attention to the need to develop the southern regions of Yugoslavia, the Cominform blockade and Soviet economic embargo dealt a severe blow to Yugoslavia's early developmental ambitions. It was not until 1957, with the adoption of the second five-year plan, that a coherent policy of stimulating the development of the underdeveloped regions of the south could be said to have existed.[3] The policy of guaranteed investments in the underdeveloped regions was introduced then, with the result that investments all too often were funneled into unprofitable prestige projects (the so-called political factories) rather than into rationally conceived objects. A further difficulty in the early period was that only a republic could be classified as developed or underdeveloped—and was so considered in its entirety. As a result, Kosovo was treated as a developed region (within SR Serbia) until 1957, whereas Bosnia, which had hitherto enjoyed preferential treatment as an officially "underdeveloped" republic, was abruptly dropped from the roster.

The Croats, plagued with their own pockets of poverty, particularly (at that time) Dalmatia, pressed the argument that the classification of entire federal units as either "developed" or "underdeveloped" was senseless, since every republic had underdeveloped zones. In 1961, the Croats, reinforced by Bosnian disgruntlement with the status quo, won their point. Portions of Croatia (Dalmatia, Lika, Banija, and Kordun), together with the southern and southwestern districts of Serbia and most of Bosnia-Herzegovina, were added to the roster of underdeveloped areas and were made the beneficiaries of special federal treatment.[4] At the same time, the system of guaranteed investments was transformed into a system of specialized funds.

But, even if this overall policy represented an advance over the more or less overtly exploitative policy of the interwar regime, it was flawed not only by repeated instances of mismanagement (resulting in the creation of factories that operated at a loss) but also by a systematic bias that, ironically, reinforced the traditional cleavage. Although light industry, even where traditional branches have been concerned, would have yielded "incomparably better results" than heavy industry in terms of impact on local income and employment, postwar economic planning emphasized investment in heavy industry in the south, thus encouraging interregional polarization.[5] Just as important, if not in fact the central reason for the failure to narrow the developmental gap between the Yugoslav north and south, was the sheer inadequacy of investment in the South. In fact, over the 1947–62 period, per capita investment in Macedonia and Kosovo—the most seriously afflicted regions at that time—was well below the Yugoslav average. Not surprisingly, these federal units grew restive, and, in the course of a drawn-out public debate over the proposed (reworked) seven-year plan for the 1964–70 period, various voices challenged the premises on which the old developmental policy had been based. For example, Kiril Miljovski, a Macedonian economist, objected that

> In the proposed texts [of the 1964–70 seven-year plan] there are plenty of measures, methods, instruments—in a word, techniques of financing. . . . Interest-free credits, credits at special rates of interest, allocated credits, renunciation of annuities, budgetary grants—all of this is very interesting, but entirely ineffective as long as it is not laid down by what deadline the relationship between the developed and underdeveloped regions must be placed on an economically and socially rational basis, what rates of growth must be assured in order to vouchsafe that goal, and what volume of investments is necessary in order to guarantee the desired rates of growth. . . . The weaknesses that we have noted thus far are not the weaknesses of financings but rather the consequences of a lack of a clear conception of time-limits, rates of growth, and the volume of investments [needed] in the insufficiently developed regions.[6]

So ineffective had federal policy been, Miljovski complained, that between 1959 and 1962 unemployment in Macedonia increased by 85 percent (reaching an unemployment rate of 18 percent in 1962), and the Republic Commission for Employment anticipated a continued worsening of the situation.

The Widening Gap

By the early 1960s, it was clear that the policy of attempting to accelerate development of the underdeveloped regions through unregulated federal grants had failed. In 1961 party politicians began to discuss the possibility of introducing a special fund to accelerate development in poorer regions. By the time this fund was introduced in its present form, however, the 1965 reforms had already been put into effect—which brought to a crashing close any immediate prospects for the continued spread of light industry to the south. Although figures fluctuate from year to year, the overall trend between 1953 and 1971 was for the underdeveloped regions to be outpaced by the developed areas in the north. Thus, per capita income in the underdeveloped regions, taken as a whole, was 65 percent of per capita income in the developed regions in 1953; by 1971, that share had shrunk to 50 percent of the northern take. The biggest decline was registered by Bosnia, which in 1953 had enjoyed per capita incomes averaging 74 percent of the developed rate but which, by 1971, retained a rate of only 53 percent. The situation in Kosovo, by this measure, was nothing short of desperate: from 42 percent of the developed average in 1953, Kosovo's average shriveled to a meager 28 percent. Macedonia's figure sank from 60 percent to 56 percent, while Montenegro's slipped only two points from an initial average of 60 percent.[7] As is suggested by these figures, Montenegro and Macedonia had succeeded in maintaining a developmental pace significantly stronger than that of Kosovo and Bosnia-Herzegovina. In fact, despite a certain advantage initially enjoyed by Bosnia in its possession of a number of industrial plants installed under the Habsburgs, Bosnia had failed, until the mid-1970s, to achieve an economic growth rate at all commensurate with the rest of Yugoslavia. Of course, in different degrees, each republic replicates the overall

Table 11. *Economic Growth Rates in Yugoslavia*
(in percent)

	1966–1970		*1971–1975*	
	A	B	A	B
Yugoslavia	18.1	14.6	25.5	15.9
Underdeveloped republics and Kosovo	14.9	14.1	26.9	27.3
Developed Areas	19.4	14.7	25.0	25.5

A = Annual growth rate of investment in fixed assets
B = Annual growth rate of gross material product

Source: Milivoje Vujačić, "Investment, 1966–1975," *Yugoslav Survey* 18 (2) (May 1977): 61–62.

pattern and has below-average sectors. In Macedonia, for example, the communes of Debar, Kičevo, Brod, Kriva Palanka, and Kratovo are sufficiently behind the rest of the republic to warrant special assistance.

Yet, from 1947 to 1966 and again throughout the 1971–75 period, the underdeveloped republics and Kosovo recorded faster economic growth rates than those prevailing in the north. The 1971–75 growth rates are contrasted with the 1966–70 rates in table 13. Even in the south there has been a narrowing of the range of growth rates. Montenegro's industrial production, which, in the 1947–74 period, grew at a rate of 14.1 percent per annum, climbed only 10.1 percent per annum in the 1974–77 period.[8] For Macedonia, by contrast, 1977 showed exceptional growth, especially in heavy industry. *Nova Makedonija* (Skopje) reported that Macedonian industry grew 52.1 percent in iron ore industry, 47.2 percent in electrical machinery and appliances, 43.5 percent in the processing of nonferrous metals, 36.6 percent in the production of base chemicals, 31.6 percent in paper processing, 27.8 percent in electrical industry, 24.7 percent in ferrous metallurgy, and 21.3 percent in the production of animal feed.[9] Moreover, the federal budget for 1978 nearly doubled the amount of money being turned over to the three underdeveloped republics and Kosovo under the rubric of general supplemental funds. Certainly, investment was disproportionately heavy in the less developed regions. On a pessimistic note, however, Ksente Bogoev, a Yugoslav economist, has claimed that the less developed regions are capable of absorbing investment at the rate of only 50 percent of what is required to exceed the overall Yugoslav growth rate and eventually catch up with the developed north.[10] As Ragnar Nurkse has observed, "economic progress is not a spontaneous or automatic affair. On the contrary, it is evident that there are automatic forces within the system tending to keep it moored to a given level,"[11] the chief of which is the tendency of capital to seek short-term investments and to gravitate toward extraction industries—with the consequent problems of achieving balanced growth. The result is that underdeveloped regions find it impossible to replicate the pattern of development set by the industrialized regions.

If, instead of looking at the growth of investment, we observe the republics'

Table 12. *Share of Republics and Autonomous Provinces in Total Investment in Fixed Assets*
(at current prices in percent)

	1966	*1969*	*1972*	*1975*
A	60.2	65.0	61.1	63.0
B	35.8	37.6	37.7	43.7
C	31.1	26.5	30.0	28.4
D	14.1	11.0	10.3	9.5

A = developed republics (Croatia, Slovenia, Vojvodina, and Serbia proper)
B = Croatia and Slovenia only
C = underdeveloped republics and provinces; beneficiaries of the Fund for the Accelerated Development of the Underdeveloped Republics and Kosovo (Bosnia-Herzegovina, Kosovo, Macedonia, and Montenegro)
D = Kosovo and Macedonia only

Source: Calculated by author from data given in Milovoje Vujačić, "Investment, 1966–1975," *Yugoslav Survey* 18 (2) (May 1977): 63.

shares of total investment, a very different picture emerges. The positive trend toward equalization disappears (see table 12). By this measure, Kosovo and Macedonia show the least progress and are therefore grouped together. This measure reveals that Croatia and Slovenia have indeed been the chief beneficiaries of the 1965 reforms and that the underdeveloped sector as a whole has stagnated. The only exception is Bosnia, which has gradually pulled itself out of the abyss.

The gap that separates the developed from the underdeveloped regions might be illustrated by various other indicators, such as numbers of vocational and technical schools, cinemas, televisions, and so on. Croatia and Slovenia constitute 29 percent of the total population, yet these two republics had, in 1972, 44 percent of the newspapers (eleven of Yugoslavia's twenty-five dailies were published in either "Croato-Serbian" or Slovenian) and 46 percent of the radio stations.[12] Kosovo, the most deprived of the federal units, had almost 7 percent of the population, but only 4.9 percent of the vocational-technical schools, 2.7 percent of the cinemas, one Albanian-language daily, and two radio stations (out of 174 in Yugoslavia).[13] Kosovo has also remained far behind in per capita television ownership.

At the same time, poverty tends to be associated with ignorance of or hostility toward contraceptive devices, and the poor, accordingly, tend to reproduce faster than those in more developed areas. Table 13 shows the rate of increase, by republic, between the most recent censuses. Those in the most underdeveloped regions are increasing the fastest—the Macedonians by one and a half times the national average, and the Albanians by almost three times the national average. As a consequence of their higher birth rates, the Albanians and Macedonians also have the largest households: respectively, an average of 6.61 and 4.68 persons per family in 1971, against a Yugoslav average of 3.80 and a

Table 13. *Population Growth by Republic* (in percent)

	1961–71	*1971–81*
YUGOSLAVIA	10.0	9.2
Kosovo	25.4	27.5
Macedonia	15.8	16.1
Bosnia	13.2	10.1
Montenegro	11.7	10.1
Serbia proper	8.3	8.4
Slovenia	8.1	9.5
Croatia	6.1	4.0
Vojvodina	5.0	3.9

Sources: Nicholas R. Lang, "The Dialectics of Decentralization," *World Politics* 27 (3) (April 1975): 322; and Slobodan Stankovic, "Yugoslavia's Census—Final Results," *Radio Free Europe Research*, March 10, 1982, p. 2.

low of 3.18 in Vojvodina (3.34 in Slovenia).[14] Unemployment is highest in these areas, skilled labor the scarcest. Illiteracy is highest in these areas, especially in Kosovo, where, in 1971, 36 percent of the Albanian population admitted to being illiterate.[15]

A related problem is the lower labor efficiency in the underdeveloped republics—rates that, as proportions of the Yugoslav average, actually declined (see table 14). The lesser efficiency of labor is partly a reflection of lower overall educational attainment and partly the result of cultural differences, and is, to a significant extent, a concomitant part of the underdevelopment syndrome. Lower labor efficiency also figures as a contributory factor to the lesser efficiency of investments in the southern regions, though the structure of the economy (e.g., fewer manufacturing industries) also has a hand in producing the higher capital coefficients of the south.

Not only has the south been poor in infrastructure, but it has also suffered from too large a proportion of capital-intensive industry in comparison with the northern republics, which have well-developed labor-intensive industry. Unemployment has thus remained a constant problem throughout the 1965–80 period, especially in Macedonia and Kosovo. In 1970, for instance, there were 31 Slovenes seeking work for every 1,000 Slovenes employed and 49 Croats out of work for every 1,000 employed Croats—the comparable figures for other nationalities were 73 Bosnians, 74 Vojvodinans, 77 Montenegrins, 97 Serbs, 216 Macedonians, and 310 Kosovars. The Yugoslav average was 83 unemployed for every 1,000 working.[16]

An *Ekonomska politika* report of April 1980 chronicled this situation and found that the four officially "underdeveloped" federal units accounted for a smaller portion of the Yugoslav social product in 1978 than they had in 1947—21.6 percent as opposed to 23.5 percent.[17] During 1947–78 average annual growth rates were smaller in the underdeveloped republics than in the devel-

Table 14. *Labor Efficiency by Republic* (in percent)

	1965	*1970*	*1975*	*1977*
YUGOSLAVIA	100	100	100	100
Slovenia	115.9	121.3	123.7	120.1
Croatia	104.9	109.7	108.9	109.2
Vojvodina	92.0	94.0	103.8	104.4
Serbia proper	103.0	95.9	91.1	95.4
Montenegro	99.7	102.5	89.5	92.5
Bosnia	89.2	87.7	89.6	86.6
Macedonia	77.9	74.6	78.2	75.2
Kosovo	81.7	77.2	76.0	74.7
Developed areas	104.4	105.2	105.2	106.1
Underdeveloped areas	86.3	84.1	85.2	82.8

Source: Momir Ćećez, "O efikasnosti društvenih sredstava u privredno nedovoljno razvijenim područjima," *Pregled* 70 (1) (January 1980): 36.

oped republics, with the inevitable result that the developmental gap continued to widen (as table 15 amplifies).

Macedonia Of all the underdeveloped republics, Macedonia derives the greatest portion of its income (72.4 percent of the total of its industrially derived social product) from light industry (as of 1977)—a statistic that points to an unmistakable transformation in Macedonian industry in the postwar era. Of those employed in Macedonian industry, 82.9 percent are in light industry, and only 17.1 percent in heavy industry. The largest sectors in the Macedonian economy are metallurgy, textiles, and tobacco. In Macedonia, as elsewhere, development has been uneven, and the republic continued to register a number of especially underdeveloped districts, which received additional assistance from a special republican fund established to supplement the federal program. These pockets of poverty, inhabited by 30 percent of the republic's population, accounted for only 18.6 percent of total fixed investments in 1980 and only 17.5 percent of the social product of the republic.[18]

Tobacco growers experienced some difficulties in the early 1980s. Development of food production has recently been the dominant strategy of Macedonian economists.

Aside from the problem of the underdevelopment of the economic infrastructure, Macedonia has also been challenged by a scarcity of trained personnel. In 1971, for example, 25 percent of Macedonian adults had three years or less of grade school education, and another 45 percent had only 4–7 years of grade school.

Because of these and other factors, between 1975 and 1986 Macedonia's economic position relative to the Yugoslav average declined steadily. In 1975, Macedonia's social product per worker was 86 percent of the Yugoslav average.

Table 15. *Per Capita Social Product of the Republics* (as a percent of the Yugoslav average)

	1947	*1965*	*1975*	*1978*	*Annual average growth rate (1947–78)*
YUGOSLAVIA	100	100	100	100	5
Slovenia	162	177	201	205	5.8
Croatia	105	120	124	127	5.7
Vojvodina	100	122	121	115	5.5
Serbia proper	101	95	92	98	4.9
Macedonia	70	70	69	68	4.9
Bosnia	86	69	69	64	4.1
Montenegro	94	71	70	71	4.1
Kosovo	49	39	33	29	3.2
Developed areas	110	118	121	124	5.5
Underdeveloped areas	77	64	62	59	4.1

Source: *Ekonomska politika*, no. 1370, July 3, 1978, p. 18; and no. 1465/6, April 28, 1980, p. 20.

This slipped to 83 percent in 1980, 73 percent in 1985, and 70 percent in 1986.[19] As of 1987, Macedonia's unemployment rate stood at 26.7 percent—the second highest in the country (after Kosovo's).[20]

Bosnia-Herzegovina In 1947, three-quarters of Bosnia's population depended on agriculture, only 14 percent were employed in industry, and 14 percent were unemployed. There were only 1,781 kilometers of railway lines, mostly narrow gauge, and no modern roads. Only one-fifth of all homes even had electricity. Yet, because Bosnia was classified as "developed" for much of the postwar period, it experienced only a 4.2 percent average annual growth rate in per capita income for 1952–68—the lowest rate of all of Yugoslavia's federal units, and significantly less than the 6.4 percent Yugoslav average.[21] And while the rural population of Yugoslavia declined 4 percent during the years 1961–68, in Bosnia rural population increased 8 percent. In spite of that, the urban population of Bosnia tallied a gradual increase, rising from 14 percent in 1948 to 28 percent of the republic's population in 1971. The figure for those employed in agriculture declined from 77 percent in 1948 to 40 percent in 1971. In education, Bosnia has lagged behind Macedonia: in 1971, less than 25 percent of the population had completed seven years of grade school and only 1 percent had completed university training. In addition, of the three-fourths with only grade school education, almost half (36.2 percent) had completed no more than three years.[22]

Bosnia's proportion of gross investments declined from 18.3 percent in the 1953–56 period to 12.9 percent in the 1957–60 period and was reduced to 12.4 percent in the 1961–64 period.[23] Bosnia's national income was 20 percent below the Yugoslav average in 1947 and sagged to 27 percent below in 1960, 34 percent below in 1964, and 38 percent below average in 1967.[24] Only in the 1970s was this slippage finally checked. During the 1971–75 medium-term plan, the republic's growth rate finally surpassed the Yugoslav average.[25] During the 1976–80 period, the rate of growth of the Bosnian economy exceeded its rate of growth during any of the three previous five-year plans. Despite that improvement, there was no narrowing of the developmental gap between Bosnia and the Yugoslav economic average during this period.[26]

Bosnia's "ace in the hole" is its raw wealth, particularly its energy resources. Bosnia accounts for 81 percent of known Yugoslav iron ore reserves, 20 percent of its coal, 28 percent of its hydroelectric potential, and 30 percent of its lumber. Notching a 6 percent rise in the production of electric energy and coal from 1979 to 1980, Bosnia recorded production of 11.18 billion kilowatts of electric energy and 13.8 million tons of coal—enough to satisfy the energy needs not only of Bosnia but also of other republics. Unfortunately, however, shortages of extractive equipment and fluctuations in the quality of the ore deposits have hindered full exploitation of Bosnia's coal reserves.[27] As already noted, the developmental pace in Bosnia has quickened by several measures in recent years. As late as September 1978, Sarajevo made a generally unfavorable impression. Public buildings were in a state of disrepair, the roads sorely needed resurfacing, a huge church across the river was in shambles and had been closed for lack of money to repair it. The overall impression was one of stagnation, decay, and deepening backwardness. By June 1980 all this had changed: the whole city, the third largest in Yugoslavia, appeared to be a huge public works project. The city plumbing system was being redone, main streets downtown were being dug up and repaired, tram lines were being torn up to be replaced by wider tracks, new sidewalks had been laid in the Bagšćaršija area, and that entire district was being paved mall-style. Various public buildings were being repaired and repainted. Even the huge church across the river was scaffolded and framed by cranes (and opened by the summer of 1982 as the Sarajevo City Museum of Art). The reason for this flurry of activity was, of course, the fact that the 1984 Winter Olympics were scheduled to be held in Sarajevo.

Yet, like Macedonia, Bosnia has its own poverty areas. At the time of the passage of the republic's five-year plan for 1966–70, 77 of the republic's 106 *općinas* were classified as especially underdeveloped and therefore eligible for additional help at the republic level. By the end of that five-year plan, only 48 *općinas* continued to be identified as especially backward. At that time, these districts covered 42.9 percent of the territory of the republic and included 38.5 percent of the republic's population but accounted for only 18.9 percent of the annual income of the republic—which means that the average per capita income in these areas was less than half the republican average and only 31 percent of the Yugoslav average.[28] Though the Bosnians have chalked up some progress in these parts, certain districts remain mired in poverty. Thus, a 1980 study prepared by the Bosnian Economic Bureau in Tuzla indicated that in the republic's three poorest communes (Tuzla, Banovići, and Lukavac), the overall economic situation and the unemployment problem were on a par with conditions in Kosovo.[29]

In the years 1981–87, Bosnia expanded its work force 3.6 percent (against a Yugoslav average of 2.4 percent). In spite of this, unemployment in the republic remained a troubling 22.7 percent in 1987.[30]

Montenegro The rugged mountainous terrain that enabled the Montenegrins to resist Turkish encroachment for centuries has proven less amenable to development. Roads and railways were long in coming; the land is largely ill-suited to farming. The latter disability notwithstanding, 72 percent of Montenegro's population was engaged in agriculture in 1948.

After the war, developmental efforts focused on exploitation of Montenegro's metallurgical resources. The republic maintained an average annual growth rate of 6.4 percent between 1947 and 1974, while Montenegrin industry grew 14.1 percent annually. Thus, industry, which had represented only 5.8 percent of the Montenegrin economy in 1947, climbed to 32.6 percent in 1974, employing 41.5 percent of the republic's work force. Simultaneously, the proportion of those employed in agriculture shrank to 27 percent in 1978.[31] Yet these impressive results are somewhat compromised by the failure to produce developmental depth. With 70 percent of its economy in capital-intensive basic industry, Montenegro has real problems. Its economy is excessively oriented toward the exploitation of its mineral wealth. Montenegro's rate of capital formation, moreover, is the second lowest of Yugoslavia's federal units, undercut only by Kosovo. Added to this is the inability of the Montenegrin economy to keep pace with projected rates: between 1976 and 1978, Montenegrin industry grew 13.1 percent, well below plan.[32]

One of Montenegro's biggest problems until recently has been the serious lack of transport infrastructure, with the result that Montenegro has been, to a certain extent, isolated from the rest of Yugoslavia. The Belgrade-Bar railway (completed in 1976) represented a decisive step toward overcoming this isolation. Montenegro's development was, however, set back by several years by the devastating earthquake of April 1979, which cost the republic more than 50 billion dinars in damage.

In the years 1981–87, the Montenegrin labor force grew 4.0 percent. But unemployment still stood at 23.4 percent in 1987.[33] In 1989, average income in Montenegro was only 48 percent of Slovenian earnings—and reportedly insufficient to maintain a minimal standard of living.[34] The average monthly salary in September 1990 was $400—$70 less than the Yugoslav average. One out of every five Montenegrins lives below the poverty line, and as of 1989, one out of every ten workers in Montenegro was employed at a firm facing imminent bankruptcy.

Kosovo Kosovo is, by all measures, the poorest, most backward region of Yugoslavia. It has the highest unemployment, the lowest levels of literacy and educational attainment, the highest birthrates, the worst roads, the least infrastructure, the least developed plumbing and electricity services, and, until

Table 16. *Structure of Investments in Industry in Kosovo* (in percent)

	Basic industry	*Light industry*
1947–56	81.6	18.4
1957–65	86.6	13.4
1966	89.6	10.4
1967	87.3	12.7
1968	91.4	8.6
1969	84.0	16.0
1970	77.1	22.9

Source: Pokrajinski Zavod za Statistiku, *Privredni i društveni razvoj SAP Kosova 1947–1972* (Priština, 1974), as adapted in Binak Madjari, "Investicije i privredni razvoj SAP Kosova," *Obeležja* 5 (3) (Fall 1967): 81.

the early 1970s, the slowest growing economy. Despite this consistent and unmistakable picture of underdevelopment, between 1947 and 1955 Kosovo was excluded, as has already been noted, from special treatment as an underdeveloped region. Even after it became eligible for special federal grants, Kosovo still had to deal with the highest capital coefficients in the country and with problems of poor management. For these and other reasons related to the underdevelopment syndrome, Kosovo registered the slowest rate of growth in social product of all the federal units over the period 1948–72.[35] Broken down into five-year periods, it is clear that until 1972 Kosovo experienced its most impressive growth in the mid-1950s and mid-1960s. Impressive as these figures may seem, two things should be noted. First, Kosovo's growth throughout this period remained below the Yugoslav average. Excluding the earliest postwar period, when Yugoslavia's economy was perilously unstable, one finds that whereas Kosovo's social product grew at an average annual rate of 7.4 percent (calculated in 1966 prices), the average annual growth rate for the Yugoslav economy as a whole during this period was 7.7 percent.[36] Thus, Kosovo could scarcely be said to be "catching up." Second, its growth took place mainly in heavy industry. Between 1956 and 1970, 63.9 percent of all investments in Kosovo went into industry, with only 12.4 percent for agriculture, 8.9 percent for transport development, and 11.1 percent for noneconomic projects. Most of the investments in this last category, moreover, had the character of building infrastructure, such as sewers and water lines, schools, hospitals, and residences. The investments in industrial projects are broken down in table 16. From this table, it emerges that some 85 percent of all industrial projects undertaken in Kosovo were in heavy industry and, thus, that more than half of all investments (about 55 percent) went into heavy industry during this period. It is true, of course, that Kosovo is rich in lignite, magnesium, asbestos, coal, lead, zinc, and other minerals. Yet it is equally true that investments in light manufactures do more to create jobs, and thereby raise the standard of living, than do equal investments in heavy industry. As a result of this investment orientation, however, almost two-thirds of Kosovo's industry is still in the area of raw materials extraction and basic industry.

These trends took a turn for the better during 1971–75, when Kosovo experienced the fastest economic growth rate among the Yugoslav federal units. During this period, industrial production in Kosovo grew at a rate of 11.6 percent per year (as compared to a Yugoslav average of 8.2 percent per year), and annual provincial agricultural production increased 30 percent during 1971–75.[37] Kosovo's social product increased at a rate of 7.3 percent annually. Between 1970 and 1975, the number of physicians in Kosovo doubled. Whereas there were only 2,712 cars registered in Kosovo in 1966, there were 34,311 in 1976. At the same time, 1,504 kilometers of new roads were laid, of which 1,007 kilometers were asphalt.[38] The employment roster expanded some 7 percent in this time frame, even as the share of agriculture in Kosovar employment fell to 45 percent in 1975. Yet, despite all this, Mahmut Bakali, president of the provincial committee of the LC Kosovo, could complain in 1976 that Kosovo was relatively more backward than it had been in 1971. The key measures corroborated Bakali's claim. In 1947, for instance, Kosovo's per capita social product stood at 49.3 percent of the Yugoslav average; by 1970, however, Kosovo's share had shrunk to 34.1 percent. In 1975, Kosovo tallied no more than 33.4 percent, and by 1976 the figure had slipped even further, to 32.2 percent. In part, of course, this measure reflects Kosovo's exploding population, half of which is still school age or younger. Again, Kosovo's share in Yugoslavia's total fixed investments actually dropped from 3.7 percent during the 1966–70 period to 3.5 percent for the 1971–75 period. In fact, the Kosovar economy had failed to meet planned growth targets. Instead of an annual average growth rate of 14 percent in industrial production, only an 11.6 percent annual growth was registered, and the 7.3 percent growth in the social product fell far short of the targeted rate of 13.5 percent annually.[39]

The Eighth Session of the LCY presidency (1970) had been intended to serve as a milestone in developmental policy in Kosovo. Yet, five years later, it was clear that the corner had not yet been turned. The new social plan devised for Kosovo for the period 1976–80 was thus supposed to fulfill those earlier promises by intensifying the effort to raise Kosovo's economic level. The plan called for annual growth rates of 9.5 percent in the provincial social product and 12 percent in the industrial sector. Instead, Kosovo chalked up annual growth rates of 7.8 percent in social product and 11.2 percent in industrial production.[40] Worse yet, instead of realizing a growth rate 60 percent faster than the national average for 1976–80, as called for by the Yugoslav social plan, Kosovo achieved a growth rate only 10 percent faster.[41] By 1980, Kosovo's per capita national income had shriveled to 28.8 percent of the Yugoslav average. Whereas in 1947 the ratio of Kosovo's per capita social product to Slovenia's was 1:3.2, in 1978 the ratio was 1:6.9.[42] The gap continues to widen.

During the plan period 1986–90, Kosovo received 48.1 percent of FADURK funds. Despite this, progress was imperceptible. A large portion of Kosovo's 406.5 thousand hectares of arable land is not being put to use, and mining-related enterprises (coal, lead, zinc, nickel, etc.) are operating well below capacity. The same is true for other sectors of the Kosovar economy. Meanwhile, Kosovo's birthrate—the highest in Europe—caused the population of the province to double in just three years (1981–84). By 1990, Kosovo had 140,000 jobless, with young people accounting for 70 percent of the unemployed.[43]

In the years 1981–87, the Kosovar work force grew by 4.0 percent, but as of 1987 the unemployment rate in the province stood at a staggering 55.8 percent—more than three times the national average (15.8 percent) and more than double that of any other federal unit. In fact, only 22 percent of Kosovars of working age held jobs in the nonagricultural sector (as opposed to 44.1 percent for Yugoslavia as a whole and 66.9 percent for Slovenia).[44]

Pockets of Underdevelopment in Other Republics. As already noted, until 1989, Yugoslavia classified various regions as "underdeveloped" for purposes of allocating developmental funds. But except for the brief period between 1961 and 1964, Yugoslavia reserved the "underdeveloped" classification in federal aid for entire federal units. As ought to be clear from the foregoing discussion, those federal units so identified (Bosnia, Macedonia, Montenegro, and Kosovo) have, without question, lagged behind the others in economic development. Yet there are pockets of backwardness in *every* federal unit. For this reason the 1963 federal constitution called on each republic and autonomous province to set up a Republic Fund for the Economic Development of Underdeveloped Districts (FREDUD), mirroring the federal fund at the republican level. The underdeveloped republics, as has already been noted, devote a portion of their own funds to alleviate this situation. Of the remaining federal units, Serbia has perhaps been the worst off—especially where the South Morava region is concerned. In 1974, 62 of the republic's 114 *opštinas* were categorized as economically underdeveloped.[45] By 1980, 14 of these had been reclassified as "developed." Among the remaining *opštinas*, some progress was achieved too. The outstanding example is the heavily Bulgarian *opština* of Dimitrovgrad, which raised its average per capita income from 44.4 percent of the republic average in 1960 to 70.9 percent in 1977. More modest gains were also recorded in Sjenica, which increased its average from 26.5 percent to 42.6 percent, in Babušnica (from 32.8 to 35.7 percent), in Bosilegrad (from 27.1 to 43.1 percent), and in Surdulica (from 40.8 to 66.3 percent). Some of Serbia's underdeveloped *opštinas*, however, were relatively worse off in 1980 than they had been in 1960.[46]

The economic decline of the 1980s hit the rural areas of Serbia hardest. In the first nine months of 1990, 2,398 agricultural collectives in Serbia recorded serious losses: their combined losses added up to 16.5 billion dinars, or ten times the level of the preceding year.[47] Much arable land is not even being cultivated. As of late 1989, for example, only 1.4 percent of Serbia's arable land was being irrigated.[48] Unemployment in Serbia in 1987 stood at 17.6 percent.[49]

Vojvodina's underdeveloped regions have a different character from those in the south, since, unlike the southern federal units, where economic underdevelopment is associated with high birth rates, in Vojvodina underdevelopment is associated with demographic stagnation or even contraction. Between 1961 and 1971, the population declined in twenty-four Vojvodinan *opštinas*, and, in many of those cases, the trend stretched back at least to 1948. Under the 1971–75 provincial social plan, seventeen *opštinas* were classified as eligible for special provincial assistance, and 100 million dinars were earmarked for that purpose.[50]

Croatia classified twenty-nine of its *općinas* as underdeveloped (as of 1982).[51] Croatia's big success story in this regard is Dalmatia, where a combination of tourism and industrial growth helped transform the area from an impoverished backwater into a flourishing Riviera. This transformation was essentially accomplished in the late 1960s. The unemployment rate in Croatia (as of 1987) is 7.6 percent.[52]

Croatia's administration of its fund has been efficient and has produced results: the underdeveloped *općinas*, which had an average per capita social product of 45.9 percent of the republican average in 1970, had a per capita social product of 52.8 percent of the republican average three years later, and this figure reached 57.2 percent by 1975.[53] Between 1970 and 1980, Zagreb reclassified 19 underdeveloped *općinas* as "developed," though two subsequently returned to the "underdeveloped" category. The republican fund was still in place at the end of 1990, even after the communists were voted out of office. But Croatia's new postcommunist authorities called an end to the earlier policy of allowing the fund to be used to bail out inefficient and insolvent enterprises and declared a firm policy of restricting funds for the development of new projects.[54]

Even the Slovenes have economic complaints and, accordingly, established their own republic fund for this purpose. In June 1971, Slovenia's executive council handed down a decision whereby eleven of Slovenia's fifty-six *općinas*, containing some 312,000 inhabitants (18.1 percent of the total population of the republic), were classified as "underdeveloped." To take one example, in the *općina* of Lenart, one of the least developed *općinas* in Slovenia, only 2,000 of its 17,000 inhabitants were gainfully employed (as of 1980).[55] When the southerners clamored too loudly about historical injustices, the Slovenes frequently reminded their compatriots that they too have had their problems with underdevelopment.

The late 1980s brought serious strains to the Slovenian economy. Despite its generally more favorable situation, with an unemployment rate of only 1.8 percent in 1987, for example,[56] Slovenia's economy suffered a 10.1 percent decline in production in the period January–November 1990, and as of November 1990, the Republic of Slovenia had a $600 million debt with hard currency countries.[57] The sense of urgency, as of late 1990, was well captured by Dušan Plut, a member of the Slovenian presidency. "The Demos government [of Slovenia]," he said, referring to the newly installed noncommunist coalition government, "will not be liked. It must rescue the bankrupt economy, solve the extremely grave employment problems, and the serious problems in farming and social services. It must resort to measures that we do not like, and therefore it cannot be a popular government."[58]

Both within and between republics, the natural tendency—in the absence of a concerted, countervailing policy—has been for developmental differences to deepen. This trend becomes dangerous where differences coincide with ethnic and republican boundaries.

Establishment of FADURK

By 1964, everyone had become disgruntled with the existing system for financing economic development. The underdeveloped republics complained that the amounts tendered were insufficient. The developed republics complained that, owing to mismanagement and poor use of funds, their contributions were being squandered. These currents came to a head at the Eighth Party Congress, which decreed that drastic organizational changes be made in the manner in which aid was funneled to the underdeveloped zones. With the bankruptcy of the centralized system of economic stimulation openly admitted, it was decided to establish a new office to coordinate developmental efforts. Finally, in February 1965, the federal Assembly passed a bill creating the Federal Fund for the Accelerated Development of the Underdeveloped Republics and Kosovo (FADURK), to be operated by a thirteen-member board of directors (one per socialist republic and seven appointed by the *Skupština*). The fund was to be financed by a 1.85 percent tax on the social product, to be paid by all federal units.[59] It was decided to treat only entire federal units as "underdeveloped" for FADURK purposes, and Bosnia, Macedonia, Montenegro, and Kosovo were declared eligible for assistance under the new program. Initially, the recipient units balked at being taxed to support the program, since they viewed FADURK largely as a means of income redistribution.[60] A more fundamental controversy concerned the distribution of the resources. According to Article 23 of the law concerning the fund, the level of credits extended was to be calculated on the basis of (a) the magnitude of per capita income, (b) the magnitude and structure of existing investments, (c) the level and efficacy of the use of means of social reproduction, and (d) other conditioning factors. Yet these broad guidelines left considerable room for negotiation, and Bosnia made it clear that it considered the proposed schedule, under which it would receive 30.7 percent of all FADURK credits and payments, unacceptable. Sarajevo demanded 34.2 percent of all funds (see table 17). FADURK's administrative committee convened to discuss the issue, which remained unresolved until 1968—that is, for three years into the five-year plan. According to an analysis conducted by the Federal Planning Commission—which the Bosnians eagerly endorsed—the most serious backwardness was to be found in Bosnia itself. The question eventually came before the Chamber of Nationalities in 1968, where it was decided (as a compromise) to grant Bosnia certain special credits

Table 17. *Disbursement Schedules Considered by FADURK during 1966–70* (in percent)

	Variant I	*Variant II (proposed by Bosnia)*	*Adopted schedule*
Bosnia	30.7	34.2	30.7
Montenegro	14.0	13.1	13.1
Macedonia	26.8	25.2	26.2
Kosovo	28.5	27.5	30.0
TOTAL	100.0	100.00	100.0

Source: Mihajlo Vuković, *Sistemski okviri podsticanja bržeg razvoja nerazvijenih područja Jugoslavije* (Sarajevo: Svjetlost, 1978), p. 59.

from fund resources approved earlier for the 1961–65 period, but to leave Bosnia's share of the 1966–70 resources at the level of 30.7 percent.[61] Ultimately, certain funds were siphoned from Montenegro and Macedonia and transferred to Kosovo—a small victory for Kosovar interests. As for Bosnia, subsequent growth patterns seemed to bear out its arguments, for while the Yugoslav social product registered an 8.5 percent annual growth rate during 1966–70, the underdeveloped regions chalked up only a paltry 6.3 percent over the same period, and Bosnia notched an even less manageable 5.3 percent. Little surprise that the question of disbursement came up again in 1970 and 1971.

The 8.9 billion new dinars disbursed by FADURK during 1966–70 were not intended to be grants, however, but low-interest loans. The terms were generous enough: FADURK allowed twenty-year repayment at 2 percent interest for investment in energy, metallurgy, basic chemical industry, cellulose, paper, and cement industry; twenty-five-year repayment at 2 percent interest for investment in communications; thirty-year repayment at 1 percent interest for investment in highway construction; fifteen-year repayment at 2 percent interest for investments in tourism; five-year repayment at 1 percent interest for technical assistance; and fifteen-year repayment at 4 percent interest for all other investments.

Although this aid undoubtedly had a positive impact in the underdeveloped south, the Kosovars gave vent to dissatisfaction. Kosovo's enterprises were, at that time, accounting for only about 20 percent of total investment capital in the province, meaning that the autonomous province was still in a position of unmistakable dependency. Moreover, by 1969, Kosovo was obliged to earmark three-quarters of its budget to service previous loans. The province felt trapped in a vicious circle of inescapable indebtedness. In an unusual gesture of solidarity, Nikola Minčev, president of the Macedonian assembly, expressed the readiness of the Macedonian leadership to support a reapportionment of the FADURK pie for the period 1970–74 in order to give special attention to Kosovo's needs, even if it would redound to Macedonia's economic detriment.

Kosovo wanted more than simply larger loans, however. In December 1969, it submitted an official request to the federal Executive Council and the federal *Skupština* for absolution from all debts incurred through acceptance of FADURK credits over the 1966–70 period and asked that subsequent credits be extended on an interest-free basis.[62] Kosovo also wanted direct representation on FADURK's board of directors.

Kosovo's demands created a minor crisis, especially since certain parties among the developed republics were becoming impatient with the entire concept of aiding the south. They were raising the embarrassing question of how much longer the underdeveloped republics would continue to receive special treatment and even broached the idea of liquidating FADURK altogether.[63] The developed republics tended to view the program as not an investment but charity. Hence, as Kosta Mihailović, a noted Serbian economist, observed at the time, "the thesis that the development of the underdeveloped regions is also in the interest of the developed regions, and accordingly in the interest of the entire economy, is more often than not accepted as an [empty] slogan rather than as the truth."[64]

In the end, Kosovo was granted two of its three demands. All credits extended during 1966–70 were written off as grants, and two members were added to the board of directors, permitting both Kosovo and Vojvodina to be directly represented.[65] The developed republics balked at the notion of interest-free credits, however, and, in the process of streamlining credit terms, actually increased interest rates. After 1970, the underdeveloped republics enjoyed repayment schedules of only fifteen years, at an annual interest rate of 4 percent. An exception was made for Kosovo, however, which was allowed a repayment term of nineteen years at an interest rate of 3 percent.

A high-ranking Macedonian official sought to have the FADURK tax increased from 1.85 percent of the social product to between 2.3 and 2.5 percent, arguing that the developmental potential of the south had been vastly underrated.[66] The levy was indeed increased—but only to 1.94 percent, with the added justification that the additional taxes would be applied against investments in Kosovo exclusively.

Kosovo had made its point and stood to increase its already large piece of the pie. Sarajevo, however, was chagrined at the prospect of laying its hands on only 30 percent of FADURK resources and demanded a reassessment. Under persistent pressure from Bosnia, the federal secretariat for finance revised the criteria according to which FADURK's funds would be distributed, but Macedonia, Montenegro, and Kosovo criticized the revised variant of the proposed federal law. Montenegro was the most distraught, since it stood to slip from a 13.1 percent share of the funds to 12.2 percent.[67] The federal authorities stood by Bosnia this time, however, forcing Montenegro and Macedonia to accept somewhat smaller portions for the 1971–75 period. Under a bill belatedly signed into law on November 3, 1972, it was agreed that, of FADURK funds raised by the 1.85 percent levy on the social product, Bosnia would receive 34 percent,

Table 18. *Disbursement of FADURK Funds, 1966–75* (in percent)

	1966–70 (Actual)	*1971–75 (Planned)*	*1971–75 (Actual)*
Bosnia	30.7	34	32.4
Montenegro	13.1	12	11.4
Macedonia	26.2	24	22.9
Kosovo	30.0	30	33.3
TOTAL	100.0	100.0	100.0

Source: Zoran Jašić, "Poticanje razvitka nedovoljno razvijenih područja u SR Hrvatskoj," in *Ekonomski pregled* 28 (5–6) (1977): 261.

Macedonia 24 percent, Montenegro 12 percent, and Kosovo 30 percent, with the 0.09 percent supplemental levy being passed on to Kosovo in full.[68]

FADURK disbursed some 25.6 billion dinars during the 1971–75 period. Montenegro received an additional 541 million dinars during this period for the financing of invalid insurance and pensions. In addition, these federal units received 1.6 billion dinars in grants from the federal budget in order to complete certain specific projects (such as the Belgrade-Bar railway and a section of the Bratstvo-Jedinstvo ["Brotherhood and Unity"] highway near Titov Veles). Montenegro also obtained loans of 510 million dinars (in 1971) and 320 million dinars (in 1974) from the National Bank of Yugoslavia for financing construction of the Belgrade-Bar railway. The Eighth Session of the presidency of the LCY (April 1970) reviewed Kosovo's backward state and decided that Kosovo must receive special treatment. (This is also important because it illustrates the taking of a binding decision on a concrete policy issue *by the central party*.) In accordance with this decision, Kosovo's share in World Bank credits was increased from 1.3 percent in 1970 to 11.7 percent over the 1971–74 period, Kosovo was given a federal grant of 89 million dinars to pay off foreign and domestic loans contracted in 1971, and Kosovo's contribution to the federal budget was reduced by 600 million dinars in the 1973–75 period.[69]

The 1971–75 social plan stipulated that the growth rate of each of the underdeveloped republics and Kosovo should exceed that of the country as a whole by 25 percent for the plan period. In fact, however, the underdeveloped units marked an overall growth rate only 9 percent greater than the national average.[70] Macedonia came closest to the mark, with a growth rate 14.9 percent greater than the national average. Kosovo came in second, at 14.2 percent. Bosnia's complaints once more appeared justified by the facts: this time the republic managed only a slender growth rate 3.7 percent greater than the national average, and Montenegro's growth rate was actually 11.2 percent lower than the national average.[71] It had been hoped that, by 1975, gross investments in the south would account for 33 percent of total gross investments in Yugoslavia; instead, they accounted for only 29 percent. The Tenth Congress of the LCY

(May 1974) evaluated the results of FADURK's nine-year program for stimulating the development of the south and concluded that the program had failed to narrow the developmental gap between the north and the south—its primary objective.

Continuing Disputes over Fund Criteria

In 1976, a new law regulating FADURK was drawn up. The new statute converted FADURK into an interrepublican agency and replaced the fifteen-member board of directors with an eight-member board—one delegate from each federal unit.[72] The amount of the contribution drawn from the basic organizations of associated labor was raised to 1.97 percent of the social product. This was to be divided as follows: of the resources represented by a 1.77 percent levy on the social product, Bosnia would receive 34 percent, Macedonia 24 percent, Montenegro 12 percent, and Kosovo 30 percent; a 0.17 percent levy would be reserved entirely for Kosovo; and a 0.03 percent levy would finance construction of the Ibar-Lepenac irrigation project in Kosovo.[73] Finally, a supplementary law established that additional resources would be raised through a 0.93 percent levy on the social product—with the lion's share going to Bosnia and Kosovo.[74] New credit terms allowed the underdeveloped republics fourteen years to repay FADURK loans, at 4.166 percent annual interest, and Kosovo was permitted up to seventeen and one half years to repay the loans, at 3 percent annual interest. Not only were these terms far more favorable than what the federal units might otherwise have obtained through commercial banks, but also the low interest rate did not nearly keep pace with double-digit inflation, which passed the 30 percent mark in 1980.

The 1976–80 social plan stipulated that the economic growth rate of the underdeveloped regions *as a whole* should exceed the average Yugoslav rate by 20–25 percent and reiterated that "the policy of the accelerated development of the economically insufficiently developed republics and Kosovo has especial meaning for the further advancement of interethnic relations and for the consolidation of the unity of the working class."[75] At the same time, it was increasingly recognized that the operative definition of "underdevelopment" as simply *development below the Yugoslav average* was becoming less relevant as that average improved. That is to say, the inequalities might well remain, but to interpret inequalities as symptoms of underdevelopment could not be justified on a priori grounds. Hence, the social plan for the period 1976–80 called on the federal units to agree on new criteria for classifying the developmental levels of the republics by the end of 1978.

The program had, in fact, been plagued from the beginning by the absence of hard and fast criteria. When the issue came up in 1971, the republics proved unable to reach an agreement, and disbursement under the 1971–75 plan period began while negotiations regarding criteria were still being carried on. The so-called Law regarding Criteria of Disbursement was finally passed in November 1972, but this law did not in fact establish criteria of disbursement—it merely determined the allocations. This situation was perhaps not intolerable at that time, but, by 1978, the growing conviction that some of the underdeveloped republics were no longer disadvantaged made the resolution of the issue a more burning need. Since the federal units were unable to agree on other criteria, the validity of the scheme based on the Yugoslav average social product was extended through May 31, 1980. As late as the end of February, republican delegates still had considerable differences of opinion on this subject. One solution, advanced by Macedonia, was to utilize a triple measure—social product, employment, and total financial resources, all adjusted on a per capita basis. A federal unit that fell below a certain standard on two of these three measures would be considered underdeveloped. The thresholds were set at 75–80 percent of the Yugoslav average social product, 85–90 percent of the average employment level, and 80–85 percent of average per capita resources. Units falling below 55 percent on two indicators (i.e., Kosovo) would receive special treatment.[76]

FADURK itself was more directly threatened by the developed republics. The Serbs, hard pressed for currency, asked that Serbia's contribution to the program be set at a significantly lower level to ease strains on the republic's ailing economy.[77] The Croats, angered as ever by the waste and inefficiency entailed in investments in the south, urged that FADURK be disbanded and replaced by an informal pool of work organizations in which cross-regional, interenterprise investment would produce development on the basis of mutual profitability.[78] Finally, the Slovenian Social Council for Economic Development and Economic Policy published a report in April 1980 that criticized the draft revision of FADURK. Urging that market mechanisms play the chief role in economic development, the Slovenes considered that FADURK's primary role in the future should be to stimulate free investment by enterprises in the underdeveloped regions. "It is crucial that the existing socioeconomic bases of FADURK be changed," the Slovenes continued, "because the Fund, as a typical state institution, cannot successfully realize its goals. . . . Professional analyses in Yugoslavia and in other countries indisputably show that [measurement based on] the social product overestimates differences in actual economic development. . . . Yet, in the draft decisions, the social product is given the dominant place, while the other two criteria in reality have only the role of corrective factors."[79] The Slovenes argued that the triple measure outlined in the Macedonian draft be adopted as the basis for FADURK eligibility but that the thresholds be set much lower: at 67 percent of Yugoslav average per capita social product, 70 percent of Yugoslav average per capita employment, and 70 percent of average per capita capital investment. The Macedonian proposal was designed to protect the status quo (since Macedonia was, by most measures, the most developed of the underdeveloped republics) and left the roster of eligible republics intact, but the Slovenian revision would have left only Kosovo

Table 19. *Three Criteria for FADURK Eligibility* (in percent)

	Social product per capita (1977–78)	*Number employed in social sector, per 1,000 available work force (1978)*	*Bulk capital in social sector, per available worker (1978)*
YUGOSLAVIA	100.0	100.0	100.0
Slovenia	196.8	171.7	197.0
Croatia	127.9	114.4	130.5
Vojvodina	122.3	103.2	100.6
Serbia proper	95.7	97.1	80.9
Macedonia	66.8	88.8	75.1
Bosnia	67.4	76.7	76.0
Montenegro	60.8	84.7	105.5
Kosovo	29.5	51.9	46.6

Source: *Borba*, April 28, 1980, p. 9.

in the program (see table 19). The Slovenes argued that, compared to Western Europe, all of Yugoslavia's federal units were "underdeveloped," but that, in real terms, only Kosovo deserved the label.

Even though it seemed unlikely that the Slovenian draft would be adopted, rumors spread that both Macedonia and Bosnia would be reclassified as "developed" after 1980.[80] The Macedonians anxiously made it known that they would not be able to meet planned goals or maintain a satisfactory rate of growth in the 1980–90 period solely on the basis of their own financial resources.[81] Likewise concerned lest it be dropped from the ranks of FADURK recipients, Bosnia invited the Slovenian executive council to send a delegation to Sarajevo and endeavored to evoke some sympathy among the Slovenes for Bosnia's situation.[82] The Bosnians also courted Croatia, entertaining a high-ranking Croatian delegation in May.[83] During the latter meeting, the Bosnians and Croats explored a number of joint projects, including certain mining projects in Bosnia in which the Croats had considerable interest. The Bosnians planned to use FADURK funds to pay for many of these projects; Croatia's interest in Bosnia's continued eligibility was therefore clear. (Vojvodina was apparently an indirect beneficiary of Bosnia's reconfirmed eligibility: within a few months after FADURK finalization, Vojvodina signed an agreement with Bosnia for cooperation in the fields of energy, metals, lumber, and chemical products.)[84]

The deadline for setting the program criteria was pushed back three times, and still the republics were unable to agree. Finally, in July, a compromise guaranteed eligibility for the same four federal units until 1985, and the deputies continued to seek agreement on new criteria.[85] By September 1980, Slovenia's

Table 20. *Disbursement of FADURK Funds, 1976–85* (in percent)

	1976–80 (Actual)	*1981–85 (Proposal, April 1980)*	*1981–85 (Proposal, July 1980)*	*1981–85 (Proposal, October 1980)*	*1981–85 (Actual schedule adopted)*
Bosnia	30.7	34.7	30.6	26.7	27.9
Montenegro	10.8	12.0	10.7	9.4	9.9
Macedonia	21.6	24.0	21.6	18.9	19.6
Kosovo	37.0	29.3	37.1	45.0	42.6

Source: *Ekonomska politika*, no. 1465/6, April 28, 1980, pp. 20–21; *NIN*, no. 1541, July 13, 1980, p. 12; *Oslobodjenje*, October 19, 1980, p. 3; and Tanjug, December 17, 1980, in FBIS, Yugoslavia, December 19, 1980.

delegate to the Chamber of Republics and Provinces, Ivo Klemenčić, frustrated by lack of progress in the negotiations, demanded a detailed explanation for the failure to agree on criteria for disbursement eligibility. Croatia's delegate, Bogdan Čuturilo, however, nonchalantly replied that there was no present need for a law on criteria, since the eligible recipients had already been determined and a law would make no difference in policy.[86]

Actually, by this time it was generally presumed that neither Macedonia nor Bosnia would require federal assistance after 1985, and perhaps not Montenegro either (although the 1979 earthquake complicated the picture). Accordingly, FADURK's total projected outlays were to be cut back from the 76 billion dinars disbursed during 1976–80 to 41 billion dinars for the 1981–85 period. Already complaints were heard that Kosovo was being prepared as a showcase; indeed, there were reports that Bosnia, Serbia, and others were becoming jealous. Hence, on the supposition that Bosnia's needs were greater than Kosovo's and that Kosovo had, at any rate, benefitted inordinately in the past, an early proposal published in April 1980 gave Bosnia a larger cut than Kosovo and Macedonia's share was not much less than Kosovo's. By July, however, under pressure from the underdeveloped republics, the FADURK purse for 1981–85 was almost doubled—from 41 billion dinars to 80 billion dinars. Kosovo managed to gather in the largest portion of the additional dinars. Its share of the FADURK kitty was boosted from 29.3 percent to 37.1 percent. By October, Kosovo's share of prospective FADURK outlays stood at 45 percent. By the latter part of December, the Kosovars had extracted all the concessions they could expect from the other federal units, and, indeed, Kosovo had even been forced to yield a little ground. Under the final agreement Kosovo received 42.6 percent of FADURK credits over the 1981–85 period.[87] Yet, as late as September, there were signs that the Slovenian representative, Ivo Klemenčić, was seeking a way to railroad the bill on FADURK and reopen discussions on meaningful criteria for underdeveloped status.[88]

The underdeveloped units were able to agree on the importance of FADURK, to be sure. But, when it came to the conditions applied to FADURK loans and credits, they fell out even among themselves. Macedonia and Montenegro wanted to retain the preexisting criteria for all underdeveloped units; Kosovo, however, wished to be the exclusive beneficiary of those conditions. Bosnia suggested a compromise under which all underdeveloped republics would enjoy the previous terms and Kosovo would enjoy even more favorable terms. Vojvodina, speaking for the developed republics, felt that FADURK credit terms should be brought more in consonance with terms prevailing on the market.[89]

Meanwhile, the constraints of overspending, insufficient exports, prohibitively high energy costs, and double-digit inflation were catching up with Yugoslavia's inefficient economy, and Yugoslav leaders reiterated the need for economic stabilization. By stabilization, the Yugoslavs meant increased exports, fewer imports, greater reliance on domestic sources of raw materials, and strict accounting of all consumption. They also planned to use greater care in investments. By 1980, with the Yugoslav standard of living declining for the first time in decades, it was clear that belt-tightening had to focus on investments. *Borba* signaled the change of policy, warning that "excessive investments remains the field in which the policy of economic stabilization is being undermined in the most drastic manner possible. Investments without proper financial backing and the use of funds, foreign exchange, and credits indispensable to the economy's current operations for investments cannot be tolerated any longer."[90] In this spirit, the federal Chamber of the *Skupština* adopted a law temporarily banning the use of social resources for uneconomic and nonremunerative investments. Some exceptions were allowed for investments in national defense, safety, basic educational needs, and hospitals.[91] But the moratorium was enough to make the Kosovars jumpy—especially in light of the traditional northern refrain about the inefficiency of Kosovo's economy. *Rilindja*, Priština's principal Albanian-language newspaper, edgily replied that it was not a question of the geography of investments but of the comparative efficiency of different sectors of industry. "From 1966 through 1975," *Rilindja* claimed,

> every dinar invested in the country's power-generating economy resulted in an increase in social production of 0.24 dinars, whereas in Kosovo the figure was 0.22 dinars. The difference is thus not very large. . . . In trade, hostelry, and tourism, the degree of the effectiveness of investments realized during the abovementioned period is approximately the same for the Kosovo economy as for that of the country as a whole. Other comparisons are also very indicative. Thus, if Kosovo had had the same structure of socioeconomic investments as the structure of investments for the country as a whole during the aforementioned 10-year period, the degree of the effectiveness of Kosovo economic investments, at the volume realized, would have been over a quarter higher than what was in fact realized.[92]

Kosovo was simultaneously finding that economic backwardness was imposing another cost—that of political isolation. Repeatedly, on issue after issue,

Kosovo opposed all the other federal units and was forced to give in. In the fall of 1979, for instance, Kosovo stood alone in resisting proposed cuts in the 1980 federal budget. The Kosovar delegation to the Chamber of Republics and Provinces (CRP) feared that the 4 billion dinars scheduled for elimination would reduce federal commitments to Kosovo. The reply proffered by one of the Slovenian delegates was ruthlessly blunt: the federal budget, he argued, must be drawn up in the same way as republican budgets, that is, aspirations cannot propel increases in budgetary outlays in excess of increases in the social product.[93] Kosovo was also isolated in year-end debates over inflation and price control in 1979. In the CRP Finance Committee, seven of the eight delegations, that is, all but Kosovo, rejected a SIV proposal that personal income be allowed to climb by a maximum of 18 percent in 1980. Instead, Croatia, Macedonia, Vojvodina, Montenegro, and Slovenia backed the Serbian delegation's alternative plan to link the growth in real wages to the growth in productivity.[94] In a meeting of the CRP Committee for Market and Prices on December 25, 1979, though it was agreed to take action to standardize prices across the republics, the Kosovar delegate, Blagoje Ivanović, sought unsuccessfully to obtain an exception in the field of energy. Such an exception he argued, was not only in the particular interest of Kosovo, but also in the interest of Yugoslavia as a whole. This recommendation was not heeded, however. Nor were those of the Slovenian and Serbian delegations, which sought exceptions for rents.[95] Moreover, the subsequent discussions of the 1981–85 middle-range plan proved the occasion for resurrection in a new form of the age-old debate over efficiency versus equality. This time the proponents of the former position advocated a return to the system of capital-intensive development, "a return . . . to the basic economic law of development." Proponents of greater equality urged emphasis on fixed quantitative targets and labor-intensive projects. No one dared challenge head-on Kosovo's demand for equality, but the gist of the debate showed increasing resistance to Kosovo's demands. Even the Serbs had come around to the Croatian and Slovenian position.[96]

Kosovo's political isolation produced certain undercurrents: in particular, a bitterness and sense of resentment on the part of the Albanians. In an article given the ironic title of Lenin's work, "One Step Forward, Two Steps Back," Miloš Antić described the failure to make progress in curbing unemployment in Kosovo, which he called the nucleus of Kosovo's quagmire. Under the social plan for 1976–80, 58,475 new jobs were to be created. But, three and a half years into the plan period, only 25,590 new jobs had been created—already 15,340 short of the projected rate. Unfortunately for Kosovo, moreover, most of the large investments based in other republics have not required the hiring of large numbers of workers.[97] Enterprises based in other republics have been chiefly capital-intensive, especially extractive, industry.

Montenegro also found itself harshly isolated in debates surrounding compensation for the ruinous earthquake that struck in April 1979. Montenegro, already classified as "underdeveloped," found it difficult to obtain sufficient compensation for damages suffered through the quake. Montenegro estimated that it had suffered some 70.6 billion dinars worth of damage and sought to obtain the corresponding figure in federal compensations. The bill was bogged down in the CRP Finance Committee, however, where the other federal units refused to ratify an agreement for this amount. By February 1980, SIV was urgently trying to forge a compromise and backed a bill to provide 60.5 billion dinars, of which 2 billion would be used to repair facilities of the JNA and other facilities under federal jurisdiction that were located in Montenegro. The seven other units nonetheless stuck to a position proposing 52 billion dinars in aid. By early March, the Montenegrins were willing to settle for 60.4 billion, slightly less than SIV's earlier compromise proposal, and SIV was supporting a new compromise figure of 55 billion.[98] Eventually, Montenegro was compelled to agree to a package of 53.637 billion dinars, of which three-quarters would be an outright grant from the other republics and provinces and the remaining one-quarter was a loan to be repaid between 1985 and 1989.[99] This final package was not significantly larger than the original amount proposed by the seven. Croatia and Slovenia may have been more sympathetic to Montenegro's needs and prepared to support a higher figure, while Serbia may well have stood at the forefront of the effort to hold compensation to a minimum. At any rate, in 1979, in the wake of the earthquake, other republics did send aid to Montenegro. The anti-Serbian faction in Montenegro—one of whose luminaries was at that time the president of the federal *Skupština*—allegedly manipulated press coverage to downplay contributions from the Serbian republic while heaping grateful praise on the republics of Croatia and Slovenia.

From the standpoint of pure economics, the prospects of the underdeveloped republics (aside from Kosovo) seemed, until the civil war of 1991 and the accompanying economic crash, fair to good—fair in the case of Montenegro and good for Bosnia and Macedonia. Yet viewed in relative terms, that is, from an interrepublican vantage point, their prospects, except possibly where Bosnia is concerned, were, even prior to the war, essentially hopeless. As a report submitted to the World Bank in 1975 noted, Yugoslavia's regional economic problem is "not a problem of economic stagnation in the less developed republics . . . [but] one of increasing regional differences between developed and less developed republics despite rapid growth in both."[100]

Kosovo's economic prospects appear increasingly hopeless. In the 1976–81 period, for instance, the social product grew at an average annual rate of 4 percent in Slovenia, 6.8 percent in Bosnia, 6.7 percent in Serbia, 5.1 percent in Vojvodina, but only 3.5 percent in Kosovo.[101] By 1982, Kosovo was unable to meet its financial obligations to the federation and asked to be released from its obligation to repay credits received during 1980 and 1981. The Kosovars also requested an increase in economic aid from the federation.[102] But, by mid-1982, it was clear that FADURK, under conditions of waxing economic duress, was in trouble. As late as August 1982, FADURK had not met its commitments for 1980, let alone for 1981 or 1982. Most of the republics had not—as of August 1982—taken any action to assume certain debts of Kosovo, as urged by the federal government, and certain federal units had failed to make their contributions to FADURK.[103] These conditions undermined the prospects for the success of the FADURK program.

Final Battles over FADURK

There were repeated efforts over the years to obtain the abolition of FADURK—naturally, on the part of Slovenia and Croatia. During 1985 and 1986, the republics were much divided over the criteria for disbursement, but finally, in April 1986, agreed on the criteria for the 1986–90 period. Yet despite the investment of $10.5 billion of FADURK money from 1965 to 1988, the underdeveloped republics were unable to narrow the developmental gap. In Montenegro and Kosovo, for example, per capita social product declined relative to the Yugoslav average from 1970 to 1986, while in Macedonia it was more or less stagnant.[104]

In January 1990, the Slovenian government (still controlled by the communists) proposed that it reduce its contribution to FADURK by about half. The Belgrade daily *Politika* attacked this decision, and Fund Director Momčilo Ćemović used the army daily *Narodna armija* as the vehicle for an interview in which he called the Slovenian move a contravention of federal law.[105]

In February 1990, the board of FADURK failed to reach agreement on a financial plan for 1990 when the Slovenian delegation refused to cooperate. The Slovenes cited the Serbian economic blockade of Slovenian goods (imposed in late 1989) as the reason for their noncooperation. Since the fund depended on Slovenia and Croatia for 45 percent of its financial means, Slovenian noncooperation was a serious blow. And in March 1990 the Federal Executive Council ordered the Federal Secretariat of Finance to freeze Slovenian accounts until the republic paid its share into FADURK.[106]

But with the entire country poised by 1990 on the brink of a choice between transformation into a confederation, dissolution of the federation, and civil war, this position could not be maintained. The first week of July 1990, the Croatian *Sabor* announced that Croatia was going to stop making payments to FADURK. Two weeks later, the Federal Executive Council announced that FADURK would cease all activity by the end of the year and that it would be replaced by a development bank that would operate according to market principles.[107] One Macedonian intellectual, contemplating this and other developments, bemoaned the fact that (in his view) Macedonia was ending up in the most difficult straits of any of the republics and commented, "Probably it's because we Macedonians are (still) on the margins of 'the broad Yugoslav public', just as, by the way, Yugoslavia is on the margins of the world public."[108]

An Airline in Every Republic

The Yugoslavs were long profoundly apprehensive of nationalism—and in the gathering nationalist maelstrom of 1989–91 some Yugoslavs remained apprehensive of nationalist energies. The Titoists viewed nationalism as embracing both the drive to separatism and the urging toward hegemonic domination over other actors in the system. It is a fundamental tenet of this work that the Yugoslav republics have been animated by a steady impulse toward self-assertion and, where possible, domination—that is, they are animated by nationalism in the sense in which the Yugoslavs define it. The repeated Kosovar demands for republican status, anti-Serbian posturing in Montenegro, and separatist sentiment in both Slovenia and Croatia reflect the centrifugal aspect of nationalism. But its centripetal guise as internal imperialism is also well exemplified—in Serbia's attitude, especially during the ascendancy first of Ranković, and more recently, of Milošević, as well as in Croatia's desires to annex parts of Bosnia and Montenegro. This self-assertive drive is also manifested at lower levels of demand articulation, mostly in the economic realm and, in particular, in the case of the republican airlines.

This is not to deny the autonomy of economics, which is the breeding ground of entirely endogenous strivings and accounts for the phenomenon of economic nationalism. But there is another side to the coin: if economic discontent can spill over into collective affectivity, the process can also be reversed, producing a sort of nationalistic economics in which a program of economic demands springs much more from collective affectivity than from economic perturbation. If the controversies over aid to the underdeveloped regions exemplify the former, the desire of Croatia, Bosnia, and Macedonia to found their own airline companies is unequivocally an instance of the latter.

Until 1961, there was only one airline in Yugoslavia—Jugoslovenski Aerotransport (JAT), which had headquarters in Belgrade. In that year, however, Adria Aviopromet was established by an act of the executive council of SR Slovenia. The new company was conceived as a charter flight enterprise, although it stood prepared to assist JAT during its peak season.[109] With the company's reincorporation as Inex Adria Aviopromet (IAA) in 1969 came a widening of services. But, although IAA has its main offices in Ljubljana, it remained, for many years, a BOAL of Belgrade's export-import firm, Interexport. IAA had seven DC-9s (as of 1983) and largely makes charter flights on Euro-Mediterranean routes, though it also has a few domestic flights.

The creation of IAA was relatively noncontroversial, since it did not represent a remonstration on Slovenia's part. That same year (1961), however, the Croats came forth with a plan to set up a Croatian airline to be operated in cooperation with Pan American Airlines. The Croats felt that JAT—whose foreign currency earnings were credited against the Serbian republic's contributions to the federation—was a Serbian airline and argued that, as an autonomous republic of the Yugoslav federation, Croatia had the right to set up its own airline. The Serbs, however, opposed the plan, as did the conservatives in Zagreb.[110] Opponents cited SAS, described as the single airline for all of Scandinavia, and challenged the proposition that there was any economic rationale behind the creation of a third airline company for Yugoslavia.[111] The battle dragged into 1962, and it seemed for a while that proponents of the Croatian airline were losing ground. Then, in 1963, perhaps as a by-product of the constitutional reform, Croatia was abruptly given the green light, and Pan Adria came into being.

The new Croatian airline started operation with a fleet consisting of three twin-piston-engine Morava L-200s (from Czechoslovakia), each capable of carrying six passengers or 450 kilograms of cargo, and a few Pipers for agricultural purposes. Yet, from the beginning, the company had to struggle to survive. Underfinanced, underequipped, underutilized, and suffering from a lack of trained personnel, Pan Adria nonetheless conjured visions of steady growth.

> People in Pan Adria stubbornly believed that the number of planes and the size of the fleet itself could resolve all its problems, and that organizational solutions were of much lesser importance. This accounts for the company's ambitious plans for the purchase of three DC-9 planes, although the company once again was not prepared for this either with respect to general organization or with respect to cadres.[112]

In 1966, Pan Adria bought four new planes—Aero Commander 500-Us, each capable of carrying eight passengers—and sold the Moravas. Four used planes were subsequently purchased from West Germany and Switzerland.

Yet Pan Adria was unable to make ends meet and, in search of passengers, began offering free flights to Trieste, subsidized in part by Trieste's airport, which was eager to acquire status as an international airport. The hope was that the gimmick would attract new customers, who would then turn to Pan Adria for domestic flights. Most of those taking advantage of this arrangement, however, were officials of Pan Adria and the Trieste airport (or members of their families), and, in the end, the Zagreb-Trieste flight was abolished altogether. Throughout this period, Pan Adria officials complained that JAT was stealing Croatia's most qualified pilots. When, in the late 1960s, JAT formed a subsidiary charter flight company, Air Yugoslavia, and Belgrade's Generalexport formed its own airline, Aviogenex, to cater to tourist groups, the Croats accused Serbia of "nationalist expansionism."[113] Nor were the Croats able to obtain the financial backing that might have prevented utter insolvency.

After hobbling along for fifteen years, Pan Adria finally collapsed in 1978 and declared bankruptcy. Within months, however, a new Croatian airline sprang up to take its place. Although the official founder is the *općina* of Velika Gorica (the small town adjacent to Zagreb's airport), in fact the republic of Croatia and the city of Zagreb were the prime movers in the resurrection of Pan Adria. Croatia's motivation was overridingly political: the republic wanted the airline as a national symbol, even if the company would not be given the wherewithal to make it into the black.[114] This new airline, which took the name Trans Adria, inherited the facilities, personnel, aircraft, and equipment of Pan Adria; it was, in fact, Pan Adria under a new name. This was even true in a financial sense, since Trans Adria's entire working capital was in the form of credits and loans to "buy" all the equipment and capital assets of Pan Adria (valued at 30 million dinars) from the bankruptcy commission. "The present assets of Trans Adria are too modest," *Vjesnik* noted, "to enable the company to pay its own way *and* repay large and expensive credits, no matter how successful it is in its business."[115] Hence, despite the expansion of its services in the first quarter of 1980, Trans Adria appeared foreordained to go the way of its predecessor.[116] The republic could not afford to write off the company's previous losses, even if it had wanted to—nor is it obvious that such a move would have sufficed to make Trans Adria a profitable enterprise. Trans Adria was, in a word, a "political factory" of the 1980s—an enterprise whose value lay not in the services it provided, but rather in its mere existence as a *Croatian* airline.

A similar process was taking place in Bosnia, rooted both in certain economic needs that did not appear to be satisfied by any of the existing five Yugoslav airline companies and in the heightened Islamic consciousness produced by the Muslim national awakening of the late 1960s and early 1970s. Bosnia has long been dissatisfied with service linking it with the Middle East, where the Bosnian republic has become involved in numerous economic projects, such as the construction of a highway connecting Baghdad and Mahmudia. The problem was especially irksome insofar as all such links were via Belgrade rather than Sarajevo, and intrarepublican air transport services were sparse. When JAT began curtailing flights to Sarajevo in the late 1970s, intimating that they would like to drop Sarajevo from their flight schedule altogether, Bosnia appealed to Slovenia for help.[117] Convinced that the flights could be made profitable, Slovenia's IAA responded in 1979 by starting a regular Ljubljana-Sarajevo-Skopje-Titograd-Sarajevo-Ljubljana flight. The Bosnians remained dissatisfied, however, and complained that, despite qualifications comparable with most international airports, Sarajevo airport accounted for only 4 percent of the total volume of air traffic in Yugoslavia.[118]

Sarajevo began to float the idea of a Bosnian airline as early as 1971.[119] Four years later, the executive council of the Bosnian republic assembly authorized feasibility studies on the subject and, in March 1978, endorsed creation of an office for the establishment of a Bosnian airline, a task entrusted to the Bosnian enterprise, Unisturist.[120] Finally, in late 1979, Sarajevo made an official decision to establish its own airline within the framework of the Unisturist organization. It is important to emphasize that this decision, like Croatia's earlier decisions to establish Pan Adria and Trans Adria, was taken by the republican government. The Serbs, convinced that there was no economic justification for the existence of multiple airlines, tried to kill the project with ridicule and circulated various ethnocentric jokes. One such joke described Bosnia's space program and its ambitious project to send a rocket to the sun—to cope with the problem of the sun's heat, the Bosnians planned to blast off at night. The Serbs also circulated rumors that Bosnia intended to illegally apply FADURK funds toward establishment of the airline, and they suggested that it could not possibly run at a profit.

None of this could deter Sarajevo, however, and in April 1980, Izet Brković, president of Bosnia's Committee for Transportation, announced that Air Bosnia's first flights were tentatively scheduled for May 1982. By the time of the announcement, Unisturist had already conducted test flights of several aircraft. Bosnia had undertaken to construct airports at Banja Luka and Tuzla (there were already airports in Mostar and, of course, Sarajevo), and its plans included air connection of these four cities, flights three times daily to Belgrade and Zagreb and service to the Middle East, North Africa, and Western Europe.[121] As of June 1980, however, Air Bosnia had yet to purchase its first aircraft, and there were no scheduled flights as of December 1982.[122] After that, the idea of an Air Bosnia gradually withered away.

American observers pointed out that there was some economic justification for Air Bosnia; nonetheless, JAT remained steadfastly opposed to the notion. JAT opposed what it called "the proliferation of airlines in Yugoslavia" and insisted that existing institutions could provide such service as was necessary. As a fallback, JAT offered a tight agreement on shared financing and close cooperation on routes, intending to let the republican lines handle the unprofitable routes.[123]

JAT used every means at its disposal to pressure the other airlines into integration. In the mid-1970s, for instance, JAT managed to acquire the legal right to veto freight transport service by foreign airlines in Yugoslavia—a superficially innocent prerogative that was designed, in effect, to allow JAT to abort the establishment of bilateral cooperation between the fledgling Slovenian and Croatian airlines and foreign companies. Since JAT lacked modern aircraft for container transport, assertion of its monopoly (Swissair pulled out, for instance) left Yugoslav enterprises with no option but to transport their goods by truck to airports in Munich or Vienna, which the JAT veto could not reach. "This . . . monopoly . . . is not useful," commented Igor Presern in *Delo*, "but is, in fact, detrimental to the national economy. . . . It causes damage not only to Slovenian interests, but also to part of the Yugoslav economy."[124] Jealous of its domain, JAT was willing to sacrifice the interests of the Yugoslav community to advance its own private interests. "JAT wants to be first in every respect," *Delo* noted dourly.[125]

JAT kept up the pressure on both the official and the unofficial level. On November 15, 1978, managers of JAT, Inex-Adria, Aviogenex, and Trans Adria came to the Yugoslav Economic Chamber at the summons of Ilija Vakić, chamber president. Vakić demanded to know why the four airlines could not combine into a single company. Dragoslav Radisavljević, director of JAT, revealed that JAT had been pressing for such an agreement for the previous three years, but that the other airlines were uncooperative. Miško Spasić, director of Aviogenex, Serbia's other airline, predictably expressed Aviogenex's readiness to integrate.[126] Surprisingly, Janez Nedog, general director of IAA, claimed that the Slovenian air transport organization endorsed the program of integration; he even claimed to have played an important role in initiating discussion of the subject.[127] But whatever their official position might have been, privately Slovenian officials expressed misgivings about JAT's motivations and about the consequences for Slovenia of the absorption of all competition by JAT.[128] JAT made another effort to annex the other airlines at a meeting in Maribor in late 1979. The meeting proved abortive, however, when some of the participants proved so reticent that they even refused to divulge details of their companies' financial transactions and plans.[129]

Symptomatic of the lack of consensus is the fact that there was no agreement on the establishment of a Self-Managing Interest Community (SIZ) for the field of air transport. Meanwhile, JAT began feeling a financial pinch, which was aggravated by a 10 percent drop in the number of domestic passengers from 1979 to 1980. Moreover, JAT's financial losses continued to mount in 1981. JAT, accordingly, became more impatient with the coexistence of other airlines. The financial woes of its competitors played into JAT's hands. For instance, in August 1980, JAT took over the twice-weekly flights to Tirana that had been previously offered by Croatia's Trans Adria.

Slovenia, Croatia, Montenegro, Kosovo, Bosnia, and Macedonia continued to voice dissatisfaction with JAT's performance and service. Macedonia began talking about establishing "independent service," and there were even rumors at one time that Kosovo might launch its own airline.[130] When separate airlines had already been established, the republican elites appeared reluctant to give up their only real bargaining chip. In March 1982, however, under the pressure of Yugoslavia's worsening economic situation, the boards of directors of JAT and Trans Adria abruptly announced a "merger."[131] Under the provisions of the merger agreement, JAT was to take over essentially all of Trans Adria's service, leaving only an agricultural spraying service in independent operation. JAT officials, expressing skepticism about the prospects of a Bosnian airline, indicated that, in their view, the annexation of Trans Adria would be only the first step in the eventual integration of all the Yugoslav airline companies into JAT.[132]

JAT was never able to realize these objectives, however. In the late 1980s, JAT engaged in an "air war" with the Slovenian airline, Inex-Adria Aviopromet, trying to invoke federal laws to assert a monopoly on certain air connections. But JAT's interpretations were judged flimsy, and Inex-Adria was able to continue its international flights.[133] Moreover, by 1990, Croatia once again had an airline—this time named Croatia Airways—established within the framework of the Bank of Croatia.[134] JAT's monopoly was, thus, further shaken.

Controversies over Road and Railway Construction

The 1965 reforms had considerable fallout in all sectors of the economy. Among the results was the decision to devolve major responsibilities for public works and construction to the republics. Thus, in 1967, the republics were given almost total control over the planning, routing, contracting, construction, maintenance, and financing of public roads within their respective juridical territories. Republican and regional funds were now the primary source for financing road construction and maintenance. Certain projects, however, particularly those connecting major cities in different republics, could obtain support from federal funds, army funds, the World Bank, other foreign sources (channeled through Belgrade), and, for those eligible, the funds for underdeveloped areas. For instance, the European Investment Bank, affiliated with the European Economic Community, approved a $600 million loan to Yugoslavia in 1977 for construction of a 1,185-kilometer four-lane highway. This supplemented credits already extended by the World Bank. In addition, Yugoslavia hoped to obtain aid for the project from both East and West. The final cost to domestic investors was still expected to top $800 million, that is, about 40 percent of the total cost.

Yugoslavia has long been plagued by a deficient transport system and is only now reaching the point at which the country can be said to be integrated by a workable system of roads, railways, and airports. In 1966, Yugoslavia had the fifth sparsest network of roads in Europe, after Norway, Sweden, Finland, and Albania. Proportional to population density, however, only Albania fell behind Yugoslavia. The problem has also been a question of routing and the distribution of roads: Sarajevo, for instance, was rejected as an alternative capital after the war because the dearth of decent roads in the vicinity made the city virtually inaccessible. Even today, the only rail connection between Sarajevo and the coast is the standard-gauge service between Sarajevo and Ploče. Some regions were markedly less developed in this respect when the partisans came to power. Montenegro, for instance, had 0.7 kilometers of hard surface roads per 1,000 square kilometers, as compared with 80.9 kilometers per 1,000 square kilometers in 1974. But even in the developed areas there were problems. The Austrians, for instance, developed communications and transport links throughout Slovenia, Vojvodina, and Croatia, but always with an eye on the dictates of military strategy and military requirements and in accordance with trade patterns of that day. As a result, the Austrians left the Yugoslavs a network of roads jutting north-south into Slovenia and Vojvodina and thus cutting across, rather than following along, the principal trade and transport routes of today. Of 54,180 miles of classified roads in 1968, just over 20 percent were paved. Most of the rest were gravel or packed-dirt roads. But the Yugoslavs have maintained a steady pace, tripling the net length of modern paved roads in less than ten years, from 12,950 kilometers in 1965 to 35,380 kilometers in 1974.[135]

A major project of the 1980s was the widening and modernization of the artery that links Zagreb to Belgrade, Niš, and Skopje and forms part of the trans-European E-5 artery that links Frankfurt to Istanbul. Partly because of poor road conditions, the Yugoslav stretches have been among the most accident-prone stretches of the highway.[136] Yet considerable parts of Croatia, Bosnia-Herzegovina, Kosovo, southern and western Serbia, and Macedonia are deficient in access roads and highways. Macedonia today has more than 150,000 registered motor vehicles, and 80 percent of commodity traffic travels by road.

Side by side with the development of roads, the Yugoslavs have been busy updating and extending their rail lines. Here a crucial problem has been antiquated tracks and stock. Much of the system consists of narrow-gauge tracks, capable of carrying only half the weight that standard gauge can bear. Only 24 percent of the standard-gauge lines were adequate for speeds over 80 kilometers per hour in 1966, and only 33 percent could handle loads of more than 18 tons per axle. This meant that freight cars were compelled to run below capacity. At that time, moreover, about half the locomotives and passenger and freight cars were more than forty years old. Add to this the fact that 70 percent of rail traffic was concentrated on 30 percent of the trackage, and it is apparent that the system was not only technically deficient but also had a warped spatial distribution that was completely inadequate for the needs of the country as a whole.[137] In 1974, 44.5 percent of all goods transported across Yugoslavia traveled by road, with railroads just barely retaining a plurality of 44.7 percent. (The remaining portion was carried either by river transport [10.8 percent] or by air.)[138]

Rail construction has been inseparable from republican competition in the development of seaports. In 1945 there were rail connections to only four Yugoslav ports: Rijeka, in the north; historic Dubrovnik; Split; and nearby Šibenik. Yet reconstruction of these ports, badly damaged in the war, proceeded at a slow pace. The Germans destroyed more than 80 percent of the port facilities at Rijeka when they withdrew from Yugoslavia, and, almost twenty years later, its capacity still had not been restored to 1913 levels, although traffic had passed the 1913 mark in 1950.[139] Rijeka and Split remain major ports for Yugoslav traffic today; Šibenik, however, has long been neglected as a recipient of investments. Work on a new terminal for handling phosphate finally began at the port of Šibenik on November 27, 1979.[140] In contrast, money has been poured into Koper (situated on the sliver of Slovenian coastline), Bar (once a negligible Montenegrin coastal town), and Ploče. The last of these, as many observers have noted, "is Croatian in name only," for its principal backers and users have been the Bosnians, and its developers have found backing through Sarajevo, not Zagreb.[141] The long Cyrillic signs and the prominent display of Sarajevo's *Oslobodjenje* at the Kardeljevo railroad station are the first clues that this major seaport—which handled a record 3.5 million tons of cargo in 1979—is more Bosnian than Croatian. And, in fact, the population of present-day Kardeljevo consists primarily of settlers from the hinterland of Herzegovina. Plocĕ/Kardeljevo's Bosnian nature was demonstrated in 1969, three years after completion of the wide-gauge electrified railway, when Sarajevo-Mostar-Ploče, the port of Ploče, despite its location in Croatia, was integrated into the Bosnian railway enterprise, ŽTO Sarajevo. Later, in October 1981, the Sarajevo railway enterprise also absorbed the nearby port of Metković, a long-time competitor of Ploče.[142]

The waxing interport rivalry inevitably acquired interrepublican hues. Rijeka, Koper, and Ploče—each backed by a different republic—competed for preponderance as the network terminal for Yugoslavia. Attempts to reach an agreement on a coordinated program of port development, such as a meeting of port representatives convened in 1974, repeatedly fell through. Rijeka argued that investment should be funneled into the port with the highest profitability of traffic—a self-serving argument, in fact. Koper and Ploče argued that each zone should have a port to serve its own hinterland, thus cutting transport costs.[143] According to one Yugoslav economic analyst, however, there was no economic justification for massive investment in all three, because there would not be enough cargo in the foreseeable future to occupy even one port at full capacity.[144] Yet Rijeka would not in fact be able to handle demand singlehandedly; Croatia's Pula and Slovenia's Koper were the obvious alternative Istrian ports. The Slovenes, who wanted to promote Koper, controlled the access routes to Pula and, taking advantage of the decentralization of authority for railway tariffs in 1966, introduced certain disproportionate tariffs for railway freight headed for Rovinj and Pula. The result was that Pula, though enjoying certain advantages of infrastructure and an excellent natural harbor and actually connected by a shorter route to both Ljubljana and Zagreb, became less attractive from a financial viewpoint.[145]

Interport competition for funding was intense, and Rijeka, for one, insisted that without financing from the federal government, necessary modernization of port facilities at Rijeka would be impossible.[146] Yet, even when funds had been allocated, the ports had to struggle to ensure that the funds were made available. Thus, for instance, a delegate from Split complained in 1978 that, although the 1976–80 plan had authorized the expenditure of 20 million dinars for technical research preparatory to reconstruction of the Split-Knin railway under the 1981–85 plan, nothing had in fact been done. He added that almost nothing had been done to improve Split's rail connections since the war.[147]

The most controversial port development project, however, has been the development of the Bar. Isolated and far from the major industrial centers of the north, the port would only be feasible if a rail connection were built. The Croats protested loudly that the money could be better spent improving facilities at Split, Šibenik, or even Zadar, all of which were located in southern Croatia, along the Dalmatian coast. The ports of Rijeka and Ploče both tried to block pursuit of the Belgrade-Bar project because they feared that development of the port of Bar and its connection by rail with Belgrade would pose a dangerous threat to their business.[148] Serbian, Kosovar, and Macedonian interests, however, lent strong support to the Montenegrins, which resulted in Yugoslavia's most expensive marine project since the war. The railway itself stretches for 296 miles and was completed only in 1976, after requiring the blasting of some 50 miles of tunnels.[149] The railroad, some thirteen years in the works, was the object of repeated Croatian complaints. From the Croatian standpoint, the development of Bar was politically motivated; the Serbs and Montenegrins wanted to have their own port and avoid having to deal with Croatia. Bar has certainly relieved Rijeka of some of its congestion, but, perhaps more important, it has also helped to open part of the south to foreign trade. In a country riddled by mountain ranges, the Belgrade-Bar railway and the development of the port of Bar has also linked the eastern two-fifths of the country with the rest of the economy and, by a 1966 estimate, would save Yugoslavia about $20–30 million annually. When the building of storage areas at the port is completed, it will be capable of handling 4.5 million tons of cargo per year.[150] It has also been argued that the Belgrade-Bar railway will open Montenegro to tourism and in time pay for itself in additional tourist revenues.[151] Yet the Croats could not fail to notice that the Serbs and Montenegrins had long enjoyed a close cooperative relationship. Serbia and Montenegro share a number of joint professional organizations, such as the Serbian and Montenegrin Bar Association, whereas in the other republics such organizations operate only within republican boundaries. There is also considerable cooperation between the universities and the academies of sciences of these two republics. Moreover, it was no secret that the idea for the Belgrade-Bar railway originated with the Serbian and Montenegrin parties—it was not a federal proposal. The two republican parties had signed a cooperative protocol in December 1963 spelling out the plans vis-à-vis Bar. Indeed, Montenegro's negligible railways were run as a branch of ŽTP Belgrade (Serbian Railways) until completion of the Belgrade-Bar railway, when, finally, the formation of ŽTO Titograd was announced.[152] Inevitably, then, the Croats view the completion of the Belgrade-Bar railway as a Serbian-Montenegrin victory, even though there is little question that the country as a whole will benefit.

If there was opposition among sectors in Slovenia, Croatia, and Bosnia to the Belgrade-Bar railroad and the Bar port project (itself a massive investment), the manner in which the two projects were to be funded provoked no less controversy. The original plan of the Serbs and Montenegrins was to use federal funds (or loans guaranteed by the federation) to construct the railroad, and the two republics, well represented by the then-dominant conservatives, were able to ram through legislation to do just that. The first investment program for construction of the Belgrade-Bar railway was drawn up in 1955 and approved by the federal Committee for Economics. Because of a lack of funds, however, the federal Executive Council (SIV) decided in 1957 to halt all work on the railway except for two short stretches—Resnik-Vreoci (37 kilometers, completed in 1958) and Titograd-Bar (51 kilometers, completed in 1959). Four years later, however, SIV reversed its decision and construction was resumed. According to an official estimate rendered in 1961, the railway could be completed by 1967 or 1968, given an intensive investment of 20–30 million dinars annually.[153] In mid-1966, the federal *Skupština* passed a law authorizing federal funding of 85 percent of the costs of construction, leaving the republics of Serbia and Montenegro to foot the bill for the remaining 15 percent.[154] But the contributions of Serbia and Montenegro were designed to play a symbolic, not a meaningful, role. Yugoslav officials were negotiating with the World Bank for a loan to aid construction of the railroad, and, after two years of discussions, an agreement was signed in March 1968 that extended a loan of $50 million at an interest rate of 6.25 percent, with repayment spread over twenty years and scheduled to begin in 1975. At this point, it was anticipated that construction could be completed by the end of 1973. Between 1966 and 1972, the federal government doled out steadily increasing sums to the two republics, while Croatia and Slovenia fumed. The total amounts involved are shown in table 21.

Table 21. *Disbursement of Federal Funds for Construction of the Belgrade–Bar Railroad*
(in millions of new dinars)

	In SR Serbia	*In SR Montenegro*
1966	47.50	22.50
1967	95.11	30.13
1968	141.15	44.40
1969	188.31	103.75
1970	149.01	144.79
1971	200.65	248.20
1972	270.05	294.65
TOTAL	1,092.58	888.40

Source: Mirko Dokić, *Ekonomika, organizacija i razvoj saobraćaja SFRJ* (Belgrade: Institut Ekonomskih Nauka, 1977), pp. 75–76.

Various problems, above all, the tortuous mountainous terrain, caused the project to fall behind schedule and ran up unforeseen expenses. Materials were increasing in price at rates not anticipated. Thus, under pressure from the northwestern republics, Serbia agreed in 1971 to assume full financial responsibility for further work in its territory. To manage this, Serbia took out a loan from the Yugoslav Investment Bank. The handwriting was on the wall, and, as 1970 drew to a close, the executive council of Montenegro decided to apply for a loan of 500 million dinars from the National Bank of Yugoslavia.[155] Croatia and Slovenia had succeeded in forcing the Serbian-Montenegrin axis to retreat.

Yet, if the northerners finally won the financial battle (albeit a partial victory, at that late date), the project backers obtained what they wanted—a multimillion dollar railroad and an extensive port at Bar, capable of handling about 4.5 million tons of cargo per year.

Not surprisingly, the Bosnians, for whom the Belgrade-Bar route had little utility, came back a few years later with what was tantamount to a rival project—a proposed railway link between Dubrovnik and Capljina. The Bosnians noted that maritime traffic had been stagnant at the port of Dubrovnik for ten years (1967–77) and that the lack of a normal-gauge rail connection meant some cargo that might have gone through Dubrovnik had gone to Bar instead. They also backed the project in hopes of attracting tourists to the blossoming Bosnian interior.[156]

The Slovenian road affair was a clash over the disbursement of federally raised funds; the Belgrade-Bar controversy represented a challenge to the legitimacy of the very principle of distribution. In both crises, accordingly, conflict arose between actors who were struggling for what they perceived as a limited good—in the first case, the World Bank loan; in the second case, cargo traffic as well as federal appropriations. After 1970, however, the federal government more or less phased out its role in the transport sector and entrusted administrative, planning, and maintenance responsibilities to the road organizations of the republics and provinces. In 1975 the federal government contributed no more than 2 percent of the total expenditure involved in highway financing. As the nature of the system was transformed, the nature of conflict was likewise transformed. No longer do the republics compete for federal funds. Rather, they clash over joint projects in which the profitability to republic A depends on the collaboration of republic B. Centrifugal conflict has been replaced by an odd kind of centripetal conflict.

The 1980 "Brotherhood and Unity" highway crisis is a case in point. At stake was the completion of the Yugoslav portion of the international highway network—linkage with which the Yugoslavs had actively sought. Yet the Yugoslav republics proved unable to hold each other to agreed timetables, and some portions of the project fell seriously behind schedule.

Some 1,200 kilometers of highway in the E-70 and E-75 sections of the international network in Yugoslavia needed reconstruction or widening as of 1975, and, under the Social Agreement regarding the Transportation Policy of Yugoslavia for 1976–80, it was agreed that 432 kilometers (or one-third of the total) would be completed by 1980, according to the following schedule: 76 kilometers in Slovenia, 148 in Croatia, 13 in Vojvodina, 145 in Serbia, and 50 in Macedonia. By the end of 1980, however, only a quarter—some 330 kilometers—was expected to be completed (by an April 1980 estimate).[157] Croatia had completed some 137 kilometers; Macedonia, another 57. Serbia completed its quota by early 1980 and planned to complete another 4.5 kilometers by the end of 1980. Yet neither Slovenia nor Vojvodina had even begun work by the end of April 1980, nor had they given any signs of an intention to do so.

Financing difficulties account for only a small part of this result, since all the republics were low in available cash. Serbia obtained a domestic loan for its section. Croatia and Macedonia financed their sections with foreign credits covering up to 40 percent of construction costs. Vojvodina also expected to obtain foreign credits; when they fell through, the Vojvodinans decided to postpone work on the highway. Slovenia had funds at hand but chose to give priority to the improvement of a network of regional roads within the republic and to the modernization of certain sections of highway other than parts of E-70: a classic case of a republic putting its own interests ahead of those of the federation. Indeed, Keti Čomovska, deputy chairman of the federal Committee for Transportation and Communication, told *NIN* that the Slovenian move would cause the federation *irredeemable* losses. [158] And though Macedonia, Croatia, and Serbia pledged to continue with their sections of the project, Gerhat Burbah of Vojvodina, even while speaking of his province's "hope" to complete thirty kilometers of roads by the beginning of 1982, cautioned that, at the moment, the situation was uncertain and no promises could be made. The success of an international highway system clearly depends on each actor completing his allotted portion. Yet Slovenia once again postponed construction on those parts of the highway that would link up with the rest of the system, arguing (1) that construction of modern highways via Ljubelj and Potkoren to the Austrian border is financially more important for Slovenia, and (2) that the Vojvodinans will not do their share anyway, so that the "Brotherhood and Unity" highway (the name sounds like a mockery) will have a "hole in the middle" in any case.[159] The entire affair is reminiscent of the old story about the five hunters who set out to capture a deer. If all five hunters cooperate, the capture is assured. But any individual hunter may abandon his post and chase rabbits instead, thereby capturing a rabbit but also ensuring the escape of the deer. Slovenia is the hunter who went after the rabbit.

By the summer of 1982, the Vojvodinans had begun work on a 17-kilometer stretch of highway (not the 30-kilometer stretch promised for early 1982), and the Slovenes had completed a 9.5-kilometer stretch of highway west of Ljubljana. The Slovenes also agreed to cooperate with Austria on the construction of the Karavanke Tunnel linking Austria and Slovenia—a 7.5-kilometer project involving 3.6 kilometers on the Slovenian side—and obtained a $31 million share of the eleventh World Bank loan (which totaled $85 million) to finance this stretch.[160] Keenly aware of their economic interests, the Slovenes again made construction of road links with Austria their priority.

Slovenia had displayed a similar proclivity to pursue its exclusive interests with ruthless vigor during the fishing waters controversy of 1972, when Slovenia demonstrated a readiness to define issues in terms favorable to itself. The controversy first appeared in June 1972, when *Ekonomska politika* reported that, for more than three months, Slovenia had been pressing Croatia and Montenegro to agree to a revision of the agreement under which Italy paid compensation for fishing in Yugoslavia's Adriatic waters. Between 1949 and 1965, such compensation had been paid directly into the federal budget. But, after 1965, these payments were made directly to Croatia and Montenegro (in 1965, 84.53 percent to Croatia, 15.47 percent to Montenegro; after 1965, 86.72 percent to Croatia, and 13.28 percent to Montenegro). As more than 17 million dinars had changed hands during 1965–72, the Slovenes were eager for a share and demanded it on the basis of their tiny, one-port coastline. Naturally, the Slovenes did not want length of coastline to be used as the criterion for disbursement and suggested that the size of the republics' fishing fleets be the criterion: under the Slovenian plan, Slovenia's take would have amounted to 17 percent of the total, while Montenegro's would have shriveled to a mere 1 percent. The Economic Commission of the executive council of Montenegro replied that the fish and, therefore, the compensation, belong to those who own the waters.[161] Such examples might easily be multiplied, but the point is clear: self-interest takes precedence over general interest; allies are sought among those with like interests or among those who are antagonistic to units with contrary interests.

Speaking to a gathering of the Federation of Veterans, on October 16, 1980, Stane Dolanc, a member of the party's central committee and a Slovene, issued a stern warning to republics that pursue self-interest to the detriment of others. "Today we feel, specifically and sharply, the consequences of [a] liberalism that is 10 years old," he charged,

> and that did not find its expression solely in the writing of one or another book but found its expression in quite specific attitudes and also economic attitudes in

> our society. . . . The republics . . . have built their own economic strategies regardless of the joint interest of Yugoslavia, regardless of the interests of the second, third, fourth and sixth republics and of the first and second provinces. . . . For that reason it comes into conflict with the interests of its own associated labor and later or even simultaneously also into conflict with the interests of associated labor of other republics and all Yugoslavia. . . . [Yet] during sessions [of committees of the *Skupština* or of the interrepublican committees] telephones ring and such questions are asked as: What should I say, what position should I adopt? This happens even though the official concerned is bound by the constitution and by [her or his] own oath to defend the interests of this Yugoslav community such as it is.[162]

Freed from political constraint, the federal units pursue their own individual interests—consistently and as a matter of policy. They cannot entirely trust each other and certainly do not wish to defer to each other's judgment—as is demonstrated by the constant demands for the establishment of control commissions to verify the rationality of investments in the south. The units are motivated by exclusive interests, and they will pursue exclusive interests whenever they can. The trick of Yugoslav federalism—if it is to work—must be to accomplish the Madisonian feat and so arrange the political order that the outcome of interrepublican debate is the same as it would have been had the republics been seeking the Yugoslav general interest.

Stabilizing the Economy, 1984–90

It used to be axiomatic that the more developed republics favored economic liberalization and decentralization and that the less developed republics favored economic centralism and the maintenance of centrally controlled state funding. By the mid-1980s, first Slovenia, then Croatia, and finally economic liberals in all of the republics came around to the idea that the return to private enterprise was necessary and inevitable if there was to be any substantial economic recovery. The Yugoslav economy, which had seemed promising and even resilient in the mid-1970s, was in deep trouble by the late 1980s. In Zagreb, capital of the "developed" republic of Croatia, some five thousand households were functioning without electricity as of 1989 because the families could not afford to pay for power.[163] Moreover, as economic conditions deteriorated, economic crime increased. In the first eight months of 1989, Croatia alone registered a record 37,000 crimes, most of them involving theft or embezzlement.[164] Wracked with problems of economic insolvency, foreign debt, unemployment, and inflation, the Yugoslav economy was further strained, in 1987, by an especially widespread rash of strikes, some of them protesting a national wage freeze decreed by federal prime minister Branko Mikulić.[165] There were large-scale protests by thousands of workers in Skopje (in November 1987) and in Belgrade (in October 1988), protesting low wages.[166] Conditions became so bad that on August 20, 1989, some 30,000 citizens—mostly local Montenegrins—demonstrated in Nikšić to protest their hunger and poverty.[167]

The Mikulić government, which had sworn to fight inflation, made no headway whatsoever. By October 1987, inflation hit 200 percent; it would eventually rise to 893.8 percent by August 1989.[168]

The massive report on economic stabilization produced by the Krajger Commission in 1986 had proven barren. Slovenia and Croatia, in particular, resented Mikulić's lame efforts to deal with the economic problems, and in May 1988 requested a vote of no-confidence in the federal *Skupština*. But the two houses of the legislature voted down the Slovenian-Croatian motion by margins of 64–23 and 125–64.[169] Mikulić stayed in office.

But on December 12, 1989, Oskar Kovač, an economics professor of the University of Belgrade who was serving in Mikulić's cabinet, resigned his portfolio (relations with the EEC and EFTA), accusing Mikulić of failing to honor a promise he had made to the IMF to keep interest rates higher than the rate of inflation. Two weeks later, *Borba* published an article demanding that Mikulić resign. Four days later, on December 30, Mikulić resigned—a year and a half before the expiration of his four-year term.

Slovenia and Croatia had won because Mikulić's power base had eroded. A financial scandal in his native Bosnia in 1987 had not helped his cause. Fittingly, Mikulić's successor was Ante Marković, hitherto president of Croatia, who had had earlier experience in industrial management. Marković gradually put together a program aimed at curbing inflation (he had brought it down to about 5 percent by early 1990, although it later once more climbed to unmanageable levels). But when Marković presented his program to the respective republic assemblies in December 1989, Serbia and Vojvodina rejected it, the former claiming that "the implementation of this program would impose the greatest burden on the most endangered strata of the population."[170] All the other republics gave their approval, although Kosovo's assembly noted some objections to the program and indicated that its delegation in the *Skupština* would try to obtain some adjustments.[171]

Pressure for privatization can be traced to mid-1986, when Judge Čedo Grbić daringly spoke in favor of private enterprise, but the drive for reprivatization gathered steam around 1988, when it became legitimate for the communists themselves to sing the praises of private enterprise. Yugoslavia's first private factory was set up in April 1986, in a village just outside Maribor. Two years later, the Croatian *Sabor* approved a widening of possibilities for private initiative in tourism.[172] Also in 1988, a private stock exchange was established in Ljubljana. By September 1990, more than 30,000 private companies were operating in Yugoslavia.[173]

In late 1988 (still during Mikulić's prime ministership), a series of measures were adopted that changed procedures in management and in the selection of managers, enabled foreigners to set up economic enterprises in Yugoslavia, and expanded the maximum size allowed for private farms.[174] By June 1989, *Borba* was calling reprivatization "the last chance for socialism"[175]—a claim not without irony. And with the election of noncommunist governments in Slovenia, Croatia, Macedonia, and Bosnia in 1990, the process of reprivatization quickened.

9

Nationalist Tensions, 1968–90: Muslims, Albanians, Croats, Slovenes, Montenegrins

Where the national question [in Kosovo] is concerned, it is necessary to keep two facts in mind. First, every nation has the right to self-determination, including secession. Second, we do not support all national movements, but only those which are really against imperialism, that is, which are for truly democratic national development. That means that the Albanians in Kosovo and Metohija have the right to do what they want, how they want.

Josip Broz Tito, in a letter to the central committee of CP Albania, dated December 2, 1943[1]

If the nationalist euphoria of 1969–71 demonstrated anything, it was that, maxims of socialist unity notwithstanding, nationalist sentiment still represents a powerful oestrus in collective behavior in Yugoslavia. By the end of the 1970s, various Yugoslav figures, such as Gazmend Zajmi, were denying that the withering away of the state would entail the withering away of the nation.[2] And yet the hope continued to be expressed that "in socialism, in the process of overcoming and transcending the division of classes and the class character of labor, national emancipation grows into human emancipation, and the national community into a direct human community."[3] Equally important was the direct challenge to the LCY's policy—contained in the efforts to legitimize nationalism; to distinguish between positive, if exclusivist, nationalism and ethnocentric chauvinism; and to carve out a new ideological watering hole at which republican etatism might nourish itself.

But if Croatian nationalism and its political consequences represented the principal threat to the integrity and stability of the Yugoslav federation in the late 1960s and early 1970s, by the end of the 1970s, Bosnia-Herzegovina and Kosovo had become the loci of new ethnocentric malaises. Indeed, the Muslim question and the persistence of separatist sentiment among Yugoslavia's Albanians were, in the mid-1980s, the chief axes of nationalist disequilibrium in the Yugoslav system. But by the end of the 1980s, under the pressure of the disintegration of the system, nationalism was stirring among the members of every nationality.

The Muslim Question

Even before Muslim consciousness became politicized, the question of Bosnia's status in the federation was recognized as critical to the stabilization of interrepublican politics. Had Bosnia been allowed to remain part of Croatia, leaving intact the eastern boundaries set by the *Ustaše* state, the Croatian republic would have been assured of overweaning economic preponderance in the federation—with 40.1 percent of the country's population (by 1948 figures), 42.9 percent of its surface area, 40.2 percent of its hydroelectric potential, 73.9 percent of its coal, 64.3 percent of its petroleum, vast stretches of Bosnian forests, and the reasonably advanced Croatian industry.[4] Yet the incorporation of Bosnia-Herzegovina into Serbia was equally unthinkable to a generation that had languished under Greater Serbian exploitation and had devoted more than two decades to the struggle against Serbianization. Nor was there any confidence that dividing Bosnia between Croatia and Serbia could provide a basis for interethnic harmony.[5] A separate status for Bosnia was as necessary to socialist Yugoslavia as was a Montenegrin republic. The legitimacy of such a status in an ethnically based federal state hinged, however, on some particular ethnic claims by the prospective regional unit. As early as July 1940, at its Fifth Conference, the CPY discussed the case for the ethnic particularity of Bosnia's Muslim population. The conference failed to resolve the issue, except to declare itself "against the attempts of the Serbian and Croatian *bourgeoisies* to divide Bosnia-Herzegovina between themselves."[6] During the war, as the Partisans were setting about the business of establishing the new constitutional order, some voices suggested constituting Bosnia-Herzegovina not as a republic but as an autonomous province attached to the Serbian republic (on the pattern of Vojvodina). Others felt that Bosnia's lack of a numerically dominant nationality that was distinct from those of the other republics deprived it of any claim to republican status. Yet, apprehensive of Serbian tutelage, they advanced an alternative proposal: establishment of Bosnia-Herzegovina as an autonomous province directly linked to the Yugoslav federation (a proposal somewhat reminiscent of Bosnia's unique status under Habsburg rule).[7] Both these proposals were felt to provide insufficient guarantees of political stability, and so, when AVNOJ proclaimed the federal principle on November 29, 1943, Bosnia-Herzegovina was listed alongside the other republics—on the supposition that the 44.7 percent Serb, 23.9 percent Croat, and 30.9 percent Muslim configuration of the republic (by 1948 figures) was sufficient justification for that arrangement.

In the early postwar period, the Muslims were viewed as the least "national" of Yugoslavia's peoples, even as potentially anational (if they did not identify themselves either as Serbs or as Croats). Some conservatives viewed the Muslims as the anational core around which the new Yugoslav nation would be formed. No one dared suggest that the Muslims might themselves have a claim to recognition as a nationality group. Ranković, who covertly admired Soviet nationalities policy and favored emulation of Russification, was openly against the notion of Muslim particularity and denied the existence, or the possibility of, a Muslim nation.[8] Throughout this period, antagonistic groups advanced rival theories about the origins of the Bosnian Muslims. The best known in the West is the Bogomil theory, which, in the variant expostulated by Croatian nationalists, held that certain groups of ethnic Croats embraced a Manichaean religion known as Bogomilism, were thereafter persecuted by both the Catholic and Orthodox churches, and converted en masse to Islam when the comparatively liberal-minded Turks subsequently conquered the region.[9] This theory contends that the Muslims are "Islamic Croats" and describes Bosnia-Herzegovina as the Croatian hinterland (more than 60 percent Croatian). An alternative theory espoused by Serbs and Serbophiles holds that the so-called Muslims are in fact Serbian settlers from the time of the Turkish occupation who abandoned Orthodoxy and adopted Islam. This theory adds, for good measure, that some Serbian immigrants in the sixteenth and seventeenth centuries converted to Catholicism, so that many of today's Croats in Bosnia are Serbs by origin.[10] Later, when the Serbianists had been squeezed out of positions of power, Avdo Humo, one of Bosnia's foremost Muslim leaders, told a party conference that the Serbian theory was an assimilationist device aimed at the Croatian and Muslim people of Bosnia-Herzegovina and that "in the policy of assimilation . . . of the Muslims there was always present an attempt by the authorities to turn the Muslim national institutions into Serbian Muslim institutions."[11]

In time, a third theory was advanced by Muslim nationalists, who argued for a Turkish origin and traced their antecedents to immigration from Anatolia. This theory contests the customary belief that the Bogomil sect was a spin-off from Christianity and contends that the Bogomils were a non-Christian sect whose doctrines were related to Islam. According to this theory, the only thing Slavic about the Bosnian Muslims is their language, which they absorbed from the indigenous population.[12]

Ranković, whose repressive Serbianization policies were concentrated in Kosovo, Vojvodina, and Bosnia-Herzegovina (i.e., against the Albanians, the Hungarians, and the Muslims), subscribed to the second theory, that is, to the notion of a Serbian origin for the Muslims. During the period of his ascendancy, Ranković and his coterie emphasized Yugoslav unity and attempted to suppress any acknowledgement or discussion of ethnic particularities. Thus, not until the Eighth Congress in 1964—that is, after the expiration of twenty-four years—was the subject of Muslim nationality once again openly broached.[13]

The fall of Ranković was not merely a victory for the Croats or the decentralists, nor even "merely" for the forces of reform: it was a victory for Yugoslavia's Muslims. Within five years of the defeat of Ranković, the status of the Muslims was significantly enhanced on a number of levels. To begin with, shortly after Ranković's expulsion from the party, Tito made an ex cathedra declaration that the national identity and national specificity of the Muslims must be recognized—a pronouncement that made possible the recognition of the Muslims as a sixth Yugoslav nationality. Tito also endorsed the concept of *organic Yugoslavism (organsko Jugoslovenstvo)*, a harmonious symbiosis between national specificity and affective attachment to the Yugoslav federal community (as opposed to the concept of *integral Yugoslavism* endorsed by Ranković, under which national specificity and affective attachment to Yugoslavia were seen as antagonistic). Tito's endorsement of all three theories of Muslim ethnogenesis must be seen as an effort to deny exclusive legitimacy to any one theory and to close the debate once and for all.

Yet there continued to be uncertainties about the Muslims, centering especially on the relationship of Islam to their national identity. Many continued to doubt, in particular, whether the Muslims could lay claim to being more than a distinct cultural community. Though the "Bosniaks" were recognized as an ethnic group in 1961, and, despite the fact that the Fourth Congress of the Bosnian party (1964) had assured these "Bosniaks" of their right of self-determination, it was not conceded that the Bosnian Muslims were as fully "national" as the Serbs or Croats. R. V. Burks credits Muhammed Filipović, a professor at Sarajevo, with being the first (in 1967) to articulate the Muslim claim to separate national status.[14] Filipović's claim was politically premature, and he was summarily expelled from the party. But just a few months later—in February 1968—the central committee of the League of Communists of Bosnia-Herzegovina resolved, at its Eighteenth Session, that "experience has shown the damage of various forms of pressure and insistence, in the earlier period, that Muslims declare themselves ethnically to be Serbs or Croats because, as was demonstrated still earlier and as contemporary socialist experience continues to show, the Muslims are a separate nation."[15] This proclamation provoked certain groups in other republics, and, at the Fourteenth Session of the central committee of the LC Serbia (May 1968), Jovan Marjanović, supported by Dobrica Ćosić, declared that "the proclamation of a Muslim nation is senseless" and sought to obtain a resolution that would prevent the category "Muslim" (in the ethnic sense) from appearing on the next census. The resolution failed to find support, however, and the majority condemned Marjanović and Ćosić for their views, expelling them from the party.[16] Avdo Humo's three-part article for *Komunist* in July 1968 (under the title "Muslimani u Jugoslaviji") was a symptom of the increasing assertiveness of the Yugoslav Muslim community—no longer on the defensive after the fall of Ranković. Humo's warning was unmistakable: "Not to see the truth about the Muslims," he declared, "not to comprehend their specificity, means to fall headlong into arbitrary and subjective interpretations of national-social relations, to lose one's balance and to irritate, unnecessarily, the national feelings of a people and of individuals."[17] Lest anyone miss the point, Humo pointedly condemned as a sign of "confusion" the assertion that Muslim communal specificity was merely a matter of religion. The Fifth Congress of the LC B-H (January 9–11, 1969) capped the process of recognition of the Muslim nation by formally endorsing its complete equality with the other Yugoslav nationalities.

The final token of the coming of age of the Muslim nationality was its formal recognition on the 1971 census forms. In the 1948 census, Bosnia's Muslims had only three options: "Serb-Muslim," "Croat-Muslim," and "ethnically un-

Table 22. *Major Nationality Groups in Bosnia-Herzegovina*

	1948	*1953*	*1961*	*1971*	*1981*
TOTAL	2,565,277	2,847,790	3,277,935	3,746,111	4,124,008
Serbs	1,136,116	1,264,372	1,406,053	1,393,148	1,320,644
of which, Serb-Muslims	71,991	—	—	—	—
Croats	614,123	654,229	711,660	772,491	758,136
of which, Croat-Muslims	25,295	—	—	—	—
Muslims, ethnically undeclared	788,403	—	—	—	—
"Yugoslavs"	—	891,800	275,883	43,796	326,280
Muslims, in the ethnic sense	—	—	842,247	1,482,430	1,629,924

Sources: "Staat und Nationalität in Jugoslawien," in *Wissenschaftlicher Dienst Südosteuropa* 19 (8) (August 1970): 114; *Statistički godišnjak Jugoslavije 1979* (Belgrade: Savenzni zavod za statistiku, July 1979), p. 413; and Tanjug, February 16, 1982, in FBIS, Yugoslavia, February 17, 1982.

declared Muslim." "Muslim" continued to be treated as a matter of religious preference rather than ethnicity in the 1953 census, but the category "Yugoslav, ethnically undeclared" was introduced. It is now more or less acknowledged that the overwhelming majority of such "Yugoslavs, ethnically undeclared" were Muslims. Whereas the original census report listed 998,698 "Yugoslavs, ethnically undeclared," the 1979 edition of *Statistički Godišnjak* lists that same figure for "Muslims in the ethnic sense" for 1953. Even in the 1961 census, when "Yugoslav in the ethnic sense" was incorporated into the census, the Muslims were still more or less ignored; most of the reporting "Yugoslavs" were once again Muslims. The 1971 census was the first in which "Muslim" was treated as a fully recognized nationality (see table 22). Inevitably, the non-Muslim nationalities of Bosnia, that is, the Croats and Serbs, felt threatened by the specter of a new ethnic force, while Muslim factions were eager to legitimize the fruit of a long campaign. The 1971 census thus witnessed considerable nationalist agitation in Bosnia, as some groups pressured citizens to declare themselves "Muslims, in the ethnic sense," while others pressured them to declare themselves "Yugoslavs, ethnically undeclared."[18]

A coalition of conservatives and other forces that felt they stood to lose by the introduction of the new ethnic category attempted to restrict the ethnic Muslim category to the republic of Bosnia-Herzegovina and the Sandžak region of Serbia.[19] This ostensible compromise was clearly a rearguard reaction, a device to block full recognition of the Muslim nationality by linking it with republican citizenship. The move failed, and the party presidium, echoed by the leading body of the Socialist Alliance of Working People of Yugoslavia, declared that the Muslims constituted a national group on a par with Serbs,

Table 23. *Distribution of Ethnic Muslims in Yugoslavia, 1981*

Bosnia	1,630,033
Serbia proper	151,674
Montenegro	78,080
Kosovo	58,562
Macedonia	39,513
Croatia	23,740
Slovenia	13,425
Vojvodina	4,930

Source: *Statistički godišnjak Jugoslavije 1989* (Belgrade: Savenzni Zavod za Statistiku, 1989), p. 453.

Croats, Slovenes, Macedonians, and Montenegrins.[20] As a result, ethnic Muslims can be found in every Yugoslav federal unit (see table 23).

In the latter half of January 1971, immediately after the census, the Muslim question fueled a dramatic interrepublican confrontation and underlined the fragility of interethnic harmony. Esad Ćimić, a professor at the University of Sarajevo, sparked the controversy when, in the course of a program broadcast over Sarajevo television, he opined that Yugoslavia's Muslims were "a national hybrid" and not a nationality, because it was "too late for them to be a people (*narod*) and too early for them to be a nation (*nacija*)."[21] Although he did not exclude the possibility that they might have certain characteristic features of nationality, at the same time he questioned whether those who declared themselves "Muslims in an ethnic sense" were in fact doing so under duress.

Shortly thereafter, the executive committee of the Socialist Alliance of Working People of Bosnia-Herzegovina (SAWP B-H) issued a sharp condemnation of Ćimić's opinions. Atif Purivatra, president of the SAWP B-H's Commission for Interethnic Relations, said that Ćimić's sentiments were at odds with LCY policy in the area of interethnic relations and denounced the recently touted designation "Bosniak." The label was unacceptable, he said, because it was a denial of specificity and a negation of the Serbian, Croatian, and Muslim national feeling within the Bosnian republic. Ethnicity, Purivatra went on, cannot be determined on the basis of place of birth or of the ethnicity of one's parents but only on the basis of the individual's group consciousness, that is, on the basis of his ethnic self-identification. Accordingly, any suggestion that the Muslims were in some way "second-rate," "incompletely developed," or "immature" was not only demeaning but historically inaccurate.[22]

Though one might argue that Purivatra's comments were in a sense defensive, they incited the Macedonians and ignited a polemical exchange between Macedonia and Bosnia-Herzegovina over the status of the Muslims. The Macedonian party was sensitive to waxing Muslim nationalism because, though the majority of Macedonians are Orthodox—to the extent that Orthodoxy is identified with Macedonianness much as Catholicism is identified with Croatianness, the alleged Orthodoxy of certain pockets of Croats notwithstanding—a certain segment of Macedonian-speaking citizens are Muslim. The LC Macedonia insisted that "Muslims who speak Macedonian *are* Macedonian" and that they were, as they viewed themselves, "Macedonians of Islamic faith." "Historically and scientifically," the secretariat of the central committee of the LC Macedonia declared, "it is quite clear that Muslims of Slavic extraction living in Macedonia, who speak Macedonian, are nothing other than Macedonians."[23] *Nova Makedonija*, the official organ of the Macedonian party, worriedly warned that "the thesis about Muslims of Slavic origin in Macedonia, as parts of a nascent Muslim nation, conceals an immediate threat of the reawakening of an old hegemonism vis-à-vis Macedonian nationality, history, and culture."[24] The LC Macedonia adamantly denied that Muslims in Macedonia have any ethnic tie whatsoever with Muslims in Bosnia. The party said there was nothing peculiar about the fact that Macedonians can be either Orthodox or Muslim, adding that Albanians living in Macedonia can be Muslim, Catholic, or Orthodox.

Before the end of the month, Slavko Milosavlevski, secretary of the central committee of the LC Macedonia, received representatives of the Debarsko-Resavski region in western Macedonia (a region heavily populated by Muslims), who affirmed their support for the party's position and underlined their own Macedonian consciousness. Milosavlevski took advantage of this occasion to stress that religion has no connection with nationality. Yet his superior, Angel Čemerski, president of the central committee of the LC Macedonia, conceded that Macedonian national consciousness is likely to be weaker among Macedonia's Muslims.

Nova Makedonija's reference to "Muslim hegemonism" naturally rankled the Bosnian party, and Purivatra replied by accusing Macedonia of meddling in the internal affairs of Bosnia. *Nova Makedonija* replied two days later, complaining that Purivatra and his colleagues had misunderstood the article but reiterating that Macedonian Muslims could not belong to two ethnic groups at once. *Oslobodjenje*'s response two days later revealed that the Bosnian party continued to be sensitive to what it perceived as Macedonian underestimation of the development of Muslim national consciousness. Recalling Vjećeslav Holjevac's book, *Hrvati izvan domovine*, which had appeared a few years earlier and had treated Muslims of both Croatia and Bosnia as "Croats of the Islamic faith," Purivatra underlined the distinction between Muslim religion and Muslim nationality and maintained that Bosnia's Muslims ought to be considered a fully formed national group.

As the verbal volleys escalated, Kosovo entered into the fray when a meeting of the presidency of the SAWP Kosovo declared that "Muslim ethnic affiliation cannot be connected with this or that republic or spoken language, because every citizen, without regard to where she or he lives, enjoys the same freedom of expressing her or his national or ethnic affiliation, which cannot be confused with religious affiliation."[25] This was, perhaps, even further than the Bosnians had wanted to go, for the Kosovars had opened fire on the Macedonian dogma that "Muslims who speak Macedonian *are*, ipso facto, Macedonian," and hence allowed for the possibility that a portion of that republic's population might indeed be Muslim—*in the ethnic sense.*

This was followed by an article in *Kritika*, in which Vladimir Blašković, a professor of economics at the University of Zagreb, questioned the degree to which the Bosnian Muslims had developed a distinct ethnic consciousness. His skepticism could only signify de facto support for Holjevac's claim that Slavic Muslims are Croats. Shaken by the renewed challenge to the claims of Muslim nationalists, Branko Mikulić, president of the central committee of the LC B-H, nervously warned that such opinions undermined the equal status of the Muslim nationality with the other Yugoslav nationalities and thereby threatened the delicate balance achieved in Bosnia.

The squabble was clearly getting out of hand. Most interesting in all this ruckus is that the position advanced by each republic—whether Bosnia, Macedonia, Croatia, or Kosovo—is the theory most appropriate to its own conditions. Each unit attempted to impose its own theory on the others, even though that theory was only appropriate to its own republic. Bosnia wanted religiocultural heritage accepted as a sufficient basis for national identity. Macedonia wanted to emphasize language and ethnic descent; Croatia, chiefly ethnic descent. Kosovo, finally, with its mixed population of Muslims of Albanian, Turkish, and Macedonian descent and Orthodox citizens of Serbian, Albanian, and Macedonian descent, preferred to articulate what superficially appeared to be the most open-minded approach.

Eventually, the Serbian party lent oblique support to the Bosnia-Kosovo coalition when Latinka Perović, secretary of the central committee of the LC Serbia, declared it a matter of LCY policy that all people in Yugoslavia must be free to determine their own ethnic affiliation. This vaguely formulated declaration amounted to a reprimand of Macedonia and Croatia and succeeded in bringing this particular episode to a close. Ironically, Professor Ćimić, whose opinions on the subject had sparked the controversy, eventually declared himself a Croat and moved to Zadar.

Whatever amity might have been established between Bosnia and Kosovo was, however, dissipated in 1977 when alleged religious persecution created friction in relations between those two federal units. According to *Preporod*, Kosovar government representatives had been illegally interfering in Muslim religious instruction in Kosovo, and, though appeals to higher courts had resulted in the rights of religious instruction being upheld, the Kosovar authorities continued to interfere.[26]

The Kosovar-Macedonian quarrel over Muslim nationality resurfaced ten years later in the months preceding the 1981 census, when a Macedonian historian, Nijazi Limanovi, published a twenty-three-installment study, in the Skopje daily, *Večer* (September 25–October 21, 1980), on "Islamism in Macedonia." He argued that the Albanians of Kosovo were utilizing Islam in a strategy to de-Macedonize Macedonia. Limanovi's conclusion was that there were some 50,000 Muslim Macedonians in Macedonia who had previously reported themselves to be Albanians, Muslims, or even Serbs and that, in the forthcoming census, they should declare themselves to be Muslim Macedonians. Ali Hadri, a Kosovar historian, shot back in the Priština daily, *Rilindja*:

> Nijazi Limanovi is so maliciously disposed toward the Albanian nation that he seeks more falsifications by borrowing the most offensive adjectives from the old arsenal of the bourgeois monarchies of the Balkans. According to him, the Albanians were "primitive," "wild," "aggressive," "domineering," "abusive," "plunderers," "killers," and so forth. . . . It seems that he thought that, by debasing the Albanian people in a harsh manner, he could successfully argue about the mistaken theory that one of the main factors for the "Islamization of the Macedonians" and of the "Albanization of the Muslim Macedonians" has allegedly been the Albanians, who in order to attain this objective, have allegedly resorted to great pressure and unequaled injury against the Macedonian people.[27]

Hadri remonstrated against Limanovi's attempt to fix the Macedonian label on this group of 50,000 and asserted that, on the contrary, ethnic identity was a matter of individual determination—a right guaranteed by the Yugoslav constitution.

Having emerged victorious both in the 1971 controversy over Macedonian Muslims and in the debate surrounding the 1971 census, Muslim nationalists gained confidence and began to agitate for redesignating Bosnia a "Muslim Republic" in the same way that Serbia is the "Republic of the Serbs" and Macedonia the "Republic of the Macedonians."[28] Under the 1974 constitutional order, however, the Serbian constitution declared that the "Socialist Republic is the state of the Serbian nation and of sections of other nations and nationalities who live . . . in it," and Montenegro's constitution allowed that "the Socialist Republic of Montenegro is the state of the Montenegrin nation and of members of other nations and nationalities who live in it"—both thus listing only one titular nationality. But the Bosnian constitution asserted that "the Socialist Republic of Bosnia-Herzegovina is a socialist democratic state and a socialist self-managing democratic community of the working people, citizens, and nations of Bosnia-Herzegovina—Muslims, Serbs, and Croats, and of members of other nations and nationalities living in it."[29] Even Croatia and Macedonia fare better, both being termed "national states," while the Socialist Republic of Slovenia was said to be "a state based on the sovereignty of the Slovene nation and the people of Slovenia."[30] The Muslim nationalists wished the Bosnian constitution to read something like "the Socialist Republic of Bosnia-Herzegovina is a state based on the sovereignty of the Muslim nation; it is the national state of the Muslim nation, and the state of the members of the Serbian and Croatian nations who live in it, as well as of the members of other nations and nationalities who live in it." The distinction between "national state" and "state" was drawn in the Croatian constitution and implied a somewhat higher status for the possessors of the "national state."

About the same time that agitation for a Muslim republic began, certain Bosnian linguists started toying with the idea that Bosanski, the language of the Muslims, should be recognized as a distinct language.[31] By 1972–73, the party had concluded that increasing Muslim ethnic consciousness was potentially threatening, and, in 1972, two leading Muslim politicians—Avdo Humo and Osman Karabegović—were dismissed from their posts for alleged Muslim "exclusivism" and "nationalism." The following year, 1973, the earliest warnings were sounded about "pan-Islamism" in Bosnia and about Muslim nationalists' aspirations toward "supremacy" in Bosnia.[32] Muslim nationalism, the party admonished, was no special case, but was just as "dangerous" as Serbian or Croatian nationalism.[33] In a four-part article for *Oslobodjenje* (February 19–22, 1974), Aziz Hadžihasanović warned of the misconception that Muslim nationalism, unlike Serbian and Croatian nationalism, was somehow "naive, harmless, . . . on another political plane." That is sheer "confusion," charged Hadžihasanović, for Muslim nationalism, even when wearing a "red veil," is a breeding ground for "antisocialist forces."[34] Hadžihasanović also condemned efforts to identify everything positive in Bosnian culture with the Islamic legacy. He upbraided Muslim nationalists for having sought, during the October 1973 war, to align Yugoslavia squarely with the Arabs and against Israel—a move that, according to him, would have compromised Yugoslavia's policy of nonalignment.[35] The Muslim clergy, the *ulema*, had become increasingly active spokesmen for Muslim ethnic interests and repeatedly sought permission to establish cultural institutions to stimulate Muslim national identity. Even before the census, *Preporod* (June 15, 1970), the official organ of the Islamic community of Bosnia, had complained that "in an organizational sense we still exist only as an Islamic community. Neither as Muslims in the ethnic sense nor as Muslims in the religious sense do we have any specific institutions through which we might develop our Islamic and Muslim activity, other than the existing institutions and organs of the Islamic community."[36] More recently, nationally conscious Muslims renewed efforts to found autonomous cultural institutions. Citing the existence of Matica Hrvatska and Matica Srpska, Muslim nationalists demanded the establishment of a Matica Muslimanska and the organization of Muslim cultural-artistic societies. But the LCY consistently blocked such endeavors, calling them efforts to obtain a "privileged status" and to establish a power base from which to pursue a policy of "discrimination against the other religions."[37] In October 1979, these "Islamic socialists," under the spell of their Arab coreligionists, tried to capture *Preporod* and use it for their own purposes. This effort failed, and in November 1979 the faction was blasted for groveling in "the pigsty of nationalism, which is only one step away from fratricidal genocide."[38]

In the late 1960s and early 1970s, attendance at Muslim religious services in Yugoslavia seemed in decline, and some mosques drew only meager attendance. But this situation changed in the late 1970s, when a new generation, educated to think of the Bosnian Muslims as a national group and encouraged by contacts with a renascent Middle East, began to look to Islam as a basis for political mobilization. In April 1983, Yugoslav authorities uncovered an illegal organization of Bosnian Muslims described as working for the creation of an Islamic republic in Yugoslavia and having illegal ties with "reactionary" Muslims abroad. Eleven persons, including two imams, were put on trial and, in the course of the month-long proceedings, were said to have described communism as a threat to Islam, welcomed anti-Yugoslav turmoil in Kosovo, criticized Yugoslav nationalities policy as aimed at the Serbianization of the Muslims, plotted to eliminate the Serbian and Croatian populations in Bosnia-Herzegovina, and manipulated the religious feelings of others in an effort to mobilize support for a militant Islam. They were ultimately sentenced to prison for terms averaging more than eight years[39] but were amnestied at the end of 1988. Among those sentenced was Alija Izetbegović, whom the authorities had previously incarcerated for Islamic fundamentalism in 1946.

Certain of the Bosnian *ulema* tried to draw a line between "positive political activity" and "negative political activity" on the part of religious organizations and thus to claim for the Islamic community a legitimate role in the political constellation. This has often been combined with a desire to stress that religion is, after all, the source of Muslim "ethnicity." But the LCY, which feared the identification of religion and nationality, wanted to have it both ways: namely, to derive a new nationality from a religion, but yet to deny that derivation and suppress demands based on it.

The rising tide of Muslim nationalism in Yugoslavia probably owed more to indigenous factors than to any influence from abroad. The nationalist renaissance of the 1969–71 period was, in particular, an important stimulus of Muslim nationalism, insofar as Croatian and Serbian calls for the annexation to their respective republics of all or part of Bosnia provided the sort of cultural threat that so quickly inflames ethnic sensitivities. In any event, Muslim nationalism in Yugoslavia predated the worldwide Islamic revival by several years. At this time, moreover, the Muslims revised the dormant "concept of Muslims as the 'only real Bosnians' and demanded the formation of separate Muslim national institutions in which the Muslim intelligentsia would gather and oppose the activity of Croatian and Serbian institutions."[40]

It is somewhat ironic that Tito, in one of his last public addresses (November 25, 1979, just before the incident that provoked Pozderac's condemnation of the "pigsty of nationalism"), should have claimed that "the nations of Bosnia-Herzegovina can be proud of their successes . . . because they have succeeded in outgrowing mutual conflicts and frictions among nationalities."[41] There was a degree of stability, but all the nationality groups in Bosnia could imagine other possibilities (e.g., proclamation of a Muslim republic, annexation of Bosnia by Croatia, annexation of Bosnia by Serbia, etc.), some of which appeared more palatable to certain people than the status quo. Edvard Kardelj once wrote that "a nation does not arise by chance, and when it does arise, it must doubtless have a social function."[42] As for this functional view of nationality, it might be argued that the Bosnian Muslims served to keep the Croats and Serbs from destroying each other. Such, at least, seemed to be the view of the LCY, even if it feared the growth of rampant nationalism.

Albanian Nationalism in Kosovo

Albanian nationalism is a problem for interrepublican relations for at least five reasons: (1) it directly affects relations between Kosovo on the one hand and Serbia, Macedonia, and Montenegro on the other (since Kosovo has long been dominated by Serbs and since many Albanians are living in Macedonia); (2) Albanian agitation for republican status for Kosovo—the central force for upgrading the autonomous provinces—has an impact on the interrepublican balance of power; (3) the nationalism of one group has an incendiary effect on the others; (4) the threat of secession is not merely a matter of concern to the federation as a whole but also to its several parts; and (5) Kosovo was the ultimate test of the Titoists' Marxist premise that economic equality causes nationalist temper to abate.

More than one-third of the 3.5 million Albanians in the world live in Yugoslavia. Most of Yugoslavia's Albanians live in Kosovo (about 1.2 million), in western Macedonia near lakes Prespa and Ohrid and in the valley of the Black Smoke (Crni Dim) (about another 350,000), or in Montenegro near Ulcinj along the Albanian frontier (yet another 50,000). There is also an important pocket of Albanians in Belgrade. During the Second World War the Kosovo region was attached to Italian-dominated Albania—a solution welcomed by most Albanians.[43] Tito's partisans, therefore, experienced considerable difficulty recruiting Albanians in Kosovo and only a few joined the partisans. Svetozar Vukmanović-Tempo, who was in charge of organizing partisan activity in Kosovo, later recalled that "the Albanian population remained suspicious toward all those who fought for the resurrection of Yugoslavia, whether it was a question of old or new Yugoslavia. In their eyes, that was less than what they [had] received from the occupiers."[44] And for several years after the war officially ended, Albanian guerrilla groups held out in Kosovo, desperately resisting reincorporation into Yugoslavia.

In interwar Yugoslavia, the Serbian-dominated government had driven out large numbers of Albanians from Kosovo and had turned their land over to Serbian and Montenegrin colonists. These had, in turn, been driven out of Kosovo in 1941. Fearing that the return of these colonists would only further aggravate what was already a delicate situation, the federal Commissariat for Internal Affairs issued a decree in 1945, barring their return.[45] But colonists or no colonists, some Albanians were determined to opt out of Yugoslavia. In July 1946, Albanian separatists ("Ballists") held an underground congress in the village of Lipovo. But gradually their ranks were decimated by arrests. Some were captured and tried in October 1946, still others were condemned to death in January 1947.[46]

As early as May 1945, Djoko Pajković, secretary of the district committee of Kosmet (as Kosovo was then called) warned that if the communists repeated the error of the interwar kingdom by assigning leadership positions in Kosovo predominantly to Serbs and Montenegrins, the local Albanians would revolt.[47] But this warning fell on deaf ears, and Serbs and Montenegrins were overwhelmingly dominant in the leadership, as well as in the state security forces and the regular police. As of 1956, Serbs accounted for some 23.5 percent of the province's population, but 58.3 percent of the members of the security forces and 60.8 percent of the regular police. Montenegrins accounted for only 3.9 percent of the local population, but fully 28.3 percent of security forces were Montenegrins, alongside 7.9 percent of regular police. By contrast, Albanians, who already numbered 64.9 percent of the population, accounted for only 13.3 percent of security police and 31.3 percent of regular police.[48]

Tension between Serbs and Albanians in Kosovo ran high in the 1950s, and the provincial police often terrorized the local population. In July 1956, several ethnic Albanians were tried in Prizren on charges of espionage (for Albania) and subversion. They were convicted and given prison terms ranging from three to twelve years. In the course of the proceedings, testimony was presented implicating several leading functionaries—specifically, Mehmet Hodža, provincial deputy in the Serbian Assembly; Fadilj Hodža, member of the executive council of Kosovo-Metohija; Šeho Hasani, provincial deputy in the Serbian Assembly; Čamilja Šarko, former deputy in the Serbian Assembly; Ismet Sačiri, member of the executive council of Kosovo-Metohija; Dževet Hamza, provincial deputy in the federal Assembly; Avdi Bakalli, former committee secretary; and Saiti Bakalli, functionary of the District People's Committee. All were said to have engaged in espionage for the Albanian secret service. Obviously, testimony to this effect was troubling to local Albanian communists, and already in 1956 the district assembly of Kosmet allegedly decided to collect all the materials and documentation related to the Prizren trial and destroy them. They subsequently declared that the entire affair had been an anti-Albanian machination of the part of UDBa (the secret police, controlled by Ranković). Until 1988, this version of the trial was almost universally accepted, and most books on the subject describe the Prizren trial as a miscarriage of justice. But in 1988, Ljiljana Bulatović wrote a book in which she argued that the case should be reexamined, claiming that the Albanians had in fact been working against Serbian domination, in effect, that the trial had been justified.[49] What really happened in Prizren in 1956? The answer to this question awaits scholarly analysis. What can be said here is that its importance for Serb-Albanian relations is clear: it seriously increased friction between the two and created yet another issue dividing the two peoples.

Ranković, the head of the secret police, deeply distrusted non-Serbs in general and Albanians in particular. He believed that surveillance was the best method for ruling Kosovo. As early as the winter of 1956, UDBa undertook to confiscate the weapons of the Albanian population of Kosovo—a project that provoked resistance and resulted in the deaths of a number of Albanians before an estimated nine thousand firearms were confiscated.[50] But the disruption of the political equilibrium in Kosovo is normally traced to 1966, when revelations of Serbian dominance of the governmental, party, and security apparatus in Kosovo inflamed resentment among the Kosovar Albanians.

Backward by all the standard socioeconomic measures, Kosovars had no reason to be grateful for Belgrade's rule. As late as 1971, 36 percent of Kosovo's Albanians were officially illiterate. Since statistics failed to distinguish between formal literacy and working literacy, however, the actual level of illiteracy among the Albanians at any given time is much worse than the statistics indicate.[51] The situation is aggravated, moreover, by a patriarchal proclivity for Albanian families to keep their female children from attending school—a practice that made the work of the authorities much more difficult.[52] There have been enduring problems of infrastructure: even in the 1974–75 school year, 564 Kosovar towns and villages lacked elementary schools, and many were hampered by the lack of good roads to bus children.

As Ranković's power base eroded and the nature of his practices in Kosovo came to light, the demand for reform became irresistible. The Sixth Session (1966) of the Serbian party's central committee (CC) issued a condemnation of "certain sections of the State Security Apparatus," that is, of Ranković's domain, for discriminatory and illegal practices "entirely contrary to the LCY program and the Yugoslav constitution," especially vis-à-vis the Albanians. The subsequent Fourth Plenum of the CC of the LCY, reviewing conditions in Kosovo, amplified this judgment and warned of Greater Serbian tendencies within the ranks of the League of Communists. The consensus was that Greater Serbian nationalism was the greater stimulus to Greater Albanian separatism and, therefore, had to be systematically expunged.[53] Albanian separatism was identified as a problem at this time, even though Kosovo had not yet been shaken by ethnic riots.

These conclusions were echoed by the provincial committee of the central committee of the Kosovar branch of the LCY at its seventh session of that year. Excoriating "Greater Serbian chauvinistic tendencies," the provincial committee warned that "every nationalism . . . represents a menace to LCY policy. . . . Communists must be alert to the man and active in the struggle against all nationalist deviations."[54] By then Ranković had slipped from power, and command of the security forces in Kosovo had been turned over to Albanian cadres. Subsequently, the Albanians were also granted permission to celebrate the 500th anniversary of the death of the Albanian national hero, Skanderbeg. But Serbs were still far more likely than Albanians to find employment in the party-governmental apparatus, and the Tenth Session of the LC of Kosovo (1967) paid particular attention to the ethnic structure of employment in the province.

These developments sent Marjanović and Ćosić into a rage. The same duo that had blasted the "senseless proclamation of a Muslim nation," Marjanović and Ćosić castigated the open promotion of Albanian nationalism and irredentism in Kosovo and lamented that Serbs had become the victims of systematic reverse discrimination insofar as employment in Kosovo was concerned. Yet, despite the resistance of Serbophile conservatives like Marjanović and Ćosić, the tide was turning. In February 1968, those Albanians who had been convicted in the Prizren trial of 1956 were rehabilitated on the grounds that the security apparatus under Ranković had rigged the proceedings, fabricated evidence, and bribed witnesses.[55] On the urging of Kosovar Albanians Mahmut Bakali and Salih Nuši, the LCY agreed in the spring of 1968 to substitute the neutral term "Albanian" for the term "Shiptar," which the Albanians considered pejorative but which had hitherto been standard vocabulary in official as well as unofficial business.

In summer 1968, the Commission for Constitutional Questions met. It consisted of delegates from all the chambers of the federal *Skupština*. Their meetings were accompanied by public discussions throughout the country. In Djakovica and Peć, local communists criticized the draft drawn up by the Provincial Committee for Constitutional Questions and demanded that Kosovo be reconstituted as a republic.[56] But this demand was not confined to local committees; it was, in fact, a sentiment shared by many Albanian communists in Kosovo. The Albanian-language daily, *Rilindja*, reflected this broad sentiment by urging the same thing in an August 1968 editorial.[57] But the provincial party apparatus itself shied away from this and pushed, instead, for an "enrichment" of the prerogatives of the province.[58]

At the plenum of the CC of the LC Serbia, held in early November 1968 (i.e., just before the 1968 Kosovo riots), it was finally proposed that the designations of the party organizations of the autonomous provinces be changed: henceforth, the League of Communists of Serbia for Vojvodina would be simply the League of Communists of Vojvodina, and the League of Communists of Serbia for Kosovo and Metohija would be simply the League of Communists of Kosovo-Metohija. The Sixth Congress of the LC Serbia (mid-November 1968) authorized the provincial party organizations to pass their own statutes. The Albanian component was immediately strengthened in the Kosovar party organization (though it must be admitted that Albanians and Hungarians were still significantly underrepresented in the respective party organizations of Kosovo and Vojvodina). The Albanians were becoming restless precisely at this point, when the slow beginnings of reform had become unmistakable—a confirmation of Machiavelli and Crane Brinton's proposition that repression becomes intolerable once reforms are begun.

There were signs of steady deterioration in Serbian-Albanian relations as 1967 drew on, including sporadic eruptions of interethnic violence.[59] By October 1968, reports surfaced of anti-Serbian demonstrations in Suva Reka, Prizren, and Peć. Participants were said to number only a "couple of hundred," and officials tried to peg the blame on "foreign [i.e., Albanian] intelligence services."[60] Officials failed to assuage Albanian discontent, and tension mounted. On November 27, the eve of Albanian National Independence Day, Kosovar Liberation Day, and the anniversary of the proclamation of the Yugoslav federal state—all celebrated, by an ironic twist of fate, on November 29—"Kosmet" (Kosovo-Metohija) exploded in violence. Demonstrators numbering in the hundreds smashed windows and overturned cars in Priština, and the anti-Serbian demonstrations quickly spread to other towns in Kosovo, leaving thirty-seven injured (among them, thirteen police) and one dead. There were reports that some rioters demanded annexation by Albania and that riotous crowds could be heard chanting "Long live Enver Hoxha!"[61] The protestors drew up a list of demands that included dropping "Metohija" (a Serbian word) from the official name of the region, its redesignation as a republic, the extension of the right of self-determination to Kosovo (the right of a republic but not of an autonomous province), and the establishment of an independent university in Priština. At the same time, the disturbances spread to the Macedonian cities of Gostivar and Tetovo, both with large Albanian populations. Haberl reports that the children of Kosovo's leading political figures took part in the Kosovo riots, but adds that this was firmly denied by those concerned.[62]

The League of Communists responded swiftly and decisively. The ring-leaders of the apparently well-organized demonstrations received jail terms of up to five years, and those held chiefly accountable for the unrest in Macedonia received sentences of up to seven years. Another forty-four persons in Kosovo received jail terms of up to thirty days. By mid-February, moreover, thirty-seven LCY members had been expelled from the party for participation in or support of the demonstrations.

The federal government was not prepared to indulge in the partition of Serbia; nevertheless, ameliorative measures had to be taken. The demand for republican status was flatly turned down. Both Kosovo and Vojvodina, however, were granted some of the prerogatives of republics, and the modifier "socialist" was appended to their official designations (hence, the Socialist Autonomous Province of Kosovo). In December, in another concession to the Albanians, Kosovo-Metohija was redesignated simply Kosovo, dropping the purely Serbian "Metohija," and the Kosovars were also given permission to fly the Albanian flag alongside the Yugoslav. Furthermore, though jailing thirty of the leading Albanian agitators for extended periods, Belgrade took steps to improve the economic situation in Kosovo and to promote more Albanians to positions of authority. Finally, there followed the creation of an independent University of Priština in 1969 and the rapid Albanianization of both faculty and student body in what had hitherto been a branch of the University of Belgrade.

Although this poured oil on the waters of discontent and eased federal regime–Albanian minority relations, Serbian-Albanian relations within Kosovo remained tense. For the Serbs, the demographic threat in Kosovo is particularly poignant because the region contains many shrines of the medieval Serbian kingdom: most important, it was at Kosovo polje (the Field of the Blackbirds) that the Serbian army was crushed by the Turks in 1389, and the battlefield has retained great patriotic value for the Serbs. The region, however, is now overwhelmingly inhabited by Albanians, who have had by far the highest birth rate of all of Yugoslavia's peoples. As a result of the turmoil, moreover, Albanian and Serbian neighbors became openly hostile and the university polarized along ethnic lines; the result—as revealed in March 1969—was that thousands of Serbs and Montenegrins streamed out of Kosovo, most of them professionals and specialists with higher education. Even the dead were not immune to the ethnic hatred, as Albanians broke up Serbian and Montenegrin gravestones in Kosovo. Meanwhile, relations between Albanians and Macedonians remained tense, as the first of some one hundred accused instigators was sentenced to seven years at hard labor on March 15, 1969.

Obviously, the Kosovo question has remained unresolved. It is worth noting, at the same time, that recurrent problems with Albanian nationalism manifest some of the same characteristics that marked the Croatian crisis. First, there were the instances of anomic and collective violence manifested in the demonstrations of 1968, the mutual incitement of the two national groups, and the Serbian exodus itself. Second, there was strong evidence that members of the local nationality were prepared to organize in defense of their aspirations: in 1975, for example, four Yugoslav citizens of Albanian nationality were imprisoned for plotting the secession of Kosovo and its attachment to Albania.[63] Third, conflict in Kosovo, as in Croatia, was transmuted to the elite level: thus, at the Twenty-ninth Plenum of the Kosovo party organization in June 1971, Serbs and Montenegrins exchanged broadsides with Albanian delegates over questions of rights for the Serbian minority in Kosovo and alleged separatist plots. Finally, the Kosovo case exemplifies conflict accommodation as practiced in communist Yugoslavia: jail the troublemakers but grant their nondisintegrative demands.

Albanian gains in Kosovo, though modest, excited a Serbian backlash. Serbs became apprehensive at Albanian inroads, dreaded the transfer of any property from Serb to Albanian, and agitatedly spoke of "losing" Kosovo. Shortly after the 1971 census, a number of periodicals began to question the validity of the Kosovo count and to spread the idea that Albanians there had pressured the indigenous Slavs to declare themselves Albanians. Stane Stanić, writing in the Belgrade weekly, *NIN*, in August 1971, followed this tack, adding that the Albanians were also exerting unrelenting pressure on Serbian and Montenegrin inhabitants to leave Kosovo. Stanić concluded that the census results were unreliable, and that the Slavic proportion had been seriously underestimated.[64] As the Albanian component of the central committee of the LC Kosovo edged upward from 61.7 percent (in 1973) to 62.5 percent (in 1974) and the Albanians registered small gains in governmental employment, Serbian nationalists clamored that the status quo in Kosovar employment and political representation was entirely satisfactory and opposed any further changes in the ethnic structure of the civil service in Kosovo. Yet the Albanians tallied some 73.7 percent of the province's population in 1971—they accounted for 77.5 percent in 1981—and they were demanding equivalent representation.[65]

Nebi Gasi, chairman of Kosovo's Committee for Interethnic Relations, told a Belgrade audience in 1977 that, although eight out of every one hundred Albanians in Kosovo had jobs in the social sector, seventeen out of every one hundred Serbs and twenty out of every one hundred Montenegrins in Kosovo were employed in the social sector. This reflected the fact that of the 128,000 Kosovars employed in the social sector at the end of 1974, 58.2 percent were Albanians, 31 percent were Serbs, 5.7 percent were Montenegrins, and 5 percent were members of other nationality groups.[66] By 1978, however, Albanians accounted for 83 percent of Kosovars employed in the social sector, with Serbs numbering only 9.3 percent. By 1980, Albanians constituted fully 92 percent of those employed in the social sector, with Serbs dramatically underrepresented at a mere 5 percent.[67]

During the 1970–71 period, when political controls were loosened, chauvinist outbursts became more frequent and more open, in Kosovo as elsewhere. The Istok region of Kosovo was identified at this time as a particular trouble spot. With anti-Serbian sentiment sweeping through Croatia and Kosovo, Mujo Krasnici, a Kosovar student, told a receptive Croatian audience in Zagreb that the Albanians were the "original" Kosovars, that the Slavs were "guests," and that the people of Kosovo wanted their own socialist republic.[68] In mid-December 1971, at the same time as Croatian students at the University of Zagreb were bringing matters in Croatia to a head, Albanian students clashed with Slavic students (mostly Serbian and Macedonian) at the University of Priština. In a stormy session of the provincial committee of the LC Kosovo, committee member Jovo Sotra observed that Albanian separatist nationalism was the principal source of instability in the province.[69]

Interethnic tension has remained high in Kosovo over the years, and distrust between the Slavs and the local Albanians runs deep. Indeed, the heavily Albanianized security forces enjoyed only a brief respite between 1969 and 1973, when Albanian separatists launched their first large-scale propaganda offensive since the demonstrations of November 1968. Yugoslav security forces discovered evidence of an underground separatist organization known as the Revolutionary Movement of United Albania, led by Adem Demachi, but were unable to uproot it. This group, together with the so-called Marxist-Leninist Communist party of Albanians of Yugoslavia, which may have enjoyed Albania's support, undertook what the regime labeled "serious propaganda actions" in 1973–75. The group called for the secession of Kosovo and those parts of Macedonia and Montenegro inhabited by Albanians and the creation of a Greater Albania that would be specifically anti-Serbian in orientation. This "Marxist-Leninist" party was apparently uncovered by Yugoslav security organs in early 1975. Another underground group, similar in nature and dubbed the National Liberation Movement of Kosovo, was discovered shortly thereafter. Two of its leading members, both students at the University of Priština and both in their mid-twenties, were given lengthy prison sentences. Five more groups, operating in Priština and Uroševac, were discovered in the course of 1979 and 1980. Security organs turned up still another such group early in 1981, which, according to Franjo Herljević, minister of the interior, had been operating in conjunction with the pro-Albanian "Red Front" organization.[70]

There were reports of student demonstrations in Priština in December 1974, in which more than one hundred ethnic Albanians were said to have been arrested. The Eleventh Provincial Conference of the CC of LC Kosovo warned that "Communists must wage a concrete and decisive campaign against particularistic-separatist Albanian nationalism."[71] In 1976, thirty-one Albanians were tried in connection with separatist activities during 1973–75 and sentenced to prison terms of up to fifteen years.[72] Another fifty Kosovar Albanians were tried and sentenced early in 1980 for subversive activity.[73] In fact, between 1974 and the beginning of 1981, the state security service had arrested more than 600 Kosovars for Albanian separatism.[74]

In addition to organized and semiorganized activity of this nature, anomic violence repeatedly broke out in Kosovo during the 1970s. In the spring of 1978, for instance, the province was shaken by massive prison riots. Albanian prisoners, claiming that their Serbian guards were racially prejudiced and guilty of brutally manhandling Albanian inmates, created a makeshift barricade from parts of the deteriorating prison. Throughout 1979, Albanian nationalists in Kosovo distributed pamphlets attacking Belgrade and stirring up ethnic passions, and, late in 1979, an angry crowd of Albanians wrecked a police station in Novi Pazar.[75]

At the same time, organized Albanian separatism was spreading to neighboring Macedonia. Between 1978 and 1981, Yugoslav security organs reportedly uncovered and suppressed two illegal Albanian separatist organizations operating in Macedonia. At its session of July 3, 1980, the High Court of Skopje convicted the alleged ringleaders of the first of these organizations of treasonous activities during 1977–80. The leaders received jail terms of three to six years.[76] The presumed leaders of the second organization, a more or less formal revolutionary party known as the National Party of Labor that was reportedly active between June 1979 and February 1981, were put on trial in Skopje in May 1981. The five accused were convicted of carrying out subversive activities in Gostivar and surrounding villages and received prison sentences of seven to thirteen-and-a-half years.[77]

The situation was complicated by another factor, however. The increasingly Albanian-dominated provincial leadership in Kosovo was loathe to allow Serbian involvement in antiseparatist efforts, partly because of a natural sympathy with the province's Albanian ethnics and partly because of a fear that the problems might incite the leadership of the Serbian republic to retract some of the political powers that the Kosovar party had—sometimes unconstitutionally—acquired. The provincial leadership engaged in a massive cover-up, the scale of which was only appreciated after the province erupted in violence in the spring of 1981. Certainly the LCY was well aware that trouble was brewing in Kosovo. The arrests of several hundred Albanian nationalists in 1979, on charges of distributing subversive material, and a telltale eruption of ethnic turmoil in Kosovo in May 1980 were powerful reminders that the festering discontent retained political significance. State security organs were placed in a state of alert in the months following Tito's demise. As early as 1977, in fact, Kardelj had warned his colleagues that if the party failed to adopt a resolute policy that would narrow the economic gap and tranquilize interethnic tensions in the province, Kosovo would explode in violence. But Belgrade had only sketchy information about the Albanian separatist movement; the Kosovar ministry of the interior, which was well informed about the strength and doings of at least some of the underground organizations, was withholding its intelligence.[78] Thus, although Albanian-language *Rilindja* warned of persistent problems with Albanian separatist groups (in 1975), the Kosovar leadership, when dealing with the Belgrade media, was far less open.[79] In 1975, for instance, Mahmut Bakali told a Tanjug reporter that interethnic "relations [in Kosovo] are good, because there is a good degree of brotherhood and unity and of trust between nations and nationalities living here."[80] Again, in 1980, Bakali, the leading Kosovar politician at the time, would tell *Politika* that "the efforts of enemies have not found wide support among the Albanian masses . . . [which] shows that the devotion of the Albanians to Tito's Yugoslavia is durable and indestructible."[81]

But the information problem involved not merely the Serbia-Kosovo relationship; it was, in fact, also an internal problem for Kosovo. As Živorad Igić noted in an article that appeared in *Obeležja* (the Kosovar party organ) in 1979, the district committees in the province were routinely withholding information from the provincial committee. In addition, the growing tendency to publish internal information in Kosovo in Albanian only tended to leave local Serbs ignorant of important aspects of basic issues.[82]

In February 1981, on the eve of a new eruption of ethnically inspired tumult, both *Komunist* and *Politika* warned of simmering discontent in the province, the latter adding that "antisocialist forces" continued to organize hostile provocations in various parts of Kosovo.[83] In spite of this, and in spite of the evident latent instability in the province, few observers were prepared for the vehemence of the nationalistically inspired riots that shook the province in March and April of 1981. In fact, when some two thousand Albanian students at the University of Priština went on a rampage on March 11, officials initially denied any ethnic link and claimed that the riot had been sparked by dissatisfaction with bad cooking in the university cafeteria. The mere fact that the riots lasted two days, producing thirteen injured (including one policeman), suggested that more than bad food was involved.[84] Indeed, a closer investigation reveals that the provincial committee of the League of Communists of Kosovo (LCK) had been scheduled to discuss the province's abysmal economic problems on March 13 and that the local press had been running a series of disturbing articles on that theme in anticipation of the committee meeting. The press reports no doubt exacerbated the already waxing resentment among university students in Priština and may have occasioned the March riots. Yet, despite the involvement of some two thousand students, the first wave of riots attracted little attention.

Further demonstrations by Prizren students on March 25 and by Priština university students on March 26 produced thirty-five injuries (twenty-three demonstrators and twelve police) and resulted in twenty-one arrests. Demonstrations followed in Obilić on March 31. Subsequently, on April 1, violent riots broke out at the University of Priština (whose full-time student body numbered 37,000 at the time). Beginning with marauding protesters who smashed factory equipment and shop windows and set trucks on fire, tensions quickly escalated into open street battles, in which some rioters used kindergarten-aged children as shields against police.[85] Miners from the nearby coal mine and workers from the electric power station in the neighboring town of Obilić joined the students as the disorder spread to Podujevo, Leposlavić, Vučiturn, Vitana, and Glogovac. By April 3, the strife had spread to Kosovoska Mitrovica and Uroševac. Hardly any municipality in Kosovo abstained from the violence. Many of the demonstrators—said to have numbered between ten and twenty thousand—were armed, and in the ensuing clashes with the riot police, perhaps as many as one thousand persons were killed and about one thousand persons injured, many by firearms.[86] The revolutionary overtones of the Albanian riots were unmistakable. Rioters demanded either republican status for Kosovo or outright secession. In the official viewpoint, these amounted to the same thing.[87] The regime rushed in tanks and armored personnel carriers, imposed a curfew throughout the province, cut off telephone connections with the rest of Yugoslavia, and established control points on all roads into Priština. Commandos and soldiers armed with machine-guns moved in to patrol the streets, and helicopters hovered overhead. Some two dozen ringleaders were jailed immediately, and a state of emergency was declared.[88] On April 5, Priština's factories were reopened, though a ban on public meetings remained in effect. Only on April 8 did the Yugoslav authorities finally lift the nighttime curfew.

But pacification failed, as local Albanians continued to scrawl anti-Serbian and anti-Yugoslav graffiti on public walls, to distribute insurrectionary pamphlets, and to disrupt instruction in schools. Trains were derailed, and the power station in Kosovo Polje, the furniture factory in Uroševac, and numerous other installations and buildings suffered varying degrees of damage in a rash of unexplained fires. Further strife flared up in Istok on the night of April 30 and at the University of Priština on May 12.[89] Eventually, the schools, closed once and reopened two weeks later, were closed for a second time, and the school year was declared over. *Borba* openly asked why the University of Priština had been encouraged to grow so large, when it was inconceivable that its graduates could find jobs commensurate with their training and ambitions.

Meanwhile, the unrest spread to Montenegro, where *Borba* reported the perpetration of "incidents" by the local Albanian minority in the capital city of Titograd and the scrawling of anti-Tito slogans on shop windows. In January 1982, it was revealed that Albanian nationalists were active in the Bar commune.[90]

In Macedonia, which had endured prolonged Albanian unrest thirteen years before, there were initially no hints of turmoil. Officials did charge that Albanian nationalists, including Muslim clergy of Albanian extraction, had exerted pressure on Macedonian Gypsies and Turks and on Muslim Macedonians, during the census taken early that year, to declare themselves Albanians.[91] The apparent calm notwithstanding, the Macedonian security apparatus was put on high alert. By the end of May, reports surfaced that local Albanians were distributing insurrectionary and irredentist literature, writing revolutionary slogans in public places, and engaging in various acts of desecration. These activities, which were especially serious in the Ohrid and Tetovo districts, prompted Yugoslav authorities to tighten security in Tetovo and the surrounding area in early July. But, by mid-July, manifestations of Albanian nationalism in the Tetovo region were said to be escalating. Skopje was rocked by "organized enemy manifestations" involving ethnic Albanians early in July. Moreover, hostile Albanian activities, such as sloganeering, were still reported in the Tetovo region in late August.[92]

Even Serbia had problems, with Albanian nationalists allegedly stirring up trouble in the communes of Bujanovac, Presevo, and Medvedja in southern Serbia. "Albanian ruffians" created disorder in Zagreb, too, while in the Slovenian capital of Ljubljana, police were able to abort a demonstration of Albanians only at the last minute.[93]

Arson, sabotage, terrorism, and pamphleteering became, overnight, a way of life in Kosovo. Some 680 fires, attributed to arson, caused damage estimated at 70 million dinars between 1980 and 1981.[94] There were again violent demonstrations in July 1981 in Djakovica, in January 1982 at the University of Priština, in February and March 1982 in Priština and Suva Reka, and in April 1982 in Uroševac. Three bombs were set off in downtown Priština between October and November 1982, the third exploding in the immediate vicinity of the headquarters of the party provincial committee. Hundreds of demonstrators clashed with security police in the February and March riots, leaving numerous injured. As 1982 drew to a close, the situation was still said to be "deteriorating," with the authorities unable to guarantee public safety or the security of property.[95]

Mahmut Bakali resigned his post as provincial party chief, admitting to the futility of past policy in Kosovo and confessing that he had attempted to sweep problems under the rug. In April 1983, he was belatedly expelled from the party. But the very ranks of the party were infected by the nationalist germ, and, by late July 1982, some 1,000 LCK members had been expelled from the party, at least some for having participated in the riots. Several basic organizations of the LCK were simply dissolved outright. More than 700 Albanians had, by this time, been put behind bars.[96] Even the party-controlled press had proven unreliable. The April 1 issue of *Fjalja*, an Albanian-language periodical, was suppressed for nationalistically provocative material, and *Obeležja* itself, the Kosovar party's Serbo-Croatian theoretical journal, was said to be treading a fine line.[97] Yet resistance to Belgrade's policy runs so deep that two years later, at a session on June 6, 1983, the Kosovar party's Provincial Committee for Information revealed that the reportage in the province's Albanian-language daily, *Rilindja*, regularly differed from that in its Serbo-Croatian daily, *Jedinstvo*; specifically, *Rilindja* was said to be allowing "alien positions" to infiltrate its pages.[98]

The LCY central committee convened on May 7 and reprimanded the Kosovar party organization for serious "weaknesses."[99] A series of purges followed. Among those dismissed were Bakali (he subsequently resigned his membership in the central committee of LC Serbia and was replaced as president of the

Kosovo party's provincial committee by his predecessor, Veli Deva); assembly president Dušan Ristić (replaced by Ilija Vakic); SAP premier Bahri Oruči; Priština television station director Fahredin Ginga; Radio Priština director Šaban Hiseni; University of Priština rector Gazmend Zajmi; and both the secretary for internal affairs (Mustafa Šefedini) and the undersecretary for internal affairs (Ismail Bajrami). Six of the nineteen members of the provincial committee presidium were expelled. Three persons were dropped from the executive council. The editors of the radio and television stations in Priština were fired, as were more than two hundred faculty members at the University of Priština.[100]

A state of siege prevailed in the province, with 30,000 troops and police—many of them sent from Croatia and Slovenia—patrolling the province as an occupation force. All incoming and outgoing traffic was scrupulously checked, and the movement of outsiders into the province was largely proscribed. Belgrade hastened to ban textbooks imported from Albania, which were now discovered to have incendiary overtones, and undertook to translate the more "reliable" Serbian textbooks into Albanian for the use of the Kosovars.[101] Party spokesmen also began to express misgivings about the radical devolution of authority to the autonomous provinces, arguing that they should coordinate their policies more closely with the Serbian republic and that some of the prerogatives they enjoyed in practice had no constitutional basis. Understandably, members of the Vojvodinan party, uncompromised in this debate, expressed strong opposition to suggestions that the prerogatives of the autonomous provinces be curtailed.[102]

The 1981 riots were a rude awakening insofar as they signified the repudiation of more than ten years of intense efforts to accelerate development in this backward region. They demonstrated the primacy of ethnic community: the demonstrators and all who sympathized with them preferred to live under an Albanian despot rather than remain part of Yugoslavia, however open the latter might be. Clearly, it was this separatist dimension, as well as the possible impact this latest outbreak might have on other discontented nationalities in the multiethnic country, that troubled Belgrade most. Rumors circulated, moreover, that at least some of the Albanian separatist groups had formed guerrilla units in the back country of Kosovo—an allegation quickly denied by Yugoslav authorities.[103]

The incipient revolt in Kosovo drove additional Kosovar Montenegrins and Serbs out of Kosovo, sparked a nationalist backlash among Macedonians and Serbs, and triggered the proliferation of nationalist excesses throughout the other seven federal units.

The 1981 census already showed an absolute decline in the Serbian and Montenegrin populations of Kosovo. There were 18,172 fewer Serbs in 1981 than in 1971, while the number of Montenegrins decreased by 4,680. As a result of the post-April turmoil, in which Albanian residents frequently "targeted" local Slavs, there was a renewed exodus of Serbs and Montenegrins from Kosovo. By one estimate, some ten thousand Serbs and Montenegrins left Kosovo between April and the end of October 1981.[104] Most of them have fled to Serbia, often to Belgrade, bearing tales of Albanian excesses.

This exodus only served to reinforce a Serbian nationalist backlash, aggravating a problem to which the party had to devote increased attention in subsequent years. It was just three years earlier, at the Fifteenth Session of the CC of the LC Serbia (April 19, 1978), that various speakers inveighed against a renascence of Serbian ethnocentric chauvinism. Mirko Popović specifically noted, on that occasion, that Serbian chauvinism had become more serious "in the last year or two." Popović charged that the Greater Serbian nationalists were exploiting every friction to further their own chauvinistic purposes.[105] Incensed by the anti-Serbian edge to these latest Albanian riots, Serbs began to speak openly of the "good old days" when Ranković was in charge of the security apparatus and claimed that it was time to put the Albanians of Kosovo in their place once and for all. Indeed, Ranković became, overnight, a hero of Serbs. Simultaneously, Serbs and Macedonians began boycotting Albanian shops and bakeries, cutting sales, in some cases, by as much as 85 percent.[106] There were even demands by Serbs that the autonomous province of Kosovo be abolished altogether—an alternative that party officials quickly labeled "unacceptable." A similar syndrome developed in Macedonia, where Macedonians started ostracizing Albanian neighbors, acquaintances, and former friends.

At the same time, the Albanians of Kosovo have found considerable sympathy among the Hungarians of Vojvodina. In a poignant expression of that sympathy, a large Hungarian crowd, which had been giving pro forma applause to dance troupes from various Yugoslav republics at a folk dance festival held in Vojvodina shortly after the riots, cheered and clapped boisterously when the Albanian dance troupe from Kosovo performed. The message was not lost on the Serbs. Shortly thereafter, *Borba* lashed out at "bourgeois-liberalist . . . Hungarian nationalism, that engages in tactical games and calculates and waits to see whether another nationalism that is rising might perhaps benefit it in some way."[107] Subsequently, nationalist incidents were reported in the Vojvodinan towns of Kanjiza, Zrenjanin, Novi Sad, Ada, Senta, Sombor, Subotica, and elsewhere.[108]

Throughout the 1980s various underground organizations of Albanians were uncovered in Kosovo, and their members prosecuted.[109] Between April 1981 and September 1987, criminal charges were brought against 5,200 Kosovar Albanians, according to official figures. In the Yugoslav army alone, some 216 illegal organizations were discovered during those years, with some 1,435 members of Albanian nationality.[110] Some 1,800 persons (1,600 of them Albanians) were expelled from the Kosovo party organization. And in June 1987, the LCY central committee convened a special two-day session to review the situation in Kosovo, describing it as "the most difficult crisis in the history of new Yugoslavia."[111] The session devoted special attention to the out-migration of Serbs and Montenegrins from the province, which had already reduced the Slavic population in the province by 22,000. By September 1988, this figure would reach 30,000.[112] The session concluded that LCY policy until then had been essentially nugatory and gave impetus to discussions about how to halt the out-migration of Serbs and Montenegrins from Kosovo. In November 1987, a program was agreed on to deal with that issue.[113]

The Belgrade media (especially television and periodicals such as *Duga* and *Reporter*) began to give play to stories about Albanian atrocities against Serbs. Meanwhile, the Serbs who had left Kosovo, including some who had left for economic reasons, began to talk of their own alleged sufferings and to demand special benefits in Kosovo in terms of housing and job placement. By 1986, Serbia (especially Belgrade) was aflame with nationalism. Overnight it became fashionable for Serbs to proclaim their devotion to the Serbian Orthodox Church, which naturally adopted a pose as the guardian of the Serbian people and culture.[114]

In October 1986, members of the Serbian Academy of Sciences drew up a seventy-page "Memorandum" bewailing Serbia's fate in communist Yugoslavia and accusing Tito and Kardelj of having conspired to "destroy Serbia." Vuk Draškovic, a Serbian novelist who would found a Serbian nationalist party three years later, addressed an appeal to the Association of Hebrew Writers in Tel-Aviv, proposing a "blood brotherhood" between Serbs and Jews. In Draškovic's view, "We Serbs are a lost unhappy tribe of Israel."[115] Eight months later, the Serbian Association of Writers issued its own appeal, accusing responsible government organs of covering up the true situation and of ignoring the plight of local Serbs.[116] Serbs complained that Albanians dominated various sectors of Kosovo society, such as Television Priština,[117] and the press became awash with poems devoted to the sufferings of Serbs in Kosovo.[118] Bora Djordjević, a self-styled rock bard living in Belgrade, sang about the corruption of the party and wrote poems expressing the Serbian spirit vis-à-vis Kosovo. These poems won Djordjević election to the Serbian Association of Writers.

While Kosovar Albanians continued to demand republic status, Serbs began to talk increasingly of the need to whittle down the prerogatives of the provincial party apparatus. In an effort to head off Serbian encroachment, Azem Vllasi, then president of the Kosovo LC provincial committee presidium, told a two-day conference of communists in January 1987,

> Our forces have strengthened to such an extent that we may essentially control the situation on the front of the struggle against Albanian nationalism and irredentism, that this nationalism no longer has either strength or a chance to consolidate itself, . . . [let alone] to essentially influence a destabilization of the situation. . . . We have to a great extent broken up the illegal organizations.[119]

As long as Ivan Stambolić headed the Serbian party apparatus, little was done, and party organs repeated vapid and vacuous phrases about the situation improving and being under control. But in late 1987, Stambolić was ousted by his erstwhile understudy, Slobodan Milošević, and the entire political picture changed overnight. (Slobodan Milošević's career and program are treated in some detail in chapter 11.)

Milošević and his adherents were angered by the steady decline in the number of Serbs and Montenegrins in the province. In 1953, these two groups combined had accounted for some 27.9 percent of the provincial population. This figure had steadily dropped—to 20.9 percent in 1971, 14.9 percent in 1981, and finally to 10 percent in 1987.[120]

Having told the Yugoslav public for years that the situation in Kosovo was being normalized, the Serbian party, now controlled by unabashed nationalists, announced that in fact the complete opposite was the case. Thus Petar Gračanin, president of the Serbian presidency, declared at a joint session of the Serbian presidency and the Serbian LC central committee presidium in September 1988,

> In all essential respects the political and security situation in Kosovo is getting significantly worse. In the past month, since the 16th LCY central committee plenum, several incidents have occurred which constitute an extremely serious warning about the negative tendencies of the continuing aggressive activity of Albanian nationalism and separatism which, if it is not ended urgently and in a radical way, will have wider and tragic consequences.[121]

The new Serbian leadership staged large-scale "spontaneous" demonstrations by Serbs and Montenegrins, to which the Albanians replied with equally large demonstrations. On November 18, 1988, in particular, some 100,000 ethnic Albanians marched through Priština in what was described as the biggest protest by Albanians in Kosovo since 1981.[122] Shortly after that protest, provincial officials in Kosovo banned any further public meetings in a vain effort to contain overt expressions of discontent.

Much of the Kosovar party apparatus had been sympathetic to the concerns and aspirations of local Albanians, as *Borba* obliquely conceded in 1981,[123] and as became clear later.[124] In the first edition of this book, I called the Kosovo crisis, "the most trying and most intractable problem on Belgrade's agenda."[125] As we shall see in chapter 11, the Kosovo crisis provided the grist for Milošević's rise to power in Serbia, provoked a dramatic showdown between Slovenia and Serbia over the place of the autonomous provinces in the federation, provided the backdrop for a general deterioration in relations between Serbia and the other republics, and fueled rising Serbian nationalism, which in turn infected Serbs in Croatia, leading to renewed difficulties in Croatia.

The Croatian Question

The purge of the Zagreb troika and the closing of Matica Hrvatska could not liquidate Croatian nationalism: it only drove it underground. The Croatian press again became, at least until the last year of Tito's reign, relatively timid about such sensitive questions as the interests of the republic and the nature of Croatian nationalism. The charismatic and popular leaders were purged and driven out of politics. They were replaced by mediocre, if pragmatic, bureaucrats who were unpopular with the people. Only one institution was available to champion Croatian national interests until 1989—the Croatian Catholic Church. Whatever it might do to Matica Hrvatska, the regime dared not suppress the church.

According to Šime Djodan, thousands of Croats were punished in one way or another. He estimates that 50,000 members of the LC Croatia lost their party cards, 12,000 enterprise directors and engineers were fired, 2,000–5,000 persons were imprisoned, 50,000 students were identified as "class enemies" and thus had a permanent blemish entered on their records that would obstruct career advancement. In addition, 270 partisan officers were expelled from the party or punished in other ways, 18 generals were punished, and 14 national heroes (including some of the aforementioned generals) were likewise punished. These sweeping penalties sowed deep bitterness among Croats. When I met Djodan in 1989, he drew attention to the fact that, shortly after the purge of the Croatian liberals, Tito was decorated, by Moscow, with the Order of Lenin.[126]

Of those Croats who received jail sentences, many were brought to Stara Gradiška, an antiquated prison known for its poor conditions and callous treatment of prisoners. Among its inmates were Croatian economists Marko Veselica and Šime Djodan, who became so seriously ill while in prison that they were finally released: they were not, however, able to find work for some time (in Djodan's case, until 1982). Neither they nor Franjo Tudjman, a leading Croatian historian who was sentenced to a two-year prison term in 1972 and was likewise unemployed, were allowed to publish in Yugoslavia. *Vjesnik* reported that some 5,806 indictments for political crimes were handed down between January 1972 and March 1973. Forty-four percent of these involved Croats, though their republic represents only 21 percent of the total Yugoslav population. Bosnia, with 19 percent of the Yugoslav population, accounted nonetheless for another 27 percent of these indictments—many of those were no doubt Bosnian Croats.[127]

The conservatives quickly quashed almost all the forums in which the nationalists had been able to publish their views, including *Tlo, Kolo, Kritika, Hrvatski književni list*, and *Studentski list*. The prestigious Croatian magazine *Encyclopaedia Moderna*, however, remained somewhat independent in its editorial policy and allowed articles of liberal shades into its pages. This oversight was corrected at the end of 1974, when the publication was belatedly suppressed. A short story by Dubravko Horvatić that refused to paint the *Ustaše* in purely negative hues served as the pretext.[128]

Deprived of any input into the politics of the society, nationalistically inclined Croats often "dropped out" altogether, adopting a forced apathy. In the rural regions of Croatia, anti-Serbian feelings became more intense than ever, and certain towns, particularly Zadar, were said to display a defiant mood.[129] In July 1974, fifteen Croats—among them three professors, a building technician, and a "distinguished member" of the Communist party—were taken into custody. After three months of interrogation, a four-month trial ensued in which the fifteen, together with Pavle Perović, a twenty-two-year-old philosophy student who had managed to escape to West Germany, were accused of having organized a terrorist organization known as the Hrvatska Oslobodilačka Revolucionarna Armija (Croatian Liberation Revolutionary Army). Perović denied that there had been any such organization or that the group had any armaments whatsoever but admitted that he and the other defendants were Croatian nationalists. *Nova Hrvatska*, the Croatian émigré publication, also pointed out that the name of the alleged organization betrayed its nullibicity, since no right-minded Croat would use the Serbian word "Armija" in place of the Croatian word "Vojska."[130] Another fifteen Zagrebers were brought to trial in 1976 for allegedly having planned to assassinate President Tito. The fifteen appealed their convictions, and, in the retrials, two of the accused complained of having been tortured and harassed by the police while in custody. In the end, the court reduced their sentences to fifteen years at hard labor.

Rumored attempts to rehabilitate the fallen troika and reinstate its members in the party inevitably failed, and the expression of sympathy for their program remained totally taboo. One Croatian farmer, Josip Česarec, who ignored this taboo and praised the troika in public, was said to have been given a four-year prison term in 1980. After Tito's passing, some thought it might be possible to obtain a certain degree of liberalization and, accordingly, in a petition sent to the federal *Skupština* and to the party presidium, forty-five Croatian intellectuals sought a general amnesty for all political prisoners. The petition, drawn up and submitted in November 1980, was signed, among others, by the former rector of Zagreb University, Ivan Supek; novelists Vlado Gotovac (restricted to Zagreb for spreading "hostile propaganda") and Zlatko Tomičić; former partisan general Franjo Tudjman; and bygone student leaders.[131]

Temporarily freed from jail, Gotovac told a foreign journalist in 1978, "We could be put in jail again at any moment, under any pretense, although we have not done anything."[132] By the end of 1980, both Gotovac and Tudjman were once again taken to court. The charge this time was spreading anti-Yugoslav propaganda, specifically, by complaining, in interviews given to Western correspondents over the years 1977–80, that the Croatian people continued to be politically, economically, and culturally oppressed in socialist Yugoslavia. Tudjman had gone so far as to provide Peter Miroschnikoff, a correspondent for ARD (a German news agency), with up-to-date statistics showing that the Serbs continued to dominate both the Croatian Communist party and the officer corps of the JNA within Croatia. *NIN*, in fact, admitted in 1980 that Serbs constituted 24 percent of the Croatian party and a majority of the Croatian police force, even though only 14 percent of Croatia's inhabitants were Serbs.[133] In February 1981, Tudjman was found guilty of having engaged in hostile propaganda and was sentenced to three years in jail. He was released early, after serving almost two years, because of illness.[134] Gotovac and former student leader Dobroslav Paraga, also identified with the Croatian mass movement, went to jail for "antistate activity," and the sickly Marko Veselica, arrested in the early spring of 1981, likewise charged with spreading hostile propaganda, eventually received a sentence of eleven years imprisonment.

There was a certain irony in the fact that, having repudiated the Novi Sad agreement and produced a separate Croatian orthography in the early 1970s, the Croats should have been forced subsequently to accept a new orthography based on the defunct Novi Sad agreement. This new Croatian orthography, the work of Vladimir Anić and Josip Silić, appeared in mid-1980. Work had begun on the project in 1976, on assignment from the Croatian Commission for Language Questions. In an interview with *NIN*, Anić admitted that, since the language of the Croats, Serbs, Muslims, and Montenegrins was a single language, he and his collaborators had consulted the incomplete Novi Sad orthography whenever possible.[135]

As a result of the purge of the Croatian liberals and the suppression of Matica Hrvatska, the Catholic church became the leading spokesperson for disaffected Croats, a role not altogether different from that acquired by the church in Poland. Several, if not most, of the Croatian upper clergy sympathize with all the traditional Croatian nationalist desiderata.[136] Archbishop Franjo Kuharić of Zagreb openly took up Paraga's cause in his Christmas sermon in 1980.[137] More recently, Jozo Zovko, the parish priest of Medjugorje in Herzegovina, went to prison on a three-and-a-half-year term, after telling his parishioners that they had been "enslaved for forty years" and that it was time to "remove the chains, [and] untie the knots."[138] Not sporadic misdemeanors on the part of isolated clergymen, however, but systematic church insistence on the legitimacy of its public role disquieted the LCY, since the LCY did not recognize such a role. "A depoliticized church does not bother the state," wrote Todo Kurtović, the chairman of SAWPY, "but the identification of religion and nationality in our conditions is sheer politicization—it is an undiluted clerical act. . . . It cannot be viewed as anything but a political act when someone claims . . . that no one can be a good Croat unless he is a good Catholic."[139] Monsignor Franjo Kuharić, archbishop of Zagreb, was guilty of this cardinal sin of "politicization," and Milka Planinc, Dabčević-Kučar's successor as president of the Croatian party, denounced the archbishop in July 1977 for using "the pulpit to appear as the protector of the Croatian nation."[140] Although relations between the Slovenian Catholic Church and the regime have been reasonably amicable in recent years, the same cannot be said for relations between the Croatian Catholic Church and the regime. The difference is that the former has been uninvolved in Slovenian nationalist currents (which are themselves far less potent and thus less threatening), while the Croatian Catholic Church has continued to act out the role of institutional bulwark against Serbianization.

Although the communists could not close down the church as they did Matica Hrvatska, the clergy enjoyed no immunity from prosecution. There continued to be reports of arrests and sentences for nationalistic clergy. In May 1980, to cite one instance, two young Croatian Franciscan monks were sent to jail: one for five years, for writing a poem treating the "oppression of the Croatian people," the other for five-and-a-half years, for possessing a copy of his fellow friar's poem and a Croatian flag that lacked the communist red star.[141]

In 1979, the Croatian Catholic Church celebrated the 1,100th anniversary of the year that Prince Branimir converted Croatia to Catholicism. The celebration took on the quality of a nationalistic event, and the church showed itself quite eager to underline the identification of Catholicism and Croatian nationality.[142] As 1981 opened, the regime, shaken by the church's renewed confidence in defending human and national rights in Yugoslavia, initiated a ferocious and slanderous anticlerical campaign, which did not stop short of identifying the archbishop of Zagreb as a fascist sympathizer.[143] Yet when, in February 1981, the archbishop celebrated a commemorative mass for Cardinal Stepinac, villified by the communists as a wartime collaborator, several thousand Croats jammed into the cathedral in a show of solidarity and defiance of the regime.

In the mid-1980s, a series of strange reports came out of Croatia. In September 1984, a group of young Croats from Duvno were arrested for having sung songs associated with the defunct wartime fascist regime of Ante Pavelić.[144] Another group of young people were apprehended for the same reason three months later. In both cases, all the accused received prison terms.[145] Other similar cases were reported in the press.

The following spring there were trials in Zagreb and Varaždin of alleged terrorists, said to have been members of an organization called the Croatian Fighting Unit and to have maintained contact with hostile Croatian exiles in West Germany. Stjepan Deglin was identified as the leader of the Varaždin group. The trials produced allegations of distribution of propaganda and the massing of weapons and incendiary devices. Members of a third alleged *Ustaše* group were put on trial about the same time in Osijek. These trials resulted ultimately in sentences of up to fifteen years in prison.[146]

Shortly after this, the party weekly *Komunist* published an article by Franjo Butorac, party secretary in Rijeka, complaining of the infiltration of purely Croatian words into Croatian schoolbooks and media (replacing words shared with Serbian). The purpose of this "strategy," according to Butorac, was "to indoctrinate young Croats with the spirit of nationalism."[147] Despite the fact that some of Croatia's most prominent nationalists were being shuttled in and out of jail, Butorac argued that

> the nationalists defeated in 1971 are mostly operating legally today, using means to push the ideas defeated in 1971; they are exceptionally well organized and linked, and are acting deliberately and "for the long," and they are doing so in a particularly sensitive sphere—language and education.[148]

The article sparked polemics in the Croatian *Sabor* and gave rise to a flood of letters to *Komunist* alleging that there was linguistic nationalism in Croatia. But when one of the chiefs of Školska knjiga, the Zagreb publishing house reponsible for most of the textbooks being attacked in *Komunist*, tried to contact the authors of the letters, he found that all the names and addresses were fake.

Table 24. *Total Residents and Serbs Living in Croatia, 1948–81*

	Total	*Serbs*
1948	3,756,807	543,795
1953	3,918,817	588,411
1961	4,159,696	624,985
1971	4,426,221	626,789
1981	4,601,469	531,502

Source: *NIN*, no. 2018, September 3, 1989, p. 23.

He surmised that the letter campaign figured as part of a "wider political game."[149]

The "Croatian question" had a particular edge because of the presence, in the republic, of several hundred thousand Serbs, accounting for about 12 percent of the republic's population in 1981. The number of Serbs residing in Croatia is shown in Table 24.

The Serbs came to Croatia in Habsburg times, when the Austrian dynasty invited Serbs to settle along the border and serve as border guards, fighting the Ottoman Turks when necessary. In exchange for this service, they were paid a state salary. This pattern resulted in Croatian Serbs abandoning agriculture, and when some of them returned to farming decades later, not surprisingly, they were far less skilled at it than the Croats. After the Old Empire collapsed, they joined the Yugoslav army or took employment in the police force, the post office, the railways, and the administration. During World War II, Croatian Serbs responded enthusiastically to Tito's call, and about 50 percent of Tito's recruits in Croatia were Serbs. After the war, many Croatian Serbs remained in the army and many joined UDBa (the secret police).[150] In the Kingdom of Serbs, Croats, and Slovenes, Cyrillic had been introduced as the official language throughout the country, but the *Ustaše* brought in the Latin alphabet in the areas under their control. After the war, the communists allowed the Croats to retain use of the Latin alphabet, although local Serbs preferred Cyrillic. Even today one can see shop signs in Cyrillic in the heavily Serbian regions of Knin, Banja, Kordun, and Lika. In Knin, as much as 80–90 percent of the local population is Serbian, while in the other regions, 45–55 percent is Serbian.

In late 1942, Moše Pijade, one of the partisans' "Big Five," proposed that a Serbian autonomous province be established in Croatia after the war. But Tito vetoed the proposal at once.[151] Yet the idea of some form of autonomy for Croatian Serbs never died and resurfaced in 1971, during the Croatian Spring. There are several issues related to Croatia's Serbs. Their overrepresentation in the police and security forces in the Titoist era was the most troubling in Croatian eyes. To the Serbs themselves, however, the real issues included the lack of special Serbian cultural institutions and newspapers, the relatively lower level of Serbian economic development, and the sheer fact of rule from Zagreb.

But to Serbian demands for special societies and autonomy, Croats have generally replied that there are also large pockets of Croats in Vojvodina and Bosnia-Herzegovina and yet no one talks of Croatian autonomous provinces in those federal units—not, that is, until 1990.[152]

From 1972 to 1987, the conservatives controlled the Croatian party apparatus. But the conservatives' policy of narrowing institutional alternatives within Croatia reinforced the very thing the communist regime dreaded most—the identification of nationality with religion—and thus reinforced latent tendencies within Croatia to reenact the Napoleonic syndrome and embark once again on a "Croatia first" course. Titoist Yugoslavia enjoyed a degree of success in conflict regulation, at least until the 1980s, and in federal relations the republics acquired wide autonomy, which permitted their elites to pursue those programs and to advance those policies that they perceived to be most in the interest of their respective federal units. It is another thing, however, to infer from this that the elites within each republic always authentically represented the viewpoints of the population whose interests they professed or, alternatively, that Yugoslavia ever managed anything resembling a "final solution" of the nationalities question. This became patently obvious (again!) in 1989–90. Repeated instances showed that tensions on the interethnic level had the potential to transform interrepublican relations, replacing one set of elites with another set that had different programmatic dispositions.

The Slovenian Syndrome

Sometime in the early 1980s, or perhaps even in the late 1970s, intellectuals and cultural elites in Slovenia began to stir. An early hint came in 1984, when Josip Vidmar told a symposium on "Yugoslavism" that Slovenian nationalism should be accepted as a normal (i.e., not evil) phenomenon.[153] That was only a straw in the wind. This syndrome went unnoticed at first, but by 1986 or 1987 it was perfectly obvious, and people began to be able to trace it back, at least part of the way. The "Slovenian syndrome" is really the Ljubljana syndrome because the political and social departures in that republic from common practice in Yugoslavia as a whole, which came into full bloom in the late 1980s, were (and are) essentially phenomena of the Slovenian capital city, even if they have consequences for the entire republic.

When people in Yugoslavia speak of the "Slovenački sindrom," they have in mind the fact that Slovenia in many ways marches to its own drummer. But more concretely the Slovenian syndrome emerged largely through three central components: Neue Slowenische Kunst (NSK), the Alternative Movement, and the confederal proclivity of the Slovenian political leadership.[154] These phenomena began as forms of dissidence, albeit at different levels, but by 1990 had become the basis for the political and cultural mainstream in Slovenia.

Neue Slowenische Kunst (New Slovenian Art) is a multimedia artistic group consisting of the Irwin group for painting, the Cosmo-Kinetic Theater of the

Red Pilot, the rock group Laibach, and a propaganda/advertising unit which calls itself the New Collectivism. NSK involves relatively few people—perhaps fifty in all—and flirts with totalitarianism, professing to be trying to foster totalitarian thinking.[155] This is all pose. NSK's real power is elsewhere, and the pop-totalitarian guise is used as an energizing medium to promote a certain image of Slovenian culture (and to market Laibach's rock albums).

NSK is deeply ironic and by nature provocative. Its members and adherents view themselves as looking back to Slovenian roots and as rediscovering the Slovenian soul. But the very choice of a German expression (it never appears in Slovenian) to denote the current was conceived as a kind of provocation: Germanization threatened Slovenian national culture for centuries, and now the project of the rediscovery of the Slovenian soul is given a German name. Laibach's 1987 album, *Krst pod Triglavom—Baptism*, is, in fact, a celebration of the Slovenian soul in music. It solemnly recreates ancient pagan music, which shifts to music darkly evocative of turmoil. Later there are lengthy citations from Johann Strauss—an allusion to Slovenia's long incorporation into the Austrian Empire—though this is inevitably sifted through Laibach's unique rhythmic prism. Then there are ponderous, dramatic-sounding but empty chords done in a mock Wagnerian style that run in circles. Still later there is an unmistakable Nazi march, frenetically sung in pseudo-German.

In fact, the Nazi style is a Laibach specialty. The group's members wear brown shirts and Nazi-style regalia, sing in German, and conduct totalitarian-style ceremonies in their performances. Even the name Laibach, the German name for Ljubljana, recalls not merely the long period of Habsburg rule, but also the much shorter, but far more traumatic, period of Nazi rule. What does it all mean? The Slovenes debated this for several years and finally gave it up, without coming to an agreement. Part of the group's meaning, certainly—as I have argued—lies in its assertion of a separate Slovenian path.[156]

The Alternative Movement, since it is not a single institution but, rather, an alliance of movements and individuals is in flux even now. One might say that the Alternative Movement is a way of thinking, and as circumstances change, the way one thinks about circumstances changes as well. The Alternative Movement was born in 1982 with the formation of the Peace and Ecology Movement. This movement became involved in protests against the country's nuclear energy program. Lilit, a feminist group, was formed by a group of female students in the humanities in April 1985. And Magnus, a gay rights movement, likewise formed in 1985, has put on gay festivals in Ljubljana annually since then.

In addition, the Slovenian student periodicals *Mladina* (Ljubljana) and *Katedra* (Maribor) and the Ljubljana station, Radio Student, offered outlets for ideas, discussions, and cultural trends that for one reason or another were not acceptable for the communist-linked and -sponsored media (up to 1990). Radio Student was somewhat anomalous to begin with, in that it was always an entirely independent radio station, never staffed or supervised by any agency of the Communist party. It was created in 1969 on student initiative; during unrest the previous year, Slovenian students had demanded the right to establish their own radio station. This was reluctantly granted, and the students literally built the station themselves. By contrast, the editorial appointments of *Mladina* and *Katedra* had to be approved by the local youth organization (until the end of 1989), but in the late 1980s such approval became more or less pro forma. Some of the people on the staffs of these three outlets were associated with the alternative scene (e.g., punk, in its heyday).

Later, in 1988, independent political parties were created that would take power in Slovenia in spring 1990. In this way, the Alternative Movement took over the government and brought its alternative into fruition.

The third component of the "Slovenian syndrome" was the confederal proclivity of the Slovenian political leadership—both of the communist leadership and of the noncommunist leadership that succeeded it. Like the Slovenian population generally, neither leadership was eager to have the republic's relatively greater prosperity milked through measures designed to support the less solvent republics in the south or to give up their policy autonomy (or "sovereignty," in the parlance of 1990) in internal matters. Predictably, this attitude aroused resentment and suspicion in some of the other republics.

In February 1987, the Slovenian journal *Nova revija* published a collection of articles devoted to the "Slovenian national program," which included, among other things, a protest against the second-class status of the Slovenian language in Yugoslavia. The issue was quickly subjected to attack in other republics in Yugoslavia, where some people expressed prescient (as it turned out) concern that the Slovenes were sliding in the direction of secessionism.[157] Eventually, there were polemics between the federal prosecutor and the Slovenian prosecutor over *Nova revija*. The Slovenes held their ground.

Slovenes started to talk of a "defensive nationalism"[158] and of how they were being milked by the other, less productive republics. Outside the republic, there was resentment of the Slovenes' tendency to look inward, or northward, rather than south, and a growing realization that Slovenes did not really consider themselves part of Yugoslavia. Moving between Belgrade, Zagreb, and Sarajevo, one encountered the same issues, the same personalities, and elements of shared culture; the Serbian, Croatian, and Bosnian environments intersected. But traveling to Slovenia, one lost all sense of the relevance of Belgrade and Zagreb. In Ljubljana, Serbia came to seem like a distant (and, of course, foreign) world.

The army did not like what was happening in Slovenia. Toward the end of March 1988, the Military Council—an advisory body to the federal presidency—prepared a report on political trends in Slovenia. The report spoke of "counterrevolution" in Slovenia, which, it said, was waging "war" against the achievements of socialism. The central committee of the Slovenian party convened a secret meeting at which it tried to refute the Military Council's accusations—but the military was not convinced. A few weeks later, rumors started circulating in Ljubljana to the effect that the army was preparing a coup in Slovenia, that it planned to clean out the liberals, that it planned executions, and so forth. In May, Slovenian party chief Milan Kučan's speech to the secret session of the central committee was leaked, confirming the truth of these rumors.[159] Ivan Borstner, a sergeant-major in the Yugoslav army, absconded with an army document outlining preparations for the coup and took it to the weekly magazine *Mladina*, making contact with journalists Janez Janša and David Tasić and editor Franci Zavrl. *Mladina* prepared to publish the material. Instead, the army arrested Janša and Borstner on May 31, and Tasić and Zavrl a few days later. On the same day that Janša and Borstner were arrested, the LCY presidency issued a completely unbelievable statement to the effect that "rumors of alleged preparations for a military coup in the Republic of Slovenia last March are absolutely groundless and represent a political intrigue."[160] In the meantime, Stane Dolanc (Slovenia's representative in the state presidency) and Milan Kučan (president of the Slovenian central committee presidium) had succeeded in thwarting the plan.

The trial sent political shock waves throughout Slovenia. The four accused became national heroes in Slovenia overnight, and in Ljubljana, crowds of ten to twenty thousand regularly convened, day after day, for the duration of the trial. The trial came to be seen in national-patriotic terms, as Slovenes turned out for the demonstrations waving the Slovenian flag and singing nationalistic Slovenian songs. Folk musicians accompanied the singing and played well-known Slovenian marches.[161] The demonstrations took on some of the character of a vigil. The Catholic Church called for the release of "the Slovenian four" and conducted an all-night prayer vigil on July 18.[162]

The Slovenian communist authorities remonstrated against the trial, and when an extralegal Committee for the Protection of Human Rights began functioning (and signing up tens of thousands of sympathizers), they entered into direct and supportive contact with the committee, even declaring their views identical with those of the committee.[163]

Janez Janša was not just any journalist, in any case. He was the author of a series of articles in *Mladina* critical of the military. He was leader of the Slovenian pacifist movement, president of the wayward Slovenian Youth Organization, and—at the time of his arrest—a candidate for the presidency of the Yugoslav Youth Organization.[164] His arrest was thus experienced as a particularly sharp, direct attack on Slovenian values, including pacifism. After his arrest Janša continued to write, and he produced an article, "War and Peace in the New Constitution," in which he argued for limiting the share of the national revenue allocated for military expenditures to 2 percent. Janša argued further,

> In the new constitution, the question of equal status of the nations within the YNA [Yugoslav National Army] should be regulated. In this very field the army lags behind most of all. . . . The constitutional changes should regulate anew: a) the question of the general plenipotentiaries of the army; b) the question of equal status of the languages in the YNA; c) the question of the extra-territorial principle of serving in [the] armed forces; d) the question of [the] even distribution of senior officers regarding their nationality, in the YNA. Among general competences, the way of financing in terms of already proposed restrictions should be regulated, military courts should be abolished, republics should have plenipotentiaries over

> military education, political parties within the army should be banned, the nomination of senior officers of higher rank on the territory of each republic or autonomous province should be in [the] competence of [the] republic.[165]

The trial was bad enough in and of itself, as far as Slovenes were concerned, and antimilitary sentiment now ran in high fever. Antimilitary graffiti adorned public walls in Ljubljana, in open expression of this tide.[166] But the entire affair was aggravated by the army's decision to conduct the trial—being held in Ljubljana—in Serbo-Croatian. The party leadership in Slovenia took the matter to the Yugoslav presidency, which ruled that the use of Serbo-Croatian in the Ljubljana military court was not unconstitutional—that is, that Slovenian law did not apply to the Yugoslav military.[167] It was a straight line from this ruling to Slovenia's 1990 declaration that its own legislation took priority over federal law. The Slovenian party leadership of course appealed the presidency's decision, but in vain. Milan Kučan commented bitterly that "Slovenes cannot regard as their own any state that does not secure the use of their mother tongue and its equality, and in which the freedom, sovereignty and equality of the Slovene people is not guaranteed."[168]

Finally, on July 27, the court found the four guilty and sentenced them to prison terms of four years (Borstner), one-and-a-half years (Janša and Zavrl, each), and five months (Tasić).

The trial had mobilized the Slovenian public, inflamed Slovenian exclusivism, provoked the creation of a human rights committee, and legitimized dissent. In the wake of the trial, a series of political initiatives were undertaken, giving birth to the Social Democratic Alliance of Slovenia, the Slovenian Democratic Union, the Slovenian Christian Socialist Movement, and a "Green" party.[169]

As a result of the trial, Slovenes began to talk in a new way. Already in June 1988, Kučan underlined the right of Slovenes to legislate for their own republic.[170] Mirjana Kasapović, a contributor to *Naše teme*, echoed this sentiment, noting, "We Slovenes did not join with other Yugoslav peoples in a common state in order to lose our soul and our national identity, but in order to defend them."[171] Then, in December 1988, Kučan introduced an entirely new element into the discourse, when, in an article penned for the party weekly, *Komunist*, he underlined that Slovenia retained the right of secession.[172] Republican leaders had not broached this subject in twenty years. There was no immediate follow-up to this, but then, in September 1989, Vladimir Rabzelj, a Slovenian lawyer, wrote an article for *Mladina* urging the secession of Slovenia and Croatia from the Yugoslav federation and the creation of a Slovenian-Croatian confederation.[173]

Mazes in Montenegro

Montenegro is a special case. Unlike the other nationalisms of Yugoslavia, Montenegrin nationalism comes in two variants—an anti-Serbian and a pro-Serbian variant—and there are Montenegrins adhering to each. Anti-Serbian nationalism follows the model of nationalism in the other republics, with the refinement that some scholars argue that Montenegrins are not Slavs at all but descend from originally non-Slavic stock, only accepting Serbo-Croatian as their indigenous language somewhat later.[174] Anti-Serbian nationalists typically want to maximize the sovereignty and juridical autonomy of the Montenegrin republic and are highly distrustful of Serbs.

Pro-Serbian Montenegrin nationalists perhaps should be called simply Serbian nationalists, since the argument they make is that Montenegrins are merely one tribe of the Serbian nation and that Montenegrins and Serbs have the same ethnogenesis, the same culture, and—allowing, of course, for the refinement of the independent Principality of Montenegro, which existed until 1918—in some "larger" sense, the same history.[175] Serbian nationalists in Montenegro complain that the "artificial" resurrection of a separate Montenegrin federal unit by the communists after World War II was a ploy to weaken Serbia that lacked any intrinsic merit.

Until the mid-1970s, the cultural infrastructure in Montenegro was weak. Only at that time were the University of Titograd and the Montenegrin Academy of Sciences founded. And only then was there a tangible development of Montenegrin media (including local television) and local scientific, cultural, and research institutes.[176] That is to say, the institutional prerequisites for the development of an articulate Montenegrin culture and identity were long in coming. By the mid-1980s, however, Montenegro was becoming sharply polarized between anti-Serbian and pro-Serbian nationalists, resulting in a worsening of the political climate among Montenegrins.[177]

In 1990, a new People's party was established in Montenegro. Its president (Novak Kilibarda) argued that Montenegro and Serbia are two Serbian states and that Montenegrins should be encouraged to think of themselves as Serbs. Although Kilibarda allowed that Montenegrins should have their own state, he also told a public gathering in July 1990 that in the event of the disintegration of Yugoslavia, Montenegro and Serbia should be united as a single Serbian state.[178]

A movement for the unification of Serbia and Montenegro was set up, and a petition to that effect was circulated that gathered more than 10,000 signatures from "citizens *of Serbia* and Montenegro."[179]

These Serbophile currents in turn provoked fear and anxiety among many Montenegrins, and one highly placed Montenegrin official claimed, in August 1990, that anti-Serbian sentiment in Montenegro had never been as strong.[180] A new Party of Socialists came into being in Montenegro and quickly issued a public warning of the threat of "Greater Serbian pretensions to the territory of the state of Montenegro."[181]

Conclusion

This chapter has highlighted the phenomenon of nationalism among five nationalities in Yugoslavia—Muslims, Albanians, Croats, Slovenes, and Montenegrins. Serbs—the most numerous Yugoslav nation and, arguably, the nation with the most complexes—are treated separately in chapter 11. But nationalism is not confined to these groups, of course. In particular, Macedonian and Hungarian nationalism have also played a certain, albeit smaller, role in recent Yugoslav politics.

Nationalism is a kind of political fuel. And as fuel, it can power different engines, driving in different directions. At various times, scholars, politicians, and polemicists have linked nationalism to fascism or democracy or political atavism—and perhaps to other things as well. But none of these linkages are automatic. They are only *possible* linkages. But in the Yugoslav context, which is also to say, in the context of communist one-party rule, this fuel powered a specific engine, namely, the engine of republic etatism. Hence, as Slovenian journalist Miha Kovač told the *New Left Review* in 1988,

> the nationalisms or local interests of Yugoslavia's six republics and two autonomous provinces became a kind of surrogate for all other political identities. You could be active within the existing political structure only on the basis of defending the interests of your republic or province. . . . Thus the system that had supposedly emerged through the defeat of Croat and other nationalisms turned out to be itself most conducive to nationalism. Nationalism is produced within the very structure of the Yugoslav system.[182]

10

Political Debates, 1980–89

As Dusan Bilandžić has perceptively noted, three developments were occurring at the transition from the late 1970s to the early 1980s that ultimately shook the foundations of the Yugoslav socialist state and created pressure for system transformation. These were the death of the founders—Kardelj (in 1979) and Tito (in 1980)—the deep economic crisis, which began to command attention already in 1979; and the eruption of ethnic tensions in Kosovo in April 1981.[1] Two further problems emerged at the same time: divisions within the party (which became a more serious problem after the death of the Great Arbiter, Tito, in May 1980) and the problem of legitimation (which was stimulated powerfully by the economic deterioration, although it certainly had other roots).[2]

As the 1980s wore on, it became clear that the fragmentation of power engineered by Tito's quasi-confederal but one-party framework was producing institutional weakness and political chaos. Chaos, of course, creates maneuvering room and uncertainty—which give the sense of freedom. And this inevitably opened the door to greater political participation by large numbers of citizens, as one could predict on the basis of Samuel P. Huntington's classic work on political order.[3] But, as I wrote in 1987, "political chaos is also the mark of stress, of transition. It is characteristic of a state in disequilibrium."[4]

The League of Communists of Yugoslavia convoked its first post-Tito congress in Belgrade from June 26 to June 29, 1982. The league had weathered the initial post-Tito transition and could congratulate itself on the stability of the system of collective decision making it had set up in the late 1970s. Yet, for a variety of reasons, the Twelfth Party Congress also became an arena for voicing various complaints and proposals, both by liberals and by conservatives. To begin with, the party was starting to become troubled about the country's deteriorating economic situation, the growing Serbian-Albanian frictions in Kosovo, spiraling nationalism (in reaction to Kosovo and to the Serbian nationalist backlash) throughout the other federal units, and a growing crisis of confidence rooted in popular despair about the party's ability to cope with the situation effectively. Although the institutions were functioning much as they had for years, there was a groundswell of criticism (both in party forums and in the press) of some of the pillars of Yugoslav stability. As early as June 1973, the presidium of the LCY central committee released a document that admitted that, in twenty-three years of "self-management," workers' self-management had not been implemented in its intended form. In the months after Tito's death, various party spokespersons charged that self-management had been "neglected," that it existed "only on paper," that workers' councils were regularly circumvented and forced to acquiesce in decisions made elsewhere, and that no large enterprises had ever introduced self-management per se.[5] Others charged that the interrepublican committees had been working inefficiently and that the state presidency was increasingly intruding into the legitimate domain of the federal executive council and the *Skupština*.[6] Even Tito was subjected to criticism—first by Bosnian General Boško Šiljegović, who accused Tito (in May 1981) of having made "great errors" in policy toward Kosovo, and later by poet Gojko Djogo, who allegedly referred to Tito as "the rat from Dedinje" in a collection of poems published by Prosveta and who was jailed for that offense in September 1981. Even the party was taken to task. *Danas* dourly charged that the Eleventh Party Congress (1978) had failed to accomplish anything and that its resolutions for decisive action had never been translated into policy.[7] Similarly, in February 1982, the Commission for the Development of the Political System of LC Serbia sharply rejected the draft political report, complaining that its authors had tried to cover up serious weakness in the party and that they had blithely described party efficacy in superlatives, even though the Kosovo problem remained unresolved.[8]

As the Twelfth Party Congress approached, centralists began to clamor for withdrawal of power from the federal units and the reinstitution of a strong center and openly fretted about what they termed the de facto federalization of the party. Throughout the summer of 1981, Serbian and Bosnian centralists blasted what they termed "unacceptable tendencies toward the federalization or even confederalization" of the party.[9] They urged that the autonomy of the regional party organizations of Kosovo and Vojvodina be reduced; that much greater coordination among republics be required in education, transport, price policy, supplies, and other policy areas; that federal agencies be given an increased role in supervising this coordination; and that general party discipline be tightened. Insofar as the centralists sought to clamp down on the increasingly open press, the liberal media found its natural allies in those anticentralist political liberals who lived in Serbia and—France Popit notwithstanding—in Slovenia. One critic even described the contemporary phase of Yugoslav political development as a kind of "refeudalization" characterized by "the absolutization of the sovereignty of the republics and provinces in spite of the trends of the modern economy." This same critic remarked that recentralization had been rejected for political reasons but might be required by economic considerations.[10]

Decentralists (or perhaps better, confederalists) responded by proposing (in late 1981)[11] that central committee members be made responsible to the republican organs that elect them rather than to the committee itself—a move that would have constituted an unmistakable step toward de jure federalization of the party—and also urged that the powers of the LCY presidium be scaled down.[12] When they followed these proposals with endorsement of a statute change retaining the principle of democratic centralism within the regional party organizations of the federal units but abandoning it at the level of the central party apparatus, party centralists and conservatives feared that the federalization program would mean the destruction of the party altogether.[13] The conservative-dominated Montenegrin central committee shot back, in November 1981, with a suggestion that republican party organizations be stripped of their power to elect members of the LCY central committee and allowed only to nominate candidates for selection by the Yugoslav party congress.[14] Other conservative circles went so far as to demand that the statutes of the regional parties be abolished and that those bodies be governed by the statute of the LCY.[15] Centralists in the Croatian, Vojvodinan, and Serbian regional parties added fuel to the fire by demanding imposition of standard mandates throughout the system—a proposal that excited considerable remonstration from the maverick Slovenes, as well as from the JNA party organization.[16] A small conservative minority from Belgrade tried, at the Twelfth Party Congress, to replace the territorial organization of the party (the basis of the quasi-federal character of the LCY) with a production principle whereby the party would be structured according to branches of manufacture.[17]

On the eve of the congress, the conservatively inclined party organ, *Komunist*, groaned volubly that, under the spell of ethnocentric nationalism and burdened by "the inertia of the unsurmounted bourgeois history of Yugoslavia" and an "irrational fixation" on the interests of their respective groups, the Yugoslav federation was dissolving into congeries of bickering regional organizations.[18] And, in September 1982, Mitja Ribičič, the newly elected chairman of the party presidium, charged (at the Third Party Plenum) that "much has to be changed" and, in particular, that the various regional leaders should agree, or be compelled to agree, on general policy guidelines for the federation as a whole.

Later, Najdan Pašić, a leading party theorist, proposed the establishment of a special commission, the Commission to Study the Problems of the Functioning of the Political System, and urged that the powers and jurisdiction of the federal units be tangibly curtailed. Predictably, Pašić's proposal met with mixed response. In March 1983, the Tanjug news agency issued a report on the conclusions of the *Skupština*'s working group on federal relations. The report criticized the federal units for autarkic behavior, charged that the republics were engaging in active dialogue only in the context of federal organs, and complained of inconsistencies, weaknesses, and deviations from the constitution.[19] This kind of institutional disarray was typified by the continued resistance by Vojvodina and Kosovo to efforts by SR Serbia to reduce their prerogatives. In January 1983, for example, the two autonomous provinces refused to allow Serbian government representatives to be present during their talks with Milka Planinc, chair of the federal Executive Council, and other federal officials.

As the party gradually came to grips with the scope of the challenge with which it was confronted, it set up two commissions to study the economic and political crises, respectively, and to recommend appropriate strategies for dealing with them. The economic commission, chaired by Slovene Sergej Krajger, delivered its report in April 1982. But interrepublican differences assured that no effective action could be taken to adopt and apply the recommendations contained in the Krajger report. The political commission, chaired by Serb Tihomir Vlaškalić, delivered its report in December 1985. The report's starting point was that republican autonomy was a given—but that meant the Vlaškalić commission continued to operate within the framework of a unit veto system and inevitably evoked criticism from centralist-minded would-be reformers.[20]

From the death of Tito in 1980 until the rise of Slobodan Milošević in 1987, the regional party organizations were factionalized along the following lines (defined by the dual issues of liberalization vs. retrenchment and recentralization vs. preservation of the decentralized system):[21] liberal recentralizers were dominant in the Serbian party, conservative recentralizers were dominant in the Bosnian and Montenegrin parties, liberal decentralists in the Slovenian and Vojvodinan parties, and conservative decentralists in the Croatian, Macedonian, and Kosovar parties.[22]

Defense of the decentralized system was especially important for the autonomous provinces, Kosovo and Vojvodina, which had the most to lose from any move toward recentralization. Serbia, by contrast, jealously eyeing the two provinces, felt it had the most to gain. Hence, in October 1984, the Serbian party issued a draft reform program calling for, among other things, the strengthening of the federal government and the curtailment of the jurisdiction and prerogatives of the autonomous provinces in particular.[23]

Slovenia and Croatia quickly came to the defense of the embattled provincial party organizations, and a Slovenian-Serbian clash at the Fourteenth Plenum of the central committee in October 1984 served as a dress rehearsal for the playing out of more serious Slovenian-Serbian tensions in 1989.[24]

But by 1986, with the deepening crisis and a growing—if transitory—consensus that Yugoslavia's troubles were somehow associated with its confederal framework, the Slovenian party had become isolated in its defense of the status quo. Typical of the mood was a statement made by Vojvodinan Vidoje Žarković, rotating president of the LCY central committee presidium, in September 1985. Žarković blasted what he called "polycentric etatism" as the chief cause of the country's problems. In his view,

> polycentric etatism is the major cause of [our] economic crisis, technological stagnation, and our financial dependence on foreign countries. . . . In the past and current year, we have witnessed serious problems concerning decision making in the federation, particularly agreement-seeking between the republics and provinces. Many difficulties, manifested in the process of coordination, for instance in the SFRJ Assembly, have been not only the result of objective circumstances, but largely the expression of the etatization of relations both in the republics and provinces and in the federation. It is unacceptable to give instructions to delegations and often to delegates in the SFRJ Assembly's chambers about how long they should discuss specific standpoints, and when and to what extent they should give in and hence, satisfy even the most trivial interests of their republic or province.[25]

The provincial party organizations were intimidated and temporarily passive, while both the Macedonian and the Croatian party organizations—though dominated by persons sympathetic to a decentralized system—had agreed to work toward constitutional reform, the purpose of which was no less than the reconsolidation of a strong central government. The tide, thus, seemed to be turned against the decentralists. And eventually (in 1988), pressured from various sides, the Slovenian Assembly even gave its preliminary approval to a set of draft amendments to the SFRY Constitution, amendments that would have had serious consequences for the autonomy of the republics.[26]

But in 1987, there was a political coup in the Serbian party apparatus, which now came under the control of Serbian nationalist Slobodan Milošević. As will be discussed in the next chapter, Milošević's centralist program ultimately pushed too far, evoking resistance and resulting in time in a complete turn in the tide—with sentiment for confederalization growing steadily throughout 1989 and 1990. Indeed, by September 1990, Borislav Jovic, president of the state presidency, would propose a nationwide referendum on the question of whether Yugoslavia should be reconsolidated as a federation or reconstituted as a confederation.[27]

The Quest for Reform, 1981–87

The political debate opened virtually as soon as Tito was buried. In the years 1981–83 it focused on reforming existing institutions, on making the existing system function effectively, on averting crisis, on reform. In the years 1984–87, by which time there was a general consensus that the system was in crisis, the debate focused on many substantive changes in the system, possibly to include amendments to the constitution or even the writing of an entirely fresh constitution. In the earlier phase, much of the debate was couched in language referring to the need for the "democratization" of the party and political institutions. In both phases, the issues of decentralism versus recentralization and liberalization versus retrenchment dominated the agenda. Since at least three parties favored any given combination (liberal-recentralizers, conservative-decentralists, etc.), motion toward change appeared to be ruled out—at least as long as those elites were in power.

Much of the debate was carried out in code. For example, recentralizers often presented themselves initially as guardians of Tito's legacy (this would change after Milošević came to power), making it appear that the decentralists wanted to loosen the system further. But at this stage, the decentralists were fighting a purely defensive battle. They would only switch to the offense in 1989.

A book by Yugoslav political scientist Jovan Mirić, published in 1984 and excerpted in *Borba* in four installments, raised the political temperature by arguing that under the system established by the constitution of 1974, the federation lacked sovereignty and derived it only from the autonomous sovereignty of the republics. Mirić considered this a weakness and criticized, in particular, the republics' enjoyment of a veto over any important decisions.[28] Many in the party, however, feared at that time that any tinkering with the system would unleash unpredictable pressures for change and for several years held to a strict defense of the constitutional order.[29] Between this fear, and the incompatibility of the sides to the debate, reform was impossible. Slovenia and Croatia feared any move that might curtail their autonomy, and when, in 1985, the federal government introduced a bill, at the prompting of the International Monetary Fund and the World Bank, that would have obliged enterprises to surrender their foreign currency earnings to the national bank in Belgrade, Slovenia and Croatia blocked the bill and succeeded in scuttling it.[30]

By 1984, it was pretty clear that some changes to the constitution were needed—even if the elites could not agree on what kind of changes. Constitutional changes to the republic constitutions were made in Bosnia, Croatia, and Montenegro,[31] while in Serbia, the pressure for change to the constitution of SR Serbia could be traced back to 1981.[32]

By 1986, the collective state presidency had agreed to authorize the preparation of amendments to the federal constitution. On October 20, the Constitutional Commission of the federal *Skupština* met and appointed a coordinating group headed by Hamdija Pozderac (who would have to resign all his posts the following year in the wake of the Agrokomerc financial scandal in his native Bosnia) to prepare specific proposals. Among the issues the coordinating group was to consider were questions of property ownership, federal relations, the unity of the Yugoslav market, the planning system, and the relationship of the autonomous provinces to the Serbian republic.

On January 21, 1987, the coordinating group finished its preliminary work and the state presidency submitted its proposal for what it considered the "minimal" changes necessary for the constitutional system to continue to function.[33] These included, above all, proposals to create a unified legal system; to bring the railroad, postal, and telephone systems under central authority; and to tighten the unity of the Yugoslav economy—at the expense of the economic sovereignty of the individual republics. "All in all," *NIN* wrote at the time, "the presidency evidently considers that the rights and duties of the federation must be widened through the constitutional changes."[34] The Serbian government quickly applauded the presidency's proposals and declared them capable of leading the way out of the crisis.[35] But in Slovenia the general reaction was outrage. Addressing a five-hour public forum organized by the Slovenian Writers Association on March 17, sociologist Dimitrij Rupel exclaimed,

> To my great surprise, I discovered that the proposal for changes in the Constitution follows word for word, so to say, the requests of the "Memorandum" [of the Serbian Academy of Sciences in 1986] for unified technological systems such as the railroad system, the post, telegraph, and telephone system, energy system, and so forth. . . . Of course, the worst is the request for a unified legal system which in fact suits those who claim that liberal-nationalist and other hostile elements have been

> tolerated too much in some parts of the country and that, for instance, this system should be simplified so that Draconian sentences such as those pronounced in Kosovo, are pronounced in Slovenia too.[36]

Ćiril Ribičič, a leading member of the central committee of the Slovenian party, rebutted the Serbian argument that the recentralizing measures were necessary to deal with the country's problems. On the contrary, Ribičič told the weekly magazine, *Danas*, in a July 1987 interview,

> I am convinced that our problems would be much smaller, and the present debate calmer and more even-tempered, if the Federation had *less* authority in the domain of economic relations and if it did not interfere so much in the laws of the market as it is doing at present.[37]

The stage was thus set for the fiercer Slovenian-Serbian polemics that erupted in 1989.

Parallel to these discussions about the reform of the governmental structure were discussions about the reform and reorganization of the party and its umbrella organization, the Socialist Alliance of Working People of Yugoslavia (SAWPY). The same issues of recentralization versus decentralism and liberalization versus retrenchment could be seen in this arena too: hence demands that the powers of the LCY central committee be dramatically enhanced, that a tighter (and smaller) politburo be created to take over work assigned to the twenty-three-member party presidium, that a single LCY statute be adopted without the possibility of separate statutes for the republic and provincial party organizations, and so forth.[38]

Narodna armija seemed especially concerned about the evident weakening and federalization of the party and claimed that

> the workers are most bothered by [the] disintegration and fragmentation of basic organizations in the territories of the republics and provinces. A composite organization of associated labor which has eight policies and eight economies, and a ninth as a compromise of the preceding eight, cannot ensure the historical interests of the working class of Yugoslavia.[39]

The Thirteenth Party Congress (June 25–28, 1986) was billed as a "congress of the strengthening of socialist self-management, a congress of the strengthening of the unity of the country and of the LCY in the struggle against waxing etatism."[40] But despite such proclamations and associated efforts to put some meat on the principle of democratic centralism,[41] *Borba* soon declared the congress a failure, noting that the federalization of the party was continuing and deepening, despite vows to halt and reverse the process.[42]

As for SAWPY, there were those who wanted to loosen its ties to the party and enhance its independence and those who wanted to increase the LCY's role in SAWPY's activity. By 1987, the latter had asserted a transitory dominance, and over the twelve-month period beginning July 1987, steps in this direction were taken.[43]

Finally, there were occasional voices like that of Branko Horvat, who advocated the adoption of a partyless form of socialism.[44] Although this idea was by and large rejected, it still had its advocates even in 1987.[45]

The Battle Escalates, 1987–89

If the years 1981–83 saw a denial of crisis and an effort to reform the existing system and 1983–87 an admission of crisis and an elevation of reform efforts to the constitutional plane, the years 1987–89 were characterized by the revival and proliferation of exclusivist nationalism throughout the republics and provinces, a growing criticism of Tito (emanating above all from Serbia) and of the "AVNOJ-system" generally, and a transformation of the two sides to the debate. The recentralizers had hitherto operated within the ideological framework of the old Titoist system and hence saw recentralization in supranational terms. With the arrival of Slobodan Milošević on the Serbian political scene, however, recentralization became associated with Serbian nationalism and Serbian interests ("strong Serbia, strong Yugoslavia," as Milošević put it). Reacting to this, the decentralists, who had hitherto largely defended the existing division of powers, became confederalists, and now sought to expand the prerogatives of the republics even further to reduce the financial obligations of their republics to the federation and, ultimately, to transform the country into a de jure confederation.

By this point, the constitutional debate revolved around five key issues:

(1) change in the status of the autonomous provinces;
(2) change in the structure of the federal *Skupština*;
(3) procedure whereby members of a proposed Chamber of Citizens would be elected;
(4) asymmetric or symmetric federation; and
(5) change in the role of the LCY in the federation.[46]

The Serbian party was responsible for putting the first three items on the agenda, the Slovenian party was responsible for the fourth item, and the fifth emerged naturally as a by-product of the crisis of legitimacy. In a nutshell, the Serbian party wanted to erode the autonomy of the autonomous provinces and to strengthen the federal center, and it saw a restructuring of the federal *Skupština* as a means of achieving the latter.

At first, other republics registered their hostility to Serbian intentions vis-à-vis the provinces. But eventually, one by one—with the exception of Slovenia—they came to the view that this was an internal matter of the Serbian republic. In August 1988, for example, the presidium of the Bosnian LC central committee discussed Serbia's proposed constitutional changes and gave them its endorsement.[47] In Slovenia, however, there was less sympathy for Serbia's point of view. Ćiril Ribičič, a member of the presidium of the Slovenian LC central committee, articulated the Slovenian position that any change in the status of the autonomous provinces was not merely a matter for Serbia to decide, but was in fact a matter for all of Yugoslavia.[48]

But the question of change in the structure of the federal *Skupština* was viewed negatively not just by Slovenia but by other republics as well. Serbia wanted to replace the bicameral arrangement (Chamber of Republics and Provinces, Federal Chamber), with a tricameral arrangement (Chamber of Republics and Provinces, Chamber of Citizens, Chamber of Associated Labor). And whereas under the former framework the deputies of the chambers were selected by the assemblies of the respective republics and provinces, the Serbian party wanted the delegates to the Chamber of Citizens to be elected on the basis of "one person, one vote." Although this solution appears natural to Americans, it was a politically charged proposal in the Yugoslav context—one that was aimed at weakening the confederal element in the system. Only Montenegro supported Serbia on this issue. Slovenia, Croatia, and Bosnia adamantly opposed it.[49] Macedonia, by contrast, took the cautious position that no change should be made until more serious study could be conducted.[50]

The Chamber of Associated Labor was, further, a Serbian proposal, while both Slovenia and Croatia opposed it because the new chamber was designed in part to increase the state's role in the economy. Slovenia and Croatia, by contrast, wanted to see a diminution in the role of the state in the economy. Serbia was not alone in wanting the federation to have a role in the economy, however; this proposal was also supported by Macedonia, Montenegro, and Kosovo. Bosnia was a more complex case, however. Economics has often been secondary to politics in ethnically troubled Bosnia. Bosnian Serbs, for example, have often endorsed Serbian proposals only because they were Serbian. Bosnian Croats and Muslims tended to oppose Serbian proposals for the same reason.

At another level, Serbia sought to have members of the SFRJ presidency elected by the federal *Skupština* rather than by the respective republic/provincial assemblies. Bosnia and Montenegro supported the Serbian proposal, while Slovenia, Croatia, Vojvodina, and Kosovo were opposed.[51]

Eventually, in August 1988, the draft amendments to the constitution were published with the idea that they would be discussed and refined and eventually passed.[52] In Slovenia and Croatia, however, these amendments ran into trouble immediately. And in Slovenia they stimulated ideas of confederation and asymmetric federation. The latter idea held that federal units in a federation do not have to enjoy the same autonomy and prerogatives; these may be tailored to circumstances and needs. This allowed Slovenes to think in terms of their obtaining additional prerogatives *even if the other republics did not want such prerogatives for themselves.*[53] The resulting system could, for example, take the form of a federation within a confederation, with Slovenia having a confederal link with a Yugoslav federation that united the rest of the country. The asymmetric idea enjoyed only a limited life-span, however—scarcely much more than a year. By the end of 1989, Slovenes were becoming less interested in asymmetric federation and more interested in confederation, and the entire atmosphere became more conducive to confederalization.

In this context, interrepublican clashes over the federal budget acquired a new intensity. In July 1989, the Federal Executive Council proposed a formula under which the republics would pay the federation an additional 61 trillion dinars in order to balance the 1989 federal budget. Only Slovenia and Croatia supported the council's proposal. Montenegro and Bosnia sought to reduce their payments, while Serbia and Macedonia claimed that their allocations from the federal budget would be "unjustifiably reduced" under the proposed distribution arrangement.[54]

There was also a growing realization that Yugoslavia's problems were not different from those of other communist systems in Eastern Europe (except, of course, in regard to the national question). Like the other countries of the region, Yugoslavia's various economic reforms had never been carried through "to the limit," with the result, as author Marijan Korošić put it, that Yugoslavia was constantly forced to adjust and readjust the system. Korošić argued, in fact, that the 1974 constitution was prolonging the Yugoslav crisis and had to be abandoned.[55]

Given all of the aforementioned issues, it will be apparent why the constitutional debate excited widespread interest among the educated public and why arguments for republic self-determination inevitably led to reconsideration of the parameters of popular self-determination, especially in the form of a multiparty parliamentary system. This broader debate in turn exerted pressure on the party's debate and eventually forced the party to rethink its premises.

An Extraordinary Congress?

By mid-1988, many communists started talking about an extraordinary congress as a way of dealing with the gathering crisis. Slobodan Milošević, as head of the Serbian party, pushed hard for such a congress. The initial impetus for the congress came, in fact, from the Serbian and Vojvodinan party organizations and won early support in Montenegro. But at first, the Slovenian and Croatian parties resisted, fearing that the convocation of an extraordinary congress could be a prelude to the invocation of "special measures" both within the party and in Yugoslavia as a whole. Miloš Prosenc of Slovenia argued that convocation of an extraordinary congress would evoke a state of political "psychosis." Nor was the Bosnian party entirely enthusiastic about the congress. Speaking to a session of the LCY central committee on April 19, 1989, Nijaz Skenderagić of Bosnia came out against an extraordinary congress, commenting that "certain leaderships and leaders behave like arsonists rather than fire-fighters."[56]

Eventually, however, the various republic organizations agreed to hold the

Fourteenth (Extraordinary) Congress in December 1989—a date later postponed until January 1990. The congress was supposed to tackle three areas: reform of the constitutional system, economic reform, and transformation of the LCY.[57] Some people pinned great hopes on the congress, but as the date drew nearer, the prospects for its success grew steadily dimmer. The Fourteenth Extraordinary Congress would prove to be the party's swan song.

11

A New Napoleon: The Rise of Slobodan Milošević

Of course, I assure everyone that Serbia will not in any way abuse its numerical size nor endanger anyone in [any] way.

SLOBODAN MILOŠEVIĆ, at the January 21, 1990, session of the LCY Commission for the Reform of the Political System

Until 1987, it seemed conceivable that Yugoslavia could continue to muddle along[1]—agreeing on long-term programs of stabilization but failing to carry them out, fretting about ethnic violence in Kosovo but being content with containing rather than defusing it, groping its way toward pluralism slowly if persistently. Yugoslavia's regional elites, governing the eight federal units (six republics and two autonomous provinces), continued to quarrel about the fundamental choices in future development. Yet as long as they quarreled, they were at least talking to each other, and that signaled a degree of consent on the rules of the game.

In late 1987, the entire political game was changed overnight. Slobodan Milošević, a former banker, succeeded in deposing his erstwhile mentor, Ivan Stambolić, and in establishing himself as the unrivaled boss in the republic of Serbia. From that bastion, Milošević started to rewrite the rules of the game and, in so doing, dramatically sharpened the growing crisis in Yugoslavia, forcing it to a head.

Before Milošević, there was a general acceptance of the principle that the two autonomous provinces—Kosovo and Vojvodina, both of which lie within the jurisdictional frontiers of Serbia—should enjoy de facto parity with the six constituent republics that make up the Yugoslav federation. Like the republics, the two autonomous provinces enjoyed wide-ranging autonomy and even conducted foreign economic relations independently of the federal government. Milošević was determined to end this.

Before Milošević, there was a strong tendency to channel power through institutional channels—chiefly the republican party organizations and republican governments. Milošević would turn to mobs and orchestrated demonstrations to marshal and apply power.

Before Milošević, there had been a string of "faceless bureaucrats" who, since the death of President Josip Broz Tito in May 1980, seemed determined to prevent the rise of a "new Tito." But Milošević's followers evidently thought of him as a new Tito—or even better—and marched down the streets, bearing his portrait and singing songs in his honor.

And finally, before Milošević, the Communist party—able to agree on little else—agreed all the same that any resurgence of nationalism would destabilize the system and promote serious political change. The party leaders, therefore, repeatedly reminded each other that "every nationalism is dangerous" and refused to legitimize *any* nationalism. Milošević changed that from the start, openly embracing both Serbian nationalism and Serbian Orthodoxy (the "Serbian" religion). For the first time since the communists had taken power, the Serbian Orthodox Church found itself coddled by the communists.

These changes had a powerful effect on the system and throttled it toward a showdown. In the gathering crisis, Milošević's Serbia was initially challenged by Slovenia and Croatia, and as the months unfolded, seemed to wax in strength, only to find itself increasingly isolated.

From Bureaucrat to Politician

As politician, Milošević has championed what he has called the "anti-bureaucratic revolution." But Milošević himself was nurtured in the economic bureaucracy and rose through its ranks.

Born in Požarevac, Serbia, on August 29, 1941, Milošević joined the Communist party at age twenty-eight. He was actively involved in party politics (as chair of the university's party ideological committee) while studying at the University of Belgrade, from which he graduated in 1964 with a degree in law. He took a post in economic management within the party hierarchy, and in 1968 was named to an executive position in the state-owned Tehnogas company; one of his colleagues there was none other than Ivan Stambolić, his later mentor and eventual rival in the Serbian party apparatus. In 1973, Milošević became general director of Tehnogas and, five years later, took the highly visible post of president of Beobanka (Belgrade Bank). In that capacity, he visited the United States several times, and, over the years, polished his English.

It was not until 1984, however, that Milošević entered politics, when he became head of the Belgrade city committee. He was forty-three years old at the time.

Meanwhile, Ivan Stambolić, his former colleague at Tehnogas, had become chair of the central committee (CC) of the Serbian party in April 1984. Milošević seemed, at the time, to be a loyal standard-bearer to Stambolić, and there were not detectable differences in their statements on policy matters. Stambolić and Milošević seemed as close as brothers; they even served as "best man" at each other's weddings. People remember, however, how at a meeting of the Serbian CC sometime in 1985, Milošević was the only speaker to address the meeting in emotional tones, and the only speaker to be given a passionate applause.[2] Later—in May 1986—Stambolić vacated his position as chair of the Serbian

CC in order to become president of the Republic of Serbia. With his blessing, Milošević succeeded him as chair of the Serbian party.

Even at that stage there were signs of a waxing Serbian nationalist backlash in reaction to the repeated Albanian riots in Kosovo and the mass exodus of Serbs and Montenegrins from the province. As early as 1983, in an overt expression of nostalgia for the "good old days," some 100,000 people showed up for the funeral of Aleksandar Ranković. And later, in October 1986, came the issuance—already described in chapter 9—of the Serbian Academy's famous "Memorandum," bemoaning Serbia's fate in Yugoslavia and calling on Serbs to reverse the tide of decentralization and halt natural processes in Kosovo. Even Stambolić found he had to pay at least lip service to the demands of Serbian nationalism. In his report to the Tenth Congress of the Serbian party (May 26, 1986), Stambolić endorsed the Serbian nationalist position that the federal constitution of 1974 was contrary to the interests of Serbs, although he also warned that "certain individuals" were "coquetting" with Serbian nationalism.[3] Stambolić straddled the fence.

Not so Milošević—and gradually differences emerged between the two men. Then in April 1987, an event occurred that had a profound effect on Milošević. The situation in Kosovo seemed to be deteriorating again, and a meeting of 300 party delegates was called in Kosovo Polje, a suburb of Priština. As head of the Serbian party, Milošević went there to attend the meeting; most of the 300 delegates were, however, ethnic Albanians. When the meeting began, some 15,000 Serbs and Montenegrins—mostly locals but also a few who had come to Kosovo for this purpose—tried to force their way into the hall. The meeting was supposed to be closed, so police blocked their way and started to beat them back with clubs. Then Milošević raised his hands, signaling the police to let the Serbs through, telling the Serbs, "Nobody, either now or in the future, has the right to beat you."[4] These words assured Milošević of a place in Serbian mythology. Milošević stayed in the building until dawn—some thirteen hours—listening to hundreds of Serbs tell him of their troubles and blame the Albanian leaders of the provincial government for allowing the situation to deteriorate. He emerged from that night a changed man. As a Serbian journalist who has known Milošević for years put it, "After that night, suddenly there was a psychological change in him. All at once, he discovered he had this power over people."[5]

In mid-December 1987, Milošević ousted Stambolić from the Serbian presidency (a post Milošević assumed somewhat later, in May 1989) and began to put a new program into effect. Whereas Stambolić had carefully balanced his speeches with veiled self-contradictions and obscure summons to action that would not be carried out, Milošević spoke simply and directly and outlined a program he in fact would try to carry out. The program involved four stages, but these stages entailed mutually incompatible prerequisites so that the program appeared doomed from the start.

The first stage in his program entailed establishing his full control in Serbia. To do so, he felt he needed a pliant press. He therefore fired a number of editors and journalists at the prestigious Politika publishing house. The daily papers *Politika* and *Politika ekspres* and the weekly magazines *Duga* and *NIN* became mouthpieces of Milošević. He also reached out for an alliance with the Serbian Orthodox Church, authorizing it to resume construction on the monumental Cathedral of St. Sava in downtown Belgrade and giving the church a new prominence and dignity in social life. Through the church, Milošević tapped one of the primordial wellsprings of Serbian nationalism. Through publications and displays and public events, Serbian society now began to revive memories of its past—especially of the Battle of Kosovo, at which the Serbian army of King Lazar had been beaten by the Ottoman army in 1389. This battle, which symbolically captures the essence of the tragedy of Serbia's conquest and occupation by Turkey, has figured prominently in Serbian mythologizing of Kosovo—now populated 90 percent by Albanians. In June 1989, Milošević joined Serbian Orthodox Church dignitaries in a joint commemoration of the battle: it was no less than a celebration of Serbian nationalism. A year later, on June 15, 1990, Milošević received a delegation of the Serbian Orthodox Church Synod to work out remaining problems in the church-state relationship in Serbia.[6]

This first stage necessarily entailed the development of a localized "cult of the personality"—the first in Yugoslavia since the death of Tito in May 1980. It was nothing to see shops and vendors and restaurants displaying photo portraits of Milošević in the front windows. At a more fundamental level, it became impossible for Serbs to criticize Milošević publicly and retain jobs of any importance. Many Serbs were buoyed by an intoxicating sense of Serbian pride, as "Comrade Slobo" began to promote criticism of Tito for having weakened Serbia. Among the alleged anti-Serbian acts said to have been committed by Tito: the removal of large amounts of Serbian industry to new locations in Croatia and elsewhere in the late 1940s and early 1950s;[7] the expansion of the prerogatives and powers of the autonomous provinces, especially after 1968; and the federal constitution itself. Some Serbs told foreigners that they had never been free under Tito but were, with "Slobo" at their head, "completely free as never before." Other Serbs quietly fretted, as did growing numbers of non-Serbs, that Milošević was patterning himself not merely after Tito, but after Stalin!

The second stage involved the reestablishment of Serbian control over its autonomous provinces and the subversion of Montenegro in order to bring it under the control of pro-Milošević forces. To accomplish this, Milošević proposed to mobilize Serbian and Montenegrin citizens and take politics "to the streets." This stage was aptly captured in the slogan, "strong Serbia, strong Yugoslavia." This slogan assured Milošević of extensive support in Serbia. But it was deeply alienating to Croats, Slovenes, Macedonians, and Bosnian Muslims, let alone to Kosovo's Albanians.

With the successful accomplishment of the tasks of the second stage, Milošević hoped, in the third stage, to bring down the old constitution of 1974, tightening up the federation and reducing the powers of the six constituent republics.

And in the fourth stage Milošević promised a reform of the by-then unified system, emphasizing the marketization of the economy and the controlled democratization of internal party life, but stopping short of the political repluralization of society. What Milošević understood by "controlled democratization" was never entirely clear, but the stress was clearly on control rather than democratization. Milošević's repeated allusions to the need for democracy and for a free market economy won him respect in the West, particularly in the United States, at first, where it was noted with approval that Milošević looked to South Korea as a kind of model. And, at that point, he won some support at home because of his reputation as a technocrat. But in the long run, he looked to political strategies, rather than economic ones, to legitimate his authority and gained a reputation as a Serbian nationalist. This image gradually eclipsed his earlier technocrat image. And in the U.S., in particular, his policies in Kosovo merely aggravated a growing public relations problem of his own making—culminating in the passage of a congressional resolution condemning Yugoslav (i.e., Milošević's) policies in Kosovo.[8]

The First Stage: Building Strength in Serbia

Milošević has boasted that he has brought Serbia "strong arm" rule (*čvrsta ruka*).[9] His rule has also been one continuous celebration of Serbia—indeed, that is the foundation and source of his strength. Milošević appeals to the passions, not to the intellect; he talks of Serbia's place in the world, of struggle, of enemies, of solutions. The spirit of his appeal is captured in the following excerpt from a speech he delivered at an outdoor meeting at the confluence of the Sava and Danube rivers in Belgrade, on November 19, 1988:

> . . . This is no time for sorrow; it is a time for struggle. (*indistinct shouting*) This awareness captured Serbia last summer and this awareness has turned into a material force that will stop the terror in Kosovo and unite Serbia. (*indistinct shouting*) This is a process which no longer can be stopped by any force, a process in the face of which all fear is weak. People will even consent to live in poverty but they will not consent to live without freedom, at least not the people gathered here and the people in Serbia, to whom I myself belong and therefore I know that they can only live in freedom and in no other way. (*indistinct shouting*) Both the Turkish and the German invaders know that these people win their battles for freedom.
>
> We entered both world wars with nothing but the conviction that we would fight for freedom, and we won both wars. (*cheers*) Now we have the unified LC stances on Kosovo and we shall implement them energetically to the very end. (*chanting: "Yugoslavia."*)
>
> We shall win the battle for Kosovo regardless of the obstacles facing us inside

> and outside the country. (*cheers*). . . . We shall win despite the fact that Serbia's enemies outside the country are plotting against it, along with those in the country. (*cheers*) We tell them that we enter every battle (*Milošević is interrupted by cheers*) with the aim of winning it. (*cheers*)
>
> We have never waged unjust and dishonest battles that would be to the detriment of other peoples. (*shouts of "that is right"*) The people, all citizens regardless of their nationality and profession, are at the head of this battle for Kosovo. And there is no battle in the world that the people have lost. (*shouts of "that is right"*) The leadership has little choice there: It shall either head the people and listen to their voice, or time will push it aside . . . (*cheers*) . . . [10]

Milošević owes his rise, above all, to the growing Serbian bitterness about the demographic changes in Kosovo and Serbian fears that the province will be "lost." Milošević's style is populist—building popular trust in him personally rather than trust in the political institutions. This aspect of his power has repeatedly been demonstrated—for example, in October 1988, 6,000 angry demonstrators peacefully dispersed moments after Milošević drove up in his car and told them that he would take up their complaints personally. Other Yugoslav politicians (outside Serbia) began to compare him to Mussolini.[11]

Milošević stoked the fires of Serbian nationalism, and in the resultant atmosphere, strange things happened. There were calls, for example, for the posthumous rehabilitation of Aleksandar Ranković (d. 1983), Tito's right-hand man until 1966, who was personally responsible for much of the repression of the Kosovar Albanians in the first two decades after the war.[12] Serbs began talking about a Vatican-Comintern conspiracy and trying to vilify the Catholic Church—the cultural champion of the Serbs' arch-rivals, the Croats. Thus, in 1987, Belgrade published a book that attempted to link the Vatican with the misdeeds of the fascist *Ustaše* of World War II, and in November 1988, the Serbian Academy of Sciences ordered a scientific meeting on the theme, "Jasenovac, 1945–1988," in order to keep alive Serbian resentments of the liquidations of Serbs at the wartime concentration camp at Jasenovac.[13] There were also reports that Serbs were reorganizing Chetnik formations—the Chetniks were Serbian nationalist resistance forces in World War II—that these Chetniks were holding demonstrations in traditional insignia and flowing beards, and that Serbian demonstrators in Montenegro were heard chanting, "Long live King Peter!" and "We want the Russians!"[14] And the Serbian Orthodox Church, which had grown accustomed to being treated like an unwelcome stepchild, suddenly found itself lauded and celebrated in the Serbian press, and its priests, inspired with new confidence, began to take part in nationalist demonstrations.

Milošević's style of rule has sometimes exploited the Serbian party apparatus as an instrument of power and, at other times, has simply bypassed it. Not without reason did he confess to a French journalist in July 1989 that he was hostile to a multiparty system, and actually preferred "a system without parties."[15] In a nonparty system, the people place their trust directly in the leader, who therefore embodies the will of the people. The formula seemed to work. Said Budimir Kostić, president of the Serbian Investment Bank: "Milošević has [in mid-1989] full support in Serbia, from the peasants to the Academy of Science. He'd get 90 percent of the vote in any election."[16]

The Second Stage: Conquering the Provinces

From early on, Milošević's supporters began saying that Serbia was a second-class republic and that the prerogatives enjoyed by the autonomous provinces of Kosovo and Vojvodina were extraconstitutional. Central to Milošević's program was the "reconquest" of these provinces. To effect this, the Committee for the Protection of Kosovo Serbs and Montenegrins was set up, under Milošević's wing, in 1988. Between July 9 and September 4, 1988, the committee organized eleven rallies, involving up to 160,000 persons at a time, and by spring 1989 had organized almost one hundred protest demonstrations, involving a cumulative total of some 5 million people, or an average of 50,000 participants per demonstration. This committee was a key instrument in Milošević's drive for power.

Chair of this committee was Miroslav Solević, who expressed the committee's philosophy quite simply when he told Radio Zagreb, "If we don't get our rights, we will take up arms."[17] Another important member of the committee was Mića Sparavalo, at one time a lieutenant to UDBa chief Ranković.

The first demonstration was modest enough and involved a seven-hour demonstration in Novi Sad, Vojvodina's capital city, in which about five hundred Kosovar Serbs were joined by several thousand local Serbs. The demonstrators shouted slogans against Vojvodina's alleged "separatism" and called the province's leaders "traitors." Vojvodina's leaders replied on July 15, accusing Milošević of making a grab for power. Three days later, at a closed session of the twenty-three-member federal party presidium, Vojvodina's leaders demanded that Milošević be fired.[18] But Milošević kept up the pressure, and in late September, a joint meeting of the Vojvodina presidency and the Vojvodina party leadership released a communiqué fretting that "an attack unprecedented in the post-World War II history of Vojvodina has been launched at the province."[19]

Such warnings were to no avail, and when, on October 6, Milošević mobilized some 100,000 supporters on the streets of Novi Sad, the entire leadership of Vojvodina resigned, including provincial party leader Milovan Šogorov and provincial president Nandor Major. Further resignations were tendered in the cities and local communities of Vojvodina.[20] In their places, Milošević installed his own people: in particular, Nedeljko Sipovac became party chief in Vojvodina, while Mihalj Kerteš took over the presidency.

In emotional terms, Vojvodina was only a dress rehearsal for Kosovo—the real jewel in the Serbian crown, despite its extreme poverty. Further rallies in Belgrade, Smederevo, and various cities throughout Serbia, as well as a march of 17,000 Serbs and Montenegrins through the streets of Priština on

August 29, 1988 (by coincidence, Milošević's birthday), helped prepare the way for a takeover in the largely Albanian-populated southern province as well. In a series of maneuvers, Milošević engineered the forced resignation of Albanians Azem Vllasi and Kolj Široka from the Kosovar leadership, placed his loyal follower Rahman Morina in the provincial party presidency, pushed through the adoption of Serbo-Croatian as the sole official language in Kosovo (making Albanian, hereafter, unacceptable for official use), and prepared a series of constitutional amendments designed to strip the provinces of much of their autonomy.[21]

The federal party central committee registered its disapproval of Milošević's actions on October 19, by taking a vote of no-confidence in Dušan Čkrebić, a key Milošević lieutenant, effectively firing Čkrebić from the party presidium. Undeterred, Milošević continued to push for changes to the constitutions of Serbia and its autonomous provinces. This was accomplished in February 1989, resulting, among other things, in the elimination of the province's authority to pass its own laws and in the establishment of the Supreme Court of SR Serbia as the highest judicial court of appeal for Kosovars, prior to appeal to the federal level. Vllasi, the former provincial party president, was eventually arrested on Milošević's orders, and put on trial on charges of organizing Albanian unrest between November 1988 and March 1989, only to be acquitted in April 1990.[22] Milošević also pledged to construct some two thousand new dwellings in Kosovo by 1993 for the use of Serbian families who decide to return to the province, funding the construction almost entirely out of federal funds.[23]

These moves by Milošević stirred federal party president Stipe Šuvar to defend the constitutional status quo against the revisionist Milošević. Šuvar had, for years, figured as a centralist and had, therefore, long been more popular in Serbia than in his native Croatia.[24] But now Šuvar criticized Milošević's use of street demonstrations. Milošević, in turn, accused Šuvar of opposing the people's will, and at a stormy session of the central committee on January 30, 1989, various Serbian delegates called for Šuvar's resignation. Šuvar suddenly became the rallying point for anti-Milošević sentiment, and former critics of Šuvar now became his loudest advocates. Milošević tried to orchestrate Šuvar's removal from office before the expiration of his term in May 1989, but failed, and Šuvar served out his term.

Simultaneously, Milošević also set in motion efforts to destabilize Montenegro and Bosnia, with the aim of installing his followers in power in those republics too. An early move came on August 20, 1988, when his action committee organized a protest involving 30,000 people in the Montenegrin capital of Titograd.[25] Further protests followed on September 18 (50,000 persons, in Nikšić) and October 7 (in Titograd). The latter demonstrations initially shook the confidence of the republic leadership, which briefly considered bowing to the protesters' demands that the leadership resign. Instead, the Montenegrin leaders sent club-wielding police to disperse the crowd. Later, to appease them, the local politicians gave the workers wage increases of up to 30 percent.

But again Milošević kept up the pressure, and finally, on January 11, 1989, following two days of renewed unrest in Titograd, the entire Montenegrin collective presidency resigned, along with Montenegro's delegates in the federal party presidium (Marko Orlandić, Vidoje Žarković, and Slobodan Filipović) and its member in the federal collective presidency (Veselin Djuranović).[26] They were replaced by supporters of Milošević.

Serbian nationalists have long tended to regard Montenegrins merely as coastal Serbs, and scholars argued back and forth throughout the 1970s and 1980s about whether Montenegrins came from the same ethnic stock as Serbs. This controversy was now revived with a vengeance, as pro-Serbian Montenegrins urged the annexation of Montenegro to the Republic of Serbia.[27] And in June 1989, Serbo-Croatian was made a mandatory subject in all Albanian-language elementary and secondary schools in Montenegro, at the same time that it was made mandatory in Serbian schools where the language of instruction was some language other than Serbo-Croatian.

By mid-1989, Milošević seemed to be in a strong position. He controlled Serbia, Kosovo, and Vojvodina outright. He had installed his people in Montenegro. Macedonia was, for the time being, allied with Milošević. And Milošević had quietly sent agents of the Serbian security service into Bosnia in order to gather intelligence and subvert the republic from within—although this did not come to light until later.[28] A confident Milošević now assumed the post of state president of Serbia (on May 8), sanctioned by a unanimous open vote.[29]

The Third Stage: Bringing Down the Constitution

Having identified himself for three years with the slogan "strong Serbia, strong Yugolsavia"—a slogan that endeared him to Serbs but alienated non-Serbs—Milošević tried, in 1989, to repackage himself in order to complete his program. He therefore tried to identify himself with what he called the "anti-bureaucratic revolution." He also talked of the need to build a "modern, efficient, stable state"—by which he meant a centralized state.[30]

But Milošević's efforts to mobilize the Serbian population in Bosnia only consolidated the anti-Serbian solidarity between Bosnian Croats and Bosnian Muslims, and the more the Belgrade media harped on "the alleged imperilment of Serbs in Bosnia-Herzegovina,"[31] the more the Bosnian leadership tended to look to Slovenia and Croatia for allies against Milošević.

In Macedonia, moreover, locals were becoming increasingly agitated already in early 1989 by the proliferation in that republic of slogans, graffiti, and songs glorifying Serbian leader Milošević.[32] Then Milošević proposed a law to allow Serbs who had land titles from the interwar period to reclaim their land. The measure was designed to provide a legal basis for large numbers of Serbs to move to Kosovo, but it also threatened to dislocate Macedonians. Relations between the two republics, accordingly, soured. And subsequently, Milošević introduced a proposal to declare December 1—the day on which Yugoslavia had been united in 1918—a national holiday. But any celebration of the old "Kingdom of Serbs, Croats, and Slovenes" inevitably hurt Macedonian sensitivities, since they recalled that the old kingdom had called them "south Serbs" and had denied them any cultural or educational guarantees.

As for Slovenia and Croatia, they were, by the latter part of 1989, rapidly moving from a defense of the quasi-confederal status quo to advocacy of a multiparty system, full-fledged confederalization of Yugoslavia, and full republic status for Kosovo and Vojvodina.[33] By September 1989, Milošević had lost his momentum and found himself on the defensive. By February 1989, the Croatian Writers Association was openly calling on Milošević to resign from office.[34] By June 1990, Yugoslav Prime Minister Ante Marković (a Croat) was found, by pollsters, to be the most popular politician in the country—with growing support even in Milošević's Serbian backyard.[35] And in mid-June 1990, a remarkable political inversion occurred: some 30,000 Serbs marched through Belgrade carrying Serbian flags with old (precommunist) Serbian insignia, chanting "Down with communism!" and bearing pictures of Milošević, with a black "X" across his face and the slogan written above, "We don't want another dictator!"[36]

The Consequences of Repluralization

Beginning in 1988, independent political parties started to form in Yugoslavia. By early 1990, there were eighty-six of them, including six in Serbia. In January 1990, the Slovenian party severed its links with the LCY. And in spring, free elections were held in Slovenia and Croatia, resulting in the electoral victories of a center-right coalition in Slovenia, and of the Croatian-nationalist Croatian Democratic Community, a party headed by retired partisan general Franjo Tudjman, in Croatia. The new noncommunist governments of Slovenia and Croatia immediately removed the word *socialist* from the designations of their republics and removed the red star from the flags, and the Slovenian parliament shortly issued a somewhat ambiguous declaration of "sovereignty" (not independence), explaining that Slovenian law overrode federal law, and that the latter would apply only when it was consistent with Slovenian law.[37] The Croatian *Sabor* likewise declared the Republic of Croatia "sovereign." Moreover, with Tanjug, the Yugoslav news agency, firmly in Serbian hands, the new Croatian government set up its own news agency (Hrvatska Novinska Agencija). On August 1, Bosnia-Herzegovina followed suit, and declared itself a "sovereign and democratic state."[38] These declarations obviously prepared the way for possible declarations of withdrawal from the Yugoslav federation.

About the same time, Bosnia announced that it would hold multiparty elections on November 18. Macedonia had already scheduled elections for that month. And in Montenegro, the government likewise promised to hold multiparty elections as soon as the republic constitution could be appropriately amended.[39] Even the Serbian leadership was eventually forced, reluctantly, to agree to promise a multiparty system in their republic too. That solution—as

Kosovo's Albanians well knew—could undermine Milošević's formula for tight control of the provinces.

Meanwhile, Milošević was faced with new competition for the Serbian nationalist "vote." Two new parties, both created in January 1990, are expressly nationalist in character—one monarchist and one populist. The former is an outgrowth of the Sava Society, set up by Vuk Drašković in Nova Pazova. Reconstituted as the Party of Serbian National Renewal, this organization calls for a restoration of the Serbian Karadjordjević dynasty at the head of a Greater Serbia, which would include the territories corresponding to the present units of Serbia, Kosovo, Vojvodina, Macedonia, and Montenegro, as well as those regions in Bosnia and Croatia (such as Knin and parts of Dalmatia) that have heavy concentrations of Serbs. In keeping with the restorationist inspiration of this program, the Party of Serbian National Renewal also promises that ". . . the state institutions(s), the economy, education, the army, [the position of] the church, and foreign policy would be restored in the form corresponding to the period."[40]

The other nationalist challenger to Milošević is the Democratic Freedom party, set up in Belgrade on January 14, 1990. While espousing democracy and Yugoslav integration into the European community in 1992, this party also pledged to work to abolish the provinces of Kosovo and Vojvodina altogether, to expel large numbers of Albanians from the country, to obtain the restoration of property lost by Serbs who were expelled from Kosovo during World War II, and, in the event of the breakup of the country, to seek the maximum extension of Serbia's borders.[41]

By late June, Milošević, who had hitherto declared confederalization "unacceptable," had to concede that this had become a very real possibility—indeed, it was probably the one route whereby Yugoslavia might have survived. But in this context, Milošević added, ominously, that in the event that Yugoslavia became a confederation, the external borders of Serbia would be an "open question".[42] Even more ominously, the draft of the new constitution of the Republic of Serbia gave the president of Serbia an unusual new prerogative—the power to declare war and conclude peace. This, of course, presumed the creation of an independent Serbian army, as Macedonian politicians were quick to note.[43] Just as obviously, this new prerogative was a dangerous escalation in a country that had been abuzz for about three years with rumors of impending civil war.

Conclusion

Milošević has had a profound effect on developments in Yugoslavia. His concerted campaign to refashion Yugoslavia along centralist lines and to erode the two autonomous provinces provoked a powerful anti-Serbian reaction throughout the rest of the country, a reaction that wedded prodemocracy sentiment to proconfederation sentiment, and probably accelerated Bosnia's ultimate embrace of political pluralism. In what appeared to be a last-ditch effort to consolidate at least his minimal program, Milošević staged a referendum on July 1, asking Serbian voters to endorse constitutional changes that would virtually eliminate any vestige of provincial autonomy. The supposedly docile Kosovo assembly replied the following day by declaring Kosovo a republic, independent from Serbia, though still a constituent part of the Yugoslav federation.[44]

The Serbian parliament replied by suspending the provincial assembly and the provincial executive council and assuming full and direct control of the province. Serbian authorities dismissed the editors of Kosovo's principal Albanian-language newspapers, as well as the station managers of radio and television stations. Albanian-language broadcasts ceased. Police even occupied the offices of the Kosovo Writers Association, which had been used by opposition circles for meetings.[45] When *Rilindja*, the Priština daily, nonetheless continued to criticize Serbian policy, Milošević closed the paper down too. On September 4, Albanians observed a twenty-four-hour general strike, virtually shutting down the province. Meanwhile, some 111 members of Kosovo's dissolved assembly—representing more than two-thirds of the body's membership—met clandestinely and drew up an alternative constitution for Kosovo that spelled out Kosovo's rights as a republic within the Yugoslav federation (or confederation) and designated Albanian as the official language of the province.[46] Milošević replied by ordering the arrest of the deputies to Kosovo's now-banned assembly.

The new governments of Slovenia and Croatia declared themselves ready for immediate negotiations on the transformation of Yugoslavia into a confederation.[47] But Yugoslavia was distinctly unstable, and the lame-duck governments of Serbia, Macedonia, Bosnia, and Montenegro were not really in a position to negotiate something so fundamental as the confederalization of the country. Yugoslavia was more anomalous than ever: one could describe it (in October 1990) as a "two-thirds communist country"—with four republics under lame-duck communist governments, two republics under noncommunist governments, the two autonomous provinces with undefined futures, and the very borders separating the republics called into question.

In spring 1984, I warned, in the policy journal, *Orbis*, that the suppression of Croatian liberalism in 1971 and the heavy reliance on Serbs to administer Croatian politics (out of proportion to their numbers in that republic[48]) had sown such bitterness and distrust between Croats and Serbs as to make civil war a real danger.[49] This danger has not been steady, and at times it has seemed to recede, but with the advent of Milošević, the mood of the country became more tense, and the country once again drifted in the direction of civil war. As bad as the situation in Kosovo has been, however, and despite the fact that Kosovo became an issue between Slovenia and Serbia in the course of 1989, thus contributing to the inflammation of interrepublican relations broadly, it is highly unlikely that any amount of trouble in Kosovo could ever have triggered generalized civil war in Yugoslavia. The most dangerous flashpoint in Yugoslavia, and possibly the only one capable of triggering civil war, was the Serbian region in Croatia. And under Milošević's influence, Croatia's Serbs started to press demands. Serbs took to insisting that if Yugoslavia were to become a full-fledged confederation, Serbs would have the "right" to create an autonomous province within Croatia.[50] In summer 1989, there was an abortive effort to set up an autonomous Serbian cultural society (the "Zora Society") in the Knin region of Croatia; the Croatian authorities immediately banned the organization and jailed its chief organizer, Jovan Opačić.[51] When the Serbian Writers Union sprang to Opačić's defense and took up the cause of political autonomy for Croatia's Serbs,[52] Croatian authorities blasted the union for seeking to change Croatia's borders and to destabilize the republic altogether.[53] In August 1990, following the May election of Tudjman's noncommunist government in Croatia, leaders of Croatia's Serbian community pledged to seek territorial-political autonomy—a solution unacceptable either to the Croatian people or to the Croatian government. But the Serbs took to issuing threats. "If the Croatian people want their own state," said Jovan Rašković, president of the Serbian Democratic party, about the proposed Serbian autonomous region, "then the Serbs will decide their own fate."[54] Rašković added that if Croatia seceded from Yugoslavia, Croatia's Serbs would try to attach their areas to Serbia. Obviously Croatian authorities would consider any such move completely unacceptable.

In mid-August, Croatian Serbs conducted a referendum on autonomy within Croatia, defying a ban by Zagreb authorities. There were maneuvers by armored vehicles of the Croatian police, and meanwhile, hundreds of Serbs, armed with AK-47 rifles and pistols, sealed the roads to Knin, felling trees to block entry. Federal army units were also sent into the Knin region, contributing to the tension.[55] Meanwhile, *Politika* blasted Croatian president Tudjman, simultaneously for trying to restore the *Ustaše* and for copying Tito, and pledged the support of Belgrade Serbs for the Serbian minority in Croatia.[56] These developments were clearly encouraged by Milošević's policies.

Officially, 756,781 Serbs took part in the August 9–September 2 referendum. Of this total, it is said, 756,549 voted for Serbian autonomy, 172 voted against, and 60 ballots were invalid. On October 1, the Serbian National Council in Croatia declared the autonomy of areas in Croatia inhabited primarily by Serbs.[57] With this move, civil order broke down in Croatia. The Croatian ministry of internal affairs, meanwhile, decided to confiscate the weapons of local militias, thereby disarming the Serbs. Resisting, Serbs raided at least one police station, burglarized gun shops, and erected barricades around Knin and other municipalities. Railway lines to Knin were also cut. Meanwhile, Serbs in Belgrade gathered in front of the Parliament building, shouting, "We want arms" and "Let's go to Croatia."[58] A similar rally took place in Zagreb. The individual republics' ever-greater assertion of control over their own military districts seemed to prefigure eventual warfare. In mid-October, the Slovenian prime minister, Lojze Peterle, even suggested that Slovenia would welcome an international peacekeeping force if the situation deteriorated any further.

Milošević has been a catalyst for crisis, his campaigns forced things to a head.

But the processes that unfolded had deep roots, and pressure for repluralization and confederalization had been building for some two decades.[59] Milošević has thought of himself as a modern, efficiency-oriented politician and likes to talk about democracy and free enterprise. But he ultimately gave priority to the nationalist components in his program and will thus go down in history as a late reactionary who tried, but failed, to turn back the clock.

12

The Transformation of Yugoslav Politics

The year 1989 was a turning point in the evolution of Yugoslav politics. Several factors entered into this. First, as already discussed, the party apparatus started crumbling at a fast pace, from the bottom up. Citizens stopped going to meetings, local committees stopped functioning and closed up, party members returned their party cards, and the party's "reach" steadily shrank. Second, inflation was soaring at 800–900 percent most of the year, and topped 1,000 percent by the end of the year. This had a tremendous impact on people's mood, attitudes, and behavior at all levels—including politics. Third, the national question, which had seemed to be under control in the late 1970s and roughly manageable in the early years of the 1980s, had clearly reemerged as a powerful force by 1989—that, to some extent, as a product of Milošević's program and strategy, as I argued in the preceding chapter. Fourth, in Kosovo in particular, after the Serbian annexation of the province in March 1989, extinguishing most of the province's juridical prerogatives, the Kosovo question alone became vastly more serious, as Serb-Albanian tensions took a turn for the worse. Fifth, the continuing constitutional debate contributed to a sense that change was not only necessary, but inevitable. And sixth, the changes sweeping through other parts of Eastern Europe—in particular, Poland and Hungary, but eventually also East Germany and Czechoslovakia—helped redouble Yugoslavs' growing impatience with their system, as they saw their neighbors make their first steps toward democratization.

As a result, by 1989, the system had lost its earlier resilience, had become, in fact, quite fragile. There was a growing sense that it was breathing its last breath.

Slovenia versus Serbia

As of 1989, the Serbian party was advocating that the federation be restructured in such a way as to incorporate the principle "one-person one-vote" while insisting that in Kosovo, the interests of 10 percent of the population took precedence over the other 90 percent. And after the Opačić affair in Croatia, Serbs advocated the rights of the Serbian minority in Croatia to enjoy an autonomous region, even though they already had a republic of their own, while denying that the Albanians had any right even to autonomy in Kosovo, let alone to their own republic.

Slovenia's view of the situation was radically different from Serbia's, and already in 1988, serious polemics divided the two leaderships. In early autumn 1988, the Serbian leadership approached the Slovenian leadership and asked for the latter's support for the proposed amendments to the Serbian constitution. The Slovenian leadership, however, refused, saying that this would amount to interference in Serbia's internal affairs.[1] But in the closing months of 1988, Slovenian-Serbian relations soured. Milošević's political style and strategy were, quite simply, unsettling to the Slovenes. "This Stalinist concept of 'democratic centralism' unavoidably leads to extolling the central figure into a living god," Slovenia's president, Janez Stanovnik, said of Serbia in a 1988 interview. "When you start worshipping a leader, you no longer have a population that is able to act democratically."[2] Slovenia's leaders accused Serbia's of "Stalinism," and Serbia's leaders accused Slovenia's of "betrayal." Hostility bred distrust, and by mid-October 1988, the two leaderships were no longer on speaking terms. On November 16, the SRFJ presidency intervened in the dispute and urged the leaderships of Slovenia and Serbia to meet.[3] But nothing came of this initiative. On the contrary, Serbs started boycotting Slovenian products. Belgrade citizens also started withdrawing their savings from the Bank of Ljubljana. And the director of the Jugoeksport work organization threatened to terminate joint ventures with some eighty-eight Slovenian partners.[4]

At this stage, the writers' associations of Slovenia and Serbia played a key role. In late February 1989, when Albanian miners at the Trepča mine in Kosovo staged a major strike, the Slovenian Association of Writers held a public meeting at Cankar Hall (Cankarjev Dom) in Ljubljana, criticizing the stationing of some 15,000 army troops in Kosovo[5] and the implementation of extraordinary measures, and expressing sympathy with the miners. On February 28, the Serbian Association of Writers broke off relations with the Slovenian Association. In the telegram sent to Ljubljana, the Serbian Association accused the Slovenian Association "of betraying the traditional, historic, and predestined friendship between our two nations."[6] The Slovenian Association refused to believe that the rupture was permanent, and when, in April 1989, a meeting of the Associations of Writers of Yugoslavia was held, Rudi Seligo, president of the Slovenian Association, attended. Seligo tried, at that meeting, to persuade the body to issue a criticism of Serbian policy in Kosovo—but this was blocked. So immediately after the meeting, the Slovenian Association decided that it had nothing further to expect from that body and ended all practical cooperation with the federation. The Slovenian Association continued to have good relations with its sister organizations in Croatia, Bosnia, and Macedonia, however.[7]

Developments in Kosovo were also prompting a politicization of the Catholic Church, and in early March 1989, immediately after the arrest of Azem Vllasi, the executive committee of the Episcopal Conference of Yugoslavia issued a statement calling for respect for human rights. The Catholic Commission for Justice and Peace issued a similar statement.[8]

In Slovenia, people started to manufacture and distribute Star of David badges, with the legend, "Kosovo"—a gesture that infuriated Serbs. And the mass demonstrations by Milošević supporters that had shaken the regional governments in Novi Sad, Priština, and Titograd were condemned by SAWP-Slovenia as injurious to democracy.[9]

During May and June 1989, various Slovenian organizations issued statements of solidarity with the Albanians of Kosovo, while a war of words raged between the leaderships of Slovenia and Serbia. Repeated Slovenian initiatives to open a dialogue were rebuffed by Milošević. After a speech at Novi Sad on May 23, in which the Serbian party boss called Slovenia a "lackey" of Western Europe and called into question its right to speak out on Kosovo,[10] the presidency of Slovenia sent a letter to the Serbian presidency, declaring, among other things,

> The Socialist Republic of Slovenia is a sovereign state of the Slovene people who, of their own free will and on the basis of their right to self-determination, have decided to live together with other peoples and nationalities of Yugoslavia in a democratic, federally organized socialist community. Therefore, it has the right and the responsibility to adopt positions and to make judgments freely and autonomously, even on the content of our joint life and our joint future, for these are parts of the joint fate of every people in a joint motherland, including the situation in Kosovo.[11]

Subsequently, in early July, the central committee of LC Slovenia issued a major programmatic statement that codified the republic's newly discovered claim to self-determination. Recalling that while still underground, Slovenian communists had, in 1923, underlined Slovenes' right of self-determination, the central committee declared that

> The right of a people to self-determination is comprehensive, lasting, and inalienable. With this right, the sovereign Slovene people, together with the two nationalities and all the other citizens of the Socialist Republic of Slovenia, ensure their independent political status and their comprehensive economic, social, and cultural development.[12]

Croatia's leadership contacted Slovenia's to express solidarity, while Montenegro's leadership faithfully followed the Serbian lead. Bosnia's leadership tried to find a middle ground but warned that the Slovenian-Serbian dispute was injurious to Yugoslavia.[13]

Then in September 1989, the Republic of Slovenia published a series of controversial draft amendments to its constitution. These included a clear assertion of the right of secession, the declaration that only the Slovenian Assembly can introduce a state of emergency in Slovenia, and the proscription of the deployment of military forces in Slovenia, except by the agreement of the Slovenian Assembly.[14] The significance of these amendments was patently clear, and the Serbian press noisily attacked the amendments as "destabilizing."[15] The amendments were passed in October all the same.

About this time, a body of pro-Milošević Serbs and Montenegrins, which called itself the Kosovo Polje Committee, declared its intention of holding a protest rally in Ljubljana on December 1. The committee planned to mobilize some 30,000–40,000 Serbs and Montenegrins from Serbia and Kosovo, and, supposedly, inform Slovenes about the "real" situation in Kosovo. There were also implied threats to destabilize Slovenia. The Slovenian government asked the SFRJ presidency to ban the proposed meeting, but the Yugoslav presidency refused. *Delo* wrote,

> In the Slovenian view, . . . the announced march would de facto be an act of civil war, because the people of one sovereign state would march against the legal and legitimate representatives of another state. The federal organs, from the state presidency and the Assembly to the government and the defense ministry, are obliged, in conformity with their constitutional and legal powers, to prevent such an intention in advance; if they do not prevent it, the question of the "purpose" of Yugoslavia arises at once.[16]

The Croatian *Sabor* expressed its solidarity with the Slovenian Assembly and demanded that federal organs prevent the meeting from taking place.[17] The Slovenian government then issued its own ban. And when the Serbian committee tried to proceed anyway, the Slovenian and Croatian railway unions stopped the trains carrying the would-be protesters and turned them back.[18]

Enraged, the Republic Conference of SAWP-Serbia cut its ties with SAWP-Slovenia, in a move the Croatian Socialist Alliance immediately condemned as "one of the most dangerous steps toward [the] disintegration of Yugoslavia," lending its firm support to Slovenia.[19] The Serbian Socialist Alliance did not stop there, however, but called on Serbian enterprises to take "revenge" by cutting all cooperative links with Slovenia. Within two weeks, Serbian enterprises cancelled business contracts with some 98 Slovenian enterprises, affecting deliveries and commerce in all branches of the economy.[20] A week later, some 329 Serbian enterprises had severed business relations with Slovenian firms.[21] The rupture was, in economic terms, an act of war.

Two months later, the Slovenian Assembly replied. It cut off those payments to FADURK that would have been payable to the now-annexed Kosovo, reduced its contribution to the federal budget by 15 percent (the amount it estimated was being syphoned to assist the Serbian economy), and declared that Slovenia would immediately stop payments to Vojvodina and Serbia in connection with rehabilitation after damage caused to agriculture and settlements in Vojvodina (by hail, in 1987) and Serbia (by flooding, in 1988).[22]

A Wildfire of Nationalism

Yugoslavia was now swept by a wildfire of nationalism. Everywhere one turned, there were intolerant actions, strangely impassioned rhetoric, discrimination, wanton violence, ethnic reprisals. The new mood was struck at an Extraordinary Assembly of the Serbian Association of Writers on March 4, 1989, to which gathering, association president Matija Beckovic declared that "There is so much Serbian blood and so many sacred relics that Kosovo will remain Serbian land, even if not a single Serb remains there."[23] Pathos, it seems, should count for more than democracy; relics may outvote citizens.

Bosnia became a political battleground. The marketplace was full of confirmable rumors about incidents between local Serbs and Croats, or between Serbs and Muslims, and as 1989 wore on, Bosnian officials began to admit that interethnic troubles were becoming serious. Serbs and Croats alike began to revive arguments that Bosnia's Muslim nation was only a political construct, and the Bosnian leadership confessed that it was worried that this could lead xnto ambitions to redraw the boundaries of Serbia and/or Croatia, at Bosnia's expense.[24] Even in Montenegro, there were currents favoring the dismantlement of Bosnia.[25] The founding of a local branch of the new Serbian Democratic party, in Trebinje (Herzegovina) in July 1990,[26] could scarcely be reassuring to the Croats and Muslims of Bosnia. In March 1990, as Serbian and Croatian irredentism gathered steam, the three chambers of the Bosnian Republic Assembly met in joint session and denounced tendencies to redraw the map.[27] That did not prevent Serbian president Milošević and Croatian president Tudjman from explicitly alluding to possible border revisions at Bosnia's expense, however.[28] By mid-summer, there were skirmishes between Serbs and Muslims, and the former were said to be organizing armed militias.

In Macedonia, too, there were grave warnings that a revival of, in this case, Macedonian nationalism was destroying interethnic harmony in the republic and destabilizing it politically.[29] Those warnings notwithstanding, on May 17, 1989, the Macedonian Assembly adopted an amendment rewriting Article 1 of the Constitution of Macedonia. In the new version, the article proclaims Macedonia "the national state of the Macedonian people," dropping any reference to the Albanian and Turkish national groups.[30] In Vojvodina, the chief issue has been the autonomist striving of local Serbs, who do not want to be dominated by Belgrade.[31] But even here, the founding of a Democratic Union of Croats in Vojvodina in July 1990 was accompanied by complaints that Croats in the Republic of Serbia have lacked their own schools, cultural-artistic societies, television, and media and pledges to work for the creation of a Croatian autonomous region in Vojvodina or Serbia-proper.[32] The move mirrored earlier demands by Croatian Serbs, and figured—at least symbolically—as a kind of reply to Serbian irredentism in Croatia.

In southern Serbia, Muslims of the Sandžak of Novi Pazar began demanding "cultural autonomy" and created the Sandžak Party of Democratic Action to promote their cause.

And then there is Croatia—the vortex of nationalism in the late 1960s and early 1970s, and ostensibly dormant through much of the late 1970s and early 1980s.[33] Croatian nationalism rebounded suddenly, in the course of 1989, and seems to have been triggered to a considerable extent by aggressive Serbian behavior. There were, altogether, three chief sparks that contributed to the rekindling of Croatian nationalism.

First, after a few years during which attacks on the Croats had died down, the Serbian press renewed the attack in late 1988/early 1989, once again talking about the *Ustaše*, the concentration camp at Jasenovac, everlasting Croatian guilt for what fascism had done to Croats and Serbs alike, and the alleged support of the Catholic Church for genocide.[34] Disgusted by the continued misrepresentation, the Catholic Church replied, finally, by publishing the transcript of the Vatican's directives to clergy in the Independent State of Croatia, dated July 24, 1941: the letter had explicitly ordered the Franciscans to desist from taking part in any forced conversions of Orthodox Serbs, from any persecution of Serbs, and from participation or membership in the *Ustaše* movement.[35]

Second, on July 27, 1989, the Italian magazine, *Il Tempo*, published the text of an interview with Serbian writer Dobrica Ćosić, which seemed to Croats to open up the question of reassigning Istria, Zadar, and the Adriatic islands to another republic, that is, of taking them away from Croatia.[36] The political fallout from this interview was enormous. For a few weeks, Croats could talk of little else, and the issue was discussed and rediscussed in the Croatian and Serbian press throughout the late summer. Local municipalities throughout Croatia met and issued condemnations of Ćosić, day after day.[37] The Association of Historical Societies of Croatia sent letters of protest to the Serbian Academy of Sciences and to the Serbian Association of Writers.[38] And the Croatian authorities claimed to see an emerging pattern, aimed at the destabilization of Croatia.[39]

And third, the mobilization of Croatia's Serbian minority, briefly described in the preceding chapter, frightened and enraged Croats at the same time. The Split weekly newspaper, *Nedjeljna Dalmacija*, echoed widespread Croatian sentiment in seeing in developments in Knin a first step in the direction of breaking up Croatia and annexing large portions of it to a "Greater Serbia."[40] Meanwhile, clergy of the Serbian Orthodox Church in Croatia complained of growing intolerance toward the Orthodox faith,[41] while the Serbian Orthodox news organ, *Pravoslavlje*, complained of discrimination, published statistics showing a decline in the number of Orthodox facilities in Croatia between 1932 and 1988, and registered a number of demands designed to change the situation to their satisfaction.[42]

The new mood in Croatia was well symbolized by the decision, in September 1989, to restore the statue of nineteenth-century governor, Josip Jelačić, to Zagreb's main square, thus finally satisfying one of the demands of 1971.[43] About the same time, the Croatian town of Zirje unveiled a bust of Jerko Sizgorić, one of the organizers of the sailors' revolt against the Austro-Hungarian monarchy in 1918.[44]

There were repeated warnings that interethnic relations in Croatia were rapidly deteriorating. One sign of this was the renewed eruption of interethnic violence at sporting events.[45] As of summer 1990, there were reports that Serbs were boarding trains in Croatia in order to beat up Croatian passengers.

The Army Debates

For years, Western observers speculated about a possible military intervention in Yugoslav politics. But, with perhaps the sole exception of the 1988 conspiracy against Slovenian liberalism—which was, in any case, scotched—the Yugoslav National Army (JNA) did little except talk—until 1991. Generally speaking, its primary concern has been to assure itself of the lion's share of the federal budget. In 1989, for example, the Yugoslav Armed Forces were allocated some 57 percent of the federal budget.[46] Understandably, with such a favorable distribution of resources, the military tended to be enthusiastic about maintaining the status quo. After all, if a multiparty system were introduced, who knows, there might be a more far-reaching debate about military expenditures. The ruling party might not be as sympathetic to military spending as the communists were.

There are other reasons for the military's general conservatism, though. The fact that 60–70 percent of the general staff consists of Serbs and Montenegrins has something to do with it.[47] Then again, the army was obliged, by the Constitution of 1974, to defend the constitutional system, and that tended to reinforce its tendency to oppose political change and to stress the importance of fidelity to the principles of AVNOJ.[48]

As the state formula started to break down in 1989 and nationalism reared its head, the military and the JNA party organization expressed concern. The military took the stance that while reform was necessary, multiparty democracy was out of the question, and the LCY would remain the pivot of any process of democratization.[49] The dangers of "bureaucratic nationalism" became a constant theme of military spokespersons, who thought in terms of restoring "the unity of the LCY and its leadership, as well as the full affirmation of Yugoslavia as an equal, socialist community of all nations and nationalities."[50] In the military's view—as expressed in September 1989—"the League of Communists must continue to be the leading ideopolitical force in society."[51]

When Slovenia adopted its controversial constitutional amendments in October 1989, there were rumors that the military would somehow intervene. There is no evidence that the military contemplated such a move at that point, although Assistant Defense Secretary Lt. Gen. Simeon Bunčić let it be known that the military was opposed to the amendments since the exercise of the right of secession "would prevent the army from doing its duty as guardian of the country's territorial integrity."[52] That literal-minded answer concealed the military's real reasons for opposition to Slovenian self-determination, which had more to do with conservatism, communist dogmatism, and Serbian interests than any fixation on carrying out specific guidelines to the end of time.

Time after time, the military reiterated its opposition to a multiparty system. In late October 1989, for example, Bunčić told a television audience,

> We favor political pluralism, but not of the multiparty type. The introduction of a multiparty system would imply the depoliticization of the JNA, which would then lose its popular character, and have to become a professional, mercenary, apolitical army in the service of whichever party was in power . . . [And consequently,] the LCY organization in the JNA, which numbers almost 80,000 [members], would also have to cease to exist.[53]

Despite its opposition to Slovenia's amendments, the military also criticized Serbia's economic blockade of Slovenia as "inappropriate" in the view of the political and economic consequences it was having. But by December 1989, as the pressure for repluralization gathered momentum, the military was sounding more flexible. For instance, Major Gen. Ivo Tominc, assistant commander of the Fifth Military District for Political and Legal Activities, told a press conference that month that the JNA would not interfere in developments, would not slow down democratic change, and would adjust to all changes in the political system.[54]

Meanwhile, voices were raised calling for a constitutional redefinition of the JNA's role in society. In July 1990, for example, the (noncommunist) presidency of the Republic of Croatia pledged to push for the complete depoliticization of the army (including the dismantlement of its party organizations and the constitutional provision tying the military to the defense of socialism).[55] Earlier, in January 1990, the new Democratic party (in Montenegro) demanded that party organizations in the army and police be abolished immediately. The party added that the generals "should particularly not be allowed to threaten us with the use of arms, which are not their property, in order to defend socialism, which is also not their property, from us democrats—as if we care about it at all."[56] This was an augur of things to come.

The Collapse of the Party

In December 1989, on the eve of the Fourteenth (Extraordinary) Congress, Slovenian party leader Milan Kučan warned that the country was on the brink of civil war.[57] Some people pinned hopes for a solution on the congress, and the draft program published in advance of the congress seemed serious about finding a way out: it promised free multiparty elections, freedom of speech, guarantees for other human rights, and efforts to obtain entry into the European Economic Community. But when the congress was convened, the Slovenian party pushed for reforms more extensive than at least some of the other regional organizations were willing to embrace. The congress appeared deadlocked, and in frustration and protest, the Slovenian delegation walked out on January 23, causing the entire congress to fall apart. The "Congress of Salvation" ended in complete fiasco. Twelve days later, the Slovenian party pulled out of the League of Communists of Yugoslavia, shattering the remaining superficial semblance of unity. The Slovenian communists renamed their party the Party of Democratic Renewal.

The Slovenian party did not stop there but proposed that the entire LCY be disbanded, that all its officers resign, and that new organizations be created with new political programs, new organizational structures, new methods of decision making, and a new recruitment and promotion policy.[58] In Slovenia and Croatia, the Socialist Alliance reorganized itself as an independent Socialist party, while in Serbia, it merged with the LC Serbia to form a new Socialist Party of Serbia. Unlike the LC organizations, these new parties were not united in any way at an all-Yugoslav level.

By this point, it was not entirely clear whether Yugoslavia even existed in any meaningful sense. "This is a strange state," Kosta Čavoški, of the Serbian Democratic party, conceded. "We have to conduct our internal relations like other countries conduct international relations."[59]

Chaos or Fragmentation

The restructuring (or rebirth) of a society is preceded by the death of its preceding incarnation. That death is accompanied by uncertainty, depression, groping, and fear—in a word, by trauma. It is also the catalyst of creative energy, which sparks the search for a new social order, which in turn makes restructuring possible. In multiethnic Yugoslavia, restructuring inevitably means change in the way the nationality groups structure their relations.

The signs of the approaching death of the self-managing socialist system could be read several years in advance of its final arrival. Writing in 1985, I observed that there had been a subtle but significant change in Yugoslav consciousness and behavior over the preceding years. The earlier confidence and self-congratulation had given way to "pessimism, gloom, resignation, escapism of various kinds," and an inward-looking quest for meanings which I call "apocalypse culture."[60] This syndrome is associated with normlessness and anomie, deriving from social decay and the deep collective insecurity to which it gives rise. "Apocalypse culture" is characterized by an "openness to radically new formulas [which] springs from the sense—whether a belief or (as more usually) merely a mood—that the system in question has arrived at a historical turning point, that it is, so to speak, the 'end of time.' "[61] Yugoslavia began to shift into an apocalyptic stage as a result of the various developments noted at the beginning of chapter 10. Doubts about the workability of the system came to the surface within a matter of weeks after Tito's death,[62] and gathered intensity over time.

Dire predictions and catastrophic visions, symptomatic of the psychology of the transitional phase associated with apocalypse culture, could be heard from time to time. Particularly striking are the comments made by Slovene Franc Šetinc on the occasion of his resignation from the LCY presidium in 1988: "In my [letter of] resignation," he told the presidium,

> I drew attention to the madness which is pushing us toward the abyss in front of our very eyes. There is a great danger that our constitutional system may be carried away with the tide, and call me to account. I have warned of the dramatic situation, the destructive lava which has spread over a large part of the country. It concerns the future of the SFRJ and in this respect, the last hour is striking when we must sober up.[63]

But if social pressure produces creativity and the anxiety that undermines dogmatism and stimulates receptivity to new ideas, the weakening of the party under pressure created conditions in which political debate became steadily more and more open, involving ever larger numbers of people in political activity, whether legal, semilegal, or technically illegal. In these conditions, independent organizations sprouted, developed, and grew into political parties. By early 1990, there were eighty-six of them: thirty-one in Croatia, nineteen in Slovenia, thirteen in Montenegro, six in Serbia, six in Kosovo, six in Vojvodina, three in Bosnia, and two in Macedonia. I have already recounted elsewhere the process of the repluralization of Yugoslavia,[64] and will not repeat the story here. It suffices to note that with the electoral victories of noncommunist parties in Slovenia, Croatia, and Bosnia in the course of 1990 (by the liberal coalition "Demos" in Slovenia, by Franjo Tudjman's nationalist Croatian Democratic Community in Croatia, and by a coalition of nationalist parties in Bosnia) and the election of a coalition government in Macedonia, an important element constitutive of the political context of the Yugoslav balance-of-power system was fundamentally changed.

Concomitant with that, the proclamation of "full sovereignty" by Slovenia, Croatia, and Bosnia,[65] together with Slovenian-Croatian negotiations about possible secession from Yugoslavia and the creation of a Slovenian-Croatian confederation,[66] rewrote the rules of the game at the structural level as well. In 1988 and 1989, Serbs continued to denounce confederalization as impractical, unwieldy, and unrealizable.[67] By mid-1990, complete confederalization appeared inevitable and was, in large part, already accomplished. Given Serbian consent, it is possible that a confederal solution could have been stabilized. Given Serbian opposition, confederalization could only figure as a prelude to complete disintegration.

Civil order continued to disintegrate in the Serbian-populated areas in Croatia, as local Serbs armed themselves, forming underground militias. Some of these were said to call themselves "Chetniks," after the Serbian nationalist formations of World War II. The army, 70 percent of whose officers were Serbian and which was expressing an ever more explicitly pro-Serbian line, began shipping arms (under a ruse) to Serbian rebels in Croatia in October 1990. Cargo trains bearing arms were unexpectedly routed through Knin and made lengthy unscheduled stops there, while local Serbs relieved the trains of their cargo.[68] Croatian Serbs also established their own "police force."[69] Both in Belgrade and in Knin, Serbs talked of detaching the Serb-populated regions in Croatia and attaching them to Serbia. The Croatian government in turn placed republic military formations under its own authority[70]—a move taken earlier by Slovenia—and set up a special "Croatian Guard," consisting of about 4,000 troops. As these developments undermined stability in Croatia, there were serious clashes between Serbs and Muslims in Bosnia and in the Sandžak of Novi Pazar (in southern Serbia).[71]

Slovenia and Croatia warned repeatedly that confederalization was the only formula under which a peaceful Yugoslavia could be preserved. These two republics prepared and published a joint proposal for confederalization in October 1990.[72] At that time, the lameduck communist governments of Bosnia and Macedonia rejected the Slovenian-Croatian proposal (although they did not side with the Serbs or the Montenegrins).[73] Later, the new noncommunist government of Bosnia-Herzegovina, led by President Alija Izetbegović (whom the communists had imprisoned in 1983 for Islamic fundamentalism), expressed some support for the Slovenian-Croatian concept. But Bosnia's multiethnic mix made it impossible for the Bosnian government to adopt a clear position.

In Slovenia, privately printed "lipa" banknotes came to be accepted as negotiable currency in a number of Slovenian shops and restaurants, and in October 1990, the Slovenian government set an important precedent by opening its first diplomatic mission abroad (in Brussels). By January 1991, sentiment in Slovenia for secession from the Yugoslav federation was overwhelming.[74]

Croatia, Slovenia, Serbia, Vojvodina, and Kosovo began withholding tax payments from the federal government.[75] As a result, by late November, income into the federal treasury was only about one-third of what had been budgeted, and federal officials described the situation as "extremely serious".[76] In addition, the Serbian government stole some $1.6 billion from the federal treasury, according to a report in the British periodical *The Economist*.[77] In a word, no government can continue to function when its funds are choked off.

Despite its earlier avowals of political neutrality, the army's largely Serbian officer corps found it increasingly difficult to remain on the sidelines. By November 1990, the army was actively involved in reconstructing the Communist party (which had been more generous with budgetary allocations than had noncommunist governments).[78] Yugoslav defense minister General Veljko Kadijević, a Serb, closing his eyes to everything going on around him, declared, "The ideas of socialism . . . belong to the future. The experience of developed countries confirms that [socialism] is one of the greatest achievements of contemporary civilization."[79] Purloined materials prepared by the Yugoslav Ministry of Defense and published in a Yugoslav newspaper on January 31, 1991, documented the army's determination to hold Yugoslavia together and its desire to bring the communists back to power.[80]

The lines of confrontation were clearly drawn. On the one side, Slovenia and Croatia, failing to bring the other republics around to a consensus on a new confederal structure modeled on the EEC, were preparing for secession and possible association in a separate confederation linking their two states. Serbia and the Serbian-controlled federal army rejected any confederal principle and insisted on the necessity of reintegrating the country firmly under Serbian hegemony, which Milošević and his followers called a "modern federation." The army, additionally, wanted to restore communism throughout the country.

On December 3, 1990, came a demand from General Kadijević that Slovenia and Croatia disarm their local defense units. If the two republics refused to comply, Kadijević warned, the army would use force to effect the desired result. The Slovenes and Croats held fast, calling up reservists, placing their units on high alert, and bracing for invasion.[81] The ministers of defense and interior from Slovenia and Croatia convened an urgent meeting in the border town of Mokrice and agreed to coordinate defense and security.[82]

There were reports that both Slovenia and Croatia had been purchasing weapons abroad and that Croatia, in particular, had imported thousands of AK-47 assault rifles and shoulder-fired antitank rockets from Hungary, as well as Singaporan SAR-80 automatic rifles.[83]

The state presidency handed down a deadline of midnight, January 19, 1991, for Slovenian and Croatian compliance. The deadline was subsequently extended by forty-eight hours. Meanwhile, Yugoslav military police arrested various persons on the territory of Croatia, including members of the ruling Croatian Democratic Community.[84] On January 25, Croatia's president Tudjman met with members of the federal collective presidency, Prime Minister Ante Marković, and high officers of the Yugoslav Army in an effort to avert civil war. At the end of the meeting, which lasted deep into the night, the storm clouds seemed to have cleared. Jović, president of the collective presidency, recognized the legitimacy of the Croatian government. General Kadijević agreed to call off the military alert at army bases in Croatia and not to interfere in Croatian internal affairs. And Tudjman, in exchange, agreed to call off the mobilization of reserve units (some 20,000 strong) in Croatia.[85] Tudjman declined to disband any of the units, however, or to turn over any of their weaponry to the army. The crisis had hardly passed, however. For Yugoslav troop movements continued in the Zagreb environs.[86] And on January 30, Kadijević ordered the arrest of Martin Spegelj, minister of defense of the Republic of Croatia, on allegations that Spegelj had made preparations for armed insurrection in Croatia. But Croatian authorities refused to arrest Spegelj. Jović threatened to use armed force to assure the apprehension of the Croatian defense minister. Tudjman, in turn, promised to employ force to prevent the arrest. By the end of January 1991, political talks between Croatian and federal leaders had broken down, with Croatia's Tudjman refusing to take part in any further meetings as long as the army was represented there. Finally, on February 8, the Republic of Slovenia declared that it had given up on Yugoslavia and would formally secede from the federation before the end of the month. The Slovenian prime minister added that Slovenia would annul all federal laws on February 20.[87]

What was evident as of early 1991—though it had surely been obvious by summer 1989, if not before—was that the old Titoist program to defuse the nationalities problem had completely failed. The question is why.

The Titoist solution consisted of four parts. First, it tried to build a sense of community around an empty core. Ultimately it was clear what the content of "Slovenianness," "Croatianness," and "Serbianness" was, in each case, but "Yugoslavness" had no content except the sum of its parts. Self-management and the myth of partisan struggle were supposed to provide some content, but these failed likewise.

Second, Titoism tried to assuage people's need for pluralization by offering regional pluralization (decentralization to regional communist elites) in place of political pluralization (the institution of multiparty democracy). This solution prevented the development of any popular-based parties that transcended ethnic lines. Under Titoism, power devolved to the republics, Yugoslavia became quasi-confederal, and when independent political parties finally developed at the end of the 1980s, they were, almost without exception, the parties of specific nationality groups. Regional pluralization, in effect, laid the groundwork for today's ethnic mobilization and political fragmentation.

Third, Tito believed that to ease interethnic tensions, an equalization of levels of economic development was necessary. What Tito did not anticipate was that self-managing socialism, far from equalizing economic levels, would cause the economic gap to widen steadily. Investment funds raised for the underdeveloped regions were often used to further political goals (e.g., investments designed to affect the interethnic mix) rather than to boost economic profit. It is possible to conclude that self-managing socialism was less well suited than free enterprise would have been to raising the economic levels in the south. Be that as it may, socialism raised expectations and failed to deliver—a dangerous combination.

And fourth, Titoism's policy vis-à-vis the army proved to be a blueprint for trouble. Tito's heavy reliance on Serbian officers to staff the upper ranks meant that the army's neutrality would be hard to achieve. At the same time, Titoism's enshrinement of the military as the "guardian of socialism" habituated the high command to think of itself as enjoying a veto right over political developments of which it did not approve.

Yet ultimately, despite these weaknesses, it took the rise of Slobodan Milošević in Serbia to bring the country from a state of confused paralysis to the brink of civil war. Milošević combined charismatic techniques with internal censorship of press and politics and the mobilization of Serbian publics in other federal units to advance his program. To mobilize Serbs, he entered into a partnership with the Serbian Orthodox Church and stirred up a mood of destiny and historicity, which sometimes took on characteristics of frenzy and which was founded on a combination of ethnic chauvinism, religious chauvinism,[88] and male chauvinism.[89] Armed with this triad of chauvinisms, Milošević converted shadings of grey into polarities of black and white and rallied Serbs to the banner of Serbian solidarity.

13
Civil War

In the early 1980s, there were troubling signs that the Yugoslav system was unraveling and that the country was sliding toward civil war. The seeds of discord had been sown, but they had not yet sprouted; to an untrained eye, it probably seemed that the society was coping well enough. By summer 1987, ordinary people in Belgrade and Zagreb were talking openly about their fears of civil war. It was not yet inevitable, but the storm clouds were gathering. The rupture first of cultural and intellectual contacts, and then also of economic and political contacts between Slovenia and Serbia, along with growing discontent among Croatia's Serbs in the late 1980s, however, set the stage for civil war.

From late 1990 through the early months of 1991, Serbia, Croatia, Slovenia, and Montenegro allegedly diverted money sorely needed for economic investment into arms purchases. The JNA is said to have approached the Soviets with a long shopping list for their army, without the knowledge of Yugoslav Prime Minister Ante Marković.[1] Hungary sold Soviet-made surface-to-air missiles to Slovenia and Kalashnikov rifles to Croatia, according to Tanjug reports; some of the rifles were reportedly transshipped via Bulgaria. Austria purchased large quantities of Spanish pistols and resold them to Slovenia and Croatia.[2] *Borba* reported that Montenegro also purchased arms.[3] Arms from Lebanon's sixteen-year civil war made their way into Yugoslavia, if accounts in American newspapers may be believed; in a matter of four months, some $100 million worth of artillery, machine guns, and ammunition were shipped from Lebanon, to unspecified groups in Yugoslavia.[4] Various private companies in Austria, Germany, Belgium, Switzerland, Italy, Great Britain, the United States, Spain, Panama, Argentina, and Israel were also said to have sold arms illegally on the Yugoslav market.[5] Various countries issued denials that they had sold any weapons to Yugoslavia's warring factions, among them Hungary, Spain, Poland,[6] and Austria (which also denied reports that it was training Croatian forces on its territory).[7]

Quantities of sophisticated JNA weaponry were delivered to Croatia's Serbs, who formed local militias. Vojislav Šešelj, the most important personality among the leaders of the Serbian "Chetnik" irregulars, stated in a *Spiegel* interview that he had received weapons from the JNA and went on to say that his group had also purchased weapons from the Hungarians.[8] Serbs in Bosnia and Kosovo also formed citizens' militias, asserting that they needed to defend themselves. Croatian and Muslim citizens in Bosnia armed themselves, although they were said to be not so well armed as the Serbs.[9] The Serbian paramilitary militias set up in the Croatian Krajina, in Slavonia, and in Bosnia-Herzegovina represented a particularly dangerous escalation.

By spring 1991, some observers[10] were certain that the explosion would come very soon. Interrepublican negotiations were deadlocked, and neither side was willing to compromise: the Serbs had refused to accept a confederal arrangement, and the Croats had refused to grant political autonomy to the republic's Serbs. US Secretary of State James Baker visited Yugoslavia on June 22 and told the republics that the United States favored Yugoslav unity and that it would not recognize the independence of Slovenia or Croatia. About the same time, NATO commander General John Galvin told the Belgrade daily newspaper *Politika* that NATO did not consider Yugoslavia within its defense perimeter and therefore would not intervene in a Yugoslav civil war.[11]

The Dispersion of Populations

Serbs can be found in all the former federal units of Yugoslavia. Even in Slovenia, there were (according to the 1981 census) some 42,182 Serbs.[12] In the same census, Croats, Slovenes, Macedonians, ethnic Muslims, Albanians, Montenegrins, and even smaller groups such as Hungarians, Bulgarians, and Ruthenes were each to be found in *all* eight federal units.[13] Since in each republic the dominant nationality gave its own language and culture a preeminent position (except in Bosnia, where no nationality is numerically dominant), local minorities could complain from time to time of the deprivation of rights: examples included complaints from the Serbs in Croatia, the Albanians in Kosovo, and, on occasion, the Hungarians in the Vojvodina. Serbs inhabiting parts of Croatia began to press more adamantly for autonomy or separation from Croatia, emphasizing that they had no desire to live in a Croatian state but reiterating their commitment to live in a united Yugoslavia. Vojvodina's Hungarian minority also complained, alleging that authorities had taken steps to seize the legitimate property of Hungarian minority organizations[14] and had banned the use of Hungarian names of towns. Hungarian sources said that a new law mandated the exclusive use of Serbo-Croatian in the Cyrillic alphabet (which few local Hungarians can read) in all official functions.[15] On the other hand, Radovan Bozović, prime minister of Vojvodina, contradicted Hungarian sources. "The position of the Hungarian minority in Serbia," said Bozović, "is good, which cannot be said of the Serbian minority in Hungary."[16]

The 1981 census recorded some 1,303,034 Albanians living in Serbia—more than twice the number of Serbs living in Croatia. On July 16, 1991, the Serbian Assembly passed a law empowering the authorities to distribute 6,000 hectares of land among Serbs wanting to settle in Kosovo.[17] The following month, Serbian sources reported that about 6,000 ethnic Albanian secondary-school teachers had been dismissed because of—as Deputy Provincial Secretary for Education Žika Nedeljković put it—their opposition to "the unified plans and programs of the Republic of Serbia."[18] Albanian and Serbian sources offered conflicting versions of what was happening in Kosovo. An Albanian source from Priština complained, for example, that "it is an everyday phenomenon for the Serbian police to beat and maltreat innocent Albanian citizens." According to this source, "The Serbian police not only impose fines [on the Albanians] but commit acts of theft and seize documents of various kinds, such as driving licenses, passports, etc. This obliges the individual to report later to the police station, where he is again subjected to violence and reprisals."[19] Serbian sources, on the other hand, called such reports fabrications and affirmed that Albanians were enjoying full human and civic rights. Slobodan Milošević, president of Serbia, for example, told visiting Austrian parliamentarians in August that the situation in Kosovo was normal and "denied that the Albanians in Kosovo suffer even the slightest disadvantage."[20]

Under the pressure of events, provocative statements were made. Croatian President Tudjman told the London *Times*, at one point, that the "division of Bosnia-Herzegovina would be the best solution to the Yugoslav crisis."[21] Later, the presidium of the Bosnian branch of the Croatian Democratic Community (i.e., the sister organization of Tudjman's party) issued a contradictory statement, upholding the sovereignty and indivisibility of Bosnia.[22] On the other side, Milan Martić, the newly elected defense minister of Croatia's Serbs, talked of wanting to separate Zadar from Croatia, because "we need a large port."[23] The majority of the population of Zadar is, however, Croatian.

Living in the Past

Psychologists have recognized that people with serious unresolved problems tend to rehash the past, and to read yesterday's meanings into today's events. When an entire society is locked in the past, such obsessive behavior is a sure sign of deep and pervasive unresolved problems at a mass psychological level. An Austrian official visiting Yugoslavia in August 1991, driven to exasperation by this syndrome, complained, "Nobody talks about the future. Everybody is obsessed [with] the past."[24]

At the center of this preoccupation with the past is the memory of the Second World War, with all the pain and hatred it called forth, and the consequent unresolved dilemmas. The chief controversy regarding the war has long been about the number of casualties.[25] World War II is central to the mythology and symbology of the 1991 civil war. The current Serbian Chetniks' long beards represent a self-conscious identification with the nationalistic Chetniks of World War II, while the privately financed Croatian "Black Legion"[26] dons black in order to recall the uniforms of the wartime *Ustaše*.

It might be helpful to examine some of the underpinnings of beliefs about the past.

After the war, the Yugoslav government estimated that the country had suffered some 1,700,000 casualties. This figure remained the "official" estimate of wartime casualties for as long as there was a working Yugoslav government

Table 25. *War Casualties by Republic, 1941–45 (in 1000s)*

	Serbs	Croats	Muslims	Total (including others)
Bosnia	170	66	78	328
Montenegro	6	1	4	37
Croatia	137	118	2	295
Macedonia	6	0	4	24
Slovenia	0	0	0	40
Serbia	211	7	15	303
TOTAL	530	192	103	1,027

The NDH comprised Bosnia and most of Croatia.

Source: Vladimir Zerjavić, *Gubici stanovništva Jugoslavije u drugum svjetskom ratu* (Zagreb: Jugoslavensko Viktimološko Društvo, 1989), pp. 61–66.

(i.e., until 1989/90). In 1989, using more accurate sources and data than had been available immediately after the war, Yugoslav demographer Vladimir Zerjavić set total war-related deaths at just over a million. Table 25 shows Zerjavić's breakdown of war casualties by republic; it reveals that almost half of all Serbian casualties occurred *outside* the NDH. Moreover, not all those killed within the territory of the NDH were necessarily victims of the Ustaše. In fact, beginning in spring 1942, Ustaše and Chetnik forces actually began to collaborate, on the territory of Bosnia-Herzegovina, in order to wage a joint struggle against Tito's Partisans.[27] In the course of this collaboration, Chetniks and Partisans inflicted losses on each other, with a large number of Chetniks (Serbs) annihilated by the Partisans in May 1945 in particular.[28] Other Serbian lives were lost in aerial bombardment by the German air force,[29] German massacres and military operations,[30] a typhus epidemic which spread in Chetnik ranks in January 1945,[31] and in Partisan campaigns against the Albanian resistance in Kosovo in 1945.[32]

The Ustaše were obviously responsible for many deaths, as were the Chetniks, the Partisans, and, of course, the Nazi occupation forces. Other active agents on the Yugoslav political scene included the Domobrani, the Albanian Ballists, the collaborative forces of Milan Nedić in Serbia, the "Russian Corps" (anti-communist Russian emigrés),[33] and the Italian, Hungarian, and Bulgarian occupation forces, all of whom inflicted casualties. In the course of 1991, however, Serbian and Croatian television produced lengthy documentary programs about World War II, dwelling on each other's atrocities and blaming each other exclusively for past sufferings.

The Road to War

In the first six months of 1991, the Yugoslav republics convened a number of conferences in an effort to find some formula on which all could agree.

Slovenia and Croatia continued to seek complete confederalization; Serbia and Montenegro insisted on recentralization. First Bosnia and then Macedonia reportedly came to support the confederal option.[34]

During this time, the federal government was rapidly decaying: its staff had been trimmed back by 15 percent by July 1991,[35] its revenues disappeared (because of the republics' refusal to pay the established subsidies), and it gradually lost control of the army. The subsequent use of the army to attack civilian populations in Croatia—over the objections of Yugoslav President Stipe Mesić—made it clear that the JNA no longer responded to federal orders. Mesić repeatedly ordered the army to cease hostilities, only to find himself ignored.

Slovenia had promised to secede "by June 26," if no agreement could be reached on the framework for a "new" Yugoslavia. Croatia had promised to follow suit. And Bosnia and Macedonia had both declared that they would not remain within a truncated Yugoslavia.

On June 25, 1991—a day before the deadline—first Croatia and then Slovenia declared their secession from Yugoslavia. The JNA responded by sending troops into Slovenia, temporarily passing over Croatia. During the ensuing ten-day military engagement, the JNA bombed the Slovenian airports at Brnik (Ljubljana) and Maribor, and tried, unsuccessfully, to seize control of Slovenia's borders.[36] The Slovenian militia fought back, capturing more than 2,000 JNA troops and contesting the federal army's efforts to take control of the border crossings.[37] The Slovenes sustained $2.7 million in damage during the brief engagement, a figure which was said to exceed the Slovenian state's annual revenue by 40 percent.[38]

A few days later, through mediation by the European Community, Slovenia and Serbia agreed on the terms of disengagement, and Serbian troops were ordered to withdraw from Slovenia (a process completed in October 1991).[39] American President George Bush's first reaction was to discourage Slovenian and Croatian independence. On June 26, he expressed "regret" at their acts of secession, adding that the United States planned to proceed as if Yugoslavia were still intact.[40] The Soviet Foreign Ministry echoed this sentiment, declaring that "the unilateral actions [by Slovenia and Croatia] have not been recognized by the Socialist Federal Republic of Yugoslavia's state bodies and cannot be regarded as promoting the solution of Yugoslavia's serious problems. As in the past, the Soviet Union consistently favors the unity and territorial integrity of Yugoslavia, [and] the inviolability of its borders, including its internal ones."[41] But on July 3, Milošević's ruling Socialist Party of Serbia issued a statement declaring, "Serbia has nothing against Slovenia's secession, it does no harm to our interests and we have no reason not to accept their separation if it is conducted in a peaceful way."[42]

The Macedonian Assembly took up the question of Macedonia's secession on June 26, at which time representatives of the VMRO–Democratic Party for Macedonian National Unity urged the immediate proclamation of independence. Other Macedonian parties urged restraint, and the Assembly adopted a "wait and see" strategy.[43] Macedonian President Kiro Gligorov cautiously told the Turkish daily *Hurriyet* on June 30, "Macedonia will remain faithful to Yugoslavia and will not follow the example of Slovenia and Croatia."[44] But events were moving rapidly, and by July 6 the political wind was shifting: the Macedonian Assembly decided that "if no agreement can be reached in a peaceful and democratic way on a union of sovereign states on Yugoslav territory, the government must put before the assembly a constitutional law whereby the Republic of Macedonia, as an independent and sovereign state, will assume and carry out its sovereign rights."[45]

By mid-July, as JNA troops began to pull out of Slovenia, Serbian irregulars (backed up by the JNA) started to clash with Croatian defense units in the Croatian "Krajina" and in Slavonia. On July 10, Croatian authorities repeated their guarantee of equal rights and full cultural autonomy to the Serbian minority living within Croatia's borders.[46]

In early July, Croatian President Franjo Tudjman expressed optimism that there would be no serious clashes involving Croatia. "Croatia is not Slovenia," he said. "We will not allow the army to become involved in the battle. Our path to freedom is different."[47] Meanwhile, clashes between the Croatian militia and Serbian irregulars increased in frequency. Within a few days of Tudjman's optimistic statement, Šime Djodan—Tudjman's defense minister—gave an entirely opposite assessment, and expressed concern that full-scale war between Croatia and Serbia could break out "in a matter of days."[48]

Within a few weeks, in July war escalated dramatically. Self-styled Chetniks, sporting long beards, traditional Serbian shepherds' caps, and royalist badges, staged rallies in the mountains of Ravna Gora, chanting, "We want war!" and recalling the "glories" of the earlier Chetniks' massacres of Croats and Muslims. Amply equipped with heavy artillery and backed by the Serbian-led JNA, they struck at various targets, including Vinkovci and Vukovar in eastern Slavonia, Glina, Banja, Tenja, Petrinja, and Osijek. Serbian forces also attacked exclusively Magyar villages (such as the village of Korogy)[49] and the exclusively Czech village of Ivanovo Selo.[50] A few soldiers deserted from the JNA almost immediately,[51] and in Belgrade there were a few scattered anti-war demonstrations by students and opposition forces.[52] But these protests were ineffectual. Meanwhile, within a matter of weeks, some 40,000 volunteers joined the Serbian Guard organized under the auspices of the Serbian Renaissance Movement.[53] Additional numbers volunteered to join Šešelj's Chetniks and other paramilitary units. Of special interest here was Tanjug's July 2 announcement that the League of Communists–Movement for Yugoslavia (the communist party organization set up within the army) was organizing guerrilla units of the People's Front of Yugoslavia and signing up volunteers. The LC-MY also spoke of its plans to create a government of "national salvation."[54]

The Croatian government claimed that the army was assisting the Serbian Chetniks. The army denied these allegations and said that it was only trying to keep the warring sides apart. Slobodan Milošević explained, "If someone wants to take a part of Serbian settlement out of Yugoslavia, by armed force, well it is logical to expect that the army must intervene."[55] Referring to Serbs' right of national self-determination, Milošević pledged to assure that all Serbs could enjoy the right to be included in Serbia. The Croatian weekly *Danas*, however, commented, "If the Republic of Serbia does not abandon the fanatical idea that all Serbs live in one state, then let Croats make the same demand. Without a doubt that would make for a new war plan on Croatia's part."[56]

War spread rapidly, as Serbian forces laid siege to key Croatian cities. Vukovar, 150 miles east of Zagreb, was bombarded.[57] Although reportedly seriously outgunned, Croatian forces held out in Vukovar, and (as of September 19) the Croatian defense there claimed to have destroyed 60 Serbian tanks and killed 800 Serbian soldiers.[58] By the end of the first week in October, after two months of heavy fighting, Serbian irregulars and the JNA controlled the center of Vukovar, but Croatian forces held onto the western portions of the city. The Slavonian capital of Osijek (24 miles northwest of Vukovar), which has been Croatian for more than a thousand years, was shelled by Serbian forces; the newspaper of the Serbian Orthodox Church, *Pravoslavlje*, gave its blessing to the campaign in a lengthy article on "the contribution of the Serbian Orthodox Church to the development of the culture of the city of Osijek."[59] The Serbian Orthodox Church also published a series of articles on the "massacres of the Serbian people" in wartime Croatia,[60] as well as a number of articles about Serbian sufferings at the Ustaše concentration camp at Jasenovac;[61] an article also recalled the attacks endured by the Serbian Orthodox Church in Croatia during World War II.[62] The Serbian Orthodox Church seemed to bless the campaign as a "holy war." Meanwhile, the Croatian weekly *Danas* published material from British archives to the effect that Tito's Partisans had liquidated large numbers of Catholic priests immediately after the war, including (according to the translation published in *Danas*) "the entire Catholic clergy" in "occupied Herzegovina."[63]

Non-strategic sites in Croatia were also reported to have been destroyed or damaged, including hospitals,[64] a veterinary station,[65] schools,[66] churches,[67] a Franciscan monastery,[68] and many of Croatia's historical and cultural landmarks. A *New York Times* editorial said that "calculated assaults" had already destroyed 116 churches, castles, and other historic monuments as of September 22, including the great dome of St. Jacob's Cathedral in Šibenik, the castle and museum in Vukovar, the historic center of Karlovac, and a number of Baroque buildings in Varaždin.[69] At the same time, Ilija Kojić, minister of the territorial defense of the Serbian Autonomous Region of Slavonia, Baranja, and Western Srem, said that "members of the [Croatian] Ministry of Internal Affairs and other Croatian storm troopers [had] attacked all [the] Serbian villages in this region. These villages are: Pačetin, Bršadin, Trpinja, Borovo Selo, Tenja, and Bogota."[70]

In mid-September, the JNA imposed a naval blockade of Croatia's coast and launched aerial attacks on the Croatian capital of Zagreb. Croatian authorities imposed a blockade of their own on thirty-three large JNA garrisons on their territory, cutting off their food supplies, water, and electricity. One by one, these garrisons surrendered, allowing the Croats to confiscate JNA equipment. Subsequently, the JNA began shelling the outskirts of the walled city of Dubrovnik. As of early October, Sisak, Šibenik, and Zadar were also besieged, and Serbian forces were within 20 kilometers (12 miles) of Zagreb. Slobodan Milošević, speaking in English at one of a number of "peace conferences" called by the European Community, said, "Serbs in Croatia are not attacking anybody. They are purely defending themselves."[71]

The Bosnian Connection

As serious as the Serbian assault on Croatia was, a number of observers expressed fear that if the conflict spread to Bosnia-Herzegovina, the result would be a Balkan Armageddon.[72] As I have previously noted, the population of Bosnia is so intermixed that it would be impossible to draw a clean line dividing it into "logical" ethnically based units. Yet, by spring 1991, the Bosnian-based Serbian Democratic Party was appealing to the principle of self-determination and actively promoting the secession of those parts of Bosnia-Herzegovina bordering on Croatia and advocating their union with Serbian-dominated sections in Croatia, to form a new "Krajina" Republic.[73] *Vreme*, a privately owned magazine published in Belgrade, reported that Radovan Karadžić, president of Bosnia's Serbian Democratic Party, had met with Milošević to discuss the timing of an eventual army attack on Bosnia.[74] Meanwhile, the Croatian Party of Law (headed by Dobroslav Paraga) demanded that all of Bosnia be annexed to Croatia.[75] Croatian President Franjo Tudjman, in his repeated allusions to the possibility of changing the border with Bosnia, was only slightly less threatening to the Bosnian authorities and, given the circumstances, was politically inept in so doing.

By July, according to a Serbian source, Milošević and Karadžić were stepping up the smuggling of armaments to Bosnian Serbs,[76] and Colonel-General Drago Vukosavljević, commander of Territorial Defense Headquarters of Bosnia, ordered the mobilization of police reservists in the ten municipalities of the Bosnian Krajina. This order was issued in defiance of instructions by the Bosnian government, leading the Muslim Bosniak Organization, the Party of Democratic Action, the Croatian Democratic Community of Bosnia-Herzegovina, and the Socialist Democratic Party to issue a joint statement warning that a de facto coup was being carried out in Bosnia under Serbian sponsorship.[77]

According to the 1991 census, the population of Bosnia was 43.7 per cent Muslim, 31.3 per cent Serbian, and 17.3 per cent Croatian.[78] The two most important Muslim parties in Bosnia are the Party of Democratic Action, whose president is, at this writing, the president of Bosnia (Alija Izetbegović), and the Muslim Bosnian Organization, headed by Adil Zulfikarpašić.[79] In July 1991, Zulfikarpašić approached Radovan Karadžić with a proposal for a "historic agreement" between the two parties.[80] Karadžić, speaking on behalf of all of Bosnia's Serbs, said that Serbs would "do their utmost for the sake of the republic's integrity, in case Bosnia-Herzegovina remains in the federal state of Yugoslavia."[81] Zulfikarpašić, for his part, said that "the interests of Serbs and Muslims [have] never clashed in any area since [the] departure of the Turks in 1878."[82]

Bosnian President Izetbegović criticized the agreement between Zulfikarpašić and Karadžić for leaving out the Croats.[83] He made no reference, critical or otherwise, to the exclusion of his own party (part of the ruling coalition of Bosnia) from the talks leading to that agreement. At the same time, the League of Communists of Bosnia-Herzegovina / Socialist Democratic Party announced its support for the agreement.[84]

Muhamed Filipović, vice chair of the Muslim Bosnian Organization, issued a brief statement on August 6. Observing that Bosnia was afflicted by "political confusion," Filipović said,

> the Serbs are armed to the teeth, they have created a state within [the] state in Bosnia-Herzegovina, relations are increasingly worse, and psychological pressure on the Muslims is growing. It is possible that a conflict between Serbs and Muslims will break out any day. To prevent this, [an attempt] is being made to sign an agreement on the preservation of the integrity of Bosnia-Herzegovina and on securing its legal status.[85]

The following day, Izetbegović reiterated his opposition to an agreement concluded without the participation of the Croats, but underlined that he supported dialogue with the Serbs.

In this context, various figures, including even the internationally known film director Emir Kusturica, staked out positions for or against the agreement.[86] The climate of controversy spread to the Bosnian presidency, where, in August, a debate arose concerning procedural questions. Protesting against an alleged anti-Serbian coalition between Izetbegović's Party of Democratic Action and the Croatian Democratic Community, and remonstrating against unacceptable procedures in the republic presidency, Nikola Koljević (a member of Karadžić's party) announced on August 8 that he intended to boycott further meetings of the Bosnian presidency, of which he was a member. His colleague, Biljana Plavšić, joined him in so doing.[87]

It might be noted that Šešelj was not a signatory to the Serb-Muslim agreement, and that (as recently as August 5) he articulated his belief that "the Muslims in Bosnia are Islamicized Serbs and part of the so-called Croats are Catholic Serbs," and his hope to see "the republics of Bosnia-Herzegovina, Macedonia, and Montenegro, and the Serbian areas of Croatia" incorporated into Serbia.[88]

On September 20, Serbian forces entered Bosnia, hoping to cross that republic's territory and open a new, southern front against the beleaguered Croatian town of Vukovar. Local Croatian and Muslim residents erected barricades and set up machine-gun nests; they succeeded in bringing a column of 60 Serbian tanks to a standstill in the vicinity of Višegrad. The following morning, the Serbian army units opened fire on Muslim and Croatian positions, and more than a thousand Muslims and Croats fled the area.[89]

Eventually, in mid-October, the Bosnian parliament held a marathon session to discuss the question of sovereignty. The 73 Serbian delegates walked out, declaring the session illegal. Thereupon, the remaining parliamentary deputies (Muslims and Croats) adopted a memorandum, preparing the way for secession and underlining that Bosnia would under no circumstances allow itself to be conjoined to either Croatia or Serbia. Commented Izetbegović, "There is no place for us in [this] Yugoslavia."[90] Radovan Karadžić commented that the memorandum set Bosnia "on the same road to hell as Croatia and Slovenia."[91]

Even prior to the memorandum, President Izetbegović lamented the intensification of a propaganda campaign directed against Bosnia—propaganda which he described as "identical with the propaganda conducted by the Nazis prior to their attack on Poland."[92] In search of diplomatic support, Izetbegović visited Libya and Iran, contacted the Turkish ambassador in Yugoslavia, and made preliminary inquiries for a visit to the United States to see Secretary of State James Baker.[93]

The Republics

In Slovenia, Croatia, Serbia, Macedonia, and Bosnia, fissures appeared within the political elites, and internal dissension grew. It would be misleading to portray the situation as if politically unified republics were engaged in controversy and debate only with each other. On the contrary, not one of these republics was able, as of October 1991, to achieve internal consensus.

The divisions within *Bosnia* have already been traced.

In Croatia, part of the controversy arose from differences of opinion as to what policy should be adopted vis-à-vis the Serbs of Croatia. In late July, for example, Zvonimir Lerotić, a close adviser of Tudjman's, said that Croatia's Serbs would soon be offered political and territorial autonomy.[94] Less than two weeks later, however, Zvonimir Separović, Croatia's foreign minister, was reported to have said that Croatian Serbs were being offered only cultural autonomy and "local self-management."[95] At the same time, the Zagreb daily *Večernji list* wrote that granting "autonomy" (presumably political autonomy was meant) would not alleviate problems; *Večernji list* argued that some people wanted to destabilize Croatia and were not interested in compromises.[96]

But there were broader issues dividing Croatian politicians. Some favored negotiations, others preferred a hard line of "no compromise" and opposed any negotiation with the Serbs.[97] Opposition extended even into the ranks of Tudjman's party, and in June three high-ranking members were expelled from that party.[98] On July 31, leaders of eight opposition parties in Croatia joined in accusing the Croatian Democratic Community of having "considerably contributed to the difficult political and security situation in Croatia." Opposition leaders said that the "postponement of democracy" in Croatia was unacceptable, and demanded that the powers of the president be curtailed and that the use of "various influential parastate organs" be curbed.[99]

Others were more critical. The Belgrade daily *Politika*, for instance, stated on August 25 that Croatian President Tudjman was planning to kill off Serbs in his republic, adding that the genocide would be carried out "silently and without any realization by the world public about what is happening in Croatia."[100] *Politika* commented dourly, "Fascism now walks openly in Croatia; an *Ustaše* regime has been reestablished in Zagreb."[101] These sentiments were seconded by Yugoslav Vice President Kostić, who argued that Croatia's Serbs were endangered by the policies of the "fascist authorities" holding power in that republic.[102]

In Macedonia, there were signs of alarm in August, when Ljupčo Popovski (of the Social Democratic Alliance of Macedonia and a member of the Republic Assembly) accused unnamed persons of having committed "high treason" by "selling" Macedonia to Serbia in secret talks. The Social Democrats demanded that the guilty persons be named, arrested, and tried on charges of treason. They also criticized Macedonian President Gligorov and Assembly President Andov of "turning Macedonia into a Serbian protectorate."[103]

At the same time, there were signs of distrust, or fear, of other republics. *Nova Makedonija*, the Skopje daily, characterized a proposal outlined by Serbian President Milošević in mid-August as "a hegemonistic stand," said to reflect "a desire for a greater Serbia";[104] yet the following day, *Nova Makedonija* also expressed its disapproval of Croatian authorities, whom it characterized as "warmongers." The Macedonian daily also criticized a view commonly expressed both in Yugoslavia and by Yugoslavs abroad—that Tudjman and Milošević shared exclusive responsibility for the crisis; *Nova Makedonija* highlighted that other people had contributed to the escalation of tensions as well.[105]

A small reflection of internal divisions in Macedonia came on August 22, when Macedonian Prime Minister Nikola Kljusev reportedly dismissed the republic's defense minister, Risto Damjanovski, ostensibly because of the latter's opposition to demands that Macedonian conscripts in the JNA should serve in Macedonia[106]—although, given the republic's steady gravitation toward independence and the consequent implication that this issue would resolve itself in time, it is difficult to imagine that no more than this was involved. In fact, a vague statement from Kljusev was reported, words to the effect that Damjanovski had "lately worked in contravention of the positions taken by the Macedonian government."[107]

In Serbia too, there were pressures and fissures. In mid-October, the *Financial Times* of London reported that Belgrade was gripped by "an atmosphere of desperation" as oil supplies dwindled, the money supply soared beyond the government's capacity to back it, and people expressed concern about an accelerating slide toward widespread poverty.[108] In this climate, criticism of the government inevitably surfaced, and divisions came into public view.

The most extreme position—at least so far as I am aware—is that taken by

Vojislav Šešelj. An excerpt from an interview he gave to *Der Spiegel* aptly captures his thinking:

> *Der Spiegel*: If you were the Serbian president, what would you do now?
> *Šešelj*: I would immediately mobilize all Serbs, amputate Croatia in a blitzkrieg, and then inform the international community of the new Serbian borders.
> *Der Spiegel*: Where would these borders be?
> *Šešelj*: The current Serbia, including the provinces of Vojvodina and Kosovo, would have to include the republics of Bosnia-Herzegovina, Macedonia, and Montenegro, and the Serbian areas of Croatia with the borders at Karlobag, Karlovac, and Virovitica.
> *Der Spiegel*: This would mean reducing Croatia to about one-third of its current territory.
> *Šešelj*: To as much as one can see from the tower of the cathedral in Zagreb. If this is not enough for the Croats, then we will take everything. Of course, we will have to resettle those 200,000 Serbs who live in Zagreb and the 30,000 from Rijeka. . . .
> *Der Spiegel*: Are you paid by Serbia's President Milošević? It is said that in reality you are his henchman.
> *Šešelj*: If I come to power, I will probably arrest Milošević. As long as the Americans try to overthrow Milošević by supporting the crazy Vuk Drašković and Mićunović's Democratic Party, however, I will help Milošević.[109]

At the other end of the Serbian political spectrum are some members of the Serbian opposition. Here one may include Serbian painter Mića Popović, who, in an interview with Belgrade's weekly news magazine, *NIN*, had sharp words of criticism for both the Serbian and the Croatian government. "All the democratic and quasi-democratic parties in Yugoslavia are led, above all, by former communists," he complained. "Even in the opposition parties. And we are not talking about just any communists, but about the most severe communists."[110] These former communists were, he said, stirring up "chauvinism" and "hysteria"; Serbia's own government he characterized as "typically communist."[111]

Somewhere between these two extremes is Slobodan Milošević, Serbia's leading figure since 1987. Milošević, who first championed the principle of "one person, one vote" in Yugoslavia's constitutional debate, told *NIN* in April that, with or without Slovenia, the international-legal continuity of Yugoslavia would be maintained: "We, as a state, have more than 8,000 international agreements, various obligations; we are a founding member of the UN, and one of the founders of the International Monetary Fund; we are an old state, not a new state."[112] But, with or without Slovenia, Yugoslavia (according to Milošević and his adherents) could not be confederal; this has been restated on many occasions.[113]

At the same time, Milošević has held to the principle that Yugoslavia's internal borders were administratively drawn and needed to be revised. In August, he set forth a preliminary plan for redrawing these borders, only to find that some of the other republics were not willing to discuss his suggestions seriously.[114] In the aforementioned interview with *NIN*, Milošević explained, "Questions of borders are essential questions of state. And borders, as you know, are always dictated by the strong, never by the weak. Accordingly, it is essential that we be strong."[115]

The federally oriented newspaper *Borba* expressed its reservations about these ideas, however. In *Borba*'s view, "It is impossible to create a greater Serbia and keep it, and it is impossible to instrumentalize Yugoslavia for one's own [Serbian] national interests . . . Slobodan Milošević," *Borba* continued, "is like his opponent [the president of the Republic of Croatia] Franjo Tudjman—in a trap. If he pursues his current policy, Serbia—great or small—is headed for international isolation, poverty, and internal unrest out of which Milošević cannot emerge triumphant."[116]

Meanwhile, in the course of summer 1991, various Serbian critics of Milošević raised their voices in protest. In July, the leaders of Serbia's principal opposition parties united in demanding changes in the government of Serbia, to include creating a government of "national unity," replacing Milošević with a "noncommunist," and appointing the majority of the ministers of the new government from outside the ranks of Milošević's Serbian Socialist Party.[117] Although Milošević ignored these demands, *NIN* opined that time was on the side of the opposition.[118] Less than two weeks later, Vuk Drašković, leader of the Serbian Renaissance Movement, told the Austrian magazine *Profil* that "Serbs and Croats should rise against the dictatorial regimes in their republics."[119] In another context, Drašković agreed with Šešelj that the western border of Serbia should be drawn along the line determined by Karlobag, Karlovac, and Virovitica.[120]

Serbian writer Borislav Mijalović Mihiz also criticized Milošević. Setting forth his ideas in a *Proposition for Reflections, In Ten Points*, Mihiz declared his belief that Yugoslavia could not be revived or sustained, because the Slovenes and Croats had essentially opted to leave. He therefore called on Serbs to set aside their self-ascribed reputation as "the guardians" of Yugoslavia, to recognize the independence of Slovenia, and to accept the legitimacy of Croatia's claim to independence, conditional upon Croatia's recognition of the right of Serb-populated districts to decide freely with which state they wished to be affiliated.[121]

Yet another critic of Milošević's—Belgrade political scientist Živorad Stojković—lamented what he viewed as "ideological, moral, and mental deformities of generations of working and unemployed people of this nation,"[122] and targeted, in particular, the simplified—as he saw it—concept of nationality which had been propagated in Serbia: "Our concept of Serbian ethnicity is linked with Orthodoxy, but not with any cultural and historical totality which is much broader and which is generally accepted [elsewhere] in Europe."[123]

Finally, one may make note of Ivan Kristan, a judge sitting on the Constitutional Court of Yugoslavia. Approached by *NIN* for his assessment of the crisis, Kristan struck a pacific pose, urging that "force cannot solve controversial questions."[124]

There was, thus, a wide spectrum of political opinion in Serbia, just as there was in Bosnia, Croatia, Macedonia, and—even though I have not discussed them here—the other republics as well. The various opinion groupings held different views about the interests of their respective republics, as well as about the appropriate policies, strategies, and instrumentalities to be adopted. Commenting on Serbia, the Swiss newspaper *Neue Zürcher Zeitung* claimed that local opposition to Milošević was placed at a disadvantage: "Every criticism of Milošević or the army is portrayed as treason or as an attempt, at a time of highest danger, to split the Serbian nation."[125]

The International Dimension

When Croatia and Slovenia first declared their independence and the Serbian army struck into Slovenia, various countries repudiated the secessionist republics and endorsed the continued existence of a unified Yugoslav state; among the countries endorsing unity were the United States, the Soviet Union, China,[126] Britain,[127] France,[128] Sweden,[129] Denmark,[130] Italy,[131] Greece,[132] Romania,[133] Poland,[134] and (cautiously) Hungary.[135] The governments of Austria and Germany, pressured by populations long accustomed to vacationing along the Dalmatian coast and, partly for that reason, broadly sympathetic to Croatian and Slovenian aspirations, nonetheless held back from recognizing the breakaway republics. The Serbian press expressed misgivings about German intentions, however, referring to alleged dangers of a "Fourth Reich."[136] "The spirit of national socialism in Germany and Austria [is] seriously increasing," said the Belgrade daily *Politika ekspres*. "Their allies in Slovenia and Croatia are trying not to fall behind."[137] *Večernje novosti*, another Belgrade daily, fretted that "Germany has always striven to expand toward the East, even to the south and the southeast."[138] At the same time, Milan Drečun, a military-political commentator for the army newspaper, *Narodna armija*, accused Austria and Germany of supplying sophisticated anti-tank and anti-aircraft weaponry to the Croats.[139] For his part, Croatian Foreign Minister Separović indicated, in an interview with Austrian television on August 12, that Croatia looked to Austria and Germany to lead the way in extending diplomatic recognition to Croatia.[140]

Albania and Hungary accused the Yugoslav Air Force of having violated their airspace, and both countries took military precautions lest the fighting spill across their borders. Hungary's precautions focused on defense of its airspace.[141] The Albanian president placed Albania's army in a state of alert as early as the beginning of July.[142] The Albanian government also declared its full support for the creation of a Republic of Kosovo "within the framework of the Yugoslav federation or confederation."[143] Meanwhile, Albania's ambassador to the SFRY, Kujtim Hysenaj, held talks with Croatian foreign minister Zvonimir Separović about "the possibilities of foreign political cooperation between Albania and Croatia," as Radio Croatia put it.[144]

Bulgaria issued a statement to the effect that the Bulgarian army would not threaten "Yugoslav" security,[145] but also intimated that it was prepared to recognize an independent Macedonian state.[146] The Sofia newspaper *Demokratsiya* spelled out Bulgarian concern quite clearly:

> If not from the territorial point of view, then at least from the historical—and this also means spiritual—point of view, Macedonia cannot be separated from Bulgaria. . . . If Bulgaria forgets Macedonia, it will disavow itself. The Bulgarians must desire the existence of the Macedonian Republic precisely as they desire the existence of the Bulgarian state. . . . Whatever direction the events in Yugoslavia take, the Macedonians in Vardar Macedonia must feel our fraternal shoulder.[147]

The Bulgarian connection assumed greater poignancy after September 9, when early returns from a popular referendum showed that 74 percent of Macedonians favored independence. At the same time, Slovenia, Croatia, and Bosnia wooed foreign capitals: Slovenia and Croatia sought support in Vienna, Bonn, Rome, and Washington DC above all; Bosnia courted Istanbul.[148] The European Community was loath to intervene and, at least as of this writing, restricted itself to sending a few dozen unarmed observers to the war zone and helping to bring about a series of futile truces. In late September, the UN Security Council imposed an arms embargo on Yugoslavia.[149]

Escalation?

Four months after its outbreak in late June 1991, the Yugoslav civil war showed no signs of abating. By that point, there had been reports that the Yugoslav air force had used napalm against the Croats,[150] claims by Serbs that Croatian President Tudjman was trying to develop a nuclear option,[151] and open discussion in the Serbian press about the possibility of an air strike against Slovenia's nuclear power plant at Krško (*NIN* cited the precedent of Israel's strike against Iraq's French-built nuclear power plant).[152] Large numbers of ethnic Croats from Canada, the United States, Australia, and various European countries were said to be returning to Croatia to fight for their homeland.[153] By late September, some 232,412 Croatian citizens had reportedly been driven from their homes. Of this number, 106,000 refugees were said to have fled to other locations in Croatia, 60,000 (chiefly Serbs) to locations in Serbia, about 30,000 to Hungary, and some 3,500 to Germany.[154]

Up to that point, despite the secession of Slovenia and Croatia, the increasingly impotent eight-person collective presidency had continued to meet. But on October 3, the four pro-Serbian delegates (representing Serbia, Montenegro, Kosovo, and Vojvodina) expelled the delegates from the other four republics and elected Montenegrin delegate Branko Kostić president of the collective presidency, thus ending the post-Tito practice of maintaining a strict annual rotation schedule, with turnover timed for each May.[155] This produced the ironic result that Slovenia and Croatia, which had declared their secession, wanted nonetheless to keep their delegates in the collective body, while Serbia and Montenegro, which did not recognize the secession of Croatia, declined to include either the Slovenian or the Croatian delegate in that body. Macedonia and Bosnia joined Slovenia and Croatia in condemning the Serbian move, which they termed a "putsch."[156] The US State Department also issued a statement characterizing this development as "a clear attempt by Serbia and Montenegro to seize control of the federal government." The State Department added, "In such circumstances, the United States does not accept that this rump group legitimately speaks for Yugoslavia."[157] One of the first acts of the "rump" presidency was to praise the work of the JNA up to then.[158]

In the wake of this development, Defense Minister Kadijević pledged "to force the 'neo-fascist leadership' [of Croatia] to its knees . . . [and called upon] all 'patriots' to defend their country against the threat of 'fascism'."[159]

A series of ceasefires brokered by the European Community fell through. The eighth such ceasefire, negotiated on October 9, was violated within a few hours, when the JNA and Croatian units resumed the exchange of artillery fire.[160] The following day, Germany's Martin Bangemann, Vice President of the EC Commission, called for Bonn to extend diplomatic recognition to Slovenia and Croatia without any further delay.[161] His initiative seemed to be ignored. But at the same time, Dutch Foreign Minister van den Broek announced that after five hours of discussions with Presidents Milošević and Tudjman and Defense Minister Kadijević, all present had agreed that all units of the JNA would be withdrawn from Croatia within a month. The following day, however, the Defense Ministry indicated that it considered the agreement non-binding and null because it had not been officially signed.[162] By that point, the Croatian city of Vukovar was said to have been "completely destroyed."[163]

High officials of the Conference on Security and Cooperation in Europe (CSCE) convened an emergency meeting in Prague on October 11 and agreed that the use of force to bring about boundary changes was "not acceptable." The delegates in attendance also condemned what they called Serbia's "cold putsch" in the collective presidency.[164] Meanwhile, the European Community–sponsored peace conference in The Hague proposed to the Yugoslav republics that they accept a loose confederation, to include a free-trade zone, common currency, a common army, the maintenance of existing internal borders, and guarantees for the protection of minorities, under international supervision. Milošević immediately rejected the proposal.[165]

The JNA continued its campaign against Croatia, sending its air force on bombing missions against the Croatian towns of Osijek, Nova Gradiška, Ogulin, Otačac, Gospić, and Pakrac.[166] At the same time, the JNA tightened its siege of the Croatian port city of Dubrovnik by mounting an amphibious assault to seize a beachhead, and then capturing several coastal villages to establish a base of operations three miles from Dubrovnik. Dubrovnik was also said to have been subjected to aerial bombardment.[167] Ninety percent of Dubrovnik's 60,000 inhabitants were Croats. In response to the siege of the walled city, the US State Department issued a protest on October 24.

The Hague peace conference offered a slightly revised peace package on October 25, but Milošević rejected this proposal as well. This second proposal would have entailed the demilitarization of all ethnic enclaves and guarantees of autonomy for Kosovo and Vojvodina. Milošević said the proposed changes would have "opened the way to new instability and tension."[168] In August, Croatian President Tudjman had told a German journalist that he ruled out any territorial compromise whatsoever: "We are not willing to give even the smallest piece of land to Serbia."[169]

The tenth ceasefire was announced on October 19, and after more than a week of non-observance, the European Community belatedly announced that this latest ceasefire had collapsed. "Ceasefire agreements have been violated by all parties," the European Community noted in a public statement. "But recent Yugoslav Army attacks are out of all proportion to any noncompliance by Croatia."[170]

Conclusion

The general direction of political developments in Yugoslavia from the 1960s through the 1980s was toward ever-greater decentralization. There were only two logical end results of this process: complete and total confederalization or civil war. Unable to agree on terms for confederalization, the Yugoslav republics slid into war.

Insofar as this book has been founded on an analogy between international and domestic politics, we may say that the eruption of war in Yugoslavia shattered this conceptual boundary, converting Yugoslavia, de facto, into a regional international system.

What will be the legacy of the war? First and foremost, the war has sown much deeper hatred between Serbs and Croats than ever existed before, a hatred that has estranged Slovenes and Serbs and that could last for generations. Second, the war has gutted the tourist trade, damaged foreign trade more generally, destroyed much of the economic infrastructure, caused serious damage to the transport system (specifically to airports, seaports, highways, and railways), wiped out Yugoslavia's credit on foreign money markets, and reduced available budgetary funds by at least 60 percent between 1990 and 1991.[171] According to estimates from the Yugoslav Ministry of Information, the Yugoslav GNP had already been sliced by 20 percent by mid-August 1991, with industrial production expected to drop by 50 percent by autumn.[172] By late August, the Yugoslav government was indicating that repayment of the $938 million in foreign debts falling due by the end of 1991 posed "an exceptionally big challenge for the Federal treasury."[173] Even food supplies have likewise been seriously affected. Third, the civil war has fueled a discussion of irredentist ideas in Albania, Bulgaria, Hungary, and even Italy (albeit chiefly in the small Italian Liberal Party). Fourth, the war has diverted public attention, in Serbia and especially in Croatia, from such concerns as economic development, environmental quality, gender equality, and cultural and artistic exchange. Fifth, as a result of the economic impact and the mobilization of ethnic loyalties, the war has seriously complicated the efforts by democratic forces in the republics to move toward stable pluralism.

In this chapter, I have tried to let the participants in the struggle in Yugoslavia speak for themselves. At a descriptive level, I have intended above all to set forth, as fairly and as completely as possible, the views of the different actors and the complexities of the political scene in each republic, to show where and how they came into conflict, and to indicate which elites advocate what kind of coalition strategy for their respective republics.

Analytically, this chapter contributes to an assessment of how political systems disintegrate. Morton Kaplan alterted us, in 1957, to the importance of analyzing the manner in which systems break down, and the consequences thereof. The events described here corroborate a point made earlier in this book: that inter-unit conflict may exacerbate conflicts *within* a given unit, and that rival elites within any given unit may (as in the Bosnian and Macedonian cases) articulate alternative coalition strategies. Finally, this chapter draws attention to the question of the stability of balance-of-power systems, the subject of some controversy in the literature. Are balance-of-power systems inherently unstable and inevitably doomed to break down; or are they potentially stable configurations, and should system breakdown be viewed, on the contrary, as the result of contingent (and therefore avoidable) factors? This is not an easy question, and the debate as to whether the civil war was inevitable—given the system and the legacy of past policies—will no doubt continue for years to come.

14
Conclusion

Princes do keep due sentinel, that none of their neighbours do overgrow.

FRANCIS LORD BACON,
"Essay on Empire"

Among the many paradoxes of Yugoslav politics that long fascinated Western observers were the apparent disjunction between Titoism's seemingly efficient mechanism for conflict regulation and its occasional lapses into acerbic crisis behavior and the contradiction between the quasi-confederal relations long prevailing among the republics and the system's long failure to fall apart. This book is, in part, an effort to explain how these ostensibly incompatible elements not only coexisted but in fact characterized a unified system of behavior, a system better known as the "balance of power." I have argued that interrepublican relations in Yugoslavia were characterized by flexible coalitions and that the political behavior exhibited by these federal units closely resembled the political behavior of states in the European balance-of-power system.

In the domestic, just as in the international, balance-of-power system, one cannot expect component actors to be moved by exhortations to the good of the community. Each group will attempt to pursue its interests by subordinating the common good to its own communal interests and also by subordinating the good of other communal groups to the good of the whole, (if not, in fact, to its own private good). Of course, an element of restraint is built into a balance-of-power system, as long as it lasts, viz., a sense that in most cases the general equilibrium (recall Kaplan's rules 5 and 6) serves the interest of each player.[1] But it is the shape of conflict that gives the system its distinctive contours. A requirement for the stability of the system is that no single actor is indispensable to the formation of a winning coalition (and therefore capable of imposing its will on decision making). Such a condition prevailed in Yugoslavia until 1990. Thus, policy outcomes in matters of interrepublican importance came to depend on the free combination of republican actors in shifting alliances and flexible coalitions. The existence of group interests may be presumed; the politicization of group interests may not. The argument has therefore consisted of three parts: establishment of politicized group interests that coincided with nationality and/or republic boundaries, demonstration that the republics and autonomous provinces enjoyed sufficient autonomy to be able to pursue these interests in meaningful ways, and confutation of simple bipolar views of Yugoslav politics.

In an ideal realm of pure abstractions, actors have no vested interests and combine in a completely free and unfettered way with no desire but to "win." And, in this spirit, the uncommitted and disinterested are expected to ally with the weaker bloc to prevent change: an international system, abstractly conceived, is said to have a built-in tendency to stagnation.[2] But, in the realm of real political behavior, the flexibility of a system is almost inevitably compromised to a greater or lesser degree by the existence of stable patterns of interests. The flexibility of a system stems in part from the overlap of interests, in part from internal contradictions (that is, competing and conflictual interests within a single republic), and in part from the willingness of partners to engage in trade-offs in the particular policy areas that most concern them (e.g., Croatian and Bosnian cooperation on the latter's eligibility for FADURK assistance). Stable communal interests among Bosnia, Macedonia, Montenegro, and Kosovo in maintaining the FADURK apparatus is an example of the overlapping of interests, while the common anti-Serbian current found in Croatian, Albanian, and Montenegrin nationalisms illustrates the role of internal contradictions in the system.

Obviously, flexibility in interrepublican coalitions may be a factor of changes in the orientation of the republican elites in power (whether because of changing issues, changing context, changing interests, or changing perceptions). It may also, however, be a factor of changes in the composition of the republican elites as certain factions edge aside their rivals. Since different factions (the chief ones being the so-called liberals and conservatives) have different perceptions of republican interests, their coalition choices will inevitably be affected by the composition of elites in the other republics. The Croatian-Slovenian-Macedonian axis of 1967–69 was possible because liberals occupied the top leadership positions in these republics. (This was not enough to vouchsafe the coalition—as was shown by the consecutive defections from the coalition of Slovenia and Macedonia, which left Croatia to seek new alliance partners.) Similarly, Croatian conservatives united with conservative forces in Serbia and Slovenia to change the balance of forces in the system; in the process, the alignments of coalitions also changed.

In recounting the several controversies and crises that have sparked interrepublican relations during the 1962–91 period, I have tried to highlight political behavior relevant to the hypotheses derived from my adaptation of Kaplan's balance-of-power model. It is now possible to take stock and see which hypotheses are confirmed and which discounted. I have discussed some thirty-two controversies (in some cases overlapping) in greater or lesser detail. These are:

C1. The reform crisis, 1961–66
C2. The status of the autonomous provinces, early 1960s–1974
C3. The Belgrade-Bar railroad, 1963–76
C4. The disbursement of FADURK's resources, 1965–72
C5. The debate on republican tax limits, 1967

C6. The status of Albanians and civil disorders, 1967 to the present
C7. The struggle over devolution, 1967–71
C8. The Slovenian highway crisis, 1969
C9. The debate on banking reform, 1970
C10. The controversy over Macedonia's Muslims, 1970–71
C11. The status of Serbs in Croatia, 1971
C12. The Croatian crisis, 1971–72
C13. The controversy over fishing compensation from Italy, 1972
C14. The debate over scope and conditions of aid to Kosovo, 1977
C15. The debate on the draft law on customs tariffs, 1978
C16. The debate over FADURK criteria, 1978–82
C17. The air transport controversy, 1979–82
C18. The controversy over inflation control—wages, 1979
C19. The controversy over inflation control—prices, 1979
C20. The controversy over compensation to Montenegro, 1980
C21. The "Bratstvo-Jedinstvo" controversy, 1980
C22. Liberalization versus retrenchment, 1980–87
C23. Decentralism versus recentralization, 1980–87
C24. Dispute over the retention of foreign currency earnings, 1985
C25. Dispute over the constitutional proposals, 1987
C26. Dispute over reform of the Assembly, 1988–89
C27. Dispute over reform of the SFRJ presidency, 1988–89
C28. The anti-Mikulić coalition, 1988
C29. Clash over the 1989 federal budget, 1989
C30. Support for Marković's economic program, 1989
C31. The "Slovenia versus Serbia" debate, 1989
C32. The confederalization debate, 1989–90

Throughout these crises, the republics and autonomous provinces displayed autonomy of decision making and willingness to realign in shifting coalitions according to perceived changes of interest (compare the patterns in appendix 1).

I have also examined ten hypotheses, set forth in chapter 1. In brief, these are:

H1. Federal units promote their own interests even when they conflict with the interests of the federal community.
H2. Federal units negotiate but provoke crisis if necessary to protect their interests.
H3. Federal units resist encroachment or ethnic assimilation and form coalitions to oppose any threatening actor.
H4. All federal units are acceptable coalition partners (though in some cases this may apply only in a faction-to-faction sense).
H5. Alliance between a federal unit and an external power is viewed as illegitimate.

H6. The federal government tries to reduce the disparities in power and wealth among the federal units.
H7. The federal government takes whatever action is necessary to resolve interrepublican disputes that threaten to upset the system.
H8. The federal government strives to be ethnically neutral.
H9. Social mobilization increases the pressure for decentralization.
H10. Conflict is effectively regulated under a concert system.

A cross-tabulation of these hypotheses with the thirty-two controversies is shown in figure 2. The results show a strong corroboration for hypotheses 1, 2, 3, 4, 7, 8, and 9—derived, in part, from Kaplan's rules 1, 2, 4, and 6—and reliable confirmation of hypothesis 9. Only twelve of the twenty-one cases were relevant tests of hypothesis 6, and, of this number, ten cases confirmed the hypothesis. But the apparent disconfirmation of the supposition of an "equalizing federal actor" in two cases is not as serious as might be supposed, since, in at least one of the two cases, the federal government "broke the rule" by limiting itself to making recommendations—a policy in harmony with the quasi-confederal character of the system. Hypothesis 5, the disallowance of alliance with foreign powers, was only explicitly confirmed in three cases, but there can be little doubt of its validity. As for the remaining hypothesis (10), it is actually neither a part of Kaplan's model nor essential to the stable operation of a balance-of-power system. Ironically, hypothesis 10, the *evaluational* hypothesis that purports to corroborate Nordlinger's favorable estimation of Yugoslavia's capabilities of conflict regulation, remains, at least insofar as the confirmatory evidence of these controversies is concerned, the most problematic.

More than seventy years ago, Arthur Bentley observed that "on any political question which we could study . . . we should never be justified in treating the interests of the whole nation as decisive. There are always some parts of the nation to be found arrayed against other parts."[3] And the foregoing case studies have manifestly demonstrated that Yugoslavia's republics do have frequent conflicts of interest. A casual observer of the Yugoslav scene might expect to find profoundly polarized alliance behavior, with the underdeveloped republics invariably coalescing around a common position, Slovenia and Croatia consistently mutually supportive, and Croatia and Serbia generally at loggerheads. Such inflexible alignments would be incompatible with a true balance-of-power system. Moreover, when the federal government plays a role, we should expect, under the conditions of the model, that more often than not it will intervene to preserve the balance. This might mean that the federal authority will come down on the weaker side, if one construes the federal government as a surrogate "balancer"; it could also come down on the stronger side, if one emphasizes instead the "concert" aspect of the federal government, that is, its self-presentation as an interrepublican arena.

Table 26 reveals the trends that emerge from a review of the twenty-one controversies. Note that virtually all of the economic controversies documented

Figure 2

	H1	H2	H3	H4	H5	H6	H7	H8	H9	H10
C1	+	+	+	+		(−)	+	+	(+)	
C2	+	+	+				+	(+)	+	
C3	+	+		(+)		+				
C4	+	+	(+)	+		+	+	+		+
C5	+	+		+						
C6	+	+	+		+		(+)	+		
C7	+	+	+	+			+	+	+	(+)
C8	+	+		+	(+)	(+)	+		+	(−)
C9	+			(+)		+	+			
C10	+	+	+	+			(+)	+	(+)	
C11	+	+	+							−
C12	+	+	+	+	+		+	+	+	−
C13	(+)	+	+							
C14	(+)			+		+	(+)	+		(+)
C15	+	+		(+)		+		+		
C16	+	(+)		+		+	+	+		(+)
C17	+	+	+	+		−				
C18	+	+	+	+						
C19	+	+	+	+						
C20	+	(+)					(+)			+
C21	+						(−)	(+)		
C22	+	+	+	+					+	−
C23	+	+	+	+					+	−
C24	+	+				+				
C25	+	+	+			+			+	−
C26	+	+	+			+			+	(−)
C27	+	+	+							(−)
C28	+	+								(+)
C29	+	+								
C30	+	+								
C31	+	+	+				+	+	+	−
C32	+	+	+						+	−

C = crisis
H = hypothesis
\+ = confirmation; (+) = partial confirmation
− = disconfirmation; (−) = partial disconfirmation
blank = crisis not relevant as measure of this hypothesis, insufficient information, or events are ambiguous

Table 26. *Trends in Alliance Behavior among Yugoslav Republics*

Condition	*Number of occurrences (out of total of 32)*	*Number of economic cases (out of total of 17)*
Serbia opposes Croatia	19	7
Serbia and Croatia ally	5	5
Underdeveloped republics operate as a bloc	8	5
Underdeveloped republics split	13	7
Croatia and Slovenia ally	17	8
Croatia opposes Slovenia	6	5
Federal government intervenes in favor of weaker bloc	2	2
Federal government intervenes on preponderant side	3	3
Actor (including the federal government) changes alliance	4	2

are relatively specific issues, in contrast to the more all-encompassing issues found under the "political" category (such as the Croatian crisis or the crisis over devolution). As often as not, Croatia and Serbia are allied in economic issues (usually as parts of a larger bloc)—reflecting system flexibility. They have been consistently at odds, however, on political issues. Second, it appears that the underdeveloped republics oppose each other more often than they stick together (in conformity with the model), and, in five of the eight cases in which they did act as a bloc, the issue was strictly economic. Indeed, little else would predispose these four units to act in unison. Third, Croatia and Slovenia appear to be mutually supportive in political issues, but, in economics, they oppose each other almost as often as they are allied. Fourth, as far as federal interventions are concerned, the federal government appears inclined to go with the preponderant bloc, though this perception may be a distortion of the issue, since what is at stake is not defeat and annexation but the general interest of the majority versus the exclusive interests of one or two republics. Seen in this light, the fact that the federal government favored the majority in 75 percent of the cases is a reflection of the workings of consensual politics within a concert mechanism. Finally, there were at least three instances among the twenty-one cases in which an actor switched sides in midstream—a recourse that lies at the heart of a balance-of-power system.

Because, as I have noted, concrete interests are at stake rather than the mere preservation of balance, it is not uncommon to find blocs of six or seven actors uniting against one or two recalcitrant federal units. The number of republics in each alliance is not so important as maintenance of the approximate equality (and formal equality) of the actors (no republic may rise to a position of preeminence analogous, even crudely, to that of the Soviet RSFSR). The system must remain at (or be restored to) equilibrium, and that equilibrium must be valued by the actors in the system. Since these conditions prevail in socialist Yugoslavia, I do not hesitate to identify Yugoslavia as a concert variant of the balance-of-power system.

I have traced the development of interrepublican relations in Yugoslavia from 1962 to 1991. During these three decades, the Yugoslav federal system passed through seven behavioral phases: (1) 1962–66, system change; (2) 1966–69, balance of power, semiconfederal; (3) 1969–71, balance of power, quasi-confederal; (4) 1972–80, balance of power, quasi-confederal, with a concert mechanism; (5) 1980–87, balance of power, quasi-confederal; (6) 1987–89, balance of power, fissiparous, with pressure toward recentralization; (7) 1989–91, confederalization. The years 1962–66 were catalytic, years when the behavioral patterns associated with the "unitarist" period broke down and dissolved the neat polarity of an age when most of the republics were politically dormant. Through the mobilization of the other six federal units into the system, the Serb-Croat rivalry ceased to be the lodestone of intra-Yugoslav politics, and the republics began to engage in a pattern of shifting coalitions. Moreover, beginning with the Janko Smole affair and the Slovenian road crisis, the republics began to consider opposition to the federal government in areas where their interests were threatened.

Mobilization of ethnic-group actors spawned a revival of nationalisms, however. Dawning awareness of the harshness of Ranković's policies, moreover, heightened the sense of collective cognitive dissonance that had already been aroused, in some cases, by feelings of relative economic deprivation. Spokespersons for the republics no longer spoke in terms of Yugoslav interests but, increasingly, in terms of republican interests. The crucial turning point came at the Fourth Plenum of the central committee of the LCY in July 1966. This plenum marked the fall of Ranković and Stefanović and the beginning of a period of increased autonomy for the republics. It also signaled a change in interrepublican dynamics. For the first time, the underdeveloped republics allied with Croatia and Slovenia and against Serbia. The Brioni plenum thus completed the process of system change begun by the economic reforms.

Between 1966 and 1969, the Yugoslav parliament was reinvigorated, the Chamber of Nationalities came back into its own, and the republics discovered that they had more political clout than previously realized. Yet this confederal tendency was limited by institutional factors and by the continued resistance of unitarist forces. The passage of far-reaching constitutional amendments between 1967 and 1968 overcame the first hurdle, and the latter retreated in the face of the growing strength of the national-liberal-technocratic coalition. After 1969, the central apparatus appears to have lost control of the situation—it was internally divided and lacked clear direction—and, consequently, the republics aggrandized their power. Republican self-interest was unabashedly touted as the highest good. In a typical comment, Miko Tripalo told *Vjesnik* in 1970 that "the League of Communists in every republic expresses and is obliged to express the interests of the working class of its nation and of its republic."[4] Ultimately, this attitude, when wedded to the nationalist oestrus, led to the formulation of nonnegotiable and totally impracticable demands and precipitated a severe confrontational crisis in the system.

Tito's "compromise," which ended the Croatian crisis and swept the liberals out of office in Croatia, Slovenia, Serbia, and Macedonia, affected interrepublican relations in an important way. Tito refused to scuttle the liberal reforms, yet he did not trust the liberals to administer them. He let the conservative factions carry out the liberals' vision, thus confirming the quasi-confederal nature of the system without allowing autonomous centers of power to become focuses of politicized collective affectivity. Ultimately, Tito hoped to hold together a "liberal" system not by force but by a common ideology, the ideology of "conservatism." In his appreciation of the importance of system homogeneity Tito may be likened to Metternich, who also stabilized a system by suppressing one of two rival ideologies. Finally, in the wake of Tito's death, the central party, shorn of the arbiter who had created unity among rival factions, proved unable to agree on a common policy and watched its control slacken as the republican parties jumped to take advantage of the new confederalism.

One of the points that I hope has emerged from this study is that multiethnic configuration and level of modernization present a regime with a narrowed field of policy options. The regime's policy "choice" may sometimes be dictated from below, by the systemic environment, including the actors in it. This does not mean the regime is helplessly determined by its environment; it does mean that the regime's ability to affect political development is limited. The LCY did choose to terminate discussion of federalization of the party on the grounds that such a debate might resurrect the multiparty system; in a multiethnic state, there is a great danger that a multiparty system (which is likely to be ideologically heterogeneous) will provoke instability.

It is incontestable that the presence of a central government distinguished the Yugoslav federal system from the classical European balance-of-power system of the eighteenth and nineteenth centuries, at least until the end of 1989. Yet, just as it makes sense to speak of polarized politics in a binational state, so is it meaningful to speak of multipolar politics in a multinational state. Where multipolar politics are characterized by a shifting pattern of flexible coalitions, the system may accurately be characterized as a balance-of-power system. Furthermore, the federal government in Yugoslavia often functioned as primus inter pares in a nine-actor universe (as in the interrepublican committees) and, in any case, is to a considerable degree an interrepublican body itself—thus warranting its characterization as a concert mechanism.

The argument of this study has proceeded at three levels to these conclusions:

(1) Yugoslavia was able to attain a measure of temporary stability by virtue of the regime's federal formula, which, one could argue, gives the system its peculiar "quasi-legitimate" character;[5]
(2) "the communists substituted regional pluralization (administrative decen-

tralization) for political pluralization (multiparty democracy),"[6] with the result that interelite conflict, during the era of the LCY monopoly, was always intra-LCY conflict, sometimes pitting factions existing within the same regional party organization against each other;

(3) the pattern of interrepublican relations that has resulted from (a) the presence of eight autonomous federal units among which no single factor predominates, (b) the combination of a viable federal system with various interrepublican bodies, and (c) the fear of the alternatives to the status quo closely approximates the pattern best known as the "balance of power"; and

(4) there are close parallels, in this instance, between the constants of internal politics and those of international politics.

The more specific findings of this work may be summarized as follows:

(1) policy is often the result of coalition politics in which republics are the actors;

(2) republican party organizations consist of rival factions with rival perceptions of interest, and coalition patterns are a function of the vicissitudes of interfaction rivalry;

(3) there is strong corroboration for the applicability of four of Kaplan's central rules to Yugoslavia, namely, (a) all actors are acceptable coalition partners, (b) actors act to restrain actors subscribing to supranational organizing principles, (c) actors unite to oppose any unit that tends to threaten the autonomy of the others or the stability of the system, and (d) actors provoke crisis rather than forego the opportunity to increase capabilities;

(4) certain trends in interrepublican behavior are identifiable, specifically: (a) Croatia and Serbia are often allied in economic issues but are consistently at odds in political issues, (b) the underdeveloped republics oppose each other as often as they stick together, and, in four out of the five cases in which they acted as a bloc, the issue was strictly economic; (c) Croatia and Slovenia are mutually supportive in political issues but often oppose each other in economic issues, and (d) the federal government, interested in stability, is inclined to side with the preponderant bloc (a factor of the concert mechanism); and

(5) the Yugoslav claim to have *affected* interethnic relations must be taken seriously.

Yugoslavia's communists tried for more than forty years to "solve" the national question. They placed their trust in strict proportionality in federal organs (though not in the military), in ethnic quota systems (which were not applied in Kosovo or always in Croatia, or even in Bosnia), in massive decentralization to the point of verging on de facto confederalization, and in a mythology that drew inspiration from the partisan war, the nonaligned movement, and, for as long as he was alive, the charismatic personality of Tito. Ultimately, they failed. But their failure was not so much a failure of confederalism, but rather a failure of the concept of limited democracy, of the idea that democracy can emerge out of one-party rule.

Models of behavior, of course, cannot substitute for either research or analysis, nor are they meant to. The best that can be expected from a model is that it will highlight patterns in real behavior, sketch relationships and state linkages, serve as a guide to meaningful and useful comparative analysis, and establish a focus for research. There is no intrinsic reason why a model of behavior developed in one context might not be adaptable to another. This study has been founded on that supposition.

APPENDIX 1

Alliance Behavior among the Yugoslav Republics, 1961–90

The reform crisis, 1961–66

Croatia	vs.	Serbia
Slovenia		Montenegro (1963–66)
Macedonia		
Bosnia-Herzegovina		
Kosovo		
Montenegro (1966)		

The status of the autonomous provinces, early 1960s–1974

Kosovo	vs.	Serbia
Croatia		

The Belgrade-Bar railway controversy, 1963–76

Serbia	vs.	Croatia
Montenegro		
Macedonia		
Kosovo		

The disbursement of FADURK's resources, 1965–72

Kosovo	vs.	Bosnia-Herzegovina
Macedonia		FADURK (subsequently)
Montenegro		
FADURK (initially)		

The debate on republican tax limits, 1967

Serbia	vs.	Federal government
Croatia		
Slovenia		

The national-liberal coalition, 1967–69

Croatia	vs.	Serbian unitarism
Slovenia		
Macedonia		
Vojvodina (associate partner)		

The struggle over devolution, 1967–71

Croatia	vs.	Serbia
Slovenia		
Macedonia		
Bosnia-Herzegovina		
Kosovo		
Vojvodina (until 1969)		

The Slovenian highway crisis, 1969

Serbia	vs.	Slovenia
Macedonia		

(Croatia remained "benignly" neutral.)

The debate on banking reform, 1970

Serbia	vs.	Croatia
Kosovo		
Montenegro		
Bosnia-Herzegovina		

The controversy over Macedonia's Muslims, 1970–71

Macedonia	vs.	Bosnia-Herzegovina
Croatia		Kosovo
		Serbia

The status of Serbs in Croatia, 1971

Serbia	vs.	Croatian mainstream
Croatian conservatives		

The Croatian crisis, 1971–72

Serbia	vs.	Croatia
Vojvodina		
Montenegro		
Bosnia-Herzegovina		

The controversy over fishing compensations from Italy, 1972

Slovenia	vs.	Croatia
		Montenegro

The debate over scope and conditions of aid to Kosovo, 1977

Federal government	vs.	Slovenia
Bosnia-Herzegovina		Croatia
Kosovo		Vojvodina (initially)
Montenegro		
Macedonia		
Serbia		
Vojvodina (subsequently)		

The debate on the draft law on customs tariffs, 1978

Serbia	vs.	Croatia	vs.	Kosovo
Vojvodina				
Macedonia				
Bosnia-Herzegovina				
Slovenia				
Montenegro				

The debate over FADURK criteria, 1978–82

Alignment unclear, but Bosnia actively courting Croatia and Slovenia and Slovenia opposed to funds for anyone except Kosovo. Underdeveloped federal units divided on some points. Croatia and Vojvodina supported Bosnian eligibility.

The air transport controversy, 1979–82

Serbia (JAT)	vs.	Croatia (Trans Adria)
		Slovenia (Inex Adria Aviopromet)
		Bosnia (Air Bosnia)
		Macedonia
		Kosovo

The controversy over inflation control—wages, 1979

Serbia	vs.	Federal government
Croatia		Kosovo
Macedonia		
Vojvodina		
Montenegro		
Slovenia		

The controversy over inflation control—prices, 1979

Federal government	vs.	Kosovo
Serbia		
Croatia, Bosnia		
Slovenia, Montenegro		
Vojvodina, Macedonia		

The controversy over compensation to Montenegro, 1980

Federal government	vs.	Montenegro
Serbia		
Croatia		
Slovenia		
Vojvodina		
Macedonia		
Kosovo		
Bosnia-Herzegovina		

Bratstvo-Jedinstvo controversy, 1980

Slovenia and Vojvodina not building their sections of highway E-70, Slovenia giving priority to highways connecting it with Austria and Italy and to improving local roads, Vojvodina doing nothing, and Macedonia, Croatia, and Serbia meeting their agreed pledges.

Liberalization versus retrenchment, 1980–87

Serbia	vs.	Bosnia
Slovenia		Montenegro
Vojvodina		Croatia
		Macedonia
		Kosovo

Decentralism versus recentralization, 1980–87

Slovenia	vs.	Serbia
Vojvodina		Bosnia
Croatia		Montenegro
Macedonia		
Kosovo		

Dispute over retention of foreign currency earnings, 1985

Slovenia	vs.	Federal Government
Croatia		

Dispute over the constitutional proposals, 1987

Slovenia	vs.	State Presidency Coordinating Group
		Serbia

Dispute over reform of the Assembly, 1988–89

Slovenia	vs.	Serbia
Croatia		Montenegro
Bosnia		

Dispute over reform of the SFRJ presidency, 1988–89

Serbia	vs.	Slovenia
Bosnia		Croatia
Montenegro		Vojvodina
		Kosovo

Clash over the 1989 federal budget, 1989

Slovenia	vs.	Serbia	vs.	Montenegro
Croatia		Macedonia		Bosnia

The anti-Mikulić coalition, May 1988

Slovenia	vs.	the rest
Croatia		

Support for Marković's economic program, December 1989

Slovenia	vs.	Serbia
Croatia		Vojvodina
Bosnia		
Macedonia		
Montenegro		

Kosovo wanted changes in the program.

The "Slovenia versus Serbia" debate, 1989

Slovenia	vs.	Serbia
Croatia		Montenegro

Bosnia took a middle position.

Confederalization debate, 1989–90

Slovenia	vs.	Serbia
Croatia		Montenegro
Bosnia		Macedonia

APPENDIX 2

Share of Yugoslav Social Product by Republic (in percent)

	1970	*1980*	*1988*
Bosnia-Herzegovina	12.2	12.1	12.8
Montenegro	2.0	2.1	1.9
Croatia	27.1	25.9	25.4
Macedonia	5.1	5.6	5.1
Slovenia	16.3	16.9	16.7
Serbia proper	24.8	25.1	24.1
Kosovo	2.0	2.0	2.2
Vojvodina	10.5	10.3	10.4
Developed regions	78.7	78.2	76.6
Underdeveloped regions	21.3	21.8	22.0

Sources: Mihailo Mladenović, "Neki rezultati privredno nedovljno razvijenih republika i pokrajine Kosovo 1971–1974," in *Jugoslovenski pregled*, 19 (6) (June 1975): 222; *Statistički kalendar Jugoslavije 1982* (Belgrade: Savezni zavod za statistiku, February 1982), p. 54; and author's calculations from *Statistički godišnjak Jugoslavije 1989* (Belgrade: Savezni zavod za statistiku, 1989), p. 42.

APPENDIX 3

Structure of Investments in Industry Financed by FADURK, by Recipient Unit (in percent)

	Bosnia	*Montenegro*	*Macedonia*	*Kosovo*	*Total*
BASIC INDUSTRY					
1966–70	74.3	85.6	64.2	80.9	74.9
1971–74	54.4	70.3	62.2	59.9	59.9
Energy					
1966–70	27.8	29.5	22.7	41.7	30.9
1971–74	11.1	30.3	17.4	15.7	16.4
Basic Metals					
1966–70	26.4	51.4	36.5	18.8	30.5
1971–74	29.0	32.5	31.0	19.1	26.5
Other branches of basic industry					
1966–70	20.1	4.7	5.0	20.4	13.5
1971–74	14.3	7.5	13.8	25.1	17.0
LIGHT INDUSTRY, MANUFACTURES					
1966–70	25.7	14.4	35.8	19.1	25.1
1971–74	45.6	29.7	37.8	40.1	40.1

Source: Mihajlo Vuković, *Sistemski okviri podsticanja bržeg razvoja nerazvijenih područja Jugoslavije* (Sarajevo: Svjetlost, 1978), p. 65.

NOTES

1. The Multinational State as an International System

1. Chadwick F. Alger, "Comparison of Intranational and International Politics," *American Political Science Review* 57 (2) (June 1963): 414.

2. Morton A. Kaplan, *System and Process in International Politics* (New York: John Wiley and Sons, 1957), pp. 21–52.

3. Ernst B. Haas, "The Balance of Power: Prescription, Concept, or Propaganda?" *World Politics* 5 (4) (July 1953): 452.

4. Kaplan, "The International Arena as a Source of Dysfunctional Tension," *World Politics* 6 (4) (July 1954): 502–3.

5. Edward Vose Gulick, *Europe's Classical Balance of Power* (New York: W. W. Norton, 1967), pp. 11–12.

6. See Winfried Frank, "The Italian City-State System as an International System," in *New Approaches to International Relations*, ed. Morton A. Kaplan (New York: St. Martin's Press, 1968); and Hsi-sheng Chi, "The Chinese Warlord System as an International System," in *New Approaches to International Relations*.

7. Clifford Geertz, "The Integrative Revolution: Primordial Sentiments and Civic Politics in the New States," in *Political Modernization*, ed. C. E. Welch, Jr., 2d ed. (Belmont, Calif.: Duxbury Press, 1971), pp. 205–6; Alvin Rabushka and Kenneth A. Shepsle, *Politics in Plural Societies* (Columbus, Ohio: Charles E. Merrill, 1972), p. 88; and Crawford Young, *The Politics of Cultural Pluralism* (Madison, Wisc.: University of Wisconsin Press, 1976), p. 95. See also Walter L. Barrows, "Ethnic Diversity and Political Instability in Black Africa," in *Comparative Political Studies* 9 (2) (July 1976): 141. Harold R. Isaacs takes issue with Geertz's view and contends that "our tribal separatenesses are here to stay" (Isaacs, "Nationality: 'End of the Road'?" *Foreign Affairs* 53 [3] [April 1975]: 447). For a refutation of Geertz's claim that nationalism represents tribal passions that will fade with modernization and for a counterclaim that modernization is itself a catalyst of ethnic nationalism, see Gary K. Bertsch, "The Revival of Nationalisms," *Problems of Communism* 22 (6) (November–December 1973): 6–8; and Paul Shoup, "The Evolution of a System," *Problems of Communism* 18 (4–5) (July–October 1969): 75. Young also challenges Geertz's theory of the effect of modernization on ethnicity. He specifically counters that "contemporary cultural pluralism is not usefully viewed as a resurgence of 'primordial' sentiments. . . . The basic units of contemporary cultural conflict, themselves fluid and shifting, are often entirely novel entities, in other instances substantially altered and transformed, in most cases redefined versions of cultural groups" (Young, *Politics of Cultural Pluralism*, p. 34). The classic statement of the case that modernization has intensified if not actually created ethnic antagonism is made by Hans Kohn, *The Idea of Nationalism* (Toronto: Collier Books, 1969). For an interesting synthesis of these two orientations, see Cynthia Enloe, *Ethnic Conflict and Political Development* (Boston: Little, Brown, 1973).

8. For a more detailed explanation of how these states illustrate the models cited, see the original version of this chapter in Pedro Ramet, "Interrepublican Relations in Contemporary Yugoslavia" (Ph.D. diss. UCLA, 1981).

9. Kaplan, *System and Process*, pp. 38–39.

10. Alex N. Dragnich, *Serbia, Nikola Pašić, and Yugoslavia* (New Brunswick, N.J.: Rutgers University Press, 1974), p. 172.

11. Frits W. Hondius, *The Yugoslav Community of Nations* (The Hague: Mouton, 1968), p. 108.

12. See Vladko Maček, *In the Struggle for Freedom*, trans. Elizabeth Gazi and Stjepan Gazi (University Park, Pa.: Pennsylvania State University Press, 1957), pp. 93–94 and *passim*.

13. Todor Stojkov, "O spoljnopolitičkoj aktivnosti vodjstva Seljačkodemokratske koalicije uoči Šestojanuarske diktature," *Istorija XX Veka* 9 (1968): 298, 302.

14. James J. Sadkovich, "Italian Support for Croatian Separatism: 1927–1937" (Ph.D. diss., University of Wisconsin, 1982) 1: 137–42, 308–18; 2: 748–65.

15. Diario Grandi Report, Roberto Forges Davanzati, 15 October 1929, as cited in Ibid., 1: 191–98. Dino Grandi, the undersecretary of state of the Italian regime, set up the meeting.

16. Andreas Graf Razumovsky, *Ein Kampf um Belgrad* (Berlin: Ullstein Verlag, 1980), pp. 365–66.

17. Conversation with Sadkovitch, April 1, 1980, Belgrade. Sadkovitch has consulted a number of hitherto untouched sources in the course of researching his dissertation: Sadkovitch, "Italian Support for Croatian Separatism."

18. As quoted in Nikola Babić, "Od ideje o autonomiji do socijalističke republike Bosne i Hercegovine," in *Nacionalni odnosi danas*, ed. Milan Petrović and Kasim Suljević (Sarajevo: Univerzal, 1971), p. 174.

19. As quoted in Fikreta Jelić-Butić, "Bosna i Hercegovina u koncepciji stvaranja Nezavisne Države Hrvatske," *Pregled* 61 (12) (December 1971): 664.

20. See Jozo Tomasevich, *War and Revolution in Yugoslavia, 1941–1945: The Chetniks* (Stanford, Calif.: Stanford University Press, 1975), pp. 23–24.

21. Babić, "Od ideje o autonomiji," p. 176.

22. *Hrvatski narod*, an *Ustaše* publication, reiterated the fixation on Bosnia on July 28, 1941. "The center of the Croatian question," it argued, "has been and remains the question of Bosnia-Herzegovina. The resolution of the Croatian question depends on the resolution of the Bosnian question. It is enough to cast a superficial glance at a map to see that [contemporary] Croatia, Slavonia, and Dalmatia lie at the periphery of historical Croatia, whose heart is Bosnia-Herzegovina" (As quoted in Jelić-Butić, "Bosna i Hercegovina," p. 669).

23. Tomasevich, "Yugoslavia during the Second World War," in *Contemporary Yugoslavia*, ed. Wayne S. Vucinich (Berkeley and Los Angeles: University of California Press, 1969), p. 78; Fred Singleton, *Twentieth Century Yugoslavia* (New York: Columbia University Press, 1976), pp. 86–88; and M. George Zaninovich, *The Development of Socialist Yugoslavia* (Baltimore: Johns Hopkins Press, 1968), pp. 28–30. Dušan Bilandžić gives a figure of 1,700,000 Yugoslav casualties during the war; Bilandžić, *Historija Socijalističke Federativne Republike Jugoslavije* (Zagreb: Školska knjiga, 1978), p. 79.

24. Kaplan, *System and Process*, p. 39.

25. Shoup, *Communism and the Yugoslav National Question* (New York: Columbia University Press, 1968), p. 241n.

26. Stanley Hoffmann, "Balance of Power," *International Encyclopedia of the Social Sciences* (Macmillan, 1968), 1: 507.

27. See Kaplan, "Variants on Six Models of the International System," in *International Politics and Foreign Policy*, ed. James N. Rosenau, rev. ed. (New York: Free Press, 1969), p. 292; Kaplan, Arthur Lee Burns, and Richard E. Quandt, "Theoretical Analysis of the 'Balance of Power,'" *Behavioral Science* 5 (3) (July 1960), p. 245; Patrick J. McGowan and Robert M. Rood, "Alliance Behavior in Balance of Power Systems: Applying a Poisson Model to Nineteenth-Century Europe," *American Political Science Review* 69 (3) (September 1975), p. 859; and Dina A. Zinnes, "Coalition Theories and

the Balance of Power," in *The Study of Coalition Behavior*, ed. Sven Groennings, E. W. Kelley, and Michael Leiserson (New York: Holt, Rinehart, and Winston, 1970), pp. 353–54.

28. Charles R. Schleicher, *International Relations: Cooperation and Conflict* (Englewood Cliffs, N.J.: Prentice-Hall, 1962), p. 359; and Hoffman, "Balance of Power," p. 507.

29. Kaplan et al., "Theoretical Analysis"; and Hsi-sheng Chi, "The Chinese Warlord System as an International System," in *New Approaches to International Relations*, pp. 407–15.

30. Gulick, *Europe's Classical Balance of Power*, p. 60.

31. As quoted in *ibid.*, p. 59.

32. Zinnes, "Coalition Theories," pp. 353–54.

33. Roger D. Masters, "A Multi-Bloc Model of the International System," *American Political Science Review* 55 (4) (December 1961): 786.

34. Savoy, for example, switched sides in the course of the War of the Spanish Succession, Russia switched partners late in the Seven Years' War, and Austria abandoned France and turned against Napoleon during the Napoleonic wars.

35. Zinnes, "An Analytic Study of the Balance of Power Theories," *Journal of Peace Research*, no. 3 (1967): 279.

36. Ibid.

37. Kaplan, *System and Process*, p. 8.

38. Ibid., p. 23.

39. Franke, "Italian City-State System," p. 452.

40. Dennison I. Rusinow, *The Yugoslav Experiment, 1948–1974* (Berkeley and Los Angeles: University of California Press, 1977), p. 136.

41. Ibid., p. 273.

2. Nationalism, Regionalism, and the Internal Balance of Power

1. See Ruža Petrović, "Etnički mešoviti brakovi u Jugoslaviji," *Sociologija* 8 (3) (1966): 91.

2. Peter Klinar, "Izvori pojavnih oblika nacionalizma u Jugoslaviji," in *Federalizam i nacionalno pitanje* (Belgrade: Savez Udruženja za Političke Nauke Jugoslavije, 1971), p. 219.

3. Stipe Šuvar, "Sadašnji trenutak medjunacionalnih odnosa," in *Udruženi rad i medjunacionalni odnosi* (Belgrade: Komunist, 1978), p. 315.

4. Petrović, "Etnički mešoviti brakovi," p. 90.

5. Šuvar, "Sadašnji trenutak medjunacionalnih odnosa," p. 317.

6. Mahmut Mujačić, "Medjunacionalni odnosi u jednom gradu: primjer Dervente," *Gledišta* 12 (7–8) (July–August 1971): 1087.

7. See Najdan Pašić, *Nacionalno pitanje u savremenoj epohi* (Belgrade: Radnička štampa, 1973), pp. 37–38.

8. See, e.g., J. Pleterski, "Vprasanje naroda v socializmu," *Naši razgledi* (Ljubljana), February 11, 1972, p. 1, cited in Rudi Rizman, "O dijalektici klasnog i nacionalnog u medjunacionalnim odnosima," in *Udruženi rad*, p. 23.

9. E. K. Francis, *Interethnic Relations* (New York: Elsevier Scientific Publishing, 1976), p. 387.

10. As quoted in Gary K. Bertsch, "The Revival of Nationalisms," *Problems of Communism* 22 (6) (November–December 1973): 15.

11. *NIN*, no. 1424, April 23, 1978, as translated in Joint Publications Research Service, *East Europe Report*, Political, Sociological, and Military Affairs, May 17, 1978 (hereafter, JPRS/EE).

12. "A World Atlas for 2024," *Saturday Review*, August 24, 1974, excerpted in *Croatia Press* 27 (3–4) (September–December 1974): 10.

13. Alvin Rabushka and Kenneth A. Shepsle, *Politics in Plural Societies* (Columbus, Ohio: Charles E. Merrill, 1972), p. 91; see also pp. 177–78, 183–87.

14. *Slobodna Dalmacija* (Split), December 27, 1977, p. 3, translated in JPRS/EE, February 9, 1978.

15. *New York Times*, February 18, 1975, p. 6.

16. Ibid., December 26, 1975, p. 3; and *Newsweek*, December 15, 1975, p. 62.

17. *New York Times*, April 8, 1974, p. 2.

18. *Oslobodjenje*, February 27, 1982, p. 20.

19. See Slobodan Stankovic, "Renewed Attack against Serbia's Most Prominent Author," *Radio Free Europe Research* December 5, 1977.

20. This occurred after a match between Split's Hajduk team and OFK of Belgrade. See *NIN*, April 13, 1975, pp. 51–52, translated in JPRS/EE, May 6, 1975.

21. *Borba*, March 6, 1966, p. 3.

22. See Stipe Šuvar, *Nacionalno pitanje u marksističkoj teoriji i socijalističkoj praksi* (Belgrade: Novinska Ustanova Prosvetni Pregled, 1976), p. 14.

23. Language is also a serious impediment to labor migration. A large proportion of Kosovo's Albanians, for example, speak nothing but Albanian. In the north, Slovenes and Magyars have been loathe to move, for a combination of economic and cultural reasons.

24. William Zimmerman, "National-International Linkages in Yugoslavia: The Political Consequences of Openness," in *Political Development in Eastern Europe*, ed. Jan F. Triska and Paul M. Cocks (New York: Praeger, 1977), p. 348.

25. Francis, *Interethnic Relations*, p. 385.

26. Crawford Young, *The Politics of Cultural Pluralism* (Madison: University of Wisconsin Press, 1976), p. 5.

27. R. V. Burks, *The National Problem and the Future of Yugoslavia* (Santa Monica, Calif.: Rand Corporation, October 1971), pp. iv, 52, 59.

28. For details on Dalmatia's economic boom, see Thomas M. Poulsen, "Migration on the Adriatic Coast: Some Processes Associated with the Development of Tourism," in *Population and Migration Trends in Eastern Europe*, ed. Huey Louis Kostanick (Boulder, Colo.: Westview Press, 1977), pp. 197–215.

29. Vladimir Dedijer, Ivan Božić, Sima Ćirković, and Milorad Ekmečić, *History of Yugoslavia*, trans. Kordija Kveder (New York: McGraw-Hill, 1974), pp. 385, 390; Jaroslav Šidak, Mirjana Gross, Igor Karaman, and Dragovan Šepić, *Povijest hrvatskog naroda g. 1860–1914* (Zagreb: Školska knjiga, 1968), pp. 157–58; Todo Kurtović, *Crkva i religija u socijalističkom samoupravnom društvu* (Belgrade: Rad, 1978), p. 139; Ivan Torov, "U crkvi uz gitare i hitove," *Borba*, February 13, 1971, p. 5; and "Sloboda i granice," *NIN*, no. 1077, August 29, 1971, pp. 37–40. See also Pedro Ramet, "Catholicism and Politics in Socialist Yugoslavia," *Religion in Communist Lands* 10 (3) (Winter 1982): 256–74.

30. Dennison I. Rusinow, "The Other Albanians," *American Universities Field Staff Reports*, Southeast Europe Series, vol. 12, no. 2 (November 1965), p. 19.

31. Edvard Kardelj, *Speech at the Plenary Session, Fifth Congress of the Socialist Alliance of Working People* (Belgrade: 1960), p. 162, as quoted in F. E. Ian Hamilton, *Yugoslavia: Patterns of Economic Activity* (New York: Praeger, 1968), p. 148.

32. For a long time after the war, industrialization in Vojvodina lagged behind that in other regions. In recent years, however, there has been a changing emphasis in the Vojvodinan economy with increasing investment in industry. Thus, in the period 1971–77, industry in Vojvodina grew by 9 percent, and agricultural production, the traditional mainstay of the Vojvodinan economy, showed only a 4 percent increase. See Stevan Bek, "Vojvodina's Economy Today," *Review of International Affairs* 29 (666) (January 5, 1978): 35.

33. Paul Shoup, *Communism and the Yugoslav National Question* (New York: Columbia University Press, 1968), p. 241n.

34. Burks, *The National Problem*, p. 54.

35. Šime Djodan, "Economic Position of Croatia," *Croatia Press* 26 (2) (April–June 1973): 14.

36. Joseph T. Bombelles, *Economic Development of Communist Yugoslavia, 1947–1964* (Stanford, Calif.: Hoover Institution on War, Revolution, and Peace, 1968), p. 148.

37. Cited in Dina A. Zinnes, "Coalition Theories and the Balance of Power," in *The Study of Coalition Behavior*, ed. Sven Groennings, E. W. Kelley, and Michael Leiserson (New York: Holt, Rinehart, and Winston, 1970), p. 365.

38. Bombelles, *Economic Development*, p. 170.

39. Fred Singleton, *Twentieth Century Yugoslavia* (New York: Columbia University Press, 1976), p. 237.

40. As quoted in Richard A. Schermerhorn, *Comparative Ethnic Relations* (New York: Random House, 1970), p. 157.

41. Eric A. Nordlinger, *Conflict Regulation in Divided Societies* (Cambridge, Mass.: Harvard Studies in International Affairs, 1972), pp. 21–29.

42. Mahmut Mujačić, *Nova dimenzija jugoslovenskog federalizma* (Sarajevo: Oslobodjenje, 1981), pp. 133–34.

43. Nordlinger, *Conflict Regulation*, pp. 31–33.

44. Franc Šetinc, *Misao i djelo Edvarda Kardelja*, trans. from Slovenian into Serbo-Croatian by Ivan Brajdić (Zagreb: Globus, 1979), p. 100.

45. *Borba*, October 30, 1967, p. 2, as quoted in Lenard J. Cohen, "Conflict Management and Political Institutionalization in Socialist Yugoslavia: A Case Study of the Parliamentary System," in *Legislatures in Plural Societies*, Albert F. Eldrige, ed. (Durham, N.C.: Duke University Press, 1977), p. 133.

46. Milovan Djilas, as quoted in "A World Atlas for 2024," p. 10.

47. Pedro Ramet, *Nationalism and Federalism in Yugoslavia, 1963–1983* (Bloomington: Indiana University Press, 1984), p. 42.

3. Yugoslav Nationalities Policy

1. Edvard Kardelj, for example, wrote that "In Yugoslavia we have in large part resolved the national question in the classical sense of that concept" (*Socijalističko samoupravljanje u našem ustavnom sistemu* [Sarajevo: Svjetlost, 1975], excerpted in *Nacionalno pitanje u djelima klasika marksizma i u dokumentima i praksi kpj/skj* [Zagreb: Centar Društvenih Djelatnosti SSOH, 1978], p. 408) (hereafter cited as *Nacionalno pitanje*).

2. *Politika*, December 23, 1982, p. 6.

3. Leopold Kobsa, Vjekoslav Koprivnjak, and Ines Šaškor, Introduction to *Nacionalno pitanje*, p. 28; see also pp. 29, 61.

4. Dušan Ičević, *Nacija i samoupravljanje* (Titograd: NIP Pobjeda, 1976), excerpted in *Nacionalno pitanje*, p. 396.

5. E. H. Carr, *The Bolshevik Revolution, 1917–1923* (Harmondsworth, England: Penguin Books, 1950), 1:414–15.

6. Stipe Šuvar, *Nacionalno pitanje u marksističkoj teoriji i socijalističkoj praksi* (Belgrade: Novinska Ustanova Prosvetni Pregled, 1976), p. 5. See also Milenko M. Nikolić, "Marx Considers That a Nation Can Be International-minded only if It Is National-minded" (Nikolić, *Ravnopravnost naroda i narodnosti u obrazovanju* [Belgrade: Novinska Ustanova Prosvetni Pregled, 1975], p. 5).

7. Carr, *Bolshevik Revolution*, pp. 416, 416n.

8. Horace B. Davis, "Nations, Colonies, and Social Classes: The Position of Marx and Engels," *Science and Society* 24 (1) (Winter 1965): 26–43.

9. As quoted in Joseph V. Stalin's 1913 work, "Marxism and the National Question," in Stalin, *Marxism and the National-Colonial Question* (San Francisco: Proletarian Publishers, 1975), p. 24.

10. Rudolf Springer [Karl Renner], *Natsional'naia problema: Bor'ba natsional-'nostei*

v Avstrii, trans. M. Bragiiskii and A. Brumberg (St. Petersburg: Obshchestvennaya Pol'za, 1909) [from the German original, *Der Kampf der oesterreichischen Nationen um den Staat*, pt. 1, *Das nationale Problem als Verfassungs- und Verwaltungsfrage* (Leipzig and Vienna: F. Deuticke, 1902)], as quoted in Stalin, "Marxism and the National Question," p. 45. For a more sympathetic interpretation of Renner's ideas on nationality conflicts, see Robert A. Kann, *Renners Beitrag zur Lösung nationaler Konflikte im Lichte nationaler Probleme der Gegenwart* (Vienna: Verlag der Oesterreichischen Akademie der Wissenschaften, 1973).

11. Rudi Rizman, "O dijalektici klasnog i nacionalnog u medjunacionalnim odnosima," in *Udruženi rad i medjunacionalni odnosi* (Belgrade: Komunist, 1978), p. 20.

12. Stalin, "Marxism and the National Question," pp. 25–27.

13. See, for instance, Dragoslav Marković's conversation with *NIN* reporters on October 2, 1977, "Akcenti nacionalne ravnopravnosti," in *Zadaci SK Srbije u razvoju medjunacionalnih odnosa i borbi protiv nacionalizma* (Belgrade: Kommunist, 1978), p. 348.

14. Cited by Šime Djodan, "Reforme u socijalističkim zemljama i položaj malih naroda," *Kolo* 7 (11) (November 1969): 1149.

15. Atif Purivatra, "Stav Komunističke Partije Jugoslavije prema nacionalnom pitanju u Bosni i Hercegovini," in *Nacionalni odnosi danas*, ed. Milan Petrović and Kasim Suljević (Sarajevo: Univerzal, 1971), p. 182.

16. "Program komunističke partije jugoslavije" (Drugi kongres kpj, June 1920), in *Nacionalno pitanje*, p. 181.

17. Sima Marković, *Nacionalno pitanje u svetlosti marksizma* (Belgrade: Narodna misao, 1923), excerpted in *Nacionalno pitanje*, pp. 197–99.

18. Marković's emphasis; Marković, *Ustavno pitanje i radnička klasa Jugoslavije* (Belgrade?: [1923]), p. 8.

19. In *Nacionalno pitanje*, p. 201.

20. Kosta Novaković, "Autonomija ili federacija," *Radnik-Delavec*, nos. 86–87 (October 28, 1923 and November 1, 1923), excerpted in *Nacionalno pitanje*, p. 207.

21. Ibid., p. 205; Gordana Vlajčić, *KPJ i nacionalno pitanje u Jugoslaviji, 1919–1929* (Zagreb: August Cesarec, 1974), pp. 20, 23.

22. "The difference between the bourgeoisie and us is not that the bourgeoisie has a national question while we do not, but that the bourgeoisie, in the framework of the capitalist social order, is not in a position to resolve the national question in a satisfactory manner, while we, within the framework of our social order, can resolve it" (Zinoviev, *Bericht der Präsidium: Protokol der Konferenz der erweiterten Exekutive der Kommunistischen Internationale* (Hamburg: Verlag Carl Hoym Nachf. Louis Cahnbley, 1923), p. 30, quoted in Vlajčić, *KPJ i nacionalno pitanje*, pp. 83–84.

23. Stalin, "Concerning the National Question in Yugoslavia," speech delivered to the Yugoslav Commission of the E.C.C.I., March 30, 1925, *Bolshevik*, no. 7, April 15, 1925, translated in Stalin, *Marxism and the National-Colonial Question*, pp. 295, 301; and Stalin, "The National Question Once Again (Concerning the Article by Semić)," *Bolshevik*, nos. 11–12, June 30, 1925, translated in Stalin, *Marxism and the National-Colonial Question*, p. 329–30.

24. Quoted in Vlajčić, *KPJ i nacionalno pitanje*, p. 125.

25. Ibid., p. 137; see also "Rezolucija o privrednom i političkom položaju Jugoslavije i o zadacima KPJ," Fourth Congress of the CPY, October 1928, in *Nacionalno pitanje*, p. 240.

26. Quoted in Purivatra, "Stav Komunističke Partije Jugoslavije," p. 184.

27. Jovan Raičević, "Savez komunista Jugoslavije i nacionalno pitanje," in *KPJ-SKJ: Razvoj teorije i prakse socijalizma, 1919–1979* (Belgrade: Savremena Administracija, 1979), p. 232.

28. Kardelj, *Razvoj slovenačkog nacionalnog pitanja*, 2d ed. (Belgrade: Kultura, 1958), p. 50.

29. Leon Gešković, "Istorijski razvoj društveno-političkog sistema Jugoslavije," in *Društveno-politički sistem SFRJ* (Belgrade: Radnicka štampa, 1975), p. 88.

30. J. B. Tito, "Concerning the National Question and Socialist Patriotism," Speech at the Slovene Academy of Arts and Sciences, Ljubljana, November 16, 1948, in Tito, *Selected Speeches and Articles, 1941–1961* (Zagreb: Naprijed, 1963), pp. 97–98.

31. Purivatra, "Tito's Contribution to the Theory and Practice of the National Question," in *Socialist Thought and Practice*, 19 (2) (February 1979): 75–76.

32. For a more detailed discussion of this aspect, see Pedro Ramet, "Self-management, Titoism, and the Apotheosis of Praxis," in *At the Brink of War and Peace: The Tito-Stalin Split in a Historic Perspective*, ed. Wayne Vucinich (New York: Brooklyn College Press, 1982).

33. See Dennison I. Rusinow, *The Yugoslav Experiment, 1948–1974* (Berkeley and Los Angeles: University of California Press, 1977), p. 106; and Nikolić, *Ravnopravnost*, p. 9.

34. Kardelj, *Razvoj*, p. 104.

35. Edmund S. Glenn, "The Two Faces of Nationalism," *Comparative Political Studies* 3 (3) (October 1970): 353.

36. Kardelj, *Razvoj*, p. 49.

37. Ibid., p. 39.

38. Predrag Matvejević, "Mit i stvarnost u našoj kulturi," *NIN*, no. 1363, February 20, 1977, p. 31.

39. As quoted in Rusinow, *The Yugoslav Experiment*, p. 167. Tito was even more explicit in *The National Question and Revolution*, where he stated "I have never favored, and do not favor now, a Yugoslav nationality in the sense of creating a single nationality. All the nations and nationalities should and can find a place in our federation" (cited by Purivatra, "Tito's Contribution," p. 77).

40. *Osmi kongres Saveza Komunista Jugoslavije* (Belgrade: Komunist, 1964), excerpted in *Nacionalno pitanje*, p. 360.

41. Personal interview, Sarajevo, June 1980; and Drago Tović, "Postoji li jugoslavenska nacija," *VUS* (Zagreb), July 1, 1970, p. 22.

42. Kardelj, *Socijalističko samoupravljanje*, p. 408.

43. Kardelj, *Problemi naše socijalističke izgradnje* (Belgrade: Kultura, 1980), excerpted in *Vjesnik*, January 21, 1980, p. 4.

44. Šuvar, *Nacionalno i nacionalističko* (Split: Marksistički Centar, 1974), p. 212; see also pp. 134, 196; and Kardelj, "Moderna nacija predstavlja integraciju društvenog rade i integraciju svijesti," in Petrović and Suljević, *Nacionalni odnosi danas*, pp. 11–12.

45. Esad Ćimić, at a symposium held at Krapinske Toplice, March 1970, remarked that "When I speak of nationality, I am prepared to understand nationalism in a positive sense" (As quoted in Vladimir Košćak, "Što je nacija," *Kritika* 3 [15] [November–December 1970], p. 872).

46. *Politika*, September 15, 1969, p. 7.

47. Quoted in Tović, "Postoji li jugoslavenska nacija," p. 23.

48. Ibid., p. 22.

49. Ibid., p. 23.

50. *Vjesnik—Sedam dana* (May 8, 1982), pp. 6–7, excerpted and translated in Foreign Broadcast Information Service (FBIS), *Daily Report*, Eastern Europe, June 11, 1982.

51. Milan M. Miladinović, *Jugoslovenski socijalistički patriotizam* (Belgrade: Novinska Ustanova Prosvetni Pregled, 1976), p. 3. See also Miladinović, "Pojam i suština jugoslovenskog patriotizma danas," *Obeležja* 7 (6) (November–December 1977).

52. Blažo Nikolovski, "Jugoslovenski socijalistički patriotizam," *Front*, June 4, 1976, p. 11.

53. See, for instance, Todo Kurtović, *Crkva i religija u socijalističkom samoupravnom društvu* (Belgrade: Rad, 1978), p. 64; and Veljko Vlahovič, "Remarks at the Second

Plenary Session of the Tenth Congress of the LCY," May 27, 1974, in *Social Consciousness and Reality* (Belgrade: Socialist Thought and Practice, 1976), p. 12.

54. E. K. Francis, *Interethnic Relations* (New York: Elsevier, 1976), p. 387.

55. See Zvonko Lerotić, "Politička zajednica i višenacionalna socijetalna zajednica," *Naša zakonitost* 28 (9) (September 1974): 805. Also relevant is Tito's speech at Bugojno, Bosnia-Herzegovina, November 25, 1979; *Vjesnik*, November 27, 1979, p. 4.

56. Tihomir Vlaškalić, at the Ninth Session of the CC of the LC Serbia (1976); *Zadaci SK Srbije*, p. 171.

57. Gazmend Zajmi, "Položaj i uloga narodnosti u SFR Jugoslaviji," in *Društveno-Politički sistem SFRJ*, pp. 379–80.

58. Rajko Djurić, "Kao u priči o miševima i gvozdenoj vagi," *NIN*, no. 1541, July 13, 1980, p. 14.

59. *Borba*, February 3, 1980, p. 7.

60. Interviews conducted by the author, Belgrade, November 1979.

61. See Kurtesh Saliu, "Neke specifičnosti ustavnog urednjena SAP Kosova," in Institut za Uporedno Pravo, *Specifičnosti republičkih i pokrajinskih ustava od 1974* (Belgrade: Savremena Administracija, 1976); and Jovan Munćan, "Specifična rešenja ustava SAP Vojvodine," in *Specifičnosti republičkih*.

62. For a specific discussion of language policy, see James W. Tollefson, "The Language Planning Process and Language Rights in Yugoslavia," *Language Problems and Language Planning* 4 (2) (Summer 1980): 141–56.

63. See *Yugoslav Law*, no. 1 (January–April 1976): 68–69.

64. Decision No. U 65/77 (October 5, 1977), summarized in *Yugoslav Law*, no. 3 (September–December 1978): 82.

65. *Vjesnik*, December 20, 1979, p. 5.

66. As quoted in Nijaz Duraković, "O 'pozitivnom' i 'negativnom' nacionalizmu," *Opredjeljenja* 11 (3–4) (March–April 1980): 133.

67. *Zadaci SK Srbije*, p. 83.

68. "Društveni Plan Jugoslavije za period 1976–1980 godine," as excerpted in *Zadaci SK Srbije*, p. 275.

69. See Kardelj, *Socijalističko samoupravljanje*, p. 413.

4. Institutional Mechanisms of Interrepublican Cooperation and Policy Making

1. The role of confederal sentiments in establishment of the Senate is confirmed by the observation that not until the late nineteenth century were senators directly elected by the populace. Until that time, they were appointed by the legislatures of the states they represented—a practice that came to appear anomalous in the American system but was consistent with the confederal spirit that inspired it.

2. Balša Špadijer, *Federalizam i medjunacionalni odnosi u Jugoslaviji* (Belgrade: Institut za Političke Studije, 1975), p. 6; and Miodrag Jovičić, *Savremeni federalizam* (Belgrade: Savremena Administracija, 1973), pp. 218–20.

3. Djordji J. Caca, *Socijalistička republika u jugoslovenskoj federaciji* (Belgrade: Radnička štampa, 1977), p. 7.

4. As quoted in Josip Sruk, *Ustavno uredjenje Socijalističke Federativne Republike Jugoslavije* (Zagreb: Informator, 1976), p. 217. See also Edvard Kardelj, *Socijalističko samoupravljanje u našem ustavnom sistemu* (Sarajevo: Svjetlost, 1975), excerpted in *Nacionalno pitanje u djelima klasika marksizma i u dokumentima i praksi kpj/skj* (Zagreb: Centar Društvenih Djelatnosti SSOH, 1978), p. 411.

5. Petar Popović, "Idemo li u konfederaciju?" *Politika*, February 11, 1968, p. 7.

6. Djuro Burašković and Miljan Komatina, "Nacionalno pitanje i federalizam," *Komunist*, April 1, 1971, pp. 18–19.

7. As quoted in E. H. Carr, *The Bolshevik Revolution, 1917–1923* (Harmondsworth, England: Penguin Books, 1950), 1:145.

8. Ibid.

9. As quoted in Jovičić, *Sauvemeni federalizam*, p. 39.

10. J. V. Stalin, *Sochineniya*, vol. 3, p. 27, quoted in Carr, *Bolshevik Revolution*, p. 147.

11. Lenin, *Sochineniya*, vol. 21, p. 419, quoted in Carr, *Bolshevik Revolution*, p. 147.

12. Wayne S. Vucinich, "Nationalism and Communism," in *Contemporary Yugoslavia*, ed. Wayne S. Vucinich (Berkeley and Los Angeles: University of California Press, 1969), p. 247.

13. Hamdija Pozderac, "Mjesto republike u jugoslovenskoj federaciji," in *Godišnjak pravnog fakulteta u Sarajevu 1976* (1977), 24:319–20.

14. "Federation cannot, in reality, be grasped, and—what is more important—cannot be properly implemented if its basic constitutive elements are not, first of all, put in order, [and] if power is not organized in an essentially democratic way" (Ćazim Sadiković, "Medjunacionalna kohezija u federaciji," *Odjek* [Sarajevo] 23 [11–12] [June 1970]: 3).

15. Jovan Djordjević, *Politički sistem* (Belgrade: Savremena Administracija, 1967), p. 376.

16. "The nation is a historical category and as such it will disappear at some point" (Špadijer, *Federalizam i medjunacionalni odnosi*, p. 18).

17. Gazmend Zajmi, "Hoće li nacija 'nadživeti' državu?" *Politika*, March 27, 1980, p. 8.

18. Sruk, *Ustavno uredjenje SFRJ*, pp. 270–71; Mahmut Mujačić, *Nova dimenzija jugoslovenskog federalizma* (Sarajevo: Oslobodjenje, 1981), pp. 95–99; and Špadijer, *Federalizam i federalni odnosi u socijalističkoj Jugoslaviji* (Belgrade: Novinska Ustanova Prosvetni Pregled, 1975), p. 12.

19. Šime Djodan, "Prilog razmatranju predloženih izmjena ustava sfrj," *Kolo* 6 (11) (November 1968): 473; and Sruk, *Ustavno uredjenje SFRJ*, p. 304.

20. Mujačić, *Nova dimenzija*, p. 71.

21. Mujačić, "Neke karakteristike procesa dogovaranja republika i autonomnih pokrajina," *Politička misao* 15 (4) (1978): 552.

22. Mujačić, *Nova dimenzija*, pp. 152–53.

23. Caca, "Društveno-politička uslovljenost podele zakonodavne nadležnosti u pojedinim fazama ustavnog razvitka Jugoslavije—s posebnim osvrtom na značaj pojmova koje ustav SFRJ od 1974. godine upotrebljava prilikom utvrdjivanja zajedničke nadležnosti," in Institut za Uporedno Pravo, *Podela zajedničke nadležnosti izmedju federacije i federalnih jedinica* (Belgrade: Savremena Administracija, 1978), p. 27.

24. See "Jedan ili dva doma," *Ekonomska politika*, no. 1022, November 1, 1971, pp. 11–12.

25. Mujačić, "O dogovaranju republika i pokrajina," *Ideje* 10 (2) (March–April 1979): 19.

26. *Izvještaj o radu SIV-a za period maj 1974–decembar 1976. godine.* (Belgrade: Savezno izvršno veće, 1977), p. 108, cited in Ibid.

27. See *Borba*, April 1, 1980, p. 1.

5. Limited Sovereignty: The Autonomy of the Federal Units

1. *Borba* (Belgrade), June 12, 1990, p. 1.

2. Dušan Bilandžić, *Jugoslavija poslije Tita, 1980–1985* (Zagreb: Globus, 1986), pp. 12–13, 21.

3. Leopold Kobsa, Vjekoslav Koprivnjak, and Ines Šaškor, Introduction to *Nacionalno pitanje u djelima marksizma i u dokumentima i praksi kpj/skj* (Zagreb: Centar Društvenih Djelatnosti SSOH, 1978), pp. 64–65.

4. F. E. Ian Hamilton, *Yugoslavia: Patterns of Economic Activity* (New York: Praeger, 1968), p. 239.

5. Paul Shoup, *Communism and the Yugoslav National Question* (New York: Columbia University Press, 1968), p. 249.

6. Ibid., p. 221.

7. As quoted in Dennison I. Rusinow, *The Yugoslav Experiment, 1948–1974* (Berkeley and Los Angeles: University of California Press, 1977), pp. 146, 295.

8. Duncan Wilson, "Self-Management in Yugoslavia," in *International Affairs* (London) 54 (2) (April 1978): 259.

9. See Pedro Ramet, "Yugoslavia's Troubled Times," in *Global Affairs* 5 (1) (Winter 1990).

10. Djuro `Gatavić, "Podjela zajedničke nadležnosti izmedju federacije i federalnih jedinica, s posebnim osvrtom na isključivu zakonodavnu nadležnost republika i autonomnih pokrajina," in Institut za Uporedno Pravo, *Podela zajedničke nadležnosti izmedju federacije i federalnih jedinica* (Belgrade: Savremena administracija, 1978), p. 127.

11. *Vjesnik*, November 17, 1979, p. 7, and December 17, 1979, p. 4.

12. Djordji J. Caca, *Socijalistička republika u jugoslovenskoj federaciji* (Belgrade: Radnička štampa, 1977), p. 26.

13. Quoted in *New York Times*, July 16, 1990, p. A7.

14. Stevan Djordjević, "Ustav SFRJ, savezna i republicke Skupštine i spoljna politika," in *Arhiv za pravne i društvene nauke* 55 (4) (October–December 1969): 564.

15. Paul Shoup, "The Evolution of a System," in *Problems of Communism* 18 (4–5) (July–October 1969): 71n; and *Hrvatski tjednik*, November 12, 1971, p. 4.

16. See Smiljko Sokol's article in *Hrvatski tjednik*, April 23, 1971, p. 4.

17. Aleksandar Fira, "Promene u ustavnom sistemu SFRJ," in *Arhiv za pravne i društvene nauke* 55, (1–2) (January–June 1969): 6.

18. Vojislav Simović, *Zakonodavna nadležnost u razvitku jugoslovenske federacije* (Belgrade: Centar za pravna istraživanja Instituta društvenih nauka, 1978), pp. 93–94; *Ustav Socijalističke Republike Srbije* (Belgrade: Savremena administracija, 1974), Article 292, p. 161; Arpad Horvat, "Sredstva za obezbedjenje ostvarivanja zajedničke nadležnosti po ustavu SFRJ," in Institut za Uporedno Pravo, *Podela*, p. 44n; and Borivoje Pupić, "Autonomne Pokrajine u ustavnom sistemu Socijalističke Federativne Republike Jugoslavije," in *Arhiv za pravne i društvene nauke* 59, (2–3) (April–September 1973): 474.

19. *Ustav Srbije*, Article 296, p. 163.

20. *Privredni pregled*, February 17, 1978, p. 2.

21. *Neue Zürcher Zeitung*, April 7, 1982, pp. 3–4, and April 30, 1982, p. 3.

22. *Frankfurter Allgemeine*, July 9, 1983.

6. The Reform Crisis, 1962–71

1. Dušan Bilandžić, "Šok nakon buma," in *Start*, no. 479 (May 30, 1987): 40.

2. Dušan Bilandžić, "Tajno pismo pred javnošću," in *Start*, no. 478 (May 16, 1987): 35; and Dušan Bilandžić, "Pet važnih koraka," in *Start*, no. 481 (June 27, 1987): 46.

3. Bilandžič, "Pet vaznih," p. 46.

4. Deborah D. Milenkovitch, *Plan and Market in Yugoslav Economic Thought* (New Haven: Yale University Press, 1971), p. 177.

5. Stipe Šuvar, "Radnička klasa i samoupravni sistem," in *Naše teme*, Vol. 5 (1968), as quoted in Slaven Letica, "O privrednoj reformi deset godina kasnije," in *Pitanja* 7, (7–8) (1978): 60.

6. Šime Djodan, "Gospodarska reforma i izbor optimalnog modela rasta," in *Kolo*, 6 (4) (April 1968): 303.

7. See Othmar Nikola Haberl, *Parteiorganisation und nationale Frage in Jugoslawien* (Berlin: Otto Harrassowitz, 1976), pp. 24–28; and Stipe Šuvar, *Nacionalno i nacionalisticko* (Split: Marksistički Centar, 1974), pp. 127–134.

8. Interviews, Yugoslavia, July 1982.

9. World Bank, *Yugoslavia: Self-Managment Socialism and the Challenges of Development*, Report No. 1615a-YU, March 21, 1978, 1:41.

10. See Leon Gešković, "Istorijski razvoj društveno-političkog sistema Jugoslavije," in *Društeveno-politički sistem SFRJ* (Belgrade: Radnička štampa, 1975), p. 99.

11. See Crane Brinton, *The Anatomy of a Revolution*, Rev. and enl. ed. (New York: Vintage Books, 1965).

12. *Borba*, February 17, 1970, p. 5.

13. Dennison I. Rusinow, *The Yugoslav Experiment, 1948–1974* (Berkeley and Los Angeles: University of California Press, 1977), pp. 112, 126, 130–31; and Paul Shoup, *Communism and the Yugoslav National Question* (New York: Columbia University Press, 1968), p. 240.

14. Kosta Mihailović, "Regionalni aspekt privrednog razvoja," *Ekonomist*, no. 1 (1962), as cited in Djodan, "Pred kritičnom barijerom," *Dometi* 2 (3) (March 1969): 5.

15. Milenkovitch, *Plan and Market*, p. 185.

16. Detailed figures on labor efficiency are given in Momir Ćećez, "O efikasnosti društvenih sredstava u privredno nedovoljno razvijenim područjima," *Pregled* 70 (1) (January 1980): 27–40.

17. "Another concept of develpment, originating in Slovenia, is that the leading area should be the most developed area in the country, which by its fast development can accumulate resources for investment in the development of other areas, which should follow the lead of the most industrially advanced parts" (Rudolf Bičanić, *Economic Policy in Socialist Yugoslavia*, postscript by Marijan Hanžeković [Cambridge: Cambridge University Press, 1973], p. 201).

18. Djodan, "Pred kritičnom barijerom," p. 6.

19. Djodan, "Robno-novčani privredni model i regionalni razvoj u našim uvjetima," *Kolo* 6 (10) (October 1968): 363. Djodan is inconsistent when it comes to Bosnia—he sometimes claims that it had "benefitted" from investment in "political factories" and at other times argues that Bosnia, like Croatia, was exploited by the "East."

20. Djodan, "Pred kritičnom barijerom," p. 4.

21. Edvard Kardelj, *Raskršća u razvitku našeg socijalističkog društva* (Belgrade: Komunist, 1969), p. 42, as quoted in Šuvar, *Nacionalno i nacionalističko*, p. 284.

22. Rusinow, *Yugoslav Experiment*, pp. 158–59.

23. Shoup, *Communism and the Yugoslav National Question*, p. 192.

24. Ibid., pp. 251, 222.

25. See Haberl, *Parteiorganisation*, pp. 28–29, 41–43. On Vojvodina's association, see Steven L. Burg, "Decision-making in Yugoslavia," *Problems of Communism* 29 (2) (March–April 1980): 4.

26. Rusinow, "The Price of Pluralism," *American Universities Field Staff Reports*, Southeast Europe Series, vol. 18, no. 1 (July 1971), p. 9.

27. Interviews, Belgrade, 1979–80; and Gary K. Bertsch, "The Revival of Nationalisms," *Problems of Communism* 22 (6) (November–December 1973): 14–15.

28. Rusinow, *Yugoslav Experiment*, p. 179.

29. Ibid., p. 180.

30. See Voja Jovanović, "Otkloniti sve sto smeta saradnji i boljem razumevanju," in *Komunist*, March 24, 1966, p. 2.

31. Boro Krivokapić, *Jugoslavija i komunisti: adresa Jovana Djordjevića* (Belgrade: Mladost, 1988), p. 55.

32. Branko Petranović, *Istorija Jugoslavije, 1918–1988* (Belgrade: Nolit, 1988), 3:387.

33. Vojin Lukić, *Sećanja i saznanja: Aleksandar Ranković i Brionski plenum* (Titograd: Novica Jovović, 1989), p. 25.

34. Ibid., pp. 23, 43–44.

35. Ibid., p. 93.

36. Ibid., p. 34.

37. J. B. Tito, *Govori i članci* 21: 100n, as quoted in Haberl, *Parteiorganisation*, p. 32.

38. *Politika*, September 13, 1969, p. 5. For a further discussion of the "Žanko affair," see Mihailo Blečić and Ivica Dolenc (eds.), *Slucaj Zanko* (Belgrade: Kosmos, 1986).

39. Stevan Vračar, "Partijski monopolizam i politička moć društvenih grupa," *Gledišta*, nos. 8–9 (1967), summarized in "Jugoslawischer Theoretiker für Zweiparteiensystem," *Osteuropäische Rundschau* 13 (12) (December 1967): 19–21.

40. See the report by Jure Bilić in *Deseti Kongres Savaza Komunista Jugoslavije (Beograd, 27–30 maja 1974)—Stenografske beleške* (Belgrade: Komunist, 1975), 2:369.

41. April Carter, *Democratic Reform in Yugoslavia: The Changing Role of the Party* (Princeton, N.J.: Princeton University Press, 1982), pp. 97–98.

42. Ibid., p. 75.

43. Radio Belgrade, June 5, 1967, translated in FBIS, *Daily Report*, Eastern Europe, June 8, 1967.

44. Haberl, *Parteiorganisation*, p. 60.

45. Ibid., p. 59.

46. Ibid., p. 94.

47. Ibid., p. 58.

48. See the reports by Avdo Humo (a liberal) and Milentije Popović (a conservative), in *Deveti Kongres Saveza Komunista Jugoslavije* (Beograd, 11–13 III 1969)—*Stenografske beleške* (Belgrade: Komunist, 1970), 3:344, 306.

49. See Haberl, *Parteiorganisation*, p. 61.

50. *Deveti Kongres* 6:406.

51. Haberl, *Parteiorganisation*, p. 97.

52. *Treća sednica predsednistva SKJ* (Belgrade: Komunist, 1969), cited in Martin C. Sletzinger, "The Reform and Reorganization of the League of Communists of Yugoslavia, 1966–1973" (Ph.D. diss., Harvard University, 1976), pp. 81–83.

53. See Dušan Bilandžić, *Historija socijalističke federativne republike Jugoslavije* (Zagreb: Školska knjiga, 1978), pp. 358–61 and *passim*.

54. *Delo*, August 1, 1969, p. 1.

55. *Vjesnik*, August 1, 1969, p. 2; and *Vjesnik*, August 2, 1969, p. 2.

56. Bilandžić, *Historija SFRJ*, p. 360.

57. See Haberl, *Parteiorganisation*, p. 105.

58. See *Borba*, September 3, 1969, cited in ibid., p. 106.

59. Interviews, Ljubljana, July 1982. See also Stevo Govedarica, "Economic Development, 1971–1975," *Yugoslav Survey* 17 (3) (August 1976).

60. Miko Tripalo, "Osnovni problemi i pravci dalje idejno-političke akcije na preobražaju SKJ," *Socijalizam* 12 (11) (November 1969): 1392–93.

61. See Bilandžić, *Historija SFRJ*, pp. 366–67.

7. The Croatian Crisis, 1967–72

1. Branko Petranović, *Istorija Jugoslavije, 1918–1988* (Belgrade-Nolit, 1988), 3:382.

2. Šime Djodan, "Gospodarska reforma i izbor optimalnog modela rasta," *Kolo* 6 (4) (April 1968): 306.

3. Djodan, "Gdje dr Stipe Suvar 'pronalazi' nacionalizam, a gdje ga ne vidi," *Kolo* 7 (7) (July 1969): 702–3.

4. See *Hrvatski tjednik*, November 26, 1971, p. 7 (hereafter cited as *HT*).

5. Ibid., November 12, 1971, p. 7.

6. Ibid., November 5, 1971, p. 7, and November 19, 1971, p. 7.

7. Paul Shoup, "The National Question in Yugoslavia," *Problems of Communism* 21 (1) (January–February 1972): 21.

8. See Djodan, "Jedinstveno tržiste, razvijenost republika i kompenzacije," *HT*, May 14, 1971, pp. 4–5.

9. Djodan, "The Evolution of the Economic System of Yugoslavia and the Economic Position of Croatia," *Journal of Croatian Studies* 13 (1972): 11.

10. Stipe Šuvar, "Društveni razvoj i medjunacionalni odnosi u tumačenjima dra Šime Djodana," *Naše teme*, no. 6 (1969), reprinted in Šuvar, *Nacionalno i nacionalističko* (Split: Marksistički Centar, 1974).

11. Ibid., pp. 238–43.

12. Djodan, "Prilog raspravi o regionalnom razvoju u SFRJ," *Kolo* 7 (3) (March 1969): 252.

13. Djodan, as quoted in Šuvar, *Nacionalno i nacionalističko*, p. 244.

14. Ibid., p. 258.

15. Šuvar, *Nacionalno i nacionalističko*, p. 255n. The central committee meeting is reported in *Borba*, May 29, 1969.

16. Djodan, "Gdje dr Stipe Šuvar 'pronalazi' nacionalizam, a gdje ga ne vidi," pp. 686, 692.

17. Ibid., p. 694.

18. "Die Sprachenstreit in Jugoslawien," *Osteuropa* 21 (10) (October 1971): A602.

19. The complete text of the declaration appears in German translation in "Der jugoslawische Sprachenkonflikt," *Wissenschaftlicher Dienst Südosteuropa* 16 (3) (March 1967): 41–43. On Moskovljević, see also *Wissenschaftlicher Dienst Südosteuropa* 15 (3/4) (March–April 1966): 41–42.

20. *NIN*, no. 1082, October 3, 1971, p. 36.

21. Cited in *Politika*, November 13, 1968, as given in ibid.

22. "Saopštenje Matica srpske o pitanjima oko izrade Rečnika srpskohrvatskog književnog jezika," *Komunist*, January 21, 1971, translated into German in "Die Sprachenstreit," p. A603.

23. Mate Simundžić, " 'Jezik, nacija i politika' Mirka Čanadovića," *Kritika* 4 (17) (March–April 1971): 353–55.

24. "Novosadski dogovor je zastario," *Komunist*, January 21, 1971, translated into German in "Die Sprachenstreit," p. A606.

25. *NIN*, no. 1082 (October 3, 1971), p. 35.

26. *The Population of Yugoslavia* (Belgrade: Institute of Social Sciences, 1974), App., Table 2.

27. Ibid., App., Tables 9–10.

28. Slobodan Stankovic, "Preliminary Report on Yugoslavia's Census," *Radio Free Europe Research*, May 18, 1981, p. 2.

29. *The Population of Yugoslavia*, App., Table 6.

30. Djodan, "The Evolution of the Economic System," p. 81. William Zimmerman confirms that "a disproportionately large share of the workers abroad had emigrated from Croatia and/or are Croatian by nationality. The fraction of Yugoslavs abroad who [were] from Croatia was particularly high during the years 1965–68" (Zimmerman, "National-International Linkages in Yugoslavia: The Political Consequences of Openness," in *Political Development in Eastern Europe*, ed. Jan F. Triska and Paul M. Cocks (New York: Praeger, 1977), p. 343.

31. M. Rendulić, "Demografska kretanja u Hrvatskoj," as cited in Djodan, "The Evolution of the Economic System," pp. 80–81. Yugoslav migratory trends are also discussed in George W. Hoffman, "Migration and Social Change," *Problems of Communism* 22 (6) (November–December 1973).

32. *Statistički godišnjak Jugoslavije 1979* (Belgrade: Savezni zavod za statistiku, July 1979), pp. 112, 413; Tanjug, February 13, 1982, in FBIS, *Daily Report*, Eastern Europe, February 18, 1982; and *Statistički kalendar Jugoslavije 1982* (Belgrade: Savezni zavod za statistiku, February 1982), 28:37.

33. Cited by Ivan Perić, *Suvremeni hrvatski nacionalizam* (Zagreb: August Cesarec, 1976), p. 185. The letter was dated July 6, 1967.

34. "Aside from Serbs, there are also a large number of *Orthodox Croats* living in

Croatia, whom the current Yugoslav government counts as Serbs, but to whom the future democratic Croatian state must guarantee full freedom of expressing their national consciousness and identity" (*Program hrvatske demokratske opozicije*, as quoted in ibid.).

35. Stijepo Obad, "Geneza autonomaštva," *Vidik* 18 (32/33) (July–August 1971): 15.

36. Tomislav Slavica, "Krivnja autonomaštva," *Vidik* 18 (32/33) (July–August 1971): 15.

37. Ibid., p. 17.

38. Andra Gavrilović, *Istorija Srpske pravoslavne crkve*, 2d ed. (Belgrade: Izdavačka knjižarnica gece kona, 1930), p. 12.

39. See *Vesnik: Organ Saveza udruženog Pravoslavnog sveštenstva Jugoslavije*, October 1–15, 1971, p. 6.

40. *Borba*, May 29, 1970, p. 7; *Politika*, June 2, 1970, p. 8; and *Borba*, June 3, 1970, p. 7.

41. *Politika*, December 31, 1971–January 2, 1972, p. 4.

42. Ibid., February 12, 1971, p. 6; and *Vjesnik u srijedu*, January 28, 1970, p. 4.

43. Slavica, "Unitarizam recidiva autonomaštva," in *HT*, May 7, 1971, p. 7.

44. *Vjesnik u srijedu*, January 28, 1970, p. 4.

45. Vlado Gotovac, "Mogućnost izdaje," *Vidik* 18 (32/33) (July–August 1971): 22.

46. Slavica, "Krivnja autonomaštva," p. 18.

47. Gotovac, in *HT*, no. 11 (1971), as quoted in Perić, *Suvremeni hrvatski nacionalizam*, p. 190.

48. As summarized in Šuvar, *Nacionalno i nacionalističko*, p. 222.

49. Interview with Miko Tripalo, former secretary of the League of Communists of Croatia, Zagreb, September 8, 1989. Tripalo also gave an interview to *Iskra*, May 24, 1989.

50. *Vjesnik*, May 1, 1968, as quoted in Šuvar, *Nacionalno i nacionalističko*, p. 223.

51. Šuvar, *Nacionalno i nacionalističko*, pp. 332–34.

52. Alvin Z. Rubinstein, "The Yugoslavia Succession Crisis in Perspective," in *World Affairs* 135 (2) (Fall 1972): 104.

53. George Schöpflin, "The Ideology of Croatian Nationalism," in *Survey* 19 (1) (Winter 1973): 133, 136–137.

54. As reported in *Borba*, July 20, 1969, and quoted in Othmar Nikola Haberl, *Parteiorganisation und nationale Frage in Jugoslawien* (Berlin: Otto Harrassowitz, 1976), p. 115.

55. Perić, *Suvremeni hrvatski nacionalizam*, p. 20.

56. Cited by Haberl, *Parteiorganisation*, p. 115.

57. Petranović, *Istorija Jugoslavije*, 3:400.

58. See *Politika*, September 13, 1969, p. 5.

59. Haberl, *Parteiorganisation*, p. 118.

60. Savez komunista Hrvatske, *Izvještaj o stanju u SKH u odnosu na prodor nacionalizma u njegove redove*, Twenty-eighth Session, May 8, 1972 (Zagreb: Informativna služba CK SKH, 1972), p. 132.

61. Cited by Vladimir Koščak, "Što je nacija," in *Kritika* 3 (15) (November–December 1970): 872.

62. As quoted in Haberl, *Parteiorganisation*, p. 143.

63. For various references to Radic, see *Hrvatski tjednik*, May 28, 1971, p. 10, June 11, 1971, pp. 1, 11–13, June 18, 1971, p. 23, and June 25, 1971, p. 5.

64. *Hrvatski tjednik*, September 3, 1971, p. 23, and November 12, 1971, p. 22; and *Borba*, February 13, 1972, p. 5.

65. *Politika*, January 3, 1972, p. 6.

66. Zvonimir Kulundžić, "Spomenik Banu Jelačiću," in *Hrvatski tjednik*, June 4, 1971, p. 10.

67. Interview with Tripalo [note 49].

68. *Hrvatski tjednik*, June 25, 1971, p. 23.

69. Yugoslav Railways had, however, done little by mid-August to bring that any closer to fruition. See *Hrvatski tjednik*, August 20, 1971, p. 14.

70. Ibid., November 12, 1971, p. 24.

71. This section draws on my chapter, "Religion and Nationalism in Yugoslavia," in Pedro Ramet (ed.), *Religion and Nationalism in Soviet and East European Politics*, Rev. and expanded ed. (Durham, N.C.: Duke University Press, 1989), pp. 320–21.

72. *Borba*, October 9, 1970, p. 6.

73. Ibid., January 21, 1972.

74. Ibid., June 6, 1981, p. 11.

75. Dalibor Brozović, "Eskalacija resprave o jeziku Srba u Hrvatskoj," in *Hrvatski tjednik*, November 5, 1971, p. 3.

76. Ibid.

77. Djurić called for similar guarantees from Macedonia, Bosnia, and Montenegro. See Dušan Bilandžić, *Ideje i praksa društvenog razvoja Jugoslavije, 1945–1973* (Belgrade: Komunist, 1973), p. 287.

78. *Ustav Socijalističke Republike Hrvatske* (1963), in *Ustav Socijalističke Federativne Republike Jugoslavije sa Ustavima Socijalističkih Republika i statutima Autonomnih Pokrajina* (Belgrade: Službeni list, 1963), Article 1, p. 272.

79. Ibid., p. 265.

80. Italics added. Quoted in *Hrvatski tjednik*, September 10, 1971, p. 1.

81. Italics in original. Ibid., p. 3.

82. Jovan Stefanović, *Ustavno pravo FNR Jugoslavije i komparativno*, 2d ed. (1956), pp. 85–86, as quoted in Ibid.

83. "Srbo-Hrvatska," in *Hrvatski tjednik*, November 12, 1971, p. 2, as reported in *Izvještaj o stanju u Savezu komunista Hrvatske*, p. 197.

84. *HT*, September 24, 1971, p. 1.

85. As quoted in *NIN*, no. 1082, October 3, 1971, p. 11.

86. *HT*, November 5, 1971, p. 12.

87. Veljko Mratović, "Prva faza ustavnih promjena u Socijalističkoj Republici Hrvatskoj," *Archiv za pravne i društvene nauke* 58 (1) (January–March 1972): 4; and *Constitutional System of Yugoslavia* (Belgrade: Jugoslovenska stvarnost, 1980), p. 85.

88. Andrew Ludanyi, "Titoist Integration of Yugoslavia: The Partisan Myth and the Hungarians of the Vojvodina, 1945–1975," *Polity* 12 (2) (Winter 1979): 251; *Borba*, December 18, 1971, p. 5; *Politika*, December 19, 1971, p. 10; and *Borba*, February 22, 1972, p. 6.

89. Dragan Vukčević, "Od vere do politike i natrag," *NIN*, no. 1016, June 28, 1970, p. 17.

90. Cited by Fred Singleton, *Twentieth Century Yugoslavia* (New York: Columbia University Press, 1976), p. 229.

91. Vukčević, "Od vere do politike i natrag," p. 17.

92. Hans Hartl, *Nationalismus in Rot* (Stuttgart: Seewald Verlag, 1968), pp. 93–95.

93. The films were, of course, in Slovenian. See ibid., pp. 96–97.

94. Carl Gustaf Ströhm, *Ohne Tito* (Graz: Verlag Styria, 1976), pp. 236–37.

95. Tanjug, April 13, 1967.

96. Report by Alojz Vindiš, in *Deseti Kongres Saveza Komunista Jugoslavije (Beograd, 27–30 maja 1974)—Stenografske beleške* (Belgrade: Komunist, 1975) 2:392.

97. *Komunist*, February 3, 1966, p. 2.

98. Ibid., January 2, 1978, p. 2.

99. *Izvještaj o stanju u Savezu komunista Hrvatske*, pp. 62, 234.

100. Ibid., pp. 61–63, 233. "Certain members of the Initiative Committee (*Inicijativni odbor*) from Zadar, at a plenum of the Main Committee in Zagreb in 1970 demanded the political autonomy of the Serbs in Croatia, and more especially 'the convocation of a Congress of Croatian Serbs' " (ibid., p. 234). See also Robin Alison Remington, "Ide-

ology as a Resource: A Communist Case Study," in *Nonstate Nations in International Politics*, ed. Judy S. Bertelsen (New York: Praeger, 1977), p. 209 n.

101. Ibid., pp. 235–36.

102. Ströhm, *Ohne Tito*, p. 257.

103. See *Politika*, May 14, 1971.

104. Interviews, Belgrade, February 1980.

105. SFRJ, Federal Executive Council (SIV), "Odluka o obrazovanju i radu medjurepubličkih komiteta" (August 19, 1971), in *Službeni list SFRJ* 27 (37) (August 26, 1971), Article 2, p. 689.

106. "Kako usaglasiti stavove," *Ekonomska politika*, no. 1019, October 11, 1971, p. 11.

107. Cited by Petar Vujić, "Kako rade 'komiteti devetorice,' " *Komunist*, March 30, 1972, p. 15.

108. *Borba*, July 24, 1972, p. 9.

109. Vujić, "Kako rade 'komiteti devetorice,' " p. 16. The coordination commission did not decide issues but performed a function often as important—drafting the proposals, which were turned over to the appropriate interrepublican committee.

110. *Borba*, August 21, 1972, p. 5.

111. Ibid., August 22, 1972, p. 5.

112. *Izvještaj o stanju u Savezu komunista Hrvatske*, p. 152.

113. The two articles are reprinted in *HT*, May 21, 1971, pp. 1, 22–23.

114. *Borba*, May 30, 1971, p. 5; and *HT*, June 11, 1971, p. 5.

115. See the discussion in Jonke, "Slovo o Matici hrvatskoj," *HT*, August 20, 1971, p. 3; and Gotovac, "Letak za Maticu hrvatsku," *HT*, June 4, 1971, p. 1.

116. Milan Kangrga, "Fenomenologija ideološko-političkog nastupanja jugoslavenske srednje klase," *Praxis* 8 (3–4) (May–August 1971): 425–26, 437, 444–45; and Gerson S. Sher, *Praxis* (Bloomington: Indiana University Press, 1977), p. 219; see also p. 311n.

117. Ibid., p. 220.

118. Interview with Šime Djodan, adviser at the Institute for Public Finances (since 1982), Zagreb, September 12, 1989.

119. *Izvještaj o stanju u Savezu komunista Hrvatske* pp. 83, 84.

120. Ibid., p. 90.

121. Ibid., p. 92.

122. *Borba*, September 16, 1971, as quoted in Slobodan Stankovic, "Die kroatische Krise—Triebkräfte und Perspektiven," in *Osteuropa* 22 (6) (June 1972): 413.

123. Cvijetin Mijatović, president of the collective presidency in 1980, admitted in the late 1960s that "in the postwar period, it was difficult to be a Croat [in Bosnia]" (Djodan, "Gdje dr Stipe Suvar," p. 695).

124. *Politika*, August 20, 1971, p. 5; and *Borba*, December 2, 1971, p. 5.

125. See *Izvještaj o stanju u Savezu komunista Hrvatske*, p. 157.

126. See *Oslobodjenje*, August 20, 1971, cited by *HT*, September 10, 1971, p. 8.

127. "Nacionalne strukture u Bosni i Hercegovini," in *HT*, November 19, 1971, pp. 10–11.

128. Hamdija Pozderac, *Nacionalni odnosi i socijalističko zajedništvo* (Sarajevo: Svjetlost, 1978), p. 96.

129. Calculated from figures in Tanjug, February 16, 1982, in FBIS, *Daily Report*, Eastern Europe, February 17, 1982.

130. Fuad Muhić, in interview with Mirko Galić in *Start*, no. 283, November 28–December 12, 1979, p. 13.

131. Morton A. Kaplan, *System and Process in International Politics* (New York: John Wiley and Sons, 1957), p. 25.

132. *HT*, June 18, 1971, p. 6.

133. See Rusinow, *The Yugoslav Experiment, 1948–1974* (Berkeley and Los Angeles: University of California Press, 1977), pp. 288–90.

134. Ströhm, *Ohne Tito*, p. 192.

135. See Schöpflin, "Ideology of Croatian Nationalism," p. 143; and Rusinow, *Yugoslav Experiment*, p. 305.

136. Symptoms of this are recounted in Šuvar, *Nacionalno i nacionalističko*, p. 291. It should be clear that the anti-Montenegrin rhetoric of Matica Hrvatska undermined the efforts of the Croatian party leadership to create a Croato-Montenegrin coalition.

137. *Izvještaj o stanju u Savezu komunista Hrvatske*, pp. 135, 204–5.

138. Ibid., pp. 204–5.

139. Ibid., p. 204.

140. *Ekonomska politika*, no. 1023, November 8, 1971, p. 12.

141. *HT*, June 4, 1971, p. 9, cited in *Izvještaj o stanju u Savezu komunista Hrvatske*, p. 205.

142. Ibid.

143. Sher, *Praxis*, p. 182; and Mahmut Mujačić, *Nova dimenzija jugoslovenskog federalizma* (Sarajevo: Oslobodjenje, 1981), p. 76.

144. Rusinow, *Yugoslav Experiment*, p. 298. See also Ströhm, *Ohne Tito*, p. 199.

145. Stoyan Pribichevich, "Tito at 80: An Uncomplicated Marxist," *New York Times*, May 25, 1972, p. 45. See also *Der Spiegel*, July 2, 1973, pp. 72–73.

146. *Borba*, December 1, 1971, as quoted in *Izvještaj o stanju u Savezu komunista Hrvatske*, pp. 118–19.

147. Rusinow, *Yugoslav Experiment*, p. 306.

148. *Borba* claimed that only about 2,000 students attended, but *HT* numbered attendance at more than 3,000; *Borba*, November 23, 1971, p. 5; and *HT*, December 3, 1971, pp. 10–11.

149. *Borba*, November 23, 1971, p. 5.

150. *Vjesnik u srijedu*, September 8, 1971, as quoted in *Izvještaj o stanju u Savezu komunista Hrvatske*, p. 107.

151. As quoted in *Izvještaj o stanju u Savezu komunista Hrvatske*, p. 58.

152. *HT*, December 3, 1971, pp. 10–11.

153. *Izvještaj o stanju u Savezu komunista Hrvatske*, p. 169.

154. Ibid.

155. Rubinstein, "Yugoslav Succession Crisis," p. 112.

156. Dušan Bilandžić, *Historija Socijalističke Federativne Republike Jugoslavije* (Zagreb: Školska knjiga, 1978), pp. 427–28.

157. Italics added; *Borba*, December 6, 1971, p. 5.

158. Bilandžić, *Historija SFRJ*, p. 428.

159. *Izvještaj o stanju u Savezu komunista Hrvatske*, pp. 114–15. Bijelić himself lost his job shortly thereafter.

160. Ibid., pp. 116–17.

161. Ibid., p. 12.

162. "Programme of Action Adopted by the Second Conference of the LCY" (Belgrade, January 25–27, 1972), *Review of International Affairs* 23 (524–25) (February 5–20, 1972): 16.

163. *New York Times*, May 23, 1974, p. 5.

164. *Izvještaj o stanju u Savezu komunista Hrvatske*, pp. 127–28.

165. These figures were provided to me by Miko Tripalo [note 49] and confirmed by Dušan Bilandžić, professor of political science, in an interview, Zagreb, August 29, 1989.

166. K. F. Cviic, "Yugoslavia," *Britannica Book of the Year 1974* (Chicago: Encyclopaedia Britannica, 1974), p. 732.

167. Rubinstein, "Yugoslav Succession Crisis," p. 109.

168. *Ekonomska politika*, no. 1040, March 6, 1972, p. 12.

169. Ibid., no. 1037, February 14, 1972, p. 22.

170. Interview, Belgrade, June 1980.

171. As quoted in Vujić, "Kako rade 'komiteti devetorice,' " p. 16.

172. *Politika*, September 12, 1972, p. 6.

173. Edvard Kardelj, "Medjurepubličko sporazumijevanje i dogovaranje—osnova funkcioniranja federacije" (1972), in *Nacionalno pitanje*, p. 451.

174. Ibid., p. 450.

175. Evgeni Dimitrov, "Novi vid jugoslovenskog federalizma," *Arhiv za pravne i društvene nauke* 59 (2–3) (April–September 1973): 413. Article 333 of the draft constitution reads as follows: "In order to ensure the participation of the authorized organs of the republics and autonomous provinces in the passage of regulations to accompany laws and other general acts that are passed on the basis of the assent of those organs, the federal Executive Council and the authorized republican and provincial organs have, by mutual agreement, established interrepublican committees for certain areas.

"The interrepublican committees are established on the basis of the equal representation of the republics and of the proportional representation of the provinces. The members of the interrepublican committees are designated by the authorized organs of the republics and autonomous provinces.

"The presidents of the interrepublican committees are appointed by the federal Executive Council from among its own members" ("Nacrt ustava Socijalističke Federativne Republike Jugoslavije," *Komunist* [June 18, 1973], p. 27).

176. SFRJ, Federal Executive Council (SIV), "Odluka o medjurepubličkim komitetima" (June 27, 1974), *Službeni list SFRJ* 30 (33) (July 5, 1974), Article 1, p. 1141.

177. Djordji J. Caca, *Socijalistička republika u jugoslovenskoj federaciji* (Belgrade: Radnička štampa, 1977), p. 217.

178. Kavčić slipped from power in October 1972, amid charges that he had conspired to have Slovenia annexed to Bavaria. No matter that Bavaria and Slovenia are not contiguous! Ströhm has called these charges "absurd." See Ströhm, *Ohne Tito*, pp. 237–38.

8. Controversies in the Economic Sector, 1965–90

1. Hamdija Pozderac, *Nacionalni odnosi i socijalističko zajedništvo* (Sarajevo: Svjetlost, 1978), p. 135.

2. Kosta Mihailović, *Nerazvijena područja Jugoslavije*, 2d ed. (Belgrade: Ekonomski Institut, 1970), p. 87.

3. Borisav Srebrić, "Neki problemi usavršavanja metoda i mehanizma razvoja nerazvijenish područja u Jugoslaviji," *Ekonomist* 22 (1) (1969): 156.

4. Bosnia had succeeded in having certain *opštinas* classified as "underdeveloped" in 1959. See Pozderac, *Nacionalni odnosi*, pp. 129–30.

5. Mihailović, *Nerazvijena područja Jugoslavije*, pp. 34, 103.

6. Kiril Miljovski, "Nedovoljno razvijena područja i sedmogodišnji plan," in *Ekonomist* 16 (3–4) (1963): 673.

7. Vinod Dubey et al., *Yugoslavia: Development with Decentralization* (Baltimore: Johns Hopkins University Press, 1975), p. 193.

8. Veselin Djuranović, "Socio-Economic Development of Montenegro," in *Socialist Thought and Practice* 16 (11) (November 1976): 81–82; and Tanjug (April 24, 1978), trans. in FBIS, *Daily Report* (Eastern Europe), April 26, 1978.

9. *Nova Makedonija* (Skopje), January 21, 1987, p. 2.

10. Ksente Bogoev, "The Policy of More Rapid Development of the Undeveloped Republics and Provinces" (from *Ekonomist*, nos. 2–3, 1970), trans. in *Eastern European Economics* 10 (4) (Summer 1972): 407.

11. Ragnar Nurkse, *Problems of Capital Formation in Underdeveloped Countries* (Oxford: Basil Blackwell, 1957), p. 10.

12. *Statistical Pocketbook of Yugoslavia*, 19th issue (Belgrade: Federal Institute for Statistics, April 1973), pp. 30–31, 103, 112–114.
13. Ibid.
14. Nicholas R. Lang, "The Dialectics of Decentralization," in *World Politics* 27 (3) (April 1975): 332.
15. Hivsi Islami, "Kretanje nepismenosti u Albanaca u Jugoslaviji," in *Sociologija* 20 (2–3) (1978): 316.
16. Ivan Stojanović, "Problemi zapošljavanja i medjunacionalni odnosi," in *Gledišta* 15 (7–8) (July–August 1974): 746.
17. *Ekonomska politika* (Belgrade), no. 1465/6 (April 28, 1980): 20.
18. *Borba* (Belgrade), June 4, 1980, p. 3.
19. Marijan Korošić, *Jugoslavenska kriza* (Zagreb: Naprijed, 1989), p. 133.
20. "Rates of Employment and Unemployment, 1980–1987," in *Yugoslav Survey* 29 (4) (1988): 35.
21. Jelica Karačić, "Ekonomski aspekti ravnopravnosti naroda," in Milan Petrović and Kasim Suljević (eds.), *Nacionalni odnosi danas* (Sarajevo: Univerzal, 1971), p. 88.
22. Robert K. Furtak, *Jugoslawien* (Hamburg: Hoffmann and Campe Verlag, 1975), p. 158.
23. Calculated in 1962 prices: Mihailo Vuković, "Neka pitanja razvoja privredno nedovoljno razvijenih republika i krajeva," in *Godišnjak Pravnog Fakulteta u Sarajevu* 16–17 (1968–69): 346.
24. Ibid., p. 340.
25. *Komunist*, January 4, 1980, p. 17.
26. *Osmi kongres Saveza komunista Bosne i Hercegovine, 18–20 maja 1982*. (Sarajevo: Oslobodjenje, 1982), p. 59.
27. *Komunist*, January 4, 1980, p. 17; *Borba*, January 18, 1980, p. 5; and *Vjesnik—Sedam dana*, April 24, 1982, p. 6.
28. Karačić, "Ekonomski aspekti," pp. 90–91.
29. *Borba*, April 7, 1980, p. 5.
30. "Rates of Employment," pp. 31, 35.
31. Djuranović, "Socio-Economic Development of Montenegro," pp. 81–83; and *Statistički godišnjak Jugoslavije 1979* (Belgrade: Savezni zavod za statistiku, July 1979), p. 414.
32. *Ekonomski politika*, no. 1390, November 20, 1978, p. 12.
33. "Rates of Employment," pp. 31, 35.
34. *Večernje novosti* (Belgrade), September 19, 1989, p. 4; and *Politika*, December 4, 1989, p. 1.
35. Predrag Cuckič, "Neki ekonomsko-politički aspekti dalje izgradnje sistema za podsticanje razvoja privredno nedovoljno razvijenih republika i SAP Kosova," in *Obeležja* (Pristina) 5 (2) (March–April 1975): 25.
36. Dušan Ristić, "Kosovo i Savez Komunista Kosova izmedju dva kongresa i dve konferencije," in *Obeležja* 8 (2) (March–April 1978): 9.
37. *Statistički godišnjak Jugoslavije 1979*, pp. 474, 500.
38. Ristić, "Kosovo," p. 12.
39. Ibid., p. 10; Nuri Bašota, "Problemi ubrzanijeg razvoja Kosova kao nedovoljno razvijenog područja," in *Obeležja* 9 (5) (September–October 1979): 41; and *Komunist*, July 11, 1980, p. 17.
40. Ristić, "Kosovo," p. 11; and *Borba*, February 12, 1980, p. 5.
41. *Vjesnik*, April 7, 1980, p. 5; and *Borba*, July 12, 1980, p. 4.
42. *Borba*, February 26, 1980, p. 5; and *Ekonomska politika*, no. 1465/6, April 28, 1980), p. 21.
43. *Yugoslav Life* (April 1990): 2.
44. "Rates of Employment," pp. 31, 32, 35.
45. Branko Kubović, *Regionalna ekonomika* (Zagreb: Informator, 1974), p. 145.

46. *Komunist* (February 1, 1980), p. 2.
47. Tanjug (November 12, 1990), trans. in FBIS, *Daily Report* (Eastern Europe), November 20, 1990, p. 53.
48. Belgrade Domestic Service (December 15, 1989), trans. in FBIS, *Daily Report* (Eastern Europe), December 20, 1989, p. 80.
49. "Rates of Employment," p. 35.
50. Jovan Miljuš, "Neka pitanja regionalnog privrednog razvoja SAP Vojvodine," in *Savremenost* 6 (26) (January–February 1976): 37–40.
51. *Komunist*, March 19, 1982, p. 13.
52. "Rates of Employment," p. 35.
53. Zoran Jašić, "Poticanje razvitka nedovoljno razvijenih područja u SR Hrvatskoj," in *Ekonomski pregled* 28 (5–6) (1977): 265.
54. *Vjesnik*, November 17, 1990, p. 1.
55. *Komunist*, February 22, 1980, p. 5.
56. "Rates of Employment," p. 35.
57. Tanjug, November 22, 1990, trans. in FBIS, *Daily Report* (Eastern Europe), November 23, 1990, p. 56.
58. *Delo* (Ljubljana), August 13, 1990, p. 1, trans. in FBIS, *Daily Report* (Eastern Europe), August 23, 1990, p. 41.
59. *Zakon o fondu federacije za kreditiranje privrednog razvoja privredno nedovoljno razvijenih republika i krajeva* (February 17, 1965), in *Službeni list SFRJ* 21 (8) (February 24, 1965): 181–84.
60. Mihajlo Vuković, *Sistemski okviri podsticanja bržeg razvoja nerazvijenih područja Jugoslavije* (Sarajevo: Svjetlost, 1978), p. 58.
61. Ibid., p. 60.
62. *Borba*, December 28, 1969, p. 9.
63. Mihailović, *Nerazvijena područja*, pp. 92, 93, 100.
64. Ibid., p. 126.
65. Agim Paca, "Fond federacije za kreditiranje privrednog razvoja privredno nedovoljno razvijenih republika i pokrajina, s osvrtom na SAP Kosovo u periodu od 1966. do 1975. godine," in *Obeležja* 7 (3) (May–June 1977), p. 571; and *Zakon o fondu federacije za kreditiranje bržeg razvoja privredno nedovoljno razvijenih republika i autonomnih pokrajina* (July 29, 1971), in *Službeni list* 27 (33) (July 30, 1971): Article 25, p. 643.
66. Bogoev, "Politicy of More Rapid Development," p. 406.
67. *Ekonomska politika*, no. 1043, March 27, 1972, p. 13.
68. *Zakon o kriterijuma za rasporedjivanje sredstava fonda federacije za kreditiranje bržeg razvoja privredno nedovoljno razvijenih republika i autonomnih pokrajina u periodu od 1971. do 1975. godine* (November 3, 1972), in *Službeni list SFRJ* 28 (59) (November 9, 1972): 1089.
69. Mihailo Mladenović, "Neki rezultati razvoja privredno nedovoljno razvijenih republika i pokrajine Kosovo 1971–1974," in *Jugoslovenski pregled* 19 (6) (June 1975): 214.
70. *Društveni plan Jugoslavije za period od 1971. do 1975. godine* (June 29, 1972), in *Službeni list SFRJ* 28 (35) (July 6, 1972): 703; and Halid Konjhodžić, "Neka pitanja finansiranja bržeg razvoja privredno nedovoljno razvijenih republika i Socijalističke Autonomne Pokrajine Kosovo," in *Godišnjak Pravnog Fakulteta u Sarajevu 1976* 24 (1977): 262.
71. Mladenović, "Neki rezultati," p. 215.
72. *Zakon o fondu federacije za kreditiranje bržeg razvoja privredno nedovoljno razvijenih republika i autonomnih pokrajina* (July 20, 1976), in *Službeni list SFRJ* 32 (33) (July 23, 1976): Articles 17–21, p. 833.
73. *Zakon o raspodeli sredstava fonda federacije za kreditiranje bržeg razvoja privredno nedovoljno razvijenih republika i autonomnih pokrajina u periodu od 1976. do 1980. godine* (July 20, 1976), in *Službeni list SFRJ* 32 (33) (July 23, 1976): Article 1.
74. See *Zakon o dopunskim sredstvima republikama i autonomnim pokrajima u per-*

iodu od 1976. do 1980. godine (July 20, 1976), in *Službeni list SFRJ* 32 (33) (July 23, 1976): Article 9.

75. *Durštveni plan Jugoslavije za period od 1976. do 1980. godine* (July 20, 1976), in *Službeni list SFRJ* 32 (33) (July 23, 1976): 806.

76. *Vjesnik*, February 22, 1980, p. 5; and *Borba*, February 22, 1980, p. 4.

77. *Vjesnik*, July 10, 1980, p. 1. An otherwise identical story in *Borba* did not carry the comments by the Serbian delegate. See *Borba*, July 10, 1980, p. 1.

78. *Vjesnik*, April 25, 1980, p. 5.

79. *Borba*, April 28, 1980, p. 9.

80. See, for instance, *Vjesnik—Sedam dana*, March 23, 1980, p. 28.

81. *Borba*, February 27, 1980, p. 4.

82. Ibid., March 20, 1980, p. 12.

83. Ibid., May 22, 1980, p. 7.

84. *Oslobodjenje*, October 18, 1980, p. 1.

85. *Politika*, July 10, 1980, p. 5; *Oslobodjenje*, July 10, 1980, p. 7; and *Borba*, July 13, 1980, p. 4. See also *NIN*, no. 1541, July 13, 1980, pp. 12–13.

86. *Politika*, September 18, 1980, p. 5.

87. Tanjug (December 16, 1980), trans. in FBIS, *Daily Report* (Eastern Europe), December 17, 1980.

88. See *Oslobodjenje*, September 18, 1980, p. 6.

89. *Borba*, November 7, 1980, p. 2.

90. Ibid., September 26, 1980, p. 4.

91. *Politika*, February 28, 1980, p. 5.

92. *Rilindja* (Pristina), November 18, 1980, p. 7, trans. in FBIS, *Daily Report* (Eastern Europe), November 28, 1980.

93. *Vjesnik*, December 21, 1979, p. 5.

94. Ibid., December 24, 1979, p. 1; and *Borba*, December 24, 1979, p. 1.

95. *Pobjeda* (Titograd), December 26, 1979, p. 4.

96. See *Vjesnik*, April 16, 1980, p. 5.

97. Milos Antić, "Korak napred, dva nazad," in *Borba*, December 28, 1979, p. 5.

98. *Borba*, February 27, 1980, p. 4, and March 6, 1980, p. 1.

99. Ibid., March 21, 1980, p. 1; and *Vjesnik*, March 21, 1980, p. 1.

100. Dubey, *Yugoslavia*, p. 192.

101. Marjan Kunej, "Deveti kongres SK Slovenije: Kontinuitet u socijalistickom samoupravljanju je nuznost, potreba i zahtev sadašnjeg vremena," in *Socijalizam* 25 (5) (May 1982): 799; Branislav Ribar, "Osmi kongres SK Bosne i Hercegovine: Kongres kontinuiteta i akcije," in *Socijalizam* 25 (5) (May 1982): 765; and Živorad Djordjević, "Deveti kongres SK Srbije: Raditi strpljivo, ali efikasno," in *Socijalizam* 25 (5) (May 1982): 812.

102. Tanjug (April 19, 1982), trans. in FBIS, *Daily Report* (Eastern Europe), April 20, 1982; and *Politika*, February 2, 1982, p. 7.

103. *Borba*, April 22, 1982, p. 3; and *Vjesnik*, August 5, 1982, p. 12.

104. Belgrade Domestic Service (September 5, 1985), in FBIS, *Daily Report* (Eastern Europe), September 9, 1985, p. 12; Tanjug (October 2, 1985), in FBIS, *Daily Report* (Eastern Europe), October 4, 1985, p. I10; *Politika*, April 4, 1986, p. 5; *NIN*, no. 1978, November 27, 1988: 12; and *Yugoslav Life* (April 1990): 2.

105. Tanjug (January 23, 1990), in FBIS, *Daily Report* (Eastern Europe), January 24, 1990, p. 83; *Politika*, January 25, 1990, p. 8; and *Narodna armija*, as cited in *Yugoslav Life* (April 1990): 2.

106. Tanjug (February 28, 1990), in FBIS, *Daily Report* (Eastern Europe), March 2, 1990, p. 77; *Borba*, March 13, 1990, p. 4; and *Vjesnik*, July 7, 1990, p. 2.

107. *Borba*, July 4, 1990, p. 1, and July 20, 1990, p. 1.

108. Ibid., July 21/22, 1990, p. 5.

109. Drago Bates, *Ekonomika saobraćaja* (Belgrade: Naucna knjiga, 1979), p. 105.
110. *Hrvatski tjednik*, April 16, 1971, p. 7.
111. Slavijan Belamarić argued that SAS was a unit only in name and that even Denmark had, in fact, six operating airline companies. See ibid.
112. *Vjesnik*, February 18, 1979, p. 8.
113. *Hrvatski tjednik*, April 16, 1971, p. 7.
114. Interview, Belgrade, March 1980.
115. *Vjesnik*, February 18, 1979, p. 8.
116. Ibid., March 25, 1980, p. 4.
117. *Delo*, January 22, 1980, p. 3.
118. *Privredni pregled*, December 10, 1979, p. 8.
119. *Borba*, May 18, 1971, p. 4.
120. *Svjet* (Sarajevo), March 4, 1980, pp. 8–9, trans. in *Joint Translation Service*, no. 5937.
121. *Politika*, January 30, 1980, p. 11; and *Vjesnik*, April 4, 1980, p. 5.
122. Interview, Sarajevo, June 1980.
123. Interview, Belgrade, March 1980.
124. *Delo*, November 15, 1978, p. 4.
125. Ibid., August 26, 1978, p. 20.
126. See *Politika*, November 16, 1978, p. 9.
127. *Delo*, July 7, 1979, p. 20.
128. Ibid., August 26, 1978, p. 20.
129. *Vjesnik*, November 18, 1979.
130. Interview, Belgrade, March 1980.
131. *NIN*, no. 1630, March 28, 1982, p. 24.
132. Interview, Belgrade, July 1982.
133. *Vjesnik—Sedam dana*, January 17, 1987.
134. *Vjesnik*, October 17, 1990, p. 9. See also *NIN*, no. 2074, September 28, 1990, p. 24.
135. Djuranović, "Socio-Economic Development of Montenegro," p. 82; and Manojlo Stanković, "Transport and Communications," in *Yugoslav Survey* 16 (4) (November 1975): 99.
136. See "E5: Terror von Blech und Blut," in *Der Spiegel*, August 25, 1975, pp. 92–101.
137. Borislav Nikolić, "Development of Transport Service," in *Yugoslav Survey* 7 (26) (July–September 1966): 3813.
138. Mirko Dokić, *Ekonomika, organizacija i razvoj saobraćaja SFRJ* (Belgrade: Institut Ekonomskih Nauka, 1977), p. 41.
139. Dennison I. Rusinow, "Ports and Politics in Yugoslavia," *American Universities Field Staff Reports*, Southeast Europe Series, Vol. 11, No. 3 (April 1964), pp. 5–6.
140. Completion of the terminal was expected by the second half of 1981, allowing Šibenik to handle two million tons of cargo a year, of which one million would be raw phosphate from North Africa. This would make Šibenik the principal terminal for the transfer of phosphate on the Adriatic. Anticipated cost was 250 million dinars (*Vjesnik*, November 27, 1979, p. 16).
141. Rusinow, "Ports and Politics," p. 17.
142. *Vjesnik*, May 19, 1980, p. 7; and *Oslobodjenje*, October 29, 1981, p. 3.
143. Dokić, *Ekonomika, organizacija*, pp. 617–18.
144. Ibid., p. 618.
145. F. E. Ian Hamilton, *Yugoslavia: Patterns of Economic Activity* (New York: Praeger, 1968), pp. 282, 293. Two other towns deserve mention—Zadar, whose annual tonnage had been negligible, and Kotor in Montenegro, whose superb natural harbor has been highly coveted by the Soviets as a desirable port for their Mediterranean fleet. Yet,

from a commercial viewpoint, Kotor is not in the running, for, as Hamilton has noted, "despite its magnificent fjord-like natural harbour, Kotor cannot become a port on account of poor site conditions and the impossibility of linking the town economically with anything but tortuous roads. The coast road to Dubrovnik and Ulcinj is difficult, but the one road inland, to Cetinje and Titograd, climbs the slopes of Mount Lovcen from sea level to about 4,500 ft. in about 30 hairpin turns. From here, too, an economic hinterland is less accessible than from Bar" (Hamilton, *Yugoslavia*, p. 295n).

146. *Novi list* (Rijeka), October 20, 1974, p. 3, trans. in Joint Publications Research Service (JPRS), *East Europe Report*, October 29, 1974.

147. Report by Marin Bakica, in *Osmi kongres Saveza komunista Hrvatske: Zagreb, 24–26, travnja 1978—Stenografske bilješke* (Zagreb: Zrinski, 1978), 2: pp. 239–40.

148. Mirko Dokić, "Društveno-ekonomska uloga i saobraćajni značaj pruge Beograd-Bar, luke Bar i priključnih pruga, i osnove razvoja turizma u užem gravitacionom području ove pruge," in *Železnice* 32 (5) (May 1976): 45.

149. "Tunnel Construction," in *Yugoslav Survey* 3 (8) (January–March 1962): 1163; Hamilton, *Yugoslavia*, p. 282; and Gordon C. McDonald et al., *Area Handbook for Yugoslavia* (Washington D.C.: U.S. Government Publications, 1970), pp. 478–79, 482.

150. Hamilton, *Yugoslavia*, p. 277; and *Privredni pregled* (February 24, 1978), p. 3, trans. in JPRS, *East Europe Report*, March 31, 1978.

151. Borislav Uskoković, "Šansa turističke valorizacije pruge Beograd-Bar," in *Ovdje* (June 1976): 26.

152. *Komunist*, January 9, 1978, p. 8.

153. Dokic, *Ekonomika, organizacija*, p. 71.

154. See Tihomir Babić, "Značaj pruge Beograd-Bar sa stanovišta saobraćajnog sistema SFRJ," in *Železnice*, 32 (5) (May 1976): 38–39.

155. *Politika*, December 11, 1970, p. 7.

156. *Vjesnik*, January 9, 1980, p. 7; and *Vjesnik—Sedam dana*, January 26, 1980, p. 9.

157. *NIN*, no. 1529, April 27, 1980, pp. 9–13.

158. Ibid., p. 12.

159. Ibid., p. 13.

160. Interviews, Ljubljana, July 1982.

161. *Ekonomska politika*, no. 1055, June 19, 1972, p. 16.

162. Belgrade Domestic Service (October 16, 1980), trans. in FBIS, *Daily Report* (Eastern Europe), October 17, 1980.

163. *Danas*, no. 394, September 5, 1989, p. 11.

164. *Vjesnik*, August 28, 1989, p. 5.

165. *Süddeutsche Zeitung* (Munich), November 21–22, 1987, p. 8.

166. *NIN*, no. 1925, November 22, 1987, pp. 12–13; and *New York Times*, October 5, 1988, p. 3.

167. *Intervju* (Belgrade), no. 215, September 1, 1989, pp. 19–21.

168. *NIN*, no. 1290, October 18, 1987, p. 9; and *Večernje novosti* (Belgrade), September 14, 1989, p. 3.

169. *Financial Times*, May 16, 1988, p. 2.

170. Ljubljana Domestic Service (December 19, 1989), trans. in FBIS, *Daily Report* (Eastern Europe), December 20, 1989, p. 77.

171. Tanjug (December 19, 1989), in FBIS, *Daily Report* (Eastern Europe), December 20, 1989, p. 77.

172. *Vjesnik—Panorama subotom*, July 23, 1988, p. 14.

173. *Politika*, September 12, 1990, p. 14.

174. Tanjug (October 15, 1988), in FBIS, *Daily Report* (Eastern Europe), October 17, 1988, pp. 52–53.

175. *Borba*, June 1, 1989, p. 7.

9. Nationalist Tensions, 1968–90: Muslims, Albanians, Croats, Slovenes, Montenegrins

1. Quoted in Miloš Mišović, *Ko je tražio republiku: Kosovo 1945–1985* (Belgrade: Narodna Knjiga, 1987), p. 170.

2. *Borba*, February 9, 1980, p. 3.

3. Muhamed Kešetović, "Edvard Kardelj—Doprinos primjeni i razradi marksističkog metoda u izučavanju nacije," *Opredjeljenja* 11 (3–4) (March–April 1980): 90.

4. *Statistički godišnjak Jugoslavije 1979* (Belgrade: Savezni zavod za statistiku, July 1979), pp. 69, 410; Vukasin Stambolić, "Položaj i odnosi republika u SFRJ" (Master's thesis, University of Belgrade, 1968), app.

5. Hamdija Pozderac, *Nacionalni odnosi i socijalističko zajedništvo* (Sarajevo: Svjetlost, 1978), p. 87.

6. Atif Purivatra, "Stav Komunističke Partije Jugoslavije prema nacionalnom pitanju u Bosni i Hercegovini," in *Nacionalni odnosi danas*, ed. Milan Petrović and Kasim Suljevic (Sarajevo: Univerzal, 1971), p. 191.

7. Pozderac, *Nacionalni odnosi*, p. 86.

8. Interview, Sarajevo, June 1980.

9. For example, Ivo Pilar, *Die südslawische Frage und der Weltkrieg* (Vienna: Manzsche k. u. k. Hof-, Verlags-u. Universitäts-Buchhandlung, 1918), pp. 170, 185, 195, 213.

10. The Serbophile theories are discussed in Kasim Suljević, *Nacionalnost Muslimana* (Rijecka: Otokar Keršovani, 1981).

11. Humo's remarks were made at a party conference on June 19, 1971, and reported in *Vjesnik*, July 5, 1971; K. F. Cviic, "Yugoslavia's Moslem Problem," *World Today* 36 (3) (March 1980): 110. See also David A. Dyker, "The Ethnic Muslims of Bosnia—Some Basic Socio-Economic Data," *Slavonic and East European Review* 50 (119) (April 1972): 238–39.

12. Carl Gustav Ströhm, *Ohne Tito* (Graz: Verlag Styria, 1976), pp. 243–44; Pozderac, *Nacionalni odnosi*, p. 66. According to Purivatra, no more than 2 or 3 percent of the Muslim population in Bosnia-Herzegovina is ethnically non-Slavic (that small portion consisting mainly of a Turkish, Arab, Persian, and Caucasian admixture); Purivatra, "The National Phenomenon of the Moslems of Bosnia-Herzegovina," *Socialist Thought and Practice* 12 (12) (December 1974): 36n. Perhaps the most sophisticated treatment of the Bogomils in English is John V. A. Fine, Jr., *The Bosnian Church: A New Interpretation*, East European Monographs (New York: Columbia University Press, 1975).

13. Interview, Sarajevo, June 1980.

14. R. V. Burks, *The National Problem and the Future of Yugoslavia* (Santa Monica, Calif.: Rand Corporation, October 1971), p. 26.

15. Pozderac, *Nacionalni odnosi*, p. 44.

16. See *Zadaci SK Srbije u razvoju medjunacionalnih odnosa i borbi protiv nacionalizma* (Belgrade: Komunist, 1978), pp. 122–25; and Branko Petranović, *Istorija Jugoslavije 1918–1988*, (Belgrade-Nolit, 1988), 3:389.

17. Humo, "Muslimani u Jugoslaviji," pt. 3, *Komunist*, July 25, 1968, p. 15.

18. Compare the 1953 census figures given in Paul Shoup, *Communism and the Yugoslav National Question* (New York: Columbia University Press, 1968), p. 267, with *Statistički godišnjak Jugoslavije 1979*, p. 112. See also Dragosavac, "O nekim aspektima," p. 127.

19. "Staat und Nationalität in Jugoslawien," *Wissenschaftlicher Dienst Südosteuropa* 19 (8) (August 1970): 119.

20. Ibid., p. 118.

21. As quoted in "Muslimani: Nacija ili vera," *NIN*, no. 1048, February 7, 1971, p. 29.

22. Milan Bulajić, "Problemi samoopredeljenja nacija i čovjeka i jugoslovenski federalizam," in *Federalizam i nacionalno pitanje* (Belgrade: Savez udruženja za političke nauke Jugoslavije, 1971), pp. 267–68.
23. "Muslimani: Nacija ili vera," p. 29.
24. Ibid.
25. Ibid., p. 32.
26. "Islamic Publication Protests Restrictions on Religious Education," summary of article in *Preporod*, nos. 19–20 (October 1977): 2, in JPRS/EE, November 18, 1977.
27. *Rilindja*, March 7, 1981, as quoted in Louis Zanga, "Kosovar-Macedonian Quarrel over Nationality Issue," *Radio Free Europe Research* (March 27, 1981), p. 2.
28. Todo Kurtović, *Crkva i religija u socijalističkom samoupravnom društvu* (Belgrade: Rad, 1978), p. 64; and Fuad Muhić, interview in *Start*, no. 283, November 28–December 12, 1979, pp. 13–14.
29. *Constitutional System of Yugoslavia* (Belgrade: Jugoslovenska stvarnost, 1980), p. 85.
30. Ibid.
31. *Borba*, April 26, 1970, p. 5, translated in *Joint Translation Service*, no. 5616.
32. *Oslobodjenje*, October 18, 1973, p. 6; and Tanjug, October 23, 1973, translated in FBIS, *Daily Report*, Eastern Europe, October 26, 1973.
33. *New York Times*, April 8, 1974, p. 2.
34. Aziz Hadžihasanović, "Muslimanski nacionalizam, šta je to?" *Oslobodjenje*, February 19, 1974, p. 5.
35. *Oslobodjenje*, February 21, 1974, p. 5; and February 22, 1974, p. 5. Yugoslavia had broken off diplomatic relations with Israel in 1967.
36. As quoted in *Borba*, May 10, 1972, p. 5.
37. Kurtović, *Crkva i religija*, p. 63.
38. Pozderac, in *Komunist*, November 23, 1979, p. 10.
39. *Delo*, May 28, 1983, translated in FBIS, *Daily Report*, Eastern Europe, June 9, 1983; *Vjesnik*, July 16, 1983, p. 8; *Archiv der Gegenwart*, August 20, 1983, p. 26903; and *Christian Science Monitor*, September 28, 1983, p. 7. See also Hamza Bakšić, "Nesudjeni neimari 'Islamistana,' " in *Komunist*, August 5, 1983, p. 7; and Nijaz Duraković, "Od 'Mladih muslimana' do panislamizma," in *Komunist*, September 23, 1983, p. 20.
40. *Vjesnik u srijedu*, February 5, 1975, translated in JPRS/EE, March 11, 1975.
41. *Vjesnik*, November 27, 1979, p. 1.
42. Edvard Kardelj, *Razvoj slovenačkog nacionalnog pitanja*, 2d ed. (Belgrade: Kultura, 1958), exerpted in *Nacionalno pitanje*, p. 405.
43. Ivo Banac, *With Stalin against Tito: Cominformist Splits in Yugoslav Communism* (Ithaca, N.Y.: Cornell University Press, 1988), p. 206.
44. Quoted in ibid., p. 207.
45. Mišović, *Ko je tražio republiku*, pp. 45–46.
46. Ibid., pp. 53–54.
47. Ibid., p. 36.
48. Branko Horvat, *Kosovosko pitanje* (Zagreb: Globus, 1988), p. 62.
49. Ljiljana Bulatović, *Prizrenski proces* (Novi Sad: Književna zajednica, 1988), esp. pp. 9–27.
50. Jens Reuter, *Die Albaner in Jugoslawien* (Munich: R. Oldenbourg Verlag, 1982), p. 45.
51. Hirzi Islami, "Kretanje nepismenosti u Albanaca u Jugoslaviji," in *Sociologija* 20 (2–3) (1978): 315–16.
52. Ibid., p. 320. See also Milenko Karan, "Žene Kosova izmedju običajnih pravila, savremenih prilika i samoupravnih zahteva," *Žena* 34 (6) (1975).
53. See documents in *Nacionalno pitanje*, pp. 500–503.

54. *Sedma sednica pokrajinskog komiteta SKJ na Kosovu i Metohiji* (1966), in *Zadaci SK Srbije*, p. 114.

55. Radio Belgrade, February 10, 1968.

56. Mišović, *Ko je tražio republiku*, p. 133.

57. Ibid., pp. 134–135.

58. Ibid., p. 136.

59. Ibid., February 12, 1968; and *New York Times*, November 28, 1968, p. 19.

60. *Borba*, October 28, 1968.

61. Enver Hozha has been ruler of Albania since World War II. See report by Dušan Mugoša, in *Deveti Kongres Saveza Komunista Jugoslavije* (Beograd, 11–13 III 1969)—*Stenografske beleške* (Belgrade: Komunist, 1970) 3: 367; also *New York Times*, November 28, 1968, p. 19.

62. Othmar Nikola Haberl, *Parteiorganisation und nationale Frage in Jugoslawien* (Berlin: Otto Harrassowitz, 1976), p. 73.

63. *New York Times*, January 16, 1975, p. 8.

64. Sensing that a natural ally agianst Serbian international imperialism was under fire, Croatian nationalists sprang to Kosovo's defense, accusing Stanić of manipulating the figures from the various postwar censuses in order to hoodwink *NIN*'s readers and accepting the official results as accurate and legitimate; Bruno Bušić, "Čudne kosovske brojidbe," *HT*, September 3, 1971, p. 3.

65. *Sednica predsedništva CK SK Srbije* (May 17, 1976), in *Zadaci SK Srbije*, p. 165; Ivan Stojanović, "Problemi zapošljavanja i medjunacionalni odnosi," *Gledišta* 15 (7–8) (July–August 1974): 747; and *Oslobodjenje*, May 14, 1981, p. 20.

66. *Bilten pokrajinskog zavoda za statistiku SAPK* (1975), cited by Nebi Gasi, "Nacionalna ravnopravnost na Kosovu i politika zapošljavanja," in *Udruženi rad, i medjunacionalni odnosi* (Belgrade: Komunist, 1978), p. 158.

67. Tanjug, March 10, 1982, translated in FBIS, *Daily Report*, Eastern Europe, March 11, 1982.

68. *Politika*, March 4, 1971, p. 6; and *Borba*, April 5, 1971, p. 6.

69. *Süddeutsche Zeitung*, December 17, 24–26, 1971.

70. Radio Belgrade, March 18, 1976, translated in FBIS, *Daily Report*, Eastern Europe, March 18, 1976; Tanjug, May 5, 7, and 12, 1981, translated in FBIS, *Daily Report*, Eastern Europe, May 6, 8, and 14, 1981; and *Times* (London), May 13, 1981.

71. Dušan Ristić, "Kosovo i Savez komunista Kosova izmedju dva kongresa i dve konferencije," *Obeležja* 8 (2) (March–April 1978): 24; *Jedanaesta pokrajinska konferencija SK Kosova* (1974), in *Zadaci SK Srbije*, p. 161; Reuters News Service, January 13, 1975, in FBIS, *Daily Report*, Eastern Europe, January 14, 1975; and *Frankfurter Allgemeine*, May 7, 1981, p. 3. See also *Yugoslav Information Bulletin* (Belgrade, January 1975), pp. 21–22.

72. *Süddeutsche Zeitung*, June 20, 1980, p. 3.

73. "Albanische Irredenta in Kosovo?" *Wissenschaftlicher Dienst Südosteuropa* 29 (4) (April 1980): 84.

74. Tanjug, May 12, 1981, translated in FBIS, *Daily Report*, Eastern Europe, May 14, 1981.

75. Interviews, Belgrade, 1980; *Vjesnik*, April 5, 1980, p. 7; *Mladost* (Belgrade), August 22, 1980, p. 6; and *Der Spiegel*, May 22, 1978, p. 182. Large numbers of Albanians were reportedly also imprisoned in the prison in Niš, in southern Serbia.

76. *Vjesnik*, April 5, 1980, p. 7; *Borba*, April 4, 1980, p. 3; *Oslobodjenje*, July 8, 1980, p. 2; and Tanjug, May 12, 1981, translated in FBIS, *Daily Report*, Eastern Europe, May 14, 1981.

77. Tanjug, May 18 and 20, 1981, translated in FBIS, *Daily Report*, Eastern Europe, May 19 and 21, 1981; and *Frankfurter Allgemeine*, May 19, 1981, p. 4.

78. *NIN*, no. 1588, June 7, 1981, pp. 11–12; and *NIN*, no. 1590, June 21, 1981, p. 13.

79. *Rilindja*, November 8, 1975, summarized in Radio Belgrade, November 7, 1975, translated in FBIS, *Daily Report*, Eastern Europe, November 10, 1975.

80. Tanjug, July 15, 1975, translated in FBIS, *Daily Report*, Eastern Europe, July 16, 1975.

81. *Politika*, March 30, 1980, p. 8.

82. Živorad Z. Igić, "SK Kosova i unutarpartijsko informisanje," *Obeležja* 9 (1) (January–February 1979): 30.

83. Tanjug, November 1, 1980, translated in FBIS, *Daily Report*, Eastern Europe, November 3, 1980; *Politika*, February 12, 1981, p. 1; and *Komunist*, February 20, 1981.

84. *Financial Times* (London), March 13, 1981, p. 18; *Times* (London), March 14, 1981, p. 5; and *New York Times*, April 7, 1981, p. A3.

85. See *Frankfurter Allegemeine*, April 24, 1981, p. 3.

86. *Times* (London), April 4, 1981, p. 4; *New York Times*, April 7, 1981, p. A3; *Frankfurter Allgemeine*, April 27, 1981, p. 3; Radio Belgrade, April 3 and 24, 1981, and Hamburg DPA, April 3, 1981, translated respectively in FBIS, *Daily Report*, Eastern Europe, April 3 and 27 and April 6, 1981; and Reuter, *Die Albaner in Jugoslawien*, p. 82.

87. See *Vjesnik*, April 7, 1981, translated in FBIS, *Daily Report*, Eastern Europe, April 13, 1981.

88. See *Frankfurter Allegemeine*, April 4, 1981, pp. 1, 3.

89. *Vjesnik*, June 11, 1981, p. 12; *Frankfurter Allgemeine*, May 14, 1981, p. 1; Tanjug, June 6, 1981, and *Vjesnik—Sedam dana*, June 6, 1981, translated repectively in JPRS/EE, June 24, 1981, and July 1, 1981.

90. *Frankfurter Allgemeine*, May 12, 1981, p. 1; and *Politika*, January 8, 1982, p. 7.

91. Tanjug, June 26, 1981, translated in FBIS, *Daily Report*, Eastern Europe, June 30, 1981; and Tanjug, July 14, 1981, in FBIS, *Daily Report*, Eastern Europe, July 15, 1981.

92. *Nova Makedonija*, June 9, 1981, p. 3; Tanjug, July 7 and 9, 1981, and Radio Belgrade (August 24, 1981), translated respectively in FBIS, *Daily Report*, Eastern Europe, July 7 and 9, 1981, and August 25, 1981.

93. Radio Belgrade, June 5 and November 12, 1981, and Tanjug, July 18, 1981, translated respectively in FBIS, *Daily Report*, Eastern Europe, June 9, November 13, and July 22, 1981; and *Frankfurter Allgemeine*, June 26, 1981, p. 3.

94. Paris AFP, November 17, 1981, and Radio Belgrade, November 24, 1981, translated respectively in FBIS, *Daily Report*, Eastern Europe, November 18 and 25, 1981.

95. *Frankfurter Allgemeine*, July 29, 1981, p. 3, and February 16, 1982, p. 1; *Neue Zürcher Zeitung*, February 17, 1982, p. 1, February 21–22, 1982, p. 3, and March 14–15, 1982, p. 4; Radio Belgrade, January 7, March 11, and April 1, 1982, and Tanjug, September 30 and October 27, 1982, translated respectively in FBIS, *Daily Report*, Eastern Europe, January 7, March 12, April 5, October 1, and October 28, 1982.

96. *Vjesnik*, April 7, 1981, and Tanjug, April 17, May 14, and June 3, 1981, translated respectively in FBIS, *Daily Report*, Eastern Europe, April 13 and 20, May 15, June 4, 1981; Tanjug, March 30, 1982, in FBIS, *Daily Report*, Eastern Europe, March 31, 1982; *Vjesnik*, July 26, 1982, p. 4; and *Christian Science Monitor*, July 27, 1982, p. 8.

97. *Frankfurter Allgemeine*, May 12, 1982, p. 6.

98. Tanjug, May 29, 1981 and June 6, 1983, translated in FBIS, *Daily Report*, Eastern Europe, June 1, 1981, and June 9, 1983.

99. "Zaključci 20. sednice Centralnog komiteta Saveza komunista Jugoslavije," *Socijalizam* 24 (4) (1981): 570–72. See also Lazar Mojsov, "O neprijateljskoj i kontrarevolucionarnoj aktivnosti u SAP Kosovu," and Ali Šukrija, "Nacionalizam i iredentizam na Kosovu," in *Socijalizam* 24 (4) (1981).

100. *Borba*, June 4, 1981, p. 4; Tanjug, June 5 and 15, July 23, and September 17, 1981, and Radio Priština, August 6, 1981, translated respectively in FBIS, *Daily Report*, Eastern Europe, June 9 and 17, July 24, September 18, and August 7, 1981; and *Neue Zürcher Zeitung*, September 27–28, 1981, p. 1.

101. *Politika*, June 2, 1981, p. 5; and *Christian Science Monitor*, September 2, 1981, p. 7.

102. See *Frankfurter Allgemeine*, September 23, 1981, p. 2.

103. Radio Budapest, April 15, 1981, translated in FBIS, *Daily Report*, Eastern Europe, April 17, 1981.

104. *Politika*, October 27, 1981, p. 7.

105. Radio Belgrade, April 19, 1978, translated in FBIS, *Daily Report*, Eastern Europe, April 21, 1978.

106. Reuter, *Die Albaner in Jugoslawien*, p. 93.

107. *Borba*, May 21, 1981, translated in FBIS, *Daily Report*, Eastern Europe, June 4, 1981.

108. Tanjug, December 10, 1981, translated in FBIS, *Daily Report*, Eastern Europe, December 16, 1981.

109. For details about these organizations, see Sabrina P. Ramet, *Social Currents in Eastern Europe: The Sources and Meaning of the Great Transformation* (Durham, N.C.: Duke University Press, 1991).

110. *New York Times*, November 1, 1987, p. 6.

111. *Večernji list* (Zagreb), June 26, 1987, p. 5. For a complete transcript of the proceedings of June 26 (the first day of the session), see *Borba*, June 28, 1987, special supplement.

112. Tanjug (September 7, 1988), in FBIS, *Daily Report* (Eastern Europe), September 13, 1988, p. 51.

113. *Danas*, no. 278, June 16, 1987, p. 30; and *Borba*, November 20, 1987, p. 3.

114. For further discussion of the Serbian Orthodox Church, see my chapter on that subject in Pedro Ramet (ed.), *Eastern Christianity and Politics in the Twentieth Century* (Durham, N.C.: Duke University Press, 1988).

115. Quoted in *New York Times*, October 24, 1986, p. A8. See also *NIN*, no. 1869, October 26, 1986, pp. 14–15.

116. *Književne novine*, June 15, 1987, reprinted in *Pravoslavlje*, June 15, 1987, p. 2.

117. *Duga*, June 13–26, 1987, p. 18.

118. For example, *Reporter*, no. 984, June 1, 1987, p. 3.

119. Quoted in *Borba*, January 20, 1987, p. 3, trans. in JPRS, *East Europe Report*, No. EER–87–030, March 2, 1987, p. 109.

120. *NIN*, no. 1939, February 28, 1988, p. 8.

121. Quoted in Belgrade Domestic Service (September 5, 1988), trans. in FBIS, *Daily Report* (Eastern Europe), September 12, 1988, p. 65.

122. *New York Times*, November 19, 1988, p. 4.

123. As reported in *Die Welt*, July 2, 1981.

124. See, for example, *NIN*, no. 1975, November 6, 1988, pp. 9–11; and *Vjesnik*, July 3, 1990, pp. 1, 3.

125. Pedro Ramet, *Nationalism and Federalism in Yugoslavia, 1963–1983* (Bloomington: Indiana University Press, 1984), p. 171.

126. Interview with Šime Djodan, adviser at the Institute for Public Finances, Zagreb, September 12, 1989.

127. *Süddeutsche Zeitung* (Munich), December 17, 1980.

128. See *Croatia Press* 27 (3–4) (September–December 1974): 6–7.

129. Ibid. 28 (1–2) (April–June 1975): 4.

130. Ibid., pp. 3, 7–8. See also *New York Times*, February 18, 1975, p. 6.

131. *Die Welt*, November 25, 1980; *Süddeutsche Zeitung*, August 5, 1980, p. 5. A separate group of Serbian intellectuals subsequently submitted a similar petition to the federal government, likewise requesting a blanket amnesty for all political prisoners in Yugoslavia.

132. *Süddeutsche Zeitung*, July 26, 1978, p. 3, translated in JPRS/EE, August 29, 1978.

133. As reported in *Frankfurter Allgemeine*, March 24, 1980.

134. Interview with Franjo Tudjman, retired general and president of the Croatian Democratic Community, Zagreb, September 11, 1989.

135. *NIN*, no. 1538, June 22, 1980, pp. 36–37.

136. Interviews, Zagreb, July 1982.

137. *Frankfurter Allgemeine*, May 22, 1981, p. 7.

138. As reported by *Svijet*, August 17, 1981, quoted in *Glas koncila*, August 30, 1981, p. 2, and translated in JPRS/EE, October 13, 1981.

139. Kurtović, *Crkva i religija*, pp. 137, 139.

140. Cited by Zdenko Antic, "Catholic Clergy in Croatia under Sharp Attack," *Radio Free Europe Research*, July 29, 1977, p. 4.

141. *Süddeutsche Zeitung*, August 5, 1980, p. 5, translated in JPRS/EE, September 9, 1980.

142. *Die Welt*, September 11, 1979, p. 5. A crowd of 150,000–250,000 Catholic Croats gathered on September 2, 1979, in the town of Nin in an outpouring of religious and national sentiment. Croatian Cardinal Franjo Šeper, prefect of the Congregation for Sacred Doctrine, represented the pope at the rally.

143. *Frankfurter Allgemeine*, July 29, 1981, p. 3. The campaign began with attacks on the character and memory of Cardinal Stepinac, broadened by criticizing current church leaders for their defense of Stepinac, and finally assumed the form of a campaign against the church per se. A particularly striking development was the arrest late in the year of the parish priest in the village of Stražeman, who allegedly had authorized the inclusion of a likeness of Stepinac in a mosaic in his refurbished church; Tanjug (October 17 and 26, 1981), translated respectively in FBIS, *Daily Report*, Eastern Europe, October 22 and 27, 1981.

144. *Vjesnik*, September 23, 1984, p. 4.

145. *Politika*, January 12, 1985, p. 6.

146. Tanjug (April 8, 1985), trans. in FBIS, *Daily Report* (Eastern Europe), April 9, 1985, pp. I7–I8; *Neue Zürcher Zeitung*, April 10, 1985, p. 4; *The Times*, April 11, 1985, p. 4; *Neue Zürcher Zeitung*, April 11, 1985, p. 2; Tanjug (April 11, 1985), trans. in FBIS, *Daily Report* (Eastern Europe), April 12, 1985, pp. I2–I4; Tanjug (April 12, 1985), trans. in FBIS, *Daily Report* (Eastern Europe), April 15, 1985, pp. I1–I2; *Neue Zürcher Zeitung*, April 14–15, 1985, p. 3; Tanjug (April 16, 1985), trans. in FBIS, *Daily Report* (Eastern Europe), April 17, 1985, p. I6; Tanjug (April 19, 1985), trans. in FBIS, *Daily Report* (Eastern Europe), April 23, 1985, pp. I14–I15; Tanjug (April 29, 1985), trans. in FBIS, *Daily Report* (Eastern Europe), April 30, 1985, pp. I21–I22; Tanjug (May 10, 1985), trans. in FBIS, *Daily Report* (Eastern Europe), May 13, 1985, p. I5; and *Vjesnik*, May 11, 1985, p. 12.

147. *The Economist* (London), September 14, 1985, p. 57.

148. Quoted in *NIN*, no. 1805, August 4, 1985, trans. in JPRS, *East Europe Report*, no. EPS–85–102, October 15, 1985, p. 132.

149. *The Economist*, September 14, 1985, p. 57.

150. Interview, Zagreb, August 30, 1989.

151. Banac, *With Stalin against Tito*, p. 106.

152. *Danas* (July 16, 1985), pp. 15–16, trans. in JPRS, *East Europe Report*, no. EPS–85–092, September 6, 1985, p. 118.

153. Josip Vidmar, in *Jugoslovensko rodoljublje danas* (Belgrade: Nova knjiga, 1984), p. 120. For early discussions, see *Politika*, January 21, 1983, p. 6; "Nationalismus in Slowenien?" in *Osteuropa* 34 (2) (February 1984): A87–A100; *Frankfurter Allgemeine*, March 16, 1987, p. 3; "Slowenien—eigenständig, aber im Rahmen der Föderation," in *Osteuropa* 37 (7) (July 1987): A366–A374; *Komunist*, September 4, 1987, p. 21; and *Borba*, October 22, 1987, p. 2.

154. On the last of these points, see *Neue Zürcher Zeitung*, September 1, 1990, p. 3.

155. Interview with Igor Vidmar, member of NSK, Ljubljana, June 30, 1987; and interview with two members of NSK who asked not to be identified, Ljubljana, Sep-

tember 1, 1989. For a discussion of the Irwin group, see *Slobodna Dalmacija*, August 28, 1989, p. 6.

156. For more on Laibach, see Pedro Ramet, "The Rock Scene in Yugoslavia," in *Eastern European Politics and Societies* 2 (2) (Spring 1988); and Sabrina P. Ramet, "Rock Music in Yugoslavia," in Sabrina P. Ramet (ed.), *Rocking the State: Rock Music and Politics in Eastern Europe and the Soviet Union*, manuscript under review.

157. The issue is summarized in *Svet* (Belgrade), September 1989, pp. 50–51. See also *Frankfurter Allgemeine*, June 12, 1987, p. 7. For an elaborate discussion of the special issue of *Nova revija*, see Mirjana Kasapović, "O slovenskom nacionalnom programu," in *Naše teme* 32 (4) (1988): 771–86.

158. *Frankfurter Allgemeine*, August 21, 1986, p. 5.

159. Tomaz Mastnak, "The Night of the Long Knives," in *Across Frontiers* 4 (4) (Winter/Spring 1989): 5.

160. Tanjug (May 31, 1988), in FBIS, *Daily Report* (Eastern Europe), June 1, 1988, p. 51.

161. *The Times* (London), July 28, 1988.

162. *Glas koncila* (Zagreb), June 26, 1988, p. 3; and *Borba*, July 18, 1988, p. 12.

163. Ljubljana Domestic Service (June 29, 1988) and (July 8, 1988), trans. respectively in FBIS, *Daily Report* (Eastern Europe), July 15, 1988, pp. 60 and 59; Tanjug (July 19, 1988), trans. in FBIS, *Daily Report* (Eastern Europe), July 20, 1988, p. 61; *Danas*, no. 354, November 29, 1988, p. 13; *Delo* (Ljubljana), July 26, 1988, p. 1.

164. AFP (Paris), June 3, 1988, in FBIS, *Daily Report* (Eastern Europe), June 6, 1988, p. 58.

165. Janez Janša, "War and Peace in the New Constitution," in *Independent Voices from Slovenia, Yugoslavia*, Special ed., Vol. 4 (October 1988), p. 27.

166. *Borba*, July 29, 1988, p. 16.

167. Tanjug (July 28, 1988), in FBIS, *Daily Report* (Eastern Europe), July 28, 1988, p. 32.

168. Ibid.

169. Interview, Ljubljana, September 1, 1989.

170. *Frankfurter Allgemeine*, June 21, 1988, p. 4.

171. Quoted in *Danas*, no. 344, September 20, 1988, p. 13.

172. Tanjug (December 17, 1988), in FBIS, *Daily Report* (Eastern Europe), December 19, 1988, p. 53.

173. *Mladina* (Ljubljana), September 1, 1989, p. 4.

174. On the concept of ethnogenesis, see *8 Novosti*, July 3, 1982, p. 33.

175. Nikola Vukčević, *Etničko porijeklo crnogoraca* (Belgrade: Sava Mihić, 1981).

176. Marko Špadijer, "Nacionalizam u Crnoj Gori," in *Socijalizam* 29 (4) (April 1986): 112.

177. Ibid., p. 113.

178. *Borba*, July 28/29, 1990, p. 13. See also *Vjesnik*, July 23, 1990, p. 3.

179. *Borba*, November 13, 1990, p. 3. See also *Vjesnik*, October 13, 1990, p. 5.

180. *Politika*, August 30, 1990, p. 10.

181. Tanjug (August 23, 1990), trans. in FBIS, *Daily Report* (Eastern Europe), August 24, 1990, p. 43.

182. "Interview/Miha Kovač: The Slovene Spring," in *New Left Review*, no. 171 (September–October 1988): 115.

10. Political Debates, 1980–89

1. Dušan Bilandžić, *Jugoslavija poslije Tita (1980–1985)* (Zabreb: Globus, 1986), p. 9. See also Ivica Josipović, "Geneza krize savremenog jugoslovenskog društva," in *Socijalizam* 30 (10) (October 1987).

2. As I noted in my earlier article, "Yugoslavia 1982: Political Ritual, Political Drift, and the Fetishization of the Past," in *South Slav Journal* 5 (3) (Autumn 1982): 20.

3. Samuel P. Huntington, *Political Order in Changing Societies* (New Haven: Yale University Press, 1968).

4. See my essay, "Yugoslavia 1987: Stirrings from Below," in *South Slav Journal* 10 (3) (Autumn 1987): 23.

5. *Oslobodjenje*, September 27, 1980, and July 26, 1981, p. 4; *Politika*, May 25, 1981; and *Start*, no. 327, (August 1, 1981), p. 19.

6. *Komunist*, July 24, 1981, p. 8.

7. *Danas*, June 22, 1982, p. 14.

8. *Politika*, February 2, 1982, p. 6.

9. *NIN*, no. 1594, July 19, 1981, p. 8.

10. *Danas*, June 22, 1982, p. 43.

11. *Komunist*, October 9, 1981; and *Politika*, March 17, 1982.

12. *Borba*, October 20, 1981.

13. *NIN*, no. 1596, August 2, 1981, pp. 15–16.

14. Ibid., no. 1601, November 15, 1981, p. 9.

15. *8 Novosti*, July 3, 1982, p. 9.

16. *NIN*, no. 1645, July 11, 1982, p. 10.

17. *Borba*, September 24, 1982; and *NIN*, no. 1656, September 26, 1982.

18. *Komunist*, July 23, 1982, pp. 12–13.

19. *Politika*, March 30, 1983, p. 8.

20. See Boro Krivokapić, *Jugoslavija i komunisti: adresa Jovana Djordjevića* (Belgrade: Mladost, 1988), p. 133.

21. No one was arguing for the confederalization of the system at that stage.

22. I argued this point and provided documentation in my essay, "The Limits to Political Change in a Communist Country: The Yugoslav Debate, 1980–1986," in *Crossroads*, no. 23 (1987).

23. For further discussion of the Serbian reform proposal, see Wolfgang Höpken, "Party Monopoly and Political Change: The League of Communists since Tito's Death," in Pedro Ramet (ed.), *Yugoslavia in the 1980s* (Boulder, Colo.: Westview Press, 1985).

24. For details of the 1984 plenum, see Ramet, "The Limits," pp. 73–74.

25. Tanjug (September 22, 1985), trans. in FBIS, *Daily Report* (Eastern Europe), September 25, 1985, p. I4.

26. *Politika*, November 23, 1988, p. 10.

27. Ibid., September 13, 1990, p. 1.

28. *Borba*, October 12–15, 1984, summarized in an editorial report for Joint Publications Research Service (JPRS), *East Europe Report*, no. EPS-84-135, November 1, 1984, p. 120.

29. See, for example, the resolutions of the party's Twenty-First Session (October 31, 1985), as reported in Tanjug (November 2, 1985), trans. in FBIS, *Daily Report* (Eastern Europe), November 13, 1985, pp. I1–I27.

30. *New York Times*, December 8, 1985, p. 12.

31. *Danas*, no. 127, July 24, 1984, pp. 22–24; and *Borba*, March 18, 1985, p. 3.

32. *Politika*, December 25, 1981, pp. 1–4.

33. *NIN*, no. 1883, February 1, 1987, p. 9.

34. Ibid., p. 11.

35. *Politika*, March 20, 1987, p. 1.

36. Ibid., March 18, 1987, p. 10, trans. in FBIS, *Daily Report* (Eastern Europe), April 7, 1987, p. I7.

37. *Danas*, July 28, 1987, pp. 12–14, trans. in JPRS, *East Europe Report*, no. EER-87-149 (October 28, 1987), pp. 28–29.

38. Tanjug (November 18, 1985), trans. in FBIS, *Daily Report* (Eastern Europe), November 26, 1985, pp. I1–I9.

39. *Narodna armija*, August 14, 1986, p. 3, translated in FBIS, *Daily Report* (Eastern Europe), August 21, 1986, p. I4.

40. *Vjesnik*, June 25, 1986, pp. 4–5.
41. Ibid., June 30, 1986, p. 2.
42. *Borba*, November 24, 1986, p. 2.
43. Tanjug (July 6, 1988), trans. in FBIS, *Daily Report* (Eastern Europe), July 12, 1988, p. 57.
44. Branko Horvat, *Politička ekonomija socijalizma* (Zagreb, 1984), as summarized (and criticized) in Miladin Korać, "Branko Horvat: 'Politička ekonomija socijalizma'—kritička analiza trećeg dela knjige," in *Socijalizam* 27 (10) (October 1984).
45. See, for example, Hamdija Pozderac, "Bespartijska demokratija kao politički ideal," in *Socijalizam* 30 (6) (June 1987).
46. Interview with Vojislav Vučković, president of the Commission for Constitional Questions of the *Sabor*, Zagreb, September 11, 1989.
47. *Borba*, August 16, 1988, p. 1.
48. Ciril Ribičič and Zdravko Tomac, *Federalizam po mjeri budućnosti* (Zagreb: Globus, 1989), p. 322.
49. Interview with Zdravko Tomac, member of the Commission for Constitutional Reforms of SAWP–Croatia, Zagreb, September 12, 1989.
50. Ribičič and Tomac, *Federalizam*, p. 48.
51. Ibid., p. 66.
52. They are listed in ibid., pp. 89–90.
53. *Borba*, June 1, 1989, p. 7.
54. Tanjug (July 6, 1989), in FBIS, *Daily Report* (Eastern Europe), July 11, 1989, p. 67.
55. Interview with Marijan Korosić, in *NIN*, no. 1959, July 17, 1988, pp. 16–18.
56. Quoted in Tanjug (April 19, 1989), in FBIS, *Daily Report* (Eastern Europe), April 20, 1989, p. 49.
57. Belgrade Domestic Service (May 5, 1989), trans. in FBIS, *Daily Report* (Eastern Europe), May 8, 1989, p. 51.

11. A New Napoleon: The Rise of Slobodan Milošević

1. I expressed some skepticism about the long-term viability of Yugoslavia's political formulas in Pedro Ramet, "Yugoslavia and the Threat of Internal and External Discontents," in *Orbis* 28 (1) (Spring 1984); and Pedro Ramet, "Apocalypse Culture and Social Change in Yugoslavia," in Pedro Ramet (ed.), *Yugoslavia in the 1980s* (Boulder, Colo.: Westview Press, 1985).
2. *Danas*, no. 354, November 29, 1988, p. 18.
3. Ivan Stambolić, *Rasprave o SR Srbiji 1979–1987*. (Zagreb: Globus, 1988), pp. 201–2. See also Ciril Ribičič and Zdravko Tomac, *Federalizam po mjeri budućnosti* (Zagreb: Globus, 1989).
4. Quoted in *Chicago Tribune*, October 17, 1988, p. 2.
5. Quoted in *Washington Post*, February 4, 1990, p. A33.
6. *Pravoslavlje*, July 1, 1990, pp. 1, 3.
7. *Duga*, no. 406, September 16, 1989, pp. 82–83; also *Intervju*, no. 215, September 1, 1989, p. 29.
8. Originally separate, but scarcely distinguishable, resolutions were proposed by Senator Robert Dole and Congressman Joseph DioGuardi. See the *Hearing and Briefing before the Subcommittee on Human Rights and International Organizations of the Committee on Foreign Affairs*, House of Representatives, Ninety-Ninth Congress, Second Session, October 2 and 8, 1986 (U.S. Government Printing Office, 1987).
9. Quoted in *New York Times*, October 14, 1988, p. 7.
10. Belgrade Domestic Service (November 19, 1988), translated in Foreign Broadcast Information Service (FBIS), *Daily Report* (Eastern Europe), November 21, 1988, pp. 72–73.

11. *Eastern Europe Newsletter* 2 (20) (October 12, 1988): 3; and *Chicago Tribune*, October 17, 1988, p. 2. See also Mirjana Kasapović, "Srpski nacionalizam i desni radikalizam," in *Naše teme* 33 (1–2) (1989).

12. *Borba* (Belgrade), May 9, 1989, p. 3, and June 14, 1989, p. 13. Also Boro Krivokapić, *Jugoslavija i komunisti: adresa Jovana Djordjevića* (Belgrade: Mladost, 1988), pp. 91–106.

13. As reported in *Glas koncila* (Zagreb), December 11, 1988, p. 3.

14. *Eastern Europe Newsletter*, 2 (19) (September 28, 1988): 7; and confirmed in many sources.

15. *Le Monde* (Paris), July 12, 1989, trans. in FBIS, *Daily Report* (Eastern Euorpe), July 17, 1989, p. 53.

16. Quoted in *New York Times*, August 6, 1989, p. 12.

17. Quoted in *Profil* (Vienna), October 24, 1988, p. 42.

18. *The Economist* (London), July 23, 1988, p. 44.

19. Tanjug (September 24, 1988), in FBIS, *Daily Report* (Eastern Europe), September 27, 1988, p. 51.

20. *Frankfurter Allgemeine*, October 8, 1988, p. 5; and *Süddeutsche Zeitung* (Munich), October 8–9, 1988, p. 6.

21. For details and background, see Sabrina P. Ramet, *Social Currents in Eastern Europe: The Sources and Meaning of the Great Transformation* (Durham, N.C.: Duke University Press, 1991), chap. 7.

22. Concerning the arrest of Vllasi and the inception of his trial, see *Start*, no. 539, September 16, 1989, pp. 32–35; and *Politika* (Belgrade), October 30, 1989, p. 6.

23. *Politika ekspres* (Belgrade), August 31, 1989, p. 3.

24. Šuvar collected many of his writings and speeches into a two-volume work published in 1988. See Stipe Šuvar, *Socijalizam i nacije*, 2 vols. (Zagreb: Globus, 1988).

25. *Vjesnik* (Zagreb), August 21, 1988, p. 3.

26. *Financial Times*, January 11, 1989, p. 2; *New York Times*, January 12, 1989, p. 6; and *Frankfurter Allgemeine*, January 13, 1989, p. 6.

27. For example, academician Vlado Strugar in the Montenegrin Academy of Sciences and Arts, as reported in *Borba*, November 19–20, 1988, p. 5, trans. in FBIS, *Daily Report* (Eastern Europe), December 5, 1988, p. 57.

28. The illegal activities of the Serbian security service became known in October 1989, and led to an immediate crisis in relations between Bosnia and Serbia. See the report in *Danas*, no. 401, October 24, 1989, pp. 15–16. See also Tanjug (October 30, 1989), trans. in FBIS, *Daily Report* (Eastern Europe), November 1, 1989, p. 68.

29. *Borba*, May 9, 1989, p. 1.

30. See his speech to the 1988 conference of the League of Communists of Serbia, reported in *Vjesnik*, November 22, 1988, p. 4. For an elaborate articulation of Milošević's program, see Radoslav Stojanović, *Jugoslavija, nacije i politika* (Belgrade: Nova knjiga, 1988). See also *Borba*, July 5, 1990, p. 3.

31. *Borba*, July 19, 1989, p. 4, trans. in FBIS, *Daily Report* (Eastern Europe), July 25, 1989, p. 45. *Politika* cited a report of the Serbian state security service that Serbs were emigrating from Bosnia in large numbers and blamed poor interethnic relations for the population movement. See *Politika*, October 27, 1989, p. 6.

32. *Nova Makedonija*, as summarized in Tanjug (March 15, 1989), in FBIS, *Daily Report* (Eastern Europe), March 16, 1989, p. 58.

33. For details and discussion, see my article, "Yugoslavia's Troubled Times," in *Global Affairs* 5 (1) (Winter 1990).

34. *Borba*, February 28, 1989, p. 2, translated in FBIS, *Daily Report* (Eastern Europe), March 3, 1989, p. 71.

35. This is a remarkable achievement considering the demands of the job and the fact that his predecessor, Branko Mikulić, had ended up one of the most unpopular politicians in Yugoslavia. See *The Economist*, June 30, 1990, p. 49.

36. *New York Times*, June 14, 1990, p. A8.

37. *Süddeutsche Zeitung*, June 23–24, 1990, p. 8, and July 7–8, 1990, p. 4.
38. *Frankfurter Allgemeine*, August 2, 1990, p. 1.
39. *Süddeutsche Zeitung*, August 2, 1990, p. 7; and *Financial Times*, August 8, 1990, p. 4.
40. Belgrade Domestic Service (January 6, 1990), trans. FBIS, *Daily Report* (Eastern Europe), January 12, 1990, p. 65. See also the interview with Drašković in *Borba* (January 16, 1990), p. 6, excerpted in FBIS, *Daily Report* (Eastern Europe), January 22, 1990, p. 102; and *Danas*, no. 414 (January 23, 1990), pp. 7–9.
41. Ljubljana Domestic Service (January 14, 1990), trans. in FBIS, *Daily Report* (Eastern Europe), February 13, 1990, pp. 89–90.
42. *Frankfurter Allgemeine*, June 29, 1990, p. 6. This is a reversal of his earlier stance. In October 1988, Milošević had declared that "Serbia has no pretensions to the territory of other republics." Quoted in *Washington Post*, October 18, 1988, p. A22. See also *Vjesnik*, June 26, 1990, p. 5.
43. *Frankfurter Allgemeine*, August 3, 1990, p. 6.
44. *Vjesnik*, July 3, 1990, p. 1. See also *Süddeutsche Zeitung*, June 23–24, 1990, p. 8.
45. *New York Times*, July 6, 1990, p. 44.
46. *Neue Zürcher Zeitung*, September 5, 1990, p. 3; and *New York Times*, September 14, 1990, p. A8.
47. *Frankfurter Allgemeine*, June 15, 1990, p. 8.
48. Serbs accounted for 11.6 percent of Croatia's population in 1981, but according to figures cited by Slaven Letica in 1989, accounted for 17.7 percent of Croatia's high-ranking politicians at the time, 12.5 percent of its economic managers, and 21.4 percent of party political functionaries at the district level. See *Danas*, no. 395, September 12, 1989, p. 19.
49. Ramet, "Yugoslavia and the Threat," p. 114.
50. See the report in *Vjesnik*, July 3, 1990, p. 3.
51. *Vjesnik*, August 28, 1989, p. 5; *NIN*, no. 2018, September 3, 1989, pp. 17–23; *Slobodna Dalmacija* (Split), September 11, 1989, p. 4; and *NIN*, no. 2020, September 17, 1989, pp. 18–20.
52. *Večernje novosti* (Belgrade), September 2, 1989, p. 18, and September 9, 1989, p. 6; *Slobodna Dalmacija*, September 10, 1989, p. 20; *Nedjeljna Dalmacija*, September 10, 1989, p. 6; *Slobodna Dalmacija* September 12, 1989, p. 17; *Start*, no. 539, September 16, 1989, pp. 28–29; *Politika ekspres*, September 22, 1989, p. 10; and *Večernji list*, September 23, 1989, p. 39.
53. *Slobodna Dalmacija*, September 12, 1989, p. 3; *Večernji list*, September 15, 1989, p. 2; and *Večernje novosti*, September 23, 1989, p. 4.
54. Quoted in *International Herald Tribune* (Paris), August 8, 1990, p. 2.
55. *Los Angeles Times*, August 18, 1990, p. A4; *La Opinion* (Los Angeles), August 19, 1990, p. 7; and *New York Times*, August 19, 1990, p. 3, and August 20, 1990, p. A2.
56. *Politika*, August 19, 1990, pp. 7, 10.
57. Tanjug (October 1, 1990), trans. in FBIS, *Daily Report* (Eastern Europe), October 1, 1990.
58. Tanjug (October 1, 1990), trans. in FBIS, *Daily Report* (Eastern Europe), October 2, 1990.
59. For elaboration, see my "Yugoslavia 1987: Stirrings from Below," in *South Slav Journal* 10 (3) (Autumn 1987).

12. The Transformation of Yugoslav Politics

1. Jože Smole, president of the Republic Conference of SAWP-Slovenia, as cited in *Politika*, September 21, 1988, p. 12.
2. Quoted in *New York Times*, October 15, 1988, p. 4.

3. *Borba*, May 31, 1989, p. 5.

4. Ibid., November 7, 1988, p. 11, and March 8, 1989, p. 2.

5. *Süddeutsche Zeitung* (Munich), April 1–2, 1989, p. 8.

6. The full text of the telegram is published in *Politika*, March 1, 1989, p. 17. See also *NIN*, no. 1992, March 5, 1989, p. 32, and no. 1993, March 12, 1989, pp. 39–40.

7. Interview with Rudi Seligo, president of the Slovenian Association of Writers, Ljubljana, September 4, 1989.

8. *Glas koncila* (Zagreb), March 5, 1989, p. 1.

9. See Tanjug (February 27, 1989), trans. in Foreign Broadcast Information Service (FBIS), *Daily Report* (Eastern Europe), March 2, 1989, p. 56.

10. See *Borba*, May 24, 1989, p. 3. Also *Delo*, May 24, 1989, p. 3.

11. Quoted in Ljubljana Domestic Service (June 2, 1989), trans. in FBIS, *Daily Report* (Eastern Europe), June 5, 1989, p. 50.

12. *Delo*, July 6, 1989, p. 3, trans. in FBIS, *Daily Report* (Eastern Europe), July 12, 1989, p. 56.

13. *Oslobodjenje*, as summarized in Tanjug (June 5, 1989), in FBIS, *Daily Report* (Eastern Europe), June 6, 1989, p. 44.

14. *Svet* (Belgrade), September 1989, Special edition, p. 7.

15. For example, *Politika*, September 20, 1989, p. 8.

16. *Delo*, November 21, 1989, p. 5.

17. Tanjug (November 24, 1989), trans. in FBIS, *Daily Report* (Eastern Europe), November 27, 1989, p. 99.

18. Belgrade Domestic Service (November 25, 1989), and Ljubljana Domestic Service (November 25, 1989), trans. consecutively in FBIS, *Daily Report* (Eastern Europe), November 27, 1989, pp. 99–100.

19. Tanjug (December 4, 1989), trans. in FBIS, *Daily Report* (Eastern Europe), December 7, 1989, pp. 115, 117.

20. Belgrade Domestic Service (November 29, 1989), trans. in FBIS, *Daily Report* (Eastern Europe), November 30, 1989, p. 84; and Belgrade Domestic Service (December 13, 1989), trans. in FBIS, *Daily Report* (Eastern Europe), December 15, 1989, p. 81.

21. *Borba*, December 22, 1989, p. 5.

22. Tanjug (February 22, 1990), trans. in FBIS, *Daily Report* (Eastern Europe), February 23, 1990, pp. 85–86.

23. *Kosovo 1389–1989*, Special edition of the *Serbian Literary Quarterly*, nos. 1–3 (1989): 45.

24. *Danas*, no. 394, September 5, 1989, p. 33; and Tanjug (December 7, 1989), trans. in FBIS, *Daily Report* (Eastern Europe), December 15, 1989, p. 87.

25. Specifically, Novak Kilibarda, president of the pro-Serbian Montenegrin People's party, said that in the event of the confederalization of Yugoslavia, Montenegro should annex the "eastern parts" of Bosnia-Herzegovina. *Borba*, November 1, 1990, p. 4.

26. *Borba*, July 16, 1990, p. 3.

27. Tanjug (March 5, 1990), trans. in FBIS, *Daily Report* (Eastern Europe), March 6, 1990, p. 64.

28. Milošević's comments are cited in chapter 11. Tudjman's comments are cited in *Borba*, June 22, 1990, p. 4.

29. *Borba*, May 10, 1989, p. 3.

30. Belgrade Domestic Service (May 17, 1989), trans. in FBIS, *Daily Report* (Eastern Europe), May 18, 1989, p. 60.

31. See, for instance, *NIN*, no. 1885, February 15, 1987, pp. 16–19.

32. *Borba*, July 16, 1990, p. 4.

33. Dennison Rusinow, "Nationalities Policy and the 'National Question,' " in Pedro Ramet (ed.), *Yugoslavia in the 1980s* (Boulder, Colo.: Westview Press, 1985), p. 141.

34. See discussions from a Croatian point of view, in *Danas*, no. 359, January 3, 1989, p. 29; and *Glas koncila*, July 30, 1989, p. 5, September 24, 1989, p. 3, and October 8, 1989, p. 2.

35. The complete text was published in *Glas koncila*, February 19, 1989. An English translation was published in *South Slav Journal* 11 (4) (Winter 1988/89): 56.

36. The text of the interview was republished in many places, including in *Večernje novosti* (Belgrade), September 7, 1989, p. 19.

37. For relevant reports, see *Večernji list* (Zagreb), September 11, 1989, p. 4; *Slobodna Dalmacija*, September 12, 1989, p. 2; *Slobodna Dalmacija*, September 13, 1989, p. 4; and *Večernji list* September 14, 1989, p. 4.

38. *Slobodna Dalmacija*, September 12, 1989, p. 3.

39. *Večernji list*, September 15, 1989, p. 5; and *Večernje novosti*, September 23, 1989, p. 4.

40. *Nedjeljna Dalmacija* (September 6–7, 1989), reprinted in *Borba*, September 8, 1989, p. 13, trans. in FBIS, *Daily Report* (Eastern Europe), September 21, 1989, pp. 56–57.

41. *Nedjeljna Dalmacija*, September 17, 1989, pp. 11–12.

42. *Pravoslavlje*, March 15, 1989, p. 5, and April 15, 1989, pp. 12–13.

43. *Vjesnik*, September 10, 1989, p. 5; *Večernje novosti*, September 21, 1989, p. 2; and *Slobodna Dalmacija*, September 22, 1989, p. 16.

44. *Slobodna Dalmacija*, September 11, 1989, p. 32.

45. *Večernje novosti*, September 11, 1989, p. 12; and *Večernji list*, September 11, 1989, p. 17.

46. Tanjug (July 19, 1989), in FBIS, *Daily Report* (Eastern Europe), July 19, 1989, p. 52.

47. Viktor Meier says 60 percent; France Tomsic says 70 percent. See Viktor Meier, "Jugoslawiens Krise wird politisch," in *Schweizer Monatshefte* 68 (2) (February 1988): 101; and interview with France Tomšić, chair of the Slovenian Social Democratic Union, in *Wiener Zeitung*, March 14, 1989, p. 3, trans. in FBIS, *Daily Report* (Eastern Europe), March 15, 1989, p. 74.

48. *Vjesnik*, June 26, 1986, p. 2; and Tanjug (October 26, 1989), trans. in FBIS, *Daily Report* (Eastern Europe), November 1, 1989, p. 74.

49. *Frankfurter Allgemeine*, July 17, 1989, p. 2; and *Narodna armija*, as reprinted in *Večernji list*, September 8, 1989, p. 2.

50. Krstan Milošević, executive secretary of the presidency of the Committee OCK JNA, as reported in *Večernje novosti*, September 26, 1989, p. 6. Also *Politika ekspres*, September 26, 1989, p. 4.

51. Ibid.

52. Tanjug (October 25, 1989), in FBIS, *Daily Report* (Eastern Europe), October 26, 1989, p. 81. See also *Narodna armija*, September 21, 1989, p. 2; and *Politika*, October 3, 1989, p. 9.

53. Tanjug (October 26, 1989), trans. in FBIS, *Daily Report* (Eastern Europe), November 1, 1989, p. 74.

54. Tanjug (December, 1989), trans. in FBIS, *Daily Report* (Eastern Europe), January 11, 1990, p. 87.

55. *Vjesnik*, July 5, 1990, p. 1.

56. Tanjug (December 22, 1989), trans. in FBIS, *Daily Report* (Eastern Europe), December 22, 1989, p. 85.

57. Tanjug (March 25, 1990), trans. in FBIS, *Daily Report* (Eastern Europe), March 27, 1990, p. 62.

58. See, for instance, Belgrade Domestic Service (March 9, 1990), trans. in FBIS, *Daily Report* (Eastern Europe), March 23, 1990, p. 95.

59. Quoted in *New York Times*, September 23, 1990, p. 15.

60. Pedro Ramet, "Apocalypse Culture and Social Change in Yugoslavia," in Pedro Ramet (ed.), *Yugoslavia in the 1980s* (Boulder, Colo.: Westview Press, 1985), pp. 3–4.

61. Ibid., p. 3.

62. See Pedro Ramet, "Yugoslavia's Debate over Democratization," in *Survey* 25 (3) (Summer 1980).

63. Tanjug (October 8, 1988), trans. in FBIS, *Daily Report* (Eastern Europe), October 11, 1988, p. 27.

64. Sabrina P. Ramet, *Social Currents in Eastern Europe: The Sources and Meaning of the Great Transformation* (Durham, N.C.: Duke University Press, 1991), chap. 14.

65. See *Borba*, June 29, 1990, p. 4, July 3, 1990, p. 3, and July 10, 1990, p. 1.

66. *Neue Zürcher Zeitung*, September 1, 1990, p. 3.

67. See Radoslav Stojanović, *Jugoslavija, nacije i politika* (Belgrade: Nova knjiga, 1988); and Slobodan Samardžić, *Jugoslavija pred iskušenjem federalizma* (Belgrade: Stručna knjiga, 1990).

68. See Zagreb Domestic Service (October 17, 1990), trans. in FBIS, *Daily Report* (Eastern Europe), October 18, 1990, p. 58; and Tanjug (October 19, 1990), trans. in FBIS, *Daily Report* (Eastern Europe), October 22, 1990, p. 53.

69. *Frankfurter Allgemeine*, January 7, 1991, p. 1.

70. *Vjesnik*, October 23, 1990, p. 2; and *Süddeutsche Zeitung* (Munich), November 10/11, 1990, p. 9.

71. Details in Sabrina P. Ramet, *Balkan Babel: Politics, Culture, and Religion in Yugoslavia* (Boulder, Colo.: Westview Press, 1992), ch.3.

72. Text in *Vjesnik*, October 12, 1990, p. 5.

73. *Delo* (Ljubljana), October 11, 1990, p. 1, trans. in FBIS, *Daily Report* (Eastern Europe), October 17, 1990, p. 53.

74. *Neue Zürcher Zeitung*, January 26, 1991, p. 4.

75. *Oslobodjenje* (Sarajevo), November 12, 1990, p. 1.

76. Tanjug (November 27, 1990), trans. in FBIS, *Daily Report* (Eastern Europe), November 29, 1990, p. 75.

77. *The Economist* (London), February 2, 1991, p. 44.

78. *Neue Zürcher Zeitung* (December 6, 1990), p. 3.

79. Quoted in *Croatian Democracy Project*, News release, December 12, 1990.

80. *New York Times*, February 1, 1991, p. A8.

81. *Daily Telegraph*, December 4, 1990, p. 11; and *New York Times*, January 20, 1991, p. 7.

82. *Süddeutsche Zeitung*, January 19/20, 1991, p. 9; confirmed in *Daily Telegraph*, January 23, 1991, p. 13; reconfirmed in *Neue Zürcher Zeitung*, January 23, 1991, p. 4.

83. *New York Times*, January 21, 1991, p. A2; *Daily Telegraph*, January 25, 1991, p. 10; and *Neue Zürcher Zeitung*, January 26, 1991, p. 4.

84. *Neue Zürcher Zeitung*, January 29, 1991, p. 4.

85. *Il Messaggero* (Rome), January 27, 1991, p. 8.

86. *Süddeutsche Zeitung*, January 26/27, 1991, p. 11.

87. *Seattle Times*, February 9, 1991, p. A5; and *Neue Zürcher Zeitung*, February 5, 1991, p. 1.

88. See my "Yugoslavia 1987: Stirrings from Below," in *South Slav Journal* 10 (3) (Autumn 1987).

89. Interview with a Yugoslav feminist, Belgrade, September 1989.

13. Civil War

1. Tanjug (July 16, 1991), in FBIS, *Daily Report* (Eastern Europe), July 17, 1991, p. 31.

2. Tanjug (July 21, 1991), in FBIS, *Daily Report* (Eastern Europe), July 22, 1991, p. 42; Tanjug (July 22, 1991), in FBIS, *Daily Report* (Eastern Europe), July 23, 1991, p. 30; and Tanjug (July 24, 1991), in FBIS, *Daily Report* (Eastern Europe), July 25, 1991, p. 49.

3. *Borba* (Belgrade), May 28, 1991, p. 10.

4. *Los Angeles Times* (July 1, 1991), p. A6.

5. Tanjug (June 13, 1991), trans. in FBIS, *Daily Report* (Eastern Europe), June 14, 1991, p. 41; partially confirmed in *Seattle Post-Intelligencer* (September 2, 1991), p. A2.

6. PAP (Warsaw), August 7, 1991, in FBIS, *Daily Report* (Eastern Europe), August 8, 1991, p. 20.

7. Austria's denial—by Peter Schieder, president of the Foreign Policy Committee of the Austrian parliament—was reported by Tanjug (August 7, 1991), in FBIS, *Daily Report* (Eastern Europe), August 8, 1991, p. 28.

8. *Der Spiegel* (August 5, 1991), pp. 124–26, trans. in FBIS, *Daily Report* (August 5, 1991), p. 52.

9. *Profil* (Vienna), June 24, 1991, p. 74.

10. Including this writer. See Sabrina P. Ramet, "The Breakup of Yugoslavia," in *Global Affairs* 6 (2) (Spring 1991), esp. pp. 97, 101–102.

11. On Baker, see *Neue Zürcher Zeitung* (June 22/23, 1991), p. 7; regarding Galvin, see Tanjug (June 1, 1991), in FBIS, *Daily Report* (Eastern Europe), June 3, 1991, p. 43.

12. This and subsequent figures come from *Statisticki godišnjak Jugoslavije 1983* 30 (Belgrade: Savezni Zavod za Statistiku, 1983), p. 439.

13. Ibid.

14. *Uj Magyarorszag* (Budapest), July 26, 1991, p. 4, trans. in FBIS, *Daily Report* (Eastern Europe), July 31, 1991, p. 58.

15. Kossuth Radio Network (Budapest), July 23, 1991, trans. in FBIS, *Daily Report* (Eastern Europe), July 24, 1991, p. 42.

16. Bozović, in an interview with the Budapest daily, *Magyar Hirlap*, quoted in Tanjug (July 22, 1991), in FBIS, *Daily Report* (Eastern Europe), July 23, 1991, p. 41.

17. Radio Slovenia Network (Ljubljana), July 16, 1991, trans. in FBIS, *Daily Report* (Eastern Europe), July 17, 1991, p. 42.

18. Tanjug (August 26, 1991), in FBIS, *Daily Report* (Eastern Europe), August 27, 1991, p. 40.

19. *Bujku* (Pristina), August 23, 1991, p. 2, trans. in FBIS, *Daily Report* (Eastern Europe), August 28, 1991, p. 38.

20. Oesterreich Eins Radio Network (Vienna), August 6, 1991, trans. in FBIS, *Daily Report* (Eastern Europe), August 7, 1991, p. 31.

21. As quoted in Tanjug (July 31, 1991), trans. in FBIS, *Daily Report* (Eastern Europe), August 1, 1991, p. 41.

22. Radio Sarajevo Network (August 1, 1991), trans. in FBIS, *Daily Report* (August 2, 1991), p. 57.

23. Quoted in *Los Angeles Times* (August 20, 1991), p. A23.

24. Quoted in *Financial Times* (August 6, 1991), p. 17.

25. See Franjo Tudjman's controversial disputations in his *Bespuća povijesne zbiljnosti* (Zagreb: Nakladni Zavod Matice Hrvatske, 1989).

26. See discussion of the Black Legion in *Manchester Guardian Weekly* (September 22, 1991), p. 13.

27. Jovan Marjanović, *Draža Mihailović izmedju Britanaca i Nemaca*, vol. 1 (Zagreb: Globus, 1979), pp. 243–51; confirmed in Jozo Tomasevich, *The Chetniks: War and Revolution in Yugoslavia, 1941–1945* (Stanford, Calif.: Stanford University Press, 1975), pp. 226–31.

28. On Mihailović's approaches to Pavelic to intensify collaboration, in the waning months of the war, see Tomasevich, *The Chetniks*, pp. 452–53. On the annihilation of the Chetniks in 1945, see Walter R. Roberts, *Tito, Mihailovic, and the Allies, 1941–1945* (New Brunswick, N.J.: Rutgers University Press, 1973), p. 307.

29. Vladimir Zerjavić, *Gubici stanovništva Jugoslavije u drugom svjetskom ratu* (Zagreb: Jugoslavensko Viktimološko Društvo, 1989), pp. 61–66.

30. Marjanović, *Draža Mihailović*, pp. 196–99.

31. Roberts, *Tito, Mihailović*, p. 306.

32. For war casualties in Kosovo, see Zerjavić, *Gubici*, p. 69.

33. On the Russian Corps, see Nikolai Tolstoy, *The Minister and the Massacres* (London: Century Hutchinson, 1986), p. 17.

34. Regarding Macedonia's endorsement of the confederal option, see *Nova Makedonija* (Skopje), June 8, 1991, p. 17, trans. in FBIS, *Daily Report* (Eastern Europe), July 12, 1991, p. 43.

35. *NIN* (July 26, 1991), p. 13.

36. Radio Slovenia Network (Ljubljana), June 26, 1991, trans. in FBIS, *Daily Report* (Eastern Europe), June 27, 1991, p. 47; Radio Belgrade Network (June 26, 1991), trans. in ibid., p. 50; Tanjug (June 28, 1991), trans. in FBIS, *Daily Report* (Eastern Europe), June 28, 1991, p. 35; Radio Belgrade Network (June 28, 1991), trans. in ibid., pp. 35–36; *Süddeutsche Zeitung* (Munich), June 29/30, 1991, p. 1; and *Neue Zürcher Zeitung* (July 16, 1991), p. 1.

37. *Neue Zürcher Zeitung* (July 7/8, 1991), p. 1.

38. Radio Slovenia Network (July 5, 1991), trans. in FBIS, *Daily Report* (Eastern Europe), July 8, 1991, p. 41.

39. *Neue Zürcher Zeitung* (July 12, 1991), pp. 1, 3, (July 14/15, 1991), pp. 1–2, (July 16, 1991), p. 1, and (July 21/22, 1991), pp. 1–2; *Frankfurter Allgemeine* (July 20, 1991), p. 1; and CNN Headline News (October 26, 1991).

40. *New York Times* (June 27, 1991), p. A7.

41. *Pravda* (Moscow), June 27, 1991, p. 5, trans. in *Current Digest of the Soviet Press* (CDSP) 43 (26) (July 31, 1991), p. 19.

42. Quoted in Tanjug (July 3, 1991), in FBIS, *Daily Report* (Eastern Europe), July 5, 1991, p. 53.

43. Radio Belgrade Network (June 26, 1991), trans. in FBIS, *Daily Report* (Eastern Europe), June 27, 1991, p. 56.

44. Quoted in Tanjug (June 30, 1991), in FBIS, *Daily Report* (Eastern Europe), July 2, 1991, p. 71.

45. Radio Slovenia Network (July 6, 1991), in FBIS, *Daily Report* (Eastern Europe), July 8, 1991, p. 56.

46. *Neue Zürcher Zeitung* (July 12, 1991), p. 1.

47. Quoted in *Pravda* (July 12, 1991), p. 4, trans. in CDSP, 43 (28) (August 14, 1991), p. 20.

48. Quoted in *Izvestiia* (Moscow), July 22, 1991, p. 19, trans. in CDSP 43 (29) (August 21, 1991), p. 20.

49. Kossuth Radio Network (Budapest), July 24, 1991, trans. in FBIS, *Daily Report* (Eastern Europe), July 25, 1991, p. 55; also MTV Television Network (Budapest), July 9, 1991, trans. in FBIS, *Daily Report* (Eastern Europe), July 11, 1991, p. 38.

50. This latter attack occurred in August. Radio Croatia Network (August 22, 1991), trans. in FBIS, *Daily Report* (Eastern Europe), August 23, 1991, p. 38.

51. Tanjug (July 13, 1991), trans. in FBIS, *Daily Report* (Eastern Europe), July 15, 1991, p. 50.

52. Radio Belgrade Network (July 2, 1991), trans. in FBIS, *Daily Report* (Eastern Europe), July 3, 1991, p. 50; Radio Belgrade Network (July 2, 1991), trans. in FBIS, *Daily Report* (Eastern Europe), July 3, 1991, p. 55; and Tanjug (July 3, 1991), trans. in FBIS, *Daily Report* (Eastern Europe), July 5, 1991, p. 53.

53. Radio Belgrade Network (July 24, 1991), trans. in FBIS, *Daily Report* (Eastern Europe), July 25, 1991, p. 55.

54. Tanjug (July 7, 1991), in FBIS, *Daily Report* (Eastern Europe), July 3, 1991, p. 36.

55. *NIN* (April 12, 1991), p. 41.

56. *Danas* (July 16, 1991), p. 8.

57. The siege of Vukovar is reported and confirmed in many sources, including the following: Radio Belgrade Network (August 26, 1991), trans. in FBIS, *Daily Report*

(Eastern Europe), August 27, 1991, p. 37; Radio Croatia Network (Zagreb), August 26, 1991, trans. in FBIS, *Daily Report* (Eastern Europe), August 27, 1991, p. 36; Radio Belgrade Network (August 28, 1991) and Radio Croatia Network (August 28, 1991)—both trans. in FBIS, *Daily Report* (Eastern Europe), August 28, 1991, p. 35.

58. Foreign Press Bureau, Republic of Croatia (hereafter, FPB/RC), Press Release 10 (September 19, 1991).

59. *Pravoslavlje* (Belgrade), July 15, 1991, p. 8.

60. Ibid. (July 1, 1991), p. 9, (July 15, 1991), p. 9, (August 1–15, 1991), p. 14, and (September 1, 1991), p. 9.

61. Ibid. (August 1–15, 1990), p. 3, (October 1, 1990), p. 10, and (November 15, 1990), p. 3.

62. Ibid. (August 1–15, 1991), p. 18.

63. *Danas* (June 18, 1991), pp. 63–65 (quoted from p. 64).

64. *New York Times* (August 27, 1991), p. A3; and FPB/RC, Press Release 21 (September 24, 1991).

65. Ibid. 42 (September 23, 1991). Note: the numeration of the Press Releases appears to be inconsistent.

66. Ibid. 18 (September 23, 1991).

67. Ibid. 7 (September 17, 1991).

68. *New York Times* (August 27, 1991), p. A3.

69. Ibid. (September 22, 1991), p. 16.

70. Radio Belgrade Network (August 26, 1991), trans. in FBIS, *Daily Report* (Eastern Europe), August 27, 1991, p. 40.

71. Excerpt on the CNN Headline News, October 4, 1991.

72. A recent book devoted to a discussion of Bosnian national identity is *Bosna i Bosnjaštvo* (Sarajevo: n.p., 1990).

73. Radio Belgrade Network (May 10, 1991), trans. in FBIS, *Daily Report* (Eastern Europe), May 13, 1991, p. 56; and Tanjug (June 11, 1991), in FBIS, *Daily Report* (Eastern Europe), June 13, 1991, p. 42.

74. *Vreme* (Belgrade, September 30, 1991), p. 5.

75. Tanjug (June 18, 1991), in FBIS, *Daily Report* (Eastern Europe), June 20, 1991, p. 43.

76. Tanjug (July 10, 1991), in FBIS, *Daily Report* (Eastern Europe), July 11, 1991, p. 42.

77. Tanjug (July 10–11, 1991), trans. in FBIS, *Daily Report* (Eastern Europe), July 11, 1991, pp. 42–43.

78. Tanjug (July 19, 1991), in FBIS, *Daily Report* (Eastern Europe), July 22, 1991, p. 48.

79. For a brief account of Zulfikarpašić's life, see *Neue Zürcher Zeitung* (June 29, 1990). For an expostulation of his ideas, see *Bosanski Muslimani: Čimbenik mira izmedju Srba i Hrvata*, Interview Adila Zulfikarpašića (Zürich: Bosanski Institut, 1986); and Fahrudi Djapo and Tihomir Loza, *Povratak u Bosnu: Razgovori sa Adilom Zulfikarpašićem* (Ljubljana: Karantanija, 1990).

80. Tanjug (July 31, 1991), in FBIS, *Daily Report* (Eastern Europe), August 1, 1991, p. 41.

81. Quoted in ibid.

82. Statement by Radovan Karadžić, quoting Zulfikarpašić, on RTV Belgrade (August 1, 1991), trans. in FBIS, *Daily Report* (Eastern Europe), August 2, 1991, p. 57.

83. Radio Sarajevo Network (July 31, 1991), trans. in FBIS, *Daily Report* (Eastern Europe), August 1, 1991, p. 40.

84. Tanjug (August 5, 1991), in FBIS, *Daily Report* (Eastern Europe), August 6, 1991, p. 44.

85. Tanjug (August 6, 1991), trans. in FBIS, *Daily Report* (Eastern Europe), August 7, 1991, p. 44.

86. Radio Belgrade Network (August 11, 1991), trans. in FBIS, *Daily Report* (Eastern Europe), August 13, 1991, p. 35.

87. Tanjug (August 7, 1991), in FBIS, *Daily Report* (Eastern Europe), August 8, 1991, p. 41; and Tanjug (August 8, 1991), trans. in FBIS, *Daily Report* (Eastern Europe), August 9, 1991, p. 44.

88. Šešelj, in interview with *Der Spiegel* (see note 8, above), p. 51.

89. *New York Times* (September 22, 1991), p. 4.

90. Quoted in *Financial Times* (October 16, 1991), p. 16. This account is confirmed in *Neue Zürcher Zeitung* (October 17, 1991), pp. 1–2. See also *Neue Zürcher Zeitung* (October 19, 1991), p. 2.

91. Quoted in *Financial Times* (October 16, 1991), p. 16.

92. In interview with *Danas* (July 16, 1991), p. 29.

93. *Danas* (July 9, 1991), p. 38.

94. *Politika* (July 3, 1991), as summarized in Tanjug (July 31, 1991), in FBIS, *Daily Report* (Eastern Europe), August 1, 1991, p. 33.

95. Tanjug (August 12, 1991), in FBIS, *Daily Report* (Eastern Europe), August 13, 1991, p. 33.

96. *Večernji list*, as summarized in Tanjug (August 12, 1991), in FBIS, *Daily Report* (Eastern Europe), August 14, 1991, p. 34.

97. *Vjesnik* and *Večernji list*, as summarized in Tanjug (August 5, 1991), in FBIS, *Daily Report* (Eastern Europe), August 6, 1991, p. 34.

98. For details, see *Danas* (June 11, 1991), pp. 26–27.

99. As summarized in Tanjug (July 31, 1991), in FBIS, *Daily Report* (Eastern Europe), August 1, 1991, p. 35.

100. *Politika* (August 25, 1991), quoted in Tanjug (August 25, 1991), in FBIS, *Daily Report* (Eastern Europe), August 27, 1991, p. 41.

101. Ibid.

102. Tanjug (August 27, 1991), in FBIS, *Daily Report* (Eastern Europe), August 28, 1991, p. 40.

103. Radio Belgrade Network (August 6, 1991), trans. in FBIS, *Daily Report* (Eastern Europe), August 7, 1991, p. 43.

104. *Nova Makedonija* (August 14, 1991), summarized in Tanjug (August 15, 1991), in FBIS, *Daily Report* (Eastern Europe), August 15, 1991, p. 45.

105. *Nova Makedonija* (August 15, 1991), summarized in Tanjug (August 15, 1991), in FBIS, *Daily Report* (Eastern Europe), August 16, 1991, p. 28.

106. Tanjug (August 22, 1991), in FBIS, *Daily Report* (Eastern Europe), August 22, 1991, p. 29.

107. Ibid.

108. *Financial Times* (October 14, 1991), p. 2.

109. Šešelj, in interview with *Der Spiegel* (see note 8, above), pp. 51, 52, 53.

110. *NIN* (April 5, 1991), p. 41.

111. Ibid., pp. 41, 43.

112. Ibid. (April 12, 1991), p. 42.

113. For example, in ibid. (July 26, 1991), p. 15.

114. Radio Slovenia Network (August 20, 1991), trans. in FBIS, *Daily Report* (Eastern Europe), August 21, 1991, p. 33.

115. *NIN* (April 12, 1991), p. 40.

116. *Borba* (August 12, 1991), quoted in Tanjug (August 12, 1991), in FBIS, *Daily Report* (Eastern Europe), August 14, 1991, p. 39, bracketed item supplied by FBIS.

117. *NIN* (July 26, 1991), p. 14.

118. Ibid.

119. Tanjug (August 7, 1991), in FBIS, *Daily Report* (Eastern Europe), August 8, 1991, p. 40. I have substituted "dictatorial" for Tanjug's "dictatorship."

120. *Neue Zürcher Zeitung* (October 4, 1991), p. 4.

121. *Danas* (July 9, 1991), pp. 36–37.
122. *NIN* (July 19, 1991), p. 15.
123. Ibid., p. 16.
124. Ibid. (April 5, 1991), p. 34.
125. *Neue Zürcher Zeitung* (October 4, 1991), p. 3.
126. Tanjug (July 15, 1991), in FBIS, *Daily Report* (Eastern Europe), July 16, 1991, p. 31.
127. Tanjug (June 26, 1991), in FBIS, *Daily Report* (Eastern Europe), June 27, 1991, p. 57.
128. AFP (Paris), June 26, 1991, in FBIS, *Daily Report* (Eastern Europe), June 27, 1991, p. 58.
129. Ibid.
130. Ibid.
131. Ibid.; and *The Independent* (London), September 16, 1991, p. 6.
132. Tanjug (June 26, 1991), in FBIS, *Daily Report* (Eastern Europe), June 27, 1991, p. 57.
133. AFP (June 26, 1991), in FBIS, *Daily Report* (Eastern Europe), June 27, 1991, p. 58.
134. PAP (Warsaw), June 26, 1991, in FBIS, *Daily Report* (Eastern Europe), June 27, 1991, p. 26.
135. Kossuth Radio Network (June 29, 1991), trans. in FBIS, *Daily Report* (Eastern Europe), July 1, 1991, p. 13.
136. The term "Fourth Reich" has become a recurrent one in the recent Serbian press. For one example, see *Politika ekspres* (Belgrade), August 2, 1991, as summarized in Tanjug (August 2, 1991), in FBIS, *Daily Report* (Eastern Europe), August 5, 1991, p. 53.
137. *Politika ekspres* (July 4, 1991), quoted in Deutsche Presse Agentur (DPA) (Hamburg), July 4, 1991, in FBIS, *Daily Report* (Eastern Europe), July 8, 1991, p. 59.
138. Quoted in ibid.
139. In an interview with RTV Belgrade (July 3, 1991), trans. in FBIS, *Daily Report* (Eastern Europe), August 1, 1991, p. 31.
140. Vienna ORF Television Network (August 12, 1991), trans. in FBIS, *Daily Report* (Eastern Europe), August 13, 1991, p. 34.
141. MTI (Budapest), August 28, 1991, in FBIS, *Daily Report* (Eastern Europe), August 29, 1991, p. 9.
142. AFP (Paris), July 5, 1991, in FBIS, *Daily Report* (Eastern Europe), July 5, 1991, p. 1.
143. As reported in Radio Croatia Network in Albanian (August 14, 1991), trans. in FBIS, *Daily Report* (Eastern Europe), August 16, 1991, p. 27.
144. Radio Croatian Network (August 19, 1991), trans. in FBIS, *Daily Report* (Eastern Europe), August 20, 1991, p. 40.
145. BTA (Sofia), July 5, 1991, in FBIS, *Daily Report* (Eastern Europe), July 8, 1991, p. 2.
146. *Neue Zürcher Zeitung* (September 10, 1991), p. 4.
147. *Demokratsiya* (Sofia), July 5, 1991, p. 4, trans. in FBIS, *Daily Report* (Eastern Europe), July 10, 1991, p. 16.
148. On Bosnia's request for Turkish support, see Tanjug (July 18, 1991), in FBIS, *Daily Report* (Eastern Europe), July 19, 1991, p. 43.
149. *Wall Street Journal* (September 26, 1991), p. A1.
150. Ibid. (September 25, 1991), p. A5.
151. *NIN* (July 19, 1991), p. 29.
152. Ibid.
153. *Daily Telegraph* (October 2, 1991), p. 13.
154. FPB/RC (September 20, 1991), p. 1.

155. *Neue Zürcher Zeitung* (October 5, 1991), p. 1.
156. Ibid. (October 6/7, 1991), p. 1.
157. Quoted in *New York Times* (October 5, 1991), p. 2.
158. *Neue Zürcher Zeitung* (October 6/7, 1991), p. 2.
159. Ibid.
160. Ibid. (October 11, 1991), p. 1
161. *Süddeutsche Zeitung* (October 12/13, 1991), p. 1.
162. *Neue Zürcher Zeitung* (October 13/14, 1991), p. 2; confirmed in *Süddeutsche Zeitung* (October 12/13, 1991), p. 1.
163. *Süddeutsche Zeitung* (October 12/13, 1991), p. 1.
164. *Neue Zürcher Zeitung* (October 13/14, 1991), p. 4.
165. Ibid. (October 20/21, 1991), p. 1.
166. Ibid. (October 19, 1991), p. 2.
167. *Il Messaggero* (Rome), October 18, 1991, p. 4; and *New York Times* (October 25, 1991), p. A7.
168. Quoted in *New York Times* (October 26, 1991), p. 5.
169. *Süddeutsche Zeitung* (August 7, 1991), p. 10.
170. Quoted in *New York Times* (October 28, 1991), p. A5.
171. On the last point, see Tanjug (July 15, 1991), in FBIS, *Daily Report* (Eastern Europe), July 16, 1991, p. 31.
172. Tanjug (August 19, 1991), in FBIS, *Daily Report* (Eastern Europe), August 21, 1991, p. 31.
173. Quoted in Tanjug (August 20, 1991), in FBIS, *Daily Report* (Eastern Europe), August 21, 1991, p. 31.

14. Conclusion

1. See George Liska, *International Equilibrium* (Cambridge, Mass.: Harvard University Press, 1957), p. 36, cited by William H. Riker, *The Theory of Political Coalitions* (New Haven: Yale University Press, 1962), pp. 163–64.
2. Riker, however, argues that "there are circumstances in which the weakest ought not oppose the strongest. Indeed there are even circumstances in which the weakest should join the strongest" (Riker, *Theory of Political Coalitions*, p. 170).
3. Arthur Bentley, *The Process of Government* (1908), as quoted in Jerry Hough, "The Party Apparatchiki," in *Interest Groups in Soviet Politics*, ed. H. Gordon Skilling and Franklyn Griffiths (Princeton, N.J.: Princeton University Press, 1972), p. 48.
4. *Vjesnik*, November 7, 1970, as quoted in Ivan Perić, *Ideje 'masovnog pokreta' u Hrvatskoj* (Zagreb: Političke teme, 1974), p. 168.
5. In his classic work on interethnic relations, E. K. Francis argues that a multiethnic political community organized on federal lines cannot hope to attain more than a "labile equilibrium," and that even that can be achieved only by establishing the institutional basis for an operative "balance of power" among the rival groups. See Francis, *Interethnic Relations* (New York: Elsevier Scientific Publishing, 1976), p. 390, propositions 31–32. For a discussion of notions of "legitimacy" and "quasi-legitimacy" in the Yugoslav context, see Pedro Ramet, "Yugoslavia's Debate over Democratization," Survey 25 (3) (Summer 1980).
6. Pedro Ramet, "Yugoslavia's Troubled Times," in *Global Affairs* 5 (1) (Winter 1990): 79.

SELECTED BIBLIOGRAPHY

Official Documents/Party (in chronological order)

Treći plenum CK SK Srbije, januar 1966. Belgrade: Sedma sila, 1966.

"Thesenentwurf zur Reorganisation des Bundes der Kommunisten Jugoslawiens" (April 27, 1967). *Osteuropäische Rundschau* 13 (6) (June 1967): 37–40.

Šesti kongres Saveza komunista Srbije. Belgrade: Komunist, 1968.

Peti kongres Saveza komunista Bosne i Hercegovine (Sarajevo, 9–11 januara 1969). Sarajevo: Oslobodjenje, 1969.

Nacrti dokumenata za Deveti kongres SKJ. Belgrade: Komunist, 1969.

Deseta konferencija Saveza komunista Srbije za Kosovo i Metohiju. Priština: Rilindja, 1969.

Deveti kongres Saveza komunista Jugoslavije (Beograd, 11–13 III, 1969)—Stenografske beleške. 6 vols. Belgrade: Komunist, 1970.

Sedma sednica Predsedništva Saveza komunista Jugoslavije. Belgrade: Komunist, 1970.

Reforma Saveza komunista Bosne i Hercegovine. Sarajevo: Studijski centar gradske konferencije SK BiH, 1971.

Dalji razvoj i idejnopolitičko delovanje Saveza komunista SAP Vojvodine. 2 vols. Novi Sad, December 1971.

Aktivnost Saveza komunista Srbije u borbi protiv nacionalizma i šovinizma u SR Srbiji. Belgrade: Komunist, 1972.

Savez komunista Hrvatske, Centralni komitet. *Izvještaj o stanju u Savezu komunista Hrvatske u odnosu na prodor nacionalizma u njegove redove*. Zagreb: Informativna služba CK SKH, May 1972.

Razgovori o platformi za deseti kongres SKJ. Belgrade: Komunist, 1973.

Sedmi kongres Saveza komunista Hrvatske (Zagreb, 7–9 IV 1974)—Stenografske bilješke. 3 vols. Zagreb, 1974.

Deseti kongres Saveza komunista Jugoslavije (Beograd, 27–30 V, 1974)—Stenografske beleške. 4 vols. Belgrade: Komunist, 1975.

Savez komunista Srbije, Centralni komitet. *Savez komunista i aktuelna pitanja idejne borbe*. Belgrade: Komunist, 1976.

Deveta sjednica CK SK Bosne i Hercegovine. Sarajevo: Mala politička biblioteka, 1977.

Osnovne teze za pripremu stavova i dokumenata jedanaestog kongresa Saveza komunista Jugoslavije. Belgrade: Komunist, February 1978.

Osmi kongres Saveza komunista Hrvatske (Zagreb, 24–26 travnja 1978)—Stenografske bilješke. 4 vols. Zagreb: Zrinski, 1978.

Osmi kongres Saveza komunista Srbije. Belgrade: Komunist, 1978.

Jedanaesti kongres Saveza komunista Jugoslavije (Beograd, 20–23 juna 1978)—Magnetofonske beleške. 5 vols. Belgrade: Komunist, 1981.

Osmi kongres SK BiH. Sarajevo: Oslobodjenje, 1982.

5. Sednica CKSKJ. Aktuelni idejno-politički problemi i zadaci Saveza komunista Jugoslavije. Belgrade: Komunist, 1983.

15. Sednica CKSKJ. Obeležavanje Pedesetogodišnjice Četvrte zemaljske konferencije KPJ. Donošenje Odluke o pripremama 13. kongresa SKJ. Belgrade: Komunist, 1984.

19. Sednica CKSKJ. Razmatranje Predloga platforme za pripremu 13. kongresa SKJ. Odluke CKSKJ o pripremi 13. kongresa SKJ. Belgrade: Komunist, 1985.

Official Documents/Government

SAP Kosova. *Ustav Socijalističke Autonomne Pokrajine Kosova*. Belgrade: Savremena administracija, 1974.

SAP Vojvodina. *Ustav Socijalističke Autonomne Pokrajine Vojvodine*. Belgrade: Savremena administracija, 1974.

SFRY. *The Constitution of the Socialist Federal Republic of Yugoslavia*. Translated by Marko Pavičić. Belgrade and Ljubljana: Dopisna Delavska Univerza, 1974.

——. *Constitutional System of Yugoslavia*. Translated by Marko Pavičić. Belgrade: Jugoslovenska stvarnost, 1980.

——. "Law concerning Supplementary Resources for the Use of Republics and Autonomous Regions from 1981 to 1985." *Službeni list SFRJ* 36 (74) (December 31, 1980): 2221–22. [Translated in Joint Publications Research Service (JPRS). *East Europe Report*. Political, Sociological, and Military Affairs. April 10, 1981.]

——. Savezno izvršno veće. "Odluka o medjurepubličkim komitetima" (June 27, 1974). *Službeni list SFRJ* 30 (33) (July 5, 1974): 1141–42.

——. Savezno izvršno veće. "Odluka o obrazovanju i radu medjurepubličkih komiteta" (August 19, 1971). *Službeni list SFRJ* 27 (37) (August 26, 1971): 689–90.

——. *Organizaciona struktura Savezne Skupštine, Predsjedništva SFRJ, Saveznog izvršnog vjeća i ostalnih organa federacije*. Šabac: GIP Dragan Srnić, [1972].

——. *Politički i poslovni imenik*. Belgrade: Tanjug, October 1978; rev. eds., January 1979 and May 1979.

——. *Statistički godišnjak Jugoslavije 1979*. Belgrade: Savezni zavod za statistiku, July 1979.

——. *Statistički godišnjak Jugoslavije 1980*. Belgrade: Savezni zavod za statistiku, January 1980.

——. *Statistički godišnjak Jugoslavije 1983*. Belgrade: Savezni zavod za statistiku, 1983.

——. "Zakon o dopunskim sredstvima republikama i autonomnim pokrajinama u periodu od 1976 do 1980 godine" (July 20, 1976). *Službeni list SFRJ* 32 (33) (July 23, 1976): 838–40.

——. "Zakon o fondu federacije za kreditiranje bržeg razvoja privredno nedovoljno razvijenih republika i autonomnih pokrajina" (July 29, 1971). *Službeni list SFRJ* 27 (33) (July 30, 1971): 641–44.

——. "Zakon o fondu federacije za kreditiranje bržeg razvoja privredno nedovoljno razvijenih republika i autonomnih pokrajina" (July 20, 1976). *Službeni list SFRJ* 32 (33) (July 23, 1976): 831–34.

——. "Zakon o fondu federacije za kreditiranje privrednog razvoja privredno nedovoljno razvijenih republika i krajeva" (February 17, 1965). *Službeni list* 21 (8) (February 24, 1965): 181–84.

——. "Zakon o kriterijumima za rasporedjivanje sredstava fonda federacije za kreditiranje bržeg razvoja privredno nedovoljno razvijenih republika i autonomnih pokrajina u periodu od 1971 do 1975 godine" (November 3, 1972). *Službeni list SFRJ* 28 (59) (November 9, 1972): 1089.

——. "Zakon o raspodeli sredstava fonda faderacije za kreditiranje bržeg razvoga privredno nedovoljno razvijenih republika i pokrajina u periodu od 1976 do 1980 godine" (July 20, 1976). *Službeni list SFRJ* 32 (33) (July 23, 1976): 837–38.

——. "Zakon o sredstvima obaveznog zajma za kreditiranje bržeg razvoja privredno nedovoljno razvijenih republika i Autonomne Pokrajine Kosovo" (July 29, 1971). *Službeni list SFRJ* 27 (33) (July 30, 1971): 644–45.

SR Hrvatske. Republički Sekretariat za Vodoprivredu. *Izvještaj o medjurepubličkoj suradnji o oblasti vodoprivrede*. Zagreb: Carbon, March 1979.

——. *Ustav Socijalističke Republike Hrvatske*. Belgrade: Službeni list, 1963.
——. *Ustav Socijalističke Republike Hrvatske*. Zagreb: Političke teme, 1974.
SR Srbija. *Ustav Socijalističke Republike Srbije*. Belgrade: Savremena administracija, 1974.

Published Sources

Aleksić, Mihailo. *Koncepcija dugoročnog razvoja saobraćaja Jugoslavije*. Belgrade: Ekonomski Institut, 1975.
Banac, Ivo. *The National Question in Yugoslavia*. Ithaca, N.Y.: Cornell University Press, 1984.
Bašota, Nuri. "Problemi ubrzanijeg razvoja Kosova kao nedovoljno razvijenog područja." *Obeležja* 9 (5) (September–October 1979): 37–50.
Bates, Drago. *Ekonomika saobraćaja*. Belgrade: Naučna knjiga, 1979.
Bertsch, Gary K., and M. George Zaninovich. "A Factor-Analytic Method of Identifying Different Political Cultures: The Multinational Yugoslav Case." *Comparative Politics* 6 (2) (January 1974): 219–44.
Bilandžić, Dušan. *Historija socijalističke federativne republike Jugoslavije*. Zagreb: Školska knjiga, 1978.
——. *Ideje i praksa društvenog razvoja Jugoslavije, 1945–1973*. Belgrade: Komunist, 1973.
——. *Jugoslavija poslije Tita, 1980–1985*. Zagreb: Globus, 1986.
Bogdanović, Dimitrije. *Knjiga o Kosovu*. Belgrade: Srpska Akademija Nauka i Umetnosti, 1985.
Bogovac, Tomislav. *Reforma obrazovanja—šta je to*. 2 vols. Belgrade: Novinska Ustanova Prosvetni Pregled, 1976 and 1977.
Bombelles, Joseph T. *Economic Development of Communist Yugoslavia, 1947–1964*. Stanford, Calif.: Hoover Institution on War, Revolution, and Peace, 1968.
Bulatović, Ljiljana. *Prizrenski proces*. Novi Sad: Književna zajednica, 1988.
Burks, R. V. *The National Problem and the Future of Yugoslavia*. Santa Monica, Calif.: Rand Corporation, October 1971.
Carter, April. *Democratic Reform in Yugoslavia: The Changing Role of the Party*. Princeton, N.J.: Princeton University Press, 1982.
Ćemerlić, Hamdija. "Državnost republika u jugoslovenskom federativnom sistemu." *Godišnjak Fakulteta u Sarajevu 1976* 24 (1977): 15–32.
Crvenkovski, Krste. *Medjunacionalni odnosi u samoupravnom društvu*. Belgrade: Sedma sila, 1967.
Diljas, Aleksa. *The Contested Country: Yugoslav Unity and Communist Revolution, 1919–1953*. Cambridge, Mass.: Harvard University Press, 1991.
Djodan, Šime. "Autonomaštvo kao recidiva unitarizma." *Vidik* 18 (32/33) (July–August 1971): 33–41.
——. "Gdje dr Stipe Suvar 'pronalazi' nacionalizam, a gdje ga ne vidi." *Kolo* 7 (7) (July 1969): 686–713.
——. "Gospodarski položaj Hrvatske." *Kritika* 4 (17) (March–April 1971): 348–52.
——. "Pred kritičnom barijerom." *Dometi* 2 (3) (March 1969): 4–13.
——. "Prilog raspravi o regionalnom razvoju u SFRJ." *Kolo* 7 (3) (March 1969): 246–54.
——. "Prilog razmatranju predloženih izmjena ustava sfrj." *Kolo* 6 (11) (November 1968): 471–73.
——. "Robno-novčani privredni model i regionalni razvoj u našim uvjetima." *Kolo* 6 (10) (October 1968): 379–87.
Djordjević, Jovan et al. *Federalizam i nacionalno pitanje*. Belgrade: Savez udruženja za političke nauke, Jugoslavije, 1971.
Doder, Duško. *The Yugoslavs*. New York: Random House, 1978.

Dokić, Mirko. *Ekonomika, organizacija i razvoj saobraćaja SFRJ*. Belgrade: Institut Ekonomskih Nauka, 1977.

Dragnich, Alex N., and Slavko Todorovich. *The Saga of Kosovo*. Boulder, Colo.: East European Monographs, 1984.

Dubey, Vinod et al. *Yugoslavia: Development with Decentralization*. Baltimore: Johns Hopkins University Press, 1975.

Dugandžija, Nikola. *Religija i nacija: Istraživanja u zagrebačkoj regiji*. Zagreb: Stvarnost, 1986.

Furtak, Robert K. *Jugoslawien*. Hamburg: Hoffmann und Campe Verlag, 1975.

Haberl, Othmar Nikola. *Parteiorganisation und nationale Frage in Jugoslawien*. Berlin: Otto Harrassowitz, 1976.

Hadžijahić, Muhamed. *Od tradicije do identiteta: Geneza nacionalnog pitanja bosanskih muslimana*. Sarajevo: Svjetlost, 1974.

Hamilton, F. E. Ian. *Yugoslavia: Patterns of Economic Activity*. New York: Praeger, 1968.

Hasani, Sinan. *Kosovo—istine i zablude*. Zagreb: Centar za informacije i publicitet, 1986.

Hondius, Frits W. *The Yugoslav Community of Nations*. The Hague: Mouton, 1968.

Horvat, Branko. *Kosovsko pitanje*. Zagreb: Globus, 1988.

Institut za ekonomska istraživanja Ekonomskog Fakulteta—Zagreb. *Autoceste i magistralne ceste u SR Hrvatskoj do 2000 godine*. Zagreb: Ekonomski Fakultet, 1978.

Institut za uporedno pravo. *Podela zajedničke nadležnosti izmedju federacije i federalnih jedinica*. Belgrade: Savremena administracija, 1978.

——. *Specifičnosti republičkih i pokrajinskih ustava od 1974*. Belgrade: Savremena administracija, 1976.

Institute of Social Sciences. Demographic Research Center. *The Development of Yugoslavia's Population in the Post-War Period*. Belgrade: Radiša Timotić, 1974.

Jelić-Butić, Fikreta. *Ustaše i NDH*. Zagreb: S. N. Liber and Školska knjiga, 1977.

Jončić, Koča. *Odnosi izmedju naroda i narodnosti u Jugoslavije*. Belgrade: Medjunarodna politika, 1970.

Jovičić, Miodrag. *Savremeni federalizam*. Belgrade: Savremena administracija, 1973.

King, Robert R. *Minorities under Communism*. Cambridge, Mass.: Harvard University Press, 1973.

Kosovo 1389–1989, Special edition of the *Serbian Literary Quarterly*, nos. 1–3 (1989).

Kosovo—Past and Present. Belgrade: Review of International Affairs, n.d. [1989].

Krivokapić, Boro. *Jugoslavija i komunisti: adresa Jovana Djordjevića*. Belgrade: Mladost, 1988.

Kubović, Branko. *Regionalna ekonomika*. Zagreb: Informator, 1974.

Lapenna, Ivo. "Main Features of the Yugoslav Constitution, 1946–1971." *The International and Comparative Law Quarterly*, 4th series, vol. 21, pt. 2 (April 1972): 209–29.

Lukić, Vojin. *Sećanja i saznanja: Aleksandar Ranković i brionski plenum*. Titograd: Novica Jovović, 1989.

Maček, Vladko. *In the Struggle for Freedom*. Translated by Elizabeth and Stjepan Gazi. University Park: Pennsylvania State University Press, 1959.

Macesich, George. *Yugoslavia: The Theory and Practice of Development Planning*. Charlottesville: University of Virginia Press, 1964.

Marković, Sima. *Ustavno pitanje i radnička klasa Jugoslavije*. Belgrade (?): n.p., n.d. [1923].

Mihailović, Kosta. *Nerazvijena područja Jugoslavije*. 2nd ed. Belgrade: Ekonomski Institut, 1970.

Mijanović, Gaso. "Ustavna reforma i proces jačanja uloge republika i pokrajina u ostvarivanju zajedničkih interesa u Jugoslaviji." *Godnišnjak Pravnog Fakulteta u Sarajevu 1976* 24 (1977): 109–33.

Milenkovich, Deborah D. *Plan and Market in Yugoslav Economic Thought*. New Haven: Yale University Press, 1971.

Mišović, Miloš. *Ko je tražio republiku: Kosovo 1945–1985*. Belgrade: Narodna knjiga, 1987.

Mujačić, Mahmut. *Nova dimenzija jugoslovenskog federalizma*. Sarajevo: Oslobodjenje, 1981.

Nikolić, Milenko M. *Ravnopravnost naroda i narodnosti u obrazovanju*. Belgrade: Novinska Ustanova Prosvetni Pregled, 1975.

Nikšić, Stevan. *Oslobodjenje štampe*. Belgrade: Oslobodjenje, 1982.

Paca, Agim. "Fond federacije za kreditiranje privrednog razvoja privredno nedovoljno razvijenih republika i pokrajina, s osvrtom na SAP Kosovo u periodu od 1966. do 1975. godine." *Obeležja* 7 (3) (May–June 1977): 561–81.

Palmer, Stephen E., Jr., and Robert R. King. *Yugoslav Communism and the Macedonian Question*. Hamden, Conn.: Archon Books, 1971.

Pašić, Najdan, et al. *Društveno-politički sistem SFRJ*. Belgrade: Radnička stampa, 1975.

——. *Nacionalno pitanje u savremenoj epohi*. Belgrade: Radnička stampa, 1973.

——. *Razvoj nacija i medjunacionalnih odnosa u socijalističkom samoupravnom društvu*. Belgrade: Marksističko obrazovanje, 1979.

Pejovich, Svetozar. *The Market-Planned Economy of Yugoslavia*. Minneapolis: University of Minnesota Press, 1966.

Peles, Aleksandar. "O postupku zaključenja medjunarodnih ugovora SFRJ, sa posebnim osvrtom na učešće republika i pokrajina." *Godišnjak Pravnog Fakulteta u Sarajevu 1976* 24 (1977): 169–77.

Perić, Ivan. *Ideje 'Masovnog pokreta' u Hrvatskoj*. Zagreb: Političke teme, 1974.

——. *Suvremeni hrvatski nacionalizam*. Zagreb: August Cesarec, 1976.

——. "Za objektivnu valorizaciju Desete sjednice Centralnog komiteta Saveza komunista Hrvatske." *Naše teme* 15 (10) (October 1971): 1651–91.

Petranović, Branko. *Istorija Jugoslavije 1918–1988*, Vol. 3. Belgrade: Nolit, 1988.

Petrinović, Ivo. "Hrvatska kao suverena država i novi smisao republičke državnosti." *Pogledi* 2 (7) (1971): 5–7.

Petrović, Milan, and Kasim Suljević, eds. *Nacionalni odnosi danas*. Sarajevo: Univerzal, 1971.

Petrović, Ruža. "Etnički mesoviti brakovi u Jugoslaviji." *Sociologija* 8 (3) (1966): 89–104.

Pozderac, Hamdija. *Nacionalni odnosi i socijalističko zajedništvo*. Sarajevo: Svjetlost, 1978.

Purivatra, Atif. *Nacionalni i politički razvitak muslimana*. Sarajevo: Svjetlost, 1970.

Rabushka, Alvin, and Kenneth A. Shepsle. *Politics in Plural Societies*. Columbus, Ohio: Charles E. Merrill, 1972.

Raičević, Jovan. "Savez komunista Jugoslavije i nacionalno pitanje." *KPJ-SKJ: Razvoj teorije i prakse socijalizma, 1919–1979*. Belgrade: Savremena administracija, 1979.

Ramet, Pedro. "Yugoslavia 1982: Political Ritual, Political Drift, and the Fetishization of the Past." *South Slav Journal* 5 (3) (Autumn 1982): 13–21.

——. "Yugoslavia's Troubled Times." *Global Affairs* 5 (1) (Winter 1990): 78–95.

——, ed. *Religion and Nationalism in Soviet and East European Politics*, Rev. and expanded ed. Durham, N.C.: Duke University Press, 1989.

——, ed. *Yugoslavia in the 1980s*. Boulder, Colo.: Westview Press, 1985.

Ramet, Sabrina P. "The Breakup of Yugoslavia." *Global Affairs* 6 (2) (Spring 1991): 93–110.

——. "Primordial Ethnicity or Modern Nationalism: The Case of Yugoslavia's Muslims, Reconsidered," in Andreas Kappeler et al., eds. *Muslims in the USSR and Yugoslavia*. Durham, N.C.: Duke University Press, 1991.

——. *Social Currents in Eastern Europe: The Sources and Meaning of the Great Transformation*. Durham, N.C.: Duke University Press, 1991.

Razumovsky, Andreas Graf. *Ein Kampf um Belgrad*. Berlin: Ullstein Verlag, 1980.

Reuter, Jens. *Die Albaner in Jugoslawien*. Munich: R. Oldenbourg Verlag, 1982.

Ribičič, Ciril, and Zdravko Tomac. *Federalizam po mjeri budućnosti*. Zagreb: Globus, 1989.

Ristić, Dušan. "Kosovo i Savez komunista Kosova izmedju dva kongresa i dve konferencije." *Obeležja* 8 (2) (March–April 1978): 7–26.

Rusinow, Dennison I. "The Other Albanians." *American Universities Field Staff Reports*. Southeast Europe Series, vol. 12, no. 2 (November 1965).

——. "Ports and Politics in Yugoslavia." *American Universities Field Staff Reports*. Southeast Europe Series, vol. 11, no. 3 (April 1964).

——. "The Price of Pluralism." *American Universities Field Staff Reports*. Southeast Europe Series, vol. 18, no. 1 (July 1971).

——. *The Yugoslav Experiment, 1948–1974*. Berkeley and Los Angeles: University of California Press, 1977.

——, ed. *Yugoslavia: A Fractured Federalism*. Washington D.C.: Wilson Center Press, 1988.

Samardžić, Slobodan. *Jugoslavija pred iskušenjem federalizma*. Belgrade: Stručna knjiga, 1990.

Schöpflin, George. "The Ideology of Croatian Nationalism." *Survey* 19 (1) (Winter 1973): 123–46.

Šefer, Berislav. *Privredni razvoj Jugoslavije sedamdesetih godina*. Zagreb: Informator, 1976.

Seroka, Jim. "Change and Reform of the League of Communists in Yugoslavia." *The Carl Beck Papers*, No. 704. Pittsburgh: University of Pittsburgh Press, December 1988.

Šetinc, Franc. *Misao i djelo Edvarda Kardelja*. Translated from Slovenian into Serbo-Croatian by Ivan Brajdić. Zagreb: Globus, 1979.

——. *Što je i za što se bori Savez komunista*. Zagreb: Globus, 1974.

Shoup, Paul. *Communism and the Yugoslav National Question*. New York: Columbia University Press, 1968.

——. "The League of Communists of Yugoslavia," in Stephen Fischer-Galati, ed. *The Communist Parties of Eastern Europe*. New York: Columbia University Press, 1979.

——. "The National Question in Yugoslavia." *Problems of Communism* 21 (1) (January–February 1972): 18–29.

Simović, Vojislav. *Zakonodavno nadležnost u razvitku jugoslovenske federacije*. Belgrade: Centar za pravna istraživanja Instituta društvenih nauka, 1978.

Singleton, Fred. *Twentieth Century Yugoslavia*. New York: Columbia University Press, 1976.

Slavica, Tomislav. "Krivnja autonomaštva." *Vidik* 18 (32/33) (July–August 1971): 15–20.

Slučaj Zanko. Belgrade: Kosmos, 1986.

Špadijer, Balša. *Federalizam i federalni odnosi u socijalističkoj Jugoslaviji*. Belgrade: Novinska Ustanova Prosvetni Pregled, 1975.

——. *Federalizam i medjunacionalni odnosi u Jugoslaviji*. Belgrade: Institut za političke studije, 1975.

Sruk, Josip. *Ustavno uredjenje Socijalističke Federativne Republike Jugoslavije*. Zagreb: Informator, 1976.

Stambolić, Ivan. *Rasprave o SR Srbiji, 1979–1989*. Zagreb: Globus, 1988.

Stojanović, Radoslav. *Jugoslavija, nacije i politika*. Belgrade: Nova knjiga, 1988.

Stroehm, Carl Gustaf. *Ohne Tito*. Graz: Verlag Styria, 1976.

Suljević, Kasim. *Nacionalnost Muslimana*. Rijeka: Otokar Keršovani, 1981.

Šuvar, Stipe. *Nacionalno i nacionalističko*. Split: Marksistički Centar, 1974.

——. *Nacionalno pitanje u marksističkoj teoriji i socijalističkoj praksi*. Belgrade: Novinska Ustanova Prosvetni Pregled, 1976.

Tollefson, James W. "The Language Planning Process and Language Rights in Yugoslavia." *Language Problems and Language Planning* 4 (2) (Summer 1980): 141–56.

Veljić, Andjelko. *Od osnovnih organizacija udruženog rada de medjurepubličkih dogovora i sporazuma*. Belgrade: Kultura, 1974.

Vlajčić, Gordana. *KPJ i nacionalno pitanje u Jugoslaviji, 1919–1929*. Zagreb: August Cesarec, 1974.

Vuković, Mihajlo. *Sistemski okviri podsticanja razvoja nerazvijenih područja Jugoslavije*. Sarajevo: Svjetlost, 1978.

Wheare, K. C. *Federal Government*, 3rd ed. London: Oxford University Press, 1956.

Ziherl, Boris. *Komunizam i otadžbina*. Zagreb: Kultura, 1950.

Collective. *Kongresi, konferencije: Pedeset godina Saveza komunista Jugoslavije*. Belgrade: Privredni pregled, 1969.

———. *Nacionalno pitanje u djelima klasika marksizma i u dokumentima i praksi kpj/skj*. Zagreb: Centar Drustvenih Djelatnosti SSOH, 1978.

———. *Udruženi rad i medjunacionalni odnosi*. Belgrade: Komunist, 1978.

———. *Ustav Socijalisticke Federativne Republike Jugoslavije: stručno objasnjenje*. Belgrade: Privredni pregled, 1975.

———. *Zadaci CK Srbije u razvoju medjunacionalnih odnosa i borbi protiv nacionalizma*. Belgrade: Komunist, 1978.

Unpublished Sources

Interviews, Yugoslavia: October 1979–July 1980, July 1982, July 1987, July 1988, August–September 1989

Birnbaum, Henrik. "Language, Ethnicity, and Nationalism: On the Linguistic Foundations of a Unified Yugoslavia." Los Angeles: University of California, 1978.

Irwin, Zachary T. "National Identity and Integration in Yugoslav Foreign Policy." Paper presented at a conference on "The Impact of Communist Modernization on National Identity and State Integration in Eastern Europe," organized by the Slavic and Soviet Language Area Center, October 30–31, 1975, Pennsylvania State University, University Park, Pa.

Rusinow, Dennison I. "Yugoslav Domestic Developments." Paper presented at a conference on "Yugoslavia: Accomplishments and Problems," October 16, 1977, at the Wilson Center, Washington D.C.

Sletzinger, Martin Charles. "The Reform and Reorganization of the League of Communists of Yugoslavia, 1966–1973." Ph.D. diss., Harvard University, 1976.

Stambolić, Vukasin. "Položaj i odnosi republika u SFRJ." Master's thesis, University of Belgrade, 1968.

Wambold, Alan B. "The National Question and the Evolution of the Yugoslav Constitution, 1971–1974." Ph.D. diss., University of Virginia, 1976.

Zimmerman, William. "Issue Area, International-National Linkages, and Yugoslav Political Processes." Ann Arbor: University of Michigan, 1977.

INDEX

SABRINA P. RAMET is Associate Professor of International Studies at the University of Washington. She is the author of *Cross and Commissar: The Politics of Religion in Eastern Europe and the USSR*, *The Soviet-Syrian Relationship since 1955: A Troubled Relationship*, and *Social Currents in Eastern Europe: The Sources and Meaning of the Great Transformation*.